CAMBRIDGE THEOLOGICAL ESSAYS

ESSAYS ON SOME THEOLOGICAL QUESTIONS OF THE DAY

BY MEMBERS OF THE UNIVERSITY OF CAMBRIDGE

EDITED BY

HENRY BARCLAY SWETE, D.D.
REGIUS PROFESSOR OF DIVINITY
FELLOW OF GONVILLE AND CAIUS COLLEGE
FELLOW OF THE BRITISH ACADEMY

καινά καί παλαιά

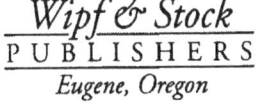

Eugene, Oregon

Wipf and Stock Publishers
199 West 8th Avenue, Suite 3
Eugene, Oregon 97401

Essays on Some Theological Questions of the Day
Early Twentieth Century Cambridge Essays
By Swete, Henry B.
ISBN: 1-59244-494-6
Publication date 1/26/2004
Previously published by Macmillan, 1906

PREFACE.

THIS volume owes its inception to a small body of Cambridge graduates who are associated for the study of Christian Doctrine. It seemed to them that the time had come when an effort ought to be made on the part of those who are entrusted with the theological teaching of Cambridge to deal in a series of Essays with some of the religious problems which are now attracting the attention of educated Englishmen. With the view of making the book fairly representative of Cambridge theology, the Association has sought the help of several well-known resident teachers who do not belong to its own ranks, and of a few non-residents who are still in touch with the life and thought of the University.

Two changes only have been made in the original list of contributors: one writer withdrew through the pressure of other work; the task of a second, the late Forbes Robinson, Fellow of Christ's College, a colleague whose early removal from us is deeply deplored, fell upon his brother, who in the midst of many duties consented to fill the vacant place.

No desire has been felt to limit the representation to any particular school or schools of theological opinion, and it will be found to include men who differ widely on questions where it is possible to disagree without disloyalty to the common Faith. Each writer is to be held responsible solely for what he has written; although the Essays have been circulated in proof, there has been no formal consultation or cooperation among the Essayists, and the Editor has generally refrained from suggesting material changes, and has made no such change without the consent of the Essayist concerned; even in the details of orthography and punctuation no attempt has been made to secure absolute uniformity. Independence carries with it certain obvious disadvantages, and the reader will doubtless observe here and there in this book something like a conflict of opinion; there may be some overlapping and occasional repetitions, and a general lack of the homogeneity which, when many writers are at work upon the same ground, can be gained only by repeated conference or by the repression of personal methods and convictions. But on the whole it has seemed better to accept these risks than to interfere with the free play of individual preferences. Such unity as this collection of Essays may possess must be sought in its general purpose.

In the selection of the subjects the Committee to whom the details were entrusted have been guided by a desire to give prominence to those which seemed to be of vital importance in themselves or under present circumstances. But they had also in view to provide an orderly treatment of the chief landmarks in the theistic and Christian positions. A brief sketch of the contents of the volume will show how they have endeavoured to fulfil their purpose. Beginning with a general view of the Christian standpoint, the book proceeds to show that theistic belief is not inconsistent with a loyal acceptance of the assured results of either physical or philosophical research. It then examines the position of Man, both as a part of Nature, and as standing in relation to God and conscious of sin; the possibility of communication between God and Man, and the means by which it is effected. The next step is to deal with certain problems which meet the student on the threshold of the Christian Revelation: the credibility of miracles, the permanence of the Old Testament, and the historical character of the Four Gospels. Some essential features of Christianity are then considered: the Person of Christ as seen in the Gospels, and the Work and Influence of Christ in History; and in the last two Essays the series is completed by a discussion of the ethical value of Christian doctrines, and the power of the Christian Ideal and the hope of the life to come.

From this summary it will appear that these Essays to some extent constitute an *apologia pro fide nostra*. To such an interpretation of our effort there can be no objection if the work of the apologist and our own relations to it are rightly understood. To be ἕτοιμοι πρὸς ἀπολογίαν, ready to answer the challenge of non-Christians, is a necessary part of the equipment of believers, and especially of the professed teachers of Christian Theology. From the first half of the second century onwards the Church has occupied herself from time to time in producing an apologetic literature, which, if not always worthy of its high aims and now partly obsolete, has upon the whole served a useful purpose. Our own time, with its wide outlook upon Nature, and searching enquiries into the origins of institutions, needs a new apologetic;

neither the efforts of Justin and Clement to correlate Christianity with the best thoughts of Greek philosophy, nor the sarcastic dialectic of Tertullian, nor Origen's brilliant reply to Celsus, nor the often acute answers of Macarius Magnes to the moribund yet militant paganism of the fourth century, nor the refutation of seventeenth and eighteenth century unbelief by English writers such as Cudworth, Butler, and Paley, can adequately meet the wants of the present age, when the case against faith is stated by a new learning of which our fathers never dreamt. We shall rejoice if this book is found worthy to suggest lines of thought to the future apologist, and we are not without hope that it may be thus used by him. For these Essays are the work of men who have lived for years, in some cases for the best part of a lifetime, in the atmosphere of an English University, and who therefore cannot be either unconscious or regardless of the problems which modern knowledge presents to theologians. It is one of the chief advantages of our academical system that the student of Theology meets, in the frank intercourse of a common life, with the student of History and Literature on the one hand and the student of Nature on the other. In Cambridge no sharp line of demarcation separates sacred from secular learning ; Theology gladly descends into the arena of the 'studies,' and learns to regard all knowledge as sacred and all truth as of God. For theologians who have lived in such surroundings it is impossible to ignore objections raised by other branches of knowledge, and no less impossible to offer answers which have not first satisfied their own intellectual needs. It is because this volume of Essays has been written by men who have in every case passed through such training that it may be expected to render some real assistance to the Christian apologist.

But while we hope that our book may not be destitute of apologetic value, we have not followed the methods of the formal apology, nor has the defence of the Faith been our primary aim. Our purpose is rather to bring certain questions connected with Christian belief into the light of modern knowledge, and to register the results of this process, whatever they may be. A special responsibility attaches to those who are called to study and teach theology under the shadow of a great University. The Master of all Christians has promised to send to His Church both Prophets and Scribes : the men of vigorous action and glowing speech, who can teach afresh to their own generation the great lessons of Truth and Righteousness, and by clearness of vision forecast the work of the near future; and the men of the cloister and the study, whose business it is to reexamine the sacred writings and to restate and hand on, enriched but essentially unchanged, the tradition which the Church received from the first generation of disciples. In England the Christian Scribe has ever found his chief home in our old Universities, and it is of good omen that the younger Universities have shown a disposition to welcome him among their teachers; it would indeed be an evil day both for learning and for religion if this happy concordat were abandoned and the theologian were led to seek shelter in an atmosphere wholly theological. For the present in any case it is to the Universities that the Church may rightly look for the "things new and old" which it is her business to bring forth out of the treasury of the Kingdom.

There is room in Theology for the new as well as for the old, and each age, as it passes, must contribute to the store and not merely preserve and pass it on. In Cambridge there is little danger of forgetting or undervaluing the great leaders of the last generation; their memories are yet green, and their work will always remain with us, a storehouse from which we thankfully borrow inspiration and knowledge. But since Lightfoot overthrew the historical position of the author of *Supernatural Religion*, the battlefield has shifted in part, and the forces of our opponents have been recruited from fresh quarters; the criticisms which are still good as against that unfortunate venture have little bearing upon some of our present controversies with unbelief. Nor do all the historical and textual results which seemed so secure twenty years ago now command universal assent. The times have moved on, bringing new workers, new facts, new ideas, glimpses even of whole fields of thought unknown to us then; and room must be found for these in our theology as well as in other departments of study. It is no disloyalty to the past to endeavour to keep pace with the present, or to prepare for a future which is already coming into sight. Theologians above other men are tempted to regard what is novel as suspect or even self-condemned; does not the Queen of Sciences teach eternal and unchangeable truth? was not the Faith, it will be asked, *once for all delivered to the saints*? But those who urge this plea forget that there is another point of view which is not to be overlooked. If there are things new as well as things old in the store of the spiritual householder, it is his duty to give prominence to each of these aspects of Truth in its own place. The New Covenant, no longer new in point of time, possesses what the Old Covenant lacked, an inherent power of presenting itself in fresh lights, and of developing points of contact with the latest revelations of human knowledge. The Logos, as an early Christian writer has finely said, though He was of old, even from the beginning, manifested Himself anew at the Incarnation, and is evermore being born into a fresh, young life in the hearts of the saints; through her progressive realization of the Christ, the Church is enabled continually to renew the vitality of her early days, whilst there are epochs in her long history when the Eternal Truth appears with the startling freshness of a great spiritual discovery. Such an epoch, answering to an age of rapid progress in other branches of knowledge, may be dawning upon us now, and it is not for us to follow the example of the Scribes of our Lord's time by overlooking or misreading the signs of the time. The disciples of the Word dare not turn away from any of the teachings of God in Nature or in History because they may be thought to involve a reconstruction of some of their cherished beliefs.

Reconstruction, however, is a serious matter, when vital truths are concerned; and in Theology it calls for the utmost care. There is grave risk lest some pearl of great price should be lost or marred in the resetting of the chain. Although new combinations are permissible, the original deposit must remain without diminution, without addition: *nove, non nova* must be the motto of the worker in this field. It is easy to state this principle, but the task of giving effect to it is one of the greatest delicacy and difficulty. How necessary it is that this should be reserved for the handling of trained students is borne in upon us by the crude pronouncements which from time to time proceed from opposite camps, and disturb the peace of the Church and the faith of not a few.

That these Essays will have succeeded in adjusting the rival claims of 'old' and 'new' is more than we hope, more indeed than can be attained at the present moment. A generation or two may barely suffice to solve outstanding problems, and as soon as they have been solved the process will begin again, through the discovery of new facts or the penetration of society by new ideas. Meanwhile in this book the reader may see the work in progress at a stage where it is still tentative and the results are therefore of uncertain value. He will bear in mind that to expect finality in such investigations is to court disappointment; it is only through alternations of failure and success, and a persistence in effort which defies discouragements, that the end can at last be reached. Nor will he look for uniform excellence in a field where many labourers are engaged upon soil of varying character. Some of the subjects are in themselves more attractive than others, or may be thought to have received more sympathetic treatment; for into the interpretation of truth the personal equation must ever enter largely, especially in a volume of this kind. The purpose of the book will have been gained if, taken as a whole, it is judged to have set forward what is perhaps the most important work that lies before the theology of the twentieth century; if it has helped to assimilate the new views of truth suggested by modern knowledge, without sacrificing any part of the primitive message, and to state in terms adapted to the needs of a new century the truths which the ancient Church expressed in those which were appropriate to its own times.

The partial Hellenizing and Latinizing of Christian thought and terminology, which began soon after the end of the Apostolic age, may not have been without danger to the Faith, but few will now doubt that valuable results have followed. If we owe to these processes certain accretions which do not harmonize with primitive simplicity, on the other hand they enriched the Christian Society with much that appealed to the thought and imagination of the centuries through which it had to pass; nor would any thoughtful believer at the present day willingly abandon the best heirlooms that the Church has received from the Greek East or the Latin West. It would be faithless to doubt that the modernizing of Theology, which seems to have begun, will upon the whole be equally productive of good. Something of the rich beauty of the ancient presentment of the Faith may be lost in the process, and the period of transition must necessarily be one of unrest and discomfort. But it needs no prophet to foresee that the time will come when ideas which to-day are strange and unwelcome will be seen to possess a beauty of their own, to be necessary to the completeness of truth, and to belong, no less than many which are long familiar, to the common treasury of the Kingdom of Heaven.

H. B. SWETE.

CAMBRIDGE,
20 *September*, 1905.

SUBJECTS AND CONTRIBUTORS.

                                                                    PAGE
I. *The Christian Standpoint* 1
    WILLIAM CUNNINGHAM, D.D., Fellow of Trinity College, Honorary Fellow of Gonville and Caius College, Hulsean Lecturer (1885), Honorary Canon of Ely; Fellow of the British Academy; Vicar of Great St Mary's, Cambridge.

II. *The Being of GOD, in the light of Physical Science* 55
    FREDERICK ROBERT TENNANT, B.D., late Chaplain and Student in Philosophy, Gonville and Caius College, Hulsean Lecturer (1901); Rector of Hockwold, Norfolk.

III. *The Being of GOD, in the light of Philosophy* . 101
    ALFRED CALDECOTT, D.D., late Fellow and Dean of St John's College, Professor of Moral and Mental Philosophy in King's College, London.

IV. *Man's Origin, and his place in Nature* . . 147
    WYNFRID LAURENCE HENRY DUCKWORTH, M.A., M.D., Fellow of Jesus College, University Lecturer in Physical Anthropology.

V. *Sin, and the Need of Atonement* . . . 175
    EDWARD HARRISON ASKWITH, D.D., Chaplain of Trinity College.

xii   Subjects and Contributors

PAGE

VI. *The Idea of Revelation, in the light of Modern Knowledge and Research* . . 219

JAMES MAURICE WILSON, D.D., sometime Fellow of St John's College and Head Master of Clifton College, late Vicar of Rochdale and Archdeacon of Manchester, Hulsean Lecturer (1898); Canon of Worcester.

VII. *Prayer, in relation to the idea of Law* . . 263

ARTHUR WILLIAM ROBINSON, D.D., Jesus College, Vicar of All Hallows Barking by the Tower.

VIII. *The spiritual and historical evidence for Miracles* 307

JOHN OWEN FARQUHAR MURRAY, D.D., late Fellow and Dean of Emmanuel College, Warden of St Augustine's College, Canterbury.

IX. *The Permanent Value of the Old Testament* . 341

WILLIAM EMERY BARNES, D.D., Fellow of Peterhouse, Hulsean Professor of Divinity.

X. *The Gospels, in the light of historical criticism* 371

FREDERIC HENRY CHASE, D.D., President of Queens' College, Honorary Fellow of Christ's College, and late Norrisian Professor of Divinity; Hulsean Lecturer (1900); Bishop of Ely.

XI. *Christ in the New Testament: the primitive portrait* 421

ARTHUR JAMES MASON, D.D., Master of Pembroke College, sometime Fellow of Trinity College, late Lady Margaret Professor of Divinity and Fellow of Jesus College, Hulsean Lecturer (1899); Canon of Canterbury.

Subjects and Contributors

PAGE

XII. *Christ in the Church: the testimony of History* 469

FREDERICK JOHN FOAKES-JACKSON, B.D., Fellow, Dean, and Assistant Tutor of Jesus College, Hulsean Lecturer (1902); Honorary Canon of Peterborough.

XIII. *Christian doctrines and their ethical significance* 527

JAMES FRANKLIN BETHUNE-BAKER, B.D., Fellow and Dean of Pembroke College.

XIV. *The Christian Ideal and the Christian Hope* . 573

HENRY MONTAGU BUTLER, D.D., Master of Trinity College, sometime Head Master of Harrow School; late Dean of Gloucester.

Ἡ πίστις εἰσάξει, ἡ πεῖρα διδάξει, ἡ γραφὴ παιδαγωγήσει.

Πῶς οὖν ἀνέλθω, φησίν, εἰς οὐρανούς; ὁδός ἐστιν ὁ κύριος, στενὴ μὲν ἀλλ᾽ ἐξ οὐρανῶν, στενὴ μὲν ἀλλ᾽ εἰς οὐρανοὺς ἀναπέμπουσα· στενὴ ἐπὶ γῆς ὑπερορωμένη, πλατεῖα ἐν οὐρανοῖς προσκυνουμένη.

Ἐκπόνει καὶ μὴ ἀπόκαμνε· ἔσῃ γὰρ οἷος οὐκ ἐλπίζεις οὐδ᾽ εἰκάσαι δύναιο ἄν.

CLEMENT OF ALEXANDRIA.

ESSAY I.
THE CHRISTIAN STANDPOINT.
WILLIAM CUNNINGHAM, D.D.

SYNOPSIS.

The Want of a Common Understanding.

I. CONFLICTING OPINIONS.
  1. Narrow Limits of Difference in the Study of Physical Phenomena.
  2. Incompatibilities of Moral Judgements.
  3. Uncertainty of Religious Principles.

II. GROUNDS FOR DISCARDING RELIGION.
  1. Materialism.
  2. Pantheism.
  3. Agnosticism.

III. COMMON SENSE OPINIONS ABOUT RELIGION.
  1. Rationalism in Theology.
  2. Analytical Enquiries as to the Essence of Religion.
  3. The protest of Religious Conviction.

IV. THE RELIGIOUS CONSCIOUSNESS.
  1. Reflection on the Contradictions in Human Nature.
  2. The Sense of Sin.

V. CHRISTIAN CONSCIOUSNESS.
  1. Conscious Reconciliation with God.
  2. Harmony with other Wills.
  3. Christian Life.
  4. The Life of Christ.

VI. THE STUDY OF THE PHENOMENA OF RELIGION FROM THIS STANDPOINT.
  1. Apprehension and Appreciation.
  2. The Spiritual Truth in the Scriptures.
  3. The Growth of Mankind in the Knowledge of God.

VII. CHRISTIANITY AND CONDUCT.
  1. Self-repression.
  2. Theistic Morality.
  3. Distinctively Christian Virtues.

THE CHRISTIAN STANDPOINT.

ORDINARY table talk, on every-day topics, brings out the curious differences that are to be found among human beings. It offers a field where bright intelligence comes to the front, by acuteness of perception, by alertness in contributing to the common thought of the company, and by adroitness in turning the stream into fresh channels when there is danger that it will stagnate. Keenness of intellect and geniality of manner show on the surface, and give a charm to talk, upon whatever subject it may turn; but other personal qualities may obstruct rather than illuminate the flow of conversation. Intimate friends have so much in common that they can speak freely, without fear of giving offence; while those who find themselves in an uncongenial atmosphere feel the duty of exercising some conscious self-repression. The Tory and the Radical have habituated themselves to look at political affairs from different points of view; each interprets the events of the day from his own standpoint, and each finds in them a confirmation of the opinions he has always held. Fruitful discussion of affairs of state between two thorough-going partisans is almost impossible; they abhor each other's principles, and deny each other's facts. There is no common ground between them, and unconvincing argument is only too apt to degenerate into mere wrangling. Nor is it only with respect to political matters that a man feels it prudent to be careful what he says among strangers. In regard to many topics of art, or of religion, one person speaks and thinks on such a wholly different plane from that which others occupy, that honest attempts to comprehend the opinion that is expressed are foiled: they only lead to mystification. The human mind recoils from the merely incomprehensible, and is not always patient enough to be at pains to try to reach the platform of those who seem to be oddities. Not a little education is needed to enable a man to interchange thought on all possible subjects of human interest, with many sorts and conditions of men. There must be some kind of common understanding, or intelligent discussion is impossible; no advance can be made towards agreement unless one at least of the disputants is prepared to try to comprehend the other's point of view.

I.

1. There are of course subjects of discussion in regard to which it is rarely necessary to take much account of different points of view; for practical purposes we are all on the same standpoint, when we are considering the objects of sense-perception in their relations to each other. The questions as to the ultimate analysis of physical phenomena, or as to their precise relations with the human mind, raise problems that many of us are ready to leave on one side; since we do not see that they have any utilitarian bearing. Those who are content to try to understand Nature, in order that they may make the most of her and control her resources for human purposes, feel that there is no need to justify their position. They are looking at the world steadily and systematically, as all civilised men take it unconsciously in every act of daily life. To find an exception, we must go to the fetichism of primitive man, which reduces nature to a chaos of capricious influences; this is a different standpoint, wholly at variance with our own; but we can trace the steps by which, with advancing knowledge, men have discarded it, and may thus find additional reason for preferring our own point of view. The conception of the physical world, as an orderly whole, gives us a sufficient basis for common action; those who are merely doing the business of life, and those who are pursuing investigations, find common ground from which to survey the knowledge acquired in the past, and to coordinate their new impressions. Differences of course there are, due

to the idiosyncrasies of particular individuals; the senses do not agree in the accuracy or character of their reports[1]; colour blindness vitiates some observations, and mere carelessness makes others worthless. But it may often be possible to account, or at any rate to allow for such divergences; there is, on the whole, one standard, in the body of knowledge about physical phenomena, to which appeal can be made, since it is a tribunal that all are ready to accept. Nor is it merely that there is a common conception in which all agree,— a dream that all dream at once; they recognise that the system of nature is *real*, because of the limitations it places on the operation of human wills; and they feel that their knowledge is growing in certainty, as their ideas come into closer correspondence with that which common sense regards as actual fact. The possibility of verifying our impressions, constantly or at stated intervals, and of fitting them into a coherent whole, renders our empirical knowledge so reliable that we do not need to take serious account of such different points of view as we may find among primitive men, or in exceptional persons.

2. When we turn to another class of phenomena and consider the relations between man and man, the variety of opinions expressed and the diversity of the standpoints adopted by different people become most startling. As Alan Breck put it to David Balfour, "I have often observed that you Low-country bodies have no clear idea of what's right and wrong[2]." The conscience seems to be capable of such strange vagaries; and there is always an interest in discovering at what precise point scrupulous persons will draw the line. Nor is there any common standard to which appeal can be made. Among non-progressive peoples the traditions of right and wrong come to be embodied in customs and institutions; there is a body of practice and observance which is right in all the relations of life, and the neglect of which is wrong. The caste system of the Hindus gives external expression to the conception of duty; but, since the close of the Middle Ages,

[1] Compare the controversy as to *n* rays, *Nature*, 29 September, 1904.
[2] Stevenson, *Kidnapped*, 177.

there has been no such generally recognised external standard among Western peoples. The pretensions of the Church to pronounce authoritatively on right and wrong in every sphere of conduct are no longer enforced; the privileges of the Head of the State, as the source of law and right, were set at nought in the seventeenth century, and the claim of every man to do that which is right in his own eyes is treated with respect.

This state of affairs has led to the diffusion of doubt as to the reality of moral distinctions and relationships; they do not seem to be given, as something which our wills cannot oppose; they are, on the other hand, to a very considerable extent affected by the individual decision. It is true that the duties of a child to a parent are thrust upon every one, but it rests with himself whether he shall undertake those of a husband, a father, or a citizen; he can remain outside them all. Not only is he free to evade these moral responsibilities, but many human relationships appear to have been constituted by individual wills. The doctrine that the State is the creation of those who agree to place themselves and their property under the protection of a common body, and to divest themselves of individual rights, removes the whole realm of law from a basis of controlling duty, and rears it instead on common expediency and individual consent to abide by a convention. The whole fabric of right becomes unreal, and the distinction between good and bad is rendered uncertain, since there is no recognised *forum externum* to which appeal may be made, or from which we can obtain clear and distinct guidance as to our conduct towards one another. We habitually admit that a man, of whose action we disapprove, may be right from his own point of view.

The differences in the ethical standpoint taken by different individuals are so great that the mere description of actual moral conditions must be greatly affected by them. The American is full of pity for the lot of the women of India, immured in zenanas and left without education—though powerful personalities have been developed and have made themselves felt under these disabilities. The Hindu would view with positive horror the preference of the American woman for an unfettered life ; and his strong sense of disapproval would necessarily colour any attempt to describe the current morality of the United States.

Even if we do not take such extreme instances as the gulf between the civilisations of the East and of the West, we find that there are striking differences between men brought up in the same country, and under the influence of Christian teaching. They may cherish very different ideals of what ought to be, and may be brought into diametrical opposition over practical issues. There are those for whom the individual is everything, and freedom for individual self-development is essential to the realising of their aims. There are others who regard the institutions which hold society together, which perpetuate the race and form the personal character, as of paramount importance, so that any individual sacrifice may be rightly demanded for the sake of maintaining them. This is the irreconcilable contradiction that underlies all conflicting views on social questions. The varieties of temperament, or upbringing, or whatever else it may be that determines a man's attitude towards the constituted order, are fundamental in affecting his point of view on all questions of human relationships ; they affect his judgement on everything connected with the family, the Church, or the State. There is so little agreement on the fundamental issues, that there is very little common ground on which such questions as the moral education of the young can be even intelligently discussed. Opinions on matters of detail of every kind are affected by the point of view from which the topic is considered.

3. While the differences of standpoint give rise to so much confusion in regard to the relations of man to man, we can hardly expect that they should be unimportant when we are considering the relations of man to the Ultimate Power in the Universe. The problems are so terribly complex ; they seem to involve elements in regard to which there is no hope of reaching a definite decision. The two poles of the relation-

ship are alike inscrutable; among all the contradictions in his disposition and character, how shall we summarise the nature of man? Are all men endowed with similar faculties, but in varying degrees, or are there differences of kind which condemn some races to occupy a lower level? Is each person immortal, or does death involve the utter disintegration of the individual life in all its aspects? And when we find it so difficult to attain to knowledge of ourselves, how shall we figure the Ultimate Power in the Universe? Our capacity for thinking does not range so far; we cannot tell what it is we are groping after. While each of the poles of the relationship is so little known, we can hardly expect to be successful in investigating the relations which subsist between them. While there is so much confusion and unreality in regard to questions of ethics, it may seem doubtful whether it is worth while to attempt to raise the deeper problems which religion presents. The problems of ethics are forced upon our attention by the practical necessity of living among our fellow-men; we must be on some sort of terms with them, and we have to decide how we will treat them, and how we will submit to be treated ourselves. But there is no such obvious and pressing necessity in regard to the issues raised by Theology; the most cursory observation shows that many men are accustomed to treat these considerations as so remote that they need only be taken into account very occasionally, if at all; and it is easy to assume an entirely negative attitude towards religion, since it seems to be lacking in reality when it does not bring pressure to bear upon the will.

II.

1. Reasons may readily be adduced in defence of this negative position; neglect of religion seems to be not only excusable, but commendable, or at least justifiable, from one or other of three different points of view.

All religious belief and practice seem to be empty and vain to those who see no reason to suppose that there are or can be any direct relations between man and the Ultimate Power in the Universe. Many of the phenomena of human life can be explained by physical conditions of climate and soil, while others can be accounted for by such influences as association or heredity. As we analyse our own conduct in the past, or look back on the history of the race, it seems as if so much was effected by material surroundings, that a little more investigation may serve to show that the residual phenomena are determined in the same fashion, and that the study of man's relations to the material universe will give an exhaustive account of his life-history, past, present, and future. Man's greatest good would then consist in examining his environment, and studying the circumstances of his lot, with the view of modifying them, so far as may be, in the interest of the species. This standpoint is materialistic, but not atheistic; it does not deny the existence of an Ultimate Power in the Universe, but it rejects religion, and hence it is in conflict with common convictions as to the nature and dignity of man. Man has been defined as a religious animal; and if he is merely an animal determined by physical environment, there is no room either for religion, or for those sides of culture which are his greatest achievement. The whole creative force, which has found expression in art and literature and civilised institutions, is a protest against this doctrine. Man's consciousness of his own personal identity and personal character rebels against the attempt to interpret him as the mere product of his surroundings. We may even come to see that the best clue for helping us to follow the development of the human race is to be found in these residual phenomena, and that neither the source of initiative nor the actual course of progress is really explicable from the materialistic point of view.

2. There is another view of the Ultimate Power in the Universe, which leaves scope for admiration and even for adoration; but it still fails, as completely as materialism does, to recognise the dignity of human personality, and thus presents a negative attitude towards religion. The various forms of Pantheism "find the ultimate and dominant idea in

some divine Mystery of the Universe, in the sense of Beauty and Power of Nature, in the immensity of the sum of Life and Matter, it may be in a pious trust in the general good of all things, be the things human and moral, or be they physical, and unconscious[1]." But such ideals are too far off and vague: they give us no *axiomata media* to serve as principles, either for thought about ourselves, or as guides for action[2]. It is, as Mr Frederic Harrison says, "the original blot on every form of philosophic pantheism when tried as a basis of religion, or the root idea of our lives, that it jumbles up the moral, the immoral, the non-human and the antihuman world; the animated, and the inanimate; cruelty, filth, horror, waste, death; suffering and victory; sympathy and insensibility. The dualism between moral being and material being is as old as the conscience of man. It is impossible to efface the antagonism between them; their disparate nature is a consequence of the laws of thought and the fibres of the brain and the heart. No force can amalgamate in one idea tornadoes, earthquakes, interstellar space, pestilences, brotherly love, unselfish energy, patience, hope, trust, and greed. No single conception at all can ever issue out of such a medley; and any idea that is wide enough to relate to the whole must be a mere film of an idea, and one as little in contact with the workings of the heart or the needs of society as the undulatory theory of Light or the Music of the Spheres."

"Try any one of these sublimities in any of the crises of life......A human heart is wrung with pain, despair, remorse; a parent watches the child of his old age sinking into vice and crime; a thinker, an inventor, a worker, breaks down with toil and unrequited hope, and sees the labour of a life ending in failure and penury; a widow is crushed by the loss of her husband, and the destitution of their children; the poor see their lives ground out of them by oppressors, without mercy, justice, or hope. Go, then, with the gospel of pantheism to the fatherless and the widow, and console them

---

[1] F. Harrison, *Pantheism and Cosmic Emotion*, 4.
[2] Compare the criticism by Maine de Biran, *Œuvres inédites*, I. ccxxix.

by talking of sunsets, or the universal order; tell the heart-broken about the permutations of energy; ask the rich tyrant to remember the sum of all things and to listen to the teaching of the Anima Mundi; explain to the debauchee, the glutton, and the cheat the Divine Essence permeating all things and causing all things—including his particular vice, his passions, his tastes, his guile, and his lust. And when social passions rage their blackest and the demon of anarchy is gnashing its fangs at the demon of despotic cruelty, step forward with the religion of sweetness and light, and try if self-culture, so exquisitely sung by Goethe and his followers, will not heal the social delirium[1]."

3. These forms of definite opposition to current religious beliefs may be congenial to men who have either an intense enthusiasm for empirical investigation, or a strongly developed artistic temperament. Of those who are lacking in these qualities, many appear satisfied to accept the ignorance to which we seem to be condemned as inevitable, and as something against which it is useless to rebel. Whatever human relations with the Ultimate Power in the Universe may be, so long as we cannot comprehend them, they can have no bearing on our lives; religion seems only to offer a field for idle speculation, and in so far as it diverts energy from practical effort it may appear positively mischievous. In lands where power and wealth are in the hands of the clergy, the feeling that these resources are wasted will easily breed an anti-clerical spirit; in any communities where religion is vigorous, its very activity may be irritating and offensive, and call forth a reaction that is consciously anti-Christian in protest against misdirected energy. Agnosticism may be positively hostile, or on the other hand it may be warmly sympathetic with definite religious beliefs, and admire the faith in which it does not participate. Mr Herbert Spencer's opinion as to the impossibility of attaining to religious knowledge appears to have remained unmodified, but he had latterly less sense of antagonism to those who cherished beliefs which seemed to him to be vain. "I have come more

[1] F. Harrison, *op. cit.* 16.

and more to look calmly on forms of religious belief, to which I had, in earlier days, a pronounced aversion....Largely, however, if not chiefly, this change of feeling towards religious creeds and their sustaining institutions has resulted from a deepening conviction that the sphere occupied by them can never become an unfilled sphere, but that there must continue to arise afresh the great questions concerning ourselves and surrounding things ; and that, if not positive answers, then moods of consciousness standing in place of positive answers, must ever remain....Religious creeds, which in one way or another occupy the sphere that material interpretation seeks to occupy and fails the more the more it seeks, I have come to regard with a sympathy based on community of need ; feeling that dissent from them results from inability to accept the solutions offered, joined with the wish that solutions could be found[1]." When it is once recognised that religion takes a permanent place in human thought, and has a practical bearing on human life, the phenomena of religion can no longer be regarded as merely futile ; they become a legitimate object of human study. The fact that some natures are insensible to this influence[2] is not a justification for waiving aside the religious consciousness, and its reports on the relations between God and man : if we do not discard religion altogether, we can go a step further and consider the points of view from which the contents of the religious consciousness may be most fruitfully studied.

III.

1. Students of the religious consciousness are inclined at first sight to assume that the phenomena are on the same plane as all other humanities, and that they may be satisfactorily investigated from the same standpoint and by the same methods. Religious opinion has found expression in theological doctrine ; religious feeling in sacred art. The canons of criticism which can be applied to other branches

---

[1] H. Spencer, *Autobiography*, II. 468, 471.
[2] W. James, *Varieties of Religious Experience*, 92.

The Christian Standpoint

of literature, the scrutiny which can be brought to bear on the history of other institutions, are ready at hand for examining the origin and character and growth of religion; it is treated as a body of opinions, on which we bring our minds to bear. There are, however, many men who are unable to adopt this mental attitude; to them religion is not an affair of other people's opinions, but a personal conviction of their own. They are unable to maintain an attitude of academic aloofness, but can only view the religious beliefs and practices of others in the light of their own convictions. The difference in the standpoint of one man, who can take a dispassionate survey of religion from the outside, and of another, to whom certain religious beliefs are a matter of personal conviction, is fundamental; though the two distinct habits of thinking may be blended in various proportions. It is not easy for anyone, however much he tries, to lay aside all personal predilection and look at disputed questions with a single-minded intellectual interest. Antipathies may distort the powers of observation, and sympathy will certainly affect the manner of expression and judgement; the decisions of the critical faculty may be obscured by a cloud of sentiment. Still the two ways of looking at religion are really distinct; and typical examples of each habit of mind may be quoted as illustrations which serve to mark the contrast. The religious controversies of bygone days are not to be lightly dismissed as mere pedantries and futilities; for these discussions have an abiding interest in so far as they bring into clear relief the particular point of view which was adopted by the disputants on either side. In this way the pamphlet literature of the end of the seventeenth and beginning of the eighteenth century marks an important epoch. The claim of the individual reason to pronounce definitely on all points of religion was strongly asserted by the Deists, and seems to have been very generally accepted by their opponents; in the tracts of that time we may find an excellent field for studying the characteristic features of this habit of mind,— as it was, and as it survives.

Rationalism in religious thought was not by any means

an isolated phenomenon in the seventeenth century, for it was closely connected with the current philosophy. It is sufficient for our purpose, however, to regard it as a product which emerged from the exigencies of theological polemics. The great struggle of the sixteenth century resulted in placing the Bible and the Church in apparent opposition, as the supreme depositaries of Divine truth on earth. Chillingworth, to whom the question was one of deep personal interest, endeavoured to define the position he finally reached in opposition to the Romanists. He held that no living infallible guide was needed, since Universal Tradition embodied in the Bible was the basis of Christian belief, and this could be sufficiently interpreted by the human understanding. He insisted that the Scripture was the only rule to decide all controversies among Christians[1], yet subject to the proviso that questions touching Scripture are not decidable by Scripture[2]. All questions as to canonicity could be settled by Universal Tradition, but private judgement was called for, since there was in fact no reliable 'traditive interpretation.' "We are ready to receive both Scripture and the sense of Scripture upon Universal Tradition," but not on the authority of the Roman Church, which had in many ways departed from Universal Tradition. Authoritative interpretation was unnecessary since private judgement was capable of applying the rule of faith which is given in Scripture. "Speaking truly and properly, Scripture is not a judge, nor cannot be, but only a sufficient rule for those to judge by that believe it to be the Word of God....what they are to believe and what they are not to believe. I say sufficiently perfect, and sufficiently intelligible in things necessary, to all that have understanding, whether they be learned or unlearned. And my reason hereof is convincing and demonstrative, because nothing is necessary to be believed but what is plainly

---

[1] He guarded himself against the misunderstanding that by Scripture all things absolutely may be proved which are to be believed, for it can never be proved to a gainsayer that there is a God, or that the book called Scripture is the word of God. *The Religion of Protestants a Safe Way to Salvation*, ch. II. pt. i. sec. 8.

[2] *Ibid.* ch. II. pt. i. sec. 27.

The Christian Standpoint

revealed[1]." Where the interpretation of Scripture was a matter of serious difficulty the precise interpretation could not be of much importance as a matter of faith. He thus insisted that the use of their own understanding by private individuals was a sufficient practical guide in religion, but he lays down somewhat narrow limits within which it may wisely operate. With the rise of Puritanism, however, the claim to put forward private interpretation ran riot; those who believed in their own personal inspiration could not submit their deliverances to any restraint, and the vagaries among different religious teachers brought this liberty of prophesying into contempt. Sober-minded men were inclined to look to reason, rather than alleged inspiration, as the guide to be followed in the pursuit of religious truth. The disordered imagination should be restrained[2] that the light of reason might assert its sway; this would give us, as they believed, a firm grasp on such fundamental principles as the existence of a God and the immortality of the soul. Disgust at the narrowness and fanaticism of the disputing sects rendered men eager to place religious controversy on a plane of thought where it could be treated calmly and dispassionately, so that there might be some hope of ultimate agreement. This was the line which was taken by the rational theologians of the seventeenth century, and especially by Tillotson, who was, both from his position and his oratorical gifts, the most striking representative of the school; it is in his sermons that the new habit of thought reaches its clearest expression. He appeals to reason not only as the interpreter of Christian teaching, but as its very basis. "All religion is founded in right Notions of God, and of His Perfections; insomuch that Divine Revelation itself does suppose these for its foundations, and can signify nothing to us unless these be first known and believed.... So that the principles of Natural Religion are the foundation of that which is revealed[3]."

"Religion begins in the Understanding, and from thence

[1] *Ibid.* chap. II. pt. i. sec. 104.
[2] More, *Enthusiasmus Triumphatus,* Cure from Temperance.
[3] Tillotson, Sermon XLI, in *Works* (1752), I. 389.

descends upon the heart and life....It is the issue and result of the best Wisdom and Knowledge, and descends from above, from the Giver of every good and perfect Gift, even from the Father of Lights[1]." "All that can be done is to set the thing before men, and to offer it to their choice; and if men's natural desire of wisdom and knowledge and happiness will not persuade them to be religious, 'tis in vain to use arguments[2]." The position which was thus taken by the Archbishop of Canterbury was singularly like that adopted by Locke in his *Reasonableness of Christianity*. He recognised Revelation, not as giving us truths of a different kind from those that could be apprehended by Reason, but as discovering truths which reason was able to confirm[3]. The untutored human intelligence was the only faculty that was needed to apprehend the leading principles of Christianity. He took the written word of God to be "a collection of writings, designed by God, for the instruction of the illiterate bulk of mankind in the way of salvation; and therefore generally and in necessary points to be understood in the plain, direct meaning of the words and phrases, such as they may be supposed to have had in the mouth of speakers who used them according to the language of that time and country wherein they lived[4]." A prominent apologist carried the reliance on men still farther. "Let what is written in all the books of the New Testament be tried by that which is the Touchstone of all Religions, I mean that Religion of Nature and Reason which God has written in the hearts of every one of us from the first Creation; and if it varies from it in any one particular, if it prescribes any one thing, which may in the minutest circumstances thereof be contrary to Righteousness, I will then acknowledge this to be an argument against us strong enough to overthrow the whole Cause[5]." It would not be easy to find a more explicit statement as to the faculty by which religious truth is to be judged or the criterion by which

---

[1] Sermon XXX. *Works*, I. 272.
[2] Sermon I. *Works*, I. 27.
[3] Locke, *Reasonableness of Christianity*, in *Works*, VI. 145.
[4] *Ibid.* 5.
[5] H. Prideaux, *Letter to the Deists* (1697), 59.

its truth is to be appraised. Individual intelligence is apparently accepted as the sole authority in interpreting the sacred writings and building up a body of theological doctrine; and the claim is put forth to survey the whole field of religious phenomena and appraise the different systems rightly.

While we may take Tillotson as a typical representative of the habit of thought which was dominant in the period from 1689 to 1750, we must remember that there were also men who were wholly dissatisfied with this point of view; they regarded his treatment of the subject as quite inadequate. Those readers to whom such a book as Law's *Serious Call to a Devout Life* appealed, could not but be dissatisfied with the placid periods of the celebrated Archbishop. In the official proclamation of Christian truth, there was a lack of earnestness which could be contrasted with the personal self-sacrifice of the Non-jurors and the fervour of such men as Whitfield and Wesley. It can hardly be a matter of surprise that strong feeling was roused by the superficial fashion in which the "letter-learned clergymen" dealt with supreme realities. To men of intense religious conviction, the famous Archbishop seemed to have been neglectful of his trust in approximating so closely to the position of the Deists, and in minimising, if he did not wholly neglect, the influence of Divine grace in the heart. The man who had regarded natural reason as a sufficient guide to the interpretation of revealed truth seemed to them guilty of a great betrayal[1]. Christianity, as they knew it, was a practical power in the heart and mind, and those who took the position of looking at it from outside seemed to be incompetent to deal with it at all.

2. The rational theologians would have indignantly disclaimed the charge that they neglected the practical working of religious belief; indeed Tillotson laid stress on the efficacy, as regards moral conduct, of the prudential arguments which may be drawn from the belief in a future state[2]. He made

[1] Seward, *Journal of a Voyage from Savannah to Philadelphia*, 62, 71.
[2] Sermon CXI, in *Works*, III. 45.

a remarkable pronouncement as to the utility of religion. "What is religion good for, but to reform the manners and dispositions of man, to restrain human nature from violence and cruelty, from falsehood and treachery, from sedition and rebellion?[1]" This school would have contended that by relying on reason they could survey a wider field, and get more forcible testimony in regard to the effectiveness of religious belief as a factor in conduct, than they would if they confined their argument to Christian lands and Christian belief. Whichcote's influence at Cambridge seems to have been largely due to the freshness which he infused into his discourses by working at this vein. He broke away from the academic pulpit tradition, and did not confine himself to elaborating his thesis from stores of Biblical and Patristic learning; he dealt with the living issues which had been raised by the teaching of Hobbes[2], and treated religion as the safeguard of morality. He valued it as a practical power for righteousness in the hearts of men, even when they professed somewhat different creeds. As Whichcote says in one of his aphorisms, "Religion has different denominations and names from different actions and circumstances, but it is one thing, viz.: universal righteousness; accordingly it had place at all times before the Law of Moses and under it, and since[3]."

The rational theologian could also hope that by this wide survey he would obtain a means of distinguishing what was essential in religion from its trivial adjuncts. Much of the discord appeared to have arisen from the way in which one party or another had treated trivialities of ceremonial, or subtleties of theological doctrine, as points of fundamental importance. The rational theologians preferred comeliness and good order in divine worship; but this was to them a matter of expediency and common sense, not in any way of principle; and on similar grounds they were indifferent in regard to many questions which had been debated between Calvinists and Arminians. They looked round on the world

[1] Sermon on 5 Nov. 1678 before the House of Commons. *Works*, I. 162.
[2] Earl of Shaftesbury, *Preface* to Whichcote's *Works* (1749), III. v.
[3] *Aphorisms*, 957.

at large, and saw that there were three great religions which had a powerful and elevating influence on conduct. They felt that the essential element in religion was to be found in principles which were common to Judaism, Mohammedanism, and Christianity alike; and that this essential element had never been entirely lacking in any age. According to this common-sense standard, the doctrines of the immortality of the soul and of the existence of God were treated as the necessary principles of religion, without which it failed to exercise an influence on conduct. The orthodox rationalist held that the adjuncts to this essential belief, which were given in the Christian religion, set forward a better morality, and by the clearness of the teaching, added to its force. But these were points which they found it hard to establish from the position they had adopted. The Deists frankly regarded revealed religion as surplusage; they might be ready to agree that revealed religion was analogous to natural theology, but this was not convincing. The superiority of Christian doctrine and practice was not so great as to render it apparent that it had any special claim to a divine origin[1]. Nor was the historical argument convincing; the ordinary understanding, applying common-sense standards, was inclined to explain away all the particular phenomena of prophecy and miracles as due to coincidence or 'enthusiasm.' The rational theologians had set out to rescue Christianity from the quarrels and follies of fanatics; but the tendency of the movement had been to discard all that was distinctively Christian. The suspicions of Whitfield and the Methodists were justified; the individual intelligence, working from the grounds of common sense and ordinary experience, appeared incompetent either to do justice to the present power of the Christian religion, or to vindicate the accepted record of its origin.

The inherent tendencies of rational theology had taken many years to show their true character; but as the movement ran its course, the views which were involved in the principles of the pioneers came into clear light. When the Bible is

[1] Earl of Shaftesbury, *Preface* to Whichcote's *Works* (1749), III. ii.

studied in the same fashion as other literature, and the history of the Church is treated as precisely similar to that of other institutions, there is a practical refusal to draw any marked distinction between various expressions of human aspiration and hope, or to regard the sacred books and the Christian society as in a special sense Divine. If religious literature and life are dealt with as part of the phenomena of human culture, in which we take an outside interest and on which we pass our judgements from the common-sense standards of expediency and probability, the claims of Christianity to stand on a level of its own are discountenanced in advance. And hence men of deep religious conviction cannot recognise that humane learning affords a suitable position from which to pronounce on the validity of their faith; to them it is not a mere opinion, and they cannot accept the 'theoretical' decision of those who are content to weigh one opinion against another. The practical force of Christianity is something they feel in their own consciousness, not a mere factor in human morality which they endeavour to analyse and appraise. In their minds it is inseparably linked with devotion to Christ; they have no confidence in a habit of mind which admires Christian morality but is content to dispense with its conscious basis. Ordinary intelligence and common-sense estimates are inclined to look favourably on religions in general, but to hesitate about the truth of any one in particular; and the man of deep convictions cannot regard this tribunal as authoritative; he claims at least to be judged by his peers.

3. In thus refusing to accept the arbitrament of ordinary human intelligence and appealing to some other tribunal, the man of religious convictions appears to put himself entirely in the wrong. To reject the voice of Reason, as expressed in the common sense of his fellow-men, seems to be a piece of arrogance that is both offensive and ridiculous. It implies a claim to have special access to sources of truth, while it pronounces human reason inadequate in a sphere in which it is habitually exercised. Still this refusal is inevitable; religious conviction has a logical character of its own; it is a personal

matter, and cannot be brought into direct line with the data on which common-sense intelligence is fitted to work. The understanding usually plays the part of the bystander who looks on and gives an impersonal decision on the phenomena before him; their characteristics and qualities and relations are presented to him, and apart from the exertion of attention, he only gives a sort of passive assent. But in personal convictions there is a definite exercise of will power[1], and the decision is the man's very own. These truths are not things that come to us ready made[2]. There is an element of personal approval in 'consenting unto the law that it is good,' and even of appropriation in deciding that it is good, as a rule for him. This personal exercise of the will is involved in all the acts of the religious life; we find it in the devotion of the Psalmist, "Thou art my God, early will I seek Thee"; and again in the faith of St Thomas when he cried, "My Lord and my God." Such convictions are fundamentally different from the religious opinions on which we pass 'theoretic' judgements, as outside observers; the peculiar force which they have for the individual mind must be taken into account by anyone who pretends to pronounce what is essential and unessential in religion. Common sense is content to consider what a man holds, and to compare his beliefs with those of other people; but from the point of view of the man of strong convictions, the important question is not *what* a man holds, but *how* he holds it,—Is it a personal thing that is ingrained in his own will? Has he got religion, or rather has religion got him? From this point of view, the ultimate decision as to the validity of religious beliefs cannot rest with Reason, or be decided by any criterion which the Understanding applies to them; the Religious Consciousness is not content to provide data for intelligence to discuss, but claims to be supreme in the interpretation of these data, and in declaring the relations of man to the Ultimate Power. The corporate religious consciousness has claimed to be independent of civil authority at sundry times and in diverse

[1] Ollé Laprune, *De la certitude morale*, 65.
[2] La Berthonnière, *Essais de philosophie religieuse*, 119; also 47.

manners; not only in the contest about Investitures, but in the recent demand of the United Free Church of Scotland for scope for self-development. In a similar spirit the personal religious consciousness refuses to submit to any intellectual authority outside itself.

IV.

1. The distinction between the points of view of those who treat religion as a body of opinions, and of those to whom it is a matter of conviction, is fundamental. The process of passing from one phase of thought to the other may be spoken of as the awakening of the religious consciousness; and some of those who have undergone this change gradually, and as the result of a long period of hesitation and unrest, have set themselves to reflect on and to record the course of their own inner experience. An admirable delineation is to be found in Pascal's *Thoughts*. No mere intellectual arguments sufficed to change the current of his moral life; for the arguments on each side were ineffective. "All the principles of sceptics, stoics, atheists, etc. are true, but their conclusions are false, because the opposite principles are also true[1]." "It is incomprehensible that there should be a God, and incomprehensible that there should not be; that there should be a soul in the body, and that we should have no soul; that the world should have been created, and that it should not[2]." There was as he insisted a deeper source of certainty in our nature. "We know truth, not only by the reason, but also by the heart, and it is from this last that we learn first principles; and reason, which has nothing to do with it, tries in vain to combat them[3]." He was distracted by the contradictions which he felt in the depths of his own consciousness[4]. "Let

[1] Pascal, *Thoughts*, translated by Kegan Paul, 111.
[2] Pascal, *op. cit.* 205.
[3] *Ibid.* 102.
[4] He felt the contradictions which Huxley observed and described, "Men are very queer animals, a mixture of horse nervousness, ass stubbornness, and camel malice— with an angel bobbing about unexpectedly like the apple in the posset, and when they can do exactly as they please they are very hard to drive." *Life and Letters*, II. 428.

man love himself, because he has a nature capable of good, but let him not therefore love the vileness that exists in that nature. Let him despise himself, because this capacity is void, but let him not therefore despise his natural capacity. Let him hate himself, let him love himself; he has in himself the power of knowing the truth and being happy, and yet has found no truth either permanent or satisfactory[1]." He had himself attempted to drown the thoughts of death, sorrow, ignorance, and all the miseries of life[2], and forget them in the enjoyments of life ; but it was only as he wearied of these that he began to find the real solution he sought. "The weariness which is man's most sensible evil is in some measure his greatest good, because more than anything else it contributes to make him seek his true healing......Man is weary of all things and seeks a multitude of occupations, only because he has the idea of a lost happiness. And not finding this in himself, he seeks it vainly in external things, without being able to content himself, because it is neither in us, nor in the creature, but in God alone[3]." "The God of Christians is a God who makes the soul perceive that He is her only good, her only rest is in Him, her only joy in loving Him. ......The knowledge of God without that of our wretchedness creates pride, the knowledge of our wretchedness without God creates despair. The knowledge of Jesus Christ is the middle way, because in Him we find both God and our own wretchedness[4]." The divine power which reconciled the contradictions within his own nature was to him the supreme reality; he was convinced of its truth. The Christian religion teaches the righteous that "it lifts them even to a participation of the

---

[1] Pascal, *op. cit.* 48.

[2] "When I see the blindness and the misery of man, when I survey the whole dumb Universe, and man without light, left to himself and lost as it were in this corner of the Universe, not knowing who has placed him here, what he has come to do, what will become of him when he dies, and incapable of any knowledge whatever, I fall into terror like that of a man who, having been carried in his sleep to an island desert and terrible, should awake ignorant of his whereabouts and with no means of escape ; and therefore I wonder how those in so miserable a state do not fall into despair." *Ibid.* 183.

[3] *Ibid.* 39.

[4] *Ibid.* 93.

divine nature; that in this exalted state they still bear within them the fountain of all corruption, which renders them during their whole life subject to error and misery, to death and sin, and at the same time it proclaims to the most wicked that they can receive the grace of their Redeemer. Thus making those tremble whom it justifies, and consoling those whom it condemns, religion so justly tempers fear with hope by means of that double capacity of grace and of sin which is common to all, that it abases infinitely more than reason alone, yet without despair, and exalts infinitely higher than natural pride, yet without puffing up, hereby proving that alone being exempt from error and vice, it alone has the office of instructing and reforming men. Who then can withhold credence and adoration to so divine a light? For it is clearer than day that we feel within ourselves indelible characters of goodness; and it is equally clear that we experience every hour the effects of our deplorable condition. This chaos then, this monstrous confusion, does but proclaim the truth of those two states, with a voice so powerful that it cannot be resisted[1]." The path which he recommended others to follow if they would attain to his conviction was that which he had himself pursued: "Labour to convince yourself," he says, "not by increase of the proofs of God, but by the diminution of your passions[2]."

The gradual awakening of religious consciousness can be traced even more clearly in the record of his inner life which has been left us by Maine de Biran. A man of keen sensibility, with a passionate interest in the analysis of mental phenomena, he continued to pursue the philosophical studies to which he had devoted himself at Bergerac, when he was called to take a prominent part in public affairs at Paris after the fall of Napoleon. He was in touch with the most eminent philosophical thinkers of his day, and was well acquainted with modern philosophy, but he possessed a singular independence. As the "philosopher of inner experience[3]," the growth of his doctrine is closely connected with the changes

---

[1] *Ibid.* 184.   [2] *Ibid.* 99.
[3] Albert Lang, *Maine de Biran und die neuere Philosophie* (1901), 3.

of personal conviction, as revealed in his *journal intime*[1]. Starting from the sensationalism of Condillac he gradually came to lay more stress on the active element in consciousness, and, as years passed on, to recognise an external source of moral vigour. "In the psychological aspect, or as regards cognition, the soul draws all from itself, or from the Ego, by reflection; but in the moral aspect, as regards the perfection to be hoped for, the good to be obtained, or the object in life to be aimed at, the soul draws all and receives all from without—not from the external world and sensations, but from the purely intellectual world above, of which God is the centre[2]." To him Christianity appealed rather as an intellectual satisfaction than as a means of redemption from evil. The sense of a want of stability of life, and the impossibility of sustained happiness weighed upon him; this was the starting-point of his reflections[3], and it occupied his mind with sombre thoughts in 1815, when he seems for the first time[4] to have turned consciously towards God. "It is too long to go on drifting with the whirl of events and opinions, with the never ceasing flux of changes without and within, and all that passes like a shadow. There is need to-day to attach oneself to the Only Being that remains Unchangeable, Who is the true source of consolation in the present and of hope for the future[5]." And his mind took an increasingly firm hold on this fixed point. "I was thinking yesterday," he writes in 1820, "as I was driving through the streets, that there are three very different kinds of temperament in the intellect or soul. The first, that of nearly everyone, consists in living exclusively in the world of phenomena, and taking them for realities; hence there is inconstancy, loathing, and perpetual unrest. The second is that of the men who reflect, and seek patiently for truth in themselves or in nature, by separating appearances from realities; but since they do not find a firm basis

[1] E. Naville, *Maine de Biran, sa vie et ses pensées*, 117—419.
[2] *Ibid.* 283. 19 Sept. 1818.
[3] 27 May, 1794. *Ibid.* 120. See also his remarks on Stoicism, 30 Sept. 1817, p. 234.
[4] Nicolas, *Étude sur Maine de Biran*, 52.
[5] 16 April, 1815, p. 178. See also 17 May, 1815, p. 185.

from this truth they despair and fall into scepticism. Lastly, there is a third group of those who are illumined by the unique and unchanging light which religion affords. None but those have found a firm support; they have courage in their convictions[1]."

2. The awakening of the religious consciousness as it has been thus portrayed is gradual, and the subject of conscious cultivation; but some of its aspects are brought into clearer view by sudden conversions, such as occurred in numbers in connexion with the preaching of Whitfield and the Wesleys. The sudden realisation of personal guilt may be called forth by the most trivial occasions; John Bunyan was conscience-stricken at his guilt in playing tipcat on Elstow Green one Sunday; but the import of such awakening is set before us for all time in the story of the Fall. We read there how man came to see his conduct, not in connexion with the motives and excuses which have urged him, but retrospectively, and dispassionately, as if from the standpoint of the Omniscient Creator. Each human act is part of an indefinite chain of cause and effect; our idle words, our careless follies may work far-reaching mischief of which we are wholly unconscious. We cannot pursue these indefinite consequences; but they come clearly into view when we sum them up in the thoughts of the Infinite God, Who sees all things, and looks at our acts in the light of His judgement upon them. Through the sense of guilt, man becomes conscious that he is part of a divine order, which he had neglected; the violation of this order by his own acts presses on him the suggestion of an existence and of relationships which he had ignored. His sense of guilt becomes the object of reflection, and his cognitive faculties are brought to bear upon it and elicit what is implied in it. The facts of the case are clear; the moral law, the distinction of right and wrong, was known to him; he accepts it and approves it, and lays it down as valid for all intelligences; and since in spite of this he is responsible for a breach of it and blames himself for his fault in failing to keep it, he recognises his own freedom.

[1] 10 June, 1820, p. 328. See also 8 Dec. 1821, p. 361.

There is more too that he feels to be immediately implied in the existence of this law, in all its dignity; he cannot account for it, in its universality and necessity, without falling back on the thought of God as the ruler from Whom it emanates, and of an unseen world in which its decisions are realised. Personal liberty, the existence of a God, and of a future life, are inferences which follow as immediate convictions from the recognition of the validity of Moral Law. The moral order, just as much as the physical order, comes to be thought of as a coherent system in which man is placed.

It is thus that by turning within himself, man becomes conscious of his own nature in all its complexity, and reaches a standpoint from which he apprehends his relation to other existences. The illustrations have been taken from modern times and from the Christian religion, but the experience of remorse and guilt is not by any means confined to those who have been instructed in the Christian religion. The tragedy of existence, the inner contradictions in human nature, the sense of a violated order and of guilt are found in all but the lowest forms of faith. The unique character of Christianity comes out in the solution it offers; in the power with which it declares forgiveness, and the restoration of man, so that he shall be reconciled to himself and to God. It shows him that by penetrating further along the path he may find, within himself, not only remorse and anguish, but the path of relief and rest. It declares to him that he need not look for his happiness in self-detachment, nor in externals, nor in enjoyment of any kind; "it is neither without us, nor within us, but in God, and thus both without and within[1]."

V.

1. The special feature of Christianity is in the sense it affords of reconciliation; and this term itself suggests the most fruitful method of procedure, if we wish to investigate the

---

[1] Pascal, *op. cit.* 49.

contents of this most highly developed form of the religious consciousness. The awakening, to which allusion has already been made, brings out a sense of a double consciousness—such as is illustrated by Clough's *Dipsychus*, or by Stevenson's story of *Dr Jekyll and Mr Hyde*. In these cases the two sides were wholly alien and repugnant to each other; and in the religious consciousness generally, they remain opposed to one another; it is only by consciously ignoring one or the other that satisfaction seems attainable. The claim of Christianity is that it affords a real method of reconciliation, so as to bring the two sides into harmony without any compromise, and without suppressing either one or the other.

We cannot get a clear view of this reconciliation by taking a single instance of religious experience, and setting our cognitive faculty to reflect on it and analyse it. We may see that the sense of guilt implies in some vague outline the ideas of a broken moral order and an offended God; but such logical inference[1] does not give us any assurance as to the reality of existences corresponding to these ideas. The exertion of the cognitive faculty in the search for truth leads us to an *impasse*. The only existence we know as real is our own, and it is by drawing upon ourselves that we give reality to our ideas. After all, in considering religion we have not to do merely with the cognitive faculty but also with the will: the gist of the Christian life consists in the reconciliation of the human will with the Divine—the control of the human will as it expresses itself in action; and in this mode of statement the severance between our subjective ideas and the real existences outside us does not arise as a sharply set opposition which we cannot satisfactorily bridge. The human will is conscious of itself as an activity; it knows itself not only as existing[2], but as doing; there is certitude in its feeling of its own doings[3]; and this certitude is extended in varying degrees to other existences. In his moral conscious-

---

[1] La Berthonnière, *op. cit.* 77 n.
[2] *Cogito ergo sum.*
[3] 'Feeling' is not used here of mere emotion, but for self-conscious activity.

ness man feels that he accepts some aim, or frames it for himself, and strives to realise it. He is aware of obstacles which balk him, and which are real to him, just because they hamper and thwart him; he is certain of the existence of an external world[1]. He may be aware, too, of a Power which cooperates with him, not as an external agent, but as a spiritual influence; which convicts him of evil when his aims are sordid and self-seeking, but which strengthens his purpose when it is something that he lays down for all intelligences as well as for himself. He may recognise a "not ourselves that makes for righteousness[2]" in the world, because he is certain of a Power that makes for righteousness in his own internal life.

Devout literature, in which various phases of the Christian consciousness are set forth fully and explicitly, testifies to two points on which it is worth while to lay stress—on the one hand the certainty of reconciliation as attainable, on the other the sense of frequent failure to maintain this harmonious relationship. There is a process of reconciliation going on, but a process that is not fully accomplished. The attempt to universalise one's action may be occasional, and it may become habitual. As the moral law is thought of as a law for all intelligences, so when I act rightly, I act from the standpoint of the Universal Will; but still it is my action, there is no force that overmasters the personal will, but rather a personal desire to come into accord with the Universal Will —to think and to do what is pleasing to God. "We have to choose whether we shall make ourselves the end of our action and the centre on which it turns, or whether we shall seek an aim and a centre outside and above ourselves. Every generous action, every effort to get out of ourselves, however rudimentary it may be, is an acceptance and affirmation of God, and at the same time a step towards the light[3]." And in this universalising of his will and activities there is no loss of his individual personal life; it is not merged in the

---

[1] Maine de Biran, *Essai sur les fondements de la Psychologie* in *Œuvres inédites*, I. 249.

[2] M. Arnold, *Literature and Dogma*, 53.

[3] La Berthonnière, *op. cit.* 135.

Universal with which it is reconciled. As a Lutheran divine urges, man is distinct from God, both in his sin and in the process of reconciliation. "The separation between God and fallen man, however deep and great it may be, does not annul for the Christian consciousness the fact—indissolubly bound up with its very existence—that even this fallen man is still God's offspring and created for God; that he, in this condition of separation from God, retains the capability of receiving influences from God, so that God can come to be for him, even as he was once and in himself for God....However great the change may be which takes place by the Christianising of the natural man, to whatever extent this effect is produced by the objective factors of the spiritual world, it is still human life and human thought, into which the Divine Life and the Divine Thought enter....It is likewise surely a fact, that the man who has become Christian is not sensible of being thereby estranged from the human nature of which he was before conscious as his own; on the contrary, he feels that by a change in himself he has passed through the evil tendencies of his human nature to its truth, and become consciously what in reality he always was and was intended to be[1]." By Christian experience there arises "a change in the centre of gravity of personality[2]," but this change takes place within the sphere of self-conscious activity; there is certitude both as regards the personal will, and about the process of coming into harmony with the Universal Will. "We have the faculty of knowing God. But God is a living reality; and the knowledge that we have of Him, if it is really a knowledge of God and not an abstraction put in His place, lives in us. We acquire the knowledge of God as we acquire the knowledge of a friend by living his life, by penetrating into his intimacy, by becoming himself. To know God it is necessary to resemble Him, and we know Him in the degree in which we resemble Him. When we make progress in the knowledge of God it is time to say that God grows in us....When He is in us, it is not we who fashion Him, but He who fashions us.

[1] F. H. R. Frank, *System der christlichen Gewissheit*, I. 78 (Clark's Theological Library), 92.   [2] *Ibid.* (Clark), 108.

But in our life of personal freedom He does not fashion us or grow in us, except in so far as we consent[1]." The Christian consciousness is not satisfied to frame demonstrations of the existence of a God Whose character is unknown, it seeks to penetrate into the nature of the God Who has brought Himself into relationship with a human personality.

2. In the same way the question as to how to demonstrate the existence of other intelligences ceases to be of much interest when we are concerned to know, as a practical thing, what attitude we ourselves take towards them in our inner consciousness. How are our activities directed with regard to them? Are we satisfied with the mere egoism of the man "who supposes himself to be a centre in which everything is united and to which it returns? He poses his individuality as the absolute on which everything depends....He professes that he only exists by himself and suffices for himself, and thus he asserts himself at the expense of everything else. One may say that he treats himself as constituting the Universe, and wills that everything should be his and exist for him[2]." Other intelligences are for us what we consent that they shall become; we may try to ignore them, or we may recognise them as partakers, like ourselves, in the power of laying down law universal.

From this point of view the world does not appear merely as a system of phenomena, or as things of which one is the centre. It appears as a system of beings, each of which is in a manner a centre, although all are interconnected together. There is a complete change of perspective[3]; "and the existence of other intelligences is no longer felt as a limitation set on ourselves, but as a sphere where we recognise privileges and responsibilities that add completeness to personal life. These moral relationships are congruent with the suggestions which we get from reflecting on the phenomena of observed and recorded experience, but they have their certitude in the manner in which they are felt, and they come into clear light as the process of Christianising the personal will goes on

---

[1] La Berthonnière, *op. cit.* 79.   [2] *Ibid.* 92.   [3] *Ibid.* 96.

increasingly. We do not begin by knowing God, or by knowing ourselves and other existences as they are. It is to this we tend, and it is to this that we ought to look as a goal[1]."

3. Personal activity is known with the fullest measure of certitude within the sphere of self-consciousness, but it is not confined to the inner life; it is externalised; and the Christian consciousness expresses itself in the world of phenomena. Faith without works is dead; and the whole history of the Christian Church is the story of the struggle of the faith once delivered to the saints, not merely to maintain itself in pious hearts but to show itself to the world in the lives and utterances of men. However chequered its success may have been, its effectiveness in holding up new ideals, in moulding individual lives, and modifying human institutions cannot be explained away. In the face of all the scandals which were the disgrace of Italy in the fifteenth century, and in opposition to the glorification of humanism which was then current, Savonarola could still point to a living witness of Divine Power present among men. He figured the march of this Power on earth as the progress of Christ through all the world, crowned with thorns, yet resplendent in the light of the Divine Trinity, and holding forth in one hand the cross and instruments of His passion, and in the other the Scriptures which record the divine message to the world[2]. The car, on which He was borne, was drawn in triumph by the apostles and heralded by the prophets, and enriched by the martyrs and doctors and saints of all ages, while multitudes of mankind followed in its wake and marked how opposition of every kind was crushed as it advanced. For the evidence of this Power he referred not to the events of a distant past, but to the familiar phenomena of his own day. "Since things which are present before our eyes are more trustworthy and reliable than bygone occurrences, we will put in the forefront those arguments for the Christian faith which rest on the deeds constantly seen in the lives of Christians in the Church[3]"—not of the unworthy, but of real Christians.

---

[1] *Ibid.* 144.   [2] *Il trionfo della croce*, I. 2.
[3] *Il trionfo*, II. *proem.*

He pointed to the devotion of souls who desired "to turn to God, to submit themselves to Him and to be made like Him, and to seek to enter into His blessedness[1]," and to the lives of men, women, and children, in all ranks of society, inspired by Christian hope and charity[2]. And since his day, there has been abundance of such evidence in the extension of the area of Christendom, and from time to time in reinvigorated intensity of conviction. This was apparent not only in Luther and Calvin, but in the heroes of the counter-Reformation,— or in such diverse movements as the rise of Methodism and the organising of the Salvation Army. The vigorous power of Christian belief, among the social conditions of modern times and in spite of widespread indifference, is patent and obvious. Like any other phenomenon it demands an explanation, and no explanation can be adequate unless it takes account of the distinctive features of the system under consideration.

Christian activity, as the expression of Christian belief, has much in common with other forms of religious life, but its distinctive traits may be more easily brought out by comparing it with the Judaism from which it sprang. The Christian to whom the Gospel message is a reality will often wish to bear testimony to the truth which has taken hold of him. It was so among the first disciples, and the same tendency reappears in modern Revivals. But this is not a mere expression of personal enthusiasm; missionary effort is characteristic of the Christian community; there has been from the earliest days organised effort to diffuse the Christian faith throughout the world, and to plant the Church in every region. And this involves a conception of a divine society upon earth to which the Jews were strangers. So long as the divinely constituted realm was conceived of as territorial, and lying round one special centre, there could be little expectation that the Gentiles would benefit, except indirectly, by a manifestation of divine triumph[3]. The new idea of the kingdom of God as a spiritual realm in which men of all races

[1] *Ibid.* II. 1.   [2] *Ibid.* II. 7.
[3] Isaiah lx.

and countries could participate fully, underlay the possibility of such missionary effort as that of St Paul. The perpetuation of the sense of a duty not merely to maintain the light, but to diffuse it, is characteristic of Christianity in the present as in many past ages, and we can trace it back to the definite charge which was given by our Lord to the Apostles.

We may also find that while there is much in common between Christian services and the utterances of Jewish devotion, there is one service which is distinctively Christian. In the Holy Communion a perpetual memorial of the Sacrifice of our Lord has been maintained in all ages of the Church; it testifies to the unchanging belief that it is in union with Christ that reconciliation with God has become possible for us. And thus we can trace this spiritual force, persisting as a living power through many ages, till we find its origin in an unique personality. It is in the work and words of our Lord Himself that the Christian consciousness has its most perfect expression in the world of space and time.

4. Before this unique personality we stand on the threshold of the very Holy of Holies; we can but recall what He has told us of Himself as it has been traditionally recorded. There was in Him a double consciousness; on the one hand the understanding of all human frailty, the comprehension of all human sin, the weakness of a human body, the limitations, as it seems, of human cognition,—and all these mark Him as the Son of Man. Yet there was also a sense of perfect harmony with the Universal Will, so that He found His true refreshment in communing with God, His ambition in seeking to please Him; it was in God that the true centre of His earthly life lay. And the conscious reconciliation, which obtained in His own person, was the inspiration of an active life: He sought by word and deed to set forth the truth that lived in Him so that it might possess the lives of all other men, and that they too might become, consciously and completely, the sons of God. In His earthly sojourning and passion He sounded the depths of degradation; in His resurrection He manifested the Divine Power to break the bonds

The Christian Standpoint

of sin and death. By this declaration of the actual reconciliation of God and man in His own personality He opened to all men the hope of becoming what He is. By training His Apostles, by enduing them with His Spirit, by instituting rites which have been perpetuated in the Church, He gave the objective means through which the life that dwelt in Him might be transfused to all future generations. This was His effort; this was what He claimed to do: and a great multitude whom no man can number have set to their seals that He is true, since they have found that His is the way that leads, in their own personal experience, to reconciliation with God.

VI.

1. If we turn from dwelling on the life and teaching of our Lord personally, to a survey of the religious history of the world, the Christian consciousness cannot be satisfied to take the negative attitude of the mere spectator. The point of view from which we look, or the attitude of mind we adopt, must affect the results at which we arrive. It is of course possible to maintain a purely scientific standpoint in regard to the literature and history of any religion; to aim at a clear apprehension of all the incidents, and at obtaining a representation of the past. But to the Christian consciousness it does not seem worth while to try to restrict the exercise of the cognitive faculties in this way. It desires to arrive not merely at an apprehension of each particular phenomenon in relation to other phenomena, but at an appreciation. We may try to appreciate any incident, or document, as regards its significance,—as for example its importance with reference to the interest of the student, subjectively, or objectively in regard to the universe of which it is a part, and the purposes which run through the whole[1]; but appreciation endeavours to take account of relations with which mere apprehension cannot pretend to deal. When we appre-

[1] W. Hermann, *Die Religion in Verhältnis zum Welterkennen und zur Sittlichkeit* (1879), 80, 81.

hend any phenomenon, we can describe its occurrence in space and time with precision, and state its relation as consequent on, or antecedent to, other groups of phenomena so as to determine its cause and effects; but we cannot pronounce on its import or significance or worth, unless we can apply to it some conception of an end towards which it is tending, or a purpose to which it gives effect, so that we may be able to appreciate it. The doctrine of development is an attempt to appreciate the significance of each animate form with reference to life as a whole. In the study of the phenomena of conscious life, it is possible to get a more intimate acquaintance with the coherence of the several parts, and a more definite view of their connexion into one whole. The idea of end and purpose is almost necessarily introduced; the whole is susceptible of a teleological interpretation, and we can get, not merely at an antecedent and consequent, but at the reasons for any change. It would be to miss the most fruitful results of the study of moral and religious phenomena if we should dispense with all attempts at appreciation, and rest satisfied with taking the phenomena into the vacuity of the empty mind. There must be an active judgement, with reference to some standard or object, if we are to pass from mere apprehension to appreciation.

It is, of course, possible to appreciate sacred literature with reference to different standards, or from different points of view. It may be considered simply as regards its artistic value; the success which attends attempts to express the deepest human feeling—the tragedy of human life in all its grandeur. There may be a critical judgement as to the skill shown by a particular poet in the employment of metre, or as to the manner in which a didactic writer handles his theme. The 'divine library of the Old Testament' and 'the sacred books of the East,' occupy a large place in the literature of the world, and we can appreciate each part with reference to artistic beauty and literary skill. From this point of view the Bible is an epic of the world. "It unrolls a vast panorama in which the ages of the world move before us in a long train of solemn imagery, from the creation of the earth and the heavens onward to the final passing away of all this material universe and the coming of a new heaven and a new earth wherein shall dwell righteousness. Against this gorgeous background, this ever shifting scenery, now bright with the hues of heaven, now lurid with the glare of hell, we see mankind strutting and playing their little part on the stage.......This may not be science and history, but it is at least an impressive pageant, a stately drama: without metaphor, it is noble literature; and like all noble literature it is fitted to delight, to elevate, and to console[1]." This mode of appreciation does not exclude the appraising of sacred literature from other points of view as well; we may consider it not only from the standpoint of the artistic, but also from that of the Christian consciousness, and estimate it with respect, not to its form, but to its content. From this point of view, the really important fact is that the literature is religious, and deals with the relations of God and man. The Christian accepts the revelation of God in Christ as giving us the most complete view of these relations as they are, and thus has a standard by which to appreciate the truth of any sacred writing. How far is it true, not merely as representing the past, but as setting forth the relations that subsist between God and man?

2. From the point of view of the simple Christian man who reads his Bible, this is the one consideration of supreme importance—the truth of the content of the books of the Bible as a revelation of the ways of God with man. He may, according to education or temperament, find a delight and an interest in the Bible for other reasons, but this is the ground which makes it worth his while to read it and get to know it better than any other book. He may be susceptible to its beauty, or he may not; he may be anxious to get the most minute accuracy about every detail of language and incident, or he may not; but matters which belong to the realm of art and of scholarship are subordinate in his mind, as compared with the effort to appreciate religious truth.

[1] J. G. Frazer, *Passages of the Bible chosen for their literary beauty and interest*, VII.

The Bible purports to be a record of the development of the religious consciousness; of the manner in which a chosen race came to comprehend with greater and greater clearness the character of God, and the relations of duty and privilege in which they stood to Him. It recognises a progressive revelation, as God by successive declarations made known at diverse times and in sundry manners more and more of His Nature and His Will. It calls attention to the unworthiness of the agents and the inadequacy of the media through which these declarations were given at first, and put on record for our learning. The inability of the agent to apprehend the full meaning of the truth he declared was the proof that he did not speak of himself, but was merely a voice inspired with a message. The messages took diverse forms in different ages and on different occasions. The worth of all, whether actual event, or vision of the night, or parable spoken, depends on the truth which it served to set forth. The plain man is quite prepared to welcome increased accuracy in our knowledge of these media as phenomena in time; he may find that the chronology he had accepted is mistaken, and that the events of which he reads took place at some other time or in some other place than he supposed. Or he may find that what he had supposed to be a description of an actual event is merely a parable; or that a piece of literature commonly ascribed to some author was not written by the man whose name it bears. For the mind that is concentrated on the spiritual import of the words these questions sink into relative insignificance. It is indeed possible to disparage them unduly; Alexandrian commentators appear to have been ready to view the whole of the Old Testament history as mere allegory which served to illustrate Christian truth[1]. But there is at all events one limitation to this comparative indifference in regard to the form which revelation may take[2]. The story of the life of Christ has an unique importance, because in Him the content of revelation is indissolubly bound up with the particular form in which it was manifested

---

[1] Cunningham, *Epistle of S. Barnabas*, xvii, ci.
[2] La Berthonnière, *op. cit.* 205.

to the world. And in seeking to grasp the teaching of the written, as of the Incarnate Word, we dare not treat it as merely spiritual to the neglect of the actual in place and time. All increased accuracy of knowledge of the phenomena is to the good, for it is almost certain to add to the vividness of some familiar truth.

The results of criticism may therefore be thoroughly welcome, even when the devout Christian is repelled by the mode in which some writers express them; to him the purely critical attitude of mind may seem offensive, in so far as it involves a concentration of thought on the phenomena, to the apparent disregard of the spiritual significance. He cannot sympathise with the absorption of scholars in questions of detail, which seem to him relatively unimportant; and he resents the air of indifference which some assume to the religious truth contained in the Bible, as at least an affectation. He finds it difficult to believe that any scholars are really satisfied with the meagre result of apprehending the phenomena better without attempting to appreciate the religious truth of the content. Such an attitude of mind is unintelligible to him, unless the critics hold that there is no religious truth contained in the phenomena, and that apprehension, without appreciation, is the only sort of study that is possible. One point at least is clear to him—that more accurate apprehension of the phenomena is not the road by which men ordinarily attain to a fuller appreciation of religious truth. When the phenomena which are recorded for us were actually present to the eye and ear, they did not in and by themselves produce conviction. The most complete success in the reproduction of the past would still show us the crowds who stoned the prophets, or from whom the Lord turned because of their unbelief. The recognition of realities behind the phenomena is not brought about by mere observation and reflection, but by coordinating recorded with present religious experience. The mere exercise of the cognitive faculties does not enable us to predicate existence, the uncertainty which attaches to arguments about existences corresponding to our ideas attaches also to any attempt of the trained intellect to pass through recorded incidents and utterances of the religious consciousness and show that the alleged relations of God and man are real. "Spiritual things" must be "spiritually discerned."

3. From the point of view of the Christian consciousness it is possible to reach a much more discriminating view of the truth and falsity of the other religions of the world than would otherwise be attainable. Those who relegate religion to a place among the other phenomena of human culture will be likely to take a sympathetic position towards all beliefs alike, and say that each is true for the man who holds it, that it is the form of religion which suits him; but this implies the opinion that no common standard can be applied; scepticism as to the very existence of religious truth seems to be involved in this judgement. On the other hand, from the point of view of Deists, all the higher religions were regarded as essentially true, and all other religions as merely false. But the Christian, who accepts the revelation made in the person of Christ as the fullest statement possible of the relations of God to man, has a standard to apply to other beliefs; and as he applies it, he finds that each of the other religions of the world has some elements of truth, and each has also some elements of falsehood.

The attitude of St Paul towards the religions with which he came in contact affords an admirable illustration of the Christian position. He recognised the truth of Judaism; he held that the Law was a true expression of God's will, and that the sense of guilt which it evoked was a true reflection of the Divine horror of sin. He held that the divinely ordained sacrifices had provided means by which the sinner could be restored to his place in the community of the faithful, and that they gave a dim expression of the fact that God is willing to forgive; but that they could never cleanse the conscience from sin, and were therefore inadequate to make a complete reconciliation. This true but incomplete knowledge of God and His will had been expressed in forms which were inadequate to serve as the medium of the full expression of the truth; that had at last been given in the person of Jesus Christ. By reference to Him it was possible to see that the beliefs embodied in the worship and practice of the Israelites were true; but the same test which confirmed the truth it contained convicted Israel of error and of falsity. Blindness had happened unto his countrymen. In so far as they persisted in their attachment to the old forms of religious truth, and regarded them as essential, they were in error; the whole of the painful controversy in which he was involved with the Galatians was the fruit of this error. In so far as they were not only unduly attached to their religious traditions, but rejected the Christian revelation and persecuted the disciples—as he himself had done—the opinions of the Jews were false. It was impossible to say offhand whether Judaism was to be approved as true or condemned as false; but it was possible to apply the touchstone of faith in Christ, and to form a discriminating judgement as to how far it was true, how far erroneous, and how far false. In a similar fashion when he turned to the Gentiles, he tried to fasten on any element of truth in their religion, such as the belief in a God of nature, while yet he denounced the forms of their worship, and sought to awaken them to their need of repentance and forgiveness.

The growth of religious knowledge in the world has consisted in the gradual passing from a more to a less imperfect appreciation of God's relations with man. The phases of progress in the world as a whole are parallel to those in the development of the individual consciousness. It is in the light of the inner life that the external history becomes most intelligible. The individual passes from knowledge of himself as guilty, to knowledge of himself as reconciled, as he learns to appreciate more truly the character of the Power not himself that makes for righteousness; and there has been a similar advance by the race in the capacity for apprehending the character of God. The possibility of change and growth among men accounts for the apparent inconsistency of the elements of truth about God which are recorded in the Bible as given in different periods. Even though God is the same in all ages, unchanging and eternal, man's ability to grasp the Divine traits brought within his cognisance has improved; knowledge has increased, as the power of appreciation has developed.

It may be difficult even for the recipient to describe the precise incidents through which a new truth has first flashed on any human mind. The Bible at least gives us a vivid presentation of each stage of progress. In the story of Abraham an early phase of religious consciousness is clearly portrayed, since we find in him a recognition of God as an unchanging Will—and therefore as One who might be trusted utterly and entirely. The sacredness of the most solemn agreement between man and man, or between tribe and tribe, symbolised the reliability which he felt to attach to an expression of the Divine Will. Amid all the uncertainties of human life—the alternatives of plenty and famine as seasons change, the mischief wrought by unfriendly neighbours, the imminent extinction as it seemed of his race and name—there was something, Some One to trust to. In the horror of a great darkness this aspect of God's character was made known to Abraham; and the faith which sprung up in his heart rendered him the precursor and progenitor of countless multitudes who have come after him and have shared in a like faith. To be delivered from constant uncertainty as to physical conditions, or the action of jealous rivals, by having Some One to trust to, in his life and beyond his life,—that was the faith of Abraham; and it is still cherished by many who do not profess or call themselves Christians.

> "It fortifies my soul to know
> That though I perish, truth is so;
> That, howsoe'er I stray and range,
> Whate'er I do, Thou dost not change.
> I steadier step when I recall
> That though I slip, Thou dost not fall[1]."

However the tribal history may be reconstructed, we cannot but feel that another step in the human power of appreciating Divine truth and a further advance in knowledge of God are marked in the Biblical account of the giving of the

[1] A. H. Clough, *Poems and Prose Remains*, II. 91.

Law. The tribes that had descended from the patriarchs had grown up in the tradition of reverencing God as an Unseen Reality; at Sinai they came to know Him as a Present Power. Moses ascended the Mount which was so carefully guarded from intrusion, and from which the thunderings and lightnings emanated, and from it he brought the Law which the Eternal God had given for His people here. In the Ten Commandments, accepted under such circumstances, there was a conscious union of religion with morality, since there was an insistence on the habitual performance of certain duties at the command of an Unseen God; the enforcement of the penalty of sin followed the disregard of breaches of these duties to man. It was a revelation for these men to learn to think of God, not merely as the Supreme Reality with Whom is no variableness, nor shadow of turning, but as one who takes such account of His creatures as to demand from them regular and habitual compliance with His righteous Will. This new apprehension of the relation in which God stands to men could not but bring out the contrast between the Creator and the creature. On the one side the people recognised God, infinite and all-holy, yet so near, with these tremendous signs of His immediate presence; and on the other was man, conscious of sin and frailty in his puny life, and crushed by the sense that God was making Himself felt to eye and ear. Throughout the narration we see that the human consciousness of sin has been awakened in its fullest form, a sense of an utter unworthiness to stand before the searching eye, or face the perfect rule of God Himself, such as the patriarchs had not felt. At Mount Sinai man could not but recognise his helplessness and his uselessness; the people shrank from such a revelation in all its appalling splendour, and besought Moses to shield them from the presence of God and the glory which manifested it.

We read that, centuries later, another great step was taken, when the human race had advanced sufficiently to be able to learn more of the character of God. There was a little company in an upper room at Jerusalem of men who had been trained by intercourse with Him Whom they recognised as the Incarnate Son of God, who had been desolated by a great sorrow, and gladdened by an unlooked-for restoration. When the Day of Pentecost was fully come they were able to appreciate the new revelation which their Master had promised them, and to find in God, not merely an Unseen Reality, not only a Present Power, but a Personal Help. They found in themselves the fulfilment of the promise that Christ would send a Spirit of Truth Who should abide with them for ever; through Him the help they needed would be supplied; and despite the weakness which discouraged and daunted them, they would be sustained by the Lord and Giver of Life. God had at length revealed Himself as willing and able to transform each frail human being by His Power into His own likeness and thus fit them to be in His Presence eternally. On Whitsunday the Apostles attained to Christian consciousness and to the full knowledge of God in His relations with man.

The various phases in the development of the religious consciousness, which are set before us in the Bible, still subsist in many parts of the world; each has its truth, yet each is enveloped in error, or charged with falsity. It is the work of Christ's ministers to-day, as it was of the Apostles at first, to be His ambassadors and declare the true knowledge of God which He has revealed. It is their wisdom to follow the example of the Apostles, and note the phase of truth any people have already attained, and the further knowledge they are able to appreciate. The message of reconciliation is not what is needed by those who have no consciousness of sin; the consciousness of sin is hardly possible to those who have no sense of spiritual realities, whose conscious life is still 'immersed in nature.' The evangelisation of the world can only proceed in the order to which God adapted Himself in the revelation of His nature and His will to the world. But the motive to make this effort and carry on this work rests on the simple obligation to declare the truth of God and make it known among men. Religion is an element in human culture; the spread of higher religions is accompanied by the diffusion of a knowledge of nobler literature and purer morality. The acceptance of one religion by the whole human race would go far to diminish mutual misunderstandings and to bring about peace and order throughout the world. These are incidental advantages, which may accrue in a greater or less degree from the successful prosecution of missionary work; but it is not because of its usefulness, but simply because of its truth that we desire to diffuse the Christian knowledge of God. The one object from which all the force and inspiration of missionary efforts come is a desire to diffuse the knowledge of God, in all its completeness, so that all men may come to be reconciled to Him, and thus to be partakers in the Christian consciousness.

VII.

1. It is claimed for the Christian consciousness that it gives a point of view from which we may obtain deeper insight into religious truth; but it has also to do with the activities of life as well as with the appreciation of the relations of God and man. Three-fourths of religion, as Matthew Arnold used to insist, are concerned with conduct and the relations of man with man. All the higher religions exercise an ennobling influence on man; there are many maxims of conduct on which they are agreed, but it is worth while to compare the point of view in regard to duty, which is taken by the Christian, with that of the Buddhist or the Theist. It would be absurd to attempt to discuss the merits of each; the success of one man in living up to his conception of life as compared with the failure of others; or the degrees of guilt which attach to those who have had clearer knowledge set before them. It is merely our part to distinguish the ethical standpoints which are consonant with one or other of the nobler forms of religious belief respectively.

There is no figure that has roused more devotion in the East than that of Buddha; and the story of his life cannot but appeal to our sympathies, and call forth tributes of admiration from the Western world to the Light of Asia.

He set forth in his own person a noble morality which was closely associated with a religion in which there was no place for God. To some of us the very suggestion of a religion without a God seems to be a contradiction in terms; but there are others who know that this is not so, because they have felt the attraction such teaching offers. The personal cultivation of devout consciousness may be pursued as an end in itself. There is so much turmoil and hurry in the world; many of us would fain be quit of it all, and pass our days in the contemplation of what is pure and noble. Life in so many cases seems purposeless and empty. The remorseless struggle for wealth and honours that are vanity and vexation of spirit, the fussiness that frets over everything or nothing, are alike despicable and tiresome. The longing to be quit of it all—aloof from all the irritation and the triviality—may be overwhelming. We may try to withdraw within ourselves, and enjoy the solitude we can create; for the power of self-seclusion may be cultivated with success, if we devote ourselves sedulously to the task.

> "As may the ear
> Hearing not hear,
> Though drums do roll and pipes and cymbals ring,
> So the bare conscience of the better thing
> Unfelt, unseen, unimaged, all unknown,
> May fix the entrancèd soul 'mid multitudes alone[1]."

This deliberate revolt against the world and all it contains—the lust of the flesh, the lust of the eye, and the pride of life—is more congenial to the Eastern than to the Western temperament; but even in England and America the strain and stress of modern life have called forth a reaction; there are signs in many quarters of eagerness to withdraw from it, and cultivate an inner life. This is an echo of Buddhism which finds expression in strange theosophies and forms of science falsely so called. Both in the East and in the West such religion has elements of noble self-renunciation, in efforts to quench the passions and master the desires; but after all a self-centred religion is only consonant with a self-centred

[1] A. H. Clough, *Poems and Prose Remains*, II. 25.

life. We can only cut ourselves free from the perturbing influences that play upon our lives by suppressing all the ties and interests that bind us to our fellow-men. If we wish to cultivate a high morality we cannot be satisfied with trying to draw within ourselves: what we need is a faith that will take us out of ourselves. And this we find in the gospel of the Incarnation; the Son of Man had a part in the sorrows and perplexities, the sins and the sufferings of our common humanity, and through it all He set forth a divine ideal. If we would do our task in the world and lead a life that is worth living, we dare not sever ourselves from all the claims of others and spend our time in mere quiescence: none of us dare set up the cultivation and training of his own consciousness as the supreme object of life. A divine sentence on this ambition has been pronounced once for all,—"He that loveth his life shall lose it"; when he has emptied it of all that can ruffle its course, he will find that he has narrowed and cramped his whole being. Salvation cannot be attained by cutting ourselves off and hedging ourselves in; that is merely to make a desert in our hearts and call it peace. By willingness to enter into the sorrows of others, and striving to rejoice in their pleasures, the best that is in us may be drawn out and developed. We may find our true lives if we strive to bear one another's burdens, and so to fulfil the law of Christ.

Without in any way disparaging the earnestness and devotion of the Buddhist saints, we may yet recognise that there is a fundamental difference between the moral consciousness of the Christian and of the Buddhist. The former recognises a Power which makes for righteousness, while the other does not. Those who are satisfied with the narrower ideal, and aim at self-subjugation and self-control may be content to trust to the cultivation of personal strength of will, as the power that can set them free. But if we are looking out on the world—out on our circle of relations with all the claims of mutual dependence, out on those who are brought in contact with us through our callings, out on those who may be influenced by the manner in which we discharge our duties as citizens, out on the posterity that will inherit the fruits of our actions—then we can have a better expectation of establishing harmony between our lives and our surroundings, if our faith and hope are placed in Some One who is greater than ourselves. It may be possible for the ascetic or the philosopher to control the little world within, and to bring it into subjection; but though we are in contact with it at so many points, we have no power in ourselves to control the great world without. Those who believe that the Universe is not a chaos, but that there is order in it all, and that in the last resort Reason is supreme, can take courage. They recognise a God who created it, a God who has a purpose in it; in so far as they succeed in making His will their own and lending themselves to be the instruments of carrying out His purpose, they can attain to calmness and confidence through all the struggles of mundane existence.

2. Not every form of Theism will serve to influence morality. It is possible to believe that God is so infinitely above His creatures, that He takes no account of them or their doings, and is entirely indifferent to the manner in which they live their lives, and to their conduct to one another; such a doctrine is a philosophy, perhaps, rather than a religion, and it can have little connexion with ethics. Any theistic doctrine, however, which recognises relations between God and His creatures, is sure to have a bearing on the conduct of human beings to one another; it gives a foundation for ideas of right and wrong, in the conception of a rule laid down for man by his Creator, and it provides sanctions and motives for living according to this rule. These sanctions may be thought of as physical, as was on the whole the case with the Israelites of old; they believed in the direct connexion of personal and national prosperity with personal and national righteousness; famine or pestilence were regarded as the direct chastisement of wrongdoing. Or the sanctions may be thought of as supermundane, and consisting of rewards and punishments in another world. Mohammedanism has a clearer hold on the doctrine of the immortality of the soul than Judaism attained; and as a consequence, the joys of paradise and tortures of

hell have a more prominent part in the enforcement of morality. In this more advanced form, Theism seemed to the moralists of the eighteenth century to give full support to the highest ethical teaching; it was the basis on which ideas of duty rested, so that the undermining of religion would be dangerous to society. As they held, theistic religion was the outcome of the exercise of the reasoning faculty on the data furnished by nature and supplemented from revelation; and morality rested on theistic religion as its foundation. They were inclined to argue that all morality was dependent on religious beliefs. This is no part of our contention; it may suffice to compare different phases of ethical life, and to show that the morality which has been built on mere Theism is defective in several important respects.

Non-Christian Theism is seen at its best in the religion of Israel and in Mohammedanism, and it has grave defects as a guide in political and social life. Pure Theism cannot give fruitful maxims for mundane affairs. The rule of the Caliphs in Spain was remarkable for the encouragement which was given to literature and science; but it is unimportant in the history of political progress. In its ultimate basis it was a theocracy, and as such it could submit to no limitations. The objects which Islam set before itself in the conquest of the world to the faith, and the attainment of paradise by fighting for it, gave no scope for any doctrine as to the responsibility of civil rulers, and their duties towards the governed[1]. The popular imagination, which filled the future life with dreams of sensuous enjoyment, gave no check to reckless indulgence in luxury here, and failed to lay down any clear teaching as to the obligations of those who were possessed of wealth; nor was there any doctrine of the value of human personality as such, to tell in favour of the gradual extinction of slavery or improvement in the position of women. Christianity has the power, which Islam has not, of bringing the highest motives to bear on mundane affairs, and of remodelling political, civic, and industrial life.

[1] These sentences are taken from my *Essay on Western Civilisation*, II. 118.

Mohammedanism is inadequate, not only as a basis for social duty, but as an incentive to the highest personal morality. Those Theisms, which put forward a rule of moral duty as revealed by God and His prophets, must necessarily rely on something of the nature of a divine code. This code may be the subject of interpretation, and the basis on which much subtle casuistry is expended; but its fundamental principles are fixed. It is imposed once for all; the aim of the virtuous man is to keep up to it, and hence there is no strong incentive to ethical progress. It inculcates conformity to an authoritative rule, rather than the development of character by a man who is free to create and adopt his own ideal. The aim of personal attainment, and the effort to pursue it, which is so characteristic of Buddhism, hardly enters into Mohammedanism; and it has no place for the recognition of higher ideals of life, and therefore none for progress to a higher plane of morality.

The defectiveness of Mohammedanism may also be indicated in another way; while it is an insufficient guide in social and mundane duty, it fails to give scope for the noblest forms of devout aspiration. In Theism the severance and opposition between the human will and the divine remain unreconciled, and the motive to right action is placed in an external reward, in this world or the next. Where real reconciliation is possible, the hope is centred, not on a possession given, but in a change effected in the individual—the blessedness of being rendered like God, and becoming a partaker in His nature. The whole conception of saintly life rests on a deeper foundation than Theism affords.

3. Christianity is a Theism, but it is more; and we shall miss what is characteristic of its ethics if we lay entire stress on the moral teaching which is common to men who profess the higher forms of religion. It is of course true that many religiously-minded men, like Locke, are content with a theistic morality and do not recognise the fact that Christian teaching is based on a distinct principle. But, nevertheless, this is the case. The Christian moral consciousness has distinctive marks of its own. "As many as received Him to them gave

He power to become the sons of God, even to them that believe on His name." That is the source of the Christian life in all its manifestations. Those who recognise a supernatural power living and working within must have a sense of the possibilities of human life, of its privileges and responsibilities, which differs greatly from that of men who do not share this conviction.

They reverence the Divine Power as an active influence for good working in the world, so that the highest conception of virtue lies in conscious cooperation with Him in His activities. The ascetic effort after self-repression is an element; passion must be mastered and desire checked, not to give scope for uninterrupted contemplation, but to remove all hindrances to an active life of self-devotion to the service of God and the good of man. And as the Divine Love has come forth freely from God to seek and to save that which is lost, so must there be no limit to the sphere where Christian charity will strive to operate, no depth of degradation which it will wholly spurn.

The faith in a Divine Influence may have another bearing on personal character and conduct; it is the source of an undying hope. Those who believe that that which is best in them cannot die, will strive to steer their course by the light which shines beyond this mundane sphere. There is wrongdoing which may seem to be harmless or even expedient, and to make for the greatest happiness of the greatest number; it is well that we should cherish an absolute standard in the thought of the life which will persist when earthly things have passed away. "We know that when He shall appear we shall be like Him, for we shall see Him as He is; and every man that hath this hope in Him purifieth himself even as He is pure." The three theological virtues, Faith, Charity, and Hope, are traits which are special to the Christian character, and which have a direct bearing in stirring up to the active doing of good.

In the criterion which it puts forward of virtuous conduct Christianity is clearly distinguished from other forms of Theism. With Judaism at least the aim is to avoid what is forbidden;

nine out of the Ten Commandments are prohibitions in form, and forbid particular kinds of wrongdoing. But Christianity inspires to the active doing of duty; and treats the neglect of opportunities as a heinous sin. Christianity sets a high ideal and an exacting standard, in the way in which it demands purity of thought as well as strictness of conduct. But the difficulty of straining to live up to the principles enjoined becomes most clear when we note the severity of the judgement on lost opportunities and omitted duties. From those to whom much is given much will be required.

While Christianity thus sets up a far sterner standard than other Theisms, it also affords the means of discriminating in many cases of conflicting duties. It suggests to us the manner in which the conflict of the claims of the individual and of society may be adjusted. The individual is of absolute worth, an undying personality; while civil institutions of all kinds, private property and civil government, are only mundane. The individual life has infinite importance; but this is no excuse for individual self-assertion. The world of institutions and conventions and ordinances is the discipline by which the individual may be subjected and trained. Mundane institutions of every kind have not an absolute, but a relative worth, since they are the means by which individual character is formed and trained. There may be frequently an opposition between the desire for individual self-assertion and the demand for the acceptance of self-discipline by submission to authority. In the cases where it is right to withhold active compliance with a human command which is in direct conflict with the Divine Will as plainly expressed, it is at least a duty to see that the manner of withholding obedience shall be so carefully considered, that the effectiveness of the authority for good shall not be in any way weakened[1].

Both in its inspiring and in its discriminating power Christian morality exhibits striking differences from that which is founded on a purely theistic basis. There is another way in which the superiority of this standpoint may become apparent; Christian teaching embraces what is best in the

[1] See my address on *Civil Obedience* in the *Path towards Knowledge*.

doctrine of those religions with which it is most often compared. Like Buddhism it insists on self-cultivation, though this is to be found, not in the mere repression of evil, but in the development of divine and undying activities. As a Theist, the Christian views external conduct in the light of a divine standard; but of one to which the man yields no slavish submission, since he has accepted it for himself and lays it down as a rule for all mankind.

It is not easy by the mere exercise of the cognitive faculty to show that one point of view is better than another, or to prove that it gives a wider range of outlook and a position for more accurate observation; but a distinction can be established, when we try to gauge the force and the aim of the influences which appeal to the human will. This is ground on which Christianity can confidently urge its superiority over other religions; and the recognition of this claim will bring us one step farther. The force and clearness of Christ's teaching on earthly things, where we can test it, may be taken as a pledge of His ability to declare aright relations which lie beyond our faculty of observation, since they subsist between man and the Ultimate and Unseen Power.

ESSAY II.

THE BEING OF GOD, IN THE LIGHT OF PHYSICAL SCIENCE.

FREDERICK ROBERT TENNANT, B.D.

SYNOPSIS.

I. *Critical.*

1. The naturalistic 'bent and trend' of physical science.
2. (*a*) The assumption that the world is 'self-existent.'
   (*b*) The argument that the world is a mechanism controlled by a Reign of Law.

II. *Constructive.*

1. Science leads up to philosophical questions which Theism answers.
2. The origin of the course of Nature. Argument for a First Cause.
3. Causality in Nature implies an all-embracing Being.
4. The characteristics of this Being are those of Mind, Will, and Unity.
5. Such idealism represents the trend of modern science.
6. The *order* of Nature implies a Supreme Intelligence whose action we can partially understand. Cosmic Teleology.
7. Attempt to explain the element of apparent irrationality in Nature. Physical evil in the light of science.
8. Conclusion. Science compatible with belief in a Personal God.

THE BEING OF GOD, IN THE LIGHT OF PHYSICAL SCIENCE.

I.

1. THE present is undoubtedly a scientific age: an age, that is, characterised by the zealous pursuit of physical science, by the application of the scientific method in various fields of thought, and by an increasingly rich and impressive harvest of results acquired by means of scientific investigation. It is claimed on behalf of physical science that it possesses a method and has obtained results which differ from the methods and results of other studies in that they are exact and also objective. Physical observations can be repeated and verified, and thus the subjective element in scientific doctrines—*i.e.* the element of individual conjecture and personal opinion—can be eliminated. Proof is therefore more possible for the theories of natural science than for those which are the outcome of speculation on matters beyond the reach of direct observation and experiment; and consequently greater unanimity is to be found amongst the representatives of science than amongst those of other branches of thought and knowledge. This success of scientific method in enriching our knowledge of Nature and applying it to practical uses, and the solid unanimity with which the great bulk of scientific doctrine is received, both rendered the more impressive by contrast with the repeated failures of philosophy to present a metaphysic of Nature and with the fundamental diversities between the philosophical schools, have not failed to produce an unbounded confidence in

whatever comes to us with the imprimatur of physical science. Indeed many scientific hypotheses and generalisations, on account of their practical effectiveness as organs of research, have come to be regarded as ultimate and necessary truths; and, in some quarters, science, 'systematised, unified, and completed,' is held to suffice for the one and the only possible system of philosophy.

It is therefore not unnatural that there should nowadays exist a widespread belief that to physical science belong both the power and the right to pronounce the last word on every question. Indeed, in view of the degree to which the popularisation of science has of late been carried, it is perhaps a thankless task to raise any doubt as to whether this prevalent opinion be well grounded. Still more ungrateful will such an inquiry seem to many readers, inasmuch as its prosecution necessitates the constant appeal from science to philosophy, or what the student of science, in proportion as he is exclusive in his devotion to his own method and line of thought, is apt somewhat contemptuously to style 'mere metaphysics.' Nevertheless, it must be remarked at the outset that scientific facts lend themselves more readily, perhaps, than any others, to shallow generalisations; and, what is more important here, that science, although most of its readers and apparently many of its teachers are unconscious of the fact, expresses itself in terms of certain metaphysical assumptions whose falsity would not in the least affect the serviceableness of scientific methods for the discovery of empirical truth about Nature, but would utterly invalidate any pretensions on its part to provide a solution of the greater riddles of the universe. Thus it is not so much the effective methods and the solid results of physical science, with which everyone is justly impressed, as its underlying presuppositions with regard to the nature of reality and knowledge, which need to be called in question before we commit ourselves to the scientific dogmatism of our day.

But, however it may stand with the popular faith in the power and the intellectual rights of physical science, there can be no doubt that the attitude of many thoughtful persons

II] *Physical Science, and the Being of God* 59

at the present time towards belief in the existence of God and of a spiritual world is determined by what they deem to be the pronouncements or the implications of science with regard to the possibility of justifying such belief. The tendency to reject any form of Theism, in so far as such a tendency prevails among votaries of natural science, is due partly to the influence of some of the representative exponents of the verdict of science as to the existence and activity of a Supreme Mind, and partly to the intellectual atmosphere in which the scientific teacher or investigator daily lives and moves, and whence he derives an habitual bent of mind disposing him to dispense altogether with theistic forms of thought.

Thus a discussion of the Being of God in the light of physical science, in order to be serviceable to readers of the present day, must embrace, in the first place, a critical estimate of the claim made on behalf of science, that it forms a court of appeal as to the validity of the theistic position, and that it finds theistic arguments untenable. Such a negative criticism will involve the raising of two questions not easily separable from each other: namely, that of the capability of science, as distinguished from philosophy and as severed from metaphysics, to decide upon the existence or non-existence of a Supreme Being, and that of the validity of the actual arguments suggested by scientific postulates and generalisations against the theistic interpretation of the universe. If such critical consideration of the scientific basis of naturalism should prove the repudiation, in the name of science, of all rational theology to be ill grounded, there will then be room, in the second place, for the positive or constructive undertaking, to furnish, from the knowledge of Nature which science affords, and in so far as such knowledge will allow, a content to the concept of God adopted by the theistic philosopher and the Christian theologian.

Before proceeding further, it must be explained that two uses of the word 'science' will need to be distinguished in the following pages; for otherwise injustice might seem to be done to some of the best representatives of scientific thought. In point of fact there are current at the present time two conceptions of the nature and the province of physical science. The 'science' of the majority of the students of natural knowledge is imbued with metaphysics. It uses terms such as force, cause, laws of Nature, as standing for physical facts, concrete entities. It speaks of atoms and ether as if these were realities—more real than the 'phenomena' presented to our senses. It regards the indestructibility of matter and the conservation of the energy of the universe as absolute and ultimate principles. It offers its mechanical description of Nature as the complete and the only explanation thereof. The reader will presently be enabled to see more clearly that this science is 'falsely so called': that it is really a kind of sandwich of genuine science between two thick layers of metaphysic, the lower of which consists of presuppositions concerning reality taken over from the language and thought of unreflective 'common sense,' and the upper of generalisations attained by scientific research and illogically identified with universally valid principles.

The newer physical science, which is slowly but surely making headway against the prejudices of scientific orthodoxy, on the other hand banishes from its terminology all such words as involve metaphysical adjuncts to what is actually presented to us by the world on the surface. It dispenses with 'force,' save as a purely mathematical relation; it replaces 'causes and effects' by equations; it recognises that 'matter,' with which the scientist deals, is very distinct from the 'substance' of the metaphysician. It insists that atoms and ether and other such implements of science are not perceptual realities, but are only useful fictions, conceptual devices for economy of thought; some of its representatives would dispense with them and rewrite physics in another terminology. It admits the shortcomings of the mechanical theory of the universe, and asserts that there is no necessity for the choice of this rather than of other methods of systematising our scientific knowledge. It proclaims that its *rôle* is not explanation at all, but only description; and, having cleared itself of all metaphysical implications, it professes to be no more than a systematised, shorthand account of natural events as they happen. With science as thus accurately delimited the earlier, critical portion of this essay has no concern. The writer confesses himself its disciple, and passes on to discuss the difficulties which are said to be put in the way of belief in the Being of God by what is more generally included under the title of physical science.

The bare facts of science have, of course, little theological interest, and they provide directly but few arguments one way or the other. The hypotheses and theories of science, however, when assumed to possess the validity of metaphysical doctrines or ultimate and universal truths, have suggested a conception of the world which, naturally congenial to the student of physical science, has sometimes been confounded with science itself, or has been said to represent its bent and trend; and the whole spirit of science has consequently sometimes been represented as hostile to the theist's faith. Thus the late Professor Huxley, though he declined to accept the name of materialist, was persuaded that the progress of science "has, in all ages, meant, and now more than ever means, the extension of the province of what we call matter and causation and the concomitant gradual banishment from all regions of human thought of what we call spirit and spontaneity." "And as surely," he added, "as every future grows out of past and present, so will the physiology of the future gradually extend the realm of matter and law until it is coextensive with knowledge, with feeling, and with action[1]." These words were delivered in 1868. We may place side by side with them the following, in which Sir Oliver Lodge describes the temper of science at the present moment:

"It is difficult to resist yielding to the bent and trend of 'modern science' as well as to its proved conclusions. Its bent and trend may have been wrongly estimated by its present disciples: a large tract of knowledge may have been omitted from its ken, which when included will revolutionise some of their speculative opinions: but, however this may be, there can be no doubt about the tendency of orthodox science

[1] Lay Sermon on *The Physical Basis of Life*.

at the present time. It suggests to us that the Cosmos is self-explanatory, self-contained, and self-maintaining. From everlasting to everlasting the material universe rolls on, evolving worlds and disintegrating them, evolving vegetable beauty and destroying it, evolving intelligent animal life, developing that into a self-conscious human race, and then plunging it once more into annihilation[1]."

Of these two scientific teachers, Huxley was typical of the men of science who have shown some interest in certain of the problems of philosophy, and who have mastered some portion, at any rate, of the history of philosophic thought. Dr Lodge has evidently reflected much upon the wider bearings of science, though he has not revealed any curiosity as to the contents or the history of what is technically called philosophy. And both these thinkers seem to have escaped the influence of the contemporary movement within the world of science which advocates examination of scientific postulates and presuppositions with a view to ascertaining their precise meaning and validity, and which demands, sometimes, their amendment or rejection. They are thus apt representatives of the standpoint of a large body of scientific men, and of the 'bent and trend' of 'orthodox' science so far as theological problems are concerned[2]. Each of them possesses the further interest for us of having sought escape from the negative, materialistic, or mechanical tendency of the science of which they are recognised spokesmen. Professor Huxley believed he had found such a refuge in agnosticism; while Dr Lodge hopes for a reconciliation of science and religion based upon a widening of the scientific survey: "the region of religion and the region of a completer science are one[3]."

Taking these writers, then, for our guides as to the trend and temper of the physical science of our time, we find that science is commonly believed to present to us a universe which is a vast machine characterised by the reign of rigid

[1] *The Hibbert Journal*, Vol. I. No. i. p. 57.
[2] It is perhaps unnecessary to state that Dr Lodge does not represent this standpoint in the sense that he wholly adopts it as his own.
[3] *Op. cit.* Vol. I. No. ii. p. 227.

Physical Science, and the Being of God

and invariable law: a universe in which the minds that investigate it are themselves dependent on matter, a product stumbled upon during the process of the world's evolution, an accompaniment bound, like a shadow, to the primary mechanism: a self-contained and self-sufficient universe, not in touch with anything beyond or above itself: a world independent of anything but itself for its origin and maintenance, its meaning and intelligibility. Nature seems, to the modern scientific investigator, as she seemed to Lucretius long ago, "to do all things of herself, without the meddling of the gods"; but to do it mechanically, and not "spontaneously."

If such a theory be really necessitated by physical science, by observable fact and logically deducible inference alone, without admixture of any questionable presuppositions whatever, it is obvious that the concept of God is not only superfluous but inadmissible: it is useless to appeal to science for guidance as to how Deity is to be conceived. It will therefore be necessary, before attempting any construction of the idea of God in the light of the natural knowledge which we possess, briefly to examine the foundations of this general view of the universe which science has suggested to certain of her exponents, and to ascertain whether they are as secure as they are sometimes represented to be.

The view in question is familiarly known as naturalism. Let it be clearly understood that it is not a product of science, in the strict and proper sense of that term, but is a philosophical system involving both science and metaphysics. Its chief component elements are a metaphysical assumption, which creeps in unawares as a pronouncement of 'common sense,' and an inference which claims to be necessitated by scientific observation and reflection. The metaphysical, or rather epistemological, assumption is that the world exists independently of experience: not only of that of any given individual, but also of the collective experience of all subjects. The material universe is supposed to be real apart from mind, prior to mind, and already waiting in its self-containedness for minds, when they have somehow been produced, to come to it and get to know it by some inconceivable process of psychological photography. The scientific inference which, more than any other, goes to build up the system of naturalism, is that this world, supposed to be existent *per se*, because it can be described, more or less, in terms of mechanical concepts, actually is a mechanism: a machine whose action is determined to the minutest particular by a system of rigid and invariable law, leaving no room for the spontaneous activity of a mind either upon it or within it.

2. These positions must be discussed in their order.

(*a*) The assumption that the world is purely objective has grown up with the human race. It is engrained in our language, employed in all ordinary human intercourse, identified with common sense; and it has very naturally been taken over by the physical sciences, whose concern is not with theoretical inquiries into the philosophical implications of natural knowledge, but with the practical business of extending one department of it. It matters nothing to science, as science, whether this assumption be valid or no; but to philosophical inquiry into the ultimate problems of knowledge and reality, such as the relation of matter to mind, or the existence of God, it matters much. The case is similar to that of the terminology in which we may describe the relative motion of the earth and sun. We still speak of the sun rising and setting; it is convenient and harmless so to do, so long as we are not pretending to scientific accuracy. So too, on the platform of science, we can conveniently and harmlessly talk of an objective world sundered from the experience of the subjects which perceive it; it does not at all follow, as the layman in philosophy commonly supposes, that if the world be not objective, in his sense, there is then an end of scientific knowledge of it. But when the man of science carries the implications of such language with him into theistic controversy, he must be reminded that he has already half begged the question at issue.

It is a delicate matter to invite the plain man to listen to

Physical Science, and the Being of God

a criticism of his belief in a wholly objective and independent external world. His courteous long-suffering may know a limit. So far has the dualism between the 'real world' and its percipients been carried in common thought, so deeply has it become entrenched in the physical sciences, that when philosophy attempts to open a discussion of the unsuspected problems which lurk beneath what appears to be the surest fundamental datum of experience, and to show the stages by which dualism and naïve realism acquired their hold upon the human mind, it labours under an enormous disadvantage. "To the plain man its teaching is a stumbling-block; to the man of science it is foolishness." And yet we must refuse any parley with the champion of naturalism until he leaves his scientific fastness and descends to the open ground of first principles of knowledge. We might urge him to do so by the argument that his dualism is discreditable because of the hopeless difficulties into which it has already led both physical science and psychology: for science has abandoned, with some little indignation, the endeavour to get from matter to mind, to derive the mental from the physical; and the history of psychology has shown that all attempts to get from mind to matter, to solve the problem (presented by dualism) of how we perceive and know a wholly external and independent world, have turned out to be blind roads. Or we might threaten him that he will inevitably be starved out of his dogmatic stronghold if he stays there: reflection will be sure to come in time and do its work. If by either means we should succeed in inducing him to give open battle, we might with much confidence point out to him how the earliest reflection on conscious experience was misled by imperfect analysis and deceptive analogies, which became embodied in common thought and language as if part of the facts instead of fictions that belie them; and, following Avenarius and Professor Ward, we might lay bare the actual stages of progress in the dualistic interpretation of mankind's experience, and their erroneousness. We might hope to convince him, by means of arguments which cannot be repeated here, but which may be studied at leisure elsewhere[1], that the objects which he collectively calls Nature and treats as implying no subject because they are independent of the experience of any individual subject, are really a factor or constituent of the collective experience of the race. They presuppose intercommunicating humanity as their subject; and this subject may be seen to be merely the individual subject extending and enlarging the range of its experience through intersubjective intercourse.

Thus it cannot be allowed to science, when the attempt is made to extract naturalism out of it, that its world of Nature is self-existent in the sense of being independent of our experience and perhaps the 'cause' of that experience. This is the thin end of the naturalistic wedge. It must be maintained that such an assumption will not bear the test of philosophic scrutiny: that, on the contrary, the 'world' with which physical science occupies itself is simply one side of human experience, and that it is the other side, after all, which is the primary.

So long as science, or rather the naturalism which seeks to identify itself with science and express its trend, builds upon faulty metaphysic and eschews epistemological reflection, it will inevitably degenerate into materialism. There will then always and necessarily be a conflict between science and religion; and no widening of the region of science will do away with it. The reconciling element, it must here be strongly insisted, is philosophical criticism of scientific presuppositions. Sir Oliver Lodge indeed will concede no such reconciling power to philosophy. He considers philosophy, in this respect, on a par with poetry. "By aid of philosophy, or by aid of poetry, a great deal can be accomplished." But this is not science. "It is a guess, an intuition—an inspiration perhaps—but it is not a link in a chain of assured and reasoned knowledge; it can no more be clearly formulated in words, or clearly apprehended in thought, than can any of the high and lofty conceptions of religion.... It is no solution

---

[1] Ward, *Naturalism and Agnosticism*, 1889, Vol. II. Part IV.

of the knotty entanglement, but a soaring above it; it is a reconciliation *in excelsis*[1]." Of some of the higher flights of philosophical speculation this may be true. All the same, there are chains of reasoned, if we may not add assured, knowledge, which have been both clearly formulated and clearly apprehended, and that by leaders of scientific thought, concerning which one may confidently make the following assertions. In the first place, such chains of reasoning reveal that the knottiest entanglements besetting the approach of scientific students to religion consist in the metaphysical crudities involved in what is mistaken for science itself; and furthermore, they serve at the same time to unravel these very entanglements, thereby giving us a science whose temper and trend is no longer one of antagonism to a theistic outlook. A reconciliation *in excelsis* need not be forced upon unwilling science; but a reconciliation *in profundis*, a reconciliation by removal of the ground for quarrel, a reconciliation through destructive criticism of those underlying presuppositions of 'orthodox science' which are not science at all: this we can insist upon, for it has already been potentially brought about.

(*b*) Upon the assumption of a wholly objective and self-existent world it is easy for science to erect the further fallacy that this world is a mechanism bound fast by inexorable laws given alike to Nature herself and to us. This theory is said to be suggested by physical science and to represent its present spirit or trend. As it is conspicuously antitheistic it calls for some consideration here.

The world, as it presents itself to the ordinary observer, is a complex of related things, living or inanimate, conscious or apparently unconscious: a complex infinitely rich in diversity of quality and meaning. Of the indefinite number of natural objects, no two, perhaps, are exactly alike, no one is permanently the same. Inanimate Nature is seemingly unlimited in its variety of colour and sound; and in the realm of living things we are presented with as infinite a diversity in point of instinct and habit, pursuit and end, interest and

[1] *Hibbert Journal*, Vol. I. No. i. pp. 48, 49.

occupation, character and personality. Lifeless things appear to act and react; living things seek and find, strive, fail, and achieve.

Such is the *prima facie* view of the world which Science seeks more narrowly to scrutinise and more intimately to understand. Her purpose in studying it, be it emphasised at the outset, is to know it in order to predict its sequences of change, and thereby to control it. To explain a particular occurrence, which means to show its likeness to previously known occurrences, she seeks to refer it to a general class of such events; she reduces the individual phenomenon to its species, and every species of change to an all-embracing physical genus. By such a method of treatment she indeed impoverishes the phenomenon she would explain. She deliberately ignores some of its aspects; possibly those which would count for most in the philosopher's view, and which would be assigned the more important place in his endeavour to construct a theory of the world as a whole and of the relations of individual things as they present themselves to him in their entirety. Science abstracts for her consideration only those aspects and relations of things which are relevant to her practical business of description, prediction, and control; only those which lend themselves or, she trusts, will lend themselves, to mathematical treatment and calculation. And the more perfectly she fulfils her end and succeeds in describing the universe as an aggregate of moving mass-elements devoid of quality, the more thoroughly, it is obvious, does she strip the 'thing' of its individuality. Concrete and qualitative diversities, of colour, for instance, or of sound, are *for her* mere differences in number: so many more or less vibrations in a second of some medium which remains the same throughout the variety of aspects presented to our senses. She describes Nature in ever more general and more simple terms, grouping her facts under a law, and laws under wider laws. She tends, in a word, to greater and greater abstraction, and increasingly parts company with the living, concrete world. In order to proceed in this course of abstraction she devises conceptual symbols, such as 'force,' 'mass,' 'ether,' which facilitate her work just as the 'straight line' renders possible the science of

II] *Physical Science, and the Being of God* 69

geometry. And further, with a view to making her description and prediction of natural events feasible at all, she postulates uniformity in their sequence, a principle of causality, an iron rule of law, a purely mechanical mode of action of one upon another of the elements into which she resolves the world. I say she *postulates* these things. Uniformity is not so written upon Nature's face that he who runs may read it; it needed first to be demanded, for practical reasons, and then to be diligently sought for before, here a little and there a little, it was found. The necessary connexion of causality, the bond of union between cause and effect, has never been *observed*. None, in fact, of these concepts has been thrust by the concrete world upon the passively receptive human mind; none is derived purely from direct experience. Nor are uniformity, causality, and the like, axioms indispensable to all thinking. They are literally postulates: postulates which science invents, tentatively applies to Nature, and finds by experience to be generally verified within the limits of actual observation.

These symbols and postulates are necessary, then, to the practical ends of science; nay, to her very existence. And so it has hitherto been very commonly assumed by her teachers that the postulates are necessary and universal truths, ultimate metaphysical doctrines, and that the symbols denote actual, concrete existences. Thus scientific analysis brings us, it has been claimed, to what is ultimately real behind the phenomena which appear to our senses.

And so, because a certain portion of one moiety of the world has been found capable of description, from one partial point of view, with some though by no means complete success, in terms of mechanical representation, the apparatus of which grows more cumbersome and is put to greater shifts the more the demands upon it are multiplied, we are asked to believe that the world *is* a mechanism and no more. It is a large demand; especially as not only the whole of the biological realm of phenomena, but even some of the physical (*e.g.* gravitation), refuse as yet to yield at all to this type of 'explanation.' In the days of the early promise of the mechanical theory, indeed, it was sanguinely believed that such outstanding and obstinate realms of fact would resolve themselves into complicated cases of the motion of elements of mass; that the blade of grass would find its Newton and gravitation its Kelvin. Nowadays, however, there are influential scientific circles in which all this hope has been abandoned; in which the search has begun to be seriously undertaken for a new foundation for all science.

Still the view obtains that the world is wholly interpretable by mechanism, living beings and mental phenomena included; that the sequence of events is determined by an iron reign of law ; that the universe is self-explanatory and self-sufficient, and offers no suggestion of spiritual reality, of originating or controlling mind.

Now obviously the tenability of such a theory of the world ultimately depends upon the answer to be given to these two questions : Are atoms or electrons, the ether, mechanical action, really concrete facts, matters of possible experience? Or are they merely *conceptual symbols*, useful only for briefly systematising our natural knowledge? And, are the postulates of uniformity, causality, law and mechanism, absolute and necessary metaphysical principles? Or are they 'working assumptions,' valid only within the limits of empirical observation, and serviceable only so far as the practical business of science is concerned?

Fully to answer these questions would require the elaborate discussion of technical scientific detail. Fortunately, however, they are questions which have of late occupied the minds of recognised masters both of science and philosophy ; and consequently they do not require to be thrashed out here. Few words, therefore, will suffice to indicate the results of such inquiry.

It may be affirmed that those scientific investigators who have at all reflected upon the validity of the postulates and symbols of which they daily make use, have, with practical unanimity, agreed that vortex-atoms, ether, mass, force, etc., are ideal things, merely shorthand formulae, not necessarily bearing any more immediate relation to what actually exists

Physical Science, and the Being of God

and goes on in Nature than that which this type bears to the writer's processes of thought. They are not things of which we have experience through our senses, and moreover they do not all seem to possess the characteristics of real things. Theories of atoms and ether have hitherto been too unstable, and not sufficiently free from inconsistencies, to warrant us in believing that in them we have found the key to the structure of the universe; and whether a mechanical hypothesis, dispensing with these inconsistencies, may be discovered, remains as yet to be seen. Further, it has been shown that the more completely the method of scientific analysis which involves the use of these symbols is developed, the more it parts company with sensible reality, the more abstract and mathematical is its nature; in the last resort it leads to a world of quasi-matter, to which no positive properties can be ascribed other than those of motion and resistance.

Again, philosophical reflection by no means justifies the conversion of scientific postulates into metaphysical doctrines. Science can only demonstrate the validity of her postulates so far as her own practical use of them goes. Indeed she has no concern with ultimate reality, and never needs, as she proceeds with her own business, to raise the question as to its nature. Her method of procedure and her achieved results would be just the same whether materialism or spiritualism were true, whether theism, pantheism, or atheism were the philosophical solution of the world-problem. And it will be obvious, from several simple considerations, that it is illegitimate and illogical to give to scientific postulates any wider significance or validity than such as is required for the immediate purposes to which natural science puts them.

In the first place, assumptions which are made in order to enable science to get on at all in her work of description, work which, as we have seen, is admittedly departmental and abstract, cannot, without proof, be regarded as assumptions necessary to thought in general. For the part is not identical with the whole: and scientific description, in so far as it advances beyond mere comparison and classification of sensible phenomena to attempt their mechanical interpretation, only applies to certain aspects of phenomena; those, namely, which admit of mathematical treatment, or are capable of reduction to matter and motion. Thought is richer than science, and reality is richer than thought. What is valid for the description of the 'outside' of phenomena and for the calculation of the sequence of some kinds of them, cannot then be assumed to be necessarily true for experience and knowledge as a whole. Thus it by no means follows that because science, if it is to exist at all, must assume uniformity in natural processes, uniformity must obtain outside the limits of experimental observation : or that causality, because its use introduces order into natural knowledge, is either necessary determination of consequent by antecedent, as naturalism affirms on the one hand, or a merely quantitative relation, such as suffices for the procedure of the newer physics on the other: or that the world, because science can only describe it tersely and systematically in terms of mechanical relations, is actually a mechanism: or that, though the assumption of unvarying law is essential to the scientific calculation of events, the reign of Law must be taken as the first of the truths that will have to be accepted by both science and theology[1]; for the use of the concept of law is by no means identical in science, of the older type, and in philosophical theology.

Further, a scrutiny of some of the leading generalisations of science which one frequently sees dogmatically stated, or rather misstated, in the text-books, such as the postulates of the indestructibility of matter and the conservation of energy, or the hypothesis of the absolute likeness of all the atoms of the same kind, reveals that these are by no means of the nature of absolute truths, but that they are approximations sufficiently near the truth to serve the purpose of what is called 'exact' science, whose absoluteness, however, admits no more of proof than of disproof. The indestructibility of matter cannot be proved, in its universal or absolute sense, by any amount of the empirical evidence upon which science adopts it as a working hypothesis. The

---

[1] Sir O. Lodge, *Hibbert Journal*, Vol. I. No. ii. p. 210.

principle of the conservation of energy, rightly formulated
and understood, can supply no knowledge whatever as to the
total quantity of energy in the universe or as to its constancy.
The doctrine of chemical atoms and their likeness is based
solely upon the statistical method of averages, and strictly
tells us nothing of individual atoms of a given element,
which may, as a matter of fact, vary widely from the average
atom without causing any need for the revision of chemical
laws. And so at all points we find scientific laws to be valid
only for the approximate methods of practical science, not
at all for the rigorously exact universal statements of the
philosopher; and we see that scientific postulates, however
productive of results, and however necessary to the existence
of science and her work of description, are by no means to be
adopted as expressions of ultimate reality. Yet it is solely
by regarding them as such that scientific thinkers have been
able to demur to the theistic position and to conceive of the
world as a self-sufficient and self-explanatory mechanism.
It is only by exchanging her *rôle* of description of phenomena
for that of dogmatic metaphysics that science has been made
to present so plausible a case against theology. But it is
just because science is purely descriptive—a fact which of
late has begun to be widely recognised within her own circle—
that she is incapable of metaphysical construction, and therefore also of theological demolition. Atomism and mechanism
are imposed on science not by reality, but simply by her
own choice of method, and by the requirements of her
abstract and mathematical procedure. If she finds no
individuality and spontaneity in things, no mind in Nature,
it may be simply because it is essential to her procedure to leave such things out of account; it by no means
follows that they are not there. And when, in forget-
fulness of her self-imposed limitations, and of her aloofness
from the concrete reality of the world, she mistakes her
abstractions and conceptual symbols for the real, and
endeavours to construct reality for us out of the abstractions
which reality alone has enabled her to form, she is, as
Mr Bradley has said, simply 'not respectable.' What is true
in science is often absurd in philosophy.

II.

1. The last remark, severed from the preceding context, might well be mistaken for a flippant paradox; especially if regarded in connexion with statements immediately to follow. For it must now be pointed out that, though it does not belong to physical science to dictate ready-made ultimate and absolute truths to the theologian or the philosopher, or to presume that her methods can cover the whole ground of research, it is her part, her very important and inalienable privilege, to contribute to philosophy the body of systematic knowledge of Nature which she has acquired, and which must not be ignored in the philosopher's elaboration of a unified and complete interpretation of the world. What is true in philosophy must be true in science, in so far as the two provinces are coextensive. In other words, a philosophical system, in interpreting Nature, in giving content to its concept of God, and in attempting to formulate the relation of God to the world, must take into account the established facts of natural science, keep in touch with them, and abide by them. If physical science, as such, cannot supply a cosmical theory, nor quarrel with one upon her own ground except in reference to particular points of fact, it must also be borne in mind that she takes her place in the council of the sciences over which philosophy presides, and whose various pronouncements philosophy correlates, unifies, and interprets. It is when absorbed thus into the wider sphere of philosophy that natural science can begin to speak as to the Being of God and the ultimate nature of the world. She does not constitute the court before which the case of Theism comes for trial: she is only a witness in the court. However, when absorbed into philosophy and taught her place in relation to the fundamental principles of knowledge, she does not wholly lose her individuality. Her utterances are still her own. Otherwise there would be no reason in attempting to discuss constructively the Being of God in the light of physical science.

Physical Science, and the Being of God

If the foregoing criticisms have sufficed to show that the methods of science are not applicable to the whole field of human thought, and that, in the light of a critique of knowledge, scientific postulates can neither be identified with metaphysical principles nor pass as substitutes for them, it must now be pointed out that physical science leads up, in many directions, to philosophical questions, the power to answer which constitutes the main claim of Theism,—that it is required for the satisfaction of our intellectual needs.

2. This is the case even if we allow, for the sake of argument, that the material world exists independently of our experience. Granted this highly disputable assumption, the view that science presents to us a world which 'goes of itself' and sufficiently explains itself without any hypothesis as to divine origin or maintenance, might have a larger claim upon our respect if science began at the beginning. This, however, is by no means the case. Ultimate causes may be undiscoverable; they are certainly not traceable by scientific research. Science, indeed, deals exclusively with existing relations, not at all with origins. Scientific explanation in terms of the causal nexus is, after all, only relative explanation; for, behind the event assigned as cause to any given phenomenon, there lies another determining that, and so on in indefinite regress. The work which made the name of Darwin immortal, for instance, tells us nothing about the real 'origin' of species. It contains no inquiry into the remoter causes of the diversity of organic forms. The world can only seem, to the upholder of the mechanical theory, to go of itself because he finds it going, and because, according to his mechanical system of interpreting it, it appears to be incapable of ceasing to go or of changing its course. It scarcely needs to be stated, however, that science is unable to represent to us how the course of Nature first started. No matter how far she takes us back—and she can carry us a long way—the actual beginning of the physical universe is involved in mystery. Yet without solving the question of ultimate origin, science 'explains,' in an absolute sense, no single event in the world's course, and therefore

falls far short of demonstrating a self-contained, self-sufficient and self-explanatory system. There are things as to which science must always continue to say not only '*ignoramus*' but '*ignorabimus*.' Even if all natural events were reduced by science to cases of motion of an undifferentiated plenum without properties, and all natural qualities were explained as arrangements and motions of such a substratum, there would remain to be accounted for, as Du Bois Reymond remarked long ago, the original motion of matter or ether and the existence of energy. And if we assume the eternity of matter and energy, we desert and transcend what is properly called science, and thereby renounce its self-sufficiency for ultimate and universal explanation. We are not, of course, casting incompetence in the teeth of science; it is of the essence of the scientific account of things that it has no beginning and no end. If her laws hold, she can put $t = \pm$ any large quantity she likes, and will get some configuration for every value of t (time). But she must begin with an already existing stock of 'simples,' such as ether (or matter) and energy. We are merely objecting, on the strength of these acknowledged facts, to the naturalistic claim that science presents us with a *self-explanatory* universe.

Science, then, does not begin at the beginning, and indeed admits that she is compelled, for scientific reasons, to utter '*ignorabimus*' as to the origin of the physical universe. Thus a positive impulse is given to philosophy to supplement the limited knowledge of Nature furnished by science, with theories suggested by a wider survey of reality than science herself is able to take. Where science ends, philosophy and theology begin; and indeed the necessity of accounting for the origin of the world has generally been the starting-point for theistic argument, when it sets out from the epistemological standpoint of the physical sciences.

Some empiricist philosophers, such as J. S. Mill, have betaken themselves, in this connexion, to the supposition that matter or force is eternal. This is not a very satisfying solution of the difficulty, even on the assumption that it is possible to assign to matter, apart from mind for which it exists, any intelligible meaning. And if, in order to account for the universe, we postulate the eternity of such things as are described in text-books on mechanics under the name of force and energy, there seems no reason, so far as physical science is concerned, for endowing these eternal entities with just the 'power to produce motion' and nothing more. Eternal mind or will would suit science at least as well as blind, unconscious force; and the minimum which science requires to postulate cannot legitimately be assumed to be all there really is. *Entia non multiplicanda praeter necessitatem* is an excellent methodological principle for descriptive science; it is irrelevant, however, in this connexion, because philosophy—and nowadays science too— denies that 'force' is an *ens* at all.

In the interests of Theism attempts have been made to discover in the world evidences of its origin by creation. If science cannot summon back to our mental view the process of beginning, one might expect that she would be able to trace in Nature evidences, or, at least, suggestions, of the creative acts of One Supreme Cause, supposing the universe to have arisen in this way. Especially might this hope be entertained of the search for such suggestions in the remoter stages through which the world is known to have passed, and in the elemental existences of which it is believed to be composed. Such a hope would, from the theist's point of view, be reasonable, though the test would not be crucial.

Now the processes of Nature, unlike those of machines made by man, are found to be of an irreversible kind. The system will not run backwards; Nature's changes proceed in only one direction. So far as we know, the transformations of energy which accompany changes in the physical world involve no loss in the quantity of energy concerned; but it is well known that though energy is not lost, it tends, during its unceasing changes of form, to become ever less available for doing 'work.' Other things being the same, this tendency of the world's energy to become unavailable points to a definite beginning and a definite end in time of the existing system of things. Provided the universe be finite in extent, the principle of the dissipation of energy implies finite duration for the world as we know it. Consequently, the order described by laws which hold good now cannot be maintained for an indefinite past. And this, it has sometimes been affirmed, is equivalent to the admission of an original creative act. As a particular case of the principle in question, it was pointed out by Lord Kelvin that Fourier's formula, representing the process of conduction of the earth's heat, implies that there must have been, at some definite past time, a thermal state of the world which cannot be regarded as the physical result of a known previous state of things. But this reasoning is hardly a secure basis for an argument for Theism. Such discontinuity cannot legitimately be identified with an absolute beginning of the finite. It merely implies that an earlier thermal state of the world did not arise by conduction of heat alone, as its later conditions did; it does not preclude the existence, before the epoch of discontinuity, of some source of heat of which our equation omits to take account.

Another sign of the definite beginning of the physical world, and of the action therein of creative power, has been sought in the alleged absolute likeness and immutability of the atomic elements into which science resolves the universe. Sir John Herschel would have had us see in the strict sameness of the atoms an essential quality of a 'manufactured article'; and Clerk Maxwell held it to be a solid result of science that the atom has been made, and made by none of the processes which we call natural. Thus the elements of which the world is built up were supposed themselves to bear witness that they are not eternal and self-existent.

As this argument stands, it is open to the criticism that the absolute permanency ascribed to atoms by the science of Clerk Maxwell's generation points at least as strongly to eternal existence as to creation in time ; and further, that the absolute likeness attributed to the atoms is ascribed without sufficient grounds. Atoms are only studied by science in the aggregate, and our knowledge of a single one

Physical Science, and the Being of God

is only such as can be acquired statistically. From this it is evident that we can know nothing as to the exact properties, the exact size or velocity, of any individual atom. This latter criticism, perhaps, may be escaped; for *absolute* likeness is not essential to the argument. Recent advances in science, however, suggest that the atom is no longer to be regarded as immutable, but as a thing which undergoes change and disintegration. This fact, while it destroys Clerk Maxwell's premise, does not in itself supply evidence either for the creation of matter or for its eternal existence. If, however, the electrons, into which science is now resolving the atoms, are to be taken as the ultimate elements of matter and as strictly equivalent and alike, the original argument reappears in new form. And it may perhaps be strengthened by dissociation from the unhappy analogy between manufacture and creation which formerly underlay it. The existence throughout vast regions of stellar space of so stupendous a number of elemental bodies exactly resembling one another is hard to explain on any supposition other than that of origin from a common source and a single cause. That this cause was the creative act of God is not an absolutely necessary inference. But if electrons are real, and not mere symbols of our making, he who is already a theist may see in their likeness one of the particulars in which the world suggests its origin by creation. For, according to his conception of the world, he would expect to find "some evidence of the origin of natural objects from a single source," and "to find the evidence stronger in the simpler and more elemental objects which composed them." "If," continues the writer from whom these words are cited, "we should find a very large number of pins or bullets that were as similar as are apparently the different atoms of the same substance, we should not hesitate to regard them as either directly or remotely sprung from one source. And if the atoms should turn out to be composed of still more ultimate elements, 'prime elements,' 'electric corpuscles,' or what not, there would be still stronger reasons to regard those more ultimate elements, which were present everywhere in space, as dependent on one ground. The logical basis for this postulate of 'one ground for similars' is simply this: The ways in which perfectly unconnected things could differ are numberless, while there is only one way in which such things could perfectly resemble one another; hence that an indefinitely great number of things should quite of their own accord *happen* upon precisely the same form, is a probability so unimaginably small as to be negligible. If, on the other hand, those elements were not independently formed, but were co-effects, their similarity would follow as a matter of course[1]." This argument cannot be offered here as sufficient to *prove* unity of origin for the elements into which science resolves the world. We are only certain of a similar origin for our pins and bullets in consequence of our knowledge that they *are manufactured* things. And it would seem that the postulate of 'one ground for similars,' if ground means origin, requires an earlier postulate to make it valid. The argument, however, suffices to confirm belief in One Source when otherwise established.

The argument for a First Cause is so familiar that it needs no elaboration here. We have seen that, however remotely back science may trace the causal series, and however simple may be its ultimate hypothesis as to the grounds of physical reality, it does not take us to a self-explanatory beginning. The undifferentiated ethereal plenum of Lord Kelvin, of which science supposes the universe to be constituted, requires an original excitation to internal motion which is not explained by the ether itself; and the existence and directing power of energy have likewise to be assumed before science can enter upon her explanatory description of phenomena. Even Herbert Spencer required for his system the assumption of a First Cause, as a necessary datum of consciousness. Adopting, then, the standpoint of science with regard to the nature and validity of knowledge, and discussing the question from that standpoint alone, we are brought to a choice between the indefinite regress of causes and the postulation of a First Cause which is *causa sui*.

[1] *The Hibbert Journal*, Vol. II. No. ii. pp. 283, 289.

The indefinite regress explains nothing, but merely restates the question to be solved; for the explanation of a given change it merely refers us to a preceding similar change, and so on indefinitely. But, as a recent writer has said, "it is impossible that what is not intelligible in one instance, should become intelligible by the mere multiplication of similar unintelligibilities." Professor Taylor, whose are the words just quoted, goes on to say that of the attempts which philosophers have made to extricate themselves from this difficulty without giving up causality as an ultimate principle of explanation, "the least philosophical is that of arbitrarily postulating a First Cause with no preceding cause"—a way out of the difficulty which "obviously amounts to an arbitrary desertion of the causal principle at the point where it becomes inconvenient to remain faithful to it."

Objection may fairly be taken to the word 'arbitrarily' in this criticism of the conception of a First Cause. For obviously, unless causality is to be identified with mere sequence and deprived of its essential implication of efficiency, a 'secondary' cause is no cause at all; it is only allowed to pass for one because of the mediate efficiency which it is assumed to derive from that which alone is efficient cause, if there be any such thing as causal action, namely the productive power of a true cause, or First Cause. It may also be urged that the principle of causality, in so far as it is a principle of systematic connexion, admittedly only applies to things which *begin to be.* 'Everything which begins to be must have a cause'—so the principle is properly stated as a postulate of scientific thought. And this postulate is perverted, surely, when it is pressed so as to include the First Cause as one among the series of similar causes; not when it expressly excludes reference to a thing or a Being of which we do not say that it 'began to be.' That every cause implies an anterior cause is a vicious interpretation of this principle, and states more than is given *a priori* and analytically bound up with the category of cause; or, in the language of the epistemology which seems destined to replace the *a priori* doctrine of Kant, it states more than is necessarily implied in the postulate of causality by means of which we have reduced our human experience to calculable order.

In so far as the cosmological proof of the Being of God is identical with an argument to a First Cause, it has often been supposed to have been invalidated by Kant's criticism, that we cannot apply the category of cause outside the realm of the empirical. This is only true, however, if cause is merely a subjective category of the understanding without any objective or concrete counterpart in the external world. Now, if cause be thus entirely subjective, simply a habit of mind forced upon us by the exigencies of our impulse to interpret our experience, we may be prepared to admit that the notion of cause, however indispensable in practice, is indefensible in theory. Everyone who has tried to think out wherein the 'efficiency' of causation consists, how 'transeunt[1]' causal action is to be conceived, what exactly causation is and how it is worked, will be familiar with the endless difficulties, paradoxes, and confusions into which his thought is thereby inevitably led. He may then conclude, perhaps, that 'cause' belongs to appearance, not to reality, and that it is an inadequate key to the complete interpretation of experience which philosophers seek. If such be the case with cause, the theistic argument for a First Cause must be abandoned; but also, along with it, one of the mainstays of the mechanical theory of the world which sees in "the extension of the province of what we call matter and causation" the completed exclusion of the theological standpoint.

On the other hand, our inability to conceive the rationale of causation is no proof that illusion necessarily lurks in our immediate experience of activity, whence the concept of cause is certainly suggested; the category of causality, however derived, may after all reflect something of what actually goes on in reality. In this case, since causation is unable to explain itself, we are authorised, and indeed driven, to seek

[1] 'Transeunt' activity is exhibited when one object is made to change by another. When a body changes uninfluenced by another its activity is distinguished as 'immanent.'

for its explanation outside the pale of physical science. And, inasmuch as science herself teaches that matter is wholly inert, and energy without the power to direct itself, it is necessary to seek for causal efficiency, whether original or derived, in mind. We are thus led to the concept of a First Cause, an absolute Being, such as is presupposed by Theism; the eternity of matter and energy, on the one hand, and blind chance (whatever that may mean), on the other, are excluded as explanations of the universe.

We here get a glimpse of the need for the concept of God which physical science has often been supposed to render superfluous or inadmissible. The special sciences do not, of course, require the use of such a concept; they would be ruined as sciences if they did. For their business is to give *relative* explanations of phenomena by tracing them causally to physical antecedents. To appeal, where gaps occur in our knowledge of the causal connexion of things, to divine activity, would be, for science, to renounce scientific explanation; while for theology to thrust such explanation into the gaps of scientific theory, with a view to vindicating the necessary existence of God, would be to mistake the functions of science and theology alike, and to play into the hand of the scientific sceptic by appearing to recognise the claim of science to metaphysical absoluteness instead of confining her to the more humble *rôle* of phenomenal classification and description.

We begin then now to see that although the special sciences can perform their work and achieve their conquests without recourse to the use of the idea of divine activity, and can perform it equally well whether Theism be true or not, there are questions raised in the mind of the philosopher by science as a whole which, the theist contends, are only satisfactorily answerable on the assumption of the existence of God.

3. So far it has been argued that if the causal relation between phenomena is real, the essential element of efficiency in the cause, which science indeed increasingly ignores as her

progress continues, inevitably carries us back to a self-existent cause, an eternal Mind and Will. Further study of the causal nexus, which science has revealed and in terms of which naturalism seeks to explain the universe, will supply another argument for the existence of an absolute Being as the ground of all individual things.

When we ask what is the bond of connexion between the cause and its effect, or, in technical language, how we are to understand 'transeunt activity,' we are led to see that something more must exist in the universe than all that science, with its particular interpretation or usage of causality, brings to light. Atomism is obviously incapable of accounting for causality at all. If the atoms, or ultimate elements into which science resolves the world, are absolutely independent of one another; if there is no spontaneity attaching to them individually and no concerted action amongst them collectively, —nothing but externally determined impacts and changes of motion: then it is impossible to explain the fact that things happen according to law, causes producing effects and like causes like effects. Nor does reduction of all kinds of causation to cases of the one most familiar to our experience, and therefore apparently the most simple, namely, mechanical action or production of motion by impact, bring us any nearer to understanding exactly how the cause produces the effect. For why, when one ball impinges on another, should motion or change of motion take place? How is the change produced? If the structure of the world is at bottom discontinuous, as is presupposed in atomistic hypotheses, how is the transition from cause to effect brought about? This question assumes a very important place in the philosophical system of Lotze, and its solution seemed to him absolutely to demand a universal Being as the background of all individual things, constituting their bond of union, and alone rendering their interaction possible. If causation is not merely conditioning, and not identical with creation out of nothing; if it cannot be conceived as a transference of influences from the cause to the effect, and yet transeunt action is not to be successfully dispensed with by theories such as those of occasionalism or

II] *Physical Science, and the Being of God* 85

preestablished harmony: then causal action must be described, as Lotze argues, in terms of the category of immanence. The passage from cause to effect, that is to say, is a development in one and the same Being. Transeunt is exchanged for *immanent activity*; pluralism gives place to monism; the One and the many are in some qualified sense identical. Thus science, or, rather, the philosophical bearings of scientifically established facts, again lead us, if change and causal action in the physical world are to be made conceivable, to postulate a single, all-embracing Being; though, so far as this argument goes, such Being is not necessarily to be identified with the God of Theism.

4. There is yet another way in which the results of physical science, when their ultimate explanation is attempted, suggest the necessary existence of a Supreme Being. In presenting this argument it will be necessary to transgress once more the limits of pure science and to enter upon the territory which belongs by right to the succeeding essay of this volume. Such trespassing, however, is inevitable, on account of the fact already emphasised, that science, *qua* science, has little or no contact with theology, and that it is only upon the common ground of philosophy that these two departments of thought can be brought into relation with each other. And in the present argument we leave behind altogether the epistemological standpoint of 'common sense' and of ordinary working science. In some of the foregoing discussions this standpoint has been retained for the sake of meeting the scientific reader on his own ground; but only, as it were, under protest. We must now act upon our repudiation of the uncritical presupposition of ordinary common sense and science, that the universe is a great machine existing objectively apart from the minds which come to it, as it were, from without: a something 'given' to those minds as ready-made reality which they are to take as it stands, along with its preexisting inexorable laws determining the sequence of its events, and are to endeavour to understand as best they can, if only understanding can find a place therein at all. If theology argue with science on the tacit assumption that the theory of knowledge adopted by

science is adequate for purposes other than those of practical life, theology will find it hard to worst its opponent. It is only by refusing to open the debate until the realistic has been exchanged for the idealistic standpoint, that Theism can entertain the prospect of ultimate success. It is precisely in repudiating the epistemological presuppositions of science that theology disarms her opponent and makes herself invulnerable.

In raising the question, then, of the reality of the physical universe, very little reflection brings even the plain man to recognise that, apart from mind, it is impossible to conceive of material existence. The properties of physical objects, as such, obviously do not inhere in them; they are made, at least in part, by our minds which perceive them. It is there, and not in the rose, that redness exists. Not even the primary properties of matter, such as extension and figure, any more than the secondary, such as colour and taste, can have any existence apart from our sensibility and thought; and so matter, as independent of mind, has no meaning. If to exist is more than to be perceived by mind,—or, rather, to be an element in conscious experience,—it certainly cannot be to possess, as inherent, qualities which require external mind to constitute them. Whether there are noumenal and unknowable 'things-in-themselves' behind 'things,' which produce on our sensibility the effects which we call the properties of matter, as Kant taught, or whether Berkeley's *esse est percipi* sufficiently defines material existence, is a question which is irrelevant in this context. In either case the world, as we know it, is made by our senses and understanding. 'Made,' however, is not 'created.' The perceiving subject does not create its objects; we do not ourselves originate our sensations. Something, then, cooperates with our mental activity to constitute reality. And of this something we can say two things: firstly, it is intelligible; for by scientific methods we are increasingly interpreting it as a cosmos: and secondly, it interacts with us active subjects; for so is our experience constituted. Either, then, it is itself intelligent and causally efficient, or

Physical Science, and the Being of God

else there is intelligence and causal activity behind it. And inasmuch as the only cause of which we have experience is mind, both of these two characteristics of the 'objective' world are also characteristics of spirit. Nature, therefore, must at bottom be spiritual. Thus does reflection on the results of science lead us to an idealistic conception of the universe. The step from such spiritualism or idealism to Theism is still, indeed, a step; but in the light of other considerations it is relatively an easy one. For science not only brings to light the uniformity and intelligibility of Nature: she no less clearly reveals the unity of Nature. "Everywhere," says a living biologist, "unities are being perceived,—the unity of vital organisation through all the varied styles of architecture in plant and animal, the unity of vital processes amid all the multifarious expressions of life, the unity of development, the unity of evolution. What the poet and the artist see instinctively, what the metaphysician and the theologian reach deductively, biology is striving to establish inductively, —the Unity of Nature." And physics has attained to the realisation of this ideal of unity far more perfectly than has biology. And thus all science approaches one aspect of the theologian's idea of God. For if Nature is one consistent whole, does it not presuppose One Ground, and therefore, in the light of what has gone before, One Supreme Intelligence and One Cause: in other words, One originating and conserving Mind? If so, God is not a superfluous hypothesis, though science may have no need of such a concept. The concept of God as Universal Mind seems indispensable for rounding off the knowledge we derive from the several physical sciences and for securing reality for the universe which science seeks to interpret.

Some of the more general truths which science has taught us about the universe have now been seen to involve inferences, necessary alike for their interpretation and for the unification of scientific knowledge, which point in the direction of theistic doctrine. The analysis of causal interaction, in terms of which science makes the universe relatively intelligible, has led us to affirm that such interaction between individual things is unthinkable without the assumption of an ultimate Being, a One embracing the many, which might possibly, though not necessarily, be identified with what the theist means by God. Further, an inquiry into what constitutes the reality of the external world has compelled us to postulate an infinite and eternal Mind. And, yet again, it has been shown that if causality is not altogether subjective, if it is the counterpart in Nature of what we mean by activity in beings endowed with will, then the argument from the course of Nature to the First Cause, which is to be identified with will, would seem to be valid. And the argument involved in this last line of thought is strengthened by the results previously mentioned. For if mind be the prior element, and matter and energy only its constructions, the ascription of the world's course to the eternal action of energy or matter becomes absurd.

If these arguments be sound, we have already reached the theistic inference that the world exists in and for an infinite Spirit, a Being characterised by Mind and Will, a Being transcending the world which exists for Him, and immanent in the world which exists in Him.

5. At this stage it may suitably be pointed out that the trend and tendency of natural science has of late years been in a direction favourable, rather than otherwise, to the idealistic view of the world which must form the starting-point for a theistic theology. The strength of materialism, which was much more prevalent among students of physical science a generation or two ago, lay in the mechanical theory of Nature, which, it has been already remarked, is now seen to be full of shortcomings from the point of view of science, and to be hopelessly inadequate from the point of view of philosophy. Biologists have insisted on the importance of mental factors, whether of the nature of mere sentience and instinct or whether of the nature of imitation and conscious choice, in the process of evolution in the organic world. But the inefficiency and irrelevancy which naturalism attributes to these mental factors is difficult to reconcile with its doctrine of the survival of only what is useful to an

organism: consequently the theory of animal automatism and of the sufficiency of matter and force to explain the whole cosmic process has been largely discredited. The change of view has been gradual, and its stages are interesting to note. The severer form of materialism, which asserted that all was matter and there was no mind, gave place to the view that matter was primary and mind was its function, phenomenally real but irrelevant to the action of the world-machine. From this the next step was to the monistic position that matter and mind are two aspects of one unknowable real: a theory which has sometimes given impartial justice to each of the two factors, but which has oftener been materialistic in all but name. This monism, which has for some time been fashionable in scientific circles, has proved, as a matter of fact, to be a position of unstable equilibrium, and may be looked upon as a half-way house on the road to idealism. The late Professor Huxley is a good instance of a scientific thinker who, in spite of his whole habit of mind, lapsed at odd moments to the side of idealism and conceded the position to the idealist's view of ultimate reality. Attention to first principles, that is to considerations as to the nature of knowledge and to the validity of scientific presuppositions and postulates, has largely been the cause of this change of position among men of science. Another cause, doubtless, is the fact that psychologists have taken up the study of organic evolution and have insisted on the due recognition of the mental factors involved in natural selection, especially in the case of the higher animals. Theories such as those of subjective selection and organic selection now find a place in the complete statement of the doctrine of evolution. One of the foremost of living physicists has expressed his belief that it is impossible to conceive of the living organism as a complicated piece of mere mechanism, and some of the leading physiologists of France, Germany, America, and our own country have revived the idea of vital force: not, indeed, in its old, crude and question-begging sense[1], but

---

[1] The ancient theory of vital force was useless mainly because of the vagueness and obscurity attaching to the term 'force.' Since the principle of the conservation of energy was discovered it has been a question

as expressive of the existence of a factor necessary for the explanation of organic life such as is not supplied by the theory that organisms are automatic mechanisms and their life-history solely determined by physical forces. In taking this step, recent science has removed itself further from the possibility of being misunderstood to be inevitably materialistic and incompatible with Theism. And in presence of the awakened interest in the study of human personality, which is now more capable than ever before of being investigated by experimental and strictly scientific methods, it is possible that our knowledge of mind and of its influence on both mind and matter may be so widely extended in the future that many of the corollaries of dogmatic materialism will be experimentally disproved. But, however this may be, it may now safely be affirmed that it is idealism and not materialism or naturalism

whether vital changes can wholly be explained as cases of transformation of known kinds of energy which are conserved. The mechanical view would represent them as entirely explicable in terms of physical and chemical change. Neo-vitalism, on the other hand, maintains that something more is required to explain growth, development, and such like phenomena. Some representatives of this school postulate a new form of energy, others a property of self-adaptation, and others a force which controls and directs physical energy, without altering its quantity (see Baldwin's *Dictionary of Philosophy and Psychology*, Arts. *Life* and *Organic*, whence the following sentences are cited). "The last view often makes consciousness the new agent, and represents a distinct tendency in discussion to restate the question in terms of a dualism between matter and mind rather than between matter and life; the additional point being assumed, or directly advocated, that life and mind are coterminous. This does not alter the essential conditions of the problem, although it is held to strengthen the position of vitalism by making accessible to it the facts and arguments in support of some sort of causal activity of mind.... Vitalism makes its strongest stand in what is called the developmental mechanics of the individual, where the facts of regeneration and organic accommodation, it is held, can only be described in vitalistic terms and illustrate the inscrutable mystery of life." The structural evolutions which take place within the cell-nucleus, the inconceivableness of a mechanical model to represent the phenomena of heredity, the response of protoplasm and nucleus to the direct action of the environment so as to cause the building up of the *appropriate* cells and tissues for each organ and part of an organ;—these are some few of the facts which at present seem to make a mechanical theory of organic processes entirely insufficient.

that is profiting most by the recent advances of science. The witness of science, in so far as science can be suggestive of philosophical theory, to that idealistic view of the universe which forms the basis for theistic theology, is increasing and may further increase; and when the survey of physical science has been widened, and its old metaphysical and epistemological presuppositions have been abandoned in the light of criticism, it may be hoped that the "trend and temper of orthodox science" will have ceased to be suggestive of a purely mechanical, self-sufficient, and self-explanatory universe of matter and motion.

6. Returning to the argument for the existence of a personal God derived by reflection on the results and implications of natural science, we take up its thread at the point where we came in view of the conclusion that the ultimate reality is a universal Mind for which all things exist, and a universal Will which is the cause of their existence. If scientific knowledge of the world seems thus to require, for coherency and completeness, the postulate of a First Cause, it may further be urged that science reveals another fact which has important philosophical implications: the fact, namely, that since the world is intelligible to the human mind, the First Cause is the First Cause of a *cosmos*.

If a world implies a First Cause, an intelligible world would seem necessarily to imply an intelligent Cause. That there is such a thing as an *Order* of *Nature*, a harmony of causes and an unvarying relation to their effects, can hardly be looked upon as the outcome of aught but intelligence. This becomes the more obvious when we reflect that natural laws cannot be self-existent, and that therefore such 'necessity' as pertains to them cannot be the necessity of blind fate, the mechanical necessity which Mr Spencer regarded as the consequence solely of 'persistence of force,' but must be rational necessity. The necessary truths which science has revealed "originate in the subject of experience, not in the object." If the objects conform to them, then all experience is rational; our reason is confronted and determined by universal reason[1]. We make the concept of law,

[1] Ward, *op. cit.* Vol. II. p. 283.

and bring it to our study of Nature; and the behaviour of phenomena is found to justify its tentative application. Mind originates the concept of the uniformity of Nature; so far we are the 'makers' of Nature. But inasmuch as we are guided by Nature to this idea of a system of laws, permanent laws being qualities of Nature as a whole, the final ground of the teleological character of the world is the relations of phenomena themselves, and their coincidence with the results of our thought. Thus, the fact that science finds Nature to be a unity characterised by regularity, a fact which increase of natural knowledge and of experience ever confirms, leads us on from the result previously reached, viz. that ultimate reality is one, and is of the nature of spirit, the actual world being real only in and for mind, to the further belief that the Mind which is the origin of things is a mind which acts in ways which we ourselves can understand. Here we arrive at the last requisite for attributing 'personality' to God.

When theology thus argues from the broad and general truth, established by natural science, that the world is an ordered cosmos, to a supreme Intelligence that framed it, she is upon safe ground. Narrower arguments than this, of the teleological class, do not possess the same cogency. The teleology which saw in each adaptation of means to end in Nature the mark of a particular purpose of an external Designer has long been discarded; the theory of Natural Selection banished it. And no argument for the existence of a Supreme Designer can be constructed out of the facts which illustrate what is called internal teleology, *i.e.* the self-adaptation of organisms to their environments; at most they serve to set a limit to the applicability of mechanical concepts within the biological field. But it is not necessary to the case for Theism that all theories which savour of the mechanical in biology should be discredited; mechanism in the means is not necessarily inconsistent with design towards the end. The end of creation in any case is not foreseen by the creature and striven for, and indeed might be perfectly well attained were the life-history of an organism simply a matter of physico-chemism. Cosmic teleology is, in fact, totally independent of the issue, whether adaptations in organisms are the outcome of their conscious and directed effort or of mechanical response to environment. If Nature pursues an intelligible and ordered course, it is enough. It is not necessary to argue further, that an organism in pursuing its own particular ends or interests is thereby necessarily furthering the great end of the course of Nature as a whole. That law obtains in biology as well as in chemistry or physics is our guarantee that purpose finds expression in the organic world. If by 'end' we mean a general end of Nature as a whole, we can extend to the lower realms, at least, of the sentient world the words in which Aquinas expressed the teleology of the inorganic: "Things which have no perception can only tend toward an end if directed by a conscious and intelligent being. Therefore there is an intelligence by which all natural things are ordered to an end[1]."

Adaptation is of course written large upon the face of the organic world. The life-history of plant or animal cannot be described except in terms of it. The chief factor is one which cannot be explained by purely mechanical processes, namely, the action of the organism in accordance with its 'interests.' But the question, who is the designer of such adaptations as we discover, is one which not everyone who admits design at all would answer alike. Some would say, the organic forms themselves; others would refer all adaptation to a supreme Mind indwelling in all. But the point to be remarked is that cosmic teleology is entirely independent of the question whether there is conscious aim on the part of living forms, directing their movements or their development. In the overlooking of this truth consists the error of supposing that the theory of Natural Selection is incompatible with a teleological view of Nature.

Natural Selection, unaccompanied by what are called Lamarckian factors, may or may not suffice adequately to describe the evolution of living things, variation being given. But, however 'mechanical' its character and however 'blindly' it may appear to act, there is no reason to assume that it, or

[1] *Summa*, I. ii. 3.

indeed the mechanism described by any other law of Nature, is anything but the means employed by the Designer of the cosmos and of the goal toward which the evolutionary process tends. If some should prefer to read the activity of purposeful mind only in processes which are not as yet, and possibly never may be, describable in terms of mechanical concepts, they may comfortably reflect upon the fact that Natural Selection, after all, only deals with the secondary 'origin' of organic forms. The true origin of species lies, of course, in the cause of diversities of variations; and by the fact that such variations must be 'definite,' or occur in single, particular directions, and that repeatedly, if they are to become fixed by selection and to form an incipient species, many thinkers have felt impelled to believe that the evolution of organic forms cannot wholly be referred to blind processes showing no directivity; that Nature, in fact, is playing her game of chance with loaded dice. But be this as it may, and be the theory of Natural Selection as inadequate as many judges, whose opinion is worthy of respect, pronounce it, it is important that the truth should be clearly apprehended that a theistic interpretation of the world would by no means be invalidated if the theory of Natural Selection proved entirely acceptable.

Similarly, it is immaterial whether the vital processes of organisms prove, in the future, to be completely explicable in terms of physico-chemical, or even mechanical, concepts, or whether they demand some form of vitalist theory adequately to interpret them. The cell-theory, which was one step towards the mechanical ideal, but only a step, has indeed proved insufficient. The phenomena of homology, of regeneration, of the growth of mutilated parts, present difficulties which many recent biologists regard as insuperable from this point of view. But it remains to be seen whether the degree to which mechanical interpretation of vital processes was once believed to have been carried by means of the doctrine of cells may not be equally attained by recourse to the theory of smaller biological units than the cell, such as histologists have of late been led by their microscopical

Physical Science, and the Being of God

researches to adopt. But, however far mechanical description may be carried within the field of biology, 'explanation' will not have been fully attained. To describe is not to explain; to calculate is not to understand. At all points science leads us ultimately to philosophy; and it is upon the latter ground alone that theological interpretations of the world can be tested, and their intellectual merits estimated.

The teleological argument from Nature, it has often been pointed out, proves the existence rather of a Framer or Architect of the universe than a Creator. But in this respect it supplements the theistic arguments previously given. That the world is an ordered and intelligible whole is a fact which science presupposes and to which its very existence testifies. And this fact leads us to endow the Being for Whom and in Whom the universe exists with intelligence which, however much it transcend our own, has so much in common with it that in His world we feel that 'spirit greets Spirit,' and that this Supreme Intelligence acts in ways which our finite souls can partially understand.

7. Yet the world is not obviously rational through and through. It is the weakness of all systems of idealism, and the most considerable difficulty inherent in theistic thought, that our experience presents us with an element in God's world which strongly suggests imperfection either in His power or in His goodness. The fuller light which science has thrown upon the processes of organic evolution has intensified our sense of the truth that the "whole creation groaneth and travaileth in pain together until now." And the more we emphasise the immanence of God in Nature; the more, that is, we insist that the minuter details of the course of Nature express His will and represent His immediate activity, as, some tell us, natural science, since the work of Darwin, has been compelling us to do, the more incomprehensible does the problem of physical evil and pain become. Certainly the apologetics which have sought to minimise animal sensibility and suffering, or to show that in man suffering sometimes justly punishes and sometimes educates, must frankly be denied to have touched much more than the fringe of this great difficulty.

Now natural science certainly suggests no teleology of physical evil. The distribution of pain appears promiscuous, and follows no plan which we can trace. In the human world "all things come alike unto all: there is one event to the righteous, and to the wicked." We are not here concerned with moral evil, which lies outside the pale of physical science. But the study of Nature seems to suggest that although pain serves no purpose in itself, it is inextricably bound up with the world's course as a whole. It would appear, in fact, to be of the nature of a necessary by-product. The earthquake and the pestilence, to which we can assign no purpose, are the outcome of the selfsame course of things, the regular sequence of events according to law, which on the whole ministers to life and health. The desert and the volcano are also looked upon as blots on the fair face of Nature; but a recent scientific writer has assured us that these things are necessary for the supply of atmospheric dust, which is a necessary condition for rain-fall; and thus they are essential to life upon our planet. Doubtless some other of the phenomena which man accounts as physical ills may be of the same order of necessity to the world-system; but many others, so far as we can see, are simply collateral products.

And this surely bears upon the theistic problem. For though Theism repudiates the conception of law which has sometimes found favour among the representatives of science, that, namely, which regards it as a fast-binding fate, independent of God and man; and though it looks upon laws of Nature as at bottom expressions of the regularly but freely acting power of the Governor of the universe, thus, in Dr Ward's expression, "letting contingency into the very heart of things": still it must be maintained by the theist, we think, that the only alternative to such regularity in God's operations as we find expressed in a reign of law, would seem to be a government of the world by means of an 'incalculable miscellany of miracles,' which would substitute chaos for cosmos and render rational life impossible for finite intelligences such as ours. When Dr Ward, in his Gifford Lectures, offers us the choice between an absolutely necessary or

Physical Science, and the Being of God

mechanical system of law, suggesting atheism, and absolute contingency, suggesting unconditioned freedom in God's causal activity: between mechanism only with no God, and God only with no mechanism, as if it were a case of 'all or none,' we may perhaps venture to ask whether it is not more in accordance with the requirements both of science and of theistic philosophy to adopt, like Martineau, as a third possibility, the idea of self-conditionedness on the part of the Supreme Being, an adherence to a coherent plan for the realisation of the world-purpose, in order to satisfy the conditions for intelligibility by finite minds. Such a plan would involve choosing certain roots for the world-equation, and abiding by all the consequences which followed upon such a choice, though they might not be of the nature of ends in themselves. Need everything in Nature, after all, be either a means to a purposed end, or an end itself, as so many idealists have asserted? Will it not be inevitable, so far as we can see, that a world-process of so highly complicated a nature as ours undoubtedly is, will, in accordance with the consistency of thought and the compatibility of being, involve contingent consequences which may have no reference to the process as a whole or to its final goal? We need not make the assumption, commonly identified with Deism, that the world, once created, is maintained by its own self-sufficiency instead of by the immanent or continuous activity of God; or that the laws of Nature are an eternal *prius* existing independently of God like the ὕλη of the ancient Greeks. Rather would we see in law the expression of the free but self-determined will of God acting in relation to the creatures to whom He has delegated intelligent and moral life. This is the view to which, as it would seem, Theism may best commit itself without danger to religion and to reason alike; and it may be added, it is one to which the facts of physical science naturally point, and in which they receive a satisfactory philosophical explanation. If, then, our knowledge of the cosmos encourage the idea that God is pledged, through Self-accommodation to finite intelligence which He would not baffle and stultify, to a definite and regular process of realising

His world-plan, we shall not be surprised to find that many of the particular details accompanying the historical execution of that plan are no essential parts of it, no ends in themselves, but only necessarily incidental epiphenomena or by-products. By this theory, which appears to the present writer, at least, to be rather a natural explanation of the facts than a far-fetched expedient of thought, the beneficence and omnipotence of the Deity are alike vindicated and reconciled; unless indeed we are rash enough to commit ourselves to the assumption that an infinite Mind could have devised a cosmic process at once sufficiently intelligible to finite minds through its regularity, free from the disturbing elements of incalculable miracle, and unaccompanied, in its realisation, by any consequences from its 'general equation' which the human mind could legitimately regard as physical evils.

Thus the moral nature of God, affirmed by Christian theology, is safeguarded against the indictments which some philosophers have put into the mouth of Nature; and thus also the reign of law, of which science is so eloquent, finds its natural place in a theistic philosophy of the world.

8. We conclude, then, that physical science has nothing to say with regard to the Being of God; to pronounce upon such a problem does not fall within her sphere. In other words, science possesses no theological creed. She is indifferent to Theism, but not atheistic. Science, however, inevitably raises a number of questions which she admittedly cannot answer, but which she can, for her own part, afford to ignore. Taking up the questions of the ultimate reality, the origin, and the orderliness of the physical world, we find that the theistic view is not only compatible with the results of science but is strongly suggested by them. Nay, we may go further and adopt Lord Kelvin's recent utterance: "We are absolutely forced by science to believe with perfect confidence in a directive Power....There is nothing between absolute scientific belief in a creative Power and the acceptance of the theory of a fortuitous concourse of atoms." For we are led, if the universe is to be explained at all, to postulate infinite Mind

as the ultimate reality for Whom and in Whom the world exists; infinite Will or Power which alone can constitute the efficiency that we associate with causation. We are guided by the discovered unity of Nature to regard its absolute Ground as One. Further, the orderliness and regularity of the cosmos, which physical science has so laboriously and so successfully traced, compels us to identify the ultimate Being with infinite Intelligence. And lastly, in the condition of accommodation to finite understandings which, as the world-order seems to suggest, the Supreme Intelligence has imposed upon Himself, we perhaps discover the compatibility of the Power behind Nature with holiness and love: attributes which complete the Christian concept of a personal God.

ESSAY III.

THE BEING OF GOD, IN THE LIGHT OF PHILOSOPHY.

ALFRED CALDECOTT, D.D.

SYNOPSIS.

§ I. HUMAN NATURE.
The whole of Human Nature is to be considered.
The central unity in Spiritual Life.
Self and the world.
Life as Intelligence.
Life as Activity.
Life as Feeling.
Life as Feeling and Activity combined.
Life as Feeling, Activity, and Thought.
Sociality.

§ II. THE INTERPRETATION OF HUMAN NATURE.
Subjectivism inadequate.
Spiritual Idealism asserted.
Mysticism and *a posteriori* Rationalism, provisional methods.
Transcendental method:
  in application to Intelligence,
    Feeling,
    Ethical Life,
    Sociality.
Interpretation offered by Pluralist Spiritualism.
Monistic Spiritualism asserted.
General Philosophy and Christian Philosophy.

THE BEING OF GOD, IN THE LIGHT OF PHILOSOPHY.

PHILOSOPHY is the interpretation of life. Its quest is the ultimate significance of the Universe, the supreme form of Reality: though concentrating upon essentials, it will fail if it leaves out any phase of life under the plea of its being unessential ; it will fail if it is unable to bring all phases into system. To other Essays in this volume falls the treatment of lower forms of being than Man, and of Man in his relation to those forms : here we are free to start from Human Nature as our datum, as the life which is to be interpreted. We shall be obliged to limit ourselves to Human Nature in its norm, at its full development in men of thought and feeling and ethical virtue, living in community as social humanity. Space will not permit of treatment of abnormality, pathological variation, imperfection ; and further, it is the study of a nature in its normal form that gives the central method of science and of philosophy. As Human Nature will be the subject-matter, so it will also be the instrument of enquiry : human philosophy is man interpreting himself. And as we shall advocate reference to a wider life than is usually suggested by the term Reason, we offer the terms Spirit and Spiritual : and state our purpose to be to show in broad outlines the Spirit of Man interpreting Human Nature.

'Theology' is here used as 'Rational Theology': related to philosophy not as concerned with a different subject-matter or a different method, but as employing a variety of terms more familiar, more expressive of practical and emotional meaning. In philosophical language many leading terms are purposely and wisely reduced in colour and in concreteness: but the reduction has been excessive by reason of the predominance of Intellectualism in the historical development of philosophy. But if all human Nature is our field and the whole human Spirit is the enquirer, we must provide for more concreteness by terms in which ethical and æsthetic aspects are plainly expressed. Force and significance will therefore be sought from time to time by associating with the intellectualist terminology the language of theology and religion.

§ I. *Human Nature.*

Philosophy is concerned to have before it human nature in its whole length and breadth and depth and height. It must, moreover, take Man as a living person, and decline every invitation to limit its view to any one elemental feature of his life. Man thinks and strives, he fears and loves, he sets valuations and works out purposes in accordance with them. He lives in the consciousness that he is a member of a community, receiving influences from an outer world and from his fellows, and in turn contributing to the changes which take place. And when he comes to knowledge of himself, he acts from his own self-conscious choice, freely; the ends that he has selected decide his modes of conduct; and he lives in union with like beings, in reciprocal activity and mutual affection, attributing to them self-consciousness and freedom like his own. Limited in time and space and in the area of the content of his consciousness as he sees that he is, yet by participation with his fellows and by entering into their spheres of life and interest and knowledge he ranges over wider and wider circles from family to village and town and nation, and, dimly, to the whole of humanity by glimpses along the records of the past, not without anticipatory forecasts of the time to be. And as his view and his interest widen, he finds in himself an ever-increasing differentiation and enrichment. Which part of this 'nature' is he to be called upon to neglect or to distrust? Why, *prima facie*, may he not have confidence in each element of it? Why may he not, with allowance for differences of value, find that in the constitution of himself as a whole every fibre of his being has its function and its right?

The amplitude of human nature has been treated with scant respect by both Philosophy and Theology; parts of the presentment have been ignored or disparaged, some in one quarter, others in another. Feeling is untrustworthy over all its range, we hear from many; the lower range of sensibility must not be brought into the final account, say some; by many it is the high ranges of intellect that are distrusted; and by others the intervention of will and choice is regarded as conducting not to reality but to delusion. Others, again, have selected some one factor of human nature, and invested it with sole constructive power. Thus it has come about that our philosophical and theological constructions are as varied as the styles of Architecture, almost as those of Literature itself. Variety has its claims and its charms, but for philosophy partiality is pathological: comprehensiveness is the breath of its life.

The first point to be fixed down in setting out human nature is the *unity of consciousness*, the singleness of the series or system of experiences we call a conscious life. We shall find ample richness of differentiation and variety, but no partition: some part of the experience will have a reference to otherness included in it, some part will lack that reference, but both parts alike are referred to the same centre; all distinctions lie within experience, though some of them point beyond. The singleness is the initial mark—the experiences of such a single centre constitute a whole: it is by no figure of speech that we use a name in the singular number, and speak of a mind or soul.

The second point is the *distinction* made in consciousness between *the thinker and other minds*. This also is fact of experience: in the higher range of consciousness we come to an emphatic and clear distinction between some changes in our mental life which we refer to ourselves, and some changes which we assign to the action of agencies other than ourselves. The mind indeed does not go out beyond itself: whatever happens outside must be capable of so operating as to produce changes of which the mind can take notice; but in taking notice of such changes it learns to distinguish them from changes of which it is itself the originator. It divides the changes into those in which there is something presented to itself, and those which it projects by its own activity. To limit the mind to what it projects from itself is to enclose it in a circle, and so, to divide the world of minds into a disconnected congeries of monads: to limit it to what it receives from outside is to dissolve the mental world altogether, since what is true of one mind is presumably true of each and all, and there can be no reception if everything is receptive only. There would be no system if every unit were either pure activity or pure receptivity. But what experience tells us is clear: over a great part of it—not over all, not in our dreams, for instance—we all refer the changes we observe to the agency of 'other than ourselves.' In the experiences which stir us most deeply the 'other' so affects us that we assign to it a personality like our own. This is so not only in knowledge but in action: only in rare cases am I occupied in carrying out plans devised by myself for ends purely of my own choice; my life is largely a choice between such forms of good and such varieties of means as I find within my compass when I look forth upon the world. Selection, not creation, is the rule. And in my proceedings I meet with other agents whose activities oppose mine, and I must adapt my actions more or less to theirs. In the world of ideas I can assert myself to some extent by moulding the experiences which come to me, but I cannot make or unmake them in their entirety. There is a stimulus in them not due to myself, and so I assign something in the experiences to other agencies than myself. This reference to things and persons at the other side of the objects of my experience to that occupied by myself is the norm of conscious life in all but the lower stages.

This distinction among my experiences is a fact of primary

Philosophy, and the Being of God

importance disclosed by observation and confirmed as experience proceeds. Its interpretation cannot be satisfied by a Realism which would regard the 'other' as so alien that in knowing it we have no contributory function; nor by a Subjectivism which refers all experience to the self and its processes: in any interpretation the two sides must both be regarded. Strange as it may seem to common sense, both of these aberrations have found frequent support, either expressly or implicitly, in the schools of philosophy, though the errors are so gross that we at once regard such attempts as marks either of premature or of decadent periods of thought. Such aberrations in Religion, amounting to the denial either of man's own reality or of that of the world and God, are plainly pathological. Urged in one direction by the determination to oppose men who were travelling in the other, ingenuity has either ignored or exaggerated this fundamental distinction found in the normal experience of the mind, the sense of self and the sense of otherness, rising in the higher experiences to a sense of other selves.

In this distinction there is no ground given for a partition of our experience. As our first point lays down, it is all the experience of a single self: that some part of it is referred to myself alone while some part also includes reference to other agencies is a distinction which lies within my experience, but the experience is all mine, belonging to myself alone as centre. The singleness within the dualism is itself disclosed as fact; of its interpretation we speak later on.

Passing now to the phases of the life of the Soul, it is due to the prominence of Intellectualism in philosophy that we should commence with *Thought*. This gives us Knowledge as the form of mental life and takes Truth as the primary guide to Reality; it speaks especially of the Being or Existence of God. The point to be emphasized here, too, is the unity of the mind through a variety of experiences. The mind in 'thinking' is engaged in various modes, but the time has now gone by for so separating these off from one another as to suggest the operation of various intellectual 'faculties.' This separatist treatment was effective in a pioneering way, but now psychology shows us graduated processes of the same fundamental activity proceeding in orderly connexion. We still conveniently speak of Sensibility and Reason and higher Intuition, but we think of them as progressive stages in mental activity. From a vague reaction to stimulus consciousness passes through stages up to an activity which almost succeeds in being spontaneous. Sensibility, as the stage of knowledge in which sensations and their images are prominent, is not purely passive and inert, as much British philosophy has assumed : in our knowing them relations and distinctions are implicit, and we soon pass higher and weave them into perceptions : and so onward until we come to conceptions and 'ideas.' The sense-data do not carry us very far, but they cannot be dispensed with in human thinking, though we come to treat them as symbols and invest them with significances of deeper quality and wider scope. The child-mind in its simplicities has already the rudiments of thinking; advancing thought distinguishes, divides, analyses, classifies, unites, consolidates, universalizes, deep and far, and we catch at the possibility of a higher immediacy beyond reasoning as we had found a lower immediacy before it.

But in neither immediacy can we live : from the lower we emerge as intelligence progresses ; towards the higher we move upwards without being able to pass into it. Hence arise the contentions between men who will insist on fixing us in one stage or the other : Sensationalism, Rationalism, pure Intuitionalism or Mysticism, each offering its own separate area. But we must insist upon them all : they must be welded together if we are to give an account of human Knowledge as a whole. The unity of the knowing mind penetrates throughout. And all down the scale of Knowledge we must stand firm to the duality of subject-object : the mind contributes, but there is something presented to it all along.

The fundamental unity of Thought in all its processes has not been the usual opinion, and on the whole it is not yet fully accepted. Rather it has been the prevalent method to assign knowledge of Reality to the higher intelligence alone; men claim to have ascended the ladder of knowledge and reached the plane of conceptions or universal ideas; for these a solitary privilege has been asserted: the Reality is Substance, it is said, or Cause, or Self-conscious Principle. These conceptions have been set out as 'Ideas' existing in a region of their own, and showing us Reality as it is; the lower ranges have been treated as hewers of wood and drawers of water. Truth has been conceived in generalities, and Reality taken to consist of necessary and universal essence or essences. But the recognition of all the ranges of intelligence, in which particulars and universals combine in varying ways in an ascending scale, and the suggestion of corresponding degrees of Reality or of participation in Reality, have the *prima facie* claim upon our attention: a claim which is now being reasserted vigorously in independent quarters of the philosophical field.

This procedure is confirmed by the reflection that in religious thought this is the view that best secures that immanence of the Divine Spirit which few of us would now exclude from any stage of the life of the soul, or from any degree of creaturely existence whatever. That the whole range of our intelligence is a unity proceeding within one mind and from one thinking centre, seems to accord with the religious conviction that in every stage of creation we find a suggestion or a symbol of all-pervading Divine intelligence.

Next there is the phase of *Activity*. Man, through his body, participates not only in being impressed by changes occurring in the external world, but also in initiating and directing such changes. And within the processes of mental life, through management of the attention, the course of changes falls partly within the conscious control and guidance of the self. Man conceives purposes, and spends himself in directing changes of activity towards their accomplishment: the course of experience is partly self-chosen and self-directed. Each of us constitutes a sphere of activity, and our several spheres of activity influence one another.

Is there such a mental experience as pure activity, activity for its own sake? On the broad ground that mind cannot be still, that its life is essentially a flux, one would suppose that there is: that, as in body, so in mind, there is purposeless exercise, purely spontaneous play, when the forces are exuberantly healthy. But even this spontaneity seeks objects to be attained, trivial and transitory though they may be, or it soon effervesces and dies down: or, rather, it subsides into that permanent will to persist in living on, which is now seen as clearly by psychologists in the life of mind, as by biologists in the life of organisms. But pure activity has so little significance for the mental life as a whole, that we may at once pass to consider the constituent which works most closely with it, previously to taking them both together.

Feeling denotes the moods or tones of the soul in its experiences; pleasure and pain, satisfaction and dissatisfaction, happiness and unhappiness, joy and misery, and the like. The separation of these tones for special study led to the threefold view of our consciousness as intellectual, emotional, active, in preference to the older arrangement under intellect and activity: and though there is again a tendency to revert to the dual division, we must avoid losing the advantage always gained when a lucid distinction is drawn. The æsthetic aspects of life have a primariness of their own, invariably concurrent as they may be with the other aspects, and specially concerned with the excitation and direction of activity.

Of the prominence of Feeling in our actual experience there is no serious question in daily life; what we find is that it is not allowed much significance for the philosophical determination of Reality or of the Divine Nature. This defect we shall consider later on: here it is only necessary to assert the presence and importance of Feeling, as fact, in a way that will require for it a more adequate treatment by philosophy. Psychological investigation has not succeeded, it is supposed, in so connecting Feeling with the structure of our nature as to lead us to trust in it as a primary factor in healthy and virtuous life, as well as to value it for its own sake; as a constituent of mental health there is much to be said for it, but the exceptions are so many that the region of chaos is as extensive as that which is brought into order by the law. Space does not allow of discussion here, but the opinion may be ventured that the exceptions are not so numerous or so important as they appear, and that further work in the promising science of psychology will tend to show that the law is operative all over the field; that Feeling is completely natural, and has its place over the whole economy of our life. Dean Swift, in one of the rare moods when his mind was unclouded by bias or bitterness, faced the great enemy of optimism, Death, with the declaration that he would not believe that an event 'so natural, so necessary, and so universal, could be opposed to the welfare of mankind.' We may, surely, urge a still more confident optimism for Feeling; in spite of our failure over large tracts to trace the law of its connexion with good life, we may have confidence that by its naturalness, its necessity, and its universality, it vindicates its place in the essence of the spiritual life.

When we think of Feeling in its higher ranges, happiness, gladness, joy, and the love of the Beautiful in all its forms, and take account of the volume of human life occupied in the production and the enjoyment of Poetry and Art, in the pleasures of social intercourse, and, finally, in the 'religious affections,' surely some perversity has possessed the minds of those who have attempted to construct philosophies without frank acceptance, to say nothing of grateful welcome, of the emotional endowment of human nature.

And yet philosophy very extensively—and theology not much less so—has taken up an attitude of opposition, or at least of neglect, towards the æsthetic side of life. For example, Locke's Essay is an enquiry into Reality on the basis of human nature, but in spite of its grip of experience at many points, it offers no answer to many serious questions which men want answered when they think of Reality; it is addressed to men of science, an exposition of what the understanding can tell us, and no more. And a similar Intellectualist tone dominated the Rationalistic philosophy of the whole eighteenth century. Is it surprising, therefore, that forms of Hedonism arose as voices protesting that it was the main business of man to be *happy*, and that philosophy meant the interpretation of that demand? And when men speak of Kant, how common it is to refer to him only as the author of the enquiry into pure Reason and practical Reason, oblivious of his final enquiry into the Beautiful. If method rendered necessary the construction of three stages of enquiry in separation, yet the total of Kant's work is to be estimated only by combining the three as a philosophy of Reality. Since Kant's day, though more recognition was at once accorded to Feeling than in the pre-Romantic period, it has been due chiefly to Lotze that philosophy is learning to lose diffidence in the æsthetic factor in human life, and to place a legitimate emphasis upon it in the interpretation of the meaning of the universe.

And for religion, it is being understood now by theologians as it has been understood all along by the people, that it is not the argument, however well-knit, that exhaustively and finally expresses our belief, but the prayer, the hymn, the ascription of glory, the solemn adoration in the worship of the sanctuary and also in the worship of the soul in its solitary devotions. The conviction in a spectatorial mind that what it sees is the work of an emotionless Creator, has its own value, and must not be despised; but it is when the heavens make us glad with their Beauty that they 'declare' the glory of God, and transform the beholder into a worshipper. It is not sufficient to say that this is 'religion,' but that it is not 'theology.' Theology, as the doctrine of God and the soul, must go astray if a fundamental element in human nature has been excluded from the basis on which the theological structure is to be raised.

But Feeling does not take place in separateness, it works intimately with Activity. When we are acting, feeling arises, and it sustains or checks us in the activity. A feeling arrested is a 'desire,' and in that state of mind the line of action that promises to satisfy the desire and bring us into experienced feeling is the line that we are impelled to take. If the desire is almost without expectation of fruition we call it a 'wish'; an 'idle wish' lying at the extreme of entire absence of expectation. But if there is expectation there arises a longing or craving which includes a sense of strain or pressure towards action; when settled or regularly recurring we

Philosophy, and the Being of God

call it 'appetite.' Desire may attach to objects of many grades and many degrees of definiteness, and we usually name our desires by their objects: ranging from trivialities of daily life to profound purposes and complicated aims: from phases of bodily sensibility to the highest concerns of personal and social welfare. Their office in the mental economy arises from their being feelings, tones, turned into impulses to action.

The recognition of the naturalness of mental Desires or Wants has followed upon the study in Biology of the *strivings* of bodily organisms: Psychology need not regard desires as signs of infirmity or defect, but as the normal forms which Feeling takes as accompaniment of the changing life. Some psychologists base Desire on the removal of Pain: this gives an abnormal character to it, indicating defect in the structure of the mind. The controversy is of long standing, as readers of Plato's *Republic* will remember. The weight of observation appears to be on the side of the view that makes most for the vindication of Nature, namely, that there are promptings and impulsive feelings in which pleasure-tone is positively operative, enhancing the activities and securing their continuance or repetition.

It is because of the operation of impulsive Feeling that our activity very rarely, if ever, works as pure activity, for its own sake. We act under the impulse of Feeling, for some interest. "To will is to bend our souls to the having or doing of that which they see to be good," is Hooker's English formulation of the doctrine of Aquinas. In Germany *Der Wille zum Güten* is the current formula for Will. Professor Stout has made the union so prominent that he suggests the category of 'Interest' as inclusive both of Conation and Feeling-attitude, over against the category of Cognition to which the rest of conscious life is assigned. The mind as active in pursuit of 'interests,' is the formula for a great part of our life. This view vindicates further the naturalness of Feeling: for if Feeling in itself has the value which is claimed for it above, it becomes even more impressively important when it is seen that it is so interlocked, as it were, with the active side of our nature.

Interest as desire for 'good' leads us to Ethics. To what point has modern Ethics arrived? This we must leave readers to decide for themselves: they may elect to stand by the Ethics which insists upon rigorous rightness in the object aimed at, stern sense of Duty in the agent, and a life of fulfilling commands and imperatives. They may eliminate all reference to 'interests' depending upon feeling, as heteronomous for morality, and insist that morality depends upon an inner freedom which realizes itself by carrying out imperatives of reason purified from all emotional considerations. To others this idea may appear as a legacy from the legalist period of both Ethics and Religion: and they may take their stand on Goodness as including power to attract the soul. It would be cumbrous to state a doctrine of human nature in two forms so as to allow for both of these alternatives, and we therefore proceed here by leaving the obligation-view for those whom it satisfies, and taking the view of human nature according to which the obligatory form of Ethics is educational only, the final position being that the Good is really *good* for Man and that its 'obligation' should be commensurate with its attractive power. By way of fortifying this position we simply recall to mind that this is really the view of the most bracing and most fertile periods of both Philosophy and Theology. Platonism and Neo-Platonism agree that the natural attractiveness of goodness for the purified and clear-sighted soul is the foundation principle of Ethics. Aquinas was Platonist in this; in England Hooker continued the tradition; and though, through the dire necessity in a hedonistic age of making control and regimen a principal aim of morals, Butler favoured the 'hard' view of the function of conscience, yet in his treatment both of self-love and of the love of God he found it impossible to suppress the naturalness of the pursuit of goodness. Shaftesbury's ethics amount to being a protest for goodness versus duty: and the Utilitarians gained their vogue by making a similar protest, though they interpreted goodness in a not very lofty way. On the other side, Kant's reversion to a rigorous view has been alluded to; and even Wordsworth, wrestling with the idea that he might trust the attractiveness of goodness, did not prevail, but let it go and gave his final word in favour of stern Duty:—

"In the light of truth thy bondsman let me live."

But in the later nineteenth century the trend was towards the more genial and inspiriting mode of conceiving our ethical life. In Cambridge, for example, Sidgwick was impelled to take up a new position because, never quitting the trust that men must be rational in a sense that the Utilitarians could not attain to, he yet never quitted another trust, namely, that the ideal must commend itself, that the good must satisfy the natural desire of man for happiness and joy.

In modern Theology it must suffice to illustrate the position by comparing a prominent theologian at the beginning of the century with some later theologians. Romanticism and the religion of Feeling owed much to Schleiermacher, yet he chose *Dependence* as the keynote of the feeling for God—a tender, loving dependence, indeed, and in great contrast with the sternness involved in Kant's ethics when moral law is brought out of the transcendental sphere into actual life; and in contrast with Carlyle's grim acquiescence in the Duty of Obedience. Later on, for Ritschl we find Dr Hugh Mackintosh saying, "It is perhaps in reaction from the exaggerated emphasis placed on this dependence, that we find Ritschl, Schleiermacher's greatest successor in constructive theology, laying so marked stress on the fact that religion confers on man true freedom." And Ritschl's position is also that of Auguste Sabatier. To these we may add a Cambridge name: it is from the grave and cautious mind of Hort that we have the words, "There is no life worthy to be called life entirely separate from joy and gladness."

It is upon an Ethics in which joy and gladness have a legitimate and not merely a permitted status, that philosophy and theology are taking their stand to-day.

Taking Activity and Feeling in combination, how does

Thought, as guide to Reality and to God, stand in relation to them? First, as to Feeling; that intellect presents to us objects and arranges them into systems and that moods or tones of feeling arise as we survey them is the simple view that first occurs to us, and it covers a great deal of the ground, ranging from the tones accompanying sensations to the æsthetic enjoyments of personal life, the affections and sentiments. But reflection shows that this is not the whole account of the matter. Feeling of some kind we must have according to the subjective condition in which we find ourselves at the moment: the objects presented to us at that moment may suggest feelings out of accord with this mood, but we do not find that we necessarily suppress our mood in deference to the objects: *e.g.* frustrated ambition does not at once perish when the possibility of success has vanished; affection will not at once subside when some unworthiness in our friend is disclosed. And the feelings which arise as appetitive impulses sometimes completely precede the presentation of any objects, sometimes are in excess over and above the intensity belonging to them as accompaniments of the imaginative representations which have to do duty for absent objects. And so it comes that intellect is often bidden to search for enjoyable objects with an imperiousness which does not consist with deference for it as superior authority.

But this is pathological, Intellectualism protests: it is actual experience, no doubt, but it is to be avoided and resisted: Feeling must be brought under control, strictly subordinated to facts and laws objective; presentations and reasonings and ideas correspond to reality, and both feeling and action which are not strictly determined by them must be suppressed. Thus, it is urged, must philosophy and theology protest, in the sacred name of truth. The claim of Intellectualism has been long before the world: and the great intellects have overawed us with their force and with the magnificence of their work. But of late the world has been impressed with the problems which Intellectualism has failed to solve, with the non-appearance of any one system commanding the support of Intellectualists themselves, and

III] *Philosophy, and the Being of God* 117

further, with the incompatibility of the several systems offered by different thinkers. And we have come to suspect that too much has been claimed for Intellect as a factor in life and therefore as a guide to Truth itself. New banners have appeared in the arena : Voluntarism or Pragmatism, asserting the primacy of Will and pursuit of Interest; Personal Idealism or Humanism, claiming some share of rights for each factor in the complex operation of life. The common ground of all is that Intellect is not the ruling factor in life, and therefore as we pursue truth it cannot be our sole guide : it is an instrument designed for service. In the construction of beliefs Voluntarism claims an inherent right to go beyond the known facts and their implications and to insist on some value being assigned wherever an 'interest' is to be served, and a supreme value whenever a primary 'good' is the aim. If these lie beyond the boundaries of proved truth, we shall not for that reason withdraw our allegiance from them, but shall insist on our natural right to follow them up : all the good is real. Intellectualism has rested in thought and what it shows us ; we may take all that is given by inductive science, historical evidence, and speculative interpretation, and we shall have the truth, it says : for us that exists, and we must neither take away anything because it seems valueless or evil, nor add anything because it is more desirable to us, or more excellent in itself. We decline the restriction, say Voluntarism and its variants; the universe partly depends on what we make it, we have creative power, and it is our high prerogative to alter the world, to call into existence forms of good and beauty and to suppress the offensive and the evil. We may therefore, and we must, carry our beliefs as far as our ideals ; we may trust in the goodness that ought to be. Much of what is presented to us is but appearance : as we have to go beyond the report of vision whenever we see a stick apparently bent when half of it is placed in water, and distrusting our own eyesight believe that it remains straight, appealing from one report to another, both within the intellect ; so with the whole compass of intellect, we are not satisfied that what it reports to us is the reality itself. When ethical conviction urges us, when desire for what is lovely and of good report is kindled, we dare not stay our steps, we must believe their objects somehow, somewhere, to be possible, and we join action to belief and put forth effort to bring them into being.

That the Voluntarists, or Pragmatists, or Humanists, have advanced to the front of the arena cannot be questioned, if we survey the philosophical literature of the last ten or twenty years. In Germany and France, as in Britain and America, they are doing much of the freshest work of the time. And they can appeal to history for support, especially when the surface is removed and under-strata of thought are uncovered. In the last generation the influence of Lotze in associating æsthetic and moral judgements with intellectual judgements, has been pervasive; his vehement declaration that to suppress them in face of intellectual perplexity would be 'intolerable,' has wakened echoes in every school of philosophy. The singularly alert and independent mind of Professor James, with his 'will-to-believe,' has been instrumental in making Voluntarism known among English-reading people, and on the Continent its prevalence is signalized by such leaders as Renouvier and Professor Paulsen, the latter of whom marks as one of the five principal features of the philosophy of the present day that "it is turning from an Intellectualist to a Voluntarist standpoint: first in psychology, under the influence of Schopenhauer and of the biologists; and then in philosophy and theory of the world."

Professor Paulsen proceeds to add that it has also entered into Protestant Theology. This, indeed, is plain enough when we remember all that Theology means by Faith. That word suffices to remind us how uncongenial Christian Theology has found the invitation to regard Intellect or Reason as the seat of sole authority for knowledge of God. In many quarters it has acquiesced in handing over Natural Theology to Reason, simply because it was reserving the central territory for other treatment. And now it cannot but be disposed to hail with some ardour the reappearance of the

Philosophy, and the Being of God

appeal to Faith in general theology. In the Ritschlian theology the dualism of Judgements of Value and Judgements of Existence has found formulation and vigorous exposition, and has attracted no small following.

Having already pleaded for the inclusion of feeling and of the ethical factor in the human nature to be interpreted by philosophy and theology, it is now open to us to urge that there is no sufficient ground for the disparagement of intellect which has set in. Nay, rather, we may feel sure that there is real danger to the cause of philosophy and of theology if this disparagement is admitted. In the common judgement of mankind, it will cause aversion from them both if it is suspected that they acquiesce in a situation in which truth occupies a secondary place. Certainly it does not appear that we are able, always and everywhere, to identify the true and the good, what is and what ought to be. But rather than abandon either the one or the other we may treat both goodness and truth as *postulates*, as the Oxford group who write as 'Personal Idealists' do, or as valid declarations of reality, even at the expense of accepting their discrepancies unreconciled.

There can be no doubt that in the individual life, at any stage, feeling and ethical sentiment may soar beyond what knowledge has to offer. But when the life is prolonged and becomes fully matured, the suspicion that the constitution of things is really other than natural hopes and aspirations had led one to suppose must give distraction and discord, and in this attitude we cannot rest. We therefore look to knowledge being brought up to conscience and to sentiment as life matures. And in the larger life of a community where continuity is preserved across many alternations of ridge and furrow, of confidence and doubt, it is not the dippings into the hollows of doubt as to the unity of things, but the successive contacts with the ridges which show the line of march. It is the types of men who were confident that truth and goodness coincided that appeal to the deepest faculties of the soul, and philosophy should be built up out of the successive expressions of such confidence. Not to speak of the great world-names which are symbols of this conviction, this is, we venture to assert, the main tradition of Cambridge thought: for Cudworth and John Smith, as for Hare and Grote and Maurice, the conviction of the unity of truth and goodness was inwrought in the very constitution of their minds. And indeed, the faith which has been generated in the Christian mind, when considered as a continuous Church, is, surely, not a faith that abandons one aspect of God in His universe, in order to enjoy a simplicity which is due to omissions, but a faith that is comprehensive; insisting on transcending the distinction, it holds firmly that the truth of all goodness and beauty, and the goodness and beauty of all truth, are now present in the mind of God, and, therefore, may some day be vouchsafed to the mind of man.

Up to this point we have been regarding human nature in the individual; *Sociality* has been brought in only when so involved that it was impossible to write without referring to it.

Consciousness is seated in individuals, in centres: these are inaccessible to one another: each of us stands within his own circle, others are *to* him. But we spontaneously make the inference that the agencies to which we refer many of the changes which thus are presented *to* us, are also, like us, *for* themselves. We make this assumption 'ejectively,' and it is scarcely to be questioned that every human individual makes it. In order of logic the signs precede the inference, but this inference begins so early, is made so spontaneously and with such assurance and becomes so radically inwoven into our whole experience, that we soon arrive at the position that the interpretation is more important in our knowledge than the sign; the other persons assume a higher order of value than their expressions, just as we ourselves are more important than any of our particular experiences or than all of them taken together. Further, our knowledge of ourselves grows by reflection from our thoughts of other persons: by 'introjection,' as it is now named, we figure ourselves to be like these other minds. The importance of others in proportion to ourselves grows upon us as we become aware of the smallness of our own contribution to the world of changes, and we end by contentedly giving ourselves a place among these 'ejectively' known minds. Then as consciousness matures and we intensify our sense of our own unity in correspondence with our conviction of a parallel unity in the universe, we apply this to the other minds with a specifically impressive force and arrive at the belief of a community of which we and they are members. This fundamental unification is the central thread of sociality—not brought into light without analysis: and along with it the phases of our mental life cooperate.

In our life of feeling, sympathy operates incessantly: our representation in our consciousness of a state supposed to be that of another mind calls up in us a tone of feeling which we take to be identical in kind with the tone of the other mind, and the sense of common feeling has a uniting effect; a common interest is ours. But this is not all: feeling is not mere passivity, in it the mind turns itself towards the object, the feeling takes an outgoing direction and becomes an affection. Further, this outgoing affection demands the response of a like affection towards ourselves: the highest range of feeling arises only in reciprocity with feeling supposed to be directed towards us by other persons. We desire the good of our friend, and we feel affection for him at its height when we are assured that he too delights in our good and that the thought of us excites pleasure in his mind. Very intense love is sometimes directed towards irresponsive persons, it may be objected: many a mother loves an unworthy and irresponsive son; the unrequited love of a Dante for a Beatrice was no fiction *qua* the existence of the affection. But it is quite open here to suppose that the mother implicitly regards the responsiveness as potential, though dormant or withheld, and that the conviction of its permanent absence or of fixed hatred would sooner or later check the love and turn it to bitterness or sad regret. But reciprocated love is acclaimed by humanity as the crowning experience of human nature. Its *vis unitiva* is manifest; it unites the centres of conscious life, each of them incorporating in its own good the good of the other. 'Otherness' is transcended by communion. And so, in various modes of genesis, feeling binds men into communities, and the individual in whom social feeling is absent or feebly developed is seen to be only potentially what he might be.

Into social union we enter by the advance of knowledge also : we become aware that our own ideas are but a portion of the ideas which human minds possess; we learn from others and are happy if we are of like service to them. And noticing differences in our several ideas, we come to distinguish between idiosyncrasies and a common element in which we agree : conceptions arise and the belief in a conceptual world which is the same for all. By such 'intersubjective' intercourse we build up the fabric of knowledge : wrought out of many minds it becomes a common possession open to all men. Modern ethics of every form is not less emphatic in its inclusion of sociality : moralists vie in their claims that they show how both personal and social good are provided for by their theory.

In social life, then, feeling expands and varies, valuations are widened and deepened, ends of action are multiplied and enlarged, and a common world enters into our intellectual vision.

It is impossible to claim that at the present time either mental science or philosophy has arrived at accord as to the relative functions of sociality and individuality in human life. Some look to one, some to the other as the primary or the ultimate concern. In the sciences, until the last twenty years, British Psychologists have unquestionably neglected the social factor in the genesis of mental life, but amends are now being handsomely made ; Sociologists on the other hand are apt to magnify their office and ignore the innate individuality. In philosophy, some Moralists place their ideals in the excellences of social order as the end to be attained ; others place the welfare of the individuals as the final purpose. But idealistic ethics on the whole acknowledges as its ideal the social community of conscious individuals, each having his own life but having it as including membership of a community in which he realizes himself as a knowing, acting, loving mind.

Recent theology has not failed to be affected by the movement in favour of regarding sociality as essential in human nature and therefore no accidental addition to religious life. As the last century closed it became evident from theological literature that in the new century the idea of the Kingdom of God would take a higher place in guiding theological reflections as well as in influencing the methods of making a religion a force in practical human life. But the conservative influence of the recent Past is still very powerful, and the force of an extreme individualism is far from exhausted in the heart of religion, for English people at least.

To what has this review of Human Nature led us? To the ideal of Man as personality, as spiritual being : a unitary self-conscious and self-determining spirit whose life is manifested in phases of thought and feeling and of action for chosen ends and purposes ; each man conscious of a world which is, at its highest finite level, a number of personalities like himself. In this spiritual world all live in reciprocal knowledge and affection and combine their individual activities for the good of the community as a whole. This is not offered as a description of actual Man. It is the character which philosophy, according to its privilege, sets forth as the norm, the essence, the ideal of Human Nature.

§ II. *The Interpretation of Human Nature.*

To man brooding over the life of the spirit there has come the thought of a higher Reality—he has 'foreboded a Mystery' —a sense of wonder has stirred, and he has become philosophical, religious. Sometimes this mood arises from inability to find rest within the sphere of his world ; questionings of the intelligence, strivings of will, and impulses of affection urge his meditation onwards towards a Beyond ; but sometimes they do no more than leave him arrested at the edge of the world he knows, murmuring interrogations—what is there besides us? why are we? whose are we? A Plato or a Dante would be required to express the pathos of the lot of the serious Sceptics and Agnostics of mankind, as it appears to the men of insight or of faith, were it not that from the Sceptics themselves voices of wistfulness are heard in the poetry, the confessions, and the *journaux intimes* of every age and country.

At the present day there are many who make their account with the affirmative disposition of their minds, when arresting themselves on the edge of experience, by declaring that the mere fact that they look beyond is itself positive, and is sufficient. They claim objective value for that outlook itself, and associate philosophy and theology with poetry and the arts, as constructions which carry sufficient justification when regarded as expressions of the life of the soul.

'Subjectivism' has won considerable ground in the philosophical and religious literature of our time. But that it offends 'common sense' is scarcely to be questioned; it comes as a surprise to the ordinary man to be invited to accept beliefs as equivalent to truths, the products of the thinking mind as the only realities, exhalations from the glowing imaginations of pious and devout souls as the things of heaven itself. Rich as our faculties may be in power of construction of what seems true and good for ourselves, it is a shock to our expectations to be told that the deepest wisdom lies in our contentedly standing alone with ourselves and our faith. We want a Reality which is for itself, whilst showing something of itself to us: we want assurance that our conceptions are not only our way of looking at it, but its way of manifesting itself to us: we feel that the universal belief in evolution justifies our confidence that the objective efficacy allowed to our ordinary thought will not fail at the highest levels. If conceptions and promptings from all the compass of our nature are to be guides to Truth, these also must be at once the thoughts of man and, in their measure, the vision of attributes of Reality. We pass, therefore, from philosophies of life which offer constructions without objective value; and from philosophies of religion which enclose it within the confines of psychological faith, or reduce it to the historical religions as the sociological products of the minds of the peoples.

The principle that we are entirely right in trusting that there is objective validity in our experience is the principle

Philosophy, and the Being of God

of Idealism: and when it issues in the conviction that the universe is, in essence, spiritual, we have 'Spiritual Idealism.' This principle we now proceed to vindicate by showing it in operation over the field of human nature as outlined in the previous section.

Spiritual Idealism is a philosophical principle, however, which is attained and employed by various methods. There is the method—or negation of method—of Ontologism, Intuitionalism, the Mysticism of Insight: our ultimate knowledge of Reality is regarded as simple vision, spontaneous, inexplicable, out of relation to all subordinate mental experience; and the ultimate Reality therefore as out of relation to all other existence. The statement of it is dogmatic, sometimes explicitly so, sometimes with a show of reasoning within the *a priori* region: direct access to Reality is claimed, unmediated communion with God. Many Mystics express themselves in terms of knowledge: they speak of intuitional insight which in lucid simplicity gives the ideas upon which all other knowledge is based; some prefer the language of feeling, of piety; others speak more comprehensively of union and communion. The beneficent influence of Ontologism and Mysticism in the history of humanity cannot be gainsaid. It has appeared in response to needs of the times: when men's attention has been distracted between Empiricisms on the one hand and partial, and therefore ineffective, Rationalisms on the other, the Ontologists have been those who at once saw what lay beyond the Empiricists' view, and were aware of the want of cogency in the Rationalists' 'proofs' as then presented. They did all they could, they affirmed the convictions of their own experience at its highest point, and found in them the tranquillity of immediate faith. If it is a question between holding firmly to faith in the eternal and transcendent, as against limitation to things of time and sense, the interests of philosophy itself must determine the course of our sympathy.

But Spiritual Idealists have also begun from the lowest ranges of experience and worked upwards to their principle. The *a posteriori* method proceeds by the application of *a priori* conceptions—themselves purely mental—to the low-grade knowledge of reality given in sense-experience, both of mental life and of the outer world. By 'application' of the conceptions to this lower knowledge higher truths are gained, and in the end Reality is demonstrated, the existence of God is proved. This method has proved acceptable over a wide range of humanity, and still has many adherents. But it lies open to one fatal objection : if the higher conceptions such as Causation, Necessity, Personality, are 'empty,' so to speak, as regards knowledge of reality, the mere application of these empty conceptions to the kind of reality disclosed by our intelligence in its lower ranges will not give us access to any higher kind of reality than we had before. We do not, for example, prove *a posteriori* a Supreme Cause, but only reach a suggestion that we should look for one; but where to look we are not told, unless it be where the Ontologists already stand, in which case it is the Ontologist who has the key of knowledge, and our 'demonstrations' have only brought us to his side.

The true philosophical method is different from both of these : it does not partition our experience into two regions, and place knowledge of Reality only in the upper region as Ontologism does, nor in an artificial combination of them, as *a posteriori* demonstration does : it recognises the authority of our nature at every stage. Even in the lower experiences there lie minor values ; and as the scale of intelligence and feeling rises, so higher values appear in the objectivity they indicate ; the whole life of the spirit is an experience, which all along its line, over its whole area, is also a manifestation of Reality ; every phase of the soul is within the compass of religious significance.

The method of interpretation of the spiritual life which is now dominant is that known as the Transcendental. It is new, and not new : it has gathered suggestions which have appeared at various times in the past and has given them new power through its explicit formulation by Kant and Hegel. It is now the most potent instrument of constructive and interpretative thought.

Philosophy, and the Being of God

A method of proof may be called transcendental, in the simplest way, when resort is made to a higher sphere than that occupied by the thing to be explained, to a sphere which surpasses it in range or excellence. We may explain a child's tentative intelligence by referring to human intelligence in maturity, for example. But if no other sphere is known, independently, then we may enquire what suppositions or conditions or principles are necessary in order that the sphere already known may be possible. In the case of our experience as a whole, what principles are required in order that the experience may be depended upon for knowledge and for guidance? It is one way of answering this enquiry to regard our highest conceptions as capable of constituting an independent sphere of knowledge, with ultimate Reality in some way directly correspondent to it; but this is Ontologism, as already indicated. The Transcendental method regards the highest conceptions as having constructive power, but as operating in and through the lower forms of intelligence, which, in turn, become fully luminous in and through the higher, so that the fabric of knowledge is constituted by the collaborative activity of higher and lower, all down the scale of intelligence. At any point in the scale an experience is illuminative for what lies below it, but is receptive of illumination from the stage above it, and the 'proof' of any one stage is the exhibition of this double function. With the highest ideas the proof is their constructive power, mediately or immediately, over the whole scale. Our knowledge of a system of forces working mechanically, for example, has its truth and value, but the value is increased when we can invest the system with teleological character also; and the value of knowledge rises further when we think of the system as constituted by conscious members. If we take our experience as a whole the highest ideas or principles are 'proved' by the total system of experience which is ordered by them, in which we may say that they are actualized or manifested. They do not present to us the objects corresponding to themselves as existing independently of the whole of the lower ranges of objects: they do not give us intuitive vision or carry us into a transcendent sphere: they work in our intelligence and raise it to its highest powers and set before our thought a Reality capable of embracing all the forms and modes of being. A special form of this claim is made by those who follow Kant in confining their force to the regulation of experience in a way which leaves them as formal conceptions, mental constructions without power to convince us of a Reality which has something more than existence *for us*. This is different from the meaning of spiritual experience as advocated in our previous section: there it has been taken as giving us real subjectivity and real objectivity, self and its life in presence and in communion with other selves and their lives for themselves. This objective validity is here claimed for the highest ideas as transcendentally regarded, and our position is that as essential constituents of spiritual experience they are to be depended upon for giving us knowledge of Reality.

Among those highest ideas are Infinity, Necessity, Self-determination, perfect Goodness, summed up in Spiritual Personality. Transcendental Idealism maintains that these ideas are indispensable factors in the construction of our experience and therefore show us necessary constituents of the nature of Reality.

We need not here elaborate the processes by which these ideas are brought into explicitness: the now familiar Hegelian 'logic' of the movement of thought is before the world, and though at points somewhat forced beyond its scope, it has no competent rival; for indeed it is only a clarification of the result of much intellectual labour of past thinkers. That we know anything to have boundaries or limits is only the part of a thought, as it were, and another part is the absence of limits, *i.e.* in its ultimate form, a negative infinity; but neither does this complete the thought: the complete conception is that of a positive infinity, of which the finite is a constituent marked out of it, or within it, by the limits we discerned. And so for the temporal within eternity, the particular space within the infinite space, the particular degree of quality within the infinite quality, the contingent within the necessary, the determination or choice which is only a relative freedom within absolute self-determination, the relative good within absolute good, and in sum, finite spirit within infinite spirit.

Looking now at the highest sphere known to us, the spirit of man, both in individual life, and in community, we find that it presents itself always on the side of the finite and its congeners: we cannot think of human spirit as fulfilling any of those completed ideas; perfection is applicable, but only in relation to a limited ideal; that is, we cannot think that man is a complete and ultimate Reality.

No unsophisticated reflection reports otherwise. Spiritual as man's nature is, in all its phases it has the marks of finitude upon it. The series of ideas which for convenience we may call the forms of the Infinite he does not apply either to himself, or to others like himself; and yet the series of ideas is there, necessary for the complete ordering of his thoughts, for the interpretation of his experience. What other course is possible, therefore, than to regard himself, together with these finitudes, as living within a Reality which has the whole series of forms of the Infinite as its attributes?

And this attribution we make in two directions—to the supreme Object of our thought in front of us, and also to the supreme Subject behind us, as it were. In both directions we know ourselves as finite, limited in our thinking and acting, and limited in the objects we grasp with our thought and in the changes we produce by our action: we remove the limits, but that is only negative, giving no resting-place; and so we pass to the idea of an infinite object before us and an infinite thinking activity behind us; and that unity of subject-object which we find in ourselves we think to exist in the infinite also. We place ourselves within this Infinite: we regard ourselves as participating in His thinking and aware of objects which are present in His thought. The fact that we stand looking upon objects at all is explained by the fact that they are His objects by whose activity of thought we think at all. We apprehend, in our mode and our degree, with His apprehension, we have our knowledge through the knowledge of Him who knows all. In Himself, being infinite, the identity of object and subject is attained: He knows all that exists, and all that exists is that which He knows: He knows Himself: otherness has no place, self-consciousness is absolute in Him. It is on this line that we can proceed to establish the whole series of attributes on the 'infinite' side of our series: necessity, substantiality, self-causality, goodness, love; summing up the whole as Infinite Spirit.

In this procedure have we gone beyond our transcendental method? have we lapsed into Mysticism after all? If we claim to have proved Infinite Spirit have we done what we said we would not do, claimed intuitional knowledge of the Transcendent? have we tried to bring Eternal Being within our finite consciousness? By no means. We have made no claim to know Him as He is for Himself: we have claimed only a mediated knowledge with finitude as the medium: and our principle obliges us never to leave out that mediating area. We may say that we have knowledge *of* Him, or *about* Him, but this is not the same as direct knowledge. We see Him through ourselves and through our world, both of which, in separation and together, the thought of His presence renders intelligible to our thought, His activity renders possible to our powers, and His love renders admirable to our affections: in His Personality we have our personal being.

In theological terms this may be expressed by saying that He both reveals Himself and withholds Himself from the intelligence of created spirits. The Pantheism which speaks only of immanence is inept, for the finite cannot exhaust infinity, and we know infinity as the mark of the series of attributes which belong, not to us and the world, but to God. Beyond the finite series, in every direction, so to speak, extends the infinite, in being, in power, in goodness. There may be other worlds than ours and other selves than ours, but they too would all fall within the sphere of God, and by no extension of them can we conceive that they are commensurate with Him. And so in our knowledge of God we may say that we know Him as immanent and believe in Him as

Philosophy, and the Being of God

transcendent. The transcendental method confirms what profound and comprehensive religious systems have more or less explicitly assumed or taken as intuitive, that man is in the presence of God, and that the world is His world, and yet that there is a sense in which man thinks of Him without knowing Him, and meditates upon Him as far exceeding all that the finite mind, expansive and progressive though it be, can ever realize.

We have been using the terminology of Intellect: looking towards the Infinite Spirit as the transcendental principle of the intelligibility of experience, and of its validity. But the method is applicable in the other phases of our spiritual life. It is indeed on the ethical side of life that some transcendentalists find a surer ground than they do on the intellectual side: but without raising any question of preference we may proceed to indicate the mode of inference from our life as consciously aiming at ideal goodness. Taking the good as the aim of our activity and ourselves as endowed with freedom to choose and to act for ourselves, we find here also that the transcendental method gives us our philosophy. However much we conceive ourselves as free in our action for good, here again the mark of finitude is obvious. We do not mean that we find badness or evil, but that in our normal, our humanly perfect ethical activity, the good we aim at remains plainly finite, related strictly to ourselves. This limit we think removed, and we think of good after good stretching forth in endless series. Then we move forward again and reach a positive idea of good as infinite, perfect, absolute. This is so for the objects we aim at: and in the other direction, for ourselves as active spirits seeking good, our freedom is known to us as limited and variable; and expansive as the energy of the soul may be, we neither find ourselves omnipotent nor do we desire to be so, and we think therefore of a negative and limitless freedom, and then, behind that, of an infinite self-determining active spirit. Here again we place ourselves and the whole spiritual world within the sphere of the Infinite Spirit. We are free with the power He entrusts to us, and our good is good because it is included in the absolute good, that which proceeds from and expresses the good pleasure of God.

The above ethical position has been stated apart from Hedonism: as it is stated alike by those who regard goodness as a category in which Feeling is at least not prominent, and by those who regard it as a category to which Feeling is altogether alien. But the 'rigorism' of the authority of the Moral Law, of the absoluteness of Right, of Duty for Duty's sake, is not now in favour; nor even the isolation of 'Goodness' as a wholly independent category. To each of these positions the transcendental method may be applicable. But neither of them is the ethical view which we are endeavouring to interpret here, as has been indicated in the outline of human nature already offered. In the conception of the good the satisfaction of Feeling is included; our good must bring us peace and joy. Yet Feeling has its own aspect and it requires some consideration for itself. Can the transcendental synthesis be applied to Feeling? The difficulty lies in the purely subjective character of Feeling: here objectivity is lost, the soul retires into its own being, all means of access to the otherness of objective Reality seem to be precluded. This is so, and if we mean only Feeling in ultra-purity of passive enjoyment it cannot offer a datum for this method, or for any other. But in our experience Feeling is, as we have seen, a subjective accompaniment or aspect of a state of mind which as a whole includes some knowledge and some activity: the objectivity must be sought in these, and from them the inference to Reality must be made. But when it is granted that we have Infinite Spirit as self-conscious and as self-determining, can we inferentially carry over Feeling into that Reality or not? If we can, it is clear that we must. And, surely, we can. For if Feeling is an expression of our life, of our very being, on the finite side, on what ground can we justify our leaving it on our side without correspondence on the other? If the finite spirit enjoys the limited life in which it manifests itself, the legitimate inference is that Infinite Spirit too rejoices infinitely in His own perfect life.

But this is not the whole case for Feeling. We have seen

Philosophy, and the Being of God

that purely passive Feeling is not the whole, that Feeling has an outgoing energy, seeking the response of like Feeling in the other-than-ourselves: that amongst finite spiritual beings love goes out to meet love coming in, love answering to love, and that it is in this reciprocity that our emotional life attains its height. At the very height of affection, however, finitude and restriction are again impressed upon us: we feel sure that we could love more and receive more love were our natures greater: we cannot be satisfied that love should remain bound and confined either to ourselves or to the whole world: surely, then, here also we may remove the boundaries first, and then pass on to the assurance that there is an all-pervading infinite omnipresence of Love, as well as of Being and of Power. If knowledge and activity have assured us of Infinite Spirit as all-knowing and mighty, we may trust the impulse of Feeling that He is also infinite Love. And especially with regard to our union with Him: we find our being to be grounded in His Being, our activity to be the expression of His Power: but the union is consummated in the reciprocity of love from us to Him and love from Him to us. And so we root and ground all love in His own love for Himself: even in loving us He loves Himself in us, and we in loving Him but reproduce that love. Our own love to one another finds, if not its spring in the order of appearance in our life-history, assuredly its ultimate ground and final confirmation in our love of God.

Dare philosophy and theology openly offer to mankind a denial that Feeling belongs to the Infinite Spirit? Is there not an irrepressible demand by humanity for a Reality which shall be infinitely loving? Let it be said openly that philosophy has no place for love in the ultimate Reality, and men will turn to the lower sphere of the finite, and finding it acknowledged there, they will leave philosophy to the schools, as they have often done before, not least in England in the century gone by, as the history of our universities—of Cambridge, in particular—proclaims. And for theology, as a general interpretation, there is the same necessity. To Christian theology it has, indeed, been impossible to wander far from the conviction that Love is of the essence of Divine Nature; but there have been times when men have proclaimed even the Gospel with intellectual and sternly rigorous ethical elements as its prominent features. For instance, men have selected from Butler his grave moods when he pondered over the Divine Government and Probation and the rigorous 'authority' of Conscience and have failed to observe that his comprehensive mind could not disallow in man the natural right to rejoice in 'self-love,' but found the ultimate privilege to be his love of God and the ultimate attribute of God to be that He is love.

Taking Feeling as entering into the determination of Goodness we get the complete sphere of 'Ethics,' the Good and the Beautiful, and we understand the man who discovering the law of the Lord rejoices therein as one that findeth great spoils, and in meditating thereon day and night experiences his soul's delight.

Transcendental method as applied to the 'good' and to 'love' has won support even in quarters where it is not regarded as cogent for 'existence' intellectually conceived. Ethical Theism has wider support than Speculative Theism; belief in God as perfect Goodness, and in the world as in its normal character created and maintained to manifest His excellences and express His good pleasure, animates many souls which are unable to attain certitude by means of the demonstration of self-conscious spirit. Kant's course in this respect greatly impressed the nineteenth century; and even after the constructive intellectual movement, sufficiently designated as Hegelian, not a few have reverted to Kant and taken their stand on the validity of transcendentalism as interpretative of our ethical nature alone. Ethical Realism in philosophy and Ethical Theism in theology had a greater volume of support as the nineteenth century closed than the Realism and Theism which was both 'Speculative' and Ethical in its structure. But thoroughgoing Transcendentalism has not failed to find powerful advocacy: and we may hope to see philosophy and theology winning back the minds of men by exhibiting not only pure Being, nor Almighty Power, nor Eternal Law, but

Philosophy, and the Being of God

the Infinite Spirit, in whose love, for Himself first, and then for those whom He has called into being, men find their life in all its phases both grounded and consummated.

So far we have been interpreting human nature primarily as individual: there remains for consideration the sociology of human nature. Our datum is spiritual beings in community, knowing one another, participating in action for common good, and united by reciprocal affections. What is the interpretation of this?

Two problems require treatment in the interpretation of the spiritual community: (i) the possibility of the reciprocal interaction of the members, and (ii) the unity of the whole.

(i) First, for interaction. Individual spirit we took to be impenetrable; the imperviousness, the inwardness, the inaccessibility of the self is rarely questioned—"impervious in a fashion of which the impenetrability of matter is a faint analogue," says Professor Pringle-Pattison. Interaction only becomes conceivable by reference to a common consciousness in which we are all grounded, so to speak; a common source of knowledge and of activity. If when I pass into some mode of consciousness there is a change in a common consciousness, then all other spirits within the range of appreciating that change will be aware of the change in me. Wireless telegraphy has given us an analogue in the physical world in which the ether is indispensable for communication; Lotze has, with his mastery of both physical science and spiritual, claimed that in neither sphere can interaction be conceived without reference to a common ground of being. For interaction of spiritual beings, the guiding law that the conclusion of an inference must lie within the same material in nature as the premise or premises, compels our inference to a spiritual consciousness as the necessary ground of its possibility.

But (ii) we have to account for the unity of the universe, a single view of the multitude of beings who constitute its highest finite manifestation. We have found that each self is a unity in all its experiences; and that each has a conviction that there is a corresponding unity in the world of objects, at the highest; for the self regards the community as a unity, a whole within which it has its life. But each self in its finitude is aware that what it knows of the whole is only the whole as it appears to itself; it is not a world so much as a world-view; and so we have as many world-views, as many myriads of facets recognised as there are impenetrable spirits. But if unity is to be objective there must be some subject to which it is objective: the unity must be for some single mind. And as a world of activities, there must similarly be some Being in which the activities are centralized. The unity of the world then requires the transcendental inference to a Monistic Spiritual Being whose universe it is, and within whose nature the individual units know and act. So for Theology; the universe is the object of the vision of God, its well-being is the expression of His will for good.

The simplest counter-interpretation is a theory of absolute 'Pluralism'; according to this the ultimate Reality may be the totality of individual spirits in their community: it may be a unity of system, where there is no centre, no place for the attribution of consciousness except to the constituent units. This conception has come into favour of late, and bids fair to attract further support. It presents the philosophy of spiritualism in a form congenial to the ever-increasing numbers of sociological workers in the empirical sphere. It also finds welcome from those who regard the ethical individual as the essential unit, and the community of ethically acting individuals as the ultimate form of humanity. And it has received an impetus by being presented as the true issue of Hegelianism—whether intended by Hegel or not—in the studies of Dr McTaggart, who holds that the Absolute is not a person, not conscious, not a monistic being for itself in a central way, but a divine city, a spiritual college, a union in which the unity is resident in the members, and rises to consciousness only in them. And so theology disappears: philosophy finds its close in cosmology.

The conditions for ultimate Pluralism would seem to be (1) as the units are finite, it must be their number which is infinite; and (2) each member of the infinitely numerous system must have a fixed character and intensity of being, it must be perfect within its limits, and always perfect, *i.e.* changeless and eternal. The Absolute Reality is an infinity of finite spirits, each perfect and eternal. This theory has in its favour that it offers to provide for both the infinite and the finite, and for system; and also for spirituality, each member being cognitive, active, and emotional, and Dr McTaggart draws out as the ultimate issue that it finds the supreme and dominating character of Reality to be Love. That it is easy to connect men as the spiritual beings we know with those eternal and perfect beings cannot be said: but we must not regard this objection as fatal, since no theory succeeds in setting human nature in all the concreteness of our life in the conditions of time and place and dependence upon bodily organisms in fully luminous relation to its essence as spiritual personality. It is with the essential features and their interpretation that philosophy has to do its work.

But Unitary Spiritualism opposes pluralistic spiritualism because this offers inadequate response to that demand for infinity which we have claimed to be inherent in the spiritual consciousness. We cannot accept the offer of an infinity of number alone as satisfying this demand: we need infinity in connexion with every ultimate category of our spiritual life. For the category of being, we must have a 'unity of centre' as well as a 'unity of system'; a central spirit from which all finite spirits issue as differentiations, in which they continue, and through which alone they can enter into system at all. Apart from this central Personality the unity of being exists only for the constituent members, and is therefore only an infinite repetition of ideas of a system. And Monistic spiritualism finds in an infinite pluralism of finite equals no satisfaction for the demand for infinity in goodness, and love, which we found to be made by our finite, emotional, and ethical nature. A commonwealth of equals all finite would leave us with ourselves—presuming that it is we who are these perfect spirits, and if we may not assume this, the theory is all in the air—as good as anyone else, with no one behind us at all, and no superior in front of us. The term 'above' is abolished: the universe although manifold to infinity would, to use a metaphor, spread out before us as a level expanse containing no one more worthy than ourselves. Either we are all as gods, whereas it is the mark of wisdom for us to prefer to be men; or else, there are no gods, and reverence, and worship, and the upward look must be eradicated from our nature. Monistic spiritualism finds it to be the nature of man to be finite in all the phases of his being; it lends no encouragement to the suppression of his inherent sense of dependence; but it consecrates it by showing him Infinite Spirit, and turns it from a feeling of oppression to a feeling of profound joy and peace in the confidence of having in every direction infinite and almighty support. For us it is health and wealth to know ourselves to be in ideal each of us an ἐντελέχεια, but with a τέλος defined in scope and an excellence proper to that scope. Indefinite progressiveness in the enrichment of our nature by internal development we look for, but neither in the present life nor in the consummation in life eternal do we aspire after the removal of all limits, much less after attainment of infinity. Man includes in his thought of infinity the recognition of absolute excellence; in his ethical nature he is obedient only to a better than himself, and only so could he be free; and at the root of his love must be the absoluteness of the Love to which his own responds.

We have dwelt at some length on the theory of a Pluralist Absolute because it seems to be likely to win some favour in the present temper of philosophy. It makes much of elements which have been neglected by advocates of a Unitary Personality. By its recognition of sociality it occupies the field lying between the two poles of finite and infinite Spirit, too often left empty, although it does so by denying the infinite pole and ranging around the other the whole sphere of absolute reality: in an age which is thinking socially this may be more congenial than the first-mentioned partial method which is essentially individualistic. But, more important still, it is a protest on behalf of finitude and differentiation against the blankness of Eternal Essence. For the time now before us the signs

III] *Philosophy, and the Being of God*   139

presage an increase of the influence of Oriental thought on the mind of the world: it is not at all likely that the consistent tendency of the thought of millions of deeply reflecting human beings will be without effect as Western peoples come more within its range. The Pantheism of Universal Essence before which all finitudes are transitory illusions is a faith of massive impressiveness for minds which have appreciated the impermanence not only of things but of persons, and the flux of changes which we call the march of history. In spite of protests, Easterns are claiming that Spinoza, Berkeley, Schleiermacher, gained their strength from coming near the light of Pantheism. There will, therefore, be a strong necessity for the Western mind to resist this movement in the interest of Personality, and to reassert vehemently the claim of some reality for the Finite. In this way Pluralistic theories will commend themselves. But it is to go to the opposite extreme to claim the highest possible place for the finite minds, to place them in their limited perfection at the summit of possible being. In Monistic Spiritualism, which regards finite spirits as derivative and created, existing within the Divine Spirit, we have a philosophy of Human Nature which refuses to relinquish its base and yet which advances to a view of Reality that both includes and transcends it. It avoids the sinister track on which selfhood is lost, and the spiritual community dissolved, and it is possessed with innate confidence in the reality of the finite in its measure. But it is assured in its confidence that the True, the Good, and the Beautiful transcend these measures and are in their perfection characters of Infinite Personality.

The plea of Philosophy against regarding finite beings as the ultimate constituents of Reality is plainly endorsed by the attitude of Religion. Religious thought in its devotion to God consecrates humility: the great religions unite in this, unless we are to except Buddhism, but even so the exception is not so extensive as it appears, for it is only to few that rigorous Buddhism has been a religion in sole sway. Over the wide field of human history the sense of humility presents itself as the first stage in the religious life: Dante is the representative of humanity when he makes Paradise begin with the souls which have as their sole virtue the spirit of resignation and contentment with what their own nature needs, because they recognise that the limits however narrow are ordained by a higher authority: they say

> "It is inherent in this state
> Of blessedness to keep ourselves within
> The Divine will, by which our wills with His
> Are one."

Christian philosophy, indeed, is not completed without a recognition of Plurality within Unity in its final conception of the Godhead, by its doctrine of God as Holy Trinity. It is one of the landmarks in the history of European thought that speculative inference to essential distinctions within the Monistic nature of Reality was active when the time came for constructing a Christian Theology. It was a time when Oriental devotion to unity was operative in combination with clear-sighted recognition of differences, in the schools of Western Asia and North Africa. The precise shares in the formulation to be assigned to the comprehensiveness of neo-Hellenic speculation and to the inner development of the original Faith a study of history alone can determine. Certainly whenever the Hellenism was weakened in the philosophy of the day the doctrine of the Trinity retreated into unintelligibility, and was regarded as truth indeed, but less as light-giving truth than as mystery. Whenever Hellenism revived the purpose of the doctrine was recovered and it resumed illuminative power, as for example with the Cambridge Platonists. When Cartesian or Lockeian philosophy became dominant theologians became Arian or Unitarian or else remitted Trinitarian doctrine to Revelation. In Hegel a fresh endeavour to unify truth was offered, in all sincerity, we may well suppose, though, no doubt, it is cogent only for those who can accept both his philosophy and his peculiar reading of the Gospel. It may be that the time has not arrived for claiming that this high doctrine of differentiation within the Unity is the united expression of both general philosophy and of specially Christian thought. But movement in that direction appears to be continually prompted both by reason and by Christian faith.

Spiritualist philosophy takes final form in theology: it constructs the doctrine of one Eternal Spirit—with possibility of differentiation within itself—as the Reality to which reason, moral purpose, feeling, sociality and the unitary nature of human spirit conduct the enquiring mind of man. This final judgement presents itself as rational, giving the rationale of our human nature : our finite thinking is real in so far as it is His thinking; our action has potency in so far as we draw upon His Almightiness; our goodness is grounded on the perfection of what He deems good; our love cannot fail to find response because it is the reciprocal of the love whereby He created us and now sustains our being. And we as men live in happy community under His gracious sovereignty, wherein we find our ground of union and mutual society. That He infinitely transcends our view is also our faith, our rational faith, for the Reason which tells us that the spirit of man is the image of the Divine Spirit tells us also that the image is not the Reality.

The conclusion of our Spiritual Idealism is not opposed to the result of such Mysticism as sees things in God without professing to see Him by immediate vision, nor to the result of *a posteriori* Rationalism, which in wise hands points to a Divine Spirit and the universe as dependent upon Him. The difference is in method.

We differ from the *a posteriori* proofs from Causation and the Moral Law because we look upon the Infinite and the finite in correlation with one another, not to be proved by inferring from one taken independently to the other in similar independence ; we support these proofs against Empiricism and endorse them as expressions of confidence in the higher Reason. In Britain the Empirical spirit, confident in the lower ranges of mind, distrustful of its higher powers, has always worked strongly ; from William of Occam to Hobbes, from Hume to Mill, it has animated men who have conferred honour on our national tradition, and, it is to be presumed, have expressed a mood inherent in our national character. Against them the *a posteriori* arguments have been offered as principal factors in a theistic view of the world. Our Transcendental method transforms these venerable methods of proof, and sets them in fresh strength and beauty as pillars of theistic faith.

For Mysticism—we know that there hovers before some of the finest minds a thought which claims to be higher than that which we are here advocating. Setting aside entirely the pseudo-mysticism which builds upon extraordinary visions, voices, apparitions, presentiments, and other phenomena of the lower ranges of experience, we mean by Mysticism the claim of some philosophers that our knowledge can rise to intuitive apprehension of unrelated and unconditioned Reality, of some religious minds that we can have wholly unmediated experience of the presence of essential Deity. Our view is that Mysticism is as illegitimately separatist in its character as Empiricism is: the Empiricist can see only things mundane, and holds that all else is illusion: the Mystic claims that we can enter into the supermundane sphere and that it is only then that we have quitted illusion and found Reality. We, on our part, urge that both of these separations are illegitimate, and must be repudiated; we cherish no desire to enter into the Transcendent regions; we look with entirely grateful contentment upon the life of finite spirit as ensphered within the uncircumferenced Reality: we look around and above and see God encompassing us everywhere; we look into our own personality and below its depths an unfathomable deep tells us of His inner presence. But in our knowing this we must never quit our hold upon our selfhood and the selfhood of our fellows; in our activity when we say we 'identify' our wills with the Divine will we must always mean not suppressing and merging, but concordant unity; in our life of feeling, the emotion is reciprocal and is from ourselves toward Him, as well as from Him to us. The Fatherhood we revere is to us unthinkable and beyond our power of appreciation, except in relation to ourselves as children.

The recent revival of attention to Mysticism of a noble

III] *Philosophy, and the Being of God* 143

kind has been beneficial—it was bound to come after a period of Empiricism—but the benefits can all be appropriated by our method. By this we fundamentally understand that the realm in which we see the immanent Spirit of God is but a part of a realm infinitely transcending all that we can know. For us, the material world indirectly, and the spiritual world directly, give us a system of signs. We rejoice in our progressive ability to interpret them, and we rejoice further in our thought that the Infinite Spirit exceeds and excels all that has been manifested to us: and it is from both what we see and what we see not but think to lie beyond that we have such a 'knowledge of God' as keeps us in serene confidence that we have the Divine permission to keep our souls as centres of spiritual life, progressive towards ideals of perfection which yet will always be finite. We are convinced that God makes no call upon us to quit our finitude, but that, instead, He deigns to invest us with the privilege of knowing Him, loving Him, and being inspired by Him, in a life which is eternal in the sense that it cannot but endure so long as He is pleased to keep us in communion with Himself.

In the general world-thought of to-day the trust in Spiritual Idealism of this transcendental type has risen to a high mark in Ethical philosophy: the advocates of Ethical Theism so grounded abound. The advocacy of thoroughgoing constructive Idealism, *i.e.* speculative or intellectual as well as ethical, is far less prevalent. But in the minds of some of us at least there is a hope that our generation will see a revival of trust in the whole range of 'Reason' as the eye and the heart of the soul: and even that some genius may presently arise to carry forward in all its magnificent comprehensiveness the constructive tradition of Aristotle and Origen and Aquinas and Leibnitz and Hegel. For those inspired with this hope the human nature on which the structure of Reality is to be built must be neither intellectual nor ethical nor mystical only, but the fulness of the life of the spirit of man, and of mankind. And the interpretation will give us the finite within the Infinite, man rejoicing in humanity, and rejoicing also in communion with God.

That the fundamental ideas of Spiritualist philosophy are congruous with the constituent ideas of the Christian Gospel is obvious. If philosophy were to issue in a materialism, in a pure pantheism, a deism, or an agnosticism, it would be incompatible with ideas explicit or implicit in Christianity; and either a dualism in the region of belief would be inevitable, or else either the philosophy or the faith must yield place. That spiritualist philosophy has won its way again to the front—the evidence lies patent to all—is partly due to the inherent force of its ideas operating in the minds of men who are as much aloof from allegiance to Christian ideas as minds can be which have been nurtured in Christian homes and have participated in Christian civilization ; and it is partly due to the influence of explicitly Christian philosophers. The allotment of the proportion due to each of these would be a problem for historical study, probably insoluble. But few will care to gainsay the claim that the Christian ideas of God and of human nature, and of the essential communion of man with God, have enabled Christian minds to contribute to the endowment of philosophy with that noble and inspiriting character with which it is now facing the demands of the people.

But having claimed this, is the Christian philosopher in a position to urge that spiritualist philosophers are bound, on their principles, to go forward to accept the Christian doctrine of God and man in its fulness? or else, as philosophy has come so far, should Christian doctrine cease to claim allegiance to any specific ideas, and allow that its differences are only secondary, derivative, symbolical, perhaps occasional, provisional, particularist, and now no longer essential? That is, should we insist that the assimilation has gone so far that the spheres should, in one of these ways or in the other, now be equated?

The sacredness of Truth permits only one answer to be seriously offered. Christian ideas claim to be *true*, all of them: we can admit of no finally differential position for them which would regard the philosophical range as true, but these specific Christian ideas as something other than

Philosophy, and the Being of God

true, whether in a region of 'faith' or of some other undefined faculty. If philosophy cannot reach them by its own inner development, it must be called upon to extend its range to admit them as revelations; and when admitted they must be fully naturalized as citizens. If they present an appearance of 'newness,' this is only what many, at least, of the present chief constituent ideas did when they first made their appearance: it has been by successive admissions that the city of ideas has been enlarged, as well as by natural increase from within: this the history of thought reports, except for a few philosophers of history who have secured but small following in their straining for a single logic of inner development. By successive admissions of new ideas changes were effected, and the present philosophy or philosophies are the result. Christians holding that the ideas of the Faith are true must expect ideas incompatible with them to give way. But to those who hold the great spiritualist ideas which are inherently compatible with specific Christian doctrines our appeal cannot be other than that they should advance to the acceptance of these also. This invitation must be made on the simple ground that truth is truth, whatever be the history of the appearance of its constituent ideas. And it is made in the further confidence that in the philosophical ideas there are latent elements and inner potencies, which render them capable of being incorporated with the new ideas, even if the new ideas are not already in them waiting for development. That these inner potencies are hidden is what offers the obstacle to advance; but it is reasonable faith to believe that in the light of the Christian ideas the latencies will be brought out, and the obstacle to advance be removed. Christian philosophy therefore calls upon general philosophy to make further effort, in order either to allow inner development to proceed, or else to recognise that there is nothing irrational in admitting new ideas on historical grounds, and looking forward to the eventual discovery of their relationship to the old, and the attainment of a single sphere for the truth that must in essence be a unity.

To the same effect is the answer if the question is put to

Christian philosophy, whether it is concerned to vindicate a specific territory for itself. Its claim to be true over its whole extent obliges it to assert itself specifically as against partial or latent truth; but its deeper trust is that the partiality may be recognised, and a single territory accepted by all. Acknowledging the progressive way in which truth has been acquired hitherto it anticipates with confidence that the future will show knowledge and faith to be one, the single truth of God. General philosophy always assumes that truth is single, and Christian philosophy must do the same. Rather, it rises to the confidence that much Christian truth hitherto held on the authority of historical revelation will be seen to be the truth which is also disclosed by philosophy as the interpretation of life. The manifestation of God in Christ is the manifestation of the Eternal at a point of time, of Infinite Spirit at a point, so to speak, of personality: but when manifested it became truth eternal. It must therefore enter into all else that philosophy has gained, and illumine with its eternal and essential light all our thought of God and of our inheritance as partakers of His nature. And our insistence upon unity is addressed not only to philosophy as guardian of truth, but to philosophy as giving us guidance for good and happy life. One is the light for our Intelligence, one the inspiration of Power and Action, one the spiritual community, one the Divine Love in which we live. In this ultimate Faith man finds God, because it is his response to God revealing Himself to man and in man.

ESSAY IV.

MAN'S ORIGIN, AND HIS PLACE IN NATURE.

WYNFRID LAURENCE HENRY DUCKWORTH, M.A., M.D.

CONTENTS.

A. The scheme and scope of the Essay.
B. The aims and method of biological study.
C. Biological evidence as to Man's Place in Nature.
  1. The evidence derived from a study of the structure of Man.
  2. The evidence of physiology.
  3. The evidence of psychology.
D. Human Evolution.
  1. Origin of Variations.
  2. Degree of Variation.
  3. Heredity.
E. Prospective Evolution of Man.
F. Origin of living organisms.
G. Conclusion.

MAN'S ORIGIN, AND HIS PLACE IN NATURE.

"Science is bound by the everlasting law of honour to face fearlessly every problem which can fairly be presented to it. If a probable solution consistent with the ordinary course of nature can be found, we must not invoke an abnormal act of creative power." (Lord Kelvin. Presidential Address, British Association, 1871.)

A. *The scheme and scope of the Essay.*

THE origin of Man, and his place in Nature, may be studied from various points of view. The present Essay will treat of these subjects from the standpoint of a student of biological science.

Scientists cannot pretend to have completely solved these problems, but they may attempt to state their present condition in the light of research. Theology, which is so nearly allied to moral philosophy, needs the cooperation of the natural sciences, and they in turn must weigh its conclusions. And I believe that such agreement is to the best interests of all concerned, provided that it be based upon a mutual determination to set prejudice aside, and to face the difficulties on either side. It is with such convictions in mind that I shall attempt to review the scientific aspect of Man's Place in Nature.

Those who embark upon the investigation of biological problems find themselves confronted at the outset with the necessity of an acquaintance with the scope and bounds of their field of work. The problems of biology consist essentially in the elucidation of phenomena presented by living organisms, in other words of the phenomena of life. The means at our disposal for these investigations consist in the first instance of those faculties of perception which in the civilised races have been brought to so high a pitch of development. And in scientific work attempts must be made, on the one hand to heighten the receptiveness of the intellect, and on the other to reduce descriptions of phenomena to the most easily apprehended forms of statement.

Yet even when the utmost has been done to secure accuracy of observation and lucidity of description, there remains a certain number of problems which will defy complete explanation from the scientific standpoint.

The great modern advances of science amount in reality to triumphs in the improvement of facilities for observation. But beyond the phenomena thus recorded, and coordinated in description, the knowledge of their *raison d'être* remains as remote as ever.

The student of biology thus finds his prime task in the collection and interpretation of phenomena connected with life. Often enough in his attempt to account for the facts observed, he is thrown back upon an appeal to the intrinsic properties of living matter. And though the range of acquaintance with the phenomena associated with life has been so immensely extended, yet there is no advance to record in the direction of a comprehension of the real meaning of the existence of living objects. Among the leaders of scientific thought, some would no doubt declare that such problems belong to the domain of philosophy rather than to that of science; but though the scientist may recognise as his special work the twofold task of collecting and coordinating data, he cannot remain entirely oblivious of these great questions, to interpret which the philosopher appears at present to be as incompetent as himself.

B. *The aims and method of biological study.*

At the risk of rendering this introduction tedious, I would venture to add a few more preliminary remarks. In the first place, scientific results (whether biological or other) have been embodied in certain conceptions of an hypothetical nature. Such conceptions or hypotheses demand constant examination and revision as our knowledge becomes more accurate and extensive. Should new facts fail to harmonise with current hypotheses, the investigator is in honour bound to submit facts and theory alike to searching criticism, and by the result of this his confidence in the theory is confirmed or shaken. From time to time modifications (occasionally on a large scale) have been found necessary in the constitution of some of these hypotheses; and it is incumbent on all to include in their surveys the extensions of horizon provided by the latest methods of research.

Secondly, everything which tends to simplify the current descriptions of our subject must be welcomed. To regard certain of the phenomena presented by living matter as closely parallel to those obtaining in lifeless matter, provides one example of this tendency. In this way conceptions of many biological problems have been considerably simplified, for physical formulae, which are comparatively easy to comprehend, have been substituted for ideas of vital forces which are often unintelligible. But when a biologist announces that he has succeeded in explaining any phenomena of life on physical principles once supposed to apply only to lifeless objects, he is liable to incur the reproach of materialism. As commonly employed, the terms materialism and materialistic appear to imply that those to whom they are applied hold views which in our estimation tend to the degradation of life and living objects[1]. I wish to record my conviction that such an implication is absolutely incorrect and misleading. The mysteries of lifeless matter are infinitely greater than most persons seem to realise. And again it will hardly be now contended that our estimate of life is lowered when we find that living organisms are composed of similar chemical elements (however complex in combination) to those of which lifeless matter is made up. It is therefore inconsistent to regard living matter as debased, when we see

[1] The term materialism is differently and definitely used by philosophers: cf. Romanes, *Monism*, 1895. But it is not necessary for my purpose that the different applications of the expression should be discussed in this connexion.

among its phenomena many processes which are identical with those found to obtain among lifeless objects.

For these reasons, it is important to bear in mind that such 'materialism' is not a deliberate attempt to degrade life, or to ignore or deny its mysterious character. Rather the tendency is to elevate what was once somewhat contemptuously styled lifeless matter to a position in our estimation more worthy of the wonderful properties now known to reside therein.

With such introductory remarks, we may turn to the immediate subject of this Essay, viz. :—Man's Origin, and his Place in Nature.

To set forth the evidence that Man is an organised being would be superfluous. The human individual is a complicated organism of the animal type. However complicated the chemical and even the physiological constitution of Man may be, it is fundamentally similar to that of other animals. The chemical constituents of the human frame are identical with those of living matter in general. The physiological processes of respiration, of assimilation of food, and of excretion of waste material are present alike in all.

Correct appreciation of the origin, and of the place in Nature occupied by a particular organism or animal is conventionally and advisedly based upon what may be termed biological evidence. And the evidence is in turn founded upon a comparison with other animals of the particular animal considered. Moreover, the comparison must take into account not only the structure and conformation, but also the functions and similar manifestations of the animal forms compared.

When these considerations are applied to the case of Man, the method and path of the present enquiry are rendered clearer. Our task is reducible to the comparison of Man with other animals, not only in respect of structure, but also in regard to function. These aspects of the case may be conveniently distinguished as the morphological and physiological sides respectively. In the latter, the evidence of psychology considered in its physiological aspects should be included.

IV] *Man's origin, and his place in Nature* 153

C. *Biological evidence as to Man's Place in Nature.*

1. *The evidence of Morphology, or evidence derived from the study of the structure of Man.*

The methods applicable to the morphological study of Man do not differ from those in general use. They may be provisionally classified in the following way:

(*a*) The comparison of the human body, part by part, with the bodies of other animals.

(*b*) The extension of this method from animals still inhabiting the earth to extinct forms of animal life now known only by their fossilised remains.

(*c*) Comparison of the mode of reproduction and the developmental history of the human individual, with other modes and histories found in the animal series.

(*d*) The further and more detailed comparison of the several varieties of Mankind.

But it is not expedient to enter here upon a lengthy discussion of the methods, material, and results of morphological study. I have however appended a summary of some important researches to make more complete the present sketch. The morphological aspects of the study of Man lack an interest presented by the psychological side, since the structural resemblance of Man to his congeners is much more evident than are similarities in respect of mental endowment.

The general conclusions from the morphological side may be summed up in the following ways:

(*a*) In structure the human body shows close similarity to those of vertebrate animals, particularly to the Mammals: and among these to the apes and ape-like animals associated by systematists with Man in the mammalian order Primates. Herein, the extraordinary development of that part of the brain known as the cerebrum confers upon Man a distinct position. At the same time, Man is not by any means in all respects the most highly specialised primate Mammal, and in numerous points of anatomical structure the human body is less specialised than those of some other Mammals, including even some of the closest relations of Man, viz. : the anthropomorphous apes.

(*b*) The human type owes its origin to a process of evolution, whereby it has been derived from a less specialised mammalian type. The exact details of the path pursued in evolution are still indistinct, but there is good reason to suppose that the more immediate human ancestors possessed several attributes (such as hirsuteness and prognathism) which are more nearly realised in the existing anthropomorphous apes than in any other known animals. For this reason, it is concluded that in those particulars the human ancestors were like apes in appearance, though certainly not identical with any kind of ape now known. Of these progenitors again, the ancestors were probably quadrupedal, but the line is quickly lost in the maze of early mammalian ancestry. As a Mammal, Man shares a common origin with other Mammalia from the vertebrate stock, and his origin is thus traceable to the parent forms of vertebrates. The ancestry of these is still in dispute, but the general results of morphology and embryology point to an origin of the multicellular vertebrate types from unicellular types of animal; the ancestry of such unicellular types again is indicated by certain persistent forms of living matter composed of undifferentiated tissues lacking even a cellular structure. Each individual human being originates in an unicellular ovum which develops *in utero*, becoming multicellular in response to stimulation provided by the advent of the male sexual element.

The minute details of this history are admittedly obscure, but the general correctness of the account cannot be doubted in view of the evidence now available. With regard to the time necessary for such an evolution as that of Man, one cannot speak with definiteness: but certainly many millennia have been required. Human civilisation extends back over the larger part of ten thousand years. The human type most probably became differentiated, and as it were recognisable as human, in the later pliocene division of the Tertiary epoch.

(c) Man is not absolutely the terminal or apical form to which all lines of animal development point. Man occupies, so to speak, the end of a particular twig on a bough of the evolutionary tree, but the tree is not of the poplar type, nor is the human twig the highest, or that which extends furthest from the trunk.

(d) The human type is not uniform; well-defined varieties still exist, though the tendency of civilisation seems to be towards a general admixture of the existing types of Mankind. Some varieties, like some of the fossil ancestors of modern men, are distinctly more ape-like than others, but it is a remarkable fact that no one race appears to be in all its characters more simian than any other.

(e) The morphological evidence as to Man's place in Nature is clear and definite. The pedigrees of some Mammals, such as Whales and Manatees, are much more obscure than that of Man. The inference is that, judged by the test of anatomical structure, Man's position in the animal series is not absolutely exceptional.

2. *The evidence of Physiology.*

In respect of physiological function the general results of morphological investigation are fully borne out. The chemical constitution of the materials which enter into the formation of human tissues is indistinguishable from that of corresponding tissues in other animals. Even with regard to the properties of the blood, the researches of the last two years, above all those carried out at Cambridge, have revealed evidence of the close relations of the higher apes and Man (a genuine "blood relationship" as Dr Nuttall puts it) which is in full accord with the results arrived at on other grounds. The mode of action of the heart and the distribution of the blood and the mechanism therewith connected are so closely allied in Man and the higher Mammals, that the differences are negligible. And the general processes of digestion, respiration, and the excretion of waste products provide similar evidence of close similarity. So it is with the general physiology of the muscular and nervous systems. With regard to the latter, a few supplementary remarks may not be out of place.

It is a matter of common knowledge that the nervous system is composed of a central portion, consisting of the brain and the spinal cord, whence offshoots in the form of nerves are distributed. Of the nerves so distributed, some are in connexion with sentient surfaces, and among these are reckoned the nerves of the special senses. All of these convey messages in the form of nervous impulses from the sentient surface, or organ of special sense, to the central part of the system. Other nerves again carry what are termed centrifugal or efferent messages or impulses from the central portion of the system to the muscular tissues and to other destinations.

The system is thus constituted by the central portion, which is in receipt of impulses arriving along one set of peripheral nerves, and which can emit impulses along another entirely distinct but peripheral series of nerves.

The nervous system of Man resembles that of other animals in these main features. It is not surprising therefore that the physiological events which manifest themselves in nerves during the passage of impulses produced by stimulation, are (so far as all the refinements of physiological research can shew) essentially the same in Man as in other animals.

Moreover, the usual effect of a centripetal nervous impulse is to give rise eventually to a centrifugal impulse, and in the human body as in those of other highly complicated animals this phenomenon may be observed. And in general too, the practical test is to apply a stimulus to a sentient surface and to observe the reaction in the form of a movement.

But now a difference in the highest forms of nervous system must be recognised, a difference of degree however, and not of kind. We have just referred to the tripartite system of centripetal path, central portion, and centrifugal path as the measure of the nervous system. In reality a complication is introduced in the higher animals by the more elaborate structure of the various parts of the central portion. In consequence of this, the simple series of events, consisting of the sequence of stimulation of the centripetal nerve followed by that of the central portion and the centrifugal nerve in succession, is held in control.

Not only may the events be controlled, but inasmuch as the connexions of various parts of the central portions of the system are many and varied, the arrival of stimuli at the central station may result in disturbance of a very complicated series of mechanisms within the central portions of the system.

In describing the human brain as more highly evolved than the brains of other animals, we refer to the higher development of this complicated series of mechanisms. From this it is intelligible that comparatively simple stimuli when impinging on the central portion of the human nervous system can cause a much more profound disturbance than in the nervous systems of less highly developed animals. And the profundity of that disturbance is indicated by the higher development in Man of psychical manifestations which in lower forms of life are rudimentary only.

Again, the existence of what has been termed the mechanism of control is asserted by another phenomenon, or series of phenomena. For in virtue of the presence and activity of that mechanism, the sequence primitively manifested—stimulation of the centripetal nerve followed successively by that of the central portion of the nervous system, and of the centrifugal nerve—may be interrupted. In such a case, even though the centripetal stimulus be applied, the other events are masked, and as regards the centrifugal impulses, may be absent. Such absence of reaction is called inhibition.

The phenomena of inhibition differ widely in their occurrence and intensity. But though extraordinarily developed in Man, they are present in all the higher animals in some degree. Moreover it is important to notice that action and inhibition provide alternative courses and the possibility of two sequels to a given stimulus. This possibility and these alternatives provide a choice of results, and investigation of the nature of this choice, and the circumstances determining the inhibition to which it owes its existence, has largely influenced the psychological conception of the nature of the Will or Volition. It is thus intelligible that the greater development of inhibitory mechanisms in the central nervous system of Man is in accord with the greater activity of the human will.

The 'automatism' of the central nervous system demands a brief notice in this place. The present tendency of physiologists is to discountenance belief in the automatic emission of impulses which at one period were supposed to pass centrifugally from the centre to peripheral parts of the nervous system. Now, on the contrary, it is regarded as probable that for the production of effects which were formerly regarded as evidence of automatic mechanisms, centripetal stimuli are really necessary. And indeed there is evidence to show that even the maintenance of consciousness is dependent upon the arrival of stimuli or impulses from without. The mechanisms whereby the heart's actions and respiration are regulated provide good examples of the importance of centripetal stimuli in this respect.

But in all these processes the nervous system of Man is closely allied to those of the more highly developed Mammals, such differences as exist being differences of degree and not of kind.

3. *The evidence of Psychology.*

We may now pass to the psychological side of the investigation. The phenomena which we here investigate differ in an important respect from the foregoing. For of their very nature, the processes of psychology are essentially transient experiences, events of which no two are precisely alike. Although, therefore, psychology offers an even wider field for experiment than the sciences first considered, this advantage is nevertheless to some extent neutralised. Moreover, exact observation, correct interpretation of results, proper control of experiments—essential preliminaries to the formation of sound judgment—can only be attained as the result of most careful and prolonged training and with the aid of wide scientific knowledge.

The study of psychical manifestations is customarily resolved into several subdivisions. Of these, the emotions, the faculties of attention, imagination, belief, abstraction, and volition, the phenomena of self-consciousness and mental individuality, the aesthetic and religious instincts may be enumerated as the chief. The view has been widely held which suggests that all mental processes are the ultimate outcome of sensory stimuli leading to perceptions, modified or 'associated' beyond recognition though the latter may be. The present trend of opinion is to recognise certain exceptions to this view, which cannot therefore be regarded as applicable to all mental processes, though it undoubtedly facilitates our comprehension of many of these.

This, however, does not amount to an identification of the mental process with the physiological phenomena by which it is accompanied. Certainly there are authors who claim that the two series of events are identical. We may aspire to a power of acquiring exact physical or physiological equivalents to mental phenomena[1]. But it should be borne in mind that even then we should not have attained to a perfect comprehension of the nature of the process. For though the tendency to identify the process with its expression in terms of physical measurement is great, yet it cannot be denied that the physical expression in this case as in others is of the nature of a measure, or property, just as the weight of a body is one measure or property whereby we may be said to know that body. For the present it seems to me preferable to distinguish mental from what are commonly recognised as physical processes, and to adopt (though without prejudice) the terms devised by Professor Lloyd Morgan. This author describes general physical phenomena as *kinetic*. These phenomena can be measured in physical terms. Other phenomena, for which we at present seem to have no physical measure, accompany mental processes. These are termed *metakinetic*. It is a matter for discussion whether such processes are susceptible of measurement in physical terms. The expression 'metakine-

[1] Psychology has here one of its most difficult tasks. Nevertheless the results obtained up to the present certainly encourage further persistence in this line of research.

tic' would seem to suggest that they are not thus susceptible. The question cannot be finally answered at this time. And in view of the uncertainty regarding the answer, it appears to me that the expressions 'parakinesis' and 'parakinetic' are more appropriate than 'metakinesis' and 'metakinetic.' Our great English pioneer[1] in this subject has suggested a threefold classification of such psychical or 'metakinetic' processes into percepts, recepts, and concepts. Of these expressions, the first is descriptive of the effect of stimulating a sense-organ or sensory nerve-ending of the simplest kind and with the simplest mechanism attached. Among the possible effects, the most important may be described as reflex actions, or again actions may be observed which are commonly described as 'instinctive.' Recepts represent an advance upon the psychical condition capable of percepts only. The term recept refers to the alteration in the mental state consequent upon the advent of a series of sense-impressions, the observed sequels of which tend to show that an 'association' of previous perceptions has been elaborated, and is now recalled, in the form of an idea. Thus in certain grades of intelligence a simple stimulus may suffice to call up a complete chain of associations in the form of ideas (recepts). But in other grades, those namely which are alluded to in the illustration of percepts, no idea would be evoked either on the first or upon subsequent applications of the stimulus.

Concepts imply that not only has the recept idea been elaborated, but that it has been abstracted, that it has been translated into a symbol, and that a name has been given to it. This comparatively simple and distinctive symbol may then be substituted mentally for the complicated association of impressions from which it originally sprang. The power of symbolising ideas is thus somewhat analogous to the process of shorthand writing.

Though distinct in the terms of classification, the three varieties of mental process pass imperceptibly into one another.

[1] Romanes. Many psychologists now deprecate this classification, and object to these distinctions as being hard and fast lines drawn in a sequence which does not admit of such arbitrary subdivision.

Man's origin, and his place in Nature

And it is noteworthy that the most perfect forms of concept are attainable only in conjunction with the faculty of speech. For herein is implied the perfection of the power of symbolising ideas, upon which the possession of a genuine concept eventually and essentially depends. Hence the pursuit of linguistic studies in relation to psychical phenomena has received a great stimulus.

One of the great difficulties in the domain of psychology has been the elucidation of the relation between instinct and intelligence. The difficulty is largely due to the loose employment of the term instinct. The net result of research is to shew that the transition from instinctive to intelligent actions is an imperceptible one; and as we shall have occasion to remark in another connexion, the force of habit or repetition may determine the transformation of what are initially intelligent into instinctive actions.

With such preliminary statements, we may pass to the consideration of some results of scientific observations in the foregoing and other branches of Psychology.

The grand general result is embodied in the conviction that the psychical manifestations of Man owe their origin to a process of evolution. This evolution is no less distinctly demonstrable than the corresponding process as regards the body of Man. Indeed, similar principles guide research in each case. And should it be desired to trace the evolution of the concept-forming intellect from a stage in which perception alone is present, the study of progress in the human mind as infancy gives place to maturity will admirably supply the demand. Moreover, not only may intelligence be observed to be superimposed upon instinct, but conversely the close relation of the two may be detected in the gradual transformation of intelligent actions, which by incessant practice and repetition become, as we say, 'instinctive.'

Nor is the study of child-life the only mode of investigation. The comparative study of the human races points in exactly the same direction. And here it must be remarked that as in morphology, so in psychology, the tendency to take our civilised neighbours as the standard of comparison is natural and insidious but absolutely unjustifiable. To obtain satisfactory results, abandonment of such a position is the first requisite. The human races must be taken in their entirety, and the range of variation they exhibit must be made the first subject of study. This path entered upon, we shall not be long engaged in our enquiry before we realise that the position of Man on the average is considerably lowered by the results of investigation in reference to other races than those most familiar to us. But a word of warning must be given in this connexion. For on the one hand, comparatively few of the lowlier races have been subjected to expert investigation by modern psychologists. And in all cases, the potentialities of even the most degraded savage for improvement (under favourable conditions and in surroundings which are stimulating) present material for careful analysis. But I believe the general result to be that stated above.

This becomes the more evident when observations are extended to other forms of life. No one can study the marvellous capabilities developed among insects without admitting the justice of the assertion that Man in his primitive state falls far behind these in respect of attributes which we deem absolutely characteristic of civilisation and even of culture. This statement applies not only to primitive human races of to-day, but, so far as can be judged, to Man as he existed in the infancy of the human race.

I have said that the general result of the researches of the last forty years leads to a belief in the evolution of the various types of human intellect from lowlier forms of intellect such as those exhibited in the other animals. But in making this statement, one is obliged to note that even ardent biologists, men of undoubted competence, have refused to accept this conclusion. Romanes has examined the positions adopted respectively by three of the most eminent of those who reject the evolution theory as thus applied. And the result of an analysis of the views held by Mivart, De Quatrefages and Dr Wallace is not a little astonishing. For it appears that the grounds upon which they severally base their rejec-

IV] *Man's origin, and his place in Nature* 163

tion of evolution as the mode of development of the human intellect are in turn mutually exclusive.

Until, therefore, greater unanimity is shown by those who demand a separate explanation for the phenomena in question, it is impossible to allow their testimony to override the very large amount of consistent evidence[1] which can be brought forward on the side of evolution.

The human intellect is no more an interruption of the course of Nature than is the human body. This consideration constitutes no obstacle to a recognition of the enormous extent to which the evolution of mind has been carried in the highest types of mankind. It is so important to realise the difference of the results when we judge by means of the psychological test from those obtained from the study of the human body, that a few words must be devoted to this difference. We must therefore revert for a moment to the morphological side of the case. As already said, Man, judged by his structure, falls naturally into place among the Primates. Among these animals, Man is distinguished by his adoption of the erect attitude in locomotion (with all the structural modifications connoted thereby), and by his great cerebral development. The latter has appeared till but recently to consist in an increased amount of substance, without such increase in complexity of structure as might indicate the wonderful functions associated with the human cerebrum[2]. It is only when we pass from the study of the artificially preserved but lifeless cerebrum, or that of the same organ as exposed in an anaesthetised patient, to observations on the psychical manifestations of the thinking living Man, that we meet with the marvellous phenomena which assign to Mankind such an exceptional position. For the psychical manifestation of the highest types of Man leave

[1] Cf. (inter alia) *Mental Evolution in Animals*; also *Mental Evolution in Man*; Romanes.
[2] Cf. Edinger's comments on the minute structure of the reptilian brain, quoted by Soury, *Le Système nerveux central*; vol. II, p. 757, l. 1. Researches on the human brain, not yet published in extenso, by A. W. Campbell, M.D., considerably modify this statement.

no room for any misconception as to their preeminence in this respect. No other form of life has ever, so far as we can judge, been able to advance beyond the stage of forming recepts. But in the more recent evolution of the Hominidae, and even among the races commonly regarded as most primitive and savage, the conceptual power has been acquired, with results which are too familiar to need recapitulation here.

We have seen that while we may aspire at some future date to attain to a measure of psychical events in physical terms, yet the two series of phenomena should not be regarded as identical. Nor is it at present possible to compare mental processes to secretions, or to refer to them as functions in the physiological sense of the term. None the less, mental processes are only known to us as inseparable from the existence of corresponding brains. To the activity of these they owe their origin, obscure though that origin may be. And upon the healthy activity of the brain, the mental process is dependent. Thus it is that the well-being of the brain is essential to the sum total of those metakinetic processes upon which personality and individuality are built. In this connexion too, the interchange and give-and-take between the brain and the rest of the body is a subject now regaining an importance which it had temporarily lost. The untoward mental effects of unhealthy conditions of the heart and liver bear in this respect familiar testimony to a general rule, while the study of the insane has, in numerous instances, revealed structural changes in the elements of the brain itself.

D. *Human Evolution.*

We must now turn our attention to the consideration of the factors which may be supposed to have determined the evolution of the human body and mind along the lines they have actually followed. Though we may feel quite assured of the correctness of evolution as the mode of development, we at once meet with the difficulty of providing a convincing exposition of the influences which have permitted the evolution to take place. As in the case of any evolution, we

IV] *Man's origin, and his place in Nature* 165

can point out the fundamental necessity of adaptation to surroundings as a condition of survival and progress. But as in the evolution of various animals, and of their component parts and organs, so here it remains to explain the origin, the preservation, and the perpetuation of the earliest rudiments of the faculty or organ destined to promote survival. For the enunciation of a belief in Evolution is not the end but the beginning of the matter.

It has long been realised that far more living individuals are actually produced than can be maintained by the resources of Nature. A surplus of these individuals fails to maintain itself in the struggle for existence. It is thus evident that a process of selection is at work. This process has been called Natural Selection. Again, the action of this process is definite. For those individuals which persist appear, so far as can be seen, to be better fitted to cope with their surroundings than those which do not persist. The selection is therefore a selection of the fittest, and though not clearly demonstrable in the case of all forms of life, there can be no doubt that selection has exercised and still exercises an influence on all alike.

The material upon which the process of selection acts, consists of the individuals which are continually being produced. At the present day, to say that naturally the endowments of all are not equal is to repeat a platitude. In order for a selective action to be exercised, it is necessary that a variety of individuals should be produced, and indeed it is not difficult to demonstrate the variability of organisms.

Our subject may now be set forth in the following way. We observe that variations occur in the individuals which are produced in successive generations. We observe that in view of the struggle for existence, a selective process determines the survival of some and the dying out of others. Our attention is thus clearly and forcibly drawn to the study of those variations. And herein there are at least three main and essential divisions of the problem.

In the first place the nature of variations and the circumstances of their origin claim attention. Again, the amount or degree of variations, and their relations to one another, provide most important subjects for research. And yet again, we must consider the nature of variations as regards the change by which a character at first constituting a variation may be reproduced in future generations as a comparatively stable and constant feature of the latter. In other words, the phenomena of inheritance demand investigation.

1. *Origin of Variations.*

The origin of Variations, *i.e.* of the material from which a selection can be made by any means (whether human or other), is ultimately bound up with the properties of living matter. The biologist can understand easily enough that variations may be infinite in degree, granted that living matter is susceptible, and that it reacts to changes in its environment. The precise explanation of how and why living matter is thus susceptible is only removed a stage further back, when we urge that such changes affect the nutrition of matter. Pressed to a logical conclusion, we find that if it be granted that living matter depends for persistence on processes of nutrition which are susceptible to the influence of external events, such as temperature, light, etc., then the production of variations is intelligible. But the key to the problem lies in a perfect comprehension of the premise, that is of the nature of life, our comprehension of which is only partial.

2. *Degree of Variation.*

In passing to the consideration of the amount or range of variations, special stress must be laid upon the researches to which the work of Mendel has recently led. It is noteworthy too, that variations are recognised which differ not only in degree but also as regards their transmissibility to offspring. Thus variations can now be subdivided into (*a*) mutations and (*b*) fluctuations. Mutations differ by wide intervals from each other, *i.e.* they are discontinuous; and they are transmitted with certainty from parent to offspring. Fluctuations are less divergent from one another, and there is no strong evidence as to their transmission. It is the more important to discriminate between the two kinds of variation, since in evolution mutations alone, and not fluctuations[1], constitute the material upon which selective actions are exercised. It may be added that while not recognising these two categories (viz. mutations and fluctuations), Darwin believed that selection was exercised among many characters now merely regarded as fluctuations, when judged by the small extent of their variability. This belief would not now be justified. But to quote a recent author[2], "How and why these mutations arise, is the great outstanding problem of Biology." The problem is therefore only narrowed within closer limits and not solved by such recent work.

3. *Heredity.*

Our ignorance regarding the ultimate cause of the production of variations (particularly mutations) extends equally to the subject of the inherited power of producing them. So that observations are for the present directed principally to the discovery of the order or rule regulating their appearance and transmission.

The importance of the study of Heredity in this connexion is not hard to grasp. For it is plain that perpetuation of such characters as have favoured parents, will, until the environment changes profoundly, tend to preserve the offspring in successive generations. Our difficulties commence however with the enquiry into, and the definition of the term 'character.' Difficult as the investigation is in any case, it is especially so in such instances as are afforded by the higher animals including Man, in which 'characteristics' are numerous and diverse, structural and psychical.

The general phenomena of heredity may be summed up in the statement that parental characters of varied nature are reproduced in the offspring. Some are reproduced with constancy: for example the essential organs of nutrition or

[1] Most of the varieties which are directly determined by food or climatic influences may be regarded as fluctuations and not mutations.
[2] Punnett, *Mendelism*, 1905.

circulation, or the normal number of eyes or limbs in animals. But beyond these, some features are not so consistently transmitted. The principal lines of investigation which have been entered upon by those whose studies have led them to this subject may be briefly indicated in the following way.

(a) In the first place, the enquiry as to the transmission and inheritance of characters acquired by a parent during the course of existence, has attracted much attention. The interest of this subject depends on its relation to the action of what has been described above as the process of Natural Selection. For if a parent may acquire advantageous characters and transmit them to offspring, the latter will from this cause, in addition to any others, be advantageously situated as regards Natural Selection. But, in fact, the present trend of opinion favours the rejection of a belief in the transmission of acquired characters, save in rare and obscure instances.

The actual work of research has followed two main paths. On the one hand, comparisons have been instituted between the parent and offspring through a series of generations; and the material for comparison has usually consisted of structural details, providing characters susceptible of measurement, although to a smaller extent, psychical phenomena have also been recorded and compared. Reference has already been made to the twofold classification of variations as mutations and fluctuations,—a distinction based upon observed differences as regards transmission or heredity. While the experiments which have revealed the constancy with which mutations are transmitted have been chiefly carried out upon lower forms of life, there is little doubt as to the applicability of similar laws to Man. The general results have thus far been applied with success to the improvement of crops or stock, but recent writers insist on the importance of their bearing upon sociological problems. One most momentous inference suggests that in combating the degenerative tendencies of certain classes among civilised societies, such remedial agencies as hygiene and education are inadequate instruments, since

IV] *Man's origin, and his place in Nature* 169

they can develop types of the order of fluctuations only, variations that is to say, which are not transmissible. By those who hold these views, the appropriate remedy would be sought in carefully restraining conjugal unions, namely in selective mating, with consequent elimination of undesirable types. The realisation of such a prospect, however desirable it may appear from some points of view, seems to-day well-nigh impossible, so complicated have the conditions of modern civilisation become. But I consider it urgent to indicate the trend of opinion upon this very important aspect of the study of heredity in general.

(b) On the other hand, enquiry has been directed to the details of the process of reproduction as revealed in the animal tissues immediately concerned. The utmost refinements of research have been employed to search out the exact part played by male and female germinal elements in the mysterious history of sexual reproduction. And yet, great as is the wealth of observed detail, the inferences are by no means clearly drawn. In this, as in so many quests, the biologist finds himself arrested by his incomplete comprehension of the nature, structure, and composition of the living cellular masses wherein he can discern changes which he is unable fully to explain.

Again, therefore, we find at the end of our investigation properties of living matter, comparable in their obscurity to those which determine variation. Unceasing though the efforts to pierce the gloom may be, failure has attended the efforts of even the finest intellects in this attempt to solve the problem.

Thus it is evident that while the biologist is convinced that Man is the outcome of an evolution, the main outlines of which are unmistakeable, yet the endeavour to render an account of the influences which have determined that evolution is far from satisfactory. There is no doubt at all as to the occurrence of variations. There is equally little doubt but that some are selected to the exclusion of others. But the weakness of the present position lies in the impossibility of providing a clear exposition of the origin of variations.

And even if to the process of Natural Selection, we add allied influences such as Sexual Selection (Darwin), Physiological Selection (Romanes), or Germinal Selection (Weismann), the difficulties are not thereby removed. In the same way, although the ascertained facts of heredity are rapidly increasing in number, the biologist's present difficulty consists in the exact application to Man of inferences drawn from the study of lower forms of life[1].

Under such circumstances biologists can ill afford to be bigoted, and must and do welcome any proffered explanations of these complex problems, provided only that such explanatory hypotheses present a fair basis of observation, open to the ordinary rules of criticism.

E. *Prospective Evolution of Man.*

As regards the future development of Man, I fail to see why the present condition of Mankind in respect of mental ability should be the final stage. Indeed I believe that in Man there is more scope for future psychical evolution than for his evolution in any other respect; for it seems improbable that the structure of Man will undergo much modification.

But to the possibilities of mental improvement it is hard to see an end, especially when one remembers the advantage conferred on each successive generation by the experience of the past, whereby each is enabled to start from a more advanced base. At the same time, I do not see that there is any very definite prospect of prolonging the normal lifetime of Man, to the extent suggested by a recent writer[2].

Whatever be the ultimate goal toward which Man is tending, we can see that one, if not the chief condition for continued progress in Human Evolution is adaptation to a social mode of existence. The great commandments of the Law were recognised long before they were so vividly recalled to human notice at the commencement of the Christian

---

[1] Farabee has recently published an interesting monograph on this subject. Cf. *Papers of the Peabody Museum of American Archaeology*, Cambridge, Mass. 1905.

[2] E. Metschnikoff.

Era. Within the limits of a civilised community the struggle for existence is much obscured, so much so indeed that Huxley declared with a good show of reason that the cosmic process of evolution and the ethical process are antagonistic. To me it appears that the difference is probably more apparent than real, and that when once a society has been evolved, its continuance depends on some modification of the process of selection within its limits, so that selection when exercised within the society might appear different from selection exercised without. I have little doubt that selection is not abolished, but only masked and restrained, within the limits of what is technically described as a social group. In the foregoing pages allusion is made to conditions under which the best and highest types may be safeguarded and perpetuated. Individual efforts in this direction may appear of infinitesimally small value. But in the special case of Man, there is increased knowledge, and this brings increased responsibility. And in this sense, responsibility is imposed on individuals so to regulate their actions that amelioration, rather than retrogression, may be the order of the day. Upon such considerations must our rules of conduct be formulated.

F. *The origin of Living Organisms.*

We have seen that Man is part of Nature, and that he occupies a definite position in the world of living organisms. The question of Man's origin brings us face to face with the question of the origin of life, and the phenomena associated with life at its earliest inception.

It must be granted that although the most carefully conducted experiments show that the living organisms known to us to-day can only be derived from pre-existing living substance, yet at every moment we may observe instances of the transformation of the elements of lifeless food into the living substance of organisms. When we study the series of changes thus presented by the phenomena of what is termed by physiologists metabolism, we shall realise the difficulty of fixing with accuracy the exact point of passage from the organic chemical compound to the living cell-substance.

And the tendency may well be excused which foresees the demonstration of the historical continuity of lifeless and living substance, both in the evolution of living organisms, and in the processes of nutrition whereby these maintain existence.

In the life of Man we perceive what is essentially a liberation of energy; and this is true, whether we identify life with energy or regard the latter rather as a measure of life. Our lives thus regarded provide demonstration of the fundamental phenomenon of nature, viz., never-ceasing transformation and redistribution of energy. Of the ultimate source of energy, of its nature, and even of its relation to matter we are at present ignorant. Indeed the very expression 'energy' is after all but a convenient symbol, whereby we designate, or recall, concepts constructed on the basis of a series of sense-impressions. Beyond these our intellectual capabilities do not at present allow us to pass. For the moment there is more than enough work for all, in the observation and attempted interpretation of those impressions. Further than this our light cannot as yet penetrate. "Science is a match that Man has just got alight. He thought he was in a room... and that his light would be reflected from and display walls inscribed with wonderful secrets, and pillars carved with philosophical systems wrought into harmony. It is a curious sensation, now that the preliminary splutter is over and the flame burns up clear, to see his hands lit and just a glimpse of himself and the patch he stands on visible, and around him, in place of all that human comfort and beauty he anticipated—darkness still[1]." To recognise the bounds thus fixed to our present knowledge, and the uncertainty beyond, is no confession of scientific failure. In the case of the subject with which we are immediately concerned, such an admission is forced from us when we pass beyond the elementary stage of realising that Man is the product of an evolution which has taken place among the Mammals.

[1] H. G. Wells.

G. Conclusion.

In the foregoing pages I have endeavoured to indicate the aspects of Man and of the Universe as these present themselves to the eye of the biologist. We may again note that the latter recognises fully the limits of the territory within which his work lies. My endeavour has been to point out the chief results of work within those limits; and to distinguish between what is sure and what is uncertain ground. With the presentation of such results the task of the biologist is at an end, and it remains for philosophers and theologians to apply those data to the solution of problems which fall within their particular domain.

If I may attempt to summarise what has been recounted, I would say that we have boldly to face the fact that, as a result of biological study, we can no longer base Man's preeminence in Nature upon grounds of physical conformation. It is by his psychical powers that his claims to supremacy are sustained. Although, in structure, Man resembles the beasts that perish, he has so far surpassed them in intellectual development that, superficially at least, comparisons hardly seem to hold. This statement is not invalidated by the admission that the human mind has been evolved from lowly beginnings: indeed, as I have already pointed out, we have only to watch the growth of the mind in the infant and child to see this evolution repeated before our eyes. But the final conclusion is that philosophers must base Man's claims to a supreme position upon his mental and not on his physical characters.

Secondly, the past history of Man fails to reveal to scientists evidence of sudden degradation like that implied in the expression 'fall.' On the contrary, the general tendency has been upwards, though the path has by no means been straight; deviations have been numerous, and mistakes frequent. We may, it is true, find instances of degeneration following as a result of over-specialisation, with consequent indulgence of the senses, with supineness and loss of adaptive power under altered circumstances. And in such special cases degradation may even proceed till the final result is extinction. But if we regard the tide of human existence as a whole, neglecting for the moment the fate of local ebb or eddy therein, we shall recognise that the general result is a rise in level. During protracted periods progress may be latent or seemingly arrested; but eventually favourable conditions obtain and coincide, leading to a further step in advance.

In no respect is this process more definite than in the evolution of the higher mental faculties. And with the higher development of these, comes the demand for corresponding modification and change in the exposition and presentation of religious doctrines. At the same time, the difficulty has to be faced, that a given civilised society will be found to include at one and the same time, an almost infinite number of intellectual types, representative of almost every phase in the sequence of human mental evolution. The problem is to satisfy the requirements of each and all.

But again at this point the scientist withdraws in favour of the philosopher, recognising that science, as Professor Wundt says of its psychological branch, "can only indicate the path which leads to territories beyond her own, ruled by other laws than those to which her realm is subject." Within those territories must be sought the clues leading to a comprehension of the essential nature of life and of those indefinable, but none the less genuine human impulses which we describe as the promptings of conscience. By the aid of such studies, we may hope to reach a fuller explanation of the phenomena of free-will, and even to gain an intelligible conception of the mysterious ultimate source of life.

ESSAY V.

SIN, AND THE NEED OF ATONEMENT.

EDWARD HARRISON ASKWITH, D.D.

CONTENTS.

I. SIN.
1. The term Sin at once religious and ethical.
2. The ground of the obligation of the Moral Law.
3. The ethically Good has meaning only in reference to Persons.
4. The Criterion of Goodness.
5. The Christian revelation of Divine Character.
6. The Divine Character explanatory of the Moral Law.
7. Sin as failure to fulfil the conditions of Communion with God.

II. THE NEED OF ATONEMENT.
1. Reconciliation of man to God.
2. Atonement the taking away of sin.
3. The need of Freedom.
4. The requirement of the Conscience an act of Divine love.
5. Christ as the Revealer of God.
6. The Divine Indwelling.
7. The Atonement and the Death of Christ.

SIN, AND THE NEED OF ATONEMENT.

THE theory of evolution has thrown not a little light on the problem of the existence of moral evil in the world. We are able to understand now, in a way that was not possible before the theory of development was reached, that moral evil is rather failure on man's part to rise higher in the scale of being, and to respond to the true dignity of his nature, than a fall from a state of perfection which was his when he started upon his history. The interpretation of the fall of man, then, has been greatly modified by the scientific conclusions of recent times. But there is perhaps a danger in our day lest an apparently simple explanation of the fact of moral evil should lessen man's sense of responsibility, and the claims of conscience should be neglected or explained away.

Moral evil is called in Christian phraseology Sin. Human sinfulness is an axiom of Christian theology. In saying this we would not imply that Christianity first introduced the notion of sin. For of course the idea of sin is pre-Christian; and among the Jewish people in particular the conception of sin rose to a high moral standard. It would be an interesting study to trace historically by a critical use of the writings of the Old Testament the growth of the Hebrew conception of sin. But it is no part of our purpose to do this in the present essay. We are more concerned to set forth what sin means, or should mean for us to-day, in the light of the Christian revelation of God, than to enquire what it has meant at different stages of religious history.

Our method then is not historical, for we have not to do principally with what has taken place in the past. Our appeal is rather to the experience of to-day. We shall indulge in no speculations as to the origin of evil, nor shall we attempt here to reconcile the fact of the existence of moral evil in the world with our faith in the absolute goodness of the Supreme Being. Speculation as to the origin of evil must fail in profit and instruction unless there be a clear idea in the mind as to its nature.

It is our intention then to insist here on the fact of sin, and to examine its nature, rather than to speculate on the how or when or where of its entrance into the world in which we live. Further, our subject, as the title of the essay suggests, is a twofold one. We have not only to treat of Sin, but of Atonement. The latter like the former is capable of historical treatment. It is not however our intention to deal historically with the subject of atonement any more than with that of sin. The conception of atonement has not been a stationary one, just as that of sin has not been stationary. But our concern is more with that to which the conception has come than with that from which it started or with the stages through which it has passed. In saying this however we would not be thought to imply that there is to-day a general consensus of opinion among Christian thinkers as to the nature and rationale of atonement. On the contrary it must be acknowledged that there is considerable difference of opinion. Such difference of opinion seems to show that the different views are but partial and not yet harmonised. On one point, however, there is a growing agreement, namely, the rejection of views which do not accord with the perfection of the Divine character. Belief in this is of supreme importance in the religious life and essential to the right development of Christian thought. Where unworthy views of God prevail it will be impossible to understand either what sin is or what is the atonement needed for its removal.

As the need of an atonement arises from the fact of sin, it is clear that our view of that need will depend on our view of sin. The nature of the atonement needed to remedy sin must be decided by the nature of sin itself. We shall then in the first part of the Essay deal with this question of the

v] *Sin, and the need of Atonement* 179

nature of sin. Of atonement we will only speak after we have reached conclusions as to the nature of that which atonement is designed to remedy.

If we were desirous of investigating the history of the development of the conception of sin we should naturally make an examination of the words used to express the idea in different languages, particularly in Greek and Hebrew. That is to say, etymology would be a necessary factor in the investigation. It would be natural that we should go back to the original meaning of the word *ḥātā* and see in what connexions it was used. Such an enquiry would lead us to the conclusion which we will express in the words of a great critical historian of Semitic religion: "The fundamental meaning of the Hebrew word *ḥātā*, to sin, is to be at fault, and in Hebrew, as in Arabic, the active (causative) form has the sense of missing the mark (Judges xx. 16) or other object aimed at. The notion of sin, therefore, is that of blunder or dereliction, and the word is associated with others that indicate error, folly or want of skill and insight (1 Sam. xxvi. 21)." And again: "In two respects, then, the Hebrew idea of sin, in its earlier stages, is quite distinct from that which we attach to the word. In the first place it is not necessarily thought of as an offence against God, but includes any act that puts a man in the wrong with those who have power to make him rue it (2 Kings xviii. 14; 1 Sam. xx. 1).......In the second place, the notion of sin has no necessary reference to the conscience of the sinner, it does not necessarily involve moral guilt, but only, so to speak, forensic liability[1]."

It is clear then that a religious conception of sin, such as is developed in the Old Testament, goes far beyond what is etymologically contained in the word which is used to describe it. And so it is in other languages.

The Christian conception of sin is far too complex to be reached or understood by any etymological process. The doctrine of sin does not stand alone, but is a part of Christian theology and is only to be appreciated in its dogmatic context.

[1] Robertson Smith, *Prophets of Israel*, pp. 102 f.

The term 'sin' as now used is essentially a theological one, or let us say, lest it should seem that we are implying that our subject is unintelligible except to theologians, a religious one. But further if the Christian idea of sin is essentially religious, its foundation is no less essentially ethical. For sin is, as we have said, the Christian name for moral evil. The fundamental ideas of ethics then are needed for a right understanding of the Christian view of sin. And we shall have to deal with these to some extent in the present Essay.

Ethics as such has not to do with sin. Accordingly in works on ethics not professedly or distinctively religious ethics, the idea of sin is not prominent, and indeed the word itself may be entirely absent from an ethical treatise. Nor can any fault be found with writers on ethics for not treating of sin, for it does not properly fall within their province. Ethics can investigate the notion of the Good independently of any religious application of it. Closely associated with the notion of Good is that of Duty, that is to say man's obligation to respond to the Good in action and to make it his own. Failure to fulfil the obligation is in the language of ethics wrong or evil. But in the language of theology it is sin. We shall hope to make clear the reason for retaining a distinctive theological term for wrong-doing.

Now moral evil or wrong-doing may be regarded as the violation of law which man is under an obligation to obey. The ground of this obligation may be conceived to be either in the *content* of the law or in its *origin*. In Kant's system emphasis is laid on the moral law independently of the lawgiver. Indeed man is regarded as his own lawgiver, because the law which he feels himself under an obligation to obey is written within him. The duty of obedience is self-evident, being an intuition of the 'practical' or moral reason.

According to Kant then the moral law is intrinsically reasonable. No external authority is needed to convince us of our obligation to live in obedience to the law. Our practical reason tells us that we ought to obey it. To disobey it is to act irrationally and therefore wrongly. Reason demands of each man that he shall "act only on those maxims which he can at the same time will to be universal laws." To act thus would be both right and good ; to act otherwise would be not merely inexpedient but positively wrong. To violate this law of reason is to fail to fulfil an obligation which we may evade but cannot deny.

It is not desirable that we should at this point go off to examine at length the ultimate reasonableness of the Kantian maxim. It is certainly open to obvious and grave criticism as it stands. Our immediate point however is not to discuss the truth or falsehood of the maxim but to emphasise Kant's important doctrine of the autonomy of the rational will.

But wrong-doing is in other quarters regarded as the violation of divine law, which man is under an obligation to obey because of its *origin*. Violation of the law is disobedience to God, the Supreme Being. He has given a law which man ought to obey. To disobey the divine law is to sin.

Now it might of course be asked by an advocate of the autonomy of the will how the divine origin of a law can be known or proved except by the intrinsic character and worth of the law itself. Conviction that a law is divinely given depends ultimately, it may with reason be contended, on the content of the law, on what it commands to be done and what it forbids. Those who find the sanctity of the moral law in its origin rather than in its content have in general a conviction, although it may not be prominent, of the ethical character of the Supreme Being from whom the law proceeds. This conviction needs to be brought out and developed if there is to be any adequate appreciation of the law as something good, in the strictly ethical sense of the word.

Even were we to grant that there is a law which a man ought to obey because it proceeds from the Supreme Being, we should still be constrained to ask what is the inner principle of the law. We cannot without impiety suppose that the moral law is based on the arbitrary will of God; for the very notion of arbitrariness is wholly alien to the conception of a perfect Being. A perfect Being can only be ethically known. This does not of course mean that His attributes are purely ethical. The power and wisdom of God can be thought of apart from His goodness. But it is only in so far as we believe that the Divine wisdom and power are exercised in perfect goodness that we have faith in a perfect Supreme Being. The moral law cannot be good because it proceeds from a Being of infinite power who is able to punish every violation of it. There is a danger lest in our desire to save people from the consequences of certain actions we appeal to them not on moral or ethical grounds but prudentially, and make the sanction of moral law depend upon the punishment that will follow upon disobedience to it. Indeed the word 'sanction' has acquired this peculiar sense, having come to mean 'that by which a law is enforceable.' But people would not in reason be persuaded that violation of moral law would ultimately meet with punishment, Divinely dispensed, unless they had within them the conviction that the law is truly ethical and its violation deserving of punishment.

It must be allowed that the Genesis story of the Fall seems to give countenance to the view that the essence of wrong-doing is that it is disobedience to a divine command considered irrespectively of its moral content. But the view we take of Inspiration does not preclude a reverent criticism of the story in the light of the Christian conscience. It is possible to discern the elements of spiritual truth it contains, and at the same time to see that it does not contain the whole truth. We need not deny that wrong-doing or sin is disobedience of a divine command, but we say that this is not a full account to give of it. It is insufficient to satisfy the Christian conscience which has been educated by the Divine Spirit to the discernment of Good in itself. It may be a necessary stage in the religious education of mankind to conceive of God as primarily a lawgiver and judge. We do not say that this is a false view, but we say that it is an imperfect one. For we are assuming that the principle of development which holds in the natural world is applicable also in the spiritual.

So then we need not be surprised if the Old Testament account of the advent of sin into the world lacks finality.

The story, as we have it, may have its use still. And that, not merely as an interesting religious document of the past, but also for its teaching, even if this be imperfect, respecting man's relation to God. Its conception of God may be anthropomorphic, but still there is expressed in the story the truth that man is meant for communion with God, and that this communion has been hindered by human failure to respond to the divine requirements. But the ethical nature of the requirements is not brought out in the story. This we must allow. And yet there is a hint of it, in that the man is represented as not only afraid when he had disobeyed, but also ashamed. He has, then, not only disobeyed, he has done wrong by disobeying. He *ought* to have obeyed.

Now in order to appreciate the Christian view of sin in all its complexity we must realise that in the condemnation of sin we have the formation and expression of an ethical judgement. To say that some one 'ought' to do anything is to imply that the failure to do it is evil. And the failure to do it can only be evil if the doing of it is good. In other words moral evil is the refusal of good, ethically conceived. Ethical good cannot be contemplated by a moral being such as man apart from the demand that it makes upon him. What is ethically good he ought, in some measure at any rate, to do. And what he ought to do must be ethically good. Otherwise there could be no obligation upon him to do it. The moral obligation to do anything rests ultimately on the fact that it is good.

Now it is of the first importance to insist on the special ethical application of the term 'good' and to distinguish what is ethically good from what is only relatively good. That is good absolutely which is good in itself. The account that we give of some line of conduct that it is ethically good is final, ultimate. For ethical good cannot be defined. If we say that such and such a thing is ethically good, we are not then defining ethical goodness but only giving an example of it. The notion of ethical good is ultimate, as that of space is ultimate. Man is distinguished from the lower animal creation in that he is an ethical being, having an idea of goodness, even if it be in some cases only a vague one. And, as has been already said, coupled with the notion of goodness is the cognition of an obligation personally to respond in conduct to that goodness. Those who regard wrong-doing as disobedience to a divine command without taking account of the content of the command as ethically good can bring their view into consonance with the ethical point of view if they take the line that obedience to a divine command is in itself good ethically. They may say that man ought, morally that is, to obey God, whether or not he discerns the principle and reason of the divine law.

But there opens out before us here the great question: What is good ethically? Let us allow for the moment that obedience to a divine command, apart from any ethical goodness that may be discerned in its content, is ethically good, it is yet clear that obedience to a divine command is not the only form of ethical goodness of which man is cognisant. For even if it be the case that a relative or created being such as man has a duty of obedience to the absolute Being to whom he owes his existence, on the ground that his being is derived from Him, and that this very fact implies indebtedness to Him from whom it is derived, it is yet true that we can and do form the conception of an absolute Being who is Himself perfectly good ethically. The absolute Being of course owes no obedience. There is nothing of which it can be said that He ought to do it on the ground of any derived existence; for He is eternal, self-existing. We can conceive of perfect goodness in the absolute Being, and therefore clearly we have some conception of goodness other than the obedience which a relative being owes to the absolute Being from whom his existence is derived.

Further it is clear that we do not necessarily feel ourselves in duty bound to do what another tells us to do on the ground that that other has done something for us, and that we owe it to him to do in return whatever he may demand of us. We certainly should not consider ourselves morally bound to make the return asked for if the person who is supposed to have benefited us had not acted disinterestedly in the matter.

The fact is that there lies behind the idea of our duty of

obedience to the Supreme Being the thought of His ethical goodness, though the idea of this may be vague. But the vaguer the consciousness of the Divine perfection is in us, the less is the consciousness of a duty, in an ethical sense, to obey Him. The 'ought' of obedience becomes more and more prudential. We ought to obey Him, because He is supreme; because He has power over us and we cannot resist that power. But that we ought to obey because obedience to Him is good—clearly discerned to be good in the strictly ethical sense—this we could not see unless we had a belief in the goodness of Him who commands.

Shall we then say of wrong-doing that it is the refusal to obey the divine law, which law we are morally bound to obey because it proceeds from the absolute Being from whom our existence is derived and who is, as we believe, perfect in goodness as well as supreme in power? Is sin to be described as the rebellion of the finite creature against the will of the Creator who is supreme in goodness? This account of sin may be true up to a point, but it is certainly not a sufficient account to give. For the old difficulty still remains: How are we to know that the so-called moral law is divine? How are we to feel assured that it really proceeds from God and that it expresses His will for us? If the content of the law is intrinsically good in the ethical sense, then we may be persuaded of its divine origin. But if we cannot discern the ethical worth of the law we shall be in danger of losing belief in it as the expression of the Divine Will.

And there is this further difficulty: How do we know or why do we believe that God is ethically good? If we are already convinced of the goodness of God, we shall require the mark of goodness on a law purporting to come from Him. If the law be found on examination not to bear upon itself the stamp of the ethically good, we shall become sceptical of its divine origin. Moreover our belief in the Divine goodness, unless it have something to rest upon, may become shaken. But if the law be seen to be ethically good we explain that goodness by its origin. The moral law becomes an argument in favour of the ethical character of the Supreme Being.

It may seem that we are here arguing in a circle. When we say that we explain the goodness of the law, seen to be ethically good, by its origin, it may appear that we are assuming that the law proceeds from God and that God is good. But we have been asking: How do we know or why do we believe that God is good? If the law is seen to be ethically good, then on the assumption that God is Himself good, we might infer the divine origin of the law. But could not the law be ethically good without being of divine origin? If this were possible, we could not from the character of the law infer the Divine goodness.

A little consideration will show that what we are really assuming is that the ethically good—even the simple conception of it—must have a cause, and this cause we cannot find to be man himself, for then the moral law could hardly present itself to him as something which he was under an obligation to obey. Obedience to it would in this case be not difficult, as in fact it is, but easy; we might almost say, necessary. The ultimate cause then of a law discerned to be ethically good must be the Supreme Being. There is nothing illogical therefore in inferring the goodness of God from the goodness of the moral law, once recognised as intrinsically good. So then our statement that if the law be seen to be ethically good we explain that goodness by its origin, and infer the ethical character of the Supreme Being, must be taken to mean that the ethically good must have a cause—even as we have said the notion of it—and this cause can be none other than God Himself, whose ethical character is hence inferred.

A careful investigation of the ethically good will make this point clearer. So far we have been speaking abstractly about the good. We are taking our stand on the view that the ethically good is incapable of definition, the notion being ultimate. But what cannot be defined is not on that account unknown. As a matter of fact we speak of certain conduct as good, using the epithet in an ethical sense. This use shows that we have a knowledge of ethical good. Even though we cannot define it we can give illustrations or examples of it. We must then now in order to elucidate our subject become

Sin, and the need of Atonement

more definite as to the ethically good. We must ask: To what can the strictly ethical epithet 'good' be applied?

And here we are at once reminded of Kant's famous dictum that there is nothing good except a good Will. This is a simple but at the same time a profound saying. Ethical goodness is the property not of things but of persons. This, if true, may at first sight appear to make much of what we have been saying valueless; for we have been speaking of good conduct, and of the moral law as good. What meaning then can such a manner of speaking have if ethical goodness can be predicated only of persons as distinguished from things? Have we been applying the ethical epithet in cases where it is properly not applicable at all?

To answer these questions we must consider more closely what we mean by a good will. Will expresses the activity of a person, purposeful activity. A person may be restricted in the exercise of his will by circumstances which he cannot control. In that case his will, supposed good, is unable to put itself forth into full activity. A person with a good will restricted in its exercise may be said to have a good intention. Good intention by itself could not satisfy a good will, which must, in order to find satisfaction, pass into action. We could not tell whether a person had a good intention unless we could see the hindrance to the activity of the will removed and observe the subsequent action. Even if the action appropriate to a good will followed, the goodness of the will might still be open to doubt, for a will not ethically good might perform the same action. Of two persons doing the same action one may do it because it is good, and the other from some other motive. Only in the first case is there the activity of a good will. A good will does good because it is good.

But if this be so, must there not be something good besides a good will? We may go further and ask: Must there not be something good prior even to the good will? If the good will does x, which is good, because it is good, must not x be good even more than the will that does it because it is good?

To give definiteness to our illustration, let us suppose that the doing of x is producing happiness in a person or a community of persons. The symbol x now stands for 'happiness in a person or community of persons.' It does not stand for '*producing* this happiness,' for the producing is allowed for in the word 'doing.' A person, then, produces happiness in a person or community of persons because it is good. Such a person manifests the operation of a good will because he does something for the reason that it is good. But what is it that is good? Is it the happiness? In our opinion the strictly ethical epithet is not applicable to the term 'happiness.' Is it then the 'producing of happiness' that is good? To this we would reply that the purposive producing of happiness may be ethically good. But 'producing happiness' unless it be purposive would not be ethically good.

It must not however be supposed that when we speak of anything as not ethically good we mean that it is evil. It is true that where there is moral evil there is an absence of ethical good; but it is not the case that where there is an absence of ethical good there is necessarily moral evil. We hope to make this point clearer further on. But it is necessary to insist at this stage that when we deny that the producing of happiness if not purposive is ethically good, we are not condemning it as evil.

What exactly then do we mean when we say that a person with a good will will produce happiness in others because it is good? Is the last epithet 'good' properly ethical? It is clear that it is intended to be ethical. For to say that a good will is active to do something because it is good would be meaningless unless the second epithet 'good' were similar in meaning to the first.

Now when we come to contemplate the real meaning of the statement that a good will does something because it is good, it becomes clear that the words 'it is good' are an abbreviated expression of the fact that the doing of the thing in question is a worthy activity of the good will *qua* good will. A good will in putting forth its activity takes account before all else of the worthiness in regard to itself of the end to which the activity is directed. It asks whether it is worthy of itself as a good will that it should be the active cause of the end contemplated. A good will expresses itself in its true character by its activities. It is active only to produce that which is worthy of itself in its character of goodness.

Kant, then, so it seems to us, was quite right in his contention that the good will is the only thing which is unconditionally good. When we speak of good conduct we mean conduct which is worthy of a good will *qua* good. And if we speak of the moral law as ethically good we mean that it is a law which prescribes good conduct in the sense just defined. To do good is to do purposively that which is worthy of a good will in its character of goodness.

In what has been written above we have taken the producing of happiness in others as a possible activity of a good will, because happiness is that which in the utilitarian system of moral philosophy is regarded as the Good. But in our argument we have refused to apply the ethical epithet 'good' to happiness, and the reason that we should give for this refusal is that happiness is a state, a mere passivity to which the epithet 'good' in the ethical sense seems inapplicable. If asked to prove this we can only reply that it cannot be proved. But it seems clear that in the statements 'Happiness is good' and 'It is good to produce happiness in others' the term 'good' has two different meanings. In the second of the two statements only is 'good' ethically used. And even then it is only properly ethical as defining an activity worthy of a good will, that is to say of a good person.

We must then part company with any who may contend that happiness is good in an ethical sense. That happiness is good in the sense that it belongs to the ideal condition of persons generally is not to be denied. We could subscribe to the statement that 'happiness is good and pain evil' with the reservation that good and evil are here not ethically used. We should dissent from the conclusion that because happiness is good and pain evil therefore happiness ought always to be sought and pain always avoided.

There will always be confusion of thought where there is

failure to recognise that the ethical epithet 'good' is properly applicable only to persons and not to things. Moral or ethical good will then tend to become confused with physical good, and moral evil with physical evil.

Possibly one reason why the failure to limit the predication of ethical goodness to the good will is not uncommon is that will is popularly conceived as contrasted with action, as when we speak of 'taking the will for the deed.' But to a good person will is no substitute for deed, nor is it an excuse for inaction. Indeed a good person if hindered from carrying the will into action would become unhappy from this very cause. To speak as if the will were everything and the deed nothing, is to mistake the very meaning of the term 'will.' A good will which has the power to carry out that which it wills must by reason of its very nature do so, otherwise it would not be good. Because there are persons who are content to be thought good rather than to be good, and persons who pride themselves on their so-called good intentions which they do not, when they can, fulfil in action, we must not transfer our epithet 'good' from persons to things and expect it to remain of ethical signification.

It must be acknowledged however that it is a matter of the first importance that ethical enquiry should direct its attention to the end to which a will, to be worthy to be called good, will direct itself and which it will labour to produce. But in so doing it is investigating what is desirable rather than what is good. Some may say that it is more important to bring about a desirable state of things than it is to trouble about the motives which prompt people to action. It is more important, they may argue, to get a thing done than to care why it is done. People must be taken as they are and enlisted in the service of the desirable; one may be actuated by one motive, and another by another; that does not matter if only the end be attained by the help of all. Well, this may be wise under certain circumstances, and even a good will may make use of the various motives which prompt men to action, in order to effect something which is desirable. But we must be careful when forming ethical judgements that we apply our ethical epithet only where it is properly applicable and not where it is inappropriate. The true purpose of moral teaching is not simply to get a thing done but to get persons to do it. This distinction, which may seem subtle, is a very real and a very important one. To grasp it is to gain some insight into the meaning of the Divine patience which bears long with the continued undesirable state of things in the world.

It is hoped that we have now said enough to make clear our position as regards the ethical application of the epithet 'good.' This we contend is properly only applicable to persons. But all this may seem to the reader a digression from our proper subject, namely, the nature of sin. It is really not so. On the contrary, it is of the first importance for a satisfactory exposition of the subject. To the present writer it has many times seemed that the treatment of the subject of sin fails often in profit and edification because of the failure to exhibit sin always as the opposite of good. Sin as we have said is the Christian name for moral evil, and we could have no conception of moral evil unless we had already some notion of ethical good. Physical evil or pain we may know apart from moral evil. The two can be thought of independently. If in our language the same word 'evil' is used for both, we yet have a distinctive word 'wickedness' to express moral evil. 'Wickedness,' if it suggests to the mind a thing, suggests it as a thing done by a person. That which we call wickedness if done by a person, can no longer be called wickedness if it be due to physical causes conceived apart from any personal causation. A wicked act can only be the act of a person having knowledge of evil just because he has knowledge of good. Moral evil is always the refusal of good, ethically conceived. It is the failure of a person to do that which is good and which he ought to do. And after all that has now been said, it will be understood that by 'that which is good' we mean that which it is fitting that a good will should perform in its character of goodness.

We have now to enquire what activity is worthy of a good will—and we again add the words 'in its character of goodness.' We add these words because in estimating the ethically good attention is usually confined to men and women such as they are in this world which we know. Now these are, it is true, *persons* having at any rate a potentiality of goodness. But certainly no human being is wholly good, or is ever likely to be in this life. We speak of certain men and women as good, and justly admire their character so far as we can read it by its outward signs, but good men and women are the very ones who would be the first to acknowledge the imperfection of their goodness. Man, though a moral being, is only in process of becoming a spiritual being. He is largely of the earth, earthy. He is first a natural being, and as such he is a part of what we may speak of as the mechanism of nature. His behaviour so far as it is mechanical is not good in the ethical sense. He may by his mechanical behaviour effect what is desirable. He may be an instrument in the Divine hand for good ends. But any ethical goodness that can be associated with him in regard to this is not his own, but must be referred to the Divine Author of his being. So then a man may act *rightly* when his conduct is not what we are justified in calling *good*. The distinction between right conduct and good conduct observed by some moralists is an important one. It is this that we had in mind above when we said that actions not ethically good are not therefore necessarily evil. When a man follows certain instincts, as for example when he eats his food, he may act rightly, but we should not call such an action good. It certainly is not evil. Actions are only evil if they are the refusal to do something which we ought to do, or the doing of something which we ought to abstain from doing.

Human persons then are in our experience only partially good. We do not find perfect goodness exemplified anywhere around us. If any pride themselves on their perfection, we can only say that they have a very poor conception of what ethical perfection is. The best of men will consider themselves sinners to the end of life, because they are conscious how far they fall below the ethical ideal. A man who is in earnest about the pursuit of goodness can never count himself to have apprehended, for the ideal is far beyond him.

But what is the ideal? What is the perfection of character? In what does it manifest itself? What is the activity of a perfectly good will? Will is, as we have emphasised, more than intention; it implies purposeful activity. So then we ask what a good person will *do*. We want an answer that will satisfy the moral reason. If there is no answer to the questions we are putting, then all that has been said about ethical goodness is meaningless.

To the question, To what will the activity of a person be purposively directed in order that we may be justified in speaking of that person as thus far good? it would of course be an insufficient answer to say that a good person will keep the moral law. This answer would not be to the point, seeing that it is our aim rather to discover whether the moral law is good; whether, that is to say, the doing of it is an end worthy of a good will. Even supposing that the moral law is good in this ethical sense we must admit that it is a law applicable to beings not wholly good but who are in process of being invited to become good. We cannot conceive of an absolutely perfect Being as governed by a law external to Himself; He is only subject to the law of His own perfection. This point is of great importance, and is only grasped when we admit that goodness is strictly applicable to persons alone.

If the moral law is good we ought to be able to discern the principle underlying it. It must be based on the principle of goodness as discerned by the moral reason. It is this principle of goodness for which we are seeking. Where can it be found?

Now in Christian theology God is set before us for our contemplation, worship, and consequent imitation, as the perfection of character. Nor is the notion of the Divine perfection lacking in definiteness. For God is revealed in Christ Jesus as perfect love. If it be the truth that God is love, then this must be the most important of all truths, and we may say too that it must be the key to the riddle of life. Without going off at this point to consider the credibility of the Apostolic dogma, we will endeavour to understand what it means and implies.

God is essentially love, and the essence of love is that it seeks to benefit others. Love cannot be interpreted as a negative thing, namely absence of hatred or readiness not to inflict injury upon others. It may be true that some of the first lessons in love which man has to learn lie in this direction. He has to be taught to obey the commandments which say 'Thou shalt not.' He must learn to abstain from that which would mean injury and privation to his fellow-men. But this is only the beginning of things. Positive love, such as we believe God essentially, and not accidentally or occasionally to be, seeks to benefit. It is not content not to hurt. The truth that God is love expresses what God will do rather than what He will not do. He will, being what He is, labour to bestow happiness upon others. He will bring into being creatures capable of happiness and spend Himself in their interest.

Now the love of God for His creatures must proceed wholly from Himself. There is nothing in us deserving of the Divine love. We may even conceive of God as loving His creatures before He brings them into existence. His purpose in creating is one of pure benevolence. He creates with a purpose of love because it is worthy of Himself so to do. In other words the Divine love expended on creation proceeds from God's own character; from what God is in Himself in the perfection of His own being. The love of God, that is to say, proceeds from the Divine Holiness.

There is no truth more precious to the human soul than this that God is love. But we have not learnt the truth, have not seen what it means, have not made it our own unless we have learnt too that God is holy. There is no opposition, no contradiction, between these truths. The one explains the other.

To the Christian the supreme truth of life is that God is love. Christ has made this known to us as we could not otherwise have known it. The cross of Jesus Christ, while it

v] *Sin, and the need of Atonement* 195

is to us a disclosure of the cruelty, the self-seeking, the selfishness of man, is also a revelation of the infinite self-sacrifice of God. We learn that God does not rule in power merely but that He reigns in love. God is love, self-sacrificing, self-communicating love. This is the Christian gospel, and it is the key to the riddle of this world's life.

It is true that the world-order is full of self-assertion. At first sight the whole character of it seems to be a contradiction of the Christian revelation of God as love. The truth of the world-order seems to be expressed in the words: "All seek their own." The creation appears to be a hiding rather than a revealing of God, if God be love. The external world seems to be at variance with our moral sense. Some have felt this acutely.

But we can admit no dualism. The world-order is a divine order. There is not one God of nature and another of revelation.

But let us ask: Does not the revelation of God as love throw light on the pressing moral problem of the world-order? Surely it does. The world-order abounds in wonderful and beautiful instances of altruism where the creature gives itself for another; and amid all the apparent self-seeking and self-assertion it remains true that nothing really lives for itself alone. We see then how, when we have the revelation of God's self-sacrifice, we are able to discern that the truth of it is all the while stamped upon His works.

The doctrine that God is love then does not seem to be wholly at variance with the facts of the world-order. Rather that order remains unexplained without the belief that God is infinite self-sacrifice. The cosmic order is full of the truth of the power and fruitfulness of sacrifice, only there it is the sacrifice of constraint, not of willing freedom. Its character is *imposed* upon it, and so in the ethical sense of the word it is devoid of character. Character results from the possession of reason and is only understood by a being of moral reason. Not until man comes on the scene with his endowment of moral reason have we in this world's history a revelation of character. Man while he comes out of the cosmic process is not limited to it. The altruism of constraint can with him become the sacrifice of love. For love in the Christian sense of the word has its root in reason. And by this it is not meant merely that love reckons the use to which it shall be put, discerning the need of the person loved. Love proceeds not simply from the consciousness of the need of some one external to ourselves, but from our own need to love. Our moral reason tells us that selfish living is a low form of living, that it is not true life. Reason demands that the person in possession of it should realise himself in living for others.

Thus moral reason and self-respect go together. And here we can see the extreme importance of the truth that God is holy. By the holiness of God we understand the Divine self-respect. God is a Being of infinite self-respect. He is love because He is holy, for only love could satisfy a perfect Being. The creation seems to become a necessity, God being what He is. Its *raison d'être* is in God Himself.

Now it is inconceivable that there can be any higher blessedness than that which must be God's by reason of what He is in character. And if God demands of man that he should learn to love, it is His own blessedness which He is offering to him. There is a danger lest we should look upon goodness principally as the condition for obtaining something which we call its reward. And against this point of view is set another which teaches that virtue is its own reward. But neither of these is properly right. That virtue is its own reward may mean that goodness neither finds nor needs reward. The satisfaction that is experienced when it is practised may be regarded as sufficient recompense. But there is a reward of goodness which it is not unworthy to hope for and desire, and that is the opportunity and capacity for more goodness. Goodness can be rewarded by greater capacity for goodness, without violence being done to the ethical supremacy of goodness itself.

On the other hand to make what we may call prosperity—other than prosperity in goodness itself—the reward of goodness is to detract from the ethical value of goodness. It is true that worldly prosperity has at a certain stage of moral experience seemed to be the fitting reward of the practice of virtue. This view may be faulty, yet it bears witness to an ineradicable instinct of the human heart that the performance of goodness should in a moral order be productive of happiness.

We have been trying to elucidate the nature of ethical goodness by reference to what we believe to be the revelation which God has made of Himself as perfect love. The whole of goodness for the absolute Being lies, so far as we are able to understand the Divine nature, in love, such love, as we have sought to explain, proceeding wholly from the perfection of the Divine Being Himself. It has been sometimes thought that to explain the moral life of man by a reference to the Divine life is useless because we are incapable of understanding the Divine nature. Questions have been propounded such as this: Is there anything in the Divine nature which would make it impossible that God should have made theft, or adultery, or murder right for man—instead of, as we now consider them, wrong and sinful? But such a question is unthinkable when the ethical basis of the moral law is once appreciated. For it is strictly according to Christian teaching to find the rationale of the moral law in goodness itself as it is conceived by the moral reason. If the essence of goodness be love, the moral law is explained, for Christian teachers from the first have taught that it is the goodness of love itself that makes the moral law good. In other words moral law inculcates love, regard for the interests of others.

Thus St Paul in his Epistle to the Romans (xiii. 10) says, "Love worketh no ill to his neighbour: love therefore is the fulfilment of the law." These words imply the negative character of law. Abstinence from injury of others is the first lesson of the moral life. But love in the Christian sense goes beyond the abstaining from injury; it seeks to benefit positively. Positive benefit includes of course the other, and so love is the fulfilment of the law of negatives which says: 'Thou shalt not.'

Even so Jesus Christ declared that He had come to fulfil the law, not, that is, merely by performing its requirements in His own earthly life but by making it binding upon the consciences of His disciples. And it was He who gave Love as the true summary of the law. When He was asked which was the great commandment in the law, His reply was, "Thou shalt love the Lord thy God with all thy heart, and with all thy soul, and with all thy mind. This is the great and first commandment. And a second like unto it is this, Thou shalt love thy neighbour as thyself. On these two commandments hangeth the whole law, and the prophets" (St Matt. xxii. 37–40).

Now it will be observed that Christ puts the love of God as the primary duty of man. And the whole strength of His appeal to men to love God lay in His own supreme effort to set forth God as worthy of man's highest reverence and love. In Christ's teaching God does not appear principally as a moral governor and judge, but as Himself the eternal and living expression of His own moral law. It was possible to say after Christ had lived and taught and died on earth, "Be ye imitators of God as beloved children" (Eph. v. 1). The imitation here spoken of is described in the words that follow, which speak of 'walking in love.' And Christ had Himself said, "Ye shall be perfect, as your heavenly Father is perfect" (St Matt. v. 48). It seems an impossible standard, but the words should make us realise that God in Christ admits us into the secret of the divine life of love, and declares that man is to be nurtured on the principle of that life. Christ called not His disciples servants, but friends, declaring unto them that all things that He had heard from His Father He had made known to them (St John xv. 15). Christianity was not the making known of a law, but the revelation of a life. Yet the putting of the world under law, until the fulness of the time, had been a necessary stage in the divine economy of the world.

The second duty of man is declared by Christ to be the love of one's neighbour. And we at once observe that while the same word 'love' is used of both duties, namely, the love of God and the love of man, there is a difference between the two. It would be impossible to speak of man's duty to his neighbour as love of him with all the heart and soul and

v] *Sin, and the need of Atonement* 199

mind. Only love towards God can be so described. Man's duty of love towards God arises from what God is in Himself, in the perfection of His own character. According to the strength of a man's conviction of the perfect goodness of God is his duty of loving God with the whole heart and soul and mind. Thus to love God is to become allied with perfect goodness, to recognise that it makes demands upon us from which it would be wrong and sinful to turn away. It is not that man has anything to bestow upon God, who is Himself the giver of all good things. But by love to man, and we may add, only by love to man can man become a fellow-worker with God in the power of the Divine life. Only by love can we get into harmony with the power and wisdom and love by which the world is directed.

As the Apostle St John teaches in his first Epistle it is simply self-deception to think that there can be love to God without love to man. For the love of God to be worthy of the name must be love of goodness, and it must carry with it a real desire to be allied with that goodness. The love of God must carry with it appropriation of the Divine, otherwise it is not what it calls itself.

Now that we have made an extended examination into the nature of goodness we are better able to understand what is the Christian view of sin. We said at the beginning of this Essay that 'sin' is a theological and religious term. It has meaning just so far as man has relationship with God. Sin is wrong-doing certainly, for it is failure in goodness. But it is at the same time failure to fulfil the conditions of fellowship with God, failure to be in harmony with the Absolute or Eternal.

To refuse the opportunities of love which God gives us, and which are made known to us by the voice of a disciplined and reasonable conscience speaking within us, is to sin. We say 'a disciplined and reasonable' conscience, for conscience is capable of discipline and it is subject to the moral reason. Conscience does not demand a blind obedience. If it did, its authority would very soon cease to be authoritative.

Christians do well to give heed to the emphasis which the modern investigations of ethics lay upon the reason in its moral aspect. We may, if we will, prefer to call what moralists speak of as 'practical reason' Conscience; but if we do so we must not regard conscience as something opposed to reason or separated from it. Conscience will cease to be authoritative in its demands if it be not according to reason. On the other hand it will appeal with an irresistible force where it gives a moral reason for its dictates.

And when we speak of a moral reason for the dictates of conscience, emphasis is laid upon the word 'moral' as much as on the word 'reason.' A moral reason is given for the conduct prescribed by the conscience just so far as that conduct is set forth as good in itself, that is to say as worthy of a good will in its character of goodness. A reason for a certain line of conduct might be the attainment of such and such an end, but this would not be a *moral* reason unless the attainment of that end were itself good.

Now this that we are saying amounts to an acceptance of the Kantian doctrine of the autonomy of the rational will. The principle involved in this doctrine is that a rational being is capable of judging for himself the moral reason of his conduct. And unless a moral reason, in the sense explained above, can be found for conduct, that conduct is not governed by the law of the will. Kant's criterion expressive of the law of the rational will seems certainly to be wanting in exactness, and it is open to obvious criticism. Thus a man might be a cobbler, though he could hardly will that all other men should be the same. But it is implied in all Kant's teaching on this point that man is under an obligation to direct his life and conduct with a proper regard for the interests of his fellow-men. To make ourselves an exception to a general law, obedience to which is seen to be for the general good, is to fail in this duty.

The doctrine of the autonomy of the will then is really a Christian one. But the recognition of this does not imply that there is no room for any external moral law; what is insisted upon is only that the ultimate appeal of any such law is to the conscience capable of discerning the moral reason of the law. The will which most insists on its own autonomy will be ready to hear the demands of external law, which however it will claim the right to judge of in the light of reason. Only we do well to be suspicious of ourselves if we find in ourselves a tendency to relax obedience to external law. We may be sure that if we do only what we find it easy to do we are not being sufficiently attentive to the demands of reason. The autonomy of the will does not mean that the will is not subject to law, but it does mean that law is only binding when it can give a moral reason for its demands.

The moral life of man is certainly not lived if the line of least resistance be followed. It is not to be supposed that God's best gift to man is to be had without strenuous effort on man's part. The paradox of the Christian life is that the self is only won by self-abnegation. But self-abnegation without the winning of a higher self is no true end, and we have to beware of caricatures of self-sacrifice. We recall the apostolic words, which justify themselves to reason: "If I bestow all my goods to feed the poor, and if I give my body to be burned, but have not love, it profiteth me nothing" (1 Cor. xiii. 3).

It may seem to some readers that we are attaching to altruism too great an importance in our estimate of what is ethically good. Is there not, it may well be asked, a self-culture which is itself good? It cannot surely be intended, someone may say, that a man should always be busying himself about others. It is right that he should attend to what he stands in need of for himself. Some degree of selfishness seems a necessity under the conditions of human life as we know it.

These objections are quite in place, and they are not unreasonable. It is surely right that we should be guided to a considerable extent by the impulses which go to determine our actions. But we must again go back to the distinction which has been made between what is right and what is good. It is of course right to use and develop the endowments which we have, and it is good to acknowledge with gratitude to the Giver of all happiness the benefits He has bestowed. If we found no joy and happiness in God's gifts we should be incapable of being agents for the extension of such joy and happiness to others. The essence of goodness lies in the communication to others of that which makes for our own happiness. If a man has no higher idea of personal happiness than the possession of what may be called physical goods, yet if he make it an end to bestow these upon others he is so far on the side of ethical good. He may be mistaken in his idea of what can give happiness to his fellow-men, but if he regard their happiness as an end worthy of his activity he is so far good.

It is clear, however, that as no human being has found perfect happiness in his life, so none is in a position to confer perfect happiness on another. It is, it would seem, ethically good to include others in our pursuit after what can bring satisfaction. Self-culture and the pursuit of knowledge, whereby we may understand the world in which we live, are right and proper. The pleasure and happiness we find in these things we acknowledge to be a good gift of God, and we find still greater happiness if we share our happiness with other persons who are as much ends in themselves as we think ourselves to be. Ethical goodness is exemplified by the recognition of other personalities, not as means to our ends, but as themselves ends. The ethically good may even be developed in us and appropriated by us when we practise kindness to dumb animals, endeavouring, as we do, by this to bestow upon them such happiness as they are capable of experiencing. But ethical goodness is wholly lacking, and is entirely absent, where a personality tries to stand alone, out of relationship to other personalities and sentient beings in general. To make myself an end selfishly and to pursue my individual happiness apart from the happiness of others is to fail utterly. To sacrifice others in our own selfish pursuits is to degrade human nature and to put ourselves out of harmony with the very principle underlying the world.

It may seem that we are here making a prudential

not a moral appeal, whereas we have at an earlier stage in the Essay objected to the degradation of the moral 'ought' to the level of a prudential 'ought.' But it is to be observed that we make no prudential appeal apart from moral considerations. What we contend for is that moral reason and prudence do really demand the same thing. To be indifferent to the principle of rational life is imprudent, for it is to be out of harmony with what is the principle of the world-order. We do need for our encouragement and support the assurance that what justifies itself to the moral reason as good must in the end prevail. It is the good that is eternal; and that which is devoid of ethical character is but transitory. Such is the verdict of faith which holds that the Absolute and Eternal One is Himself the perfection of goodness.

The very conditions of life in a civilised community make it imperative that at any rate most of its members should give and not only take. The obtaining of the means of livelihood is dependent on service rendered to other members of the community. Nor can we doubt that this is a wise provision of the eternal Providence to teach moral truth. It is of course possible for us to fail to learn the lesson. But to those willing to be taught it is plain and unmistakeable. It certainly is not the perfection of goodness that we should need the incentive of reward to make us fulfil our service, but we take a step in the right direction if we humbly and indeed thankfully acquiesce in the wise providence which makes the fulfilment of service the condition for the obtaining of physical goods.

So then the organised social order may, if we will only have it so, become to us a valuable aid in the practice of goodness. Not that the doing of anything for the sake of reward is in itself good. But as that for which reward can be had is the doing of something which, if rightly regarded, may be itself good—that is, as before, worthy of the activity of a good will—our very desire for reward may in the process of the exercise of the activity which is worthy of us be subordinated, and by a gradual discipline be corrected. We need not deceive ourselves into imagining that we have attained to goodness when we do things that may be worthy of a good will. For a careful analysis of the motives which prompt us to action will reveal to us how imperfect if not unworthy these often are. Yet we shall be thankful if what we do, even if it be from motives not the best, benefits those who are affected by it.

Motive, it should be hardly necessary to insist, is of fundamental importance in the practice of goodness. But there is a tendency in some directions to disparage motive, and to care, as we have said before, more about getting a thing done than about the persons who are to do it. Our point has been that Kant is quite right in his insistence on the fact that ethical goodness is properly predicable only of the will. And our conclusion is that the will is not necessarily good when it does what is worthy of a good will, but only so far as it does this because it *is* worthy of it. A good motive is the property of personality. A good motive is the principle of action of the good will. The difficulty of the practice of goodness lies just in this, that it has to be done for its own sake. What we call temptation to evil would have no meaning unless there were at the same time a temptation to good. Something is set before us by the conscience as alone worthy of us under the circumstances; to fail to fulfil this would be to sin. We are being tried in goodness when we are tempted to sin. This thought throws much light on the terrible fact of the presence of moral evil in a world which we yet believe to proceed from a Being as supreme in goodness as He is in power. But we cannot deal with this subject in the present Essay.

Our aim thus far has been to bring out the ethical conception of sin which could only be done by enlarging on the nature of ethical goodness. The perfection of goodness is realised, according to Christian belief, in God Himself. The ultimate motive of the Divine action, so far as we are able to think of it, lies in the character of the Eternal Being, which character we designate as Holiness. Further, according to Christian teaching God reveals Himself as our Father. And by this very revelation He teaches us the possibility of our attaining to a share in the Divine character. God is the creator of things and of sentient existence, but He is more than the creator of personalities. He is to persons a Father. In them He is reproducing Himself. When those who have the potentiality of goodness, the potentiality of personality, resist the demands which goodness makes upon them, they are all the while rejecting the supreme gift of God. They sin in that they refuse the good; they sin, in that they do that which forfeits the blessing of communion with the Eternal Himself.

"That which we have seen and heard," writes St John, "declare we unto you also, that ye also may have fellowship with us; yea, and our fellowship is with the Father, and with his Son Jesus Christ.......And this is the message which we have heard from him and announce unto you, that God is light, and in him is no darkness at all. If we say that we have fellowship with him, and walk in the darkness, we lie, and do not the truth: but if we walk in the light, as he is in the light, we have fellowship one with another, and the blood of Jesus his Son cleanseth us from all sin. If we say that we have no sin, we deceive ourselves, and the truth is not in us. If we confess our sins, he is faithful and righteous to forgive us our sins, and to cleanse us from all unrighteousness" (1 John i. 3–9).

The quotation of this passage makes a fitting transition from the first to the second part of our subject. We have written on the nature of sin; we must pass now to say something of the need of Atonement as a remedy for sin.

It is impossible in the space of a few pages to treat of the subject of atonement at any length. It is a subject of immense difficulty, as is shown by the many and various theories which have been and still are held respecting it. It is not our intention here to deal historically with these different theories. All we can do is to emphasise a few points which arise out of what we have been maintaining and which must be taken into account if we are to reach a view of the atonement which shall satisfy the Christian reason and conscience. Some views of the atonement fail to commend themselves because they are unworthy of and inconsistent with the perfection of the character of God Himself.

A very important part of the Christian doctrine of sin is, as we have seen, that it is a hindrance to man's communion or fellowship with God. By his sin man is alienated from God. Hence if his true destiny is fellowship with God this cannot be attained without some remedy for the sin which has interfered and does still interfere with this end.

Now our first point is this: that no view of the atonement can be sufficient unless it implies this fact that man is intended for fellowship with God. To sin is to hinder this fellowship and not simply to forfeit Divine favour. It is insufficient to think of sin as something in man, or something done by man, which incurs the Divine displeasure. In other words sin is not to be thought of simply as failure to fulfil the conditions for the obtaining of Divine favour. Regard must always be had to the ethical nature of the conditions, and to the ethical nature of the Divine favour. The purpose of atonement is not the obtaining of Divine favour, regardless of its nature, but the effecting of communion with God.

By atonement we understand reconciliation; and this reconciliation is the reconciliation of man to God, not that of God to man. We reject the view of atonement which may be summarised thus: Man by his sin has forfeited the Divine favour and incurred the Divine displeasure; some offering then is necessary to turn away the Divine wrath, and to make the forgiveness, that is in this connexion the Divine overlooking, of sin a possibility; the Divine justice must be satisfied before the Divine love can forgive; the penalty of sin must be paid, just as crime in a well-governed state must be punished; Christ on the cross bore the penalty of all human sin, and for His merits God forgives the sins which men have committed; they are restored to the Divine favour for Christ's sake. This view we reject, though we do not deny that it contains elements of truth. As it stands it does not give prominence to the ethical purpose and effect of atonement. For this reason it cannot be accepted as a full account of the matter.

But it is far from our intention to depreciate the merits of Christ's passion and death. The last thing we would do is so to explain the atonement as to explain it away. We are not going to say that the Christian doctrine of atonement is no longer necessary, that it belongs to the earlier and cruder stages of man's religious development, and so on. This is not our view at all. Quite the contrary. We adhere strictly to the doctrine of the Creed that it was "for us men and for our salvation" that Jesus Christ "came down from heaven, and was incarnate by the Holy Ghost of the Virgin Mary, and was made man, and was crucified also for us." The life and passion and death of Christ wrought a deliverance for man which he could not effect for himself. But exception is taken here to any view of the atonement which puts Christ outside God, and regards Him as paying the penalty of sin to God. Whereas the scriptural view is that "God was in Christ reconciling the world unto Himself" (2 Cor. v. 19). And again: God "spared not His own Son, but delivered Him up for us all" (Rom. viii. 32).

The purpose of atonement is the *taking away of sin*. The remedy for sin is not forgiveness, if by this is meant only the overlooking of the sins that have been committed. It is not the scriptural gospel that God could not overlook the sins of the past until the penalty had been paid by one able to pay it. It would be no good news to men to tell them that the sins of the past were by the mercy of God overlooked unless at the same time they could be told of a deliverance, a salvation, from the bondage of sin.

We do not mean to imply that forgiveness, interpreted as the overlooking of the past, is not a necessary part of the remedy for sin, but we do mean that it is only a part of the cure. Forgiveness in this sense may be a remedy for the distress of mind which the conviction of sin brings with it, but it can be no remedy for sin itself. The only true remedy is its removal; the rendering of it impossible; the annulling of it. And this can only be by the bringing in of its opposite.

Evil can only be overcome by the genesis of good. Evil as we have been arguing, possibly with wearisome reiteration, is the negation, the refusal of good by a will which knows that good is its true expression. The true remedy for sin lies in the freedom of the will, release from the bondage of the lower self-seeking self.

But at this point we shall probably be met by objections. It will be at once said, If the will of man be not already free can he properly be said to be responsible for his actions, can he be accounted guilty of sin? He may be sinful in the sense that he does what he sees to be a refusal of what is good; he may be sinful too in the sense that by his actions he is separating himself from communion with God. But is this in any sense the man's fault unless he be all the while a free agent? Sin implies guilt, and only a free agent can be accounted guilty.

Perhaps difficulties of this sort are best met by an appeal to personal experience. Say that I have done such or such a thing (which we will call x), and that deliberately. Suppose that I have the consciousness before doing x that I ought to do a, the doing of a and x being mutually exclusive. I have failed to do what I knew that I ought to do and done what I ought not. Now the question is: Could I have done a as easily as x? It is well known to myself that I could not. I will not say that I could not by any possibility have done a; for clearly my knowledge in regard to this point is strictly limited, and I cannot repeat the experience under precisely the same conditions as before. Say, for the sake of argument, that I could have done a, but that the inducement to do x was much stronger than that to do a. I was then free to do a, but clearly not as free to do a as to do x. For to do x was to follow the line of least resistance. That was the line of least resistance to me, being what I am, or rather being what I then was. It was I who did x in preference to a. I cannot lay the blame on another. It was my choice to do x, and I feel now that it was an unworthy preference. My conscience tells me that I did wrong, and though I may try to forget the voice of my conscience, still, whenever I remember it, it speaks the same message to me and tells me that I ought to have done *a*. It is I that am at fault; I myself am not what I ought to be. For my outward action is an expression of what I am. My action which is contrary to that which I know it ought to have been shows me to be a slave and not properly free. I have done that which I did not properly speaking will to do.

For I am not really free unless I prefer to do that which I ought to do. To be free I must find pleasure and delight in doing for its own sake that which I see to be good. But when I fail to do that which my reason tells me is good, and which my conscience tells me I ought to do, it is I who thus fail. I am not coerced into failure; but I turn away from that which is properly speaking my freedom. For freedom is self-identification with goodness. And self-identification with what is good cannot by its very nature be coercion. In the natural world coercion is the rule, in the spiritual sphere it is not. It is of the essence of a spiritual being that he should have good commended to him in reason, and should of his own free choice fulfil it. That which we call Holiness in God and which we have ventured to define as the Divine self-respect is potentially ours too, by reason of the fact that we are children of God. Holiness is not ours because of our physical nature, but only through our spiritual nature, and then it is only ours by reason of the Divine mercy which bestows it. And we can see that it was a part of the wisdom of God to prepare man to be a sharer in the Divine holiness by placing him under law, which law is commended to us gradually as the expression of what is good, but which, so far as we are still carnal, is not the expression of what we are, but of what we ought to be. In so far as we self-conscious beings, having a knowledge of good, do not fulfil it we are enslaved and are not in the enjoyment of the true spiritual freedom. If asked whose fault it is that we are not free, we must attribute the blame to ourselves. We are not doing that which alone we see to be worthy of us.

We shall probably never understand the great mystery of freedom until we are ourselves properly free, in the sense that we have attained to self-identification with goodness[1]. We shall then see that when in past times we failed to do what we knew that we ought to do we were all the while rejecting a good which God in His love was offering to us. The turning away of God's favour, as we felt it to be at the time, will be seen to have been an act of highest wisdom. God casts not His pearls before swine; and as we proved ourselves unworthy of the gift, He withdrew the blessing, because we could not then see it to be a blessing, but regarded it rather as an exaction of what we were not prepared to give. Only after long discipline were we in a state to be appealed to once more, and God again made us the offer which, through the change wrought in us by His discipline, we were able to accept.

But whatever be our attitude of mind towards God in all His dealings with us, we cannot suppose that there can be any change in His love towards us. What a heart of infinite pity must be the heart of God who is Love! With what compassion must He view us with our selfish views of life, seeing that the law of His Being is His Holiness which only love can satisfy! God needs no propitiation to make Him favourable to us. His own pitying love supplies the reconciliation which He would effect in man towards Himself. Nor is any sacrifice too great for Him the law of whose Being is infinite self-sacrifice. We cannot for one moment think of the sacrifice of Christ as needed in any way to appease the wrath of God; rather is that sacrifice a revelation of Divine self-sacrifice, intended to win man, to make him forgiveable and to declare him forgiven. Man is made forgiveable when he is made to see sin in its true light and to desire a deliverance from it. Forgiveness is not the remission of a punishment, but the remission of sins. As Bishop Westcott well put it: "True forgiveness is the energy of love answered by love. The forgiveness which remits a punishment may leave the heart untouched. The forgiveness which remits a sin includes by its very nature the return of responsive gratitude[2]."

---

[1] See the excellent chapter in Moberly's *Atonement and Personality*, on 'Human Personality.'
[2] *Victory of the Cross*, p. 85.

v] *Sin, and the need of Atonement* 211

And again: "There can be no discharge of the sinful while they keep their sins[1]."

We may say that when God has once appealed to a man by the revealing to him something of what goodness is, that man can never afterwards find peace until he has yielded himself thereto. He may for a time regard the requirement of goodness as an exaction, but he will have to learn that it is really asking for the true expression of himself, and that fulfilment of goodness alone can bring him satisfaction. It is because the destiny of man is so high that he cannot find a lower satisfaction. He thinks that he can, but he cannot. He takes too low a view of himself when he imagines that he can.

The purpose of atonement then is the bringing of man into that relationship with God which He in His love eternally meant for him. We cannot for a moment suppose that God in creation was in any way ignorant of the course which things would take before His great purpose of love towards mankind could be accomplished. The Son, who has been manifested to us in time, was eternally the Mediator between God and man. He is the Lamb slain from the foundation of the world. God must have known the cost of the work which He undertook. He must have known that the spiritual could only be developed out of the carnal by Himself bearing the burden of it all. He, who is Himself Spirit, can alone understand the greatness of the work of the production of spiritual beings, who are to find their destiny in communion with Him. His patience knows no limits. This belief is our confidence in the presence of the apparent failure of the race of man through sin.

In the fulness of time the Son of God was manifested to proclaim and to effect the sonship of humanity. He took upon Him the whole burden of human sin, that is the failure of mankind in goodness, with infinite pity for those who knew not the things belonging to their peace. In a people prepared by the discipline of a moral law, which had been regarded by them as divine in origin, He unfolded the principle of that law, not in any way relaxing its claims, so far as these were

[1] *Ibid.* p. 87.

strictly ethical, but rather making it more stringent than before. But He does not lay it upon mankind as a burden which they are to bear ; He reveals it in its spiritual meaning as the true expression of a spiritual being. The moral law— the law which proclaims that our fellow-men should be as much ends in themselves for our consideration as we ourselves are—He shows to be the way by which we can be partakers of the Divine life. The inner principle of the law is the principle of the Divine life. Goodness is displayed as love, love springing from holiness, the consciousness of one's own worth and dignity. Here, at any rate, in the ethical teaching of Christ is a part of the atonement. In His doctrine He taught us not only what we ought to do, but what God is. He is our atonement by teaching us to know God ethically, and to interpret ourselves ethically. God is through Christ proclaimed to be love, and love is declared to be the principle of all true life.

But Christ not only taught men about God so that His words could be handed down to be their own interpreters. He is Himself so perfectly identified with mankind that He dwells in men spiritually to give them fellowship with God, to work out in them the goodness of God Himself. The operations of the Holy Spirit in the human heart and conscience and reason are the result of the work of Christ—the result not simply of His teaching but of His self-sacrifice. For the Holy Spirit was not given until Jesus was glorified ; and Jesus was not glorified until He had first been rejected, had suffered and died. And, according to Christian teaching, His glorification was no selfish glorification. It was in no sense for Himself that He was glorified. He came out of glory to exalt man to glory. In His glorification after death man was exalted to communion with God.

And man is not invited in Christ to have an independent goodness of his own, but he is so to be identified with Christ that he may be in all things the recipient of the Divine goodness of character. He is not to offer to God anything concerning which he can say : For this I deserve Thy favour. What goodness he has is not his own, but his only by the mercy of God. So long as goodness is conceived of as something deserving Divine favour, which favour is not strictly ethically interpreted, legalism will still prevail. It was to combat legalism that St Paul set forth his great doctrine of justification by faith, which faith identifies him who has it with Christ Himself in a life of holiness. The Pauline doctrine of justification by faith gives no countenance to lawlessness. Quite the contrary. "Shall we continue in sin that grace may abound? God forbid" (Rom. vi. 1). It is true that St Paul's teaching is capable of being wrested in support of lawlessness. And any apparent contradiction there is between the teaching of St Paul and St James arises from the different aims of the writers. As St Paul combats legalism, so St James condemns lawlessness. Both these things are alien to the spirit of the Christian life.

The Christian doctrine of atonement sets forth the fact of man's fellowship with God in Christ, and tells us that this fellowship can become possible to man in spite of the fact of human sinfulness. But it gives no countenance whatever to any view that man is secure in the Divine favour by reason of something which has been done for him by a Mediator apart from the cooperation of the man himself. St Paul teaches: "Work out your own salvation with fear and trembling; for it is God which worketh in you both to will and to work, for his good pleasure" (Phil. ii. 12, f.). So that the working of the Divine Spirit in the human heart in no way destroys the personality—on the contrary it develops it. Man in Christ is not deprived of his independence or of his freedom. Quite the contrary, he does not know freedom until he is in Christ by the indwelling of His Spirit. The pain and anguish that man experiences when he finds himself in the possession of an independence whereby he can refuse obedience to the Divine will, discerned by the conscience, are removed by the atonement which Christ has effected in bringing him into his true relationship with God. "Who shall deliver me out of the body of this death? I thank God through Jesus Christ our Lord" (Rom. vii. 24, f.).

We have now emphasised what seem to be two very important aspects of the Christian doctrine of atonement. We are taking atonement or reconciliation to mean the removal of all barriers which hinder man's oneness or fellowship with God. A first and important feature of atonement then is the imparting of the knowledge of God, the revelation of Him in terms of character, rather than in terms of power. This the historic Jesus brought to man. The revelation of what God is ethically is a disclosure of the real nature of sin in all its hideousness. No one can have any sense of the blackness of sin until he discerns the goodness of its opposite. Christ convicted the world of sin by revealing the holiness of God. But in convicting of sin He proclaimed a gospel of forgiveness, which could only be of use to man when he was in a position to respond to the demands which goodness made upon him. This, then, was the second point that we emphasised: the imparting of a new life, which results from the glorification as man of the Mediator between God and man.

But we have now in conclusion to speak of the connexion between atonement and the death of Christ. By some thinkers the sufferings and death of Christ have themselves been regarded as the atonement. According to them Christ has by His death upon the cross borne the penalty of human sin, so making it possible for God to forgive; the sufferings of the innocent availed for the clearing of the guilty; and so far as we look with faith and acceptance to the cross of Christ, who there bore the penalty of our sins, is the guilt of our sin removed.

Against this way of regarding the matter there has naturally been a protest and a reaction. It has been felt that the division which is thus disclosed in the Godhead is really unthinkable. If the Father is only able to forgive when the penalty of sin has been borne, we may indeed ask whether there is any such thing as Divine forgiveness at all. The essence of forgiveness is that it is not vindictive. The debt is forgiven not because some one else has paid it, but out of pure mercy because the debtor cannot pay it. And we cannot solve the difficulty by regarding the Divine forgiveness as

v] *Sin, and the need of Atonement* 215

something entirely different from human forgiveness, for this would be to render meaningless the conditioned petition of the Lord's Prayer respecting forgiveness—'forgive, as we forgive.'

Against this, which we may call the penalty view of atonement, it was inevitable that a protest should be made; but there is danger lest in protesting against an erroneous view of the matter the cost of atonement should be lost sight of. It is insufficient to see in the cross of Christ nothing more than an evidence of Divine love, or an example of humility. For it is extremely difficult on close examination of the matter to see how the cross of Christ can attest the Divine love, unless there be some good bestowed on man through it. The love of God to man is only proved by the bestowal of Divine benefits upon him. What is the benefit in this case? If there be none, then the cross is no evidence of Divine love. Some may say that the benefit is the lesson of humility, which the cross teaches. But readiness to endure suffering for its own sake is no evidence of humility, any more than it is a proof of love.

It is one of the merits of the late Dr Dale's work on the Atonement that he makes this point clear. The love of God is not manifested by the cross of Christ unless by it some blessing is bestowed upon mankind. But Dr Dale's view of the benefit which the cross of Christ bestows, thus proving it to be a manifestation of Divine love, is open to most serious criticism. He advocates the punishment theory. According to him the justice of God could only be satisfied if the penalty of sin were borne. This penalty Christ bore by His sufferings, and so our sins can be overlooked by God, who otherwise could not have forgiven. The cross thus witnesses at once to the justice and the love of God.

This way of regarding the Atonement is defended by Dale with considerable skill and force. But his defence is open to grave objection, in that it is supported by an appeal to the practice of human societies in the administration of justice, as if, indeed, that could be regarded as an ideal to which the methods of God must conform. A man guilty of a crime against the laws of an earthly State must, even if he become penitent, bear the penalty of what he has done, that the sanctity of the law may be vindicated. This is true. But we must remember that the punishment of crime in an earthly State does not aim principally at the good of the individual punished—though in the providence of God we believe it to have this end—but it is for the protection of members of society from injury that may be done to them by their neighbours. In administering penalties the State cannot take account of the fact that the wrong-doer is penitent or the contrary. It would be incapable of deciding this point, seeing that penitence is a thing of the heart which God only can discern. Its rule then is rigid and mercy finds no place in its application. The State inflicts punishment because it exists to enforce the principle that man shall not injure his neighbour. A criminal may bear his punishment so that it becomes to him a discipline of penitence. This matter is the concern of the Church, which cares for the individual in spite of his wrong-doing.

Now let us put to ourselves the question : If a man were condemned to death for a fearful crime would any Christian State allow a fellow-man to step in and bear the penalty instead of the offender? The question has only to be asked to be answered unhesitatingly in the negative. Yet is not this just what the penalty view of the Atonement requires us to accept as right in principle?

The State in administering punishment for crime does not regard the crime committed as an injury done by the offender to himself, but as an injury done to his neighbour. But spiritually regarded, the offender has done a great injury to himself—not a bodily injury in that he must suffer in the flesh for his misdeeds, but a spiritual injury in that he has acted unworthily of his true manhood.

The Christian atonement belongs to the spiritual sphere, and cannot be interpreted by an appeal to earthly modes of administering justice, which are necessarily imperfect, although right and proper in their own sphere. The rulers of the kingdoms of this world are, unconsciously it may be, ministers of God, in so far as they impartially administer law which has for its end the protection of members of society from injuries selfishly inflicted by their neighbours. But a criminal, if he is in the eyes of the law to be condemned, is in the eyes of spiritual mercy a being worthy of pity. Revenge is the law of earthly states, but not personal revenge. The natural desire for revenge in an individual is of course better than indifference. We may say that personal revenge for injury is a natural stage in human development. But it is not a final stage. It belongs to the carnal state. The spiritual man pities the offender, even when he feels acutely the injury which has been done to himself. It is the height of spiritual perfection to be able to forgive personal injury done to oneself, and to look with pitying eye upon the person who has inflicted it. Christ was able to pray without any reserve: "Father, forgive them, for they know not what they do."

In effecting a work of atonement, or reconciliation of man to God, Christ, we must believe, had a heart of love which enabled Him to enter with infinite pity into the misery of sinful human life, and to labour to rescue the sinner from his sin. He, with the perfect consciousness of His own Divine Sonship, desired nothing more than to make that Sonship effective for the race of man, with which He identified Himself. There is no minimising on His part of the Divine demands if man is to attain his true destiny. There could of course be no withdrawal on God's part from the moral requirements already testified in the human conscience, and Christ's teaching made the moral law more strict than before. But by His disclosure of the beauty of the Divine character of holiness and love— each explanatory of the other—He so set forth the spiritual principle of morality that it is seen to be man's true expression of himself, that wherein he finds his true freedom. He gave Himself, so that the Divine life might belong to man in a sense in which it had not previously been his. He took humanity to Himself that He might spiritualise it. And the condition for the giving of His life for mankind was, in the wisdom and providence of God, the cross, which Christ endured for the joy that was set before Him of regenerating humanity. If it be asked whether the new spiritual life which Christ came to impart to men could not have been given otherwise than by the way of the cross, we can only reply that we are incapable of answering such a question, but we can see the appropriateness and fitness of this way. "It became him, for whom are all things, and through whom are all things, in bringing many sons unto glory, to make the author of their salvation perfect through sufferings" (Heb. ii. 10). The perfect consecration of human life to God demanded for its consummation an obedience even unto death. By His faithfulness to the cause of God and His truth Christ incurred the hostility of the carnal minds of men. This He did deliberately, knowing all the time what should come upon Him. His obedience and faithfulness were tested to the uttermost, so that of Him it can be said that He knew no sin. By His obedience even to death He consecrated humanity to God, and for it God exalted Him, as Man, to supreme power, whereby He could sway the hearts and consciences of mankind. The fruit of His conquest has been and is the indwelling of the Divine Spirit in men. This is the true atonement, that man should know God and be in communion with Him in goodness:

"This is the covenant that I will make with the house of Israel
After those days, saith the Lord;
I will put my laws into their mind,
And on their heart also will I write them:
And I will be to them a God,
And they shall be to me a people:
And they shall not teach every man his fellowcitizen,
And every man his brother, saying,
Know the Lord:
For all shall know me,
From the least to the greatest of them.
For I will be merciful to their iniquities,
And their sins will I remember no more."

ESSAY VI.

THE IDEA OF REVELATION, IN THE LIGHT OF MODERN KNOWLEDGE AND RESEARCH.

JAMES MAURICE WILSON, D.D.

All thy children shall be taught of the LORD, and great shall be the peace of thy children. Is. liv. 13.

Reason, following in the wake of faith, grasps the great conception that the religious life is a life at once human and divine—the conception that God is a self-revealing God, that the Infinite does not annul, but realises Himself in the finite, and that the highest revelation of God is the Life of God in the soul of man; and, on the other hand, that the finite rests on, and realises itself in the Infinite; and that it is not the annihilation, but the realisation of our highest freedom, in every movement of our thought, in every pulsation of our will, to be the organ and expression of the mind and will of God.

JOHN CAIRD, *Gifford Lecture*, II.

ABSTRACT.

Limitation of the scope of this Essay: Revelation may be regarded either as the growth of the Divine Life within man, or as God's progressive enlightenment from without. Modern thought tends towards the former conception. Illustrations of this tendency. The characteristics of subjective revelation. Revelation the working of the Divine Reason in man; compatible with the objective Revelation in Jesus Christ. Consideration of some objections to this view. The need to reconsider the popular presentment of the method of revelation.

THE IDEA OF REVELATION, IN THE LIGHT OF MODERN KNOWLEDGE AND RESEARCH.

This Essay on the idea of revelation is concerned with beliefs that have sprung up in all religions, and arise out of regions of consciousness and feeling which have not been completely explored. It is therefore not possible to begin by defining the terms we are compelled to use, unless we are willing also to predetermine our conclusions; for the simple reason that the facts and feelings which are grouped under those terms have in reality as yet indistinct outlines, and undetermined and growing boundaries. A definition, as Mill says, comes at the end, not at the beginning of the study of a subject; and the world is still at the beginning of the study of the nature of revelation. I offer then no attempt at a definition of Revelation. Happily there is no authoritative definition of Revelation given by the Church.

I may however begin by narrowly limiting the scope of this Essay.

I have first to rule out from my treatment the metaphysical elements of the question. Of course any discussion of the idea of revelation will imply assumptions as to the nature and origin of knowledge; and for complete treatment such assumptions as these should be explicitly stated and justified. Moreover the idea of a revelation from God assumes the existence of a God whom it is not misleading to think of under the terms of Personality. I pass over however the whole of this important side of the subject because others are better qualified to deal with it.

And I must next exclude any systematic treatment of the historical side. As the idea of revelation involves metaphysics, so, even more obviously, do its realisation and expression involve history. The idea of revelation, and the facts and modes of revelation, cannot be separated. We cannot speak or think of revelation without calling up before our minds some picture of the long and world-wide history in which, "at sundry times and in divers manners," God appears to have made Himself known ; and without some assumptions as to the methods by which He has made, and is now making, Himself known to men. But it is obvious that to treat this section adequately needs a volume, not a few paragraphs in an essay. In broad outline it is familiar to us ; other writers have moreover dealt with it. I must pass it over; not as irrelevant, nor as unimportant. The omission, however, is not wholly loss. Studies help one another. Some degree of knowledge of the history and experience of revelation has been essential to form our idea of revelation ; but, conversely, the study of the idea of revelation may help us to reinterpret what we have read as its history ; for all history, and especially the history of revelation, is the story of an evolution of thoughts, as well as a chronicle of events, and on that account each stage needs constant reinterpretation in the light of what follows it.

The only further limitation that I need specify is that this Essay is not intended to be apologetic,—a defence of any theory of revelation against real or imaginary opponents of Christianity ; still less is it a polemic. I wish that it may be written, and I hope that it may be read, in no controversial spirit.

Having thus briefly indicated what this Essay might have been in other hands, and will not be in mine, I will even more briefly state what I wish it to be.

My sole aim is to express, with the greatest truthfulness that I can attain, the conception of the substance and method of revelation which has finally, as I believe, established itself consciously or unconsciously in the minds of many thoughtful Christian people. I believe that anyone who can faithfully express what is true to himself, may be drawing from a region of universal consciousness; and may help others to interpret, even if not exactly in the same way, their own experience, and thus advance true knowledge.

One more prefatory remark. The view of revelation which I shall put forward is not precisely the view which, from its being at present dominant with the majority of earnest-minded Christian people, is therefore popularly regarded as orthodox. On the other hand it is not contrary to any other and more permanent standard of truth; and it is by no means new. It is widely diffused, even if unformulated. It is moreover not inconsistent with the retention and use, in its right place, of customary language about the method of revelation. The right place for that language is in popular exposition, and in practical enforcement. There is a right place for speaking of the sun rising on the earth, where it would be pedantry to insist that it is the earth that turns to the sun. It is only when popular language is insisted on as being not poetry but prose, not approximate but scientific, not parable but dogma, that it becomes misleading and mischievous. If revelation, or indeed any other truth, is best presented to a child or man in one stage of education by one method, and in another by a different method; and if it is the revelation, and not the method, that is primary in the teacher's aim, it is open to him to use either method. As Pascal says, "We must have a hindmost thought, and judge all things by it, and yet must we speak as do the people[1]."

"In the light of modern knowledge and research." What have modern knowledge and research to do with anything so transcendental and spiritual as the idea of revelation? They affect that idea in two ways, by their general spirit, and by some of their specific results. The spirit of modern science and philosophy has compelled us to regard the universe as a whole—as a continuous, purposeful, reasoned whole—evolving itself under conditions of unbroken law. There is, I know, *prima facie* ground for holding in suspense this conviction of purpose. The universe is too vast. No one man can

[1] *Pensées de Pascal*, xvii. 109.

arrange all experiences in reasoned sequence. Neither in national nor in universal history, nor in the interaction of natural laws, can we yet find clear proof of a purpose in the whole. It is as in stellar astronomy; no mind has yet grasped the complexity of the sidereal universe, so as to see all its motions and changes as those of an ordered system. Yet I think that anyone who is penetrated with the scientific spirit must assume that, as in the stellar system, so in the universe of matter and life and mind, there exists, even if beyond his imagination to grasp, a fundamental unity and purpose. I do not know from what source, or by what channels, this conviction has come to the world. That is a question for the metaphysician. It may be an intellectual inference from observation. But our inveterate habit of finding reasons for 'conclusions' which were rooted in our minds prior to any reasons warns me that here also our 'conclusions' may come first, and our reasons second. This conclusion, this conviction of unity, may be an intuition arising out of our very nature, as it is being slowly and unequally developed. It may itself be the witness of the Indwelling God in our reason. It may be the most essential element in man. It may be the most real knowledge we possess. Whatever its origin, I believe it to be a growing conviction in the world of science, a conviction of unity and purpose, consolidating itself in leading minds, that is determining the form which the idea of revelation is now taking.

For there are two ways of throwing into a systematic form our imaginations respecting the universe.

We may, on the one hand, regard it as essentially one continuous whole, in which, from hidden sources of life within, which we call Divine, mysterious and ordered movements spring up, progressing towards some remote end. Such a development in the spheres of matter and of physical life is popularly called Evolution; in that of the intellect it is called Knowledge; and in the realm of conscience and will it may be called Revelation, though perhaps there is no real distinction. Revelation, from this point of view, is regarded as the growth or evolution of the Divine Life, and of the knowledge of its own nature, in the human race. The earth has been slowly turning to the sun.

Or, on the other hand, we may think of this phenomenal world and of the Personality of God, as of two things apart, objective to each other, external to each other. From this point of view Revelation is regarded as a history of God's successive gifts *ab extra* to man whom He created; and in particular the word is associated with His gradual enlightenment of man in consciousness of Himself. First individuals, then a family, then a nation, and then a Church, are the Divinely selected channels and depositaries of God's revelation to man in the past. That Revelation reached its climax, if not its completion, in the manifestation of God in Christ. That is the other way of regarding the facts. The sun has been slowly rising on the earth.

These two ideas of revelation are clearly distinguishable, though they have very much in common; and the change in the modern thought of revelation that must be first explained is the substitution of the first for the second. Whether they are mutually exclusive time may show. But to modern thought the second, as an exclusive or dominant theory, is becoming impossible. Nevertheless it is still very strongly entrenched in our minds. It may be described as being 'in possession.' It has the sanction of ancient as well as of popular language; it possesses an apparent simplicity and usefulness and authority. I must endeavour to show why the older conception so long held the field, and why the pendulum has, as I believe, swung finally away from the older conception and towards the newer, and to show the modifications resulting in the scientific idea of revelation.

The older conception has, in the first place, a stronghold in the very word *revelation*. Great is the power of words to preclude thought. It seems impossible to abandon a familiar word, though on reflection we see that it begs the question; and equally impossible to enlarge its meaning. We cannot shake ourselves entirely free from the misleading connotations of many familiar words in theology, which were selected, and got their popular meaning indelibly stamped on them, at a time when they expressed accurately enough the prevailing thought. Still less can we get rid of the words. The thought may have passed away in reality, but the word remains, not only as a witness to past thought, but as a temple that gives it shelter and sanctity and keeps it alive—a temple which is thought to be desecrated by anyone who attempts to justify a change in thought. Revelation is such a word. It carries with it in its popular use, whenever it is uttered, the inseparable connotation that what is so described is, at any rate, not in any sense a development of human ideas,—that it has not come through man. "All religions," says a popular writer of to-day, "are made by man; and therefore there is 'no revelation.'" This argument is to him conclusive. So completely is his thought in bondage to a word, that he thinks he is logical. And in this respect he represents a considerable section of the Christian public. From the mere uttering of the word 'revelation' it has come to be assumed as self-evident, as admittedly unquestionable, that revelation is the communication to men, by some external agency, of truths which they could not arrive at by internal processes of their own minds; and, it is often added, which they do not possess the faculties for verifying or criticising. It is assumed that what grows in man springs from a separate root of human ignorance, and not from the one root of Divine wisdom.

Upon this impression—that a 'revelation' must be *ab extra*—is built up the edifice with which we are so familiar, the popular but very crude conception of revealed religion as a scheme of truths added from outside to natural religion; a scheme of dogmas about God and man, beyond our reason to establish; dogmas originally introduced with miraculous credentials, and now stored in a supernatural authority, Bible or Church. Natural religion takes us, it is represented, a certain distance; it consists of what man can discover for himself; revealed religion takes us further. Or, to use another metaphor, one lays the foundation, the other adds the indispensable superstructure. God begins where man leaves off. This presentation is so familiar, and is so immediate a consequence of what is implied or suggested by the word 'revelation,' that it requires an effort even to think of the series of truths which constitute what are called 'natural and revealed religion' as in any other and closer relation to one another.

The origin and form of this conception, however, may be traced to a large extent to other than Christian sources. It has often been remarked that Roman law moulded the forms of mediæval theology; and the later influence of the Deism of the 17th and 18th centuries is also clearly perceptible. It will give us less of a pang to part with this conception when we remember its parentage, and when we reflect that it is regarded as orthodox chiefly because it is familiar.

If, then, the assumption, which modern thought and science have been led to make, respecting the fundamental unity and purpose of the whole, corresponds with the facts so far as known; and if it is the former, not the latter, of the two conceptions above described into which our idea of revelation must at last fit itself; we are led to surmise that revelation may be the wrong word for the group of experiences we mean to denote by it; and that we might more correctly call that group of experiences the quickening of the spirit, the illumination of the reason, or the guidance of the will of man by the universal indwelling Spirit of God. We may call it inspiration, if we use that word correctly, as belonging to minds, not to truths apprehended by minds. We are led to regard the experiences which we have called revelation as rather an intuition of truth and of God, inherent in the nature of man, springing from his sharing the Divine life, and as a result of his continuous growth in power and clearness of vision, than, under the more imaginative form, as an unveiling of new truth *ab extra*. Revelation is the expression of the Divine Wisdom taking varied form in the thoughts of man, corresponding to the varied expression of Divine Life in living organisms. It is a more complete, more varied, more continuous phenomenon than in our simplicity we thought.

Moreover, it is plainly an intuition, arising from man's

sharing of God's nature, which is the prerequisite of his capacity to receive what has been assumed to be an external revelation. Only through the union already existing between God and man is man able to form the conception of God at all, or to be assured of His existence. "Thou could'st not seek me hadst thou not already found me." Logically, therefore, if there is any distinction at all, revealed religion—that is the divine illumination and preparation of the soul of man—precedes anything that can be called natural religion. The eye that receives, and the brain that interprets, impressions of light must be given before the light can affect us, or external objects be perceived. It is the Divine in man that hears God's voice. "The Spirit of man whereby he knows God is simply the Spirit of God Himself," as Hegel said, repeating St Paul.

The popular conception of the method of revelation as consisting of transactions in the phenomenal world is clearly responsible for most of the disbelief in any revelation at all. For there is no freshly renewed experience to be appealed to as verifying this conception; it rests on testimony; and the testimony, when examined, is incomplete, uncertain. Such an examination over-stimulates the faculties which deal with the phenomenal and the intellectual, and makes little demand on those which are spiritual, in which revelation really takes place. It therefore shifts religion to a different plane. It lays stress on the wrong thing. By making revelation objective[1], it therefore makes it scientifically

---

[1] The words 'objective' and 'subjective' seem to me to be as incapable of ultimate scientific definition as is the word 'revelation' itself. They can only be ultimately defined when the regions which they respectively designate are exhaustively known. But I may attempt to outline the general sense in which I endeavour to use these words.

By the word 'objective' as applied to revelation, I mean any communication of truth that comes to a mind in and through the phenomenal world. By the word 'subjective,' applied to revelation, I mean communication of truth in and through the world of personality. It will therefore include the action of God regarded as Transcendent and as Immanent, so far as this distinction is valid, on the human mind. The contrast between the words is not one of revelation to the subject by God, and of revelation to the subject by itself; but a contrast of revelation

VI] *Revelation, and modern knowledge* 229

demonstrable or the reverse. It turns the eye of the mind away from that which is within, which alone can give meaning to that which is without. For the outer fact is dead, non-existent, unless there is the sensitive organ within. If that sensitive organ is atrophied by disuse, what are called the facts of 'revelation' are, as we see daily, powerless to give it life; and as a result all revelation—exclusively thought of as having come from without to reveal an external God—is earnestly and confidently denied by good and sincerely truthful men. They have had their attention distracted from the region in which revelation takes place.

Once more, the conception of revelation or of revealed religion as a graduated series of objective communications from God forces on us the difficulty of understanding why it is so imperfect. Imperfect, to say the least, it confessedly is. In order therefore to reconcile the finality which would be expected in an objective revelation with the obvious fact of imperfection, we formulate the further hypothesis of a progressive revealing from without, rather than one of a growing of the Divine Light within; and we picture God as standing apart from man, and educating mankind gradually according to His will; 'accommodating,' as we say, His teaching to man's capacities—an accommodation which in matters of science seems unnecessary and unaccountable, and in matters of conduct and belief sometimes shocks our moral sense. It explains the facts which it is formulated to explain, but it throws no light on other problems. It is an arbitrary and supplementary hypothesis, and requires further hypotheses to support it. "It is a tangled web we weave"; and it ought to be a warning that we may be weaving badly. The theory of a 'progressive revelation' has been a useful stage in thought; but it is so no more. It is not final.

by God to the subject through phenomena or through personalities. In either case *Dominus illuminatio mea*. It is a distinction in the method, not in the source, of revelation. But it must be noted that the distinction is not exhaustive: for the Person of Jesus Christ was both a revelation in the phenomenal world, and a revelation through personality to personalities. See p. 249 ff.

The old conception of revelation is also in conflict with our growing conviction of continuity and progress. Not only is revealed religion to be regarded under this conception as a separate thing with separate origin from natural religion, but mankind is apparently to be sharply divided into two classes, whether of nations or of individuals; one to whom revelation is given directly, and another whose duty it is to believe on their testimony. History proves that nations differ in degree of spiritual insight, and therefore as media of revelation to the world: but history does not prove that they differ in kind. Modern knowledge and research demand an idea of revelation expressed in terms compatible with continuity, with evolution, and with unity.

In fact the whole conception of an external revelation is felt to be untenable, when once it is realised. We cannot really conceive the tables of stone written with the finger of God, nor a voice from heaven declaring in audible words some revelation of God to man. Such modes of presentation are poetical, and have their use; but must not be pressed into statements of physical fact, and made a basis for scientific deduction.

The externalisation of the idea of revelation offers on reflection a striking parallel to idolatry. Both are results of the weakness of the human mind; of its need of the concrete to give firmness of outline to the abstract, to give permanence to high thoughts and lofty imaginings. Both seem inevitable in certain stages of growth. Men make a material image, in the first instance, we may well believe, in order to fix their thoughts, to assist and concentrate their devotion, not to be the object of it; but such a use passes easily into worship, with themselves or with those who follow them; and it is far better that men should worship these symbols of God, than never think of Him at all. So it is better, it is indeed necessary, till men can trust their highest intuitions as sacred, and have learned by obedience to them to recognise their authority, that they should embody these intuitions in some imagined phenomenal revelation in order to give them the sanction they needed. So it was with the

VI] *Revelation, and modern knowledge* 231

law said to be given on Sinai. So it has been with the Bible. But the time comes when such conceptions are intellectually impossible ; and if teachers then insist that revelation is an event in the phenomenal world, and not an outward projection of the Divine Light within, the historical character of which is of minor importance, they challenge denial, and at last suspicion of their honesty. They undermine the real foundations of faith.

The work of sceptics and unbelievers, as they are called, seems therefore to be as essential to progress in our present condition as that of believers. They compel believers to reconsider what they really mean in the light of their other knowledge, and thus enable them to get a more vital hold on their beliefs. They are perhaps doing as much for the restoration of faith to-day as are its apologists. For this insistence on reconsideration is very necessary. Men very soon get into the habit of contentedly worshipping idols, not of wood and stone, but thoughts of God, once inspired by reverence, but now unworthy. This is the sin forbidden in the second commandment. The refusal of earnest men to accept revelation, in the form in which it has been presented, is then another call on us to reconsider our popular conceptions of the method of revelation, and justify the ways of God to men.

It will be seen that the questions raised about the idea of revelation in our day are not new. But they are raised more widely, more confidently, and with more historical and critical learning at their back. Is there any authenticated evidence of a revelation made to man which can be rightly called external, phenomenal ? Is there any direct and explicit communication *ab extra* to men of facts of science, or history, or ethics, or theology ? The whole trend of modern knowledge and research surely compels us to answer 'no,' with the reservation that appears later on.

But to the further questions which are now being asked— Has there been a revelation given to man otherwise than externally ? Have men received an access of power of seeing for themselves ?—modern knowledge and research will not answer 'no'; but are more and more disposed, with due reserves as to the terms used, to answer 'yes.' There is a strong positive side to the modern thought of revelation.

This was not the trend of science and philosophy in the eighteenth century, and the early part of the nineteenth. The answer then given to these questions would have been 'no.' But it would have been so because, among other reasons, the prevailing conception of God which was in the minds of religious people at that time was that known as the Latin or Western—a God apart from, remote from, the universe; manifesting Himself only by an occasional interference. Scientific minds were driven to deny this as an impossible theory of God; and to deny this was to deny the only conception of revelation then current. I do not of course pretend that such a comparison of the centuries is strictly accurate; but it is, I think, true that the popular denial of revelation by thoughtful sceptics of the period referred to was induced by the denial of the prevailing theory of God. That theory, though still dominant, is no longer held to be so exclusively orthodox as it was. And with that theory of God is also passing away the confident denial of revelation. The conception of God, and the conception of revelation, are of course closely connected. The whole matter is, therefore, being reopened from the historic and scientific points of view. What are the facts, what is the idea, of revelation to man from God, coming *in* man, *through* man?

Such in brief have been the causes of the swing of the pendulum away from the old and apparently simple conception of a revelation made from without by God to man.

It may however further help us to understand better the nature of the change that has taken place in the idea of revelation if we try to note not only such difficulties as I have mentioned, which are involved in the old conception, and are causing its abandonment, but also some of the reasons which are attracting men to the new.

One reason is the impossibility, under the theory of phenomenal or external revelation made to man, of answering satisfactorily the first and obvious question, 'What is it that has been revealed?' If revelation were of this nature, this question must, it would seem, admit of a clear answer. But clear answer there is none. Widely different answers have been given in successive ages of the Church, and are given now by different branches, sections, or parties in the Church, by contemporary individuals of equal learning and character, and by the same individual in successive stages of his spiritual growth. And the differences in these answers are not diminishing. Now this could scarcely be the case if revelation was wholly or mainly objective. The diversity of the replies is plainly not to be regarded as an accident, a transient stage due to ignorance; it must be of the essence of revelation, arising out of its nature. This consideration suggests—I think it demonstrates—a large subjective element in the method and substance of revelation as the cause of the indefinability of the truths revealed. Let anyone endeavour seriously to answer in writing, the simple question, 'What has been revealed?' and he will appreciate the argument. "The whole of the Bible" would be, or would have been, one answer; but apart from all difficulties about texts and canons of Old Testament and New, let the reader think what this implies. The origin of man, and of woman, and of divers languages, down to the heavenly city with its streets of gold. It is of course conceivable that a book beginning with legend and containing rudimentary ethics and theology, and ending with symbol, might be as it stands an objective revelation from God, though its ethical and spiritual value resides wholly in the interpretation of it by each age in accordance with its own light. It might be in this sense objective in itself, though to us its value is accessible only through processes which neglect its objectivity. But is this a truthful and profitable way of regarding it? Is it not rather suggested by a desire to retain old forms of thought alongside of the new? "The whole of the Church's Creeds and Doctrines" would be, or would have been, another reply. Witness the Biblical Theologies that have been constructed. But such an answer would scarcely bear cross-questioning. Or shall we say that reasonable selections must be made from both? But on what principle? If 'reasonable,' will not the selection be subjective? Is it not subjective for us all? Is it not increasingly so as we grow older, and as we take a wider survey of the world and its history? If we replied "The Person and character of our Lord Jesus Christ and His teaching about God and man," we do not escape the difficulty. We see Him with different eyes. We cannot escape from our personality.

Moreover the area of accepted objective revelation, which can be expressed as dogma, is dwindling; and that in an age which is not to be described as averse to religion.

We are driven to the conclusion that the weary so-called conflict of science and religion has been largely misunderstood. It has really been a conflict between science and a theory of a revelation made objectively; and in the region of objectivity science rightly claims to be supreme. Science is therefore expelling an unintentional and mistaken trespasser.

Then again there is a reaction from the diversity, the complications, the confidence, of the dogmatic statements about God made in the name of objective revelation, and as logical deductions from it. Some text-books of dogmatic theology look like a handbook of astronomy based on the theory of epicycles. They are logical and complete, and amazing in the intimacy of their knowledge of God's purposes, and the confidence of their assertions about His will; but they have too many unverifiable assumptions to be trustworthy. Slowly a conviction has set in, for which scientific method is responsible, that the pegs on which logical deductions hang, in any and every science of observation, can bear little but their own weight.

This is true even in the physical and natural sciences; and even more plainly so in theology, and its kindred studies. The lesson can scarcely be better put than it was by Huxley in a letter to Darwin. "The great danger," he wrote, "which besets all men of large speculative faculty, is the temptation to deal with the accepted facts of natural science, as if they were not only correct but exhaustive; as if they might be dealt with deductively in the same way as propositions in Euclid may be dealt with. In reality every such statement, however true it may be, is true only relatively to the means of observation, and to the point of view of those who have enunciated it. So far it may be depended upon. But whether it will bear every speculative conclusion that may be logically deduced from it, is quite another question."

This thought, familiar to men of science, has great influence on their way of regarding the nature and so-called 'proofs' of revelation, and is leading men towards a more subjective view, and a resulting modesty and differentiation of certainty in statements about God.

The conviction of continuity in all things has moreover a strong hold on the modern mind, which is deeply, though half unconsciously and indirectly, affected by scientific influences. Continuity is demanded in the idea of revelation; revelation should be regarded as the evolution of the knowledge of God which is life eternal. All other knowledge is won by the human intellect with slow and toilsome steps, or by human insight and genius. If this evolutionary growth is true of the arts and sciences and philosophies, on what ground, it is asked, can we finally except theology? Surely all branches of human knowledge grow by virtue of the divinely implanted powers of man. Thus men are led from regarding revelation as a transaction due to some external agency, a transaction in which man is the passive recipient, to regard it as a quickening process within, in which man is the active instrument.

The historical method also, applied to the Christian revelation, throws light on all revelation, and is leading men in the same direction. For if anything has been revealed all will agree that Christianity has been revealed. And the historical method can be applied to Christianity; for Christianity at any rate had a definite beginning; there was a time when it was not. Historical enquiry is throwing much light on the appearance, the nature, the growth, the continuous development of Christianity, and on its relation to the thoughts and literature of the age and country in which it appeared. And although the result of this enquiry is far from complete, and is not negative as regards the objective and historical character of the substance of the New Testament narratives, yet it has, on the whole, assisted in the recognition of a strong subjective and continuous element in revelation. The revelation of Christ is looked for less in a series of novel truths of any kind to be gathered in their final forms from His words, and more in His quickening and illuminating influence on the souls of His followers, continued in the world by His spiritual presence. It is not less Divine because it is more continuous in its method.

The nature of evidence from prophecy has also changed under historical criticism. It was once thought to be an evidence of a distinct prevision of the future granted to some of the Old Testament prophets; such that passages could be selected from them which fitted more or less accurately into a detailed picture or mosaic of Christ's life. That whole conception has passed away. The revelation to the prophets is seen by us now to have been a quickening of their ethical insight, of their spiritual apprehension, of their sense of close filial unity with God in this life. The fulfilment of their hopes truly was in Jesus Christ; but not as was till lately thought. The function of the prophets was to make it plain that the Spirit of God speaks in and through the hearts of men; and that the illumination of the conscience is in itself a revelation of the Indwelling God, and of His message. The historical method has directed our eyes to search in every age for God's message to that age, as shown by the best thoughts of that age. God is to be sought for here and now, as the prophets sought Him, and if we cannot find Him now, but relegate Him to the past or the future, our thoughts about Him are not likely to be true.

Again, the literary criticism of the Gospels is directing our thoughts inwards, by slowly unfolding Christ's method, and preparing men's minds to see its essential nature. We begin by its aid to realise how He changed the centre of religion from without to within; from observances to filial love; from a national institution to brotherliness; from a mediated to a direct approach to God; from the authority of a sacred tradition and text-book to that of a pure and enlightened conscience. He utters truth, and He awakes the response which proves it true. Plato said that the teaching of Socrates was a 'maieutic' art. It is the method of every true teacher. He is ever striving to bring to the birth the infant intellectual life. Supreme among teachers of the spiritual life was Christ; precisely for this reason, that He more than all others brought, and still brings, to conscious birth the infant spiritual life—the filial love of God, and the brotherly love of man—that lie in the womb of the human heart. This bringing to the light is revelation. Literary criticism thus explains Christ's amazing freedom, and His apparent want of didactic method. Story and parable, action and proverb, discourse and silence, all are meant to evoke the inner spirit of man, to bring to life. Such criticism shows that Christ's revelation, and by inference all revelation, has, at any rate, in large measure consisted in opening men's eyes to see. Revelation is education, not instruction, to use a hackneyed contrast. It therefore never grows old. Christ and His revelation are verily "the same yesterday, and to-day, and for ever."

So the pendulum has swung. The facts of religious experience remain the same; our knowledge of them has been greatly extended. The past interpreted them as results of an external objective origin; and slowly, remorselessly, much of the objectivity is filched away. And why? Simply because subjectivity seems better to explain and connect the facts observed and their diversity. The revelation of God, like the Kingdom of God, is within; evoked, it may be, stirred into life and birth, by what is external but acting from within. We are forced to the conclusion that just as the word revelation was not, as was suggested, the right word; so the question 'What has been revealed?' has been put in the wrong form. The first and primary question is not 'What has been revealed in the darkness?' but 'What is the light, and what is the eye, that enables us to see anything?' When this is answered we may go a step further, and compare what we see.

We have in fact to take a fresh metaphor. Put aside the picture of God lifting a veil; of God showing to the gaze of man a clear vision; of God whispering in the ear of some sage the narrative of what has been in the far past, or what shall be in the far future, or explaining the secrets of His nature and His designs for men. Put these pictures aside, and think of man as we know him, in this mysterious world of matter and spirit, of physics and metaphysics; in these two worlds, I would rather say, of which he is the solitary link; living in both, able to think of both, to know something of both, but only to know a little, where everything indicates that infinitely more is to be known. Think of man as peering out into the darkness; from one point of view, from another, and from yet another, as amid mists on dark mountains a traveller might try to realise his surroundings. Day seems slowly and doubtfully to be dawning; some of his earlier impressions as to shapes guessed at in the darkness are being modified. And then let him ask himself, 'What is the source of light by which he is able to see anything, and what the indwelling eye and faculty by which he sees it?'

If then this is the new idea of revelation which appears destined to modify the old, we must proceed to examine it somewhat more closely.

We may be quite sure that in its essence the revelation of God to man must be something very simple, very universal, very recognisable; we have not to fetch it from the heights above or from the depths beneath. It can be the product of no extended research, a prize for few. It must be now and here. "The word is very nigh" us. The simplest ways of thinking about God—such as Christ's sayings about God recorded in the Gospels—must be the truest and highest. Revelation must carry its evidence within itself. And the criterion of a divine revelation must be its fruits. They should be "love, joy, peace." But there is something else. The test of a revelation must be its life-giving power; and life means growth, and growth means change. "I am come," said our Lord, "that they might have life." And a revelation from the Father of all flesh must surely be universal, though varying, like all else, in degree. Every thought of God, and of duty and of love, in the saint, in the child, in the heathen, in the most brutalised product of civilisation, is truly a revelation of God within. It is light within the soul. No one may despise its crudest form, or its darkest surroundings. There are no hard and fast lines in nature. There are none in humanity. We are so united by a mysterious solidarity that the presence of the Divine in one is a proof of its presence in all. What we call progressive revelation is an increasing presence and influence, we may call it an evolution, of the Divine in man. There is an evolution of the soul as well as an evolution of the body.

Revelation, under this idea, is not regarded as a body of truths of any kind made known to the intellect, but as consisting in an awakening of personality; not as a reminiscence, on Divine authority, of the forgotten past, nor a semi-disclosure of the unknown future, but as a growing intuition of what *is*. Events in the past are in the world of facts and transactions, and for ascertaining and verifying them we have other faculties. Revelation is in another order of ideas. It interprets facts, it does not communicate them. Under this idea, again, revelation is not regarded as a body of speculative truth; such statements are meaningless till the mind is ready for them. Rather it is the enlightenment of the whole man, the intensifying of the feeling, the stimulation of the conscience. It is in a word the δύναμις τοῦ πνεύματος, the power of the Spirit; God in action upon us— in us. The life in us is connected with the life of God, as the little pools and creeks on the sea-shore are one with the unseen and infinite ocean.

The only conception therefore of revelation possible to science is that it is made through persons alone, by the immediate operation of mind on mind. This is a part of the old doctrine of the Logos, that the reason in man is the manifestation of the Divine Reason, or that the Divine

Reason manifests itself in the illumination of the minds of men. The answer then to the questions as to the nature of subjective revelation, given to-day by one who can make no break with scientific method in his treatment of theology, is not inconsistent with the answer which the Christian philosopher would give. Both would practically say with St John that it is "the Light which lighteth every man"; a Light still "shining in the darkness"; an indwelling in the material and animal nature of every man of some share of the Divine Reason. This is at once the Light, and the power of vision also.

The transference of the idea of Revelation from without to within has been described as a characteristic of Christ's teaching, and it must have startled His hearers. They had heard of the "still small voice"; of the word 'written in the heart.' But it was inconceivable to them that the sacredness of Jerusalem or of Gerizim as places of acceptable worship was not a permanent reality, but only a transient phase of religious thought. The passing away of Jerusalem, of the temple, of sacrifices, and Christ's whole treatment of tradition and of Scripture, must have seemed to that generation to be the extinction of all that was tangible in religion; and now, as then, men confuse the tangible with the real, and thus mistake the temporary for the eternal.

And if we test this theory by examining how far to our Lord's disciples, and to the first generation of Christians, Christ's revelation appeared as an objective revelation, we cannot fail to be struck with the fact that the mind of the Apostolic age, so far as we can judge, dwelt but little on the life of Jesus of Nazareth, or on any creed or code which He bequeathed to them. His revelation was primarily an immense illuminating and quickening power given to man; a "transformation by the renewing of the mind"; a seeing with Christ's eyes, and therefore seeing for oneself what He saw; it was in very truth "Christ in" them "the hope of glory." And "Christ in us" means "God in us." It is the living indwelling Christ, it is the spirit of Christ in him, and not the Jesus of the Synoptics, that we see in St Paul. It seems as if the

Divine Jesus, who lived among men after the flesh and died and rose again, had revealed or brought to the birth, in the human hearts that loved Him, a corresponding self, a spirit of Christ, nay "Christ" Himself, as St Paul says; a Christ with whom they also died and rose again; and that this was a real unveiling, a showing what was there before, but unknown. The faith committed to the saints is the new Life.

We may test this thought of revelation by the Church; for the Church also is a revelation. Its faith in the Divine goodness has revealed gradually, as the light in it has grown, both the indwelling and the historic Christ. But has it revealed anything objective, external? Is it not rather a revelation because it has preserved, and illustrated, and fostered a new ideal of life, the Christian ideal? How much we owe to "the collective consciousness of a Christian Society"! It is an expression of the Divine power working within; it is still the $\delta\acute{u}\nu\alpha\mu\iota\varsigma$ $\tau o\hat{u}$ $\pi\nu\epsilon\acute{u}\mu\alpha\tau o\varsigma$. It is a revelation because it strengthens and purifies our power of seeing. And this is plainly subjective.

We may further test the theory by applying it to the Bible; for the Bible is unquestionably a revelation of the first importance. But is the revelation here really a statement of final truth made by God in this concrete form? Who can venture to say so? To anyone who has realised the progressive education of the world it must seem as unscientific to look in the Jewish Scriptures either for accurate information about physical facts, or for final statements of truth of any kind, ethical or theological, as to search Babylonian records for truths not yet brought to light in astronomy. And in reading the New Testament we must never forget that we have but very fragmentary records of Christ's life and teaching; and those only after they have passed through the sifting process of the imperfect minds and memories of His followers. How much He may have said that they did not understand, and therefore did not repeat! Some part of what they did repeat they may have imperfectly or wrongly understood. How little we should have suspected the mystical aspect of Christ's teaching had St John's Gospel not been preserved!

When every deduction is made, the New Testament shows us indeed the mind and character of Christ, if we have eyes to see, and is an assurance of His historical character; but we cannot claim even the New Testament as an objective revelation of the complete Christ in the sense and degree it was once thought to be. It evokes our spiritual life. It is a revelation because it 'finds' us. But this is to say that, as a revelation, it has a large, a preponderant, subjective element.

This theory of a revelation in the main subjective has then strong arguments in its favour. And they are not inconsistent, and will not, I think, be thought by anyone, on full reflection, to be inconsistent with the objective revelation in Christ of the Divine Logos. The identification by St John of the Divine Reason with the Master whom he had known and loved on earth, was, in fact, a philosophical, a metaphysical theory. It was to him the key to all his experiences past or present. Jesus of Nazareth had illuminated the world as none other had done. He was therefore "the Light." Of the absolute truth of that identification there cannot, in the nature of things, be a demonstration to our human reason. The proof of a theory is that it explains and comprehends all the facts old and new. The Church, if I understand its history aright, has never professed to demonstrate. It states; and each must decide for himself as to the acceptance of such a statement, by such a faculty for discerning spiritual truth as God has given him, trained and exercised by a single eye to truth and by a pure and loyal life. That is the test of truth—experience. The scientific theory of a subjective revelation is not inconsistent with the conviction that though man always stood in the relation of child to God our Father, and always shared His nature, yet that historically it was only in Jesus Christ that this relation was fully manifested; nor inconsistent with the further conviction that in Jesus Christ alone God did give an objective revelation of Himself, as the ever present Light—the Word with man, as with God, from the beginning, but in Jesus alone fully revealed. Modern knowledge and research can never demonstrate, but it can never disprove, and it will never discredit, this belief. If there is a teleology of the universe it is summed up in the hope of the kingdom of God, and of man's ultimate full participation in the Divine nature, anticipated in the Person of Jesus Christ.

I do not think that this view of revelation differs appreciably from Bishop Westcott's careful definition of Christian Doctrine. He defines it as "a partial and progressive approximation to the full intellectual expression of the truth manifested to men once for all in the Incarnation." His words clearly imply that the relation between God and man, though manifested fully at one epoch in one Divine Person, was and is eternally true, and will be more and more manifestly true in all men. Revelation has been well defined as "the becoming explicit of what is implicit."

The theory of a subjective revelation is therefore, as I hold, entirely compatible with a belief in Jesus Christ, as a manifestation to the world in His Person of the nature of God. And there is a further modification to be made in the purely subjective theory, by the recognition of objective elements in His teaching. But before proceeding to this point I wish to meet some of the obvious objections that will be felt by those to whom the theory is not already familiar.

It may be felt that this theory involves a reversal too complete, too revolutionary; that the world cannot have been all wrong till the nineteenth century after Christ; and that the old view is the safer.

But I would reply that the thought of revelation as subjective is no new idea, though it presents itself once more reinforced, and in new terms. It has, as theologians know, always existed side by side with the other. Yet, even were it a reversal, history has proved the necessity of such reversals of theory in all departments of human thought. Epicycles gave way to the ellipse; vortices to the more subtle and less obvious laws of motion and gravitation; geocentric to heliocentric astronomy, in face of strong prejudice and the evidence of the senses; atomic theories are already giving way to something new. So it is in all human experience. The Messiah came, but not as He was expected; the promises were not reserved to the children of Abraham; one interpretation of the Atonement succeeds another. Our thought of the Bible is not quite that of our fathers. The expectation of Christ's speedy return was not fulfilled. There is nothing new, in science or philosophy or religion, in a complete reversal of the interpretation of facts. There is perpetual readjustment as the world swings on into fresh points of view. This is the lesson taught by the Epistle to the Hebrews. God has "provided some better thing concerning us." And if we are distressed or angry at new views, it is well for us to examine whether that distress is not a sign that we adopted our old views without much examination; or whether what we thought to be our reasons for them have not in reality already passed away. We are sometimes disposed to fight hardest for what, if we try to handle it, we find is but a shadow.

Others again will feel that to abandon any claim, like that of an external act of revelation, that has ever been made in the name of religion is a sign of weakness, even a treachery; it is a surrender of outworks, to be followed by a surrender of the citadel. It seems to them like a retreat in face of the enemy, accompanied by a humiliating petition to be permitted to exist a little longer in some inconspicuous corner, till a convenient moment comes for extermination. They think the existence of Christianity is staked on the old theory of revelation. And so the trumpet is blown, and the old warriors put on their armour, and prepare for battle with the infidel. But do not these metaphors of outworks and citadel mislead us? Apologists for Christianity need never surrender, and never take low ground. Nor are we doing so in advocating a subjective view of revelation. On the contrary we are surely preferring a great claim; claiming nothing less for humanity than did St Paul—the power of the Indwelling Spirit—to "be filled with all the fulness of God"—"according to the power that worketh in us" (Eph. iii. 19, 20). To advocate a subjective view of revelation is a surrender in no other sense than was St Paul's claim for the freedom of the Spirit in place of the bondage of the law a surrender of

VI] *Revelation, and modern knowledge* 245

the law. It was a surrender of the sign when the thing signified had come. It is the fighting for a symbol, not a reality, that brings us on low ground, and involves questionable methods.

A further and important question may be asked. Does not the subjective theory of revelation abolish all certainty? May it not be said that to accept subjectivity in revelation is in fact to say that there exists no authority, no ground, for faith except individual experiences? But is it true to say that such a faith would rest on one's own individual experiences, when one sees its wide and firm hold on human nature? Does it not rather, as shown by this fact, rise out of the solid and permanent substratum of our common— may we not say Divine?—humanity? and has it not therefore perhaps a better right than anything else to be called a reality, a certainty?

And when the thought has once become familiar to us that what has been represented as an event, a phenomenon in the natural world, was often, in its origin, an inner fact of consciousness, projected without, and interpreted as phenomenal from the exigencies of imperfect language and of primitive modes of imagination and thought, or from the practical need in teaching of giving form and permanency to the thought, we shall not feel that the subjectivity of revelation lessens the weight of its claim upon us.

For the same reason, to have such a theory as "our hindmost thought" may make the presentation of Christianity more effective. One secret of effective preaching is the conviction that there is a Word of God speaking in every heart; and he who can show that man has always heard this Word has the power of hushing the clamour of external voices, so that every man may listen for that inner voice in his own. Such a one unveils, reveals, the Divine within his hearer, and thus helps to transform. It is the presence of God in every heart that is, as it were, the conducting element that allows the current of conviction to pass from heart to heart.

Surely then it is not uncertainty, not insecurity, that

comes with such a conception of revelation. If Christian Revelation is presented and accepted, not as a supplement to Natural Religion and as resting on a different kind of evidence, but as the completion and confirmation and satisfaction of the deepest, simplest, and most universal experiences of man, it wins a confidence that no external attacks can ever weaken.

To some it may seem as if such a conception of diffused and, so to speak, natural revelation brought the loss of a glorious vision of dramatic Divine action, and no compensating gain. There is a loss. Perhaps "it is expedient."

I think the sense of gain comes later. But can we not even now at least sympathise with the gain, and with the truth to fact, in recognising a revelation in the normal life of the many? It is the same sort of incommunicable gain and repose that comes to men of science when they have finally come to see God's presence in natural law rather than in miracle. It is the same sort of gain that comes when prayer is no longer thought of as an attempt to bend the will of God to ours, but as the effort to merge our will entirely in His. It is a recognition of the universal God, the universal Christ. Every virtuous, kindly life becomes a witness to eternal truths. Is the starry heaven less able to declare the glory of God to us than to our fathers because the telescope and the camera have revealed oceans of diffused and nebulous light, and myriads of suns behind and among the stars they saw? Is natural life on earth less a witness to God since its variety has been multiplied and its continuity grasped? No more is the marvel of spiritual insight diminished by our regarding revelation as a gift more widely distributed, less consciously possessed, and less precisely defined, than we had thought.

Consider again what room this conception of revelation offers for growth and expansion, and how necessary this is to give unity and meaning to history. Millenniums have been spent in prehistoric gropings after God and the meaning of the world; millenniums under the ancient religions of the world; a millennium or so may have been spent by one nation under the Mosaic law, as a schoolmaster to bring men to Christ; and then it passes away, when the Christ comes. A few millenniums more may be spent as now in the training of men under the symbols of the external to fit them for the spiritual autonomy which is our acknowledged goal, the law written in the heart, "the measure of the stature of the fulness of Christ." Nothing short of this can be permanent. Let us at any rate pitch our ideals high. The final stage of the evolution of the soul must be something other than a magnified present. It is premature to put a limit to our ideals. This was the mistake of the Jewish teachers. But Christ showed, and St Paul saw, a higher truth; and He taught us that what His contemporaries held dearest was but a parenthesis in the long evolution of man, the goal of which we cannot yet define. Such parentheses are not at an end. "The end is not yet."

But some may ask, "Will not the adoption of a subjective theory of revelation resolve religion into emotion, or into an unpractical and contemplative mysticism?"

Emotion and mysticism in religion are elements in human nature, and must not be overlooked. They are elements very unequally developed in different individuals; but in humanity as a whole, and in the story of the Christian Church, they are of much importance as regenerating and moving forces, and as springs of a higher life. It is scarcely a scientific spirit which desires to minimise or preclude these elements in religion. All facts merit the closest attention; any one fact may give the clue to great mysteries. The least obvious phenomena, as a score of instances might be adduced to prove, have been the key to solutions of physical and biological problems.

When Joan of Arc during her trial at Rouen was rudely asked, by an English soldier, why he could not see visions as she did, she at first gave no answer. But when again and again pressed, she at last replied, *submissa voce*, as the record says, "Perhaps it was because you were not good enough."

The possibility that this is true should prevent our disparaging exceptional intuitions and feelings, and should prepare us to admit that there are many degrees in human capacity for revelation. And is such a spirit in religion unpractical? When I think of Christ's teaching, and of the emphasis St Paul lays on the working of the Spirit of God in man, of his most practical "therefores," and of the immense practical results that follow, it seems strange that it should have come to be thought that revelation, if it is to be practical, must be regarded as a thing of the past, embodied finally in a book or in creeds and institutions, rather than as the indwelling of a Light and Life that should continuously inspire our lives.

And let it not be thought that a conception of revelation as subjective dispenses with discipline. Of course if a man starts by identifying discipline with obedience to an external authority, and by identifying the freedom of the Spirit with uncontrolled license, to him it is manifestly impossible to think of revelation as the recognition of the growing autonomy or self-discipline of a soul which has surrendered itself to Christ's spirit and will. Such a one must reconsider *de novo* the nature of discipline. Moreover discipline is not the same for all. Some have thought that there could be no religious and disciplined life outside the cloister. Others have found that obedience to an inner rule is severely disciplinary. Obedience to an external rule has indeed helped to make saints; but it would be a strangely prejudiced limitation of sainthood to confine it to those who have placed themselves under such a rule.

But though there might be no extravagance in conduct, would a united worship, it may be asked, based on a common creed, be possible, if that creed came to be regarded not as a revelation from outside, authoritative, final, indisputable, but only as an approximate summary of such truths as the best minds had, under God's guidance, as yet reached?

On this much might be said. Prophecy on such matters is hazardous. We must try, regardless of consequences, to think and speak truly, and trust the God of truth. The compensation that comes with a sense of joint search and effort for truth, involving the cooperation of all thoughtful Christians and an increasing moral thoughtfulness and responsibility, and with the unexpected unity of Christians and the joy of common service, may be greater than we imagine. And perhaps among the older and more thoughtful and truly loyal members of our Church, there is more of this subjectivity and relativity in their adherence to the Creeds than we commonly realise.

I have left to the last, in order that it may have a somewhat fuller treatment, that which will be felt by many as far the greatest difficulty in any theory which regards revelation as primarily subjective. "Does it not do away with, or make completely subordinate, the objective revelation which Christians believe was made to the world in Jesus Christ, and by Him?"

The question must come sooner or later, "What think ye of Christ? was He Himself, were His life and words, His death, resurrection and ascension, a real and also an objective revelation?" On this there must be surely a plain answer, yes or no. And my answer must be a convinced 'yes.'

I have already shown that the theory of a subjective revelation is not inconsistent with regarding our Lord as an Incarnation of the Divine Word. It is indeed wholly compatible with that essential Christian doctrine. To many this theory will indeed seem to be the necessary presupposition to make the doctrine credible or even intelligible.

But further, the theory of revelation as essentially subjective in its operation in man leads directly to the belief in the objective revelation made to men in and by Jesus Christ.

For we must consider His operation on the souls of men under two aspects which we may distinguish in thought. First there is the action of the Divine and Eternal Word, the Light of the Soul, indwelling from the beginning in man; that Divine Life which in some mysterious way we share with Him as the Eternal Son of God : and, secondly, the action by the influence, example, teaching of the historic Jesus of Nazareth, which made His work in time. These two actions upon us are felt as one ; they are simultaneous, concurrent. They appeal unequally to different temperaments ; but both are real. And it is plain that our Lord regarded His indwelling life in the soul of man as the higher. "It is expedient for you that I go away." The removal of the visible Christ after the flesh made possible the indwelling Spirit, and brought about the transformation of the apostles. It is plain too that to St Paul the revelation in Christ was not mainly the words or the life of Jesus. It was something closely connected with Him; manifested, symbolised, made objective in His Person. But in its essence that revelation was the awakening of the human consciousness to a Divine Life, which has in its totality to go through those experiences which Jesus Christ went through—the death to sin, the rising to new life. He is always conscious that all which is most characteristically Divine in our Lord has its counterpart and potentiality in us. The cross of the Lord Jesus Christ was that on which the world was crucified to Paul, and Paul to the world. It is by the combination of the contemplation of the Divine in Christ, as truly an objective manifestation, with that of the existence of the same Divine Life in ourselves, that we really get into communion with God. To St Paul, we may say, the love and self-sacrifice of Christ would have been unintelligible, if seen in Him alone. And they are so still to many minds. They need the life of the Church as their interpretation in human experience. The revelation of God needs the whole creation as its sphere. It cannot be isolated. There is a continuity even here.

In defining the objectivity of the revelation of God incarnate in the historic Jesus surely all violent affirmations or negations are strangely unsuitable. There are depths here which we cannot fathom. On the one hand we may frankly and gladly admit that the statements of fact in the Gospels are wholly and solely matters for historical and rational investigation. The historic truth of events related about our Lord is not a matter for "spiritual discernment,"—for any subjective revelation whatever. The illumination of the conscience imparts no discernment of past events, no critical acumen as to the value of evidence. For the history of Christ, so far as it consists of events, we are dependent on our normal faculties of reason. On the other hand this limitation "so far as it consists of events" is a very important one. For our understanding and entering into Christ's teaching, our feeling and reverence for His character, our acceptance of the ideas we associate with His name—all this depends on quite other qualities. Spiritual discernment is essential for entering into the revelation of a character. A biographer, or a reader of the life of a great man, must have much in common with the life if he is to see all or nearly all that is to be seen in it. The revelation to us of the character, of the Divine, in Christ is in this sense subjective. But it is neither sympathy nor love that is needed to state or to verify dates and incidents, or weigh the evidence for traditions, most important as this work is. We must in all honesty remove from the sphere of subjective revelation the power to affirm the historical accuracy of any recorded event or any spoken words in our Lord's life; and we may be thankful that the rational evidence is as strong and convincing as it is. This is the claim on us of the historical method, and it must be granted without reserve.

But we resolutely claim for ourselves what we grant to others. There must be no appeal to subjective certainty on either side. If faith is ruled out of court in the study of history, as likely to disturb the judgement, so must all other bias be ruled out of court. It is one of the results of modern knowledge and research that history can only be studied successfully by men of wide human sympathies, possessed of a varied knowledge of human nature even in its rarer manifestations; men who feel human nature as the expression of something greater than it seems. The same demand must be made from science. Much has been assumed to be incredible which further research in science is proving credible. History cannot be studied on the presupposition that nothing can have happened outside our normal experience. The appeal is to reason, and to reason we will go; but it must be to a reason sufficiently enlightened to know how insecure are many of the generalisations, founded only on a normal experience, and drawn by men, it may be, of ordinary powers.

It is not possible in this Essay to enter at all on the momentous questions closely involved,—the actual nature of the Incarnation, the Resurrection and the Ascension of our Lord regarded as revelations through facts. But it must not be forgotten that these events constitute, and have from the beginning constituted, an essential part of the fact of revelation as accepted by the whole Christian Church. And perhaps "the idea of revelation" might fairly be extended so as to include them. But if these subjects are to be dealt with "in the light of modern knowledge and research," they will require a volume, not a paragraph.

Readers, however, of this Essay have some claim to know in general outline how I regard these questions, in order that they may rightly interpret the rest of the essay.

I hold it to be not inconsistent with either the results or the spirit of modern knowledge and research to accept a complete continuity of the natural and the supernatural, to acknowledge complete ignorance of the ultimate nature of mind and matter, and to regard the ordinary and present limitation of our powers, senses, and understanding as neither universal nor final. Our physical laws are only provisional. I hold that the Resurrection, to take that event alone, was an event in the phenomenal world, but one both taking place and witnessed in some plane of consciousness higher than the normal, and admitting of no explanation on the lower plane. If these events so took place, and were so witnessed, they could only be made known to ordinary men by narratives such as those in our Gospels, which appear miraculous as transcending normal experience. And in some of us the narrative evokes faintly the same consciousness of the presence of God in the world that the original witnesses felt at the events themselves.

We may now go back to the question. Were not Christ Himself, His life and words, His death, His resurrection and His ascension a real and also an objective revelation? And to this the answer is 'yes'; though the qualification is repeated that we have no right, "in the light of modern knowledge and research," to postulate the historical accuracy, or on the other hand the historical inaccuracy, of the New Testament records respecting these alleged facts.

Nevertheless this qualification is plainly not the whole nor the final result of a century's study of everything that bears on the Person of Christ, His surroundings, and His work. Whatever were the hopes or fears of a generation ago, the result of the concentrated study of Christ, in this new and critical spirit, which takes nothing for granted, and looks through no coloured glasses, has been the very reverse of belittling Christ. Beyond all question the gaze of the world is concentrated on Him with profounder interest and reverence and belief than ever before. The world looks on the Church, it might truly be said, with less awe and less hope, as it looks on Christian theology with less confidence, than before. To the Church and to theology the world is more indifferent, where it is not scornful or hostile. But nothing is plainer than that the world is not indifferent, and not scornful or hostile, to Christ. Every effort has been made in the name of science, in the name of philosophy, and in the name of criticism, to interpret Him in the terms of ordinary or slightly extraordinary human personality, evolved from His environment: and with what result? Can it be doubted that He stands before the world, as a great Historic Person, with a Personality unfathomed, more clearly than He ever did before? The result of this close study has not been to rend away the halo, the luminous veil of mystery, that surrounded Him. It has been rather to show that much of the ecclesiastical and dogmatic scaffolding through which we have seen Him has been shown to be removable, and to show more clearly, more intelligibly to our consciences, to our critical judgements, the radiant figure within. The result of criticism has been to establish the history of Jesus Christ. Much might be said in confirmation of this result from many quarters; but it is familiar and obvious. The serious attacks on Christianity are not attacks on Christ, but on the use that is made of His name, and on our affirmations about Him. The Christ of theology is a remoter figure from the world than he was, but not the Christ of Galilee and Jerusalem,—and not the spirit of Christ as a motive to action. There is a half-formed and growing belief that if we could really recover

His revelation of Himself and of God's will, and live in His light, all would be well. Myriads who cannot think of Christ as the pre-existent and eternal Son of God, or as the second Person in the Trinity, sent down from Heaven to reveal God to man, can and do think of Him as the Son of Man who lived on earth to reveal God in man as the germ of the kingdom of God. They will not deny, but neither will they affirm, that He is more.

Such is one of the positive results of a century of study. It is the affirmation of a revelation in Christ of what some will speak of as the ideal of humanity, others as the Divine in man, others as the Son of God. But He is ever more and more clearly a Revelation.

Now this faith, for faith it is, is surely a fact of absolutely first-rate significance; though what it may portend, and ultimately lead to in world-history, no man may foresee. It may be the spring of a new and popular revival of religion. It may have far-reaching social and political results, when it has formulated itself as clear knowledge. But it is only with reference to the idea of revelation that it can now be considered; and for this the significance of the fact seems to lie here.

That which has concentrated of late, and is now holding more strongly than ever, the reverence and love of the world is the character of Christ. More than ever that is the human ideal. He has been a stimulus and a light to the human conscience in consequence of the standard, an objective standard of perfection, that He has given to it. Our capacity for that reverence and love presupposes, as has been shown above, our possession of the elements, the rudiments, of that character. If it were wholly alien to us it could not move us to love or reverence. We love it because it is our ideal self. Granted this initial and rudimentary power in us, this eye to see the Divine, this indwelling of the Divine in us, then the Christ of the Gospels embodies for us, more plainly in this century than ever before, the ideal which the world recognises as its own. And it is this recognition that a revelation without is identical with the revelation within, that is the only proof open to us of its truth. This is the fundamental intuition. But this is to say that Christ put before the world in visible form, or that He is, the objective Revelation of God from Whom we came into being, Whose children we are. Without that inner subjective revelation of God in human souls which enables us to recognise the Divine, a historic Christ could never have been known, never have founded a Church; and without the historical Person of Christ the Christian ideal in the hearts of men could never have taken the concrete, commanding, and permanent form needed to found a religion. It would have been, as it was in 'Christians before Christ,' a beautiful dream, or a philosophy, no more. As it is, the idea and the fact of revelation have met, and are being acknowledged to have met in the character of Christ, as the supreme revelation.

This is utterly independent of any details of criticism. The historic validity of early traditions as to events in our Lord's life, the speculations of theology as to His precise nature, the relations of history to doctrine, are of great philosophical interest, but they are not part of revelation, and are precarious deductions from it. The more we contemplate Jesus Christ as a revelation of Divine character to lift and save mankind, and as a stimulative pattern which men are not unwilling to accept and acknowledge, the more, I think, we shall feel that He was an objective and real revelation of God in the phenomenal world. It is the old conception of revelation in a new form. "The Word became flesh, and dwelt among us."

But this is by no means all. For it is quite impossible, as I believe, to think of Christ's character as a true revelation of the Highest or the Divine, and to dissociate from that character all His fundamental beliefs and teachings about God and a future life. His character is the embodiment, and at once the cause and consequence, of those beliefs. His character therefore, as an objective and phenomenal revelation, is so bound up with His doctrine of God, that we must accept His doctrine of God as an equally objective revelation. That seems to me the logic of the idea of revelation; and a logic which modern knowledge and research is tending to accept.

How far into detail of theology this will take us may be doubted. We cannot demonstrate that we ever have Christ's actual words. We possess but fragments, occasional fragments, of His teaching; and deductive theology, like intuitive criticism, as was remarked above, is insecure. But there is enough of certain knowledge for our life and guidance. If we try to take Christ's thought of His Father, and make it ours; to see God and man through Christ's eyes, and therefore as He saw them, we shall not desire much detail in our theology. Enough to see a trustworthy revelation of God the Father, a God of love and holiness, drawing the world of man to Himself in Jesus Christ, and a Holy Spirit guiding and sanctifying the hearts of men. Christ's revelation of Himself, and of God's nature and presence in man, in a word His Incarnation and teaching, form an objective revelation, interpreted ever more truly by the light and power of the continuous and growing subjective revelation in the hearts of men. The identification of Jesus of Nazareth with the Divine Word, is, we may say, the identification of revelation, objective and subjective, witnessed to by experience.

I have reserved till now, at the close of this Essay, the consideration which some may think ought to have come first, and to have guided the whole treatment. But it must now be very brief. What do we learn from the Bible itself as to the nature of revelation? Does it support the theory of a subjective revelation? Does it not plainly speak of revelation as objective?

Undoubtedly in the time of our Lord the Scriptures of the Old Testament, and the incidents of the Old Testament, were appealed to as an objective revelation of God's will. "The Scripture saith"—"It is written,"—such phrases are definitive, and leave no doubt as to their implication.

But it is not less plain that Christ Himself treated the Old Testament as not final, and therefore as not, except in some modified sense, an objective revelation from God. The words "It was said to them of old time"—"But I say unto you,"

VI] *Revelation, and modern knowledge* 257

and the promise that the disciples would be led into "all the truth," and His allusion to the "hardness of their hearts," are sufficient proofs of this. He claimed that His words and teaching were a revelation on a higher level than that of the Old Testament; and, what is more, that the disciples, the Church, should have the power given to them of learning truth for which they were not even yet prepared. A detailed discussion of our Lord's words as appealing to the inner revelation is impossible here. But let us think what is implied in the awful saying, "If the light that is in thee be darkness, how great is that darkness." It is the inner light alone that can illuminate. Why should He refuse to work signs, charge His disciples not to say who He was, give special blessing to those who had not seen and yet believed, except to teach that the only real evidence lies in moral union with Him arising from love? If we look for this thought we see it everywhere; in the promise of the Spirit of the Father to speak in them; in the revelation to babes; in His finding the greatest faith in a Roman centurion; in the testimony that not flesh and blood had revealed to Peter who He was; in His saying that the Kingdom of God is within; that the well of living water is within; that he alone who desires to do God's will shall know of the Teaching whether it be of God. It is not too much to say that the final appeal of our Lord's teaching, then no less than now, is that each of us should show by his life that we really are the children of our Father, who is in heaven.

To pass to St Paul, I think that when one has read his Epistles with due care, and weighed his carefully chosen phrases, not disparaging and dismissing them as 'mere metaphor,' we shall see that the spiritual revelation of the Divine Christ in himself, and the conviction that there was a Christ to be formed in everyone, were more intensely real and important than anything else. We shall see the thought everywhere as a key to his full meaning.

Slowly this revelation of the Christ within—this living presence of God in the human heart, by which the soul is helped to come to its true nature, seems to have been lost sight of, in spite of the Sacrament of the Body and Blood. The Christ within was lost in a metaphor; and the Christ on earth, or the Christ in the heavens, became the main object of Christian thought.

The call comes to us from many sides to look once more for the revelation of the Christ within.

It comes from without our Church and from within. From without is the challenge of the agnostic who denies that human reason can ever by searching find evidence of God or of the divinity of our Lord, and proclaims that to believe without evidence is unworthy of a man. He is right; but to him the reply is in substance that the Spirit of God in man may know God and Christ, not by evidence from without, but by unity of nature with Him, and that in such knowledge, not in belief in certain statements, is eternal life.

It comes from within, from all who are made uncertain of the grounds of their faith by doubts historic, critical, scientific, as to the Gospel narratives. To these the reply is: You know enough of the historic Christ, enough is established by the soundest criticism, to have aroused your own consciousness of the Divine life, of eternal life, within. You are called to follow that revelation; you have no doubt to what sort of life it calls you. Do God's will, and you will assuredly know His teaching, so far as is necessary. True religion is "righteousness and holiness of life."

It comes from the perplexed in faith; for there is no other view of revelation that throws light on this great and ancient world with its millions of souls passing through their short and troubled and often dark lives, from one eternity to another. What does it all mean, if it is not the manifestation of the Divine and universal Life, still groaning and travailing in pain, but waiting for the fuller manifestation of the sons of God? It enables us to see the millions who live and die in other religions, as, like ourselves, the children of God, with less light than we possess, but as taking part with us in that stream of life which shall one day pass into the presence of

VI] *Revelation, and modern knowledge* 259

God Himself. It gives hope, incentive, encouragement. It is the faith of many who have given it no expression in words. It is the faith of all workers; for it cannot be held along with the spirit of fatalism and acquiescence in evil which is the curse of some conceptions of the revelation of God. There is no limit to the transforming power such a faith may exercise on civilisation. Christ has revealed an ideal, and stimulated the growth of all ideals, when we have learnt that the Christ is within.

It may be said that Christianity itself illustrates the method of all revelation. All revelation, we have said, comes from within. When therefore God wished to redeem and illuminate man, He sent Christ to be one of us, that He might redeem the world from within; and so He redeems and has performed every work of individual redemption in every age from within. For Christ's redeeming work did not begin when He was born in Bethlehem; it had begun as the Word of conscience, the Word "very nigh" to man, in all men, in all ages. That which is universal in man was manifested, concentrated, in the historic revelation of Christ. In Him the universal subjective became the unique objective revelation. But in all time He was "the Light which lighteth every man."

We are told triumphantly that there was a Christianity before Christ, as if this disproved our faith. How could it be otherwise? The scientific idea of Christian revelation is not of some discontinuous inrush of the real into the phenomenal, out of relation to the past continuous growth; but of a concentration of the real always present in the phenomenal: a development, however exceptional; a further intertwining of the two strands implicit in human nature ages before. To those who accept this idea of revelation, and of the New Testament as a fragmentary history of that exceptional development, the popular attacks of to-day on Christianity seem strangely wide of the real mark.

Finally, it is quite certain that the limitation of our faculties renders impossible to us a complete understanding

17—2

of ourselves. There will always be room for theories of human nature, and for differences of opinion. The God whom nature reveals is indifferent to good and evil. The God whom conscience manifests is a God of righteousness and holiness. It is for us Christians, one and all, to make the venture of faith and declare, what we cannot prove, that these are One. And we think that experience justifies the venture. The world without, and conscience within, act and react on one another. The Divine within sees a fresh indication of the Divine without; and straightway that Divine revealed without stimulates the Divine within to new efforts of vision. They are the warp and woof out of which what we call revelation is woven. Or, to put it otherwise, a reaction from speculative dogmas about God sends us back to the study of man, and results in the discovery in man of precisely that consciousness of God which formed the basis of dogma. The problem of priority of origin is insoluble. The implicit consciousness of God and of the infinite is of the essence of human nature, and the point of convergence at which all contrasts meet. But it is out of sight, and its acceptance remains a venture of faith.

But apart from all differences of opinion, which can never cease while we "know in part," we are all called to united work, and if such differences of opinion were not so bound up with political, social, and personal antagonisms, they would not of themselves keep us apart. It is not religion, but the want of it, that divides us.

No one can look on the melancholy failure of mankind in spite of all its civilising influences, all its religion and philosophy and science, all its practical common sense, all the motives of kindly feeling and self-interest that urge it to do away with the curses of our political and social life; the awful contrasts of luxury and starvation, militarism, the drink-traffic, religious jealousies, corruption, slums, and the ceaseless growth of the unemployable,—without feeling that some fresh impulse is needed for human nature. The great engines of our civilisation-factory want a larger steam supply.

We may be brothers in our efforts to diminish these evils, though we admit different motives for making those efforts. May it not be that new life will come from an evergrowing recognition of the power of every human spirit to know God and to be like Him; from a belief in a revelation not of old time only but of to-day ; the Divine within cooperating with the Divine without to bring man to that knowledge which alone is eternal life, and to that service which alone is perfect freedom?

ESSAY VII.

PRAYER, IN RELATION TO THE IDEA OF LAW.

ARTHUR WILLIAM ROBINSON, D.D.

ANALYSIS.

I. The growing recognition of the witness borne by the instincts and emotions of human nature: the demand that this should be allowed full weight in attempts to give a logical account of the universe. The instinct and habit of *prayer* universal. Aim of this Essay, to inquire whether prayer, in the sense of petition, is in harmony with what we know of the order which exists in the world. The principle of that order is what we mean by *Law*. Origin of our conception of law: how far derived from the constitution of our minds, from civil legislation, and from scientific investigation of nature.

II. Is the idea of law inconsistent with the first postulate of prayer—the existence of a Supreme Ruler? Source of the popular impression that it is. Failure of attempts to get rid of the natural interpretation of causation. Second postulate of prayer—the possibility of alteration in the course of events as the result of our appeals. The objection as to presumption on our part. Difficulty of conceding that interference is possible where the regularity of the natural order is concerned. The controversy of 1872. Prayer was admitted to possess an efficacy in the spiritual, but not in the physical sphere. The grounds upon which this denial was based. The philosophical argument involved an unwarrantable addition to the scientific definition of law, led to an intolerable dualism, and was refuted by the most elementary facts of experience. The doctrine of psychological parallelism.

III. Is it true that any interference with the physical order must inevitably upset the balance of things? We have a power of interference, without, it would seem, any violation of law. The slightest change in antecedents must produce an altered consequent, in accordance with the principle of law. It is the unvarying character of laws that enables us to use them. Why the analogy from the "stoppage of an eclipse" is fallacious. Why we may pray for recovery from sickness. Sir G. Stokes on prayers for a change in the weather. The objection of the determinist. On strict principles of necessitarianism there can be no ineffective prayers.

IV. How far our views of prayer are likely to be affected by the teachings of psychology. Naturalistic explanations of answers to prayer. Limits to the influence that can be exerted by human wishes. A fresh motive in prayer. Attitude of our Lord to spiritual forces and prayer.

V. The freedom to pray must be used constitutionally. Public spirit in prayer. The *raison d'être* of prayer, to secure the accomplishment of the Divine purpose. The more we understand of Law, the more confident and reverent Prayer will become.

PRAYER, IN RELATION TO THE IDEA OF LAW.

I.

THERE seems good reason to hope that the reverence for facts, which has been the distinguishing characteristic of modern inquiry, is at last about to be extended ungrudgingly to the facts of which we may reasonably be supposed to have the closest and most trustworthy knowledge.

For many a day men's minds have been principally occupied with the investigations which have been going forward with extraordinary success in the realm of external nature. The engrossing interest of these investigations, and the seeming certainty of the results that have followed from them, have disposed multitudes to acquiesce in the opinion that this realm of external nature is preeminently the region of fact. In vain have the metaphysicians pleaded for the recognition of realities much nearer home, realities moreover upon which all knowledge must be ultimately based. The physical filled the horizon, its claims were insistent; there was no time or inclination to look within.

But now there are signs of a change. Perhaps the discoveries in the physical sphere are not quite so startling as they were, though that indeed will scarcely be maintained; perhaps we are realising more clearly that matter after all can only be made intelligible to us when it is interpreted in terms of mind : perhaps, upon third thoughts, the world is beginning to suspect that the initial step in philosophy is to "know thyself." Whatever the explanation, there can be no doubt that there is at the present time an increasing readiness to accept the primary affirmations of consciousness, and to attach importance to the evidence afforded by the fundamental instincts and emotions of human nature. Increasingly it is being felt that the business of the intellect is to explain and justify, rather than to arraign and condemn, these emotions and instincts.

But, while this is so, we may not imagine that there is likely to be any abandonment of that demand for logical and systematic completeness which had been encouraged and strengthened by successive advances and triumphs in the previous field of research. On the contrary, the demand is likely to be larger and stronger than ever. What will be sought will be the wider completeness that embraces all the facts. All must be exhibited as constituting a recognisable order, a consistent whole. If none are to be excluded, none can be allowed to remain isolated.

To be reverent and to be rational, to bring the evidence of the spiritual instinct into accord with the requirements of the intellectual judgement, that is the problem which is before us more distinctly than ever; and it will be to the various aspects of that problem that those who wish to render the best service to their generation will have to address themselves.

In the present Essay we are to attempt to deal with the problem as it presents itself in the very important instance of Prayer.

No one to-day is likely to question that prayer is a veritable fact of human experience. Among the higher instincts none can be named more natural, more universal, more persistent, than the instinct of prayer. Men have prayed always and everywhere. "We unroll Egyptian papyri, and find them filled with forms of prayer. We unearth Babylonian tablets, and amid all their sorceries and superstitions there is prayer. We translate the ancient books of India, of Persia, and of China, and they too are replete with prayers[1]."

[1] Illingworth, *University and Cathedral Sermons*, p. 164.

Of the classical peoples of the West a like account can be given. "They began nothing without prayer for Divine aid; journeys were not commenced without supplication, nor voyages without sacrifice; the opening of popular and senatorial assemblies was preceded by religious rites; colonies were not planted without inauguration; the history of some ancient cities is now almost limited to the ruins of their temples. The most sublime poem [the *Iliad*], and the most eloquent oration [the *De corona* of Demosthenes] commence with invocations of heavenly assistance. When was an ancient general known to set forth on a military campaign without an enquiry whether heaven was propitious to his enterprise[1]?"

There is no state of life but has felt its dependence upon an unseen aid. The mother prays. The child prays. Most men die praying. Whole sections of communities have devoted themselves to prayer. "Wherever man lives," it has been said not less truly than eloquently, "under certain circumstances, at certain hours, under the dominion of certain impressions of the soul, his eyes raise themselves, his hands seek each other, his knees bow, to petition or to give thanks, to adore or to deprecate. With joy, or with fear, openly or in the secrecy of his heart, it is to prayer that man betakes himself, in the last resort, to fill up the void of his soul, or to bear the burdens of his destiny[2]."

Amongst those who have prayed the most have been our bravest and best. If a list were to be written out of great thinkers, and great statesmen, and great artists, and great discoverers, who have believed firmly in the power of prayer, there is not one of us who would not be able to suggest a number of names that ought to be added to it. We must all have known men and women who could have abandoned any other practice more easily than the practice of prayer. Prayer to them was the supreme effort towards which all their energies turned: without it their whole existence

---

[1] Bishop Chr. Wordsworth, *Discourses on Public Education*, xii.
[2] M. Guizot, *L'Église de la Société Chrétienne*, p. 22, as quoted by Dr Hessey, *Boyle Lectures*, 1873.

would have seemed stunted and mutilated. And, above all, we remember the teaching and example of Him to whom men have looked as to no other for the expression of what is highest and most abiding in manhood. Upon nothing did He insist more eagerly than upon the value of Prayer.

It is inconceivable that an instinct so universal, so dominant in our nature, can be foolish and vain. Οὐδὲν μάτην ἡ φύσις ποιεῖ. Even if we omit the appeal to any authority above us, or to any more than mundane influence within us, we are constrained to affirm that, with enlarging experience, there has come the growing conviction that 'Nature makes nothing in vain.'

The external evidence for the success of particular prayers may not be decisive. It is capable of being explained until it is virtually explained away. With our very limited and uncertain understanding of historical antecedents, it is generally open to us to make several conjectures as to the causes which have led to an event; and consequently it must always be difficult, if not impossible, to secure agreement as to the nature of the forces which have been at work in any specified case. Tests that at one time might have been deemed satisfactory, at another would be distrusted and disallowed. Thus, for example, it may safely be predicted that the hospital-ward test will never again be proposed, as it was in 1872. In view of our extending knowledge of what can be effected by telepathy, it could no longer be regarded as conclusive. It would not now be doubted that a number of persons, who directed their thoughts and wishes in prayer towards a group of sufferers, might be the means of producing a remarkable change in their condition. What might be questioned would be the inference that anything more than human intervention was necessary in any instance to explain the result.

In a remarkable sermon preached to the Wakefield Church Congress, in 1886, on the "Reasonableness and Efficacy of Prayer," Bishop Reichel boldly asserted that "we can have no knowledge of the hearing and answering of prayer, *such as shall be capable of being proved to others. All attempts to demonstrate the efficacy of prayer must fail.*" "But," he added, "certainly one thing may be said with perfect truth : and that is, that no one who has been in the habit of praying in the way in which a creature ought to pray to his Creator, with the due measure of commingled reverence and awe, will say that his doing so has been useless and ineffective."

More and more it will be realised that the true and sufficient evidence for the validity of prayer is to be found, not in the history of particular answers, however remarkable, nor in the convictions, however absolute, of individual suppliants ; but in the broad fact that human nature, through all the stages of its evolution, has looked to a source above itself, and has believed that it could derive help by appealing to that source. The universality of the tendency and the invincibility of the habit compel the conclusion that prayer is a deeply implanted necessity of our being, and that it has been found to be efficacious over long reaches of our experience.

If it is hard to sustain an indictment against a nation, it is harder still to carry a conviction against humanity at large. *Securus judicat orbis terrarum*[1].

But, when we have thus satisfied ourselves that prayer is a great fact of life, we are only at the beginning of our task. To admit prayer to be a fact is tantamount to challenging our intelligence to tell us in what way it is related to the multitude of other facts. However it may have been in the past, it is certain that those who to-day are most fully persuaded of the efficacy of prayer are not less sincere than others, though possibly they are somewhat less impatient, in their desire to ascertain the relation in which prayer stands to the order and constitution of the universe.

It is true, no doubt, that, in proportion to the willingness with which we accept the evidence of the spiritual instinct as

---

[1] See further the Additional Note on pp. 305 f.

to the power of prayer, all intellectual inquiry in regard to its interpretation becomes for us largely speculative in its character: but nevertheless it does not cease to be of most real importance. For very many it is well-nigh impossible to continue to retain a belief which must be upheld against a perpetual discontent of the critical faculties: for nearly all, the effort to do this is painful and exhausting.

Prayer can scarcely become increasingly an element in the lives of educated men and women so long as they have in their minds a lurking suspicion that prayer, in the sense in which it has been commonly understood, is irreconcilable with what science is showing us of the working of the universe. And, on the other hand, nothing does more to encourage prayer, and to make it confident and hopeful, than the conviction that such a suspicion has no sound basis to rest upon.

Prayer, we say, in the sense in which it has been commonly understood. If we build our argument for the effectiveness of prayer upon the common consent of mankind, we must be prepared to accept the common consent of mankind as to what has been intended by prayer. Now, beyond question, what has been intended has been *petition*. The cry that has gone up from innumerable souls through all the ages, pagan and Christian, has been a cry for some kind of good, or for deliverance from some kind of evil, addressed to a higher Power which it was hoped could be moved to give the good, or to ward off the evil. It is prayer in this sense to which the deep instinct and long habit of the soul has borne witness. And it is prayer in this sense that specially calls for justification by the intellect. It is certainly about prayer in this sense that any suspicions and difficulties have arisen.

We are free, of course, to maintain that prayer is more than petition; that it is contemplation, communion, realisation of the unseen, even a mode of self-education: but we are not free to resolve prayer into any or all of these, while at the same time we rest our case for prayer upon the inborn necessity that has compelled men always and everywhere to

Prayer, and the Idea of Law

lift their hearts and their hands to a source of help above them.

Prayer, then, in the sense in which it has been commonly understood, is petition. It is for us to inquire whether prayer, so understood, is in opposition to, or in harmony with, what we may reasonably think we know of the arrangements which prevail in the universe.

Naturally, and indeed unavoidably, we employ such terms as order, constitution, arrangement, when we attempt to describe the world, the cosmos, the universe. And when we are pressed to explain what is implied in these terms we fall back upon a single term—*Law*. Law is the underlying and unifying principle. It is by conformity with Law that a settled order is rendered possible. Having decided what we mean by Prayer, we must next decide what we mean by Law.

And, to begin with, we had better ask, From whence do we derive the idea? Is it a part of the essential framework of our minds, a something that the mental eye brings with it to all that it sees? or is it acquired by experience from the social constitution around us, in the maintenance and development of which we all have a share? Or, again, has it been derived by us from the constitution of the physical world with which we are brought into contact through our senses?

The true answer would seem to be that we are indebted for the idea to all these sources. And it is necessary, therefore, when we are endeavouring to arrive at the full content of the idea, that we should try to estimate the measure of our debt to each of them.

That we do bring with us a tendency, original or inherited, to arrange and unify the data of experience, will not be disputed even by those who may hesitate to dogmatise as to essential and inevitable categories of the logical understanding. Many to-day would maintain that this *a priori* belief in an ordered uniformity is still the most potent influence in determining the view which we take of facts and occurrences in nature. "We believe that our experiences, in spite of their apparent irregularity, follow some (perhaps) unknown rule, because we first believe the world to be governed by immutable law." "Perfect uniformity is never observed[1]."

That an impression of "perfect uniformity" is by no means always made on the mind, when first brought into contact with new departments of facts, was strikingly illustrated by a remark of Professor J. J. Thomson at the recent meeting of the British Association. "There was one law," he said, "which he felt convinced nobody who had worked on this question [the radio-activity of matter] would ever suggest, and that was the law of the constancy of nature[2]."

When men attempted to form a clear idea of the order which, in spite of all the contradictions of experience, they were nevertheless disposed to find in the world, they were naturally led to think that it must bear some resemblance to the legislation administered in the State. "We know that prescientific man assumed the prevalence of a divine law and order in nature analogous to that existing among men. We know, too, that this assumption was at least the origin of the conception of scientific law[3]."

The enrichment of the idea of law which resulted from the use of this analogy brought with it the conviction that the order observed in the natural world might most reasonably be regarded as the manifestation of arrangement by a supreme Mind and Will. Mr J. S. Mill freely allowed that "the expression *law of nature* has generally been employed with a sort of tacit reference to the original sense of the word law, namely, the expression of the will of a superior[4]."

When we inquire as to what special development of the idea of law has been due to modern scientific thought and observation, we become aware that it has lain chiefly in the direction of differentiation and analysis. The general conception has been seen to include the thought of a vast number of particular *laws*. "The first point to be noted,"

---

[1] A. J. Balfour, *Foundations of Belief*, pp. 132, 131.
[2] *Times'* report, Aug. 24, 1904.
[3] J. Ward, *Gifford Lectures*, II. pp. 248 f.
[4] *System of Logic*, III. 4, 1.

VII] *Prayer, and the Idea of Law* 273

said Mr Mill, "in regard to what is called the uniformity of the course of nature is, that it is itself a complex fact, compounded of all the separate uniformities which exist in respect to single phenomena. These various uniformities, when ascertained by what is regarded as a sufficient induction, we call in common parlance, Laws of Nature[1]."

The process of analysis has been carried still further until the single law is defined to be the principle according to which a certain consequent is connected invariably with some particular antecedent, or set of antecedents. In more ordinary language, the invariable consequent is spoken of as the effect, and the invariable antecedent as the cause. Where there are several antecedents it is common to single out one only as the cause, and to describe the others as being merely conditions[2].

It will be necessary that we should return later to some points in this rapid statement of the history of the growth of the idea of Law. Our immediate concern is to note the general bearing of what we have seen upon the broad question of the legitimacy of petitions for any modification of the order which we believe to exist in the world. Such petitions involve the postulates (1) that there is a Power—a personal Power—above and behind the course of nature, to whom appeals can be made; and (2) that He is a Power by whom events can be influenced. Any attempt to provide an intellectual justification of acts of Prayer in a world of law must show that these postulates are capable of being reconciled with such requirements as may reasonably be deduced from what we have learnt of the nature and character of law.

---

[1] *Ibid.*
[2] See Mill's *Logic*, chap. v. Mill refused to follow Comte in "his objection to the *word* cause." "I consider him," he said, "to be entirely wrong" (chap. v. 6). Comte, like Hume before him, had wished to reduce causation to conjunction.

II.

Does, then, we must ask, the idea of Law, in any of the senses in which we have been taught to conceive it, or in all of them combined, preclude the possibility that there is in the universe a directing Power such as that to which the instincts of men have led them to turn, in all ages, with requests for help and deliverance?

The fact, if it be a fact, that we bring with us to all experience an expectation that events will be found to conform to some regular order—so that we are dissatisfied and ill at ease until we can discover its existence—if it is not conclusive evidence that such an order exists, certainly points to the probability that it does, and that it is of a character such as might emanate from a mind that is not unlike our own.

If the belief that this is the case has its beginnings in the very constitution of our nature, it plainly must gain in strength as we proceed to trace out the resemblance between the order of nature and that which appears in society. When once this resemblance has been suggested, it would seem to be impossible to banish altogether the notion of authority from our thoughts of the signification of law; and indeed we cannot point to any time at which any considerable number of men have conceived of the universe as subject to law in any other sense. We are assured that this was "the original sense of the word law, namely, the expression of the will of a superior[1]."

So far, then, we may confidently claim that nothing has entered into the meaning of law which could make it in the least degree unnatural to regard law as the outcome of mind and the expression of personal will. Nay more, it is allowed that, for the vast majority of those who have entertained it, the thought of law has carried with it, avowedly or tacitly, the thought of a lawgiver.

Has the case been altered by any modification which the idea of law has undergone through the influence of modern

---

[1] J. S. Mill, *ut supra*.

VII] Prayer, and the Idea of Law 275

science? It is often popularly supposed that it has. This has been largely the result of a loose and unguarded manner of speaking. We very commonly hear the expressions "governed by law," and "reign of law." Such expressions, vivid and picturesque as they are, cannot be defended when accurate thinking is in question. They may become seriously misleading. Years ago Dr W. B. Carpenter challenged the propriety of the first of them, and urged that what was intended would be more satisfactorily conveyed by saying, "governed according to law." Law is not an entity in itself, nor is it a force which we have any right to invest with the attributes of personality. It is simply a principle of arrangement, a method of procedure. "Law," said Professor Huxley, "means a rule which we have always found to hold good, and which we expect always will hold good[1]." Law of itself can have no governing power. At the most its existence can suggest, or imply, a personality behind it. But does it really do this, when it is interpreted in the sense in which we moderns have come to think of it in connexion with natural phenomena?

Certainly many of those who have done most to make "law" the watchword of scientific progress have never concealed their desire to rid the idea of personal associations of every kind. Such associations they have regarded as tending to disturb the mathematical exactness of their calculations. They have aimed at eliminating from their minds everything like anthropomorphic bias, and at reaching a standpoint as far removed as possible from human limitations. For most of us these endeavours seem like the attempts of a man to detach himself from his own shadow; and it is, of course, to be remembered that, when such thinkers present us with their conclusions, they are still *their* conclusions in spite of all their efforts to depersonalise them.

Let us try, however, to understand what does become of the idea of law when it has been subjected to the process. To state the result shortly, we are left with a notion of invariable sequence. Law so presented is pallid and ab-

[1] *Collected Essays*, vol. I. p. 193.

stract enough, and very far removed from contact with any characteristically human interest. But then the idea has become so unsubstantial that we are unable to rest upon it. Our minds are simply incapable of contenting themselves with so bare a substitute for an explanation. And things are not bettered when invariable sequence is defined to be inevitable connexion of antecedents and consequents. We are compelled to ask "Why inevitable?" and "How connected?" Sooner or later we must arrive at Mr Mill's proposition :— "The inevitable antecedent is termed the Cause; the invariable consequent, the Effect." And then we are obliged to ask what is involved in causation? And from causation we are sent back to that which alone can make it intelligible, to our own constitution. Without a doubt we derived our idea of causation from our own constitution and its experiences. Mr Mill quite frankly admits it. "The succession," he says, "to move a limb and the actual motion is one of the most direct and instantaneous of all sequences which can come under our observation." "Accordingly, our voluntary acts, being the most familiar to us of all cases of causation, are, in the infancy and early youth of the human race, spontaneously taken as the types of causation in general, and all phenomena are supposed to be directly produced by the will of some sentient being[1]."

Mr Mill is content to dismiss this tendency as nothing more than "original Fetichism"; but, when we seek to discover what wiser account our modern science can give of causation, we are merely informed that there are "efficient" causes and "physical" causes, and that science as such has only to do with the latter, and cannot be concerned about "a cause that is not itself a phenomenon." "Of the efficient causes of phenomena," he says, "or whether any such causes exist at all, I am not called upon to give an opinion[2]."

It would appear, therefore, that we must either penetrate behind the processes of nature until we arrive at the hypothesis of a Will which could originate and direct them—a

[1] *Logic*, III. 5, 11.   [2] *Logic*, III. 5, 2.

Will which is the motive force of Causation, which in its turn must be presupposed if we are to give any intelligible account of the ordered sequences that betoken the presence of law; or we must try to be satisfied with the assurance of those who tell us that this, the natural explanation, has to be set aside for no explanation at all.

If the attempt to arrive at the genesis of causation leads us inevitably back to a point at which we find it natural to predicate the influence of Will; so also we may say, with an equal certainty, that the consideration of orderly arrangement in the world leaves us face to face with the possibility, and more than possibility, that such order is an outcome of the action of Mind.

What is plain is, that, neither the idea of Law which we may be supposed to bring with us as a necessary condition of experience, nor the idea which we have gained from our observation of civil government, nor yet the modified conception which is now accepted by scientific thinkers, is in the least degree irreconcilable with the belief that there lies behind Law the mind and will of a Lawgiver. What may fairly be said to be doubtful is whether any idea of law can be rationally entertained which does not lead us eventually to this belief.

But, suppose it to be granted that the idea of Law is by no means irreconcilable with the faith that there is a great Ruler of the universe; what is to be said in regard to the second postulate of Prayer, that He is to be thought of as ready to direct, and if need be to alter, the course of events in response to our petitions?

It is against this most persistent affirmation of the religious consciousness that the most determined attacks have been directed, both from the moral and from the intellectual side.

The moral objection has made much of the fact of our relative unimportance in the universe. That beings so petty, so ill-informed, so incapable of judging, should presume to dictate, or even suggest, to the Supreme Wisdom what course should be adopted or avoided, has been denounced as the very height of irreverence and presumption.

We have to deal with this objection only in so far as it can be said to affect our view of what may, or may not, be rightly considered possible and suitable in a realm that is subject to law. And perhaps it may be enough to submit that a careful consideration of the history of the relations between a ruler and his subjects has made it more and more apparent that despotism, however it may simplify those relations in some respects, is never again likely to be regarded as the ideal goal towards which a true progress tends. Government in accordance with law has been recognised as the right way of escape from the narrowing and degrading effects of personal tyranny—not the less tyranny, and scarcely less disastrous, when exercised by the best of men, and from the best of motives. We have gradually learned to realise that the highest administration of government is that in which the central authority is most accessible to the needs of the lowest of the governed, most ready to grant liberty for the expression of opinion, and most prepared to move, slowly if need be, by means of the cooperation of the greatest number towards the attainment of the common good.

Must we not admit, then, that it is possible that, under the government of the Supreme Ruler, there may be room made for such freedom as will grant even to the humblest the right to a hearing; and will permit of the education of human minds and wills by allowing, and even enjoining, the exercise of a considerable degree of responsibility in regard to thought and action? Must it of necessity be presumptuous to imagine that there should be this freedom, and that it may be a duty to use it?

Can we dare, then, to say that the idea of Law is irreconcilable with the belief, for which we have the highest spiritual authority, that we may without irreverence carry our desires to the Ruler of all, and feel assured that it is His wish that we should do so? Such a belief will certainly never seem impossible so long, at all events, as we continue to think of Law in its larger and "original sense."

But how does the matter stand when we pass on to consider it in the light of the strictly scientific, and exclusively intellectual, conception of the meaning of Law? Here the problem is removed from the ambiguities and uncertainties that are more or less inevitable in a moral discussion. Here it becomes a question, not of proprieties, but of possibilities. Law, in its scientific sense, is held to be immutable. Any suggestion of interference with its operations must therefore, it is supposed, raise formidable difficulties for the scientific mind. In particular, any thought of interference with the undeviating regularity of the physical order has been declared to be wholly inconsistent with what has been ascertained to be the nature and working of natural law.

It was in order to direct attention to these difficulties that Professor Tyndall and an anonymous writer, afterwards acknowledged to be Sir Henry Thompson, opened a famous attack upon the traditional doctrine of Prayer rather more than thirty years ago. A good deal has happened since then, and the ground taken by the objectors, and by those who replied to them, is not in all respects that which would be occupied by either side at the present day. Nevertheless this discussion is still full of significance, and should not be overlooked by any who are anxious to follow the modern mind in its dealings with the issues involved. It is to our advantage that we can view the controversy from a distance, for thus we are helped to observe impartially, and should be able to distinguish what was of permanent interest in it.

The attitude of the critics was by no means disrespectful. There was no refusal to allow that any efficacy belonged to prayer. On the contrary, there was an evident wish to concede as much as possible. "The value of prayer to the Deity," said the anonymous writer, "has been recognised in all ages and by all nations[1]."

"It is not my habit," wrote Professor Tyndall, "to think otherwise than solemnly of the feeling which prompts prayer. It is a potency which I should like to see guided, not extinguished, devoted to practical objects instead of wasted

[1] *Contemporary Review*, June, 1872, vol. xx. p. 206.

upon air. In some form or other, not yet evident, it may, as alleged, be necessary to man's highest culture. Certain it is that, while I rank many persons who resort to prayer low in the scale of being—natural foolishness, bigotry, and intolerance being in their case intensified by the notion that they have access to the ear of God—I regard others who employ it as forming part of the very cream of the earth[1]."

The position adopted was that, while important effects might conceivably be produced by prayer in the region of inward disposition and moral character—these effects were described with great clearness and fulness by a subsequent contributor—it was to be strenuously denied that prayer could exercise any direct and immediate influence upon the external course of things. "No good," Professor Tyndall said, "can come of giving it a delusive value by claiming for it a power in physical nature."

In fact it was roundly asserted that it needed only a little more of the intelligence and knowledge, which now prevent most people from praying for certain physical changes, to prevent them from praying for any. "No one," it was maintained, "even slightly acquainted with scientific methods and results, can for a moment brook the idea of any interference with the laws of external nature produced by human prayer[2]."

The replies called forth by this challenge were well-nigh innumerable. Some of them appeared immediately in the pages of the periodical which gave publicity to the attack: others of a more weighty description followed in the shape of pamphlets, and volumes of lectures and essays.

Naturally a great deal was made of the theoretical consequences which flow from the concession to prayer of an influence in the spiritual sphere; and it was often assumed, rashly as we shall see, that those who made it might be credited with the opinion that this sphere is outside the operation of law.

Naturally also, the practical value of the concession was asserted for all it was worth: and, certainly, if Mr Knight's

[1] *C. R.* Oct. 1872, vol. xx. p. 766. [2] Rev. W. Knight, *C. R.* Jan. 1873.

interpretation might be pressed to its logical conclusions, there are few results for which men are accustomed to pray that might not be looked for as the indirect effects of spiritual influence. "We pray," he wrote, "for a friend's life that seems endangered. Such prayers can never be an influential element in arresting the physical cause of disease by an iota. But it may bring a fresh suggestion to the mind of a physician, or other attendant, to adopt a remedy which, by natural means, 'turns the tide' of ebbing life, and determines the recovery of the patient." "The latent power that lies within the free causality of man may be stimulated and put in motion from a point beyond the chain of physical sequence; and crises innumerable may be averted through human prayer[1]." Obviously, a great deal has been granted when so much is allowed.

But the point of real importance was not the concession, however inconsistent or significant it might be shown to be. The concession was made with varying degrees of assurance and hesitancy by the different writers[2]. Where all were agreed was, in confidently asserting that a belief that prayer could effect any direct change in the physical order was absolutely irreconcilable with the scientific idea of the nature and operation of law.

When we set about to discover the precise grounds on which this confident assertion was based, we find that the reasons given were two—one of a philosophical, the other of a practical character. The philosophical objection implied a definite doctrine of cause and effect; while the practical objection amounted to an attempted *reductio ad absurdum* of the opposite view. It will be necessary to examine both these objections with some care.

[1] *C. R.* vol. XXI. p. 196.
[2] To what lengths Professor Knight was prepared to go may be gathered from the following extraordinary statement. "In the region of the spiritual there is conscious disorder, moral chaos, which is at once an evidence of the need, and a vindication of the reasonableness, of an interference with it. Since, then, it *can* be altered for the better (which physical nature cannot)... why should men not petition for that help?" (*C. R.* vol. XX. p. 192.)

The philosophical objection was stated with commendable clearness. "A spiritual antecedent," it was said, "will not produce a physical consequent." The actual words were those of Mr Knight, but there is abundant evidence to show that in using them he but succinctly expressed the thoughts of those whom he was explaining and supporting. Indeed it was this doctrine that pervaded and gave consistency to the entire argument. Prayer could be allowed to produce effects in the spiritual order, for there a spiritual cause would be followed by a spiritual effect: but when this condition was not fulfilled, the thought of an "intrusion of supernatural power" was not to be tolerated. Accordingly prayer was declared to be "a power altogether removed from the sphere of physical causation."

It will be noted that there was no denial of the existence and efficacy of spiritual causes themselves ; the assertion was that a scientific idea of law required that their action should be restricted to their own proper sphere.

There are several observations to be made upon the doctrine which was thus proposed for acceptance. The first is suggested by what has been already said in this Essay as to the modern definition of law.

Accepting Mr Mill's careful account of the matter, we said that law, in its strictly scientific sense, is the principle according to which a particular consequent is connected invariably with some particular antecedent, or set of antecedents. Now the first thing that strikes us, when we read the arguments of those who promoted the controversy to which we have referred, is that they would oblige us, if we accepted their guidance, to make a radical alteration in this definition of law.

To say that law requires an invariable connexion between a consequent and the antecedent, or antecedents which produce it, is one thing. To say that these antecedents and consequents are to be divided into two separate classes, so distinct in their nature that an antecedent belonging to one could not possibly have a consequent belonging to the other, is a very different matter. Something more than a mere assertion is needed to persuade us that such an alteration is legitimate.

In the next place we may observe that this doctrine would inevitably land us in a condition of dualism naked and unrelieved. That dualism is to be the last word of our philosophy of the universe, is a conclusion which the human intellect is as yet by no means generally inclined to accept. Since the cruder attempts to state the whole problem of existence in terms of matter alone have been repudiated and abandoned, the choice has appeared to lie between two alternatives. Either there must be a bold advance to an avowedly spiritualistic interpretation, and towards this many of our acutest students are being led, if only because they are becoming convinced that "mind, though perhaps neither completely known nor completely knowable, turns out less of a fiction than matter[1]"; or, failing that—it may be, pending that—a halting-place must be found in a theory of monism which would resolve both mind and matter into a single something, not exactly like, and yet not essentially different from, either.

For ordinary purposes we shall continue to think and speak of the spiritual and the physical; but we shall not easily be induced to rely upon any reasoning which requires us to suppose that they stand for two spheres so sharply divided that no sort of causal connexion is possible between them.

Moreover, the doctrine that "a spiritual antecedent will not produce a physical consequent," can be brought to a most simple and convincing test. As the Duke of Argyll said at the time, "this proposition we know to be untrue in the case of an organism." The "theory of a fundamental separation between the physical and the spiritual is a theory entirely unsupported by any evidence in observation or in consciousness[2]."

No reasoning will persuade us that, in the case of our own bodies, mind does not somehow direct the movements of

[1] J. Ward, *Gifford Lectures*, II. p. 211.
[2] *C. R.* XXI. pp. 466, 471.

matter. To quote again the words of Mr Mill, "the succession to move a limb and the actual motion is one of the most direct and instantaneous of all sequences which can come under our observation." To the plain man it seems inconceivable that any question should have been raised as to whether or not such a relation between thought and act is a genuine relation of cause and effect. And, if he has the patience to read through a discussion of the subject, he is only bewildered by it, and may be pardoned if he comes to the conclusion that those who would instruct him are even more confused than himself. He opens, let us say, a volume by Professor Tyndall, and reads the "Apology" for the famous Belfast Address. He sees this question propounded:—"Do states of consciousness enter as links into the chain of antecedence and sequence which gives rise to bodily actions, and to other states of consciousness; or are they mere *by-products* which are not essential to the physical processes going on in the brain?" That is intelligibly asked, and what is the answer? "Speaking for myself, it is certain that I have no power of imagining states of consciousness interposed between the molecules of the brain, and influencing the transference of motion among the molecules. The thought 'eludes all mental presentation'; and hence the logic seems of iron strength which claims for the brain an automatic action, uninfluenced by states of consciousness"—a truly remarkable deduction, and scarcely "of iron strength," to make from a simple confession of ignorance! The Professor proceeds: "But it is, I believe, admitted, by those who hold the automaton theory, that states of consciousness are *produced*[1] by the marshalling of the molecules of the brain: and the production of consciousness by molecular action is to me quite as inconceivable on mechanical principles as the production of molecular action by consciousness. If therefore I reject one result, I must reject them both." There, indeed, we seem to have arrived at a sound logical result; but what do we read? "I,

---

[1] The italics, here and above, are Professor Tyndall's own.

however, reject neither, and thus stand in the presence of two Incomprehensibles, instead of one Incomprehensible."

Does that mean that he is going to withdraw his previous inference? Not at all! "While accepting fearlessly the facts of materialism dwelt upon in these pages, I bow my head in the dust before that mystery of mind which has hitherto defied its own penetrative power, and which may ultimately resolve itself into a demonstrable impossibility of self-penetration[1]." This may be magnificent, but it is not argument. All we can gather from such a statement is that interchanges of influence between mind and matter are inexplicable; but that the influence of mind over matter is not a whit more inexplicable than the influence, the admitted influence, of matter over mind.

Since Professor Tyndall wrote, elaborate pains have been expended upon an attempt to demonstrate that the relation between spirit and matter is most correctly expressed by saying that a state, or condition, of either is not the product, but only the concomitant, of the other. This is the doctrine of psychophysical parallelism. But, when all has been said and done, it seems impossible to avoid the somewhat obvious conclusion that, "invariable concomitance means causal connexion somewhere[2]."

From all which it may be confidently deduced that the philosophical doctrine of the writers in 1872 would meet with less acceptance to-day than it did when it was first enunciated.

III.

But the objectors did not rely only upon their doctrine of the relations between the spiritual and the physical. They advanced another line of argument, less subtle, and more practical in its character. Apart altogether from the question as to the possibility of an influence of spirit upon matter, it seemed to them that the least interference, however effected, with the physical order necessarily involved the

---
[1] *Fragments of Science*, p. 222.   [2] Ward, *Gifford Lectures*, II. p. 93.

violation of physical law; and this, if it were not in itself an impossibility, would inevitably be followed by the most widespread confusion. No one part of the fixed order of nature, they were convinced, could be interfered with, without upsetting the balance of the whole.

"The Italian wind," wrote Professor Tyndall, "gliding over the crest of the Matterhorn, is as firmly ruled as the earth in its orbital revolution round the sun." "The dispersion of the slightest mist by the special volition of the Eternal would be as much a miracle as the rolling of the Rhone over the Grimsel precipices down the valley of Hasli to Meyringen and Brientz." "Without the disturbance of a natural law, quite as serious as the stoppage of an eclipse, or the rolling of the river Niagara up the Falls, no act of humiliation, individual or national, could call one shower from heaven, or deflect towards us a single beam of the sun[1]."

The objection thus raised has a formidable appearance, but again it will be found upon consideration that it is by no means unanswerable.

It has to be remembered that we are all of us perpetually interfering—no weaker word can be substituted—with the physical order about us. "What is it that most distinguishes human intelligence in its relation to Natural Law? Most assuredly its utilising ability—its power to direct the natural forces to the accomplishment of special ends...The mind of man, considered thus as a natural cause, is certainly of all single natural causes the most influential: not, of course, in respect of the magnitude of its effects, but in respect of their number and diversity[2]."

It may be worth while to add a similar statement made by Professor Huxley in one of his latest essays; and the more so because he did not scruple to use the very term "interference." "The history of civilisation," he wrote, "details the steps by which men have succeeded in building up an

---

[1] "Prayer and Natural Law" (in *Fragments of Science*). These often quoted words were written before the *Contemporary* controversy, but they well express the thought of those who initiated it.

[2] G. J. Romanes, *Christian Prayer and General Laws* (1872), pp. 161 f.

artificial world within the cosmos...As civilisation has advanced, so has the extent of this interference increased; until the organized and highly developed sciences and arts of the present day have endowed man with a command over the course of non-human nature greater than that once attributed to the magicians[1]."

As a matter of fact, then, we can and do interfere with the forces of nature: and by our interference we achieve results that, before experience, might have seemed improbable enough. As Sir Oliver Lodge has put it, with direct reference to the passages from Tyndall quoted above, "We ourselves are readily able, by a simple physical experiment, or by an engineering operation, to deflect a ray of light, or to dissipate a mist, or divert a wind, or pump water uphill[2]."

What we can do, with our limited knowledge and power, could, we must suppose, be done on a much vaster scale by one who was vastly our superior in these respects. Indeed it would be the height of rashness to attempt to set any bounds to what would be possible in such a case.

Nor is there any reason for thinking that such interferences occasion a violation of law. There would be less chance of misunderstanding on this point if the distinctions laid down by Mr Mill were more constantly borne in mind. We have already referred to these. When speaking of the invariable sequence which constitutes any single uniformity, or law, he is careful to explain that what is meant is that "every consequent is connected with some particular antecedent, or set of antecedents." He adds, "It is seldom, if ever, between a consequent and a single antecedent that this invariable sequence subsists. It is usually between a consequent and the sum of several antecedents; the concurrence of all being requisite to produce, that is, to be certain of being followed by, the consequent." "The uniformity of the course of nature is...a complex fact, compounded of all the

---

[1] "Evolution and Ethics," *Collected Essays*, IX. pp. 83 f.
[2] *Hibbert Journal*, Oct. 1902.

separate uniformities which exist in respect to single phenomena[1]."

It follows that a change in one of the antecedents, be it never so slight, will produce a change of result, and that, not in violation of the principle of Law, but in the strictest accordance with it. When, therefore, we interfere with the course of nature, we do not violate any physical law. The violation, or even suspension, of a law of nature is, so far as we know, a thing beyond our power. What we plainly can do is to utilise existing and ever-acting laws. If they were not inviolable we could do nothing with them. "It is the very certainty and invariableness of the laws of Nature which alone enables us to use them and yoke them to our service[2]."

If, then, we are convinced that we are able to interfere,

---

[1] *Logic*, III. v. 3. Compare the Duke of Argyll's words:—"There is another fact quite as prominent as the universal presence and prevalence of laws—and that is the number of them that are concerned in each single operation of Nature. No one Law—that is to say, no one Force—determines anything that we see happening or done around us. It is always the result of different and opposing Forces nicely balanced against each other. The least disturbance of the proportion in which any one of them is allowed to tell, produces a total change in the effect." "There are no phenomena visible to Man of which it is true to say that they are governed by any invariable Force. That which does govern them is always some variable combinations of invariable forces." "In these senses...Law is not rigid, it is not immutable, it is not invariable, but it is, on the contrary, pliable, subtle, various." "It cannot be too often repeated that phenomena are not governed by Invariable Laws; because phenomena are never the result of individual Forces, but are always the result of the conditions under which several forces are combined, and these conditions are variable." (*Reign of Law*, People's Edition, pp. 76, 98, 318.)

[2] *Reign of Law*, p. 99. It does not seem necessary to introduce here any discussion of the bearing of the doctrine of the "Conservation of Energy" upon the question of interference with the physical order. "It is plainly impossible," as Dr Ward has said (*Gifford Lectures*, II. p. 76), "to prove that the phenomenal energy in the universe is fixed in amount. And this the physicists themselves are beginning to see more clearly, and frankly to admit." And, even if it could be proved that the existing amount of physical force is incapable of being increased, this would not affect the fact that it is capable of being directed with infinitely varied effects.

in proportion to our knowledge of the laws of nature, and in conformity with the principle elucidated by the father of modern science—"non nisi parendo vincitur[1]"; if, without the infraction of any law, nay in reliance upon the invariability of all laws, we can manipulate and make use of the forces around us; if, in short, *we* have the power of doing much that we wish, or that others may ask us, to do: it is manifestly impossible to conceive that the acceptance of the universality of Law can be any barrier to a belief that physical changes may be made in answer to Prayer.

But attention to Mr Mill's caution as to the number of antecedents which may be needed to produce effects, would help us also to detect a fallacy in any comparison that would represent the smallest physical change as an undertaking wholly on a par with the "stoppage of an eclipse," or the rolling of a world from its orbit.

It is interesting to find Mr Mill himself writing as follows: "The causes or forces, on which astronomical phenomena depend, are fewer in number than those which determine any other of the great phenomena of nature. Accordingly, as each effect results from the conflict of but few causes, a great degree of regularity and uniformity might be expected to exist among the effects: and such is really the case: they have a fixed order, and return in cycles[2]."

If it were really true that to ask for any modification of the course of events, such as the relief of a sickness, or a change in the weather, must be regarded as in all respects as serious as to expect that the stars should be stopped in their courses, then we might well pause before venturing upon such a petition, and might be constrained to admit that any alteration of a physical character in answer to prayer was, to say the least of it, highly improbable.

There are physical changes which, so far as we can judge, would be more momentous in their nature and effect than others. For these we should rightly be slow to pray, because we should realise that, although they might not be impossible in themselves, yet the reasons that could make them advisable

[1] *Nov. Org.* I. 3.   [2] *Logic*, VI. 2.

and suitable would need to be more imperative than any which it is in our power to urge. We may allow, therefore, that there was some measure of truth in the conclusion drawn by the anonymous writer of 1872:—"It plainly follows that what a man will pray for depends precisely on the extent of his intelligent acquaintance with the phenomena around and within him." But we are not bound to agree with him when he goes on to add:—"the more ignorant he is of them, and of their modes of recurrence, the larger his field for petition; the more intelligent, the smaller must be his range[1]."

It is true that a fuller insight might in some cases show that a change ought not to be asked for, and perhaps ought not to be made; but, on the other hand, it might very well happen that instances would present themselves in which a more perfect understanding of phenomena, and "their modes of recurrence," would lead to a different conclusion. A deeper knowledge might diminish, rather than intensify, the feeling of difficulty in regard to them.

The position was admirably defined, in the very year of the controversy, by a preacher who was not then so well known as he afterwards became. Speaking of the different attitudes to be adopted in dealing with different cases he said:

"We recognise, without murmuring, that gravitation is a principle for the maintenance of the universe which God has made. We have no wish to change it, and therefore do not pray that it may be changed. In consequence of our recognition of this fact, we are sometimes told by those who investigate the laws of nature that it is useless to pray for the sick, because their condition depends on natural laws which cannot be altered. Are all diseases the same? Does every sick man die within a certain time as surely as a stone thrown in the air falls down again within a certain time? If it were so, we would not pray for the sick;......we should no more pray for them than we should pray that the sun might set.......Our prayers proceed from our desires, our desires from

[1] C. R. xx. p. 776.

VII] *Prayer, and the Idea of Law* 291

the uncertainty of the event; if the uncertainty were to disappear so would the desire; men who would not hesitate to say in a private talk, 'I hope my friend may recover,' need not hesitate to say, 'O Lord, look down from Heaven, behold, visit, and relieve this Thy servant[1].'"

The instance of prayer for a change of weather has often been singled out for special emphasis by those who have thought that it supplied a typical illustration of the difficulty of interfering with nature without thereby violating natural law. It may therefore be useful to give the carefully considered opinion of one who was preeminently qualified to form a judgement on this subject.

Sir George Stokes goes very fully into the question in his *Gifford Lectures* (1891). "Is it lawful, or possible," he asks, "to pray for fine weather, with a view, suppose, to a plentiful harvest? Those who are disposed to give a negative answer to this question might urge such considerations as the following :—The weather is determined by solar radiation taken in conjunction with the warming of the earth's surface by the absorption of radiant heat, the emission of heat by warmed bodies, evaporation, the precipitation of vapour in the form of cloud, rain, etc., and the rotation of the earth, which besides causing the alternations of day and night, with the corresponding thermal changes, has, for dynamical reasons, such a powerful influence in causing the winds. All these are carried on in accordance with perfectly definite physical laws, as regular as those which determine the places of the planets in their orbits, places which, from our knowledge of the laws, can be calculated years beforehand.......

"But does our physical knowledge authorise us in saying that the course of the weather is as much fixed as that of the planets in their orbits? I doubt it. There is much tending

[1] From a sermon on Prayer, preached by Mandell Creighton in 1872. *University and other Sermons*, pp. 43 f. Something more will be said, before this Essay concludes, as to the limitations which reverence and intelligence may rightly suggest in the case of petitions for both spiritual and physical changes.

to show that the state of the atmosphere depends a good deal upon a condition of unstable equilibrium...Now the character of unstable equilibrium is, that it is a condition in which the very slightest disturbing cause will suffice to start a movement which goes on accumulating till it produces a complete alteration of position. It is perfectly conceivable that a child, by lighting a bonfire, might produce an ascending current of air which in particular cases might suffice to initiate a movement which went on accumulating till it caused the condition of the atmosphere to be widely different from what it would have been had the child not acted as I have supposed. It is not, therefore, by any means certain that the condition of the weather is solely determined by physical conditions the effect of which could even conceivably be calculated beforehand. Hence it is conceivable that a change in the future of the weather might be made without any interference with the physical laws actually in operation[1]."

Once more, then, we seem to be justified in saying that the assertion that prayer cannot be answered where physical changes would be involved, because any physical interference must necessitate the violation of law, is an assertion which cannot be sustained. We ourselves are able to produce physical changes, most astonishing changes, by an act of volition and the employment of appropriate means, without contravening, so far as we can tell, any existing law ; nay, rather, by the help of existing laws. And we do it, evidently, without upsetting the balance of nature. What we can do on a small scale could most certainly be done on a much larger scale by a mind and will wiser and more resourceful than our own.

But there is yet another ground upon which an intellectual

[1] pp. 217 foll. Arago, many years ago, when discussing the question as to how far it was likely that science would ever be able to predict the weather with certainty, gave it as his opinion that it was in the highest degree improbable that this could be done, because, among other reasons, the weather is in part the result of man's actions. (So J. H. Jellett, *Donellan Lectures*, 1877, who refers to the *Annuaire* for 1846, p. 590.)

Prayer, and the Idea of Law

objection to the efficacy of prayer has been rested. It is the ground that has been taken from very early times by those who have denied to mankind any freedom, or power, of volition whatsoever. Their reasonings have varied greatly. Some have argued that the universe is ruled by a blind and inexorable fate; some that it is under the sway of a Divine sovereignty which, if more favourable in its character, is not less absolute in its methods. In our own time the determinist objector has usually declined to express any view as to what is, or is not, behind the order of phenomena, though his persistent use of that term might seem to commit him to the view that there is something behind. He has been contented to maintain that this order is a vast unalterable mechanism in which all the constituent forces, human volitions included, play their inevitable parts. For him every event that happens is the result of the working of laws, and of law, whose action might have been predicted beforehand. No room therefore is left for contingency, or change, of any kind.

This form of objection has been recently revived with considerable vigour in the course of a popular discussion. We can scarcely think, however, that it is more likely to find permanent acceptance than those others which we have considered.

The mechanical theory of nature has been subjected to most searching criticism from more than one quarter, and is allowed to have been seriously discredited. Apart from such critical investigation from the side of metaphysics and physical science, the necessitarian doctrine is not such as can ever commend itself to the judgement of thoughtful and practical men. It is too directly opposed to the verdict of consciousness, and to the moral sense.

We are fully aware that our actions are actuated by motives which are prior to them: and we can easily conceive that these motives may be accounted for by reference to yet earlier acts and conditions. But we can never dispossess ourselves of the conviction that we, and others, have at the least the power of selecting and emphasising, and so of rendering effective, a particular motive. And we are convinced that, by virtue of this power, we incur a responsibility for our actions which is irreconcilable with the notion that we are merely the parts of a machine. As a matter of fact, we can only continue to act, or get others to continue to act, while we dismiss from our minds the paralysing thought that we may be mere creatures of fate.

But, even suppose it could be proved that we are integral parts of an all-embracing and all-sufficing Nature, of a fixed order of things that goes, as we say, by clockwork; and that our imagined interferences are not in any true sense interferences at all, but only the necessary links in an iron chain of unalterable cause and effect—being merely the results of conditions depending upon other precedent conditions over which we can have no conceivable control—so that what happens through our instrumentality could not possibly have happened otherwise: even suppose this made out, are we therefore shut up to the conclusion that prayer is useless and absurd?

Certainly not, unless we are also to conclude that all the efforts we make, and all the wishes we entertain, are also useless and absurd. These are rescued from absurdity, in the view of the determinist, because they fulfil their functions, and are indispensable to the evolution of the assumed inevitable sequence; they are necessary contributions to the predetermined progress of the whole. Why, then, not say the same of our prayers?

Professor Huxley's words about necessity have often been quoted. "It does not lie," he said, "in the observed facts and has no warranty that I can discover elsewhere. For my part I utterly repudiate and anathematise the intruder. Fact I know, and Law I know; but what is this Necessity save an empty shadow of my mind's own throwing[1]?"

But in any case, whatever may be the strength or weakness of the theoretical arguments, the most resolute theorist is driven to admit that Bishop Butler was right when he insisted that "the opinion of necessity considered as practical

[1] *Collected Essays*, I. p. 245.

is false[1]." In the words of Kant, "Even though the speculative proof [of freedom] should not be made out, yet a being that cannot act except with the idea of freedom is bound by the same laws that would oblige a being who was actually free[2]."

In actual life, then, we are driven either to abandon the doctrine of necessity altogether, or so to interpret it that it shall find place and room for our volitions, by conceding that they too are a necessary element among the determining causes of conduct. If we introduce the notion of necessity or fate, we must apply it to all the parts of the problem. When we do so we can only conclude, with Mr Romanes in his early essay, that "if Prayer for physical benefits is ever answered (as we believe to be the case), the prayer and the answer must have been foreordained to coincide[3]."

Let our conception of nature be as rigid as it may, at the least we have to admit that prayers, since they are made, have their place in the economy of things. We might, indeed, quite reasonably go further than this, and claim that, on the principles of necessitarianism, it is impossible that there should be any ineffective prayers. Since every act has to be followed by its consequence, it would appear that prayer not only may, but must avail; possibly not precisely as the petitioner wished, though in that case it might not be easy to explain why the practice of praying for definite objects should have been continued as it has been.

We can only say, therefore, that the objection to Prayer, arising from a conception of nature as a vast mechanism in which we fulfil our inevitable parts, is not more securely based than the other objections which we have already considered.

---

[1] *Analogy*, I. 6.
[2] *Fundamental Principles of the Metaphysic of Morals*, p. 80, ed. Rosenkranz: see J. H. Bernard, *Butler's Works*, vol. II. p. 108, *note*.
[3] *Christian Prayer and General Laws*, p. 217.

IV.

So far, then, we have been occupied with difficulties that have been raised, from the moral and intellectual standpoints, and have been thought to militate against the belief that the human soul is free to pour forth its petitions to a Supreme Ruler in the confident hope that those petitions will be heard and answered.

We have endeavoured to show that this belief is not inconsistent with a belief—for such it rightly is—in the general uniformity of nature; whether we derive our conception of that uniformity from the constitution of our own minds, or from the social order, or from the observed sequences of physical phenomena. We can find nothing in the idea of Law that would forbid the conclusion that Law is the expression of mind and will. Indeed the more we think about it, the less possible it seems that any clear idea of Law can be entertained at all if Law is to be entirely dissociated from the thought of a Lawgiver.

Then, next, we entered upon an examination of the objections that, even granted the existence of a supreme Lawgiver, it must ill become such creatures as we are to make suggestions to Him; and that the operation of law must render interference with the established order impossible, at all events in the physical sphere.

We need not recall the details of our examination further than to say that the analogy of civil government encouraged us to suppose that the highest administration may rightly provide for such a cooperation on the part of the governed as would allow for the full expression of their thoughts and desires: and that a careful analysis of the scientific definition of law failed to furnish the reasons that would warrant our maintaining that spiritual causes are incapable of producing physical effects; or that physical changes must necessarily involve the violation of law, with endless consequences of confusion.

Passing on to the objection put forward from the side of determinism, it was a comparatively simple task to show that the most rigidly mechanical view of the world has to find a place and a value for all our efforts, and therefore for our prayers as much as the rest. Since these also contribute to the predetermined result, they not only may be, but must be, availing.

The difficulties of which we have been thinking are such as have chiefly attracted attention in the past. For the most part, no doubt, it is wise to confine what is said about difficulties to those which have been actually felt and definitely formulated. It is safest, as well as easiest, to write of what has been : whilst it must always be hazardous to forecast and describe the thoughts of the just opening future. In one particular direction, however, it is becoming clear that the discussion as to prayer will be provided with a new problem, and, consequently, there would seem to be some good reason for stating that problem, and for making a few suggestions in regard to it. The problem is to be forced upon us by the advent of the psychologist, with his fresh information as to the action and influence of mind. Those who have followed the lines along which psychological inquiry has of late been moving are aware that there are indications which point to the necessity of reconsidering much that has been hitherto accepted in regard to the nature of personality, and the limits within which its influence can be exerted. We are told that we must no longer think of personality as the bounded and isolated thing we had taken it to be: nor may we continue to suppose that its area, so to speak, is co-extensive merely with our consciousness. Each of us, it would appear, is capable, in his degree, of making his presence felt beyond the bounds of his body. Mind acts upon mind, overleaping the barriers of space. There is transference of thought, and communication of suggestion. "The sub-conscious can achieve results the conscious can by no means understand or perform." "We can operate on each others' minds through our physical envelope, by speech, by writing, and in other ways, but we can do more : it appears that we can operate at a distance, by no apparent physical organ or medium ; if by mechanism at all, then by mechanism at any rate unknown to us[1]." "The subjective mind, or entity, possesses physical power; that is, the power to make itself heard and felt, and to move ponderable objects[2]."

But, perhaps, some will be inclined to say, Surely this extension of view will not create a fresh difficulty for those who believe in the power of prayer; but will rather tend to strengthen the conviction that intervention on the part of mind and will is both possible and natural. Does it not look as if the tables were about to be completely turned, and the primacy so commonly claimed for the physical forces would ere long be ascribed to the psychical?

Most decidedly there is truth in this account of the matter, and in time it may be seen that there is little that has to be urged against it on the opposite side. But, nevertheless, we may not shut our eyes to the fact that the advance of mental science, if it puts more completely out of date than ever some of the old arguments, will also stir fresh questionings that may occasion for a while not a little perplexity.

To illustrate what is meant let us take concrete examples. We have already suggested that the hospital-ward test is never likely to be put forward again, because it would not now be disputed that a number of persons might, by steadily concentrating their thoughts and wishes upon a group of sick people, be able to effect a remarkable change in their condition. The difficulty for us would be to distinguish how much of the result could properly be traced to prayer, and how much might be due to the influence of mental suggestion and will power.

So, again, we are all of us familiar with cases in which very extraordinary things are said to have been achieved by the prayers of the founders of certain great philanthropic institutions. They themselves have assured us, with undeniable sincerity, that the necessary funds have been sent to them without fail for years, although they had made it their invariable practice never to appeal, publicly or privately,

[1] Sir O. Lodge, *Hibbert Journal*, Jan. 1903.
[2] T. J. Hudson, *The Law of Psychic Phenomena*, p. 208.

VII]   *Prayer, and the Idea of Law*   299

to any human being for them. Hundreds of thousands of pounds have come solely, as they were persuaded, in answer to prayer. Here, as before, the facts will be freely accepted. The prayers were offered, the money came, and no requests were addressed to those who gave it. But the difficulty will be to know how much can with certainty be assigned to any power that is peculiar to prayer, when all has been subtracted which might conceivably be explained by the telepathic influence exerted by the conscious, or possibly sub-conscious, mental action of these unusually sympathetic men.

In short, the new objection will be founded upon the contention that the influence claimed for prayer, so far from its being incredible in view of what we know of the working of natural law, is to be regarded as merely an instance of a particular part of that working.

It would be premature to attempt a detailed explanation of the bearing upon the problem of Prayer of our knowledge of forces, which are only now for the first time being systematically investigated. The writer of an essay ten years hence will be in a far better position to furnish such an explanation than any one of us can be to-day. Those forces are in all probability greater, and more mysterious, than we have been wont to imagine. For a while the rapidly accumulating evidence of what mind and will can effect may lead in some quarters to an exaggerated estimate of the results that might be attained by a deliberate cultivation of functions and capabilities which have been little understood and very generally disregarded. Until we know much more about the limitations of these powers, we can form no trustworthy conclusions as to how far men's unaided efforts can reach. And then, of course, the more we do become aware of the scope of the influence of individual minds and wills, the more clearly we shall realise also how formidable must be the obstacles to their working which are continually presented by a similar activity on the part of other minds and wills.

The tendency to exaggeration will be met, we may be sure, by correctives enough. The futility of human schemes, and the disappointment of human desires, will supply ample matter for reflection in the future as in the past. "If wishes were horses, beggars might ride." We shall surely not need to have it formally demonstrated to us that there are limits to the power which our wills can exert in the world.

That some new light will be thrown upon the manner in which the spiritual activities of prayer are exercised, we may confidently hope. Already there have been opened fresh glimpses into unsuspected possibilities of fellowship and communication, not only between one human being and another, but between ourselves and the One who is "never so far off as even to be near."

Is it overbold to suggest that in one direction we may see how an advance might be made in the understanding of the service to be fulfilled by prayer? May not the popular estimate of the value of prayer have been in the past too exclusively associated with the sense of human weakness? That a consciousness of weakness has been, and will continue to be, the primary motive compelling men to bow their knees and lift their souls in prayer, no one can question: but because this is the first motive, it does not follow that it is the only motive, or the noblest. Can we not feel that it might be a yet nobler prayer which sprang from the realisation of entrusted power, and from a sense of the responsibility which such power involves?

Above all we shall do well to remember that He, who exercised as no other the mental and spiritual forces into which we are only now beginning to get any intelligent insight, was absolutely confident when He spoke, as He did continually, of the mighty influence of Prayer[1].

We may await the results of the new studies without impatience, and without misgiving.

---

[1] Special interest attaches, in this connexion, to such a saying as that recorded in St Mark ix. 29: "And He said unto them, This kind can come out by nothing, save by prayer."

V.

The purpose of this Essay has not been to prove the reality of the power of Prayer. This has been taken for granted, on the testimony of the invincible instinct of the soul, operating through long ages, among all peoples, and all conditions of men and women, ranging from those who are "low in the scale of being" up to "others who form part of the very cream of the earth." What has been chiefly aimed at has been to show that no reasonable exception can be taken to the right of a free exercise of this power on the ground that such freedom is inconsistent with the idea that we live in a world that is ruled in accordance with quite definite and, in many cases quite well-known laws.

But to assert, and even to vindicate, the claim to this freedom is after all scarcely more than a preparatory service; and the treatment of the relation of Prayer to the idea of law would be seriously incomplete if nothing at all were said with reference to the sort of action required from us in the large field of practical employment upon the borders of which we find ourselves when the obstacles to our entrance have been removed.

It is of the first importance, no doubt, to be assured that the freedom to pray is ours, and that the threatening prohibitions, which have from time to time been issued to forbid it, are in reality unauthorised and invalid, howsoever they may invoke the rigours of Law. But it is not less important that we should ascertain how and in what way the right is to be properly exercised. Liberty is a very different thing from license. In a world which is governed constitutionally—and this after all is what is really meant when we speak of our world as the realm of law—freedom must be used constitutionally. Prayer, in such a world, stands upon the same footing with deeds in this respect. If it is not legitimate to do anything and everything in virtue of the liberty accorded to us, so neither can it be right that we should exercise unconditionally the privilege of appealing to the Supreme

Ruler. If our prayers are to be good prayers, that is to say, acceptable and availing prayers, we must rely not merely upon the emotion that prompts them; we must learn to bring them more and more intelligently into harmony with the conditions which a study of the laws under which He has set us may reveal; we must pray, not "with the spirit" alone, but "with the understanding also."

It may remain a mystery to us that the Divine Disposer should have made our prayers a part, and a needed part, of His administration; but, when we do believe this, we are constrained alike by humility, and by the desire to discharge our function with success—a desire as natural to us in this instance as in any other—to seek for a clear understanding of the principles upon which our requests should be framed.

Without attempting anything like a full consideration of this, which we may describe as the art of prayer, enough may be said here in a few words to indicate the general lines that such a consideration might follow.

It may almost seem to go without saying that truly *constitutional* prayers must, before all else, be loyal prayers. They must have for their keynote the desire for God's honour, and for the advancement of His Kingdom; and for that, moreover, in His own appointed way.

We need constantly to be on our guard against what has been described as the "fanaticism which would like to see the Supreme Good active in some other way than that which it has itself shown, or which believes that Good to be attainable by some shorter path than the roundabout way of formal orderliness which it has itself entered upon[1]."

The conviction will deepen in us that the perfect petition is that which has been expressed in the familiar words, "Thy Will be done." But we shall discover, as indeed we must have already discovered, that it needs all our intelligence, and the utmost self-discipline, to use those words with any full sense of their meaning. It is no more easy to make them

---

[1] Lotze, *Microcosmos*, (E. T.) II. p. 727.

the rule of our prayers than it is to make them the rule of our deeds.

Whilst the knowledge of the Divine purposes must be sought from the higher sources of revelation, both without us and within, we shall realise also, possibly more than we do at present, that a careful attention is due to that source which has been opened to us, as to none who preceded us, through the modern discoveries in nature. "If we look on the order of nature as carried on in accordance with the will of God, then, according as we know more or less of the laws of nature, we may regard it that we know, in a certain department, more or less of His will[1]."

In prayer all such knowledge is power. "This is the confidence that we have in Him, that, if we ask anything according to His will, He heareth us[2]."

It is, then, the first axiom of a true prayer that it shall be offered to secure the accomplishment of Divine ends, by the employment of the Divine methods. All other considerations must be expressly subordinated to these.

It will follow that spiritual desires should occupy a larger and more prominent place in our prayers than requests for material and temporal things: though these also are to be included, as forming an integral part of the great problem of life and its needs.

Then, clearly, constitutional prayers must be unselfish in their character. The strong sense of the all-importance of the commonweal must make it seem unfitting to urge any petition for a purely individual good, for a merely private gain. More and more the words "me" and "my" will drop out to make way for "us" and "our."

And, lastly, so far from there ever being any notion of a wish to substitute any other order for that which the Divine Wisdom is seeking to set forth in the world, it will be increasingly realised that the very *raison d'être* of prayer is the securing the victory of that order in its mysterious conflict with forces which, in ways beyond our comprehension, are

[1] Sir George Stokes, *Gifford Lectures*, I. p. 217.
[2] 1 St John, v. 14.

banded to resist and defeat it. Prayer may exist to make possible the voluntary acceptance of law[1].

When we pray thus constitutionally we are not greatly troubled by questionings as to whether God could, or could not, do this thing or the other, under the conditions which He has imposed upon the universe in which He rules. We believe that, without the breach or suspension of a single law, He is able to effect all that the fulfilment of His purposes can possibly demand. This is what we mean when we address Him as "Almighty."

We shall be careful how we use the word "impossible" in regard to any request that we might conceivably make. We shall bear in mind that "when we are dealing with the works of God, with the whole constitution of nature...it is absolutely impossible...to say what is, or what is not, an impossibility in the nature of things[2]."

At the same time, we shall reverently recognise that He may, and even must, have set limits to His own action in the very act of creation—limits which may be more and more clear to us as we gain a growing insight into the nature of moral and physical laws. Consequently it will often be right to preface our appeals by the words "if it be possible."

We shall investigate God's methods in order that we may gain increasing sympathy with them. Our petitions will be confident in proportion to our assurance that His granting of them will conduce to the progress of the good that He intends. When we ask for peace, for victory, for health, for fine crops, or fair weather, we shall ask what we judge to be expedient in active submission to His higher Wisdom. We shall ask, because we believe that a place has been assigned in His order to the expression and education of our desires. "Our aim in praying is not that we may change God's appointment, but that we may procure by our prayers that which He has appointed" (oratio nostra non

---

[1] It will be noted that this account of the elements of a true prayer is just that which we might arrive at from an analysis of the nature and order of the petitions of "The Lord's Prayer."

[2] Sir G. Stokes, *op. cit.* pp. 27 f.

ordinatur ad immutationem divinae dispositionis, sed ut obtineatur nostris precibus quod Deus disposuit[1]). The more we believe in the power of Prayer, and the more we understand the meaning of Law, the more reverent, and conditional, in a word, the more Christian, will our prayers become. Whilst we claim the freedom to pray, our prayer will be that we may use it lawfully.

To sum up our conclusions in the very simplest terms— we shall rejoice as we realise that we need no longer fear any notice warning us off as trespassers from a field of high activity which the inner voice is prompting us to enter; but we shall not on that account be blind to the fact that there are intimations, not less worthy of attention because gently conveyed, that require us to "*keep to the paths.*"

Additional Note.

It is right that we should remember that the argument from the universal instinct and habit of mankind has been challenged; but we need not fear that its force will be materially weakened. Probably there has been no more uncompromising indictment of it than that which was made by Mr Galton in the *Fortnightly Review* for August 1872. "A *prima facie* argument," he wrote, "in favour of the efficacy of prayer is to be drawn from the very general use of it. The greater part of mankind, during all the historic ages, have been accustomed to pray for temporal advantages....The argument of universality either proves too much, or else it is suicidal. It either compels us to admit that the prayers of Pagans, of Fetish worshippers, and of Buddhists who turn praying-wheels, are recompensed in the same way as those of orthodox believers; or else the general consensus proves that it has no better foundation than the universal tendency of men to gross credulity."

Not a few of Mr Galton's readers must have been considerably astonished at the readiness with which he supposed that they would feel bound to impale themselves upon one or other of the horns of his dilemma. In truth, the dilemma itself breaks down upon examination. Why may we not allow that the evidently earnest and oft-renewed prayers of even the least enlightened human beings should find some justification and encouragement in experience? why not allow that they

[1] Aquinas, *Summa*, II. 2. 83. 2.

may be "recompensed in the same way," and possibly sometimes to the same extent, as our own, while at the same time we concede that the best of us may have more of "credulity" than we have yet of intelligent faith?

For a juster estimate of the value to be attached to the testimony of imperfect religious ideas and practices we may refer to one of the later works of Mr Herbert Spencer (*Principles of Sociology*, §§ 659 f. quoted by Dr Ward). After discussing the development of the "consciousness of the Unknowable from what he maintained were its earliest stages of gross superstition"—so gross as to appear "absolutely false"—he raises the question whether any worth could be allowed to a belief of which such was the history. And he replies, "Unexpected as it will be by most readers, the answer here to be made is that at the outset a germ of truth was contained in the primitive conception— the truth namely, that the power which manifests itself in consciousness is but a differently conditioned form of the power which manifests itself beyond consciousness."

Similarly we may conclude that "a germ of truth," if no more, "was contained in the primitive conception" which led men to think that they might carry their needs and desires to the often but dimly apprehended Power above them, in the hope that He would do for them all, and more than all, that they were willing and able to do for one another.

Even if we had no more than the belief and practice of the least advanced peoples to base our induction upon, we should be justified in arguing that a belief and practice so prevalent and persistent could not have been entirely foolish and vain.

ESSAY VIII.

THE SPIRITUAL AND HISTORICAL EVIDENCE FOR MIRACLES.

JOHN OWEN FARQUHAR MURRAY, D.D.

ANALYSIS.

Introduction.
  Some difficulties in the way of discussion.
  The object and plan of the Essay.

I. THE DEFINITION OF A 'MIRACLE.'
  (*a*) From the point of view of Science a 'Miracle' is an 'extremely wonderful event' waiting to be fitted into its place in the order of Nature.
  (*b*) From the point of view of Theology 'Miracles' are events which suggest the immediate action of God.
   (1) They involve the action of a power controlling the forces of Nature, but not violating the laws of their working.
   (2) They are for the race what 'special providences' are for the individual. For this end they need objective evidence.

II. THE EVIDENCE FOR A 'MIRACLE.'
  (*a*) *Internal.*
   (1) 'Miracles' in the Theological sense tested by the Revelation they contain;
   (2) requiring a spiritual, as well as a strictly historical, faculty of apprehension.
  (*b*) *External.*
   (1) Historical evidence for 'Miracles' the same in kind as for any other events, but needing specially careful examination.
   (2) Various objections to the Christian evidences considered; especially the alleged lack of 'scientific training' in the witnesses to the Resurrection.
   (3) Various estimates of 'antecedent probability' in specific cases from the Scientific and from the Theological standpoint.

III. THE EVIDENCE FOR THE RESURRECTION OF OUR LORD.
  (*a*) The extent of the evidence.
  (*b*) The indirect evidence from its place in the history of Israel.
   (1) 'Prophecy' as a proof of a special relation between God and Israel.
   (2) The presence of a unique element in the personality of Jesus.
      (i) The argument from the Pauline Epistles.
      (ii) The argument from the Gospels.
  (*c*) The direct evidence.
   (1) St Paul's list of witnesses.
   (2) The accounts in the Gospels.
      (i) The Empty Grave.
      (ii) The Appearances after the Resurrection.
  (*d*) Summary, and Conclusion.

THE SPIRITUAL AND HISTORICAL EVIDENCE FOR MIRACLES.

THE subject of miracles has for at least two centuries been the chosen battleground between opposing forces, who rightly or wrongly range themselves under rival banners bearing the sacred names of 'Religion' and 'Science,' 'Reason' and 'Revelation.' If the controversy has at any time seemed to die down, the cessation of hostilities has been due rather to exhaustion than to any real *rapprochement* between the combatants. It is hard to trace any sign of progress on either side as a result of all this fighting, still less of any growth in mutual understanding. So the whole discussion seems unutterably wearisome and barren. It is a trial to our patience to be asked to tramp once more along the old familiar round.

At the same time, when we are once more embarked on it, it is as hard as ever to preserve a judicial temper throughout the discussion. The question at issue is of fundamental importance. The differences that correspond to the different points of view of the opposing parties are real and vital. No logical subtlety can explain them away. Nor has anyone as yet succeeded in resolving their discord into a deeper harmony. Meanwhile neither side can pretend to be indifferent as to the issue. And when both sides feel keenly it is hard to discuss dispassionately.

Again, it is, of course, always 'ill arguing on fundamentals.' For the opposing arguments can only be brought to our notice one by one. And even when we do not see our way at once to a conclusive reply, we are apt to regard it as 'a regrettable incident,' 'a mere affair of outposts.' Our position is that of a general working on 'interior lines.' We instinctively concentrate the whole of our forces to resist an attack on any particular point. Our confidence in the strength of our main contention remains unchanged even after a succession of such 'reverses.' The truth is that our fundamental convictions rest ultimately on immediate experiences and intuitions which no words can fully express. We can therefore always take refuge in the thought that there is an element in our position to which full justice has not yet been done. In fact processes of reasoning and reflection can help us to interpret and define our fundamental convictions. But they can neither create nor destroy them. And the storm and stress of controversy is more likely to quench than to generate the light of the reconciling truth by which alone they may be transfigured. Indeed at this stage in the controversy with regard to 'miracles,' however conscious we may be of the incompleteness of our own solution of the problem, we have almost lost hope in the possibility of the dawning of such a light. Our minds are no longer 'open.' We have taken our side. Any progress that we can hope to make must be along the path we have already chosen.

Under these circumstances the last thing that I wish to do is to approach the subject in a controversial spirit. I cannot indeed profess to be ready with a final solution which shall be acceptable to both sides, nor to be indifferent as to the side on which I stand. But I think that I should help the cause of Truth, which is the cause of both sides, best by an attempt to restate the problem as I understand it, and to indicate with as little polemic reference to the opinions of others as possible the direction in which I think a solution is most likely to be found.

The subject proposed for our consideration by the title chosen for this Essay raises two preliminary questions to

which we must find an answer before we can approach it directly:
 1. What do we mean by a 'miracle'?
 2. What evidence, if any, can justify us in believing that a 'miracle' has actually occurred?

I propose therefore to take these questions first—and then to apply the principles brought to light in the course of our investigation of them to the solution of the specific problem of the Resurrection of our Lord.

I.

What then do we mean by a miracle? In the eighteenth century the answer accepted without question by both sides would no doubt have been, to quote Hume's definition, "A transgression of a law of nature by a particular volition of the Deity or the interposition of some invisible agent." If the nineteenth century contributed nothing else to the discussion it did at least demonstrate the inadequacy of this definition. Nothing (at least from the scientific point of view) can be added to Huxley's trenchant criticism in ch. vii. of his Essay on Hume. "Nature" to the man of science "means neither more nor less than that which is; the sum of phenomena presented to our experience, the totality of events past, present, and to come. Every event must be taken to be part of nature until proof to the contrary is supplied. And such proof is from the nature of the case impossible."

Again, criticizing Hume's statement, "It is a miracle that a dead man should come to life: because that has never been observed in any age or country," he writes, "That is to say, there is a uniform experience against such an event, and therefore, if it occurs, it is a violation of the law of nature. Or, to put the argument in its naked absurdity, that which never has happened never can happen without a violation of the laws of nature. In truth, if a dead man did come to life, the fact would be evidence, not that any law of nature had been violated, but that those laws, even when they express the results of a very long and uniform experience, are necessarily based on incomplete knowledge, and are to be held only as grounds of more or less justifiable expectation."

"To sum up, the definition of a miracle as a suspension or a contravention of the order of nature is self-contradictory, because all we know of the order of nature is derived from our observation of the course of events of which the so-called miracle is a part. On the other hand no conceivable event, however extraordinary, is impossible; and therefore, if by the term miracles we mean only 'extremely wonderful events,' there can be no just ground for denying the possibility of their occurrence."

On the second part of the definition he writes, "Upon what sort of evidence can we be justified in concluding that a given event is the effect of a particular volition of the Deity, or of the interposition of some invisible (that is unperceivable) agent? It may be so, but how is the assertion that it is so to be tested? If it be said that the event exceeds the power of natural causes, what can justify such a saying? The day-fly has better grounds for calling a thunderstorm supernatural than has man with his infinitesimal fraction of duration to say that the most astonishing event that can be imagined is beyond the scope of natural causes."

In brief, then, the scientific attitude towards 'miracles' to-day amounts to this. No phenomenon can be regarded by a man of science as intrinsically, on *a priori* grounds, incredible. Only, as soon as the fact of its occurrence is established on sufficient evidence, it must take its place in the order of nature. No evidence available to science can demonstrate the intervention of any invisible (that is unperceivable) agency.

This result seems to me inevitable from the necessarily 'agnostic' attitude of science while it keeps to its proper sphere. Science, as Romanes points out in his 'Thoughts on Religion,' deals strictly only with proximate causes. In other words, as an earlier writer in this volume has reminded us,

VIII] *Spiritual and historical evidence for Miracles*

"from the scientific point of view the hypothesis of a direct action of God in any physical phenomenon is inadmissible." To accept it as a solution in any case would be a confession of failure—or a sign that science had reached its limit.

A theologian has, as far as I can see, no reason to quarrel with this conclusion. It leaves the field entirely open for historical investigation. It only becomes antagonistic to theology when science trespasses beyond her province and claims to dominate the whole range of human thought or to control all the avenues by which men attain to the knowledge of ultimate truth.

When a leading scientist like Sir George Stokes or Lord Kelvin publicly confesses his need of the hypothesis of God for the ultimate solution of the problems with which he finds himself confronted, his brothers are ready enough to remind him that he is wandering from his proper sphere. They are not however, as far as I have noticed, equally alive to the fact that the same charge on precisely the same grounds lies against anyone who on purely scientific grounds decides in favour of an antitheistic or any other ultimate philosophy.

Let us turn now from a scientific to a theological examination of Hume's definition. The change in standpoint naturally produces a change in the relative importance of the different elements contained in it. The relation of 'miracle' to 'law' remains of course a problem of abiding interest for the theologian as well as for the scientist. But the interest of the theologian centres in just that element, the reference to 'the particular volition of the Deity,' which the scientist would rule out as irrelevant or at least incapable of verification.

For it is as much the business of Theology to deal with the ultimate, as it is the business of Science to deal with the proximate, cause of any phenomenon. As the scientist is bound to find a place for any duly certified event in the constitution and order of nature, and if necessary to revise his whole conception of nature to make room for it, so the theologian cannot rest until he has found the key to the harmony between 'the particular volition of the Deity' expressed by a miracle and the revelation of the character and purpose of God contained in the general course of Divine Providence, that is, in the history of His previous dealings with men. The significance of any event lies for him precisely in the light which it throws on or derives from the Being of God.

Now if this be so, it is clear that every event must for the theologian have God at the heart of it. But we are so constituted that in some events, especially in some 'extremely wonderful events' this deepest significance comes nearer the surface than in others. Indeed it is in this quality that the true *differentia* of a miracle from the theological point of view would seem to lie. It[1] is an event or phenomenon which suggests the immediate action of God, and brings a man who witnesses it or reflects upon it either in itself or in its attendant circumstances directly into His presence.

If we ask next, as we are bound to ask, what elements in an event will give it this power, a little reflection will make it clear that the question admits of no simple answer which will fit all cases. All evidence is relative. It can only appeal to those who have eyes to see it. Divine oracles are always φωνᾶντα ξυνετοῖσιν. To the Hebrew Psalmist thunder was the voice of God. Linnaeus fell on his knees when he first beheld the glory of the broom. To us both of these are merely natural phenomena. The wonder in them has been worn off by use and wont, even though we may feel that fuller life would enable us to be conscious again of the freshness and the awe of common things. The poet to whom 'the meanest flower that blows' gives 'thoughts that do often lie too deep for tears' sees, we cannot doubt, more truly than Peter Bell or the man in the street. It is no small part of our debt to Wordsworth and his compeers that he is able now and then to lift the veil for us that we also may see 'the infinite in things.' Indeed one main function of 'miracles' may be by their very strangeness, as James Hinton suggests in an essay in his *Art of Thinking*, to help us by the logic of

---

[1] Cf. Westcott, *Gospel of Life*, p. 207.

VIII] *Spiritual and historical evidence for Miracles* 315

facts, as the poet helps by the magic of his verse, to realize afresh the wonder of the commonplace.

My immediate point, however, is that though there is an element of strangeness and mystery, something unexpected to startle us out of the familiar routine, inseparable from the idea of a miracle, there is nothing in it, from the theological any more than from the scientific standpoint, that necessitates any violation of 'law' or any interruption of the natural sequence of 'cause and effect.' The result which we have seen to be characteristic of a miracle is produced most effectually by any event in the life of an individual or of a nation or of the race that suggests an intelligent, purposeful control of natural forces by a spiritual power, not ourselves, using them, as we ourselves are conscious of using them, each in obedience to its own law, and directing them to an end.

If we ask how we are to conceive of the mode of operation of this power, we must admit that no complete answer is as yet, or perhaps ever may be, forthcoming. We are still very far from any solution of the difficulties involved in the attempt to correlate the spontaneous action of a spiritual force with the action of the physical forces which we naturally conceive of as mechanical. The fact, to which allusion has already been made, that we ourselves possess the power of controlling the operation of physical forces, must be accepted as proof that such a relation exists, unless we are prepared to refuse any power of origination or self-determination to the human will. But this fact only shows that the difficulty is not created by the perversity of theologians. The difficulty itself remains. Perhaps all we can say is that the difficulty is less, not greater, in the case of the Divine Will, of which, if there be a Divine Will, all physical forces must be the expression. And if a deeper philosophy leads us, as it seems that it is leading us, to the conviction that all force, under whatever form we perceive it, is essentially spiritual, the difficulty will be in a fair way to disappear altogether. Universal 'contingency,' as Professor Ward rightly and boldly warns us, is a necessary corollary from his philosophical position. But, if the contingency be dependent on the Divine

Will, this will not bring us back to chaos, though it may well make it impossible to give a concise and complete account of the universe in any terms of 'conceptual shorthand.'

If then we may grant that such a control of natural forces by the Divine Will, however we may conceive of the mode of its operation, is in itself possible, we have still to ask how it can come within our range of perception. Have we any criterion by which to distinguish effects due to the overruling action of the Divine Will from effects produced by the normal action of natural forces? I do not think that we need have any hesitation as to the answer to this question. We are so constituted as to be capable of recognizing the traces of the operation of intelligence and will. If we are confident, as we have every right to be, in the capacity of an experienced antiquarian to distinguish between, let us say, a worked flint and a stone fractured casually or by the action of natural forces, why should we doubt man's capacity to distinguish special tokens, if such should be provided for him, of the action of God either in his own life or in the more extensive field of the experience of the race?

We are familiar enough with the fact that in individual cases combinations of circumstances do from time to time bring home to a man the conviction that the hand of God has been laid on him—that, in the words of Hamlet, none the less true that their felt appropriateness to universal experience has made them over-trite, "There's a Divinity that shapes our ends, rough-hew them how we will."

In such cases the impression on the subject of it is irresistible—though the evidence is for the most part too purely personal to be capable of being adequately presented to anyone else. So 'special providences' of this kind can never be brought forward for general discussion as typical 'miracles.' It is a question, however, whether there may not be analogous instances in the history of the race to which this limitation does not apply—events of world-wide significance suggesting the operation of a power controlling the whole course of human history. In such cases, as the lesson would *ex hypothesi*

VIII] *Spiritual and historical evidence for Miracles* 317

be meant for the guidance of all men, the evidence must be capable of being laid before them. The tokens of the Divine action must be strictly objective. Such an event or series of events so attested, however commonplace the details, would be rightly regarded as 'miraculous.'

The experience of centuries combined with a careful study of all that led up to it, and all that followed from it, would be necessary to reveal its full significance. But in itself it is difficult to see how it could stand any chance of attracting the attention of mankind, either at the time or after, in any degree proportionate to its importance, if it were not accompanied by the appearance of a force unexampled in human experience. In the circumstances attending the origin of Christianity this feature was not lacking.

To sum up the results attained so far. From the scientific point of view 'miracles' are simply 'extremely wonderful events' waiting to be fitted into their place in the order of nature. From the theological point of view they are events which primarily suggest the direct action of God, and which may or may not include an 'extremely wonderful' element.

II.

We must pass on now to our second question. What evidence, if any, can justify us in believing that any alleged 'miracle' actually occurred, and bore the character ascribed to it?

This question is clearly one which has a peculiar interest for theologians, because if we are right in our analysis, any alleged miracle must have a direct bearing on our conception of the character of God. If it be genuine, it must be charged with a special revelation of His Mind and Will towards mankind. If it be false, we are, to use the language[1] of St Paul, "found false witnesses against God" if we ascribe it to Him. For our conception of His character depends directly on the acts which we believe to be rightly attributed to Him.

We shall do well therefore to preface this part of our

[1] 1 Cor. xv. 15.

study by a brief examination into the relation between 'miracles' and 'revelation.' Here again we shall find that Christian thought has passed through a remarkable transformation in the course of the last century. In the eighteenth and indeed well on into the nineteenth century the popular conception of this relation was that which found its clearest and ablest expression in Professor Mozley's Bampton Lectures for 1865. It may be summed up in the formula 'Miracles are the proper proof of a revelation.' Miracles from this point of view were regarded as essentially manifestations of Almighty Power granted by God to give public attestation to those whom He sent to speak in His Name. Faith in Christianity, for example, was held to be based directly on the evidence that Christ and His Apostles worked 'miracles,' quite irrespective of the character of the miracles in themselves, and of the contents of the revelation which they were to attest.

At the present time a Christian apologist if he wished to express the relation between 'miracles' regarded as 'extremely wonderful events' and the revelation which they contain or attest would prefer to transpose the terms in Professor Mozley's formula. The proper proof that an 'extremely wonderful event' may be rightly ascribed to the action of God is derived directly from the teaching conveyed by it. We accept a miracle to-day on the strength of the revelation that it brings, rather than the revelation on the strength of the miracle.

An excellent illustration of this fact in modern psychology is provided by Huxley's treatment of the account given by St Mark of the healing of the Gadarene demoniac. He prefaces his examination of the miracle by recording the evils which have in fact followed from the belief in witchcraft, and seeks to create a prejudice against an incident, which he cannot rule out as scientifically impossible, on the strength of the consequence which in his judgement would follow on its acceptance.

It would have been interesting to read his criticism of a Christian apologist who prefaced his examination into the fact

VIII] *Spiritual and historical evidence for Miracles* 319

of our Lord's Resurrection by an examination into the effect on human life produced by faith in immortality.

But whether the temptation to score a controversial point against an antagonist would have been too much for his consistency or not, there is no doubt that his instinct was right. If belief in the healing of demoniacs by Christ is the source of, and not the safeguard against, the terrible abuses of popular superstition, we cannot go on believing in the accuracy of the narratives that record it.

Nor is the feature in our present attitude to which I am calling attention really due to a weak concession to the spirit of the age. It is deep-rooted in the true conception of a miracle. As Dr Westcott, among others, was never wearied in pointing out, the criterion of 'a sign' really sent by God for the instruction of His people was always, if we are to believe the express teaching of Holy Scripture[1], to be found in the consistency of the teaching that accompanied it with the whole course of the revelation that had preceded it. The message must no doubt have novel features in it. For revelation grows. But unless the message is felt to come from our fathers' God, it will be darkness to us, not light. We are surely right then in concluding that, while 'a miracle' is a natural instrument or vehicle for a further revelation, it cannot strictly be regarded independent of the revelation as a 'proof' of it.

If we come back to the question of 'evidence' from which we started it will be clear now that the answer must include a spiritual as well as an historical element. The essence of 'the miracle' lies not in its strangeness, in its apparent 'lawlessness,' but in the message that it brings us from God. So the appeal lies in the end not merely to the intellectual side of our nature, the purely critical faculty, by which we judge of truth or falsehood in regard to matters of external fact and experience, but to the whole complex of spiritual faculties, the heart, the conscience, and the will, as well as the reason, by the combined action of which a man becomes

[1] *E.g.* Deut. xiii. 1—5.

conscious of and enters into communion with God. For it is worth while reminding ourselves here that, while a 'miracle' may quicken, define, and develop an embryonic faith in God by throwing fresh light on His character and on His relation to and ultimate purpose for mankind, it cannot of itself bring a man into the immediate presence of God if, apart from the miracle, he sees no reason for believing in His existence.

It by no means follows, however, that the purely critical faculty has no place in the process by which we attain to this as to any other fundamental truth. If the 'extremely wonderful event' never took place, the fact that men once believed in it may be interesting to the student of psychology, but it can have no message from God for the race. The mere fact that we have to speak of 'evidence' shows that we cannot, if we would, escape the necessity of an appeal to reason. Reason is not for us, whatever it may be for some seekers after truth, a purely negative, destructive faculty. It could not help us to reject what is false if it did not at the same time enable us to recognize what is true. The highest sphere for its exercise lies, we believe, in the examination of the records of God's past dealings with men contained in the facts of history. A true historian is for us a prophet. It will not therefore be easy to persuade us, even with the prospect of preserving 'religion,' to give up the search for historical truth.

What then, we must ask finally, is it reasonable to demand in the way of historical evidence to justify belief in the actual occurrence of any particular 'miracle'?

Any phenomenon however wonderful is, as we have seen, from the scientific point of view *a priori* possible. And our knowledge of the scope of natural causes is so limited that we are not justified in doing the least violence to any fragment of solid evidence to make it fit our canons of probability.

It is therefore impossible to maintain that 'extremely wonderful events' require evidence different in kind from that which would be sufficient to establish the occurrence

VIII] *Spiritual and historical evidence for Miracles* 321

of any other events. Still in face of the natural tendency of the human mind to weave legends and marvels out of a very slender basis of fact, it is no doubt right to remind ourselves that phenomena of an unparalleled kind require exceptionally strong evidence. At any rate the evidence for any such phenomenon, if it carries with it far-reaching consequences, is sure to be scrutinized with peculiar care. Only we have to be on our guard lest the fear of blind credulity make us the prey of a spirit of suspicion that is none the less blind because it is always boasting of the keenness of its powers of vision.

Hume's famous epigram for example, "It is contrary to experience that a miracle should be true, but not contrary to experience that testimony should be false," in spite of the "naked absurdity" of it exposed by Professor Huxley[1], still beguiles the unwary by its smartness. There are still writers who take credit for making full allowance for the *a priori* possibility of miracles, and yet assert that no sufficient evidence can be produced to justify us in accepting them, so that we have no right to believe them, even if they are true.

Closely akin to this is the position taken up by Professor Gardner in his *Historic View of the New Testament*. He regards it as unreasonable that he should be asked to prove that the miracles recorded in the New Testament did not occur. He asks us to accept his assertion that such miracles would be sure to be recorded whether they occurred or not, as a sufficient justification for refusing to take any account of them. He would find some difficulty in proving his assertion in face of the fact that 'no such miracles are recorded' of St John the Baptist. But even if he could get over that difficulty, the records would still remain, and with them an imperious necessity to examine the evidence for ourselves and see whether we can satisfy our own minds on the question 'whether these miracles did or did not occur.'

The most serious form of the objection taken to the evidence for the miracle which is to be the subject of special study later, the miracle of our Lord's Resurrection, affects

[1] See extract on p. 311.

the competence of the witnesses. They were, we are told, not 'scientifically trained' experts, and we have no means of cross-examining them. This seems a particularly safe method of discounting their evidence. At any rate it opens a way of escape from a difficulty which is beginning to press seriously on the opponents of Christianity. It can no longer be denied that the Apostles were themselves genuinely convinced of the Resurrection of their Lord. No one now seriously contemplates accusing them of conscious deception. But, it may still be urged that we have no means of ascertaining the grounds of their conviction, and, even if we had, it would be of no use. It was their misfortune to be born nineteen hundred years too soon to be qualified witnesses of such a fact.

It is perhaps worth while remarking here that even if this objection were securely established, if the Gospels were proved to be utterly untrustworthy, so that we really had no knowledge of the evidence to which the Apostles appealed, and if we were sure that the fact could only be proved by evidence out of reach of an untrained observer, we should not have proved that the Resurrection never took place. We should only be driven back on the question of the intrinsic credibility or incredibility of the fact.

We should have to consider, on the one hand, whether it is in itself easier to believe that the career of a personality demonstrably unique ended in an unexampled way — or whether the impression made during His Life on earth created the conviction of His immortality; and on the other, whether it is consistent with our belief in the fundamental rationality of the universe to believe that the mightiest spiritual force which has appeared in human history should have been based on a delusion.

I do not wish to foreclose these discussions, or to assume that the questions suggested have only one possible answer. I only wish to call attention to the fact that, even if the contention which we are considering were to be generally accepted, we should still have them before us.

Meanwhile I should myself seriously challenge the validity of the contention.

VIII] *Spiritual and historical evidence for Miracles*

No doubt if we were endeavouring to ascertain the manner of the Resurrection and the exact sequence of physical changes that accompanied it, or the nature of the Resurrection Body, supposing it capable of description in any terms at present available to science, we should require the assistance of highly trained faculties of observation. But if the fact to be established is the fact of an empty tomb, why should we doubt the evidence of eyes that were searching for the Body that had lain in it as the most precious treasure that the world contained?

If the essential truth to be conveyed was the personal identity of Him who died and was buried with Him who was raised and appeared, what evidence is to be compared with that of intimate personal friends?

But, we shall be told, we have not got this evidence.

We must of course consider that objection presently. My present point is that such evidence, if it be producible, is sufficient. The *a priori* objection from the lack of scientific training on the part of the witnesses will not stand examination.

To sum up: the conclusion which I would draw from the study of the question of evidence is this.

From the scientific point of view the evidence required to establish any 'very wonderful event' is essentially the same as that required for any other historical event; only it must be scrutinized with special care, proportionate to its antecedent improbability judged from that point of view.

From the theological point of view our judgement on the 'miraculous' character of the event, where the fact of its occurrence is established, will depend on the light which it throws on the character and purpose of God.

And from this point of view it is worth while bearing in mind that a theologian's judgement of the *a priori* probability of any event may vary very considerably from that of a man who looks on the same event merely in the light of its relation to our present knowledge of 'the scope of natural causes.'

For instance, he who sees reason to accept the Christian view of the Person of Jesus Christ would regard it as antecedently probable that special powers would be manifested by Him in the course of His ministry.

A man who believes in God cannot be surprised that God should in a marvellous way have shown Himself worthy of the trust reposed in Him by One who did not shrink from surrendering Himself to death in obedience to what He felt to be His Father's will.

He will not on that account scrutinize the available evidence with less scrupulous care. He more than others must feel the solemn obligation to "guileless workmanship." But he cannot pretend to say that his faith does not affect his judgement on the antecedent probability of an event like the Resurrection of Jesus Christ. He is more sure of the capacity of man's moral judgement to determine what is or is not worthy of the character of God, than of his intellectual qualifications for deciding a question of scientific probability.

III.

Let us come then finally to an examination of the historical evidence for the Resurrection.

This evidence cannot, without risk of serious misrepresentation, be limited to the brief accounts contained in the Canonical Gospels and in the Acts of the Apostles, and to the incidental allusions in the other books of the New Testament.

The event is not isolated. It stands in the closest relation to the whole course of God's dealings with the people of Israel, and to the life and death of Him who was crucified, and with whom Christians believe that they can still hold communion because He is alive for evermore.

Even the direct evidence for the particular fact cannot be fairly estimated apart from its whole context.

We cannot however do more than indicate very briefly some few points in the evidence in this wider sense.

VIII] *Spiritual and historical evidence for Miracles* 325

We must begin with the evidence for a special relation between God and the people of Israel. The solid basis of fact bearing on this point, of which historical criticism is bound in any case to give account, is supplied by documents composing the Old Testament. The result of a century of strenuous criticism devoted to the elucidation of these documents has not been fruitless, even though students may still be far from general agreement on many important points. And no doubt the Christian argument needs restatement in the new light. But the determination to read each book as far as possible historically, to understand it in the first instance as the writer and first readers of it must have understood it, while it has rendered the old argument from isolated prophecies as antiquated as the argument from 'special design,' has yet established the fact of the inspiration of the Prophets on a broader and deeper basis[1].

[1] See A. B. Davidson, *Old Testament Prophecy*, pp. 153 ff. W. Robertson Smith, *The Prophets of Israel*, p. 16.

I should not, however, wish to imply that the whole argument from 'special predictions' is worthless. My feeling with regard to it can best be indicated by a fuller consideration of the analogy to which I have just referred. From the scientific side the case is stated with equal clearness and cogency by Romanes (*Thoughts on Religion*, p. 59). After explaining how the phenomena of a coast-line each apparently due to 'special design' can be seen to be the result of the automatic action of well-known natural causes, he writes:

"He" (the observer) "would therefore be led to conclude that if the teleological interpretation of the facts were to be saved at all, it could only be so by taking a much wider view of the subject than was afforded by the particular cases of apparent design, which at first appeared so cogent. That is to say, he would feel that he must abandon the supposition of any *special* design in the construction of that particular bay, and fall back upon the theory of a much more *general* design in the construction of one great scheme of nature as a whole. In short, he would require to dislodge his argument from the special adjustments which in the first instance appeared to him so suggestive, to those general laws of nature, which by their united operation give rise to a cosmos as distinguished from a chaos."

'Special predictions' with their apparently literal fulfilment seem to me from this point of view to correspond closely to the 'special adjustments' in nature. After all, the 'special adjustments,' while unable to bear the weight of the whole argument, yet point in the right direction. They suggest the idea of a cosmos, and in their turn are

If we are here, as I believe, in touch with an objective fact capable of being established by the ordinary methods of historical investigation, the way is open for the examination of the special view of the philosophy of the history of Israel formulated in the opening sentence of the Epistle to the Hebrews. If God did speak to Israel in old times *in divers portions and in divers ways in the prophets*, it is worth considering whether He did or did not crown His previous revelations by speaking at last in One who stood in an even nearer relation to Himself as Son.

We come then to our second point, the evidence for the presence of a unique element in the Person of Jesus Christ.

Here again the facts, that we have in any case to give an account of, are the books of the New Testament.

In dealing with these facts it is well to begin our study with the Pauline Epistles. The most recent discussion of those documents in the articles contributed by a Dutch professor, H. van Manen, to the *Encyclopaedia Biblica* has a significance the importance of which it is, I believe, difficult to overrate. With more than Teutonic "rigour and vigour" he pressed his principles to their logical conclusion utterly regardless of received opinions. So his work has at least the merit of bringing into clear light the real issue raised by this part of the New Testament.

Starting from a frankly humanitarian view of the Person of Jesus he was struck by the fact, to which indeed Bishop Lightfoot and others had long ago called attention, that in every one of the Epistles ascribed to St Paul, even in the little letter to Philemon, an office and dignity are attributed to Jesus as a source of Divine Grace in some real sense coordinate with the Father, which St Paul could not have attributed to one whom he believed to be merely man.

justified by the idea of a cosmos. What is true of the whole can hardly be false of the parts.

The bearing of this idea on special predictions was suggested to my mind many years ago by a striking essay by Professor Cheyne, *Commentary on Isaiah*, vol. II. on 'The Christian Element in the book of Isaiah' (1881).

He maintained, therefore, surely quite correctly, that the view of the Person of Christ involved in the Pauline Epistles could not have been developed out of the facts of the life of Jesus, *as he conceived them*, within the lifetime of St Paul.

He was in consequence bound either to modify his view of the Person of Jesus or boldly to impugn the genuineness of the whole collection of letters attributed to St Paul. He chose the latter desperate alternative—boldly challenging the claim of the documents to be regarded as in any sense 'letters' at all. They are really dogmatic treatises, the work of a School or Party rather than of an individual, and addressed early in the Second Century to no one in particular.

It is not surprising that his critics found it difficult to take this conclusion seriously.

It revolts our literary conscience. No one could have been betrayed into it except under the tyranny of *a priori* considerations. But it has at least this merit that it brings into clear light the strength of the testimony of the Pauline Epistles to the presence of a 'supernatural' element in the Person of Jesus.

We must pass on now to consider the evidence supplied by the Gospels. The subject has already been treated at length under different aspects in two of the Essays in this volume, so I gladly content myself with calling attention very briefly to the one point of special importance to my present argument.

The four Gospels as they stand imply throughout a 'supernatural' element in the Person of Christ.

By this I do not mean merely that in each of them mighty works are attributed to Jesus. I agree with Professor Tyndall that we have no right to infer that the powers put forth in even the mightiest of them could only be wielded by One who was essentially more than man. What I mean is that the Person depicted in them is supernatural in the essential features of His personal character, *e.g.* His sinlessness, and the relation in which He claims to stand both toward God His Father and His brother men.

This is true, I maintain, of each of the Evangelists, of the Synoptists no less than of St John. The only hypothesis that can account for the calm matter-of-fact way in which they describe the most wonderful of His works and words is that the writers regarded them as in the strictest sense natural and normal as coming from Jesus as they conceived Him. Certainly any attempt to eliminate the supernatural element reduces the work of each of them to a chaos of incoherent fragments[1].

It is true also of those for whom the Evangelists wrote. Though two at least of the four may fairly be said to write with a dogmatic purpose, there is no sign that any of them is putting forward a view of the Person of Jesus which he regards as likely to affect his readers as strange and unfamiliar.

These statements are independent of any judgement that we may form as to the date or authorship or historical value of the documents before us.

They describe a common characteristic into the origin of which it is the business of historical criticism to enquire.

Whatever view we take of the sources of information accessible to the different writers and of the use that they made of the material before them we are, I believe, bound to admit that there is at once a distinct individuality in the portraits of Jesus which they severally present to us, and at the same time a wonderful harmony between the different portraits. They are, we feel no hesitation in saying, portraits of the same Person. If so, is it not irrational to account for this result on the supposition that the Person so depicted is a purely imaginary being, an Ideal evolved by something vaguely conceived as the Christian consciousness out of a slender basis of 'natural' fact?

I maintain therefore, as I said, that the four Gospels as they stand imply throughout a supernatural element in the Person of Jesus.

In other words they present us with just the background which we require to render the Pauline Epistles intelligible.

[1] See generally F. D. Maurice (*The Unity of the N.T.* vol. I.).

VIII] *Spiritual and historical evidence for Miracles*

We can pass on now to the examination of the evidence for the specific fact of the Resurrection.

Here again we shall do well to begin with St Paul because the materials on which our judgement has to be formed are less open to question, though experience shows that they may be very variously interpreted.

The cardinal passage is of course 1 Cor. xv. In this passage St Paul is preparing the way for an argument on the general resurrection of the dead. He is going to treat the truth of a general resurrection, which some of the Corinthians were denying, as an inevitable deduction from the fact of our Lord's Resurrection, which had been an article of Faith among them from the beginning. He prefaces his argument therefore by recalling the primary articles of the Christian Creed as he had delivered them when he founded the Church in Corinth four or five years before. He begins with the Death "for our sins according to the Scriptures," and the Burial. He is not engaged in considering the dogmatic significance of these articles, so that the reference to them must, it would seem (if he is not quoting mechanically from a stereotyped formula), be meant to lay stress on the fact that Christ had entered completely into the human experience of death.

In any case the separate reference to the burial, in so concise a passage, is remarkable.

He then passes on to the Resurrection on the third day, this also being "according to the Scriptures," and to the appearances to Cephas and to "the Twelve."

The other appearances in the list, "to upwards of five hundred brethren at once, to James, to all the Apostles," and "last of all" to St Paul himself, may or may not have formed part of the early preaching. St Paul does not expressly include them in it. But there is no indication that he is communicating any facts not already familiar to his correspondents. If the list as a whole is in any sense formal and complete, it is unlikely that he should have communicated only a part of it on his first visit. He records it now in full, not because the fact of Christ's Resurrection was questioned at Corinth, but because, in view of the polemical use he was going to make of the fact, it was important to give a clear conspectus of the evidence by which it was supported.

What then is the significance of this list for us to-day? Let us examine first into its date. We find it in a document the date of which may be approximately fixed at 55 A.D. But the substance of the list, the germ if not the whole, had been familiar to the Corinthians for five years, and to St Paul at least for twenty. It was not his creation. He had received it, and whatever differences there may have been between him and the original Apostles, he claims this at least as common ground : "so we preach, and so ye believed."

It will probably seem to many mere trifling to examine further into the possible antecedents of the list so accredited. But if the list has the fundamental importance in regard to the whole evidence for the Resurrection with which it is generally credited, time spent on it cannot really be wasted, and the points to which I wish to call attention have a bearing on the whole problem which is apt to be overlooked.

In the first place it is impossible to doubt that the discussion of the evidence for the Resurrection must date from the moment that Christianity first began to attract public attention. Whatever may have been the case with the little band of original disciples, it is simply incredible that they could have attempted to claim for the Crucified the dignity of Messiah on any other ground than that of a triumphant Divine vindication. Whatever may be the general historical value of Acts i. to v. we cannot doubt that the Apostles appealed from the first, as they are represented in those chapters as appealing, to the fact of the Resurrection. They must therefore from the first have had to stand cross-examination on the grounds of their conviction.

If so, is it antecedently improbable that a list should very soon be drawn up of the witnesses to whom public appeal could be made?

How far then does this carry us? St Paul's conversion, according to Harnack's chronology, took place within a year of the Crucifixion.

VIII] *Spiritual and historical evidence for Miracles* 331

The greatest interval, that it is possible to allow for it, is that given by Mr Turner[1], and it is only six or seven years. And St Paul's study of the evidence for the Resurrection must go back at least to the ministry of Stephen.

Let us leave now the question of the date of the list, and come to questions of its interpretation. These require for their elucidation a criticism a little more historical than that which is content to isolate the document altogether from its context, and then to deal with its language as lawyers, rightly or wrongly, deal with the rubrics.

For instance, if we are right in our contention that we are dealing simply with a *list* of the witnesses for the Resurrection, we must go astray if we persist in calling it a *narrative*, and laying stress on its omissions, when we wish to find 'contradictions' between St Paul's account and that of the Evangelists.

To take a single example. It is really trifling to lay stress in this connexion on the absence of reference to the empty Tomb or to spoken words.

Even the significance of the absence of any reference to the appearance to Mary Magdalene depends on the purpose for which the list was drawn up. St Paul himself may well have been ignorant of it. It is not mentioned in St Luke, and St John[2], who describes it, does not count it in reckoning up the appearances to the Disciples.

Again, the list by itself tells nothing as to the nature of the appearances which the witnesses attested. The only points about which we can be certain are that St Paul regards his own experience on the way to Damascus, in spite of some abnormal features, as substantially the same in kind as that of the other Apostles, and that he uses the list as a whole as the basis of an argument on behalf not merely of personal immortality, but of a resurrection of the dead which is in some real sense corporeal, though he has to strain language almost to the breaking point to find a phrase "a spiritual body" to intimate his conception of the new organism.

[1] See *Article* 'Chronology' in Hastings' *B.D.*
[2] St John xxi. 14.

One last point before we pass on. The list is not a list of witnesses to the Resurrection, but of witnesses to the appearances of Christ after the Resurrection. We are often reminded, and reminded rightly, that none of our witnesses claims to have seen our Lord leave the Tomb. The silence is certainly remarkable. If the accounts of the events at the Tomb were as legendary as the most recent criticism would have us regard them, I could not but account it as inexplicable. A faith that was capable of creating, with absolutely no basis in fact, so circumstantial an account of the emptiness of the Tomb, would assuredly not have left without a witness the one moment on which the significance of its whole creation seems to depend. The portentous account in the *Evangelium Petri* brings into clear relief the self-restraint of the Canonical Gospels in this respect.

But the point to which I wish to call attention is this. St Paul prefaces his list by a reference to the Resurrection as a fact by itself, independent of the appearances, a fact too which was capable of being precisely dated "on the third day." If all that he meant was that "He appeared on the third day to Cephas," why did he not say so?

To sum up then, St Paul gives a list, which may fairly be regarded as formal and precise, of accredited witnesses who claimed to have seen the Risen Lord. With two of the most important he had had close intercourse three years after his own conversion. And their witness had even before his conversion been sufficient to start a movement which had not only attracted the attention of the authorities at Jerusalem, but had spread to some distance beyond the limits of the Holy Land. And he regarded their experience, in which he claimed to have shared, as the proof of a Resurrection which in some sense could be called corporeal.

Let us come now to the narratives in the Canonical Gospels, and see whether there is anything either in the character of the appearances themselves or the attendant circumstances, to help us to understand the grounds on which this conclusion was based.

The narratives come to us from five different sources. Of these it is now generally agreed that the account in Mark xvi. 1—8 was published first, and was actually in the hands of the other three Evangelists substantially[1] in its present shape.

To this extent it may be fair to say that the other Evangelists were dependent on St Mark. At the same time it is clear that each of them possessed access to other sources of information which enabled them to supplement and even modify the account in St Mark xvi. 1—8.

The fifth source to which reference is made above is contained in St Mark xvi. 9—20. In this the relations seem to be reversed and the writer most probably drew his materials from St Matthew, St Luke, and St John.

The account in St Mark xvi. 1—8 is unfortunately imperfect, breaking off in the middle of a sentence. It describes the visit of three women to the Tomb, and the appearance of an angel who announces the Resurrection, bids them examine the place where the Lord had lain, and promises an appearance in Galilee. In the unfinished state of the Gospel arguments from silence are unusually precarious. It would be rash to rest anything even on the authority of the express statement in the broken sentence. It is impossible to take it *au pied de la lettre*. For if they had never said anything to anyone the Evangelist could never have recorded their experience. It is perhaps worth while to call attention to the fact that St Mark has a curious habit of qualifying his universal negatives.

St Matthew records a visit of the two Marys to see the Tomb on Saturday evening. Then, without further note of time, there follow an earthquake, and the rolling away of the stone by an angel of Jehovah ; the terror of the Roman guard ; the utterance of the angel (apparently outside the Tomb) to the women, substantially the same as that found in St Mark ; the flight of the women to report to the Disciples.

---

[1] Dr A. Wright maintains that the narrative has been twice revised, and leaves to the original St Mark nothing that is not represented in St Luke.

The whole story concludes with an appearance of the Lord to the women on their way and the report of the soldiers to the chief priests.

St Luke records not the purchase but the preparation of spices on the Friday(?) evening: a visit of certain women early on Sunday morning, and their entrance into the empty Tomb; an appearance of two angels who recall the predictions of the Resurrection given in Galilee. The women (it is not clear which) report to the Apostles and are disbelieved. The disciples on the way to Emmaus (v. 24) seem to have heard nothing of any vision of the Lord.

St John describes a visit from Mary Magdalene to the Tomb "while it was yet dark," and her report of its emptiness to St Peter and the other disciple whom Jesus loved.

They verify the fact and notice especially the condition of the grave-clothes. After their departure Mary Magdalene sees first two angels in the Tomb and then the Lord Himself outside.

Now we must freely admit that we have not the means for harmonizing completely these different accounts.

But the points on which they differ must not blind us to the strength of their testimony to the one point on which they agree. Not one but all these accounts must be rejected as pure inventions if the Grave was not empty.

Let us see what this involves.

The account of the Ministry in St Mark, as we are assured on the evidence of one of the disciples of the Lord, embodies notes of St Peter's preaching. The special reference to Peter in the message given through the angel (which is a peculiar feature of St Mark's account) is one out of many remarkable confirmations from internal evidence of the substantial accuracy of this tradition. Yet if the Grave was not empty, we must believe that here we pass (without the slightest indication in the structure of the Gospel) altogether away from the region of historical reminiscence to pure legend, created by some pious Christian fancy to supply a foundation for a material view of the Lord's Resurrection, a legend which not only could have had no sanction in St Peter's

VIII] *Spiritual and historical evidence for Miracles* 335

genuine reminiscences, but which must have supplanted those reminiscences before it could have gained acceptance.

Similarly the account in the fourth Gospel claims to come to us on the authority of an eye-witness. Even those who still resist the evidence which leads us to regard it as the work of St John himself are for the most part ready to admit that it must embody genuine reminiscences of his teaching. It is at least in a secondary sense Johannine. Here, again, if the Grave was not empty, the genuine Johannine reminiscence must have been ousted by a new and even bolder exertion of the legend-creating fancy. For it not only substitutes fictitious experiences of the faithful women for the genuine experience of St Peter, but it invents fresh Johannine corroboration.

Again, there is good evidence for identifying the author of the third Gospel and the Acts with a companion of St Paul. He claims to write on the authority of eye-witnesses. Has he also been deceived into giving us here legend for fact? Can we believe that his account was fundamentally different from that which St Paul had received and preached?

Nor is this all. The differences between the accounts in St Luke and St Mark may or may not be due to the fact that they are describing the experiences of different parties of women. They are certainly enough to show that St Luke had independent information. Was he also mistaken as to the character of this source also?

How comes it that the account of the appearance on the way to Emmaus presupposes the emptiness of the Tomb? Is that also a later creation of the same pious fancy?

Lastly, we come to St Matthew. His differences from St Mark when the two Evangelists are covering the same ground present here as in one or two instances in other parts of the Gospel special difficulties. But in this connexion he supplies us with an entirely independent addition to the Marcan narrative dealing with the guard of Roman soldiers. We have no means of estimating the value of the source from which this is taken. But whatever that may be, there is no reason to doubt the accuracy of the note with which the section closes, "And this saying is commonly reported among the Jews until this day." And this is enough to show that even in unbelieving Jewish circles the fact of the empty Grave was admitted. If so, the evidence for it must have been too notorious to be denied.

Now surely this concurrence of testimony is remarkably strong. There is nothing like it for any fact of the Evangelic history except the Crucifixion.

Let us now turn to the appearances of the Risen Lord recorded or implied in the Gospels or the Acts.

Here the independence is carried so far that the narratives hardly even overlap. It is in fact only in the account of the appearance to the assembled Apostles on the night of the Resurrection that we can be sure that any two writers (leaving out of account the last twelve verses of St Mark) are describing the same appearance.

At the same time the superficial differences between the accounts taken as wholes are striking. Too much stress must not be laid, as we have seen, on the omissions in an incomplete narrative like St Mark's. To say for instance that "St Mark knows nothing of any appearances of the Risen Lord," implying that his evidence may be cited against that of the other Evangelists, is incautious.

Still it is noteworthy that the only references to an appearance which are contained in that part of the Gospel which has come down to us refer expressly to Galilee.

In St Matthew, though an appearance to two women in Jerusalem finds a place, the main stress is laid on the promise of a Galilean appearance, and its fulfilment.

St Luke, on the other hand, not only says nothing of any appearances away from Jerusalem, but seems at any rate in his Gospel to leave no room for them.

But this turns on questions of interpretation and reading, which we need not pause to discuss here. For even granting that St Luke, when he wrote his Gospel, believed that the Ascension took place on the day of the Resurrection, and

VIII] *Spiritual and historical evidence for Miracles* 337

therefore could have known nothing of any appearances in Galilee, yet before he wrote the Acts he had become conscious of an interval between the two events which at least leaves room for appearances outside Jerusalem.

The closing chapter to St John's Gospel supplements appearances in Jerusalem with an appearance in Galilee.

These differences are due no doubt to distinctness in the sources, and perhaps to ignorance on the part of one or other of the Evangelists, but they give us no ground for rejecting one series of appearances in favour of the other. At the same time, as the accounts describe different appearances, we cannot appeal to them for mutual corroboration; each account must stand or fall on its own merits in the light of internal evidence.

We cannot of course examine the different narratives here in detail. But it will be worth while to call attention to one or two characteristics more or less common to them all.

Let us take first the style in which they are written. Regarding them for the moment merely as a collection of 'ghost stories,' is there anything like them in literature? They are told as simply and unaffectedly as all the stories that precede them, with the same absence of any straining after effect. Except in the case of the conversion of St Paul the appearances are marked by no external manifestations of supernatural glory. The conflict of emotions in the hearts of those who behold their Risen Master is the only indication that we are in the presence of a Visitor from the world beyond the grave. The result is a series of pictures which are either direct transcripts from life, or the creations of a very high order of literary genius.

It may help us to decide between these alternatives, if we notice next that the narratives are clearly not written to create a belief in the Lord's Resurrection in the minds of men to whom the fact was unfamiliar. They record quite freely the doubts and hesitation of the first witnesses, and are at no pains to explain in every instance how the doubts were removed. It would seem therefore that at least the earliest of the narratives must have taken shape, as indeed

St Luke's Preface is sufficient to assure us, while the memory of the facts recorded by the first preachers of the Gospel was still fresh and vivid.

If we pass now from the style to the substance of the narrative and reflect on the wonder of the personality of Jesus as revealed in the records of His earthly ministry, and on the peculiar power of the words that fell from His lips, it is surely no slight corroboration of the truthfulness of these records that the appearances should be always in character, and that the words that fall from His lips should be no feeble echoes of previous utterances but new revelations, at once the crown and the consummation of the old.

These general characteristics of style and contents are no doubt incapable of being brought to a mechanical test, and therefore depend for their cogency on independent verification. I cannot help feeling, however, that taken together they will be found to constitute a strong case on behalf of the substantial accuracy of the narratives of the Appearances after the Resurrection.

I have said nothing of the physical aspects of the phenomena described. If the narratives themselves are true, the physical conditions must have been unique, and we have no criterion by which to judge the accuracy of the descriptions.

It is quite arbitrary therefore to rule out as belonging to some secondary source just those elements which offend our *a priori* canons of probability.

According to the accounts as they have come down to us, the Risen Lord not only rendered Himself visible (in a shape which was ultimately, though not always at first, recognisable) and spoke in familiar tones, but also offered His Body to the test of touch, and still more strangely brake bread with His own hands and ate in the presence of the Apostles after entering the room with closed doors.

It seems natural, if not inevitable, to regard the whole of the material side of these phenomena as a condescension to our limited powers of apprehension, and to the consequent necessity that the truth should be brought home to us by the concurrent use of all our faculties. We naturally, however wrongly,

VIII] *Spiritual and historical evidence for Miracles* 339

imagine that the sense of touch is less likely to be deceived than any other, evidence is granted through it to assure us that the form taken by the life that triumphed over death, though not subject to the laws of matter as we understand them in this order, is yet solid and substantial (whatever the words may mean under the new conditions), the exact antithesis to the empty, shadowy existences with which popular imagination, whether Jewish or Gentile, had peopled the world beyond the grave.

Such then are the narratives in the Canonical Gospels by which we can judge of the kind of evidence on which the faith of the Apostles in the Resurrection of their Lord rested, and out of which they must have developed their view of the nature of the resurrection body. There is no likelihood that any of them was put into writing till ten years after the writing of 1 Corinthians. Yet surely it is a strong confirmation of their historicity that as they stand they supply in this respect also a natural background for St Paul's argument. They help us to understand not only how St Paul was able to fix the date of the Lord's Resurrection, but also how natural it was for him to connect with the list of appearances his very remarkable doctrine of the nature of our resurrection bodies, the origin of which, in all its startling boldness and originality, would apart from this be left shrouded in a veil of impenetrable mystery.

Such are some at least of the elements of the case for the truth of our Lord's Resurrection, so far as it depends on the documents contained in the Christian Bible. If we deny the fact, it is not too much to say that we reduce the whole literature to a mass of incoherent fragments for the origin of which we can only account by the aid of a series of violent and arbitrary hypotheses, which owe what plausibility they possess partly to their vagueness, and chiefly to the supposed necessity of forcing all historical events to fit into the limits fixed by our present knowledge of the forces of Nature.

If we accept the fact, difficulties and perplexities in detail no doubt remain, for which we can at present suggest no certain solution, both in the documents themselves and in the phenomena they describe: but at least the fundamental harmony is clear.

We can see how (1) in the midst of the nation which God had chosen out of the nations of the world, that they might be trained through the prophets whom He raised up in the knowledge of Himself, and (2) in the Person of Him in whom that revelation was consummated, when He had surrendered Himself to death in obedience to His Father's will, God did by a mighty act at once set His seal on the Revelation that He brought, and bring life and immortality to light for all mankind by raising Him from the dead.

The physical laws in obedience to which, the particular force by the operation of which, this result was attained, are at present unknown to us, and it is possible that they may remain unknown. No one can wish anything but God-speed to those who press onward in the hope that a fuller knowledge of the constitution of matter and a closer study of psychic phenomena may enable them in the end to lift the veil. The revelation contained in the fact does not depend on our ignorance of the method by which it was wrought. No possible growth in our knowledge of the force by which it was effected can touch the grounds of our conviction that in this act the hand of God is seen by those who have eyes to see it, working His Will in the history of mankind.

ESSAY IX.

THE PERMANENT VALUE OF THE OLD TESTAMENT.

WILLIAM EMERY BARNES, D.D.

Male sentiunt, qui veteres tantum in promissiones temporarias sperasse confingunt.

ANALYSIS.

Christianity claims to be historical.

There can be no history without continuity.

The Old Testament attests the continuity of Christianity with the Past.

This continuity is manifested chiefly through the Messianic element in the Old Testament.

Other services of the Old Testament are that (1) it testifies to the paedagogic value of pre-Christian religions, (2) it illustrates the method of Divine Revelation, (3) it proclaims to us under the most vivid forms the dependence of the Universe upon one Creator, (4) it preaches with unsurpassed power the necessity of Social Righteousness.

THE PERMANENT VALUE OF THE OLD TESTAMENT.

THE Christian religion is an historical religion. It rests not on what its Founder taught, but on what He was, and did, and suffered. The Christian Creed may be summed up in the statement that Jesus the Christ worked out at a certain time in a certain country and under certain outward circumstances a certain dispensation of God, which He alone by reason of His very nature could so work out. In other words, the Creed consists of the chief facts recorded in the four Gospels. The Christian is not bound to the letter of the Evangelists' record, nor to the accuracy of every statement; but unless the general outline of the story told in the New Testament is true, the Christian religion is nothing but a dream, forcible, full of suggestion, not to be easily put aside indeed, but yet in fact a dream. Christianity is based on history; it rests not on ideas, but on facts. Herein lies its strength.

But if we assert that the Creed of Christianity is historical, we commit ourselves to a statement which is wider than appears at first sight. History is the manifestation not of isolated events, but of an evolutionary progress. If therefore we connect Christianity definitely with a period of thirty years, *i.e.* with a definite part of the First Century of our era, we cannot pause at this step. Whatever is historical reaches backwards and forwards. The 'forwards' is represented by the Christian Church and its achievements, but what of the 'backwards'? If there be no 'backwards,' if Christianity was truly a new thing nineteen hundred years ago, then Christianity appears as a late afterthought in the history of the World, not as a portion of the Universal Providence of God. If Christianity be thus new, it can hardly be true. But it is not new; Christianity is indeed far older than the beginning of the Christian era. For the main proof of this we appeal to the ancient literature of the people amongst whom the religion of Christ was born, to the books of the Old Covenant.

This appeal is different in important respects from the appeal which used to be made to the (supposed) literal correspondence of the Old Testament with the New. It is not enough to compare the two books as books apart from the religious life to which they testify. This comparison was made in the Past, and was found to have its value for past generations. It was not in itself untrue, but it was wholly insufficient. It was a comparison of shadow with shadow, not of substance with substance. Further, a proceeding which treats the Old Testament mainly as a collection of foreshadowings and predictions, and the New Testament as the historical account of the 'fulfilment' of those 'types' and 'prophecies' leads to most unsatisfactory results. Careful study shows that the amount of prediction in the Old Testament in general and in the Prophets in particular is very small. There is a deeper correspondence between the Old and the New than one of words.

The main object in making a fresh appeal to the Old Testament is to discover whether we are contemplating merely broken threads of human thought, or whether we find that the separate manifestations point to one great progress of Revelation which is worthy of a superhuman author. The question cannot be answered in words; no man can judge what is and what is not $\theta\epsilon o\hat{v}$ $\check{a}\xi\iota o\nu$, and yet from such a contemplation a spiritual conviction may arise which is not indeed independent of thought, though it soars beyond the realm of logical proofs. The question is whether the contents of the New Testament and the Old Testament do indeed agree in testifying to an actual dispensation of God wrought in this world by the hand of a Mediator. Such an

Permanent Value of the Old Testament

agreement (if it can be found) running through so varied a history would be at least an impressive moral fact, a fact not to be set aside on any but the most weighty grounds.

Our most convenient method of procedure is to summarise (as far as possible) the main substance of the Old Testament revelation, and to compare this summary with the main teaching of our Lord and His Apostles. Modern research has brought out into stronger light the fact that the utterances of the Old Testament came πολυμερῶς καὶ πολυτρόπως[1] —by many parts and in many manners—and it is open to an investigator to ask, Is there unity in these scattered messages? Is it possible to sum up the teachings scattered over so many centuries? May we speak of the message of the Old Testament as one?

Our task does not involve the reconciliation of every passage of the Old Testament with all the rest; it is not necessary to fit every detail into one great scheme. The Old Testament on one side is National Literature and not pure matter of Revelation; it contains lower as well as higher elements. We have to do with the spirit, not the letter. We do not identify Revelation with the Old Testament; we look for Revelation *in* the Old Testament; we enquire whether the Revelation which is given us in many parts may be said truly to make up one whole.

The difficulty of this larger task, *i.e.* the task of comparing the Revelation which is made in the Old Testament with that which is made in the New Testament, has not been seriously increased by the work of recent 'Higher Criticism' on either Literature. The force of the old appeal to the letter of the Old and New Testaments has indeed been blunted, if not broken; but the Old Testament as a whole stands as it always did, a witness to an ancient Divine Revelation. Such is at any rate the main contention of this Essay.

Now the Old Testament literature is divided into three periods, each of which has its own well-marked character. Each is unique in its political and social circumstances.

[1] Heb. i. 1.

During the first (Pre-exilic), Judah was still a kingdom, ruled by an ancient line of kings. During the second (Exilic), the national life lingered on under most disadvantageous circumstances on a foreign soil, but fostered by religious influences exerted chiefly through the great prophets. During the third (Post-exilic), the remnant of a nation strove to nourish its national consciousness on memories of former greatness reinforced by the joy of a partial Restoration.

We have now to ask whether any great unifying element is to be traced through all these periods. Is this Literature to be considered as a Collection of fragments, or is it on the contrary a Unity of a special kind? Is it (to expand the latter half of the question) a Unity which is deeper than any merely national Unity, a Unity which is due not to the fact that the Literature is national, but to the fact that it is spiritual? Such, I believe, is the case.

The element which gives Unity to the varied Literature contained in the Old Testament is nothing less than the doctrine as to the relation of God to man. This great central doctrine running through the Old Testament as a whole binds its separate messages together and links itself inseparably with the main message of the New. The doctrine is almost startling in its simplicity. For when we put aside for the moment the words of the students of 'Wisdom[1]' together with those of the writers on ritual[2], and turn to the utterances of the Prophets and of the prophetically minded historians, of which the greater part of the Old Testament consists, a doctrine of the relation of God to man stands out in the simplicity of greatness. God is presented not in the form of a Master, not as an Object of fear, not even as an Object of worship. In each of these presentations there is something that is (if we may use the word) artificial, whereas the characteristic doctrine of the Old Testament relating to God is that God stands towards man in a relationship which is truly natural. Man was created *in the image of God, after*

[1] As contained in Proverbs, Ecclesiastes, part of Job, and a few of the Psalms.

[2] Large parts of Exodus, Leviticus, and Numbers.

God's likeness[1]; there is a certain close relation between God and man which cannot easily be defined, though it may be illustrated from natural human kinship[2].

The force of this teaching of the closeness of the relation between God and man is not seriously weakened by the fact that such a nation as the Greek had many stories of the gods which seem at first sight to convey the same teaching. That Zeus is the father of gods and men is a well-known commonplace of the *Iliad*. That *the gods have come down to us in the likeness of men* is very good Greek doctrine of an antique and poetic type. The *Iliad* portrays gods making favourites of particular cities and individual men, intervening in Trojan battles, and receiving painful wounds while defending human favourites. But the doctrine of the Old Testament does not submit to be compared with these poetic phantasies. There is indeed no common ground for comparison. The gods of the *Iliad* are too plainly demigods, human beings raised a little above their fellows. Homer arrays god against god in conflict, and endues god and goddess with human passions in language which no kind of exegesis can satisfactorily explain as metaphorical[3]. Take away the human nature from these gods, and nothing remains.

There is indeed nothing surprising in these stories of the intercourse of Greek gods with Greek men. The moral nature of the two is one. There is nothing *holy* about the gods to distinguish them from sinful men. In fact we may leave out the words 'holy' and 'sinful' altogether from our account. Two classes of beings of like passions meet together; only the possession of certain unmoral qualities such as power and immortality marks off one class as superior to the other.

On the other hand there is something more than surprising in the teaching of the Old Testament, that the God who gave the Law to Israel is capable of drawing near to men. The Old Testament writers themselves seem to utter the truth one

---

[1] This phrase though it comes from Gen. i. 26, which is ascribed by critics to P, is itself certainly much older than P.

[2] Cf. Gen. v. 3.

[3] I do not think that the attempt of the philosopher Porphyry will satisfy any modern mind.

moment and to shrink from its contemplation the next. Moses speaks with God "face to face, as a man speaketh unto his friend[1]," but he is told only a few verses later by God, *Man shall not see me and live*[2]. Certainly the early writer who joined together the two strands, E and J, into one narrative, felt with one thrill on the one side the nearness and on the other the awfulness of God.

Further this nearness of God to man as taught in the Old Testament was no abstract doctrine; on the contrary it received the most practical applications. The literature of the Old Testament presses upon the children of Israel the fact that God is near to *them*. They are 'chosen' by God, they are God's particular portion or 'inheritance[3].' The boldest metaphors are employed to enforce this teaching; Israel is God's *son* or *firstborn son*[4]; or even God's *spouse*[5].

This second metaphor is pressed still further when God is spoken of as a *jealous* God[6]. This metaphor of a special nearness of God to Israel is not however so pressed as to assert that other nations are to be kept at a distance. On the contrary, Israel is the medium through which all nations are to experience the blessings of this nearness, *And all the families of the earth shall gain blessings in thee*[7].

But further, the nearness of Jehovah to a nation can be expressed in terms of His nearness to an individual belonging to the nation or to a succession of such individuals, in fact to a kingly house. In the Old Testament the choice of God is represented not only as general, affecting a particular nation, but also as special, affecting one particular family. Yet *general* and *special* in this case are not mutually exclusive. The choice of David, described in 2 Sam. vii. 1—16, is not a choice of exclusion; on the contrary it is made for the ultimate inclusion of others. David is chosen for the sake of "my people

---

[1] Exod. xxxiii. 11 [E].
[2] *Ibid.*, ver. 20 [J or E].
[3] סגלה Exod. xix. 5 [E], λαὸς περιούσιος.
[4] Exod. iv. 22; Hos. xi. 1; Jer. xxxi. 20.
[5] Hos. ii. 16, 20; Jer. ii. 2.

[6] Exod. xx. 5, xxxiv. 14; cf. Isa. ix. 7.
[7] Gen. xii. 3; cf. Isa. xix. 23—25, a prophecy which has been referred on insufficient grounds to a writer of the Fourth Century B.C.

IX] *Permanent Value of the Old Testament* 349

Israel[1]." The special choice of David presupposes the general choice of Israel.

We find here the starting-point of the Messianic doctrine. God sought of His own purpose, *proprio motu* (if the phrase may be used), a man fit to be king over Israel[2]. The same thing has been said no doubt of heathen kings; indeed the words used of Cyrus "king of Persia" are no whit less emphatic than those used of David king of Israel[3]. Only, similar terms are used of kings of another line displaced by Cyrus, *e.g.* of Merodach-baladan II. The unwavering choice of the House of David to rule over Judah has no parallel, so far as I am aware, in other nations.

But even if a parallel were found, the doctrine of the choice of the House of David would still need to be considered in its wider context. It tended to become spiritual as time went on and passed by a natural development into a doctrine of Messiah. The doctrine of Messiah indeed from its earliest appearance in the Prophets (Isaiah and Micah) was a spiritual, not a mere political idea. Messiah is connected indeed with a temporal deliverance from Assyria, but the real subject of Messianic prophecy is Messiah's spiritual reign. The Old Fathers did not look only for mundane and transitory promises, for safety from invaders and oppressors; they looked (it may be said) for a righteous kingdom, a City of God.

This becomes clear when the chief Messianic prophecies are examined each by itself. The passages thus to be treated are (1) Micah iv. 8—v. 6, (2) Isa. ix. 1—7, (3) *ibid.* xi. 1—10, (4) Jer. xxiii. 5, 6; xxxiii. 15, 16[4], (5) Isa. lii. 13—liii. 12.

In our study of these great prophetic utterances very great caution is needed. The old expositors spiritualised every

---

[1] 2 Sam. vii. 10, 11.
[2] 1 Sam. xiii. 14. The collocation "a man after his own heart" is contrary to Hebrew idiom.
[3] "Marduk (Merodach) took compassion. All lands he inspected, he passed in review, and sought for a righteous prince after his heart, that he might take him by the hand. Cyrus king of Anshan he summoned by name," etc. Schrader, *Die Keilinschriften*, p. 381 (third edition).
[4] Ezek. xxxvii. 22—27 stands in some sense by itself; it is briefly discussed below in connexion with Jer. xxiii.

phrase; the modern find little or nothing spiritual in any one. Both may claim some support for their results from the nature of the passages themselves. What we call 'political' is blended with what we call 'religious,' present with future, the kingdom of Judah with the Kingdom of God. We must beware of ignoring or of minimising either the natural or the spiritual. Both are present and each must be considered. But we may say briefly that the prophets saw, each under a form suited to his own age, a vision of God's presence with men, realised to a new degree and 'specialised' (if the word may be used) in Israel through the instrumentality of a visible leader of Israel. The ideas of a chosen people and of a chosen leader upon whom the Spirit of God rests are found in all these prophetic passages.

We begin with the passages of more general contents, *i.e.* those found in Jeremiah and Ezekiel. Jeremiah's main prophecy is given in chapter xxiii. and repeated with some variations in chapter xxxiii. The context in each case is a promise of the return of Israel and Judah from captivity. The text of chapter xxiii. is as follows :—

Behold, the days come, saith the LORD, *that I will raise up to David a shoot, a righteous One, and* [*a king shall reign and deal wisely, and*[1]] *he shall do judgement and justice in the earth. In his days Judah shall be saved, and Israel shall dwell securely, and this is the name by which He shall be called,* JEHOVAH OUR RIGHTEOUSNESS (vers. 5, 6).

That chapter xxiii. preserves in substance the original form of Jeremiah's prophecy there is good reason to believe. The reference to captivity[2] is natural in the mouth of one who believed that the best of the land had gone into exile with Jehoiachin. The definite reference to a person, and that person a king, suits the time of Jeremiah better than any later time. The prophet of Anathoth had seen great things done under a king, Josiah, and faith relying on the analogy of the Past might hope for still greater things under a Davidic king yet to come. Moreover it is not fanciful to

---

[1] Omitted in xxxiii.; perhaps an early gloss.   [2] *vv.* 2, 8.

see allusions to kings contemporary with Jeremiah in the words, *I JEHOVAH will raise up a shoot*[1], and in the words, *JEHOVAH our righteousness*[2].

This prophecy of Jeremiah, though not so far-reaching as some utterances of Isaiah and Micah, is in essence Messianic. The prophet does not look to the fulfilment of promises that are merely temporary. A reign of a new kind, not a mere act of deliverance, is that which Jeremiah announces. The king is Davidic. The reign is not merely one of peace, but also one of righteousness and judgement. The duration of the reign is not mentioned, but the ideal reign must necessarily be thought of as prolonged; indeed the use of the word 'shoot' (Heb. *çemaḥ*), which can be used as a *collective*, rather than the word 'son' (Heb. *bên*), suggests that the prophet is thinking of a Davidic line rather than of a single king. The word king (Heb. *melech*), if the clause in which it occurs be genuine, catches a collective sense from the context.

A somewhat similar utterance of Jeremiah's contemporary, Ezekiel, illustrates Jeremiah's great prophecy. The prophet in Babylon, like the prophet in Judah, begins with a promise of the return of both Israel and Judah from captivity. He then continues:

And I will make them one nation in the land upon the mountains of Israel; and one king shall be king to them all...they shall also walk in my judgements, and observe my statutes, and do them...and David my servant shall be their prince for ever....My tabernacle also shall be with them; and I will be their God, and they shall be my people[3].

It is clear that Ezekiel has in his mind a vision of a future kingdom essentially the same as that which Jeremiah described. But on one point the exile of the river Chebar speaks more definitely. Jeremiah, it was said above, tells us nothing regarding the duration of the Messianic reign, though it is difficult to believe that he thought of it as of a merely human

---

[1] The meaning of *Jehoiakim* is *JEHOVAH raises up*.
[2] The meaning of *Zedekiah* is *JEHOVAH my righteousness*. Geiger's opinion that xxiii. 5—8 belongs to Hasmonean times has met with some acceptance, but there is very little to be said for it.
[3] Ezek. xxxvii. 22, 24, 25, 27.

span. But it is otherwise with Ezekiel. His central phrase suggests definitely the absence of a limit of time. The prince is to be *David my servant*, a person who in this connexion has neither beginning of days nor end of life. His reign is to be *for ever*.

This teaching of the Coming of a Righteous Kingdom (a City of God), which Jeremiah gave amid the falling ruins of the Judaean State, and Ezekiel amid the depressions of the Captivity, is traceable to earlier times. For we must look upon the prophets as a spiritual succession, as bearers of successive portions of the truths of Revelation; they are indeed a *goodly fellowship*; their central teaching is continuous from age to age; it is held in common by them all.

Probably both Jeremiah and Ezekiel derived the doctrine of the Righteous Kingdom from the very similar teaching given by Isaiah. The fact (if it be a fact) in no way throws doubt on the reality of their Divine commission. Their worth as prophets depends not on the newness of their doctrine, but on the spiritual insight which taught them that an old doctrine was fitted for the needs of new times, and also on the spiritual courage which was faithful to received truth in the darkest days.

The vision as we have it in Isaiah is described at greater length than in Jeremiah and Ezekiel. The passage, however, is so well known that only its chief phrases need to be repeated here:

And there shall come forth a rod out of the stock of Jesse, and a sapling (Heb. *nēçer*) *from his roots shall bear fruit. And the spirit of* JEHOVAH *shall rest upon him, the spirit of wisdom and understanding, the spirit of counsel and might, the spirit of knowledge and of fear of* JEHOVAH.... *With righteousness shall he judge the poor, and reprove with equity for the meek of the earth....The wolf also shall dwell with the lamb, and the leopard shall lie down with the kid....They shall not hurt nor destroy in all my holy mountain, for the earth*[1] *shall be full of the knowledge of* JEHOVAH[2].

[1] Or, *the land*.   [2] Isa. xi. 1, 2, 4, 6, 9.

IX] *Permanent Value of the Old Testament* 353

This is a fuller picture than that given either by Jeremiah or by Ezekiel. It is the expression of the mind of one who has received an earnest of his hope; it is indeed very much that which we should expect from Isaiah *after* Judah had been delivered from the Assyrians. The person of the king with his splendid endowment of spiritual and intellectual gifts is more fully realised here than in the two later prophets. He is a Davidic monarch endowed with a sevenfold dower of Divine grace. His reign is a reign of perfect wisdom and perfect righteousness.

It must not be thought that we have here merely a vision of temporal glories. It is true that the continuation of this passage[1] connects the Messianic Reign with the return of Israel and Judah from Assyrian bondage. But the prophecy itself is not concerned with the Assyrian oppression, but with things which lie beyond it. As in Jer. xxiii. the main thought is of the coming of the Kingdom of God. What remains is illustrative detail intended to help the contemporary hearer (or reader) to a fuller realisation of the blessings of the Kingdom.

But the vision of a Messianic reign was not confined to the later years of Isaiah, when a past deliverance from a terrible danger might suggest thoughts of peace. As early as the Syro-Ephraimite war, in the reign of Ahaz, under the stress of civil war[2] Isaiah had received a revelation of the Messianic King:

For to us is born a child,
To us is given a son,
And the government falls upon his shoulder,
And his name is called:
Wonderful Counsellor, Mighty God;
Eternal Father, Prince of Peace.
Great is his government, and peace hath no end upon the throne of David and upon his kingdom; he cometh to establish it and to uphold it in judgement and in righteousness from henceforth even for ever[3].

---

[1] Isa. xi. 10—16. [2] *Journal of Theological Studies*, vol. IV. pp. 17—27.
[3] Isa. ix. 6, 7.

This prophecy, like that of chapter xi., lays the stress on the Person of the Messianic King. The description given him in the fourfold name brings him very near to the Person of JEHOVAH. In chapter xi. the Spirit of JEHOVAH rests with sevenfold energy on the scion of David's House; here the Davidic king receives a title (*El gibbor*, "Mighty God") which might be given to JEHOVAH Himself. The quality of timelessness is added to the description; the Son of David is an *Eternal Father* to His people. Thus the most exalted realisation of the Person of Messiah is given in the earliest of Messianic prophecies.

The passage of Micah which speaks of the ideal ruler of Israel is near akin in its ideas to Isa. ix. 6, 7. Its starting-point is the Assyrian trouble, its immediate promise is of relief from the tyrant's yoke, but the prophet looks on to something greater, that is, to a Messianic age and a Messianic King:

And thou, Bethlehem Ephrathah, which art little to be among the thousands of Judah, out of thee shall one come forth unto me, one that is to be ruler in Israel; whose goings forth are[1] *from of old, from everlasting....And he shall stand, and shall feed his flock in the strength of the* LORD, *in the majesty of the name of the* LORD *his God: and they shall abide; for now shall he be great unto the ends of the earth*[2].

This prediction must of course be read in connexion with the earlier passage in which Micah[3] speaks of the future glory of Mount Zion. The fuller description of the Messianic Reign is to be read there. But the main elements of a Messianic prophecy are all found in Mic. v. 2, 4. We find the Davidic king, the endowment with Divine grace, the permanence of the reign, and the world-wide extent of the kingdom.

The persistence of the prophetic teaching as to a Messianic Reign to which the five passages discussed above bear witness

---

[1] Or, *whose origin is*.
[2] Micah v. 2, 4. For a study of Micah iv. 8—v. 6 see the *Expositor*, Sixth Series, vol. x. pp. 376—388.
[3] Micah iv. 1—7.

IX] *Permanent Value of the Old Testament* 355

is a most impressive fact. From Isaiah and Micah prophesying towards the end of the Eighth Century B.C. on to Jeremiah and Ezekiel labouring at the beginning of the sixth, from the triumphs and escapes of king Hezekiah down to the catastrophe of Jerusalem under Zedekiah and even beyond, the doctrine of the Advent of a righteous Davidic Ruler, the Saviour and Father of His people, always maintained itself. The unideal Present even in its darkest hour never availed to quench the hope of the ideal Future. The reigning king might be an Ahaz, a Jehoiakim, a Zedekiah, or even a monarch good but weak like Hezekiah, yet the prophetic vision was never lost. The House of David might *weary God* and *weary men*[1], and yet with it was bound up the hope of the Advent of the Kingdom of God.

It is to be noticed further that the doctrine of the Advent of the Messianic kingdom persists from prophet to prophet as a living doctrine. It is not a dead tradition handed on in a rigid formula from teacher to teacher. On the contrary each prophet expresses it in a form of his own. In Micah and Isaiah the details which form the setting of the picture are taken from the times of Ahaz and Hezekiah; in Jeremiah and Ezekiel the corresponding details are drawn from the beginning of the period of the Exile. The subject of the picture can be presented in several forms because it is a thing which lives in the hearts of the successive prophets.

But a very important question still remains. In the five prophetic passages discussed above there is a striking unanimity. The same doctrine of the Messianic kingdom is presented to us by all the prophetic teachers. But as regards the Person of the Messianic King, this unanimity is not reached. One passage seems at first sight to stand apart from the rest.

In Isa. ix. 6 the King is named by four names, the second of which is *Mighty God*. The remaining passages have nothing like this, unless we make an exception of Jer. xxiii. 6, "This is the name whereby he shall be called, JEHOVAH *our righteousness*" (or JEHOVAH *is our righteousness*). The question therefore arises, Do the Messianic passages

[1] Isa. vii. 13.

yield a consistent picture of the Person of the King, and, if so, what is it?

We may say at once that on any interpretation four of the passages agree as to two features of his person[1]; the king is in the first place of Davidic origin, in the second, the grace of God rests in unwonted measure upon him, or he is (in some sense) himself Divine. Some closer analysis however of the phenomena of these passages is necessary.

Looking back we see that Isaiah has two views, a 'higher' and a 'lower,' of the Person of the Messianic King. According to the first, which is peculiar to Isaiah, the king is Divine; according to the second, which agrees with the representation given by Micah, he is one upon whom the Divine spirit rests. Yet the two views are not mutually exclusive, for a thousand years intervene between Isaiah and the Council of Nicaea, and we must not look upon the prophet's expressions as rigid doctrinal statements. We may doubt whether Isaiah, if he had been asked whether the ideal King of his vision was human or Divine, could have answered the question at all. He recognised that Hezekiah the king of the grey Present was utterly human in his weakness and in his reliance on an "arm of flesh," but he could not see the person of the King of the golden Future of his vision with equal distinctness. The glory of the sight in part blinded the prophet. The fact which stood out most clearly before him was that the Son of David, the King of his Vision, stands very near to JEHOVAH Himself, stands indeed in a relation which is closer than any other known to men.

The modern theologian may ask, Does not such a conclusion represent Isaiah as holding a view which is inconsistent with the doctrine of the Unity of the Divine Nature, which presumably was held by the prophet? A further caution is therefore needed. We must not imagine that Isaiah had a philosophic conception of the unity of JEHOVAH. As contrasted with the gods of the heathen the God of Israel was doubtless *one*, but the prophet could nevertheless attribute to Him the words, *Who will go for us?*[2] It cannot

---

[1] The fifth passage (Ezek. xxxvii.) gives the first only of these features.
[2] Isa. vi. 8.

be shown that the doctrine of the Divine Nature had yet received a rigid form in Israel; certainly we find no trace in Isaiah's age of a metaphysical confession of JEHOVAH as a Monad. Rather the acknowledgement of JEHOVAH as the One God of Israel was as yet found compatible with a kind of dualism by which His Angel could at one moment be identified with, and at another distinguished from Himself.

During the century which separates Isaiah and Micah from Jeremiah and Ezekiel some progress seems to have been made in the definition of Doctrine. In the interval Deuteronomy was published and in it the great formula, *JEHOVAH our God, even JEHOVAH, is one*. Jeremiah seems always to be conscious of this principle; he mentions no angels, no cherubim; he stands himself alone in the presence of a God who is one.

Accordingly the name which the later prophet gives to the Messianic King is one which tells us nothing concerning the king's person, but something concerning the work of God. *JEHOVAH zidkenu* ("JEHOVAH is our righteousness") is a name descriptive not of the person of Messiah but only of the work which God will do through him. JEHOVAH will bring *righteousness* to His people by the hand of His Messiah. Messiah is a special instrument, a chosen vessel, for a great work; beyond this we learn nothing from Jeremiah concerning his person.

Ezekiel describes the future king with startling brevity as "David," the king given of old to Israel by special Divine gift. This title however does not fix our attention on the king himself but on his kingdom. It suggests, *first*, that the Divine Goodwill towards the subjects of the kingdom is assured, because JEHOVAH gives to them the ideal king, and, *secondly*, that the Messianic kingdom will be lasting, because God's faithful promises are with David. Of the person of the King, only enough to challenge thought is said.

It may be that both Jeremiah and Ezekiel shrink consciously from Isaiah's description of Messiah as *Mighty God*, as a title conflicting with the new exactness of definition given in the Seventh Century B.C. to the doctrine of the oneness of the God of Israel. It may be that in referring to the future King these two prophets purposely limit themselves to language which can be used of one who is purely human. But these concessions when they are made only throw into clearer light the fact that Isaiah does describe Messiah in terms too high to be applied to one who is merely man. The doctrine of the person of the Future King is not identical in the three great prophets. Once more we must remember that we have no formal doctrinal treatise before us, but three great Divine messages, each intended primarily for its own time and place. The person of Messiah is mysterious in the utterances of Jeremiah and Ezekiel, but in the teaching of Isaiah it is Divine. The future king is the agent of a world-wide Dispensation of Good, to be worked out in the sphere of the Coming Kingdom of God, and among the titles assigned him by the prophet who gives the fullest description of his work, is one which caused a difficulty to Isaiah's successors in the prophetic office, and causes a difficulty to some critics at the present day, the title of *Mighty God*.

The mystery of the Incarnation is foreshadowed in Isaiah; Deutero-Isaiah adds a vision of the Conquering Cross:

Behold, my servant shall deal wisely,
He shall be exalted and lifted up,
And shall be very high.

He shall sprinkle many nations.

He was despised, and rejected of men ;
A man of sorrows, and acquainted with grief.

The Lᴏᵍᴅ *hath laid on him the iniquity of us all.*

He was oppressed,
Yet he humbled himself and opened not his mouth ;

He was cut off out of the land of the living.

*If thou shalt make his soul an offering for sin,
He shall see his seed, he shall prolong his days,
And the pleasure of the LORD shall prosper in his
  hand.*

*I will divide for him the great,
And the strong he shall divide as spoil*[1].

The change in the description of the person of Messiah, as the Messianic vision is handed on from Isaiah to Jeremiah and Ezekiel, prepares the student of the Old Testament for the further change which first shows itself in the prophecy of Deutero-Isaiah. In Isaiah Messiah is Divine, in Jeremiah he is simply *a shoot of David*, in Ezekiel he is *David my servant*. No doubt the two later prophets think of the future king as one fully endued (like David) with the spirit of JEHOVAH, but they do not follow their predecessor in giving him a title higher than any which can be given to any merely human hero. Messiah is—for all that Jeremiah and Ezekiel say to the contrary—*human*. And it is just on this side—the human—that a fresh revelation was about to be given. Hitherto the leader of Israel had been portrayed as a prosperous king, now he is to be described as suffering under oppression. Perhaps the sufferings which the nation as a whole underwent during the Exile prepared the way for the thought of a leader for Israel who suffers, but in any case the transition is made, and it is the more easy since the future king is never represented even in the earlier prophecies as a Conqueror in war, but as a Prince of Peace. JEHOVAH fights his battles for him. In Deutero-Isaiah the character of the king has become merged in that of the sufferer. There can be no doubt of the identity of the central figure with the king of the earlier prophecies, though in this last passage there is no express mention of the House of David, nor of any kingship.

The *Servant of* JEHOVAH according to Old Testament thought is always a leader of men, a prophet at least[2], if not

[1] Isa. lii., liii. [2] Amos iii. 7.

a Moses[1] or a David[2]. The *Servant of* JEHOVAH *who shall deal wisely*[3] *and be exalted and lifted up and shall be very high* is a Prince in spite of any depth of humiliation to which he may be for a time exposed.

But what is to be said of the *work* of the *Servant of* JEHOVAH? At first sight it appears to be utterly different from that of the Davidic King spoken of by Isaiah, Micah, Jeremiah, and Ezekiel. Certainly our first impulse is to deny that it has anything in common with the work of the King of the Fourfold Name. The earlier prophets speak of the administration of a kingdom, but where is the mention of a kingdom in the prophecy of Deutero-Isaiah?

The contrast is more apparent than real. It is striking only as long as we regard the Kingdom spoken of by the earlier prophets as purely mundane, and as long as we search Isa. lii. 13—liii. 12 for the word *kingdom*, and not for the signs of kingly rule. The contrast however loses almost all its significance in the light of two considerations. In the first place the future Kingdom spoken of in Isa. ix. 7 (and the kindred passages) is not "of this world." The prophet ascribes to it the three qualities of *permanence, peacefulness*, and *righteousness*. It is a kingdom without fortresses and without chariots, a kingdom of moral, not material, forces. It does not coerce, but attracts, it does not impose a yoke, but teaches to willing scholars *the ways of* JEHOVAH[4]. Such an institution as this cannot be tied to the name of *kingdom*; it is a new cosmos, a *civitas Dei*, though it is presented by Isaiah in the guise of an Israelite state under a Davidic king.

The second consideration which helps to diminish the contrast between Isa. ix. and Isa. lii.—liii. is that the latter passage does contain elements which suggest a kingdom, albeit a spiritual one. The Servant of JEHOVAH, it has been said above, is a Prince and leader of men. In this passage he claims many nations for the God of Israel by sprinkling[5] them

[1] Num. xii. 7.
[2] 2 Sam. vii. 5.
[3] Cf. Jer. xxiii. 5, "shall reign and deal wisely."
[4] Micah iv. 2.
[5] The emendation of the Hebrew word *yazzeh*, "he shall sprinkle," is a desperate device, though it has

IX] *Permanent Value of the Old Testament* 361

with cleansing water or blood (lii. 15). The power of JEHOVAH is manifested through him (liii. 1), and the pleasure of JEHOVAH is carried out by his hand (*ibid.* ver. 10). The spiritual kingdom is found in this passage in fact though not in name. The only contrast which remains between Isa. ix. 1—7 and Isa. lii. 13—liii. 12 is one of a difference of framework, not of essential contents. In the first passage, written while the kingdom of Judah was still standing, the imagery of the temporal state is borrowed in order to give expression to a spiritual message. In the second passage, written half a century after the fall of the Jewish state, all such imagery is discarded as useless for illustration. Something which is in fact a spiritual kingdom is described, but the name of *kingdom* is not given to it. The passage makes clear to us the fact that the Messianic idea is not inseparably bound up with a victorious king of Judah.

But the special significance of Isa. lii. 13—liii. 12 lies still deeper. The passage shows us the means by which the King builds up his spiritual kingdom. It is by *sprinkling many nations*; it is by *justifying many* (or *making many righteous*). The work is done not on the battlefield, but in the spiritual sphere, the sphere in which God meets with the soul of man. The Servant *poured out his soul unto death*, and so in his own person reconciled the rebellious to God (liii. 12).

We find then that there was growing up in Israel from the end of the Eighth Century B.C. to the end of the Sixth a doctrine of a coming Kingdom of God. To this doctrine successive prophets made their contributions, not formally or scholastically, but naturally as to a faith by which men live. The message was re-stated in each prophecy according to the circumstances of the age in which it was delivered. Usually some fresh element was added. At first sight it seems that the several portions of prophetic teaching cannot

commended itself to some good scholars. The word is a common word, and is used in its ordinary sense. The omission of a preposition ('*al*) after the verb can be defended by sufficient parallels. No argument for emendation can be based on the LXX rendering, which indeed is very bad for the greater part of this passage.

be united into an homogeneous body of teaching. A more careful examination however proves their harmony. The differences are of the outward form. There is a progress, but no disunion. A Son of David, Divine on one side of His Nature, reigns over a Kingdom of Peace[1], the knowledge of JEHOVAH prevails everywhere in it[2], the Man from Bethlehem is great even to the ends of the earth[3], He bears the symbolic name, *JEHOVAH our righteousness*[4], He is a Prince for ever[5], and the means by which He wins this splendid position, and gives peace to His people is by pouring out His soul unto death, a sacrifice which is accepted by JEHOVAH as a sacrifice for sin[6].

This living doctrine of the prophets which prevailed more than five hundred years before the Coming of our Lord is in itself sufficient proof that Christianity is no new faith, but a republication and perfecting of an old. The permanent value of the Old Testament consists in the first place in this, that it is a witness to the fact that Christianity is part of the World-Scheme.

As compared with this great service of the Old Testament to Religion, all other services must seem relatively small. In an essay like the present it is sufficient to mention them briefly. In the first place then not the least of these further services of the Old Testament consists in its witness to the value of many elements in the faiths of the Pre-Christian World. It is sometimes said in disparagement, as it were, of the religion of Moses, that most of its ordinances and not a few of its doctrines are to be found in the religions of Israel's neighbours. The sacrificial system of Leviticus resembles in some points that which prevailed among the Phoenicians. The Sabbath was in some form perhaps derived from Babylon. There are signs moreover that in practice (as distinct from theory) the monotheism of the Hebrews was not always easily to be distinguished from the devotion of

---

[1] Isa. ix.   [2] *ib.* xi.   [3] Micah v.
[4] Jer. xxiii.   [5] Ezek. xxxvii.   [6] Isa. liii.

IX] *Permanent Value of the Old Testament* 363

Moab to Chemosh, the national God of Moab, and of Assyria to Asshur the eponymous God of Assyria.

Thus viewed with modern eyes the religion of Moses loses a good deal of the *originality* with which it was once credited. But this loss is a gain to the thoughtful religious man. If *Mosaism* (to use an ugly but useful word) was the only light shining in the world before Christ's coming, how are Christians to understand St Paul's assertion that God *left not Himself without witness* among the Gentiles in the earlier days[1], or that passage of the Epistle to the Romans which speaks of the Gentiles as having no law, and yet being a law to themselves, their conscience bearing witness with a law written in their hearts[2]?

Points of contact between the Jewish religion and the faiths of their neighbours are not evidence that all these early religions are equally false (as some insinuate); rather they enable us to see that if one imperfect religion was helpful in preparing the way for the Christian Revelation among the Hebrews, other imperfect faiths might perform the same office among the Gentiles. Accepting this view of the religious history of the world, to which the Old Testament itself points us, we find ourselves in accord with some of the best of early Christian thought, with the following sentiments of Origen for instance:—

"When God sent Jesus to the human race, it was not as though He had just awoken from a long sleep, but Jesus, though He has only now for worthy reasons fulfilled the divine plan of His incarnation, has at all times been doing good to the human race. For no noble deed among men has ever been done without the Divine Word visiting the souls of those who even for a brief space were able to receive such operations of the Divine Word[3]."

It is true that there are many passages of the Old Testament which pass an unqualified condemnation on all other religions than the Mosaic. It is true, but not the whole truth. "Blood is thicker than water," and the life-blood of

[1] Acts xiv. 17.
[2] Rom. ii. 14—16.
[3] As translated in Hort's *Ante-Nicene Fathers*, p. 133.

the Old Testament (if I may use the phrase) is found flowing in the veins of these other religions. The prophets were bound to protest against the influence of foreign religions, in spite of the truth which was bound up in them, for they found that these religions were apt to communicate their worst elements and not their best, when their influence was brought to bear upon the people of Israel. Practices such as Soothsaying and Human Sacrifices were easier to transmit than Faith and Love and Honesty. But in modern days we see in Assyrian penitential psalms and in Vedic hymns a side of the old Gentile faiths which perhaps the prophets never saw, a side which has kinship with the teaching of the Hebrew prophets themselves, and through the prophets with the teaching of Evangelists and Apostles. The links are complete; we see a Way, a Truth, and a Life which was not confined to a few centuries, not to one small people. The second service of the Old Testament to the cause of Religion is that it stands as a permanent witness to the fact that God gave light to many nations, and not to one only, before the coming of Christ.

Again, the Old Testament is valuable to religious men of all ages for the illustration it gives of God's method of Revelation. Revelation is not a sudden act, but a gradual process. Its full daylight does not come with one blinding world-wide flash, but with the gradual broadening of a tiny ray of light, a broadening which many men think too slow. Adam in the Garden (not Milton's Adam, but the Adam of Genesis) is a creature evidently fit to receive only the simplest teaching. He is shown his duty, one thing to be done—a garden to be kept; one thing not to be done—a particular tree not to be touched. It is the kind and the degree of moral discipline to which the veriest savage might be put. Later on we come to the revelation—a somewhat fuller revelation—given to Noah after the Flood. All the living creatures are delivered into Man's hand for his use or to slay for his food. Only Man is taught that the shedding of blood, even of the blood of a beast, is an awful thing. The blood of a beast is not to be eaten, the shedding of a man's blood is to be punished

Permanent Value of the Old Testament

with death. Still very few and simple commands, only the beginnings of a moral law, and yet sufficient to train man. The development is still slow when we reach Abraham. Abraham *was called the friend of God*[1], but we shall entirely misunderstand both the man, and God's dealings with the man, unless we realise at what a low state of morality he stood at the beginning, and even towards the end of his career. The Mosaic law was not yet given, much less the law of Christ, and Abraham must not be judged by them. Two facts mark the moral stage at which the patriarch stood, first, his denial of his wife, secondly, his temptation to offer up his son. The denial of Sarai was an especially revolting act, since it was accompanied with Abraham's own enrichment, an enrichment contemplated in advance by the patriarch. The temptation to offer up Isaac could only have happened to one whose moral condition was below that of the generation which Prophets taught. Such an act as a human sacrifice is never mentioned later in the Bible[2] without a tone of horror in the telling. But Abraham acted up to his light, such as it was. He obtained and deserved a blessing for being willing to surrender his chief treasure to his God, but the same willingness in a man who had heard the prophecies of Micah or Isaiah would have been a defiance of morality in the name of superstition.

We judge Abraham, then, by his own age, and not by later times, but judged by his own age what a splendid figure he is! This half-savage man, journeying to and fro in a savage land which knew no law but force, a stranger with no hold on life except by the sword of his servants and no foothold in the land except a burial place bought from the Hittites, bought when towards the end of his days the inhabitants had learned to respect the increase of his strength,—this half-savage man learned to look forward to the fulfilment of God's promises, and upwards to God as his protector. He became the Father of the Faithful, the pioneer (so to speak) of the men of every age who hear the voice of God amidst the tumult and terror of the earth. He was a learner in morality and a learner in

---

[1] James ii. 23.   [2] With the difficult exception of Jephthah.

religion; he had to learn God that his descendants might learn virtue. Imperfect as he is, he towers above the men of his time, and—in the matter of faith—over most men of all time.

We need not go below Abraham in tracing out the method of God's revelation. The rest of the narrative of the Old Testament surely confirms the conclusion about to be drawn. The method of God's revelation, then, is marked by two features. In the first place, God does not hurry (be it reverently said). *A thousand years* of moral evolution *are with Him as one day*:

"So many a million of ages have gone to the making of man."

The other feature of God's revelation is that He reveals Himself, before He reveals the whole moral Law. Throughout the Old Testament we are shown a double revelation in progress, a revelation of God growing fuller and fuller, and a revelation of duty growing wider and wider.

The value of the Old Testament in this respect lies in the light it throws not only on the history of religion in the past, but also on the religious circumstances of the present day. Man—even religious man—still answers to the poet's characterisation,

"The piebald miscellany, Man,
Bursts of great heart and slips in sensual mire."

And we shall be perplexed, perhaps daunted by what we see, unless we learn the lesson of the Hebrew Scriptures, that the moral nature of Imperfect Man is very slowly perfected in the providence of God. Startling contrasts remain even in those whose religious sincerity is past question, and there exists perhaps no better reminder of this important truth than the story of Abraham, whom the Old Testament holds up not indeed for a perfect example, but as a hero of Faith.

Again, the Old Testament has been and is most helpful to simple souls by reason of the story of Creation. It may be granted that the first chapter of Genesis contributes nothing to modern Natural Science. But the Origin of the Universe is quite as much a theological question as a physical one.

IX] *Permanent Value of the Old Testament* 367

If the modern religious man is to be free from superstition[1], he must be assured that the mysterious world in which he lives is the creature of one Almighty God. The first chapter of Genesis devotes itself to giving such an assurance.

How welcome this assurance has been to man at all times is a fact which needs no laboured proof, but one testimony to the opening verses of Genesis must not be withheld. About the year 150 A.D. there came from the mountains of Northern Mesopotamia a heathen named Tatian travelling westward to Greece and Rome in search of religious truth to satisfy a gnawing spiritual hunger. Somewhere in the Grecian lands he was told that the sun was a glowing mass, the moon a world, that there were three tenses, past, present, and future, and that his own Greek pronunciation left something to be desired. Very good information, but not of much value to a man whom a desire to find the true God had driven from his home! Leaving Greece he pushed on to Rome. There he was recommended to the worship of Jupiter Latiaris and of Diana, but his simple provincial soul revolted at the discovery that these two deities delighted in human sacrifices. He was driven in upon himself; his own words may tell the sequel:

"Now as I was considering what was best to be done I "chanced to light upon certain barbarian books, older than "the opinions of the Greeks, and too divine to be compared "with their errors. And it happened that I was persuaded "by these because of their unpretentious style, and the "simplicity of the writers, and the plain statement of the "creation of all things,...and the unity of the divine govern-"ment over all....And I perceived that these writings bring to "an end the bondage that is in the world, and rescue us from "ten thousand powers that would fain lord it over us[2]."

The Old Testament again is of abiding value in the tremendous moral issues which lie now before the world, and it may be that the splendid ideals of a Messianic kingdom

---

[1] The modern cult of "Christian science" in America and England shows that the danger of superstition is not an unreal danger in the present day.
[2] *Ad Graecos*, § 29.

which the prophets of Israel announced will play no small part in the movement now going on towards Social Righteousness. On this point the words of a non-theological writer may be quoted: "Throughout the history of the Western World" (so he writes) "the Scriptures, Jewish and Christian, have "been the great instigators of revolt against the worst forms "of clerical and political despotism. The Bible has been the "*Magna Charta* of the poor and of the oppressed ; down to "modern times no state has had a constitution in which the "interests of the people are so largely taken into account, in "which the duties, so much more than the privileges, of rulers "are insisted upon, as that drawn up for Israel in Deuteronomy "and Leviticus ; nowhere is the fundamental truth that the "welfare of the state, in the long run, depends on the upright- "ness of the citizen so strongly laid down. Assuredly the "Bible talks no trash about the rights of man ; but it insists "upon the equality of duties, on the liberty to bring about "that righteousness which is somewhat different from "struggling for 'rights' ; on the fraternity of taking thought "for one's neighbour as for one-self."

These words are those of Professor Huxley[1].

The permanent value then of the Old Testament reveals itself in four particulars. In the first place the Old Testament supplies the chief part of the pre-Christian history of Christianity. Without the presentation of such a history Christianity is left with a serious gap in the evidences of its truth. If no worthy *Praeparatio* of Christianity can be pointed out, then the proof that Christianity is part of the Universal Divine Providence is left seriously incomplete, and therefore weak. But we find in fact on the contrary in the Old Testament an expanding revelation of Truth, which the experience of more than eighteen centuries shows to have found its only fitting continuation in the Christian Faith.

But in the second place the Old Testament, besides containing the chief part of the History of the Divine Preparation for Christianity, points to other parts of the same history, which it does not itself contain. As we study the Old

---

[1] *Essays upon some Controverted Questions* (1892), Prologue, pp. 52—3.

Permanent Value of the Old Testament

Testament more deeply, and compare its teaching with the information we possess regarding Gentile religions, we are led upwards to a still grander view, a more complete view, of the work of Divine Providence in preparing for the Gospel. The points of resemblance between the revealed religion of the Hebrews and the other religions of the pre-Christian world, which a comparison yields, supply a proof that the Almighty Father provided in addition to one 'tutor' for the Hebrew people many other tutors to lead the nations of the world to the same Christ.

In the third place part of the permanent value of the Old Testament lies in its witness to the imperfections and incompletenesses of the Old Revelation. Even under the Christian revelation we have to confess that *we know in part and prophesy in part.* Many of the difficulties in accepting and in holding our Faith disappear when we realise the truth which the Old Testament illustrates so fully, namely, that God's way is to speak *by many parts and in many manners.*

Lastly, it should be said that the witness of the Old Testament to God's demand for Social Righteousness can never lose its force. The Christian Socialists of the middle of the Nineteenth Century after Christ were moved by the words of the Prophets of the Eighth Century before Christ. The teachers of the Old Jerusalem have made it possible for later seers to see a vision of *the New Jerusalem descending out of Heaven from God.*

ESSAY X.

THE GOSPELS IN THE LIGHT OF HISTORICAL CRITICISM.

FREDERIC HENRY CHASE, D.D.

ANALYSIS.

Introduction. Aim and method of historical study.
Application of the historical method to (1) the Old Testament; (2) the Origins of Christianity.
Relation of the Gospels to the Gospel.
The documents (the Four Gospels).

I. The record of our Lord's sayings.
Their preservation conditioned by three influences: (1) memory; (2) translation; (3) the editor's hand.
Conclusions.

II. The record of our Lord's life on earth.
Light thrown by the comparative study of the Gospels on their character as historical witnesses.

(I) The Resurrection. Evidence of (1) St Paul; (2) The Gospels. Consideration of objections: (i) The accounts formless and inconsistent; (ii) The Gospels at variance as to *time* and *place*; (iii) The disciples unscientific.
Other considerations: (i) Christ's character; (ii) The sequel of the Resurrection.
Conclusions.

(II) The Miracles. Present state of the question. Considerations now urged: (1) Two classes of miracles (works of healing; nature-miracles); (2) Analogy of miracles in other religious movements.
Considerations urged in this Essay: (1) Character of the earliest Gospel; (2) Nature-miracles in the earliest Evangelical stratum; (3) Absence of reference to our Lord's miracles in the Epistles; (4) Scope and motive of the miracles.
Do miracles involve the suspension of natural laws?
Conclusions.

(III) The Virgin-birth. The evidence differs from that of the Resurrection.
Sources of information open to the writers of the First and Third Gospels.
Discrepancies between the two accounts.
Consideration of important points in the two accounts.
Review of theories as to the genesis of the history in (i) Gentile-Christian circles; (ii) Jewish circles: (*a*) Isa. vii. 14; (*b*) Philo's allegories; (*c*) The history of Isaac's birth.
A priori expectations as to the mode of the Incarnation irrelevant.
Conclusions.

Conclusions. Effect of historical criticism on Christian belief: (i) Desire for truth; (ii) Varying degrees of certitude; (iii) Faith, not demonstration.
Danger of alienation. The mutual duties of 'simple Christians' and students.

THE GOSPELS IN THE LIGHT OF HISTORICAL CRITICISM.

THE title of this Essay brings us face to face with a group of problems which are felt to be of increasing importance to every thoughtful Christian. Many of the questions which are most vehemently discussed among religious people do but ruffle the surface of the Church's life. These affect permanently its deepest currents. The burden of dealing with them seems to be laid on this generation. They cannot be disposed of by the easy method of dogmatic assertion. They clearly demand long and patient consideration on the part of many students, regarding them from different points of view, and bringing to bear on them varied experience and knowledge. Yet probably no one approaches the subject free from bias, either the bias which springs from a tendency (however acquired) to question, or the bias which springs from a tendency (however acquired) to affirm, traditional views. In the providence of God both types of students may serve the cause of truth. The one is an effective witness against a slothful acquiescence in what has been received. The other offers a protest always needful against that temper of mind, a parody of intellectual candour, which with inconsiderate haste catches at the new. Progress towards truth is attained by the correction of inherited views of truth. And this process of correction from its very nature must be slow and painful and tentative.

From what has been said it will be clear that my aim here is not to attempt anything like a final verdict on these momentous questions. Nor, within the necessarily narrow limits of an essay, will that minute discussion of details be possible which is essential for a full and complete treatment of the subject. It must be sufficient to indicate the conditions of the problem, to state principles, and to offer in regard to certain aspects of the whole problem such a solution, however proximate and provisional, as the evidence at our disposal seems to warrant.

The study of history has now become a science, both in regard to its aim and in regard to its method. An historian of the old school was content to glean from his authorities a picturesque, or a majestic, or an instructive story. Finished pictures of events, life-like portraits of great men, the interpretation of the past as a prophecy of the present—such was the work on which he spent his strength. But it lacked the security which comes from the recognition of clearly defined principles and of a single aim. In a word, the historian was lost in the politician or in the man of letters. The historian of to-day, on the other hand, is primarily a student pledged to the work of research. His method is precise. He conscientiously collects his authorities; he analyses them; he compares them; he weighs them in the balances of his critical judgement. From a consideration of the evidence which he has accumulated, he reconstructs the life not only of the period with which he is dealing, but also of that to which his authorities belong; and in the light of this reconstruction he estimates the value of the accounts, whether contemporary or traditional, on which he bases his results. Thus chronicles become documents—a term which itself suggests severe and prosaic repression; and these he interprets and reduces, so far as he can, to their original elements of fact and romance. Further, if he is dealing with an early period, especially if questions of social custom or religious belief are involved, he claims the aid of anthropology.

And if the historian's methods are thus precise, so his final aim is simple. It is not grandeur, or pathos, or artistic beauty, but historical truth. Truth is the one and only thing which it is his business to discover and to present—words

x] *The Gospels in the light of historical criticism* 375

which were really spoken, events which really happened and which became the cause of events that followed them. At the same time it must ever be remembered that, from the very nature of the evidence from which the historian draws his conclusions as to a distant past, he must be content with probable results. In historical studies demonstration is impossible.

It may be truly said that such a rigid method of historical enquiry involves loss. In this attempt to get back to the bare truth of the past we surrender much that is beautiful. We gain only a relative accuracy: we sacrifice poetry. It must sometimes seem to us that

> "Our meddling intellect
> Misshapes the beauteous forms of things:
> We murder to dissect."

Yet here, as elsewhere, we believe that time will redress the seeming wrong; that truth, at least the whole-hearted search for truth, has in the end some better things in store than any of which it threatens to rob us. Science in the province of history works on in the belief that in due season there will come a great reward in pure and trustworthy knowledge.

A few years ago attention was concentrated on the application of historical criticism to the literature of the Old Testament. To speak broadly, calmness has now succeeded panic. A feeling of antipathy and dismay has given place to a sense of reassurance and hope. It would be too much to say that earnest and thoughtful men are in complete agreement as to the results of Old Testament criticism. But at least something like a consensus of opinion has been attained. A large number of serious and devout Christians thankfully allow that methods of investigation which seemed at first to threaten revolution have in truth taught them fruitful and abiding lessons. Such men do not think of the early chapters of Genesis as their fathers thought. Their views as to the way in which God unfolded Himself to Israel and through Israel to the world, and as to the historical character of some portions of the literature of the Old Testament, have been sensibly modified; and this modification has been found to remove many ancient stumbling-blocks in the way of an intelligent faith.

It was not difficult to foresee that the time would soon come when in a new sense and with a new cogency the principles of historical criticism would be applied to the origins of Christianity. Christianity is an historical religion; a religion, that is, which, though it must needs be tested by present human experience, yet as a matter of fact is based neither on philosophical speculations nor on spiritual intuitions, but on alleged events, the events of the earthly life of the Lord Jesus Christ. The record of these events is contained *for us* in the literature of the New Testament, and of course above all in the Gospels.

The relation of the Gospels to the Gospel is obvious; but it is worth while explicitly to state it. The Gospels were not the source of the forces which, to speak of course from the historian's point of view, created the life of the Church. They were themselves the outcome of that life. The Christian Society existed before the Gospels, and *essentially* is independent of them. The faith of that Society has been watered and matured by the devout study of the Gospels; but it was not planted by that study. The evidence of those Epistles of St Paul the genuineness of which is not impugned by serious critics leaves no possibility for doubt that the alleged facts about the Lord, which are the essence of the Christian faith to-day, were also the substance of the message which was proclaimed by the first Christian missionaries. It cannot be maintained that this Gospel was the creation of the genius of St Paul. The Church was in existence before his apostolate; for he tells us that he had himself persecuted it. And those who were Apostles before him, as he explicitly asserts, proclaimed in the same way as he himself the Lord's death and the Lord's resurrection (1 Cor. xv. 3—11). In this connexion the evidence of the Epistle to the Romans is of special importance. The Church at Rome included among its members many personal friends of St Paul; but it was not a Pauline Church. The precise circumstances of its origin are lost in obscurity. It no doubt gradually grew up, as converts,

x] *The Gospels in the light of historical criticism* 377

whether Jews or Gentiles, found their way to the capital of the Empire from centres of trade where the Gospel had been already preached. If any Church, surely the Church at Rome represented the average belief of the Apostolic age. But in writing to this Church which owned no Apostle as its evangelist or its teacher, which sprang up we know not how, St Paul refers to the great *momenta* of the life of Christ— His human birth, His redemptive death, His resurrection— not as matters which were unfamiliar and which needed explanation, but as facts a knowledge of which he could as a matter of course assume on the part of all who were members of a Christian Church. Thus the belief in the birth, the crucifixion, the resurrection of the Lord, and the conviction that He stood in an absolutely unique relation to God are shown to have been universal and (in the strictest sense of the word) primitive. The faith of the Christian Church was prior to, and independent of, the Gospels. And it must be added, however far from practical issues the statement may be, that, as the Gospels were not necessary for the genesis of the Church, so the discovery that they were unhistorical in their presentation even of important elements in our Lord's life would not of itself cause the dissolution of the Church. The Eucharist, the Christian Sunday, the existence of the Christian Church itself are evidences of Christ's earthly life, of His death and of the view which His first followers took of His death, and lastly of a belief in the Resurrection which can only have originated in the days which immediately followed His Crucifixion[1]. Let us then for the sake of argument imagine a result, which I am deeply convinced that sober criticism will never bring about; let us suppose that Christian men have been obliged to surrender their trust in the Gospels as substantially true records of the Lord's life on earth. They have become unspeakably poorer; the historical Christ is for them a thin and unsubstantial figure; but Christ Himself, as the One who died for their sins and rose again from the dead, has not been taken from them.

The application of the methods of historical criticism to

[1] See Salmon, *Non-miraculous Christianity*, pp. 13 f.

the Gospels is a process which we cannot ignore or hinder. It will rather be welcomed by all who believe in the providential ordering of the intellectual advance of the world, and who are convinced that the Holy Spirit is to-day sent forth to guide the mental activity of seekers after truth. Such men will regard with honest sympathy and appreciation, albeit with vigilant caution, the handling of the records of our Lord's life on earth that is based on those methods of investigation which during the last few years have proved fruitful of result in other fields of enquiry.

The first duty of historical criticism is to examine the documents which it recognises as the authorities for any period. It is still busily at work on the records contained in the New Testament. In regard to the comparative study of the Gospels it would be obviously premature to speak of final and comprehensive results. But certain conclusions seem already established beyond the reach of reasonable doubt. If I may summarise a large and intricate subject, they are these. (1) In the First and Third Gospels we can trace two chief strata corresponding to what appear to be the two main sources, whether written or oral. The one of these, in the main identical with the Second Gospel, contains the story of the Lord's Baptism, His ministry in Galilee, the last week at Jerusalem, the Passion, and the discovery of the empty tomb. The other comprehends sayings and discourses of the Lord. (2) The authors of these two Gospels arranged and edited the materials on which they severally worked, sometimes interpreting them, sometimes giving them new point and fulness, sometimes adding information which, as we may believe, either one of them derived from some authority unknown to, or unused by, the other. (3) The sources themselves, in the period which elapsed before we have knowledge of them, must have been gradually taking shape; and this process of formation must have been analogous to the process of editing which we can discern in the First and Third Gospels, when we compare them with the Second. (4) The Fourth Gospel stands apart from the Synoptic Gospels. It appears

x] *The Gospels in the light of historical criticism* 379

to presuppose them, to supplement them, and sometimes to correct them. It opens with a theological statement as to the Word of God, and as to the Incarnation of the Word; and the earthly life of our Lord is presented to us in a form which vindicates and explains this position. The writer, whom the Church from the second century onwards has identified with St John, tells the story of the Lord's works, and records His words, not on the authority of others, but as one who himself had 'seen and believed.' (5) If a question be asked in regard to the date of the Gospels, the general answer may be given that the average opinion of scholars places the date of the Synoptic Gospels in the decade immediately preceding, or in the decade and a half immediately following, the Destruction of Jerusalem, and assigns the Fourth Gospel to the last fifteen years of the first century, though those who abandon the Johannine authorship commonly consider that it belongs to the first two decades of the second century[1].

The traditions as to the First Gospel are meagre and obscure, and we can make no positive assertion as to its authorship and early history.

The Second Gospel, according to what appears to be a trustworthy tradition, was written for Roman readers by John Mark, the companion and 'interpreter' of St Peter, and embodies the substance of that Apostle's reminiscences of his Master's works and words.

There is much internal evidence which confirms, and (so far as I can see) no internal evidence which leads us to question, the constant tradition of the Church, which we can trace back to the last quarter of the second century, that the Acts and consequently the Third Gospel also were the work of St Luke, the companion of St Paul[2]. We learn from an incidental notice in the Acts (xxi. 15 ff.) that the author of the Book, in company with St Paul, visited Jerusalem some

[1] In regard to the Synoptic Gospels I am referring to the opinions of what may be termed the moderately conservative school. A useful table giving a conspectus of opinions will be found in Moffatt, *The His-torical New Testament*, ed. 2, p. 273.
[2] I may be allowed to refer to my Hulsean Lectures, *The Credibility of the Book of the Acts of the Apostles*, pp. 9 ff.

twenty-five years after the Crucifixion, that he became known to St James and to the Elders of the Church there, many of whom must have seen and heard the Lord. Further, since he went to Jerusalem with St Paul and, after the latter's two years' imprisonment at Caesarea, embarked with him from that port on the voyage to Rome, it is a fair inference that he spent the whole or some portion of those two years in Palestine and in Jerusalem. I may perhaps be forgiven for adding my own view as to the chronological relation of St Luke's two Books. It is, so far as I know, universally assumed that the Gospel was written first, and afterwards at some later date the Acts. It is of course true that the respective subjects of the two treatises determined their relative order, the Gospel, the 'first treatise,' dealing with the earlier and creative period, the Acts, the 'second treatise,' treating of the later and secondary period. But it by no means follows that the two Books were planned and composed in this order. The probabilities are, I think, in the other direction. As early as the time when he wrote the Epistle to the Galatians, St Paul was fully aware of the necessity for some authoritative statement as to the main facts of his own life, and especially as to his relation to the Apostles at Jerusalem. The sense of the need of some true record of his work, as the fulfilment of a great commission, would not lessen as the years brought fresh controversies and increased the complexity of the Church's life. When then the Apostle was contemplating his last journey to Jerusalem, with the solemn consciousness that it would not improbably cost him his life (Acts xx. 22 f., 25, Rom. xv. 30 ff.), what more likely than that he should at this crisis entrust to his friend and fellow-traveller, whose literary power could hardly have escaped his notice, the task of telling in outline the story of his apostolate? On the supposition that St Luke had already taken this responsibility we have a natural explanation of the care and fulness which characterize in so marked a degree the last ten chapters of the Acts. Subsequently, as we may suppose, the opportunities of obtaining information from those who had been "eye-witnesses and ministers of the word," and on the other hand a growing sense that St Paul's apostolate could not be understood apart from the apostolate of the Twelve, and still more that St Paul's life and work had their root in the life and work of his Master, led to two successive enlargements of the original plan. In the first place the treatise must comprehend, not only the acts of Paul, but also the acts of the Apostles. In the second place another treatise must be written containing the acts of Jesus Christ. Such a theory as to the composition of the two Lucan Books does not admit of proof; but it is in itself natural; it gives a reasonable account of the genesis of the two Books; it harmonizes with the facts. In particular it explains the relation between two very important sections of St Luke's writings—the closing section of the Gospel and the opening section of the Acts. The history of the Ascension, including the statement as to the Lord's appearances during forty days, which forms the almost necessary introduction to the Acts of the Apostles, is naturally summarised and not repeated at the close of the later treatise on the works and words of the Lord Jesus.

The Fourth Gospel presents problems a *complete* solution of which has not been found, and probably never will be found. What are we to say of the difficulties which confront the traditional view, more especially of the marked contrast between the Fourth Gospel and the Synoptic Gospels? If, assuming that the author of the Fourth Gospel was himself a primary authority, we suppose that the relation of that Gospel to the Synoptic Gospels was designedly supplementary and corrective, we have given a reasonable account of many differences in matters of detail. But more fundamental variations still remain unexplained. In the Synoptic Gospels, for example, we trace the slow and halting recognition of our Lord's true character even on the part of the Twelve. The Fourth Gospel on the other hand in the opening scene of the great drama brings before us the Baptist pointing to Jesus as "the Lamb of God, which taketh away the sin of the world"; Andrew making the great announcement to his brother, "We have found the Messiah"; Nathanael confessing Jesus as "the

Son of God, the King of Israel." It may, I think, be fairly urged that a disciple, whose mind was deeply spiritual and keenly sensitive of the mystical significance of words spoken under deep emotion, would treasure what other men of less subtilty and less insight would fail to notice or would at once forget; while at the same time, as he often meditated on them, the form of mysterious sayings would insensibly coalesce in his memory with the interpretation which in the light of later belief he put on them.

"What first were guessed as points, I now knew stars."

The history of a great movement will be told long years afterwards with the nearest approach to truth, not by the prosaic observer who noticed only what lay on the surface, but rather by one who at the time discerned something of its grandeur, and who as he recalled it instinctively idealized it. Idealization is perhaps a necessary condition for the preservation of the memory of a momentous spiritual crisis.

Very similar is the position which, I believe, a large-minded criticism will take as to our Lord's discourses presented to us in the Fourth Gospel. Here too we may reasonably believe that remembrance was moulded by meditation. But there are other considerations which ought not to be overlooked. A man of the highest genius has a wide range of utterance. The character of his thoughts and words will vary almost infinitely with his mood, his subject, his surroundings, his audience. Can we conceive that less than this was true of Him to whom the application of the term 'genius' is an impertinence? Moreover the record of our Lord's words in the Synoptic Gospels is not an absolute standard. The version of His utterances preserved by the Synoptists cannot but have been limited and shaped by the memories through which they passed. It may well be the case that the higher prophetic element in the Lord's teaching, which was not comprehended at the time, was eliminated in the remembrance of those hearers on whom the Synoptists ultimately depended, and that this element has been preserved for us with substantial faithfulness in the pages of the Fourth Gospel. And there is

x] *The Gospels in the light of historical criticism* 383

another consideration to which in my judgement the greatest weight ought to be given. The conscience of men with singular unanimity approves of some at least of the utterances recorded in this Gospel as being in substance the words of Christ. Anyone who has had the honour of doing pastoral work remembers that not once or twice but again and again he has been asked by the suffering and the dying to read to them the parable of the Good Shepherd and the discourses of the Upper Room. These words come home to the spirits of men, educated by the profoundest of human needs, as no other words do even of those which the Gospels record as the words of Christ. To such they embody the thought of Christ. This is evidence which I dare not put aside as invalid. This seems to me a deeper, a subtler, a more human judgement than that of the critical intellect. The verdict may conceivably be wrong; but it is the unquestioning verdict of the highest court of appeal.

Against these difficulties in the way of the traditional view of the Fourth Gospel, lessened though not wholly removed by such considerations as have been here suggested, must be set positive arguments which support that view. On these it is not necessary to dwell at length. In the first place there is external evidence, early in date (*e.g.* the testimony of Irenaeus, who came from Asia Minor and who through Polycarp was the spiritual grandson of St John), manifold, and (with the single exception of the somewhat nebulous sect of the Alogi) unanimous. In the second place this external evidence is reinforced by evidence derived from the internal characteristics of the Book itself. This aspect of the question was some thirty years ago very fully and carefully investigated by Dr Lightfoot, Dr Westcott, and Dr Sanday; and in some recent discussions of the Johannine problem the contributions of these scholars, as it appears to me, have been strangely overlooked. The cumulative force of the external and of the internal evidence in favour of the traditional view as to the authorship of this Gospel has been lately admitted and indeed earnestly insisted on by Dr Drummond in his remarkable book on *The Character and Authorship of the Fourth Gospel*.

With a candour which it would be inappropriate to praise he accepts the Johannine authorship of this Gospel, with the important proviso however that this position is compatible with the recognition in the Fourth Gospel of "the presence of a large ideal or allegorical element" (p. 426). This proviso brings us to what, I believe, will be seen with increasing clearness to be the real centre of the Johannine problem. Few scholars in the present day would refuse to find in the Fourth Gospel *some* signs of a process of idealizing. An attempt to gain a clearer view of the extent to which this tendency has operated, this, if I may venture to prophesy, is the form which in the future the Johannine problem will assume.

At this point the subject of this Essay bifurcates. The Gospels possess two aspects. They contain (1) records of our Lord's sayings; (2) narratives of His life on earth. We proceed then in the light of historical criticism to consider separately each of these two elements in the Gospels.

I.

The Gospels contain records of our Lord's sayings.

We have already touched upon the problem which the Fourth Gospel presents in this connexion. In the main therefore we shall now deal with the Lord's utterances as they meet us in the pages of the Synoptic Gospels. Within what limits do these Gospels preserve for us a true and genuine record of what our Blessed Lord said when He was on earth? It is without doubt a momentous question. Yet in trying to answer it we must turn to prosaic and commonplace facts. The preservation of our Lord's words was, so far as we can see, conditioned by three influences.

(1) There was the moulding influence of memory. The Lord Himself wrote nothing. He left on earth no record of His teaching to compel assent. Nor is there any indication that any one of His disciples till long afterwards put into writing what they had heard from His lips. His words then have

come to us through the channel of human remembrance. Those who were 'eye-witnesses' and who afterwards became 'ministers of the word,' and many others, treasured His sayings with the tenacity which is characteristic of Oriental memories, and which, we do not doubt, was in this case strengthened by reverence for their Master and by the divine illumination of the Spirit. And here it is all the more necessary for us to notice what cannot but have been the habit of our Lord as a teacher of men, because this consideration is commonly lost sight of. A human teacher who is deeply conscious that he has a message to proclaim, and who is intent on bringing home that message to the men of his generation, does not fear to repeat himself. If he speaks to multitudes, he knows that his audience changes and that, even if his hearers are always the same, the only way of deeply imprinting his teaching on their minds and consciences is to rehearse it again and again. We may be sure that our Lord, who perfectly knew human nature, in this respect must have been like all teachers who have made their mark on the world. If harmonists are fatally ready to multiply occasions on which a given incident took place, critics are no less fatally ready to simplify their task by assuming that there was but one particular occasion on which the Lord uttered a given saying. They take it for granted, for example, that there was one and only one delivery of the Lord's Prayer. Such an assumption is purely artificial. It is far removed from the observed realities of life. Our Lord must have repeated again and again His characteristic utterances sometimes in the same form, sometimes in slightly differing forms. And this habit of the Teacher must necessarily have had a twofold effect. It would assist His hearers to remember the general scope of any one of His sayings. On the other hand one hearer would connect it exclusively with one occasion, another with another; one would recall it in one form—"Blessed are the poor"; another in another form—"Blessed are the poor in spirit." This very obvious consideration appears to me to be of the first importance for a sound criticism of the Gospels.

But how was the remembrance of our Lord's sayings

preserved in the Christian Church? Chiefly, we may answer, in two ways. In the first place the Brethren must often have spoken to each other, in the sacred privacy of fellowship, of what they had once heard the Master Himself say. Secondly, the Lord's sayings must have formed the basis of 'the discourses of exhortation' in the Christian synagogues. We can hardly doubt that the Epistle of St James gives us the substance of that Apostle's discourses in the public assemblies of the disciples at Jerusalem; and that Epistle is a mosaic of 'oracles of the Lord.' In these ways various lines of tradition would gradually take shape. It follows that these lines of tradition, ultimately embodied in the Gospels, were the result of the interaction of many fallible memories, each unconsciously affected by the formative influences of daily life and thought.

(2) There was the moulding influence of translation. Our Lord's words were uttered in Aramaic. We possess them in a Greek dress. Translation, especially when it is the work of unskilled minds and when it is undertaken for an immediate purpose of edification, in the process of reproduction refashions and changes. In the case of our Lord's sayings, translation must have been a necessity almost from the beginning, directly, that is, Hellenists at Jerusalem became 'obedient to the faith.' The comparative freedom and ease of the representation of our Lord's words in the Greek Gospels, as contrasted with the rendering of Old Testament sayings in the LXX., is an indication that here we have the outcome of a long process, and that constant repetition has rubbed smooth the rough places which must have characterized the earliest attempts at reproducing our Lord's sayings in Greek. On the other hand the fact that we are able at times to discern the original Aramaic through the Greek, and in this way to restore a paronomasia or to bring kindred sayings into verbal relation to each other, is a warning to us that we must not exaggerate the influence of translation on the tradition of our Lord's utterances. Such an influence cannot have acted uniformly. If sometimes it is a curtain, perhaps oftener it is a thin veil. Criticism must take account of its presence.

x] *The Gospels in the light of historical criticism* 387

(3) There was the moulding influence of the editor's hand. The attempt to put a saying of Christ into literary shape, and to fit it into a literary context, cannot have been without effect on its form. And in some cases, we cannot doubt, an Evangelist deliberately amended the words which came into his hands. That this sometimes happened is clear from the following instance. St Mark's record of the opening words of the dialogue between our Lord and the rich young man is as follows (x. 17 f.): "Good Master, what shall I do that I may inherit eternal life?...Why callest thou me good? None is good save one, even God." With this St Luke's account (xviii. 18 f.) coincides. But in St Matthew (xix. 16 f.) a significant variation confronts us. The word "good" reappears indeed, but its reference is wholly changed—"Master, what *good thing* shall I do that I may have eternal life?... Why askest thou me *concerning that which is good?* One there is who is *good.*" Here it is clear that the wording of the dialogue has been altered to avoid the appearance of our Lord's calling in question His own goodness and of His refusing to accept the attribution to Himself of what is Divine.

The comparative study of the Synoptists, especially in those passages in which they record, in divergent forms, sayings of our Lord which from the nature of the case could only be appropriate to a single occasion, and the more general considerations discussed above are sufficient to convince us that seldom indeed can we venture to say: "Here we have a precise and exact representation of what the Lord actually said." Too often in the past the practice of theologians has been to assume that in a particular conversation, or in a particular saying, the very words of Christ have been reproduced, and on the frail foundation of that assumption to build a superstructure of doctrine guaranteed by the sure authority of the Truth Himself. To take one example, what a tremendous weight of inference as to the mystery of the κένωσις has been made to rest on our Lord's part in the dialogue about Psalm cx. 1, as it is recorded in the Synoptic Gospels (Mark xii. 35 ff., Matt. xxii. 42 ff., Luke xx. 41 ff.)! But that inference is only valid if we have the dialogue exactly and completely before us. No one would have drawn any inference as to our Lord's ignorance, if we had read in one of the Gospels: "Jesus said unto them, Which of the Prophets said, The Lord said unto my Lord, Sit thou on my right hand till I make thine enemies the footstool of thy feet? They say unto him, David. He saith unto them, How then say the Scribes that the Christ is the son of David? David himself calleth him Lord; and whence is he his son?" Such a question as, for the sake of argument, I have ventured to put into the Lord's mouth is very similar to the question, "Whose is this image and superscription?" The disciples who were listening, and on whose remembrance the version given in *e.g.* St Mark's Gospel ultimately depends, had, we may be certain, no suspicion that this Psalm or any Psalm was written by anyone but David. The supposed question of the Lord would have been pointless to them and would have made no impression on their minds. Further, the difference between the dialogue in the form supposed and the record in St Mark is no greater than the difference between the record in St Mark and the record in St Matthew. I do not of course maintain that the version of the dialogue suggested is the true version, nor am I arguing that our Lord had formal knowledge on questions belonging to literary criticism. I only wish in a concrete instance to point out the peril of drawing far-reaching conclusions from the report of our Lord's words, when neither by a consideration of the way in which that report must have been handed down nor by an examination of the different versions given in the several Gospels are we justified in concluding that we have a complete and absolutely accurate account of the conversation.

Criticism then enforces the lesson of caution on all who are tempted to base important conclusions on the exact phraseology of the report of our Lord's words in the Gospels, and to claim for those conclusions the authority of Christ Himself. While criticism confirms us in the belief that the Gospels preserve for us a record of the Lord's teaching sufficient for the purposes alike of spiritual edification and of history, it warns us that in this record God has not given us an infallible oracle, from which, apart from the exercise of our own intellectual and moral judgement, we can seek immediate and decisive guidance. Few things in the Apostolic age are so remarkable as the fact that the Apostles and their companions, so far as their teaching is preserved for us in the New Testament, do not, except on one or two occasions (Acts xx. 35, 1 Cor. vii. 10, 25, ix. 14), appeal to the authority of their Master's sayings. They rely not on their own remembrance or on the living tradition of the words of Christ, but on the Spirit of Christ to guide them to a right judgement on questions of belief and of conduct.

II.

The Gospels contain narratives of the Lord's life on earth.

A full discussion of the bearing of historical criticism on the trustworthiness of the Gospels, considered as historical documents, would necessitate a much wider investigation than is here possible. We must therefore sacrifice completeness and concern ourselves only with what would be the goal and climax of an exhaustive treatment of the subject, viz., the supernatural element in our Lord's life on earth.

The only preliminary which must detain us is the attempt briefly to answer the question, "What light does the comparative study of the Gospels throw on their character as historical witnesses?" We accept the testimony of a document till it is proved unworthy of credit. We are concerned therefore rather with reasons for caution than with reasons for confidence. Concrete instances or groups of instances will be the best form of statement. (1) St Matthew (xxvii. 34) describes the "myrrhed wine" (Mark xv. 23) in the story of the Crucifixion as "wine mingled with gall" plainly in order to connect the incident with the words of the Psalm (lxix. 21). (2) St Mark ascribes to our Lord such strong human emotions as surprise, anger, horror (iii. 5, vi. 6, x. 14, xiv. 33). St Matthew and St Luke appear deliberately to omit or to tone down such notices as unbefitting our Lord's Divine Person. (3) St Mark (i. 34), picturing the scene at the door of Peter's house, says that the Lord "healed *many* that were sick with divers diseases." St Matthew (viii. 16) and St Luke (iv. 40) heighten the description of the Lord's works of healing, the former telling us that "*all* that were sick he healed," the latter that "on *each one of them* he laid his hands and healed them." Again, in St Mark's account (xi. 12 ff., 20 ff.) the Lord rebukes the barren fig-tree as He goes from Bethany to Jerusalem, and not until His disciples are accompanying Him along the same road on the following morning does St Peter notice that the fig-tree was withered. In St Matthew (xxi. 18 ff.) however "the fig-tree was *immediately* dried up." The disciples at once see and wonder at what had happened. And the immediate efficacy of the Lord's word becomes the point of their question: "How is it that the fig-tree was *immediately* dried up?" (4) When in St Matthew (xxviii. 2 ff.) we read the description of "the angel of the Lord" who "descended from heaven, and came and rolled away the stone" of the sepulchre, "and sat upon it"—"his appearance was as lightning, and his raiment white as snow"—we can hardly resist the feeling that here we have something akin to what we find in the Jewish apocalypses, and in particular to the story of the Resurrection as told in the so-called Gospel of Peter. Again, from the same Gospel (xxvii. 51 ff.) we take the reference to the resurrection of many bodies of the saints and their appearance to many after the Resurrection. The notice obviously presents peculiar difficulties: it has no parallel in, or support from, the other Gospels. Few will maintain that it has an authority equal to that of the narrative of the Last Supper or of the Passion. It is permissible for us to suppose that the writer of this Gospel incorporated a story which was current among some early Christians, the origin and the significance of which it is vain to attempt to conjecture. These instances appear to reveal a tendency on the part of the disciples of the first age, however narrow the limits within which it worked, to mould the narrative of the Lord's life in accordance with a current view of prophecy, of our Lord's Person, and of the character of His life on earth, to enhance the wonder of His miracles, and even to include in the record something analogous to legend.

x] *The Gospels in the light of historical criticism* 391

The way has now been prepared for the discussion in the light of historical criticism of the witness of the Gospels to the Resurrection; to the Lord's miracles; to the Virgin-birth.

(I.) The Resurrection. The earliest witness is St Paul. In the first Epistle of his which has come down to us he asserts the fact of the Resurrection—"to serve a living and true God, and to wait for his Son from heaven, whom he raised from the dead" (1 Thess. i. 10). And this Epistle was written little more than twenty years after the Crucifixion. But what was St Paul's conception of the Resurrection of the Lord? "Did the apostle," Professor Harnack asks, "know of the message about the empty grave?" His answer is, "While there are theologians of note who doubt it, I think it probable; but we cannot be quite certain about it. Certain it is that what he and the disciples regarded as all-important was not the state in which the grave was found but Christ's appearances[1]." I venture to think that the matter is placed beyond doubt by St Paul's own words. We note in the xvth chapter of the First Epistle to the Corinthians the juxtaposition of the Burial and the Resurrection—the latter is the reversal of the former; the mention of "the third day"; the assertion not that He "was seen on the third day" but that He "hath been raised on the third day"; and lastly the inference as to the future resurrection of the bodies of men which the Apostle draws from the resurrection of the body of Christ. To recognise and give due weight to the significance of St Paul's words and arguments is to be convinced that he believed that on the third day the Lord's body was raised from the grave; that he believed that the grave was found empty as well as that the Lord Himself was seen by His disciples.

But what was St Paul's evidence for the Resurrection on the third day? Clearly his own sight of the glorified Christ was rather a proof of the Lord's life than of the Lord's historical Resurrection. A belief in the historical event could be confirmed or rendered possible, it could hardly be created,

[1] *What is Christianity?* p. 161.

by it. For testimony as to the event itself he would have to depend on others. Who were they? Now in his enumeration of the witnesses to the Resurrection (1 Cor. xv. 5 ff.), besides bodies of men (the Twelve, the five hundred brethren, the Apostles), St Paul specifies just two individuals by whom the risen Lord was seen—" He appeared to Cephas " : " He appeared to James." Clearly Cephas and James had a unique place in St Paul's thoughts about the Resurrection. An incidental notice in the Epistle to the Galatians explains this. In that Epistle (i. 18 f.) he tells us that three years after his conversion he went up to Jerusalem; that he stayed there a fortnight; and that he then saw these two Apostles, Cephas and James, and none other. Since St Paul, as he assures us, undertook this journey for the express purpose of "seeing Cephas" ($\iota\sigma\tau o\rho\hat{\eta}\sigma\alpha\iota$ $K\eta\phi\hat{\alpha}\nu^1$), it is a reasonable conjecture that he earnestly desired to learn from him the details of the story of the Resurrection. It is surely impossible to doubt that during the fortnight spent at Jerusalem he received from those two primary witnesses, Cephas and James, whom alone he mentions by name among those who had seen the Lord, the facts which he records as to the Resurrection itself and the successive appearances of the risen Lord. The two passages from the two Epistles mutually explain each other. It is further worthy of remark that in reference to his subsequent visit to Jerusalem fourteen years later St Paul tells us (Gal. ii. 9), not only that he again saw "James and Cephas," but also that John as well as they gave him "the right hand of fellowship." These facts are of the first importance. On the one hand, since St Paul's earliest visit to Jerusalem after his conversion must be placed from five to eight years after the Passion, we have the clearest evidence, contained in documents which no reasonable critic disputes, as to what the belief of Cephas and James was within the first decade after the alleged event, viz., that the Lord died and was buried and on

[1] St Paul had certainly been living in Jerusalem during the early days of the Church's life, and it is clear that he must have known much about the disciples. When he singles out Cephas as the one Apostle whom he wished "to see" (see Lightfoot's note), he gives a strong confirmation of the Acts as to the position attributed in that Book to St Peter.

x] *The Gospels in the light of historical criticism* 393

the third day was raised. On the other hand, through St Paul we are brought into immediate contact with three of the primary witnesses to the Resurrection, St Peter, St John, and St James.

From the witness of St Paul we turn to the story of the Resurrection as contained in the Gospels. That whole story consists of two parts, both of which, as we have just seen, were recognised by St Paul—the Resurrection itself (that is, the empty grave), the appearances of the risen Lord.

The Gospel of St Mark abruptly breaks off as the first part of the Resurrection story is passing into the second. It tells us that the grave was found empty and that the Lord had been raised—ἠγέρθη, οὐκ ἔστιν ὧδε· ἴδε ὁ τόπος ὅπου ἔθηκαν αὐτόν (xvi. 6); and then either the Evangelist, for some reason which it is vain to surmise, left his work unfinished, or the copy, from which all extant copies are derived, was mutilated at this point. The last authentic words of St Mark record that the women "fled from the tomb ...and they said nothing to anyone, for they were afraid[1]." There are good reasons for thinking that the First Gospel, which has close points of verbal contact with St Mark in this section up to the point where he breaks off, gives us in substance the concluding portion of the Petrine memoirs[2]. But, whatever may be thought of this theory, the point on which I wish to insist is this—the Gospel of St Mark, which embodies the Petrine account, and the Gospel of St Luke who, as we saw reason to believe, visited Jerusalem about the year 56 A.D., and was brought into contact with James and the Elders of the Church there (Acts xxi. 18), are clear in their testimony to the Resurrection itself.

[1] It has been maintained that the last words are in contradiction to what is said in St Matthew (xxviii. 8) and in St Luke (xxiv. 9, 22) of the women, and in St John (xx. 18) of Mary Magdalene. But surely it is rash to judge of the meaning of the words οὐδενὶ οὐδὲν εἶπαν in the absence of the succeeding context. It may well have been made plain by what followed that the meaning is that the women told nothing to anyone whom they met in the way.

[2] I have given my reasons for holding this view in an article in the *Journal of Theological Studies*, July, 1905.

Against the accounts of the appearances of the risen Lord certain objections are urged; and these, or at least the chief of these, we must now, however briefly, consider.

"It has been repeatedly shown by critics," writes Professor Gardner[1], "that the mass of testimony as to the physical appearances of Jesus Christ after the crucifixion is formless and full of inconsistencies." "Who of us can maintain," asks Professor Harnack[2], "that a clear account of these appearances can be constructed out of the stories told by Paul and the evangelists?" It is of course true that the accounts are partial and the information which they give is incomplete. There are many questions which it is possible to ask and to which St Paul and the Gospels supply no answer. But to make completeness a condition of trustworthiness involves a confusion of thought. It is of small and common-place events that an approximately exhaustive description can be given. The greater and the more startling the event, the more certain it is that we can know it only in part, even in its outward aspects. Some of the inconsistencies which have been pointed out as between the several accounts of the Resurrection and of the appearances of the Lord will be dealt with in greater detail below. In general it must be urged that to scientific criticism, that is, to educated common sense, a large measure of divergence between the authorities is neither a matter of surprise nor an indication of untruthfulness. On the contrary, when we have to do with several records of a time of intense emotion and excitement, if the actors in the drama were many, if the documents were put into writing many years after the event itself, and if, in the case of at least some of the writers, we have no reason at all for thinking that any eye-witness was near at hand to explain uncertain points in the 'sources' (whether oral or documentary), we should account it strange if there were no variation in details. Divergence in details, when it does not involve contradiction

---

[1] *A Historic View of the New Testament*, p. 166. As I shall quote Professor Gardner several times, I may be allowed to record my sense of the reverent and considerate tone which pervades the book.

[2] *What is Christianity?* p. 161.

in essentials, is *pro tanto* a pledge of truth. A candid student of the Gospels claims for them substantial veracity, not infallible accuracy.

An examination of the passage in the First Epistle to the Corinthians (xv. 1—8), in which St Paul deals with the Resurrection of Christ and the witnesses to it, will bring before us many of the most important difficulties which have been raised as to the accounts of the Resurrection in the Gospels. We will consider the salient points in St Paul's statement one by one. (1) St Paul is not here primarily an apologist. He is not consciously writing a *locus classicus* as to the evidence for the Resurrection. He is not giving fresh information; but, insisting on the doctrinal significance of the Lord's Resurrection and especially on its relation to the future resurrection of men, he summarises what he had himself told the Corinthians by word of mouth. The passage is a recapitulation of oral teaching. The grammatical structure of the sentence demonstrates that the first two appearances are included in the recapitulation (*vv.* 3 ff. παρέδωκα...ὅτι Χριστὸς ἀπέθανεν..., καὶ ὅτι ἐτάφη, καὶ ὅτι ἐγήγερται..., καὶ ὅτι ὤφθη Κηφᾷ, εἶτα τοῖς δώδεκα); and, though the construction changes (*v.* 7 ἔπειτα ὤφθη Ἰακώβῳ), it is natural to suppose that the recapitulation extends to the end of the series, the appearance of the Lord to St Paul himself. The recognition of the nature of the passage alone supplies a complete answer to the difficulty which some have found in the fact that, whereas the Evangelists speak, *e.g.*, of the Lord eating with His disciples, St Paul is silent even as to whether the Lord spoke to those who saw Him. (2) "By his careful enumeration with 'then... next...next...then...lastly,'" Professor Schmiedel writes[1], "he guarantees not only chronological order but completeness." It is doubtless true that St Paul gives the appearances to

---

[1] *Encyclopaedia Biblica*, iv. 4058. It must be noticed that (1) ἔπειτα denotes that a given appearance was subsequent to the one just mentioned; it does not imply that no appearance took place in the interval:

(2) ἔσχατον δὲ πάντων is wider than "lastly": if it does not precisely assert that other appearances not mentioned by St Paul took place, at least it leaves room for such appearances.

which he refers in a precise order. But there is nothing to show that his enumeration is exhaustive. He mentions as witnesses the leaders of the Church whose names were well known to the Corinthians—Cephas, the Twelve, James, all the Apostles, himself; and he further refers to what we may call a great public manifestation of the risen Lord to "more than five hundred brethren at once." Such an enumeration was sufficient for his purpose. He could not have referred to the appearances to the women, to Mary Magdalene, and to Cleopas and his companion, without explanations unsuited to a rapid summary. (3) St Paul's language (ὅτι ὤφθη Κηφᾷ, εἶτα τοῖς δώδεκα) links closely together the appearance to Cephas and that to the Twelve. Hereby he confirms the narrative in the Pauline Gospel (Luke xxiv. 33 f.). The fact that the grammatical construction continues unbroken to the end of v. 5 (ὅτι ἐγήγερται τῇ ἡμέρᾳ τῇ τρίτῃ...καὶ ὅτι ὤφθη Κηφᾷ, εἶτα τοῖς δώδεκα) and then changes (ἔπειτα ὤφθη κ.τ.λ.) seems to denote that the Apostle regards the appearances which he mentions as falling into two groups; and it is natural to infer that he places the appearance to Cephas and that to the Twelve among the events of "the third day." At any rate these two appearances he places first. Here too he is at one with St Luke. (4) It is difficult to suppose that the appearance to "more than five hundred brethren" took place at Jerusalem. It seems to demand as its fitting scene some secluded spot, far removed from the vigilance of the High Priests, like the mountain in Galilee (Matt. xxviii. 16). It becomes necessary therefore to examine the account of the appearance of the Lord on the mountain of Galilee given in St Matthew's Gospel (xxviii. 16—20). It has been already pointed out that here St Matthew is almost certainly following the lost section of St Mark. The first reference to this meeting occurs in the history of the night of the betrayal (Mark xiv. 27 f., Matt. xxvi. 31 f.): "All ye shall be caused to stumble: for it is written, I will smite the shepherd and the sheep shall be scattered; but after that I am raised up, I will go before you into Galilee." Here the metaphor of the shepherd and the flock seems to be continued in the words προάξω ὑμᾶς—"I will go before you" (comp. John x. 4); and it is natural to regard the entire passage as intended to look forward to a gathering of the whole flock around the Shepherd in Galilee after the Resurrection. When we turn to the account of the meeting itself as given in the First Gospel, it is obvious that it is related in the briefest terms. The interest lies wholly in the words of the risen Lord. That others however besides the Apostles were present seems clear from the phrase, "But others doubted" (v. 17). The manifestation of the risen Lord on the mountain in Galilee, and the revelation of His will to those who were with Him there, seem to be intended by the Evangelist as a counterpart to the gathering of the multitudes round the Lord on 'the mountain' and to the great sermon at the beginning of the Ministry. The impression produced by the narrative is that it deals with an appearance of the Lord to a great company of His disciples and with a communication to them, as representing His Church, of His final commands. Though then the identification of the two appearances cannot be proved, there is much to be said in favour of, and nothing (so far as I can see) against, the supposition that the appearance of Christ on the mountain, with which the Gospel of St Matthew ends (as did probably that of St Mark also), is the same as the appearance to "more than five hundred brethren" mentioned by St Paul. (5) The appearance which St Paul places immediately before the manifestation granted to himself is an appearance "to all the Apostles." Such an appearance is recorded in the Acts, and, as I believe, in the Gospel of St Luke also[1], as the prelude to the Ascension. Thus it is a simple matter of fact that the appearances recorded by St Paul (with the one exception of that to St James) correspond exactly to appearances recorded in the Gospels. The following alone meet us in the Gospels but not in St Paul's Epistle—the appearances to the women, to Mary Magdalene,

---

[1] In my *Syro-Latin Text of the Gospels*, p. 130, I have given reasons for doubting the soundness of Dr Hort's theory of 'Western non-interpolations,' and for holding that his rejection of the words καὶ ἀνεφέρετο εἰς τὸν οὐρανόν in Luke xxiv. 51 cannot be sustained.

to the travellers to Emmaus, to St Thomas and his fellow-Apostles on the second Lord's day, to certain of the Apostles at the Sea of Tiberias. The probable reason of the omission by St Paul of the first three in this series has already been indicated. The appearance on the second Lord's day and that by the Sea of Tiberias were of interest less as vouchsafed to Apostles than as dealing with individuals. The two important appearances to the Apostles, that apparently on the day of the Resurrection and that which (apart from the appearance to St Paul) ended the series, have a distinct place in St Paul's enumeration. It is not too much to say that the enumeration in St Paul's Epistle anticipates the Gospels; and that the Gospels give us details connected with the several appearances referred to by St Paul.

It is further urged that the Gospels are at variance with each other in regard to the history of the period succeeding the Resurrection both in regard to *place* and in regard to *time*.

In regard to *place*. It is pointed out that, whereas St Luke and the Acts speak only of appearances in Jerusalem and the immediate neighbourhood, St Matthew and St Mark are ignorant of any meeting of our Lord with His disciples except in Galilee. I fully allow that, if the words of the Angel of the sepulchre (Mark xvi. 7, Matt. xxviii. 7) were all we had to guide us, we should conclude that we were intended to think that the Apostles did not see the risen Lord till they saw Him in Galilee. But on the one hand we may understand the message of the Angel as meant to forecast a meeting in Galilee between the Lord and not the Apostles only, but the disciples generally. And on the other hand the assumption that the silence of St Matthew (following probably his source, St Mark) as to any appearance to the Apostles in Jerusalem means ignorance, and that such ignorance implies that the appearances at Jerusalem were a later addition to the earliest form of the Resurrection story, which spoke only of Galilee, proves too much. St Matthew indeed only mentions Galilee; but in Galilee he only mentions one single appearance. Can we possibly conclude that he and his 'source' knew of no other

x] *The Gospels in the light of historical criticism* 399

appearance? It is worthy of remark that the words "the mountain where Jesus had appointed them" seem to imply a consciousness on the writer's part that this was not the first meeting between the Apostles and the risen Lord. But apart from this, we have the clearest evidence in St Paul's Epistle, who drew his information from Cephas and James, that many appearances were known widely in the Apostolic Church from the very earliest times, and that this subject formed part of the instruction given in the Churches (1 Cor. xv. 3, 11). This last fact may well be thought to offer a sufficient explanation of the silence of St Matthew and of his 'source.' If any facts about our Lord were familiar to their readers, the appearances after the Resurrection were so. An Evangelist was at liberty to hasten on to record, as the goal and completion of the Gospel history, that interview in which the Lord laid on His disciples the final crowning commission.

In regard to *time*. It is often said that St Luke places the Ascension on the day of the Resurrection. I have already pointed out that there are grounds for thinking that the section of the Acts which speaks of appearances at intervals during forty days was composed, or planned, before the closing section of the Gospel. But be this as it may, we again appeal to the evidence of St Paul. No one, I think, will argue that the five appearances mentioned by him were crowded into one day. The Pauline Evangelist must have written with the consciousness that facts notorious in the Church would render impossible any such interpretation of his words. It is quite in St Luke's manner to move rapidly on without explicitly noting changes of time and place. He frequently records sayings of the Lord without defining their relation to the previous context (xii. 22, 54, xiii. 6, xvi. 1, 19, xvii. 1, xviii. 1, 9). We are justified therefore in supposing that there is a break at xxiv. 44, and that the phrase εἶπεν δὲ πρὸς αὐτούς introduces sayings which were spoken at a later time than the evening of the day of the Resurrection.

It would be unreasonable to demand as a necessary condition of the evidence for the Resurrection contained in the New Testament being regarded as trustworthy that every contradiction as between the several Gospels and the passage in St Paul's Epistle should be certainly and convincingly removed. Of the most important of these variations I believe that a natural, though in some points a necessarily hypothetical, explanation has been offered. My conviction is that critics who come to negative conclusions on this great subject are in reality much less impressed by difficulties connected with the testimony of the New Testament than by those which lie further back in the chain of evidence. "The great difficulty," Professor Gardner says[1], "in regard to the physical resurrection arises from the unscientific frame of mind of the early disciples, who did not in the least understand how to test or to value evidence, and who looked on the events of the visible world through a thick haze of preconceived notions, which made many simple occurrences seem to them vague and monstrous." It is true that the early disciples were, in the strict sense of the term, unscientific. They did not know anything of the laws which govern the world of matter or of mind. We cannot but ask whether any of their contemporaries possessed such knowledge, and remind ourselves that to-day those who have made the furthest advance in these regions of science are the most ready to confess that their knowledge is partial and incomplete. But it is more pertinent to note that, while lack of scientific knowledge, and of the instinct which springs from the consciousness that such knowledge is possessed by others, may limit men's powers of observation; while it may prevent men from attaining to an adequate interpretation of phenomena; yet it does not betray a group of truthful men and women into a wholesale invention of events which in fact never took place. It is true also that the early disciples were not experts in sifting evidence, and did not rise above the conceptions of their generation as to the spiritual world. But it is at least a rational position that the testimony of St Paul and of the Gospels justifies us in thinking that the evidence of the Lord's Resurrection on the third day was too positive and too direct to need elaborate investigation; and further that the thought of that age could not

[1] *A Historic View of the New Testament*, p. 165.

The Gospels in the light of historical criticism

have produced ideas so majestic, so subtle, so divine, and so deeply human as are involved in the story of the Resurrection. It is important to observe in this connexion that the phrase 'the physical resurrection,' which some writers use in a tone of disparagement, falls far short of expressing the teaching of the New Testament. If we seriously believe in the Resurrection, we regard it as an event in which the ultimate realities of the world and of life are involved; it is a reconciliation of the antithesis of spirit and matter.

Of two further considerations historical criticism is bound, if it faces the whole position, to take account. It cannot overlook the fact that the Lord was morally no ordinary man; that He claimed to be in a unique relation to God and to men, and to reveal God to men. And in the second place it must take into account the sequel of the Resurrection. The Resurrection is the one explanation of the existence of the Christian Church. On the basis of a belief in the Resurrection the Christian Society arose and has lived, at times seeming to sin against its first principles, yet surviving; again and again in the hour of its apparent decrepitude renewing its youth, proving itself a moral power able to regenerate men of every type, of every race, of every age. The Resurrection cannot be separated from the effects which have flowed from it through all the Christian centuries.

The whole historical evidence for the Resurrection of our Lord, critically examined, is, I solemnly believe, adequate. But no historical evidence can compel men to believe that an alleged event in the past actually took place. From the nature of the case such evidence can only establish its probability. If the alleged event belongs to the sphere of religion, when historical criticism has done its work, the result becomes the material on which religious faith works. Faith in the living God alone enables us to discern the congruity of the Resurrection, to realise it, and to know in our own lives its power.

(II.) The Miracles. In the second place we turn to a subject which is subordinate to the question, vital as it seems to me, of the Resurrection—the record in the Gospels of miracles attributed to our Lord.

It can hardly be questioned that the miracles were regarded by the Evangelists and by the men of that age as in the fullest sense interruptions of the common course of nature, and therefore as immediate signs of a supervening Divine power. What is our position in regard to them in these days? On the one hand it may be said that the old rationalistic view which reckoned the miracles as "the result of imposture in the Master, and easy credulity in the disciples," or else as the outcome of pure deliberate fraud on the part of Christ's followers, has passed away. On the other hand few would now maintain that the miracles are *to us* proofs of the Divine mission of Jesus Christ. Their evidential force, supposing them to have been wrought, was immediate: they appealed to those who originally saw them. And the conviction aroused in the primary witnesses could not be communicated to later generations. Thus the problem presented by our Lord's miracles is for us less theological and apologetic and far more historical and literary than it used to appear to our fathers.

The considerations to which attention is now commonly called are these:

(1) The miracles are divided into two classes. In the one class are placed the works of healing; and these, speaking generally, are regarded as authentic. "Jesus as a healer of disease is historic," so writes Professor Gardner[1], "and the tales told of His cures, though doubtless deformed by exaggeration and distorted by very imperfect physiological knowledge, rest on a basis of fact." To the other class are assigned the so-called nature miracles, such as the feeding of the multitudes and the walking on the sea.

(2) It is urged, if I may again quote Professor Gardner[2], that "whether we investigate the history of the past, or turn our attention to the less civilised countries of the world in which we live, we find that no class of phenomena

[1] *A Historic View of the New Testament*, p. 146.
[2] *Ib.* p. 146.

x] *The Gospels in the light of historical criticism* 403

is a more constant concomitant of the story of the rise and progress of religions than the miraculous ; that a prophet will scarcely be listened to in any land, unless he is credited by his followers with the power of reversing or superseding the laws of nature ; that marvels follow the steps of the saint by an inevitable law of human nature." Thus the so-called nature miracles are regarded as accretions to the authentic story of Christ's life, and as analogous to observed phenomena in the rise and growth of other religious movements.

These positions must be fairly and candidly faced ; and in this connexion the following considerations seem to me important.

(1) The Gospel according to St Mark, which appears to be the earliest and simplest of the Gospels, presents the Lord far less as the teacher than as the healer and succourer of men. In the portrait there drawn it is the characteristics of pity and of power which stand out in special prominence.

(2) We can draw no distinction between the accounts of the miracles of healing and those of the so-called nature miracles. The latter class of miracle, as well as the former, is found in the earliest stratum of the Evangelical narratives.

(3) The New Testament outside the Gospels contains two references and only two references to our Lord's miracles. In Acts x. 38 St Peter is represented as alluding to our Lord having gone about "doing good and healing all that were oppressed of the devil" ; but these works are not in dispute. Again, St Luke makes the same Apostle on the Day of Pentecost appeal to "mighty works and wonders and signs, which God did by him in the midst of you" as pledges of the Divine mission of Jesus of Nazareth (Acts ii. 22) ; and this appeal is made in the one place in which it could naturally and rightly have been made, *i.e.*, in the presence of those who are alleged to have themselves witnessed the works—"even as ye yourselves know." Elsewhere in the New Testament, though St Paul is deeply conscious that the Jews whom a crucified Messiah "offended" "demand signs" (1 Cor. i. 22), and though he (Gal. iii. 5 ; 1 Cor. xii. 9 f., 28 ff. ; 2 Cor. xii. 12 ; Rom. xv. 19) and the writer of the Epistle to the Hebrews

(ii. 4) allude to "signs and wonders" wrought in Apostolic times, there is a complete and unbroken silence as to the miracles of our Lord. A similar statement may be made as to the Apostolic Fathers. The fact is most significant. It constitutes in my opinion a strong historical argument against the position that in the days when the Evangelical tradition was in process of formation, and when the Gospels were written, there was a tendency at work among the disciples which impelled them to decorate the story of their Master's life with fictitious miracles.

(4) The motive and scope of the Lord's miracles recorded in the Gospels are ever the same. The notices of the miracles are scattered up and down over the Gospels. But, when they are considered in relation to each other, we discover in them an undesigned unity. Together they cover the whole ground of our Lord's work as the Saviour, renewing each element in man's complex being and restoring peace in the physical order[1]. They are not presented in the Gospels as primarily designed to enhance His dignity and His power[2]. If they had

---

[1] Two incidents in the Gospels may perhaps be adduced against this statement. (1) The destruction of the Gadarene swine (Mark v. 11 ff., Matt. viii. 30 ff., Luke viii. 32 ff.). I call attention to two points. (*a*) The man, believing that his thoughts and words were the thoughts and words of the devils, asks from our Lord permission that the devils should go into the swine. That the man should be convinced that the devils had found another home was probably essential to his cure. (*b*) St Mark says simply ἦν δὲ ἐκεῖ πρὸς τῷ ὄρει ἀγέλη χοίρων (*v.* 11; comp. Luke viii. 32). St Matthew introduces a notice of the distance of the swine from the man (μακρὰν ἀπ' αὐτῶν, *v.* 30)—probably his own interpretation of his 'source.' It is likely that our Lord's word of permission was followed by a frenzied rush of the man, still identifying himself with the devils, towards the swine; hence their panic and destruction. (2) The withering of the fig-tree (Mark xi. 12 ff., Matt. xxi. 19 ff.). Our Lord, noting perhaps signs of decay, saw in the fig-tree a parable (comp. Mark xiii. 28, Matt. xxiv. 32, Luke xiii. 6, xxi. 29). The disciples thought that our Lord cursed the tree (Mark xi. 21); or at least this was the view of their thoughts which the Evangelist long after records. Those who do not hold that in the Gospels we have an exact representation of our Lord's words are free to believe that our Saviour did not curse the tree but foretold its fate. Such a position does not in the least degree involve any questioning of divine δικαιοκρισία in cases where there is moral responsibility.

[2] Partial exceptions to this statement are perhaps to be found in John ii. 11, xi. 4.

x] *The Gospels in the light of historical criticism* 405

been the invention of pious fancy, yearning to illustrate by imposing stories His greatness and His glory, it is a moral impossibility that this subtle unity of purpose should have been so consistently and so unobtrusively observed.

It is impossible at this point not to ask the question whether, if we regard the miracles of our Lord as historical, we must consider that they involve a suspension of the so-called laws of nature. Physical science teaches us a twofold lesson. On the one hand everyone knows that science reveals to us a universe, vast in relation to space and in regard to time, in which forces are found to act according to fixed and undeviating laws. The inference drawn from the investigation of all known phenomena is that these laws are constant in their operation. On the other hand science startles us by the revelation that beneath the surface of the familiar world there are forces, hitherto unsuspected, ever ready to operate when we have learned the secret how to set them in motion. And further it is true, I think, that psychology justifies us in assigning a far larger province than men once allowed to the will of man as an agent in the world of men and perhaps also in the world of nature. But we have no experience which enables us to form any conception of the essential potency of a will never weakened by sin and always controlled and quickened by uninterrupted communion with God. This is a consideration which the historical student, who desires to take into account all the conditions of the problem, cannot justly overlook. And further, if we accept the doctrine of the Divine immanence in nature, and connect that doctrine, as the New Testament encourages us to do, with the Person of the Lord, then miracles, as Dr Illingworth has pointed out, may well be regarded as a strictly 'natural' element in our Lord's life on earth.

That there was conspicuously present in the Lord's life an element of activity transcending common experience is a conclusion which rests on amply sufficient evidence. At the same time there are considerations to which we cannot honestly shut our eyes. The accounts of particular miracles come to us in records written by ordinary men; and these

406   *Cambridge Theological Essays*   [x

records are based on the reminiscences of ordinary men, whose observations were conditioned by the ideas of their age. The comparative study of the Gospels shows us, as we have already seen, that there were tendencies in operation among Christ's followers in the earliest days which might conceivably transfer this or that event across the boundary which for most minds separates the memorable from the miraculous. If then it is unreasonable to maintain that the whole of the so-called supernatural activity of our Lord was due to a mythopoeic tendency among His followers, yet criticism must be free to examine the accounts of the several miracles in the light of the ascertained characteristics both of the evangelical writers themselves and also of their race and age. We have no right peremptorily to decide beforehand that every narrative involving miracle will stand the test of careful and thorough investigation. It is as unfair for the defender as it is for the assailant of the so-called miraculous element in the Gospel history to maintain that Christian belief, or even the substantial veracity of the records of our Lord's life, depends on the accuracy of every detail of every narrative, or even on the general accuracy of every narrative, in which miracle has a place.

(III.) The Virgin-birth. In the last place we have to consider the difficult and anxious question of the Virgin-birth.

In several important respects the evidence for the Virgin-birth differs from the evidence for the Resurrection. (1) The history of the Lord's birth was not part of the original Gospel. The earliest of the Gospels, that of St Mark, begins with the Baptism of John. So did the Gospel of St Luke as at first written or at any rate as at first planned[1], though it must

---

[1] The position taken up in the text above must be justified in a note. In the opening sentence of the Acts St Luke defines the subject of the πρῶτος λόγος (*i.e.* the Gospel) in these words: περὶ πάντων...ὧν ἤρξατο Ἰησοῦς ποιεῖν τε καὶ διδάσκειν ἄχρι ἧς ἡμέρας...ἀνελήμφθη. The meaning of these words is "all things which Jesus began to do and to teach and continued to do and to teach until that day in which He was taken up." For the brachylogy ἄρξασθαι ἀπό...ἄχρι compare Luke

x] *The Gospels in the light of historical criticism* 407

be at once emphatically stated that the evidence of style is decisive that the first two chapters of that Gospel are the work of the same writer as the rest of the Book. There is no allusion to the circumstances of the Lord's birth in any Book of the New Testament except the First and the Third Gospels. St Paul (1 Cor. xv. 2 f.) defines the Gospel which he preached as comprehending the Death, the Burial, and the Resurrection of Christ. No reference to the Virgin-birth is found in the doctrinal teaching of St Paul, St Peter, or St John. (2) There is no clear evidence of a tradition on this subject in the Church independent of the Gospels of St Matthew and of St Luke. A confession of belief in

xxiii. 5 ἀρξάμενος ἀπὸ τῆς Γαλιλαίας ἕως ὧδε: Matt. xx. 8 ἀρξάμενος ἀπὸ τῶν ἐσχάτων ἕως τῶν πρώτων. It is carried still further in Luke xxiv. 27 ἀρξάμενος ἀπὸ Μωυσέως καὶ ἀπὸ πάντων τῶν προφητῶν διερμήνευσεν. Hence Chrysostom's brief paraphrase of Acts i. 1—ἀπ' ἀρχῆς μέχρι τέλους— is absolutely correct. What this ἀρχή (cf. Mark i. 1) was is plain from other Lucan passages, Acts i. 22 ἐν παντὶ χρόνῳ ᾧ εἰσῆλθεν καὶ ἐξῆλθεν ἐφ' ἡμᾶς ὁ κύριος Ἰησοῦς, ἀρξάμενος ἀπὸ τοῦ βαπτίσματος Ἰωάνου ἕως τῆς ἡμέρας ἧς ἀνελήμφθη (a parallel to i. 1 which seems to put the interpretation given above beyond doubt): x. 37 ἀρξάμενος ἀπὸ τῆς Γαλιλαίας μετὰ τὸ βάπτισμα ὃ ἐκήρυξεν Ἰωάνης. The proof is completed by the emphatic insertion of the word ἀρχόμενος in reference to Jesus immediately after the account of the Baptism: Καὶ αὐτὸς ἦν Ἰησοῦς ἀρχόμενος ὡσεὶ ἐτῶν τριάκοντα (Luke iii. 23). Two important inferences must be drawn from Acts i. 1. (1) The πρῶτος λόγος included, or was planned to include, the Ascension—an inference which has an important bearing on the reading in Luke xxiv. 51 and on the relation of Luke xxiv. 50 ff. to Acts i. 6 ff. (2) It began, or was planned to begin, with the Baptism of John; and therefore it did not include the story of the birth and of the childhood. I have already pointed out reasons for thinking that the Acts was written, or planned, before the Gospel. It seems probable that, when St Luke wrote Acts i. 1, the plan of the Gospel had formed itself in his mind, and that he intended to follow his source (*i.e.* the Marcan Gospel) and begin the history with the Baptism of John. The fact that there is absolutely no textual evidence against Luke i. ii. (contrast the case of [Mark] xvi. 9 ff.) at once negatives the possible suggestion that the two chapters were added in a second edition of the Gospel. We conclude that before the Gospel was published one of two things had happened: *either* the Evangelist had received information as to the Lord's birth which he had not possessed before; *or* he had for some reason become free to use information which he already possessed but might not disclose.

the Virgin-birth has a place in the earliest forms of the Creed. It is insisted on in the Epistles of Ignatius and in the earliest Apologies, those of Aristides and of Justin. But it seems clear that our Gospels were known in the Christian Church many years before the date of the earliest of these writings and of the earliest form of the Creed. We cannot therefore assert that the Church's belief in the Virgin-birth was not derived from these Gospels.

It may indeed be urged with the highest degree of probability that silence could not but be maintained till the death of the Lord's mother, and that in this hypothesis we have a satisfactory explanation of the absence of the history of the Lord's birth from the original Gospel. But an explanation of the want of evidence does not create evidence. And thus the only testimony which we have is supplied by the Gospels according to St Matthew and St Luke. What then are we to say of these two authorities and of the two forms of the story which they respectively present?

It has been remarked by Bishop Gore[1] and others that the narrative of St Matthew views everything from the side of Joseph, and "bears upon it undesigned but evident traces of coming from the information of Joseph"; that the story in St Luke regards the events from the side of Mary and thus supplies internal evidence of being derived ultimately from her. From a critical point of view we must regard the First Gospel as anonymous; and thus we have no clue at all to the source whence the writer derived the substance of the first two chapters. But the case of the Third Gospel is altogether different. There are, I believe, very strong critical reasons for accepting the tradition that the Acts and consequently also the Third Gospel were the work of St Luke[2]. The Acts affords evidence, as we have already seen, that the writer spent some time in Jerusalem and in Palestine, and further that he was known to James, the brother of the Lord. It is not an extravagant conjecture that he derived his knowledge of the birth and infancy of our Lord from St James and other members of the Holy Family. As regards St Luke's story,

[1] *Dissertations*, pp. 18, 27 f. [2] See above, p. 379.

x] *The Gospels in the light of historical criticism* 409

therefore, the inference that it is ultimately derived from the Lord's mother is in agreement with what we independently infer from a study of the other Lucan document as to the sources of information open to the Evangelist.

When we compare the two versions of the story of the Lord's birth, it must be allowed that, though the discrepancies between them are often exaggerated, it is not easy to harmonize them. But the difficulty caused by the variations between them are only serious to those, whether defenders or assailants of their historical character, who postulate the inerrancy of the Gospels in matters of detail. They do not appear, either in magnitude or in character, to be other than we should naturally expect in the case of two independent writers who edited different accounts of events which had taken place more than sixty years earlier, and who had themselves no personal or complete knowledge of the facts and, when they wrote, were probably far from those who could assist them.

Some of the more important points in the two narratives it is necessary, however briefly and baldly, to notice. (*a*) I cannot think that there is a shadow of justification for regarding Luke i. 34, 35—the question of Mary, "How shall this be?" and the answer of the angel—as an addition to the original document, inserted either by St Luke himself or by some unknown interpolator, and for thus eliminating the idea of the Virgin-birth from the genuine Gospel. The authenticity of these verses is not, and cannot be, impugned on the ground of any lack of external evidence; they have, from the point of view of textual criticism, as good a right to a place in the Gospel as any verses. The arguments brought forward against them are wholly subjective[1]; and I hope that it is not arrogant to say that these arguments appear to me both far-fetched and mechanical. (*b*) St Luke connects our Lord's birth at Bethlehem with peculiar circumstances created by the enrolment under Quirinius. On this subject of perennial controversy it must here be sufficient to say, *first*,

[1] See the article of Professor Harnack in the *Zeitschrift für die neutestamentliche Wissenschaft*, 1901, p. 53 ff.

that St Luke is entitled to have taken into account that character for historical accuracy which the evidence of the Acts establishes; *secondly*, that, while it cannot by any means be maintained that all difficulties have been cleared up, it is certainly true that the investigations of Professor Ramsay have advanced by many stages the probability that St Luke's reference to the enrolment is historical. (*c*) It is said that St Luke's assertion that Mary and Joseph did not understand the words of the Holy Child, "Wist ye not that I must be in my Father's house?" (Luke ii. 49), is inconsistent with the story of the Annunciation. I do not myself feel the difficulty; if I did, I should plead that the notice may well be one of those editorial comments, which are not infrequent in the Gospels, and which embody a common-place of the history. (*d*) Unless the secret of the Lord's birth had been made widely known from the first, it was necessary that He should be regarded as Joseph's son, and that Joseph's genealogy should be accounted as His genealogy. (*e*) It is difficult to see why the announcement of the Divine Sonship at the Baptism should be in conflict with the story of the supernatural birth, so that, as it is alleged, these two histories must be regarded as two independent methods of deifying a revered teacher. It may be reverently asserted that it was psychologically natural (if the word 'natural' may be used in such a connexion) that at a great spiritual crisis of His life our Lord should become conscious of His unique relation to the Father. (*f*) I have reserved for the last place the consideration of an important and difficult subject. The two narratives of our Lord's birth have one characteristic in common, not peculiar indeed to these sections of the Gospels but specially conspicuous in them. What are we to say of the Angelic appearances which play so large a part in these narratives? To some minds these manifestations cause no difficulty. But to others, who are far indeed from denying the existence of created spiritual beings, they are a stumblingblock and seem to give an air of unreality to the history in which they form incidents. The sight, for example, and the sound of a multitude of the heavenly host singing in the sky have nothing analogous to

x] *The Gospels in the light of historical criticism* 411

them in the experiences of the most spiritually minded men in these days. The difficulty—and to some it is very real and oppressive—is mitigated, even if it is not wholly removed, by three considerations which are closely related to each other. In the first place to the mind of a pious Jew the world around him was peopled with spirits, good and bad; and to him, therefore, an intense spiritual impression, as we should say, would naturally present itself as the message of an angel, and he would with 'the eyes of the heart' and so, in his own belief, with the eyes of the body see angelic visitants. Secondly, we cannot but think that Divine revelation is conditioned as to its methods by the beliefs of those to whom it is vouchsafed. Thirdly, some at least of these details in the story may be due to the influence of poetic instinct and of the literature of the Old Testament in the case both of the Evangelists themselves and of those through whom the history came to them. Thus, the story is told in the Gospels in the form in which, if we assume its truth, it would naturally and perhaps inevitably shape itself in the minds and on the lips of the first actors and of those who heard them and repeated their tale.

But the question must be asked, How, on the supposition that the story of the Lord's birth is due to a mythopoeic tendency, are we to account for its genesis? In what circles did it originate? And here a choice between two main alternatives is offered to us. The story must on this assumption be the embodiment either of Gentile or of Jewish ideas.

"For the whole birth- and childhood-story of Matthew," writes Professor Usener[1], "in its every detail it is possible to trace a pagan substratum. It must have arisen in Gentile-Christian circles, probably in the province of Asia, and then was to some extent legitimated by its narrator." "The Jewish-Christian representation of Luke," according to this theory, "had to be heightened by the introduction of the angelic messages and so brought into conformity with the demands of faith." Against such an hypothesis two objections, decisive in my judgement, at once suggest themselves. In the first

[1] *Encyclopaedia Biblica*, iii. 3352.

place, if time is to be found for the complicated interaction between paganism and Christianity which this theory involves, the First and Third Gospels must be placed at a date which, I believe, is quite untenable. In the second place, the story in St Matthew, like that in St Luke, moves within the circle of Eastern conceptions. Its Jewish character is not a veneer which lies on the surface. The narrative is essentially Jewish. The solution offered by Professor Usener is directly at variance with the primary conditions of the problem.

If the story is not a loan from paganism, it must have grown up, if it be a romance, on Jewish soil. Here three possible theories present themselves.

(1) The story has been regarded as the expansion in a concrete form of the idea conveyed by the mistranslation in the LXX. of the passage in Isaiah (vii. 14)—ἡ παρθένος ἐν γαστρὶ λήμψεται καὶ τέξεται υἱόν. But there appears to be absolutely no evidence that this passage in Isaiah, so familiar in this connexion to ourselves, was ever interpreted by the Jews in a Messianic sense. It is easy to understand how it might be adduced to illustrate a history already current; it is difficult to see how it could be considered so relevant to Jesus the Messiah as to lead to the fabrication of a particular story about His birth.

(2) It is sometimes urged that the language of Philo as to the birth of some of the heroes of the Old Testament suggested the story of our Lord's birth[1]. Philo, pressing the words of the Scriptural narratives and giving to those narratives an allegorical meaning, speaks of the birth of these heroes as due to a Divine generation. But Philo regards the whole transaction in each case and all the persons concerned in it as constituting a philosophical parable. The several

---

[1] See e.g. Dr E. A. Abbott's article in the *Encyclopaedia Biblica*, 1778. The passages of Philo (ed. Mangey) referred to are i. 131, 147 f., 215, 273, 598 f. As an example of Philo's method I quote the first of the above passages: γέλωτα ἐποίησέ μοι ὁ κύριος· ὃς γὰρ ἂν ἀκούσῃ, συγχαρεῖ- ταί μοι. ἀναπετάσαντες οὖν ὦτα, οἱ μύσται, παραδέξασθε τελετὰς ἱερωτάτας. ὁ γέλως ἐστὶν ἡ χαρά, τὸ δὲ ἐποίησεν ἴσον τῷ ἐγέννησεν, ὥστε εἶναι τὸ λεγόμενον τοιοῦτον· Ἰσαὰκ ἐγέννησεν ὁ κύριος· αὐτὸς γὰρ πατήρ ἐστι τῆς τελείας φύσεως, σπείρων ἐν ταῖς ψυχαῖς καὶ γεννῶν τὸ εὐδαιμονεῖν.

x] *The Gospels in the light of historical criticism* 413

characters symbolize different virtues. There is a great gulf between the Platonic mysticism of the Alexandrian thinker and the simple and purely Jewish ideas embodied in the Evangelical stories of the Lord's birth. The Christological language of the Gospel of the Infancy closely resembles the Messianic language of the Psalms of Solomon and of the Eighteen Benedictions[1]: "He shall be great, and shall be called the Son of the Most High : and the Lord God shall give unto him the throne of his father David : and he shall reign over the house of Jacob for ever ; and of his kingdom there shall be no end " (Luke i. 32 f.). Such anticipations cannot be the invention of men who borrowed their ideas from Philo, with whom the Messianic hope had dwindled to a vanishing point. Nor, on the other hand, can they be due, I will not say to the Gentile Evangelist, the friend of St Paul, but to any believer in the Messiahship of Jesus in days when the Jews had rejected Him, and when the Resurrection and Ascension had raised the conception of His Messiahship to that of a spiritual and universal sovereignty. The Christology of these chapters is a decisive proof that they are Palestinian in origin and absolutely primitive and even pre-Christian in character.

(3) A third alternative must be considered. Is the story of the Lord's birth a romance intended, in point of wonder and of Divine interposition, to raise His birth above the birth of Isaac, the child of promise, to which the birth of the Baptist is analogous? Such a theory at any rate would not be in conflict with the simple and non-pagan character of the narrative of the Evangelists. But two lines of thought are specially relevant here. In the first place, if we put aside the esoteric doctrines and practices of the Essenes, there is nothing which suggests that the Jews exalted virginity above the married state. Many passages of the Old Testament at once occur to our minds which indicate that Israel held marriage in special honour. The story of the Lord's birth is, we may say with confidence, alien in its very nature

[1] See Ryle and James, *The Psalms of Solomon*, Introduction, pp. xci f.; also my *The Lord's Prayer in the Early Church* (Texts and Studies, i. 3), pp. 147 ff.

to Jewish ideas. In the second place, it was in large measure as a power making for truth that Christianity gained its victories. It was conspicuous as creating a new standard of truth : it set a new value on truth. In the first age it could not afford to be in conflict with its own first principles. Historical criticism cannot leave out of sight the influence of moral sentiment. A love of truth, reinforced by a deep sense of reverence for the Lord Jesus, cannot but have been a power restraining His disciples from taking liberties with the story of His earthly life. I know that there are many strange surprises in the history of religion. But I confess that I find it very hard to believe that in the inner circle of the earliest disciples at Jerusalem (*i.e.* within forty years after the Passion) there grew up and took shape, not poetical and idealized adjuncts to the story of the Lord's birth, but a story itself wholly fictitious.

One objection of a more general character still remains. The real difficulty which many feel has been expressed in these words : "We should not now expect, *a priori*, that the Incarnate Logos would be born without a human father[1]." But surely we can have no *a priori* expectations of any kind as to the way in which the Incarnation would be brought about. We have no exact knowledge, so far as I am aware, of the laws of heredity as they affect moral character, or, in regard to the entail of sinful propensities, of the relation of the father's to the mother's influence. Still less have we any acquaintance with, or experience of, any analogous event to inform and guide our ideas as to the way in which "the Word became flesh." We cannot say that it was necessary, however congruous it may appear to many devout and thoughtful minds, that the Word, when becoming Incarnate, should be born of a Virgin mother. Neither on the other hand can we assert that it was natural that one who stands alone among men, as being truly Divine as well as truly human, should enter the world in the common way of human generation. A little reflection must convince us that we are

[1] *Contentio Veritatis*, p. 88. Mr Inge is giving a *résumé* of "the difficulties which many people now feel."

x] *The Gospels in the light of historical criticism* 415

not in a position to dogmatize as to what was either necessary or natural in relation to an event so uniquely unique as the Incarnation. In such a matter *a priori* assumptions in this direction or in that are emphatically irrelevant.

Two conclusions, from the point of view of historical criticism, seem to me to be beyond doubt. On the one hand it is not too much to assert that there are very serious difficulties as to the genesis of the story of our Lord's birth, if we give up its historical truth. On the other hand the evidence is slight. That must be candidly admitted. But to estimate the force of this admission we must ask the question—Can we, if the truth of the history is assumed, conceive of the evidence being essentially different from what it is? We keep our birthdays; we veil all that concerns the first beginning of our physical life in reverent silence. It cannot have been otherwise in the Holy Family. The story, if true, must have rested ultimately on the word of the Lord's mother. It can only have been known to very few, and their lips must have long been sealed.

The discussion of some of the most important among the problems which historical criticism raises as to the Gospels leads us finally to the question what is at the present time, and what in the future is likely to be, the effect of historical criticism on Christian belief.

One view of the general position finds expression in the following words of Dr Rashdall[1]: "We may be quite confident that for minds which have once appreciated the principles of historical criticism, or minds affected by the diffused scepticism which has sprung from historical criticism, neither religious faith in general, nor any doctrine of primary religious importance, will ever depend mainly upon the evidence of abnormal events recorded to have happened in the remote past." To speak frankly, the attribution of such a result as this to the recognition of the principles of historical criticism appears to me to be legitimate only on the assumption *either* that the "abnormal events"—whether any event is in an absolute sense abnormal depends on its antecedents

[1] *Contentio Veritatis*, p. 58.

and environment—are of such a nature that historical criticism, if it has not done so already, must eventually pronounce clearly and decidedly a negative verdict, *or* that religious faith can only be based on demonstrated knowledge. The former of these assumptions is, to say the very least, premature. The latter neglects the lesson which is enforced on us by common experience, namely, that in departments of life which are of the deepest and most intimate concern to us we rest on probabilities, and we act on probabilities. The theistic position itself is incapable of strict proof. Though the science of history, as we have seen, cannot attain to other than probable conclusions as to an alleged event in the past, yet the probability of a given conclusion may be of so high a degree that theories and actions are legitimately based upon it on which, for instance, the welfare of a nation may depend. The whole evidence, for example, for our Lord's Resurrection (I am not now referring to the details of the story of the Resurrection or of the appearances of the risen Lord), while of course it does not compel intellectual assent, does appear to be of such a nature as to form a secure foundation on which rational faith can repose, and on which religious philosophy can rationally build a superstructure of doctrine.

Yet without controversy the student of Christian doctrine is profoundly affected by the recognition of the validity of the principles of historical criticism. "Several of these articles [*i.e.* of the Christian Creed] relate to historical facts, and our belief in these must be obtained by evidence of the same nature as that on which we believe other historical facts....It is impossible to evolve a historical fact out of our inner consciousness, or to have any real belief that anything took place 1800 years ago, merely because we wish it did and because we find such a belief comforting and consolatory"—so Dr Salmon wrote nearly a quarter of a century ago[1]; and such a position as this is becoming more and more a common-place of educated religious thought. Our acceptance of it must be no mere otiose assent: it must be real and practical. It seems to me to involve three chief consequences.

[1] *Non-miraculous Christianity*, p. 6.

(1) It quickens the desire for truth as opposed to an easy contentment with traditional ways of thinking. The loyal seeker after truth is sure to meet with perplexities and trials of faith; he may even be saddened by what at first appear to be losses. That it is possible that he will find some readjustments and some restatements needful, cannot beforehand be absolutely and categorically denied. But I at least believe that in the end he will hold in reassured possession all that is deepest and most fundamental in the orthodoxy of the past.

(2) It will, I believe, be more and more clearly seen that, in regard to the events of our Lord's life on earth recorded in the Gospels, there is a wide difference between the amount and the nature of the evidence available in the several cases, and a corresponding difference between the degrees of certitude or (to speak strictly) of historical probability which can be attained. All evidence is not the same evidence. All belief is not the same belief. Christianity is an historical religion; and therefore, as in the natural order, so in the world of faith there must needs be twilight as well as noontide splendour. Inability to rank all articles of the Creed on the same level in regard to historical evidence is not equivalent to the denial of any.

(3) The thoughtful Christian will recognise more clearly than in past days that he lives his religious life by faith, not by sight, not by that demonstrated certainty which in the intellectual sphere corresponds to sight. He will also be content to admit that round his central beliefs there lies a margin of admittedly open questions. The cry 'all or nothing' is the confession of despair. In his last letter, in answer to an invitation from his life-long friend Archbishop Benson to write a paper on Inspiration, Bishop Lightfoot said: "There is nothing so dangerous on such a topic as the desire to make everything right and tight. I do not know whether it is that my mind is illogical, but I find that my faith suffers nothing by leaving a thousand questions open, so long as I am convinced on two or three main lines[1]."

[1] *The Life of Edward White Benson*, ii. p. 289. The date of the letter is Dec. 14, 1889. The Bishop died on Dec. 21.

In days like these a preeminent practical danger is lest, as at Alexandria at the close of the second century, so among ourselves there should grow up a feeling of alienation between those who (to adopt the phraseology of Clement) may be called simple believers and those who may be called Christian Gnostics. Such a temper is strictly schismatical, and sins against the unity of the Body of Christ. The one side must allow to an intellectual and spiritual movement, of which they themselves do not feel the need, reasonable freedom. Mistakes in the application of historical criticism to the records of the New Testament are sure to be made; and in so serious a subject even trivial mistakes are serious. But the spirit of suspicion must be kept in check. The mistakes of an earnest seeker after truth must not be treated with harshness. It is certain that the criticism of those without cannot be satisfactorily dealt with, unless the criticism of those within is honest and courageous as well as cautious and reverent. The other side must see to it that the liberty which they rightly claim does not become license. The Church, like every other society, must define its conditions of membership and of admission to office. At the heart of these lies the confession of the Apostles' Creed. No good can come from a light view of serious obligations. But quite apart from license in this extreme sense, nothing involves greater danger to the cause of Truth than rash, crude, defiant pronouncements on subjects which touch men's deep and sacred convictions. The Apostle's maxim ἀληθεύοντες ἐν ἀγάπῃ is binding on no one more conspicuously than on the Christian critic. The student must bring the results of his investigations, more or less certain, and submit them to those who are trained in the school of practical religious life. *They* must take their part in the progress towards a final verdict. The conclusions of the critical intellect must be reviewed, and, if need be, revised in the light of the widest experience and the fullest knowledge. For indeed the subject with which I have endeavoured to deal in this Essay is not the exclusive possession of the specialist. It is one in which the whole Christian Society is vitally concerned. To the whole Christian

x] *The Gospels in the light of historical criticism* 419

Society is given the promise of the Holy Spirit as a guide into "all the truth." Those who are called to be students and whose special duty it is—a difficult, anxious, and perilous duty—to examine these problems and to strive for their solution, need, no less than the evangelist and the missionary, the intercessions of their brethren that the Spirit of Truth may teach and control them, that they may be endued with the spirit of intellectual discernment and honesty and with the spirit of reverence and godly fear.

ESSAY XI.

CHRIST IN THE NEW TESTAMENT:
THE PRIMITIVE PORTRAIT.

ARTHUR JAMES MASON, D.D.

ANALYSIS.

It was impossible for Christ to be understood at His first appearance; the knowledge of Him is progressive; nevertheless it must be based upon the earliest evidence.

The earliest evidence that of St Paul.

Scantiness of biographical references in St Paul due to his desire to draw attention to Christ as He now is.

St Paul's view of His Person common to the Apostolic writers.

Sources of the Apostolic Christology; the actual life of Christ must have been such as to lead up to it.

The account of Christ in Acts, and in St Mark; St Mark does not attempt an exhaustive biography, but a "Gospel."

The Christ of St Mark; His emotions; the impression produced by His energy; His miracles.

The novelty of His teaching; parables; His breach with Judaism; the religion of the Spirit.

The kingdom of God; Himself the Christ, but a suffering Christ; His death the beginning of a new Covenant; His resurrection.

His Person; His sovereign relationship to men. The Son of Man; the Son of God; the Son.

Similar teaching in St Matthew and St Luke.

St John and the Synoptic Gospels.

The Christ of St John profoundly human; His redeeming purpose; His descriptions of Himself; His Sonship; His pre-existence; "the Word." Christology of the Apocalypse.

The Gospels only intelligible on the theory of Christ's Person set forth by St Paul and St John. It "became" an Incarnate Son of God to be born of a Virgin; to ascend into heaven; to allow the knowledge of His nature to be gradually learned.

The historical Christ is no mere man.

CHRIST IN THE NEW TESTAMENT:
THE PRIMITIVE PORTRAIT.

A GREAT scholar has recently told his hearers that, in order to show what Christianity is, it is not enough "to exhibit the mere image of Jesus Christ and the main features of His Gospel[1]." Every great and powerful personality, he says, reveals something of itself in those whom it influences. We must look at the man's reflexion in those whose leader and master he became. Even the impression which he made upon contemporaries is not an adequate standard to judge him by. It is a true saying. Jesus Christ cannot be appreciated until we have taken fully into account the effects which He has produced upon the history of mankind, and is still producing and to produce. In the language of St Paul, "the measure of the stature of the fulness of Christ" is not yet reached. Any attempt even now to estimate what Christ is must be provisional; at best it can only hold good for the time being. No portrait can depict its subject except at that stage of his development at which it was taken; and Christ is still growing.

Later generations are, for this reason, in some ways, in a better position to understand Christ than His own contemporaries were. Men were better qualified to say what Christ is towards the close of the apostolic age than they were during His earthly ministry. It was not possible, except in a dim and prophetic sense, for those who knew Him only in infancy or boyhood to discern what became manifest to the witnesses of His crucifixion and His resurrection. To see the end, and

[1] Harnack, *What is Christianity?* p. 10 (E. T.).

not to mistake the unfinished career for the finished, is as necessary a caution for the student of Christ's history as for those to whom Solon first addressed it. Nevertheless, in order that the later judgement may be sober and true, it must be based upon the earlier. Much as we may learn of Christ from the experience of two thousand years, from the experience of our own time, our knowledge of Him rests ultimately upon the evidence of those who saw Him. If our present conceptions of Him are not the outcome of those which were formed by His first disciples, they must be imaginary, speculative, unsubstantial, without warrant in fact. There must be agreement between the last and the first, or we delude ourselves with an idealised figure instead of the real Jesus Christ. It is of the utmost importance to examine again and again the testimony of the earliest Christians as to what they saw in Him.

When we begin to examine that testimony, it becomes apparent, as we should have expected beforehand, that not all who observed Him saw in Him precisely the same thing. Some men, of course, saw nothing but what they abhorred and condemned. But even among those who loved and believed there were different degrees of appreciation. Various aspects of His life and character appealed to this disciple and to that. No disciple, it may be safely affirmed, thought of Him at the beginning of his discipleship as he did at the end. Men's opinion of Him underwent a development, and they wondered afterwards to think how little they understood Him when first they were with Him.

It happens that the earliest estimate of Jesus Christ which we possess, so far as the literary chronology can be ascertained, is the estimate formed by one who never saw Jesus Christ before His death, though he spent a life of astonishing devotion, amidst trials perhaps unparalleled in history, in maintaining that he had seen Him after He was risen from the dead, and in propagating his own convictions concerning Him.

It is to be observed that in the writings of St Paul which have come down to us the Apostle does not often refer to the life and ministry of Christ. He speaks of His being born of a human mother; of His Jewish origin; of His Davidic descent "after the flesh"; of His having "brethren," of whom James was one; of His providential subjection to the Jewish law, of His circumcision. If we may trust the reports of his speech and practice in the Acts, he spoke of the testimony borne to Jesus Christ by John the Baptist. But he leaves much unsaid which he might have been expected to say. No reference to the miracles of Christ is contained in his Epistles. To His teaching St Paul refers but seldom. He mentions that Christ had laid it down that the preachers of the Gospel should be supported by those to whom they preached, and that wives should not quit their husbands, nor husbands put away their wives. In a speech recorded in the Acts he quotes the words of the Lord Jesus, how He said, "It is more blessed to give than to receive." These are his only direct references to Christ's teaching[1]. A less infrequent subject of mention is the character of Christ. St Paul says that He "knew no sin." He speaks "of the meekness and gentleness of Christ"; of His self-humiliation, of His unreserved obedience to the will of God; of His love towards men, which the Christian ought to imitate. But the allusion, even in such passages as these, is not mainly to the character exhibited throughout the life of the Master, but rather to the condescension which first brought Him down into human conditions, and to the final self-sacrifice of His death.

The last scenes of the Saviour's earthly history are more prominent in St Paul's writings than earlier events. He gives a whole narrative of the institution of the Eucharist on the last night of the Lord's life. He mentions that in that same night the Lord Jesus "was betrayed[2]." If the Pastoral Epistles may be quoted as his, he refers to the "good con-

---

[1] There is no ground for considering 1 Thess. iv. 15 as a quotation of words of Christ. St Paul claims there to speak by direct revelation, as himself a prophet, and uses the language of the ancient prophets (1 Kings xiii. 2, xx. 35). Cp. 1 Cor. xv. 51.

[2] The exact meaning of the word has been disputed; but the choice must lie between the action of Judas in "betraying" Him to the Jews, and that of the Jews in "delivering Him over" to Pilate.

fession" borne by Christ Jesus "before Pontius Pilate." His writings are full of what followed,—of Christ's crucifixion, His blood, His death, His burial, His resurrection, His appearances after the resurrection, His ascension, His future coming. But for the most part St Paul's references to these things are large and general, without mention of details. They are introduced with a view to drawing out their doctrinal significance, not with a historic interest. The only place where the historic interest is markedly present is the famous passage where St Paul recounts the successive appearances to the official witnesses of the resurrection, in accordance with the tradition which St Paul had himself received, ending with the appearance which had violently transformed his own life and its aims[1].

This absence of what may be called biographical material in St Paul's Epistles is to be accounted for in several ways. It is to be accounted for partly by the relation in which St Paul stood to those to whom he was writing. He was not giving them their first lessons in Christian doctrine. In most cases he had himself given them those lessons. He not infrequently alludes to the careful oral instruction which he had imparted— instruction in the history of Christ, as well as in the doctrine founded upon it. "I delivered unto you first of all that which I also received." "I received from the Lord that which also I delivered unto you." "Remember ye not that when I was yet with you I told you these things?" In other cases the instruction had been given by others than himself; but he could always assume that it had been given, and that, by whomsoever given, it was practically identical. "Whether therefore it were I or they, so we preach, and so ye believed." There was therefore no necessity for him in his Epistles to go again over the teaching of the evangelical events which had been imparted at the outset.

This reason might seem in itself to be enough to account for the fact which has been observed. But St Paul himself

---

[1] St Paul may or may not have known of other appearances: it is clear that those to which he appeals are appearances either to "Apostles," or to the assembled Church.

calls attention to another reason. Among his less loyal converts there were some who appear to have disparaged his authority on the ground that he had not been acquainted with Jesus Christ during His earthly life, as other Apostles had been. The objection was one which seems not wholly unreasonable. But St Paul repudiated it with vehemence. To have "known Christ after the flesh" was in his eyes a comparatively unimportant thing. It might even become a hindrance to the knowledge which was vital for the Christian and for the Church. Christ was not a memory, like the saints who were dead and gone. Christ was alive; and the thing which concerned all believers, and all mankind, was to know Christ, not as He had been, but as He was and is. The historical occurrences of some years back were not, indeed, to be neglected; for they were the means by which Christ had manifested Himself and shown what He is—by which God had declared His eternal purposes for mankind and had wrought out our salvation; but it was essential for the welfare of the world that the Church should not keep her eyes fixed upon the past. Christ is a present Christ. His power is to be felt at every moment;—not merely the power of His example, of His former teaching, of the principles expressed in His earthly life, but His own personal power, still exerted out of the midst of His exalted conditions, through the agency of His Spirit. To know this exalted Christ, to understand the present direction of His will, to be governed by Him as an active force, to be so lived in by Him as to lose self in serving as a vehicle for the life of Christ, this was worth more than any reminiscences of what He had said and done in other days.

St Paul's conviction about Jesus Christ was that He was a being of heavenly origin. Not that St Paul had any fantastic notions about the unreality of His human nature: His death and resurrection could not have had the meaning which they bore for St Paul if they had been to him anything but realities of the most entirely practical kind. But St Paul had no doubt that Jesus Christ was something higher first, and man afterwards. It was by His own astonishing condescension, it was of His own self-sacrificing desire for the glory of the Father and for the salvation of mankind, that He had submitted to become what we are. His own eternal right was to be on an equality with God; but He had not clung to His right. He freely waived it, and entered—knowing what He was doing—upon the course of human experiences, the experiences of servitude and of suffering. Other men have no choice but to be what they are; Christ voluntarily abandoned His "riches" for our "poverty." Upon the fleshly side He belonged to us, He sprang of Israel: but antecedently, in Himself, He bears the incommunicable name; He "is over all things God blessed for ever[1]"; He is the Son of God's love; He is the image of the invisible God.

If such was St Paul's conception of the person of Christ, it is not to be wondered at if his conception of the place of Christ in history is on a similar scale. Christ not only existed before the world. The world owes to Him its origin and its unity. He is "the beginning"; "He is the first-born of all creation." In Him, and through Him, and for Him all things were made. Without Him, if there could be a world at all, it would not be the world of order and consistency in which we live. It was the eternal purpose of God, before the work of creation began, to gather up all things and persons in Christ. Until He came, the world did not know what it was making for. God knew, but He kept the secret to Himself. The Jewish law and its institutions, in ways too manifold to enumerate, were preparing the Chosen People. Nature,

---

[1] Other interpretations of this passage (Rom. ix. 5) have been offered, but they do not bear examination. See any of the Commentaries, e.g., Sanday and Headlam, or Gifford. Mr Burkitt's recent attempt (*Journal of Theol. Studies*, April, 1904) to make the words a solemn attestation of the preceding "I say the truth in Christ, I lie not" (ver. 1) fails for two reasons if not more:— (1) the distance between the assertion and its supposed attestation, —to which we may add that the assertion itself was not of sufficient importance to return to in this manner after all that has intervened; (2) the obvious incompleteness of the impassioned sentences which, on that hypothesis, would end with τὸ κατὰ σάρκα. Τὸ κατὰ σάρκα evidently calls for a mention of what Christ is from another point of view. Applying the words ὁ ὢν κ.τ.λ. to Christ, some other contentions of Mr Burkitt's have much to recommend them.

and what appeared to be the unguided course of history, were preparing the rest of mankind. Christ came, and the secret was disclosed. Christ was the key to the riddle of the universe. In Him the divisions of the human race were abolished. Man in Him was recreated and placed on a new level. His cross and blood were the reconciliation of men to God and to each other, and not of men only: things heavenly as well as earthly were won back and brought into harmony by His death.

Such is the earliest presentation of Christ which is preserved for us. Nor does it differ in any important features from the presentation conveyed by the writers of the almost contemporary First Epistle of St Peter and of the Epistle to the Hebrews. These Epistles, it is true, dwell with especial fondness upon the sufferings of Christ in detail, and upon the fullness of His human sympathies, based upon the trials through which He once passed. But in both He is as much above humanity as He is to St Paul. The Epistle of St Peter again and again applies to Him the language of the Old Testament about "the Lord," "the Lord of Hosts," without betraying any consciousness of doing a daring thing. The Epistle to the Hebrews speaks of Him as the effulgence of God's glory, the impress of His essence,—as the Son through whose agency God made the worlds, and as the force by which the whole cosmic order is borne along upon its mighty way. It is to Him that the Psalmists address themselves when they say, "Thy throne, O God, is for ever and ever," and "Thou, Lord, in the beginning hast laid the foundation of the earth, and the heavens are the works of Thy hands." Well may Harnack say that "within two generations from His death Jesus Christ was already put upon the highest plane upon which men can put Him[1]."

In no other religious movement has there ever been anything to compare with this wonderful development of

[1] *What is Christianity?* p. 154 (E.T.). As Harnack puts the Epistle to the Romans between 52 and 54, and the Epistles to the Philippians, Colossians, and (more doubtfully) Ephesians in the years 57–59, or perhaps 56–58, he might have said "within one generation."

belief in Christ. Buddha, Muhammad, are not even now exalted by their followers to any similar position; and certainly neither of them was thus exalted within so short a space of time, and in circumstances of which the history is so well known. The opinions entertained by the friends of Socrates as they looked back upon the career of their martyred master are of a very different order. None of the great prophets of Israel were regarded in this manner; not Abraham, nor Moses. High as was the veneration with which the Apostles themselves were regarded by the following generations of Christians, there was never the least tendency to deify them. If in later ages a place has been assigned in the thoughts of many Christians to the Virgin Mary which may in some degree be compared to that which St Paul and his contemporaries assigned to Jesus Christ, it was only many centuries after her death that such notions concerning her began to be held, and they are only held because of her relationship to the Lord Jesus.

How came such views to be entertained concerning Jesus Christ while men were still living who had been intimate with Him, and even—if St Peter's Epistle and the writings ascribed to St John are genuine—by His disciples themselves? This is the question which needs to be solved, and at which all students of the origins of Christianity are working. A partial answer may be found in conceptions of the Messiah which were current at the opening of our era,—a partial answer in speculations like those of Philo with regard to the relations between God and the world. But such answers are only partial. Assuredly the doctrine of a St Paul concerning Christ was not mainly constructed out of those sources. He knows nothing of a Messiah in the abstract[1]; he has nothing to do with a cosmical necessity *a priori*. It is the historical, the living personality of Jesus which calls forth his adoring devotion.

Nor was his doctrine the result of a process of baseless

[1] Herein lies the fallacy which vitiates the otherwise useful and interesting essay of M. Brückner, *Die Entstehung der paulinischen Christologie*.

Christ in the New Testament

idealising. That it was formed by thoughtful reflexion is, of course, indubitable, but the process of reflexion was not arbitrary, nor conducted, so to speak, in the air. It took place under Divine guidance. Without question there was amongst the early Christians an experience known as "receiving the Holy Ghost," which produced upon their imaginations, as upon all other faculties, an extraordinary effect, creating in its highest examples an audacity of religious thought only equalled by the sobriety and depth of the practical morality which it enforced. That men under the influence of this novel inspiration should have seized upon those elements in the thought of their time which lent themselves to a philosophy like St Paul's is natural enough. The Christian doctrine of Christ is, no doubt, the product of prophetic activity, of intelligence carried beyond itself by an illuminating and transporting force. But the material upon which the illuminated intelligence went to work was not mainly to be found in Alexandrian speculations or in Jewish apocalypses, nor even in Old Testament prophecies, but in the facts of the life and teaching of Jesus as remembered by those who knew Him. After all allowance has been made for minor influences, it still remains to be asked, whence came that strange *afflatus*, which was universal, so far as we know, among the first Christians, though limited to them, and how did the high mysticism which it brought fasten for its main object upon the Galilean Teacher who had been crucified under Pontius Pilate? No satisfactory answer can be given to these questions, except that the "coming of the Holy Ghost" was the direct result of the life and death of Jesus Christ, and was the extension to His disciples of that power of insight into Divine truth which had been exercised by Jesus Christ Himself, and that the main purpose of it was to enable those who received it to value aright the person of Jesus Christ, and what He had done for them.

Accordingly we are forced to assume that the life and character of Jesus Christ were really such as to affect men's minds in the way in which we see them to have been affected. After all legitimate deductions have been made in view of the general tendency of men to idealise and to weave poetical legends about great and cherished personalities, there must have been in the history of Jesus Christ that which made it possible for men to believe within thirty years of His death that He was what St Paul made Him out to be. No estimate which reduces the life of Jesus Christ to that of an ordinary religious leader will meet the requirements of historical science. The nucleus for the legends, if legends there were, must be sufficiently great to have gained acceptance for the legends.

The wonder is, when we come to examine the primitive records of the life of Christ, that they are so little influenced by the developed theology of the age at which they were written down, and that they reflect so faithfully the impressions made at the time of the occurrences which they relate, while the convictions of men with regard to Jesus Christ were still in process of formation. The Acts of the Apostles, if not as a whole the work of St Luke, the companion of St Paul, must of course be ascribed to some later writer, to whom doubtless the Pauline Christology was familiar and accepted; but his picture of the historic life, in the speeches which he records, is simplicity itself. "Jesus of Nazareth, a man approved of God unto you by mighty works and wonders and signs, which God did by Him in the midst of you,...Him, being delivered up by the determinate counsel and foreknowledge of God, ye by the hand of lawless men did crucify and slay... This Jesus did God raise up, whereof we all are witnesses." "The God of Abraham and of Isaac and of Jacob, the God of our fathers, hath glorified His servant Jesus, whom ye delivered up and denied before the face of Pilate, when he had determined to release Him. But ye denied the holy and righteous One, and asked for a murderer to be granted unto you, and killed the Prince of life; whom God raised from the dead, whereof we are witnesses." "The word which He sent unto the children of Israel, preaching good tidings of peace by Jesus Christ (He is Lord of all)...which was published throughout all Judaea, beginning from Galilee, after the baptism which John preached; even Jesus of

Nazareth, how that God anointed Him with the Holy Ghost and with power; who went about doing good, and healing all that were oppressed of the devil, for God was with Him...whom also they slew, hanging Him on a tree. Him God raised up the third day, and gave Him to be made manifest, not to all the people, but unto witnesses that were chosen before of God." The author of the Acts must have felt that there was no discrepancy between the loftiest flights of Pauline Christology and this simple and primitive teaching.

The three speeches from which these words are taken are attributed to the Apostle Peter, and their delineation of the person and function of Christ is in close agreement with that which is displayed by the Gospel which ancient tradition connects with St Peter and his interpreter. Even in reading St Mark's Gospel it may be necessary for the critical student to be on the watch for occasions where the opinion of a second generation of believers may have influenced the narrative and caused it to deviate from historical exactness. But all attentive readers can recognise the primitive character of this precious document as a whole, and feel that it would not be easy to imagine a record more unsophisticated, a portrait more convincing. What then should we know of Jesus Christ, if the Gospel of St Mark were our sole source of information?

It is not the object of St Mark, any more than it is the object of the author of the Fourth Gospel, to give a biography of Christ, but rather to present a picture of Him in His living activity, and in His last sufferings. The author evidently knew many things which he did not formally record. For instance, he tells us nothing of Christ's parentage and early life, except incidentally. It is in this way only that we learn that He was by origin a Galilaean, an inhabitant of Nazareth. It is in this way that we learn that He had once followed a trade. A later Evangelist, who has made use of St Mark's narrative, has for some reason of his own, altered St Mark's language upon this point, and made the people of Nazareth ask in astonishment, "Is not this the carpenter's son?" In St Mark they ask, "Is not this the carpenter?" They had known Jesus Himself in that capacity[1].

There are many points connected with the Lord's ministry upon which St Mark is silent where we should be glad of certain information. What was His age when He began His public career? How long did His public career last? How many times in the course of it did He visit Jerusalem and its neighbourhood? It has been frequently—perhaps we might say generally—assumed that St Mark conceived definitely of a ministry which lasted but a year, and of only one visit to Jerusalem, at the close of it. Such a conclusion would be natural enough if we could be sure that St Mark had written down all that he knew about our Lord's life. But he nowhere states the duration of the ministry, and nowhere affirms that Jesus visited the capital but once. It is but a deduction from silence, and deductions of the kind are always precarious. Any positive evidence to the contrary is sufficient to shake such a deduction; and in this case not only is there some degree of evidence,—the likelihood lies all that way[2]. St Mark himself may well have been

---

[1] Perhaps if St Mark had said "the carpenter's son," and St Matthew "the carpenter, the son of Mary," the latter might have been suspected of altering his text in order to suit the virgin birth, which he relates, while St Mark does not. St Mark probably calls Him "the son of Mary," rather than of Joseph, because Mary was still alive and at hand, while Joseph was dead; so that his language cannot be used as evidence either for or against the belief in question.

[2] The evidence is to be found not only in St John's Gospel. It is implied in such language as that which St Matthew and St Luke have taken out of the primitive document which they employed—ποσάκις ἠθέλησα...καὶ οὐκ ἠθελήσατε (Mt. xxiii. 37, Lk. xiii. 34), according to which not only had the desire often come into the mind of Jesus, but the people of Jerusalem had often had the opportunity presented. In view of this language it is not fanciful to see a reference to a ministry of more than one year in Lk. xiii. 7 f. and 32 f. Thus even supposing that St Mark was under the impression that there was but one year and one visit, St Luke's and St John's Gospel are independently agreed to suggest a different view. If we may for the moment number witnesses without weighing them, there are at least two to one in favour of the longer period. But St Mark's Gospel itself offers at any

aware of a ministry of three or four years without giving a sign of it in the arrangement of his material. His interest in writing was of a different order. He was writing a "gospel," not a "life."

The figure which he presents to us is that of "a man approved of God." It is no colourless apparition of a being from another world, enveloped in a misty pretence of human nature; it is one who lives His life in the same way that we do. It is little to say that the Jesus of this Gospel, as of all the rest, eats and drinks and sleeps like other men. He hungers, is overpowered by weariness, finds it necessary to escape from the pressure of the crowds that seek to Him, and to gain a breathing space for Himself and His disciples in a brief holiday. He has all our feelings, emotions, passions. He is tempted, sometimes for many days together, sometimes in sudden and dangerous bursts which make Him turn sharply upon His tempter. Pitying sympathy, the rush of affection for a mistaken but well-intentioned youth, tenderness for little children, whom He clasped to His bosom, are combined with sternness and severity, with indignation and anger. He glances round about Him in wrath and grief, disappointed at the hardness of heart which He encounters. He is surprised at the unbelief of the people whom He had known from childhood; it fills Him with wonder, and reduces Him for the time to comparative impotence. As He approaches the crisis of His passion, amazement takes possession of Him, so that His faculties are almost lost in swoon. It would scarcely be doing violence to the language of the Evangelist to say that for the moment he describes Him as under the influence of terror. Only an agonizing struggle with Himself brings Him into frame to go on with the work which He had taken in hand, the cost of which is suddenly seen to be so great. Throughout His active life information reaches Him through the same channels as it reaches us. He learns; He discovers; He perceives; He hears,—sometimes He

rate one indication of a ministry which included two springs. It is contained in the notice ἐπὶ τῷ χλωρῷ χόρτῳ (vi. 39, cp. John vi. 4, 10), and is none the less important for being minute and perhaps unintentional.

"overhears"; He asks questions; He goes to see whether a thing is really as it appears to be. There are some matters about which He disclaims all right to know and to decide, and is content to wait upon His Father's as yet unmanifested will. Prayer—solitary and long-continued prayer—is a marked feature of His life, especially at great junctures; and when He recommends to His disciples faith and a forgiving charity as the conditions for successful prayer, He is plainly drawing upon His own experience. When a man approaches Him to ask Him to prescribe an action or course of action which by its intrinsic merit may secure for the doer eternal life, and appeals to Him on the strength of His goodness, Jesus disclaims all separate goodness of His own, referring the man to the One Source of all goodness, from whom His questioner may derive that goodness in something like the same way that He Himself did.

With this rich endowment of human temperament the Jesus of St Mark's Gospel goes about His work with a vivid energy which impresses all who meet Him. There is a perpetual ferment of the people round Him. All is movement where He comes. Whole populations are seen rapidly carrying their sick about in beds where Jesus has been observed to land. From far off men run towards Him; they leap to their feet at the sound of His voice; pursue Him at full speed, and fall to the ground before Him. Astonishment, amazement, even terror, strike the spectators. The disciples themselves are frightened at what they see Him do, and at the air of determination with which He marches at the head of them. The members of His family think that He must have taken leave of His senses; His enemies say that He is possessed by the chief of the devils. When He comes into a house full of hired mourners making a noise, He casts them all out, as if He were the master of the house, in spite of their angry derision. When He clears an unholy traffic out of the temple, the temple authorities dare not interfere, and He takes command of the sacred precinct so that no one should carry a burden through it. When He stands before Pilate, the heathen magistrate is filled with wonder at His behaviour. When He dies, the heathen centurion catches up the language which he has doubtless heard on the lips of others[1], and exclaims that He was indeed the Son of God.

The work which He goes about in this impressive fashion is a work of miraculous activity. It is sometimes affirmed by modern writers that the age was an age when miracles were supposed to be of every-day occurrence. That is not the impression which we gain from the Gospels. In the Gospel of St John the Jews comment upon the absence of miracle in the life of the Baptist. In that of St Mark the people of Capernaum exclaim that they never saw anything like what Jesus does. Wherever Jesus goes He heals the sick, the blind, the deaf, the dumb, the lame. Fevers, and palsy, and that frightful scourge of His country, leprosy, disappear at His compassionate word and touch. Once, at any rate, He brings back to life a little girl who was believed to be dead. Above all other forms of disease He wages war upon that half-mental, half-bodily ailment which was known at the time as being possessed of devils. Jesus Himself treats the possession as a reality. He speaks to the evil spirits[2]; He silences them when they attempt by the mouth of the possessed to say what He is; He gives them leave occasionally to seek a fresh field of mischief; He speaks about their ways of action like one who considers them to be more than personifications of a distressing malady. He casts them out upon pagan territory as well as among the sacred people. But His miraculous activity is not confined to the healing of diseases. Winds and waves obey His command. He walks upon the rough waters of the lake. Twice over He gives an abundant repast to a great multitude with the slenderest of materials. A word from Him withers an useless tree.

---

[1] So far I disagree with Dean Robinson's interpretation of the words, given in *The Study of the Gospels*, p. 59.

[2] It ought, however, to be observed that in St Mark's Gospel He also "rebukes" the wind, and speaks to the sea as to a living being, and treats the barren fig-tree as a thing which had a duty and had left it undone. In St Luke He "rebukes" a fever.

The miracles, however, are always distinguished by their instructive, and usually by their directly beneficent character. This life of miraculous energy is by no means the life of an ordinary wonder-worker. Jesus Himself does not make much of His miracles. He frequently tells those whom He has healed that the healing is the effect of their own faith. Faith, He declares, would work wonders quite as great in the hands of His disciples as in His own. He imparts freely to them the power to do as He does, and on one occasion shows marked displeasure with them because they had failed to use the power effectively.

If people are astonished at what Jesus does, they are at least as much astonished at what He says. The very first effect of His early miracles is to make men cry out "What is this? A new teaching!" In a world which had become accustomed to the scrupulous repetitions of a traditional lore, timorous of the least departure from what had been said by teachers of established reputation, the appearance of anything so fresh and unconventional as the teaching of Jesus was altogether startling. "They were astonished at His teaching; for He taught them as having authority, and not like the scribes."

The form of His teaching was novel. Other men, of course, had spoken in parables before Jesus; but parables were a characteristic of His teaching beyond that of all other teachers. St Mark gives but a sample or two of the parables with which he was acquainted, and has no intention of offering a collection of them; but he is careful to impress upon his readers that this was the Lord's constant method of teaching. "With many such parables spake He the word unto them, according as they were able to hear it; but without a parable spake He not unto them, and privately He expounded all things to His own disciples." His purpose, as St Mark explains it, was to conceal His meaning from those who were not prepared to appreciate it. The form of a parable was well suited to stimulate thought and enquiry on the part of those who had ears to hear; it did not force a revelation upon the understanding of those whose hearts were too hardened to profit by it.

But there was a great deal of teaching given in a form which it was impossible for the dullest to mistake. St Mark's is not the Gospel to which we should turn to find the fullest exhibition of it, but it contains enough to show that the hearers might well be startled. A new religion had come to birth. It was not only that Jesus, like John the Baptist before Him, began by preaching that the long expected moment was come, and that the Kingdom of God was near, and by calling upon men to repent and to believe in the glad tidings. The new order of things, of which His miracles were a token, did not begin, it is true, by abrogating the old: the first leper who was healed was bidden to comply carefully with the prescriptions of the Mosaic law, for a testimony to the principles of his benefactor. But although the requirements of the law were not repealed, Jesus soon showed that He had no intention of inculcating only a reformed Judaism. To those who complained of Him for not making His disciples fast at a time when the Pharisees and even the disciples of John were fasting, He answered that it would spoil both Judaism and the new religion to seek to combine the two; it would be putting a patch of new cloth upon an old garment, pouring new wine into an old wine-skin, to the detriment alike of old and new, of the wine and of the skin. Others might fast; but it was not possible to impose a discipline of the kind upon His followers, when they were all full of the joy of having Him, the Bridegroom, among them, and were beginning the fruition of the marriage feast.

There were worse outrages than this in store for the convention-ridden religion of the day. In healing a palsied man, Jesus pronounced him absolved from his sins; and when the not unnatural objection was made that the forgiveness of sins was a prerogative of God alone, Jesus combated the opinion. The authority to forgive sins here upon earth, as God forgives them in heaven, belonged to the Son of Man. No part of the law was more strictly obeyed and observed than the commandment which forbade all labour on the Sabbath-day; the disciples of Jesus on that day made a way for themselves through a cornfield, plucking the ears as they went. This was considered to be reaping; but Jesus defended the law-breakers. They were doing no worse than David and the high-priest of his time, who gave and who ate the shewbread, which was not allowed by the law to be eaten by any except the priests. Humanity was above all such arbitrary laws. The Sabbath was made for man, not man for the Sabbath; and the Son of Man was lord of it. A man with a withered hand attended the synagogue on a Sabbath-day when Jesus was present. He healed him, knowing that the action would be an affront to received opinions. To abstain from doing so, when it was in His power to heal, He declared with an angry glance around Him, would be to do evil, to destroy life, which was far less fitting to the Sabbath than to do good and to save. The distinction between permitted and prohibited meats was as fundamental a part of Judaism as it is of Indian caste, and to guard against all possible defilement in eating an elaborate system of washings had been long established. But the disciples of Jesus broke the rules of the system; and when His attention was called to the matter, He acquitted them of all blame. He affirmed that what a man ate had no effect upon character, and was therefore a matter of indifference. At one stroke He made all meats clean and lawful; and not content with this revolutionary proceeding, He carried the war into the enemies' country, and showed how the rules which had been invented for the safeguarding of the law had in practice come to be a means of evading its plainest and most important requirements. The Mosaic law allowed a considerable freedom of divorce after marriage, and on various pretexts the Pharisaic teachers had enlarged that freedom. They came and asked Jesus whether He approved of divorce. He told them very plainly that He did not, and that the law which allowed it, though excusable in the circumstances in which it was given, because men were not educated up to anything better, was a departure from the Divine intention and ideal, and that for married men or women to avail themselves of the liberty which it allowed was to commit adultery. He lost no opportunity of declaring His opposition to the ways of the dominant parties among the Jews. There was nothing from which He was more anxious to keep His disciples free than from the leaven of the Pharisees and the leaven of Herod. With publicans and sinners He vouchsafed to be on familiar terms, accepting their hospitalities in the hope of winning them to better ways, and He cared little what offence was taken by strict people at the company which He kept; but St Mark's Gospel never shows us, like those of St Matthew and St Luke, Jesus at meat in the house of a Pharisee.

In these and similar ways Jesus, according to St Mark, showed Himself as the introducer of a new religion, which was not the religion of the Scribes, nor yet the religion of the Law. What the new religion was is sufficiently indicated by the words of John the Baptist, which stand as a kind of preface to the Gospel: "I baptized you with water; but He shall baptize you with the Holy Ghost." The religion of Jesus was a religion of the Holy Ghost. Immediately after the record of the Baptist's words we are told how the Holy Spirit came upon Jesus Himself, and how He was immediately led forth by the Spirit to His great conflict in the wilderness. All His miraculous works were wrought in the power of that Spirit: Jesus said that those who affirmed that they were the effect of demoniacal possession blasphemed against the Holy Ghost. He promised that His disciples, when dragged to persecuting tribunals for the sake of their religion, should be enabled to speak with an inspiration similar to that of the ancient prophets: "It is not ye that speak, but the Holy Ghost." It was unnecessary for St Mark to give any further account of the work of the Holy Ghost. He was writing for Christians, who knew by experience what that work was.

It may be said that this description touches rather the conditions of the new religion than its substance,—the inward character and force by which the followers of Jesus, like their Master, were to live and feel, rather than the kind of direction which their actions and thoughts were to take. It is true. Christianity is first and foremost a religion of inward and vital experiences. It has its own theology and its own institutions; but both the theology and the institutions are subordinate and subservient to the spiritual life of Christians, and cease to have any value if they are not used for that end. Participation in the Holy Ghost is the great and distinguishing mark of Christ's religion. Of positive ordinances in the new religion St Mark's Gospel in its present form mentions but one as established by Jesus Christ, and that on the last night of His life. St Mark does not even state expressly that it was to continue as a permanent institution of the Christian religion. The ordinance was so firmly established when he wrote that it was unnecessary to record more than the circumstances of its first celebration. Perhaps if we still had the original ending of St Mark, we should have found in it the institution of Christian Baptism; but this is only conjecture, however probable. That Jesus was not indifferent to the advantages of organization among His disciples is plain not only from St Mark's account of His "making" of "the Twelve," and of their authoritative mission, but also from the stress which He laid upon the need of union in a kingdom which is to stand. He who made such careful arrangements for grouping those whom He was about to feed in companies and rows, of a hundred and of fifty, was not likely to be less methodical in matters of greater importance. Any rivalry among the Twelve for superior positions was sternly discouraged, but nothing that Jesus said implied that all His followers were to be on the same level of function or of privilege.

For the rest, the general teaching of Jesus, as contained in St Mark's Gospel, presents not many salient features. Undoubtedly the emphasis which it laid upon principle as compared with detail made a great difference between His moral teaching and that of the Scribes; but there was little that had not been said by the Old Testament writers before Him. The same may be said of His teaching about God's character and dealings with men, about sin, and about the future both of the good and of the bad. It was the manner of it which surprised men rather than the matter. His teaching, whatever were the subjects upon which He touched, is everywhere marked by absolute certainty and freedom.

There is no trace of wavering or hesitation. No problems of existence weigh upon His spirit, and cause Him to falter, as they do with other men. If people ask Him questions which deserve to be answered, the answer comes with a decision and a clearness which leave no room for doubt. He speaks as one who knows. He shirks no difficulties. "Is it lawful to give tribute to Caesar, or not?" "Whose wife shall she be of them?" "Which is the first commandment of all?" So men ask; and Jesus replies to each with words which lay bare the principle involved, together with the inmost thoughts and aims of the questioners. "Why tempt ye Me?" "Ye err greatly." "Thou art not far from the kingdom of God." Men who asked with a dishonest animus were soon discouraged by the swift directness of such responses.

But if we see how little novelty there was, according to St Mark, in these parts of His teaching, the more startling are the proportions which His language about Himself and His own place in history assumes. It is clear that He regarded the coming of the Kingdom of God as identified with His own coming. That new order of things, in which the will of God was to be universally known and obeyed, in which good was triumphant and evil no longer had any power, was already begun, because He Himself was amongst men. To John the Baptist, as to all earlier prophets, the Kingdom of God was still an expectation, a vision of the future; but with Jesus it was a present fact.

So far is it from being true that Jesus Christ has no place in His own Gospel—only God and the soul, the soul and God—that the "good tidings" and Himself are one and the same thing. "For My sake and the Gospel's" is a phrase which resounds again and again in His discourses. Not indeed that the Kingdom was as yet established in all its power and supremacy; far from it. The Kingdom had its unvanquished foes to contend with, and was still a long way from its completion. It was as yet like a tiny grain of mustard seed, the smallest of seeds upon earth. It was like the corn thrown upon the ground by the sower, with a long growth before it which no human effort could hasten. As with Himself, so with the Kingdom: the Son of man was already come, and yet His coming was a thing of the future, the subject of apocalypses which it was hard for the first Christians to unriddle, and perhaps is yet harder now. The Kingdom of God likewise, in some aspects, was still far off. But there was a sense in which the Kingdom had already come; and the reason was that Jesus was there. So far as anyone received and believed the glad tidings, that man had entered into the Kingdom, and was in the enjoyment of its ever expanding benefits.

What was the meaning of this identification of the coming of the Kingdom with His own, except that Jesus was Himself all that the Jews in their best moments associated with the title of the Christ? That Jesus was the Christ—that is, the cynosure of all the prophetic hopes of their nation—was the most certain of all the convictions which shaped themselves in the minds of the disciples with regard to Him. They stood in no doubt whatever that Jesus regarded Himself as being so. How He came to think of Himself as the Christ was not a matter with which St Mark, at least, was concerned. The descent of the Spirit at His baptism, and the voice which accompanied it, were enough to awake in Jesus the consciousness of the fact. That Jesus forbade His disciples to proclaim that He was the Christ, and even forbade in many cases those whom He healed to proclaim the miracle which might tell in the same direction, is no sign that He rejected the title[1]. He welcomed, and even courted it, on His last journey to Jerusalem. He expressly claimed it when driven to do so at the end by the adjuration of the high-priest, at a time when no further misunderstanding was possible. He accepted it at an earlier date from the lips of His disciples. The reason why He would not allow it to be published abroad lay, no doubt, in the ambiguous content of the title, which varied indefinitely with the speakers who

[1] Wrede's attempt to make out that the injunction to keep the Messiahship a secret is unhistorical, is well characterized by J. Weiss as a "morbid scepticism" (*Das älteste Evangelium*, p. 53). Cf. also Sanday in *J.T.S.*, April, 1904.

XI] *Christ in the New Testament* 445

used it, and in its liability to be distorted by the people. Among them there was a danger lest the name should encourage worldly and unspiritual aspirations and a fanatical excitement. Jesus could not allow it to be thought that He was a Christ such as the Jews in general expected. He was indeed the Christ, but a Christ of a wholly different kind.

There was one element, in particular, in the Christship, of the most profound importance, which had lain undiscerned in the sacred writings of the ancient dispensation, and which ran counter to every Jewish prepossession. The final acceptance of the title by the disciples, and by St Peter as their spokesman, was the signal for Jesus to reveal it to them. From the moment that St Peter, severing himself and his fellow disciples from the opinions of the Jewish public, declared his unshaken adhesion to the belief that Jesus was the Christ[1], Jesus "rebuking" the inclination which He saw in them to speak of Him as such, "began to teach them that the Son of man must suffer many things, and be rejected by the elders and the chief priests and the scribes, and be killed, and after three days rise again; and He spake the word openly." More and more from that point onwards He spoke of suffering as the distinguishing mark of Himself and of His followers, and sternly reproved the Apostle who presumed to exhort Him to take a more cheerful view. The Transfiguration itself, with its mystical anticipation of glories to come, only led up to a reiteration of Jesus' statement, and to the intimation that the coming sufferings were all foretold in Scripture. That the Christ was to be a suffering Christ was thenceforth the great contention of those who believed in Jesus as against those who rejected Him; and their rejection became in itself an argument in favour of the belief.

Nor did Jesus leave His disciples without some key to understanding why the Son of man was thus to suffer. Divine providence had not decreed it without a reason. It was to be His supreme act of service for men. When two of the Apostles—in spite of His warning that what they asked

[1] There is nothing in the Gospels to justify the assumption that the disciples had never before considered Jesus to be the Christ.

would involve drinking of the cup that He drank, and being baptized with the baptism with which He was baptized —sought ambitiously to obtain the highest positions "in His glory," Jesus told them, and the rest who felt aggrieved at them, that high position among His followers meant only the most self-sacrificing service of others; that such had been the law of His own life, and that so it would continue to the last and the worst. His own was, of course, the highest position of all; but it carried with it the obligation of the uttermost cost. "For even the Son of man did not come to be served, but to serve, and to give His life a ransom in the stead of many." The words were not interpreted. They were left to await the interpretation of events, and of the enlightening Spirit which the disciples were afterwards to receive. But the impression made by them was deepened, when on the last night of Jesus' life, after He had told His disciples of the impending betrayal by one of their own number, "He took bread, and blessed it, and brake it, and gave it to them, and said, 'Take, eat; this is My body.' And He took a cup, and gave thanks, and gave it to them, and they all drank of it; and He said to them, 'This is My blood of the covenant, which is poured out on behalf of many.'" The pouring out of His blood was to form and ratify a new relation between God and men, making as great an advance (to say the least of it) upon anything that had preceded, as the advance made by the Mosaic covenant upon the unformed religion of the earlier world. Animal sacrifices were at an end; the new bond between heaven and earth was effected by a love which gave itself freely to death for men.

It was plain that Jesus saw in His own death something far more than the inevitable consequence of a reformer's activities, amidst a people unwilling to be reformed. But Jesus looked beyond the cross which He carried, and which He said that His disciples must carry, to a glorious future. Time after time He assured His followers that He should rise again from the dead. Sometimes He gave them the resurrection as a fixed date to go by; they were not to mention

XI] *Christ in the New Testament* 447

His transfiguration till the Son of man were risen from the dead. Unless the event has coloured the record of His prophecy, which there is no reason to suppose, He told them how long He should remain among the dead: He would rise "after three days." He appointed them a trysting place before He departed from them : "after I am risen," He said, "I will go before you into Galilee." The disciples did not understand His language. They were accustomed to hear Him speak in parables, and they supposed that this was a parable. Among themselves they discussed its interpretation, but they did not dare to ask the Master Himself. They waited ; and at length to their astonishment the parable was found to be a literal fact. The predictions of Jesus were not falsified. We have lost the conclusion of St Mark's Gospel: but the truncated last chapter contains the record of the tomb found empty on the third morning, and the announcement that Jesus was risen. There is no doubt that the missing portion contained an appearance of the risen Lord on the appointed scene in Galilee ; otherwise the words of the angel to the women, "There shall ye see Him, as He said unto you," would be unmeaning.

The Resurrection was to St Mark, as it must have been to any early Christian, the climax and culmination of the whole narrative. If the Cross threw back a light upon Christ's character and purposes, the Resurrection threw back a light upon the manifestation of His person and His nature. St Paul says that it was by the Resurrection that Jesus Christ was defined as the Son of God with power. Never until the Resurrection does the Fourth Gospel represent any of the disciples as discerning that Godhead of the Lord Jesus which it begins by affirming. It was the greatest of the miracles of Christ. The theological language of Christendom varies in ascribing it to God, through the agency of the Spirit, or to Christ Himself. In St Mark's Gospel, unless the false witnesses at the trial misrepresented Jesus more completely than there is any need to suppose, Jesus claimed to raise Himself. "We heard Him say, 'I will destroy this temple that is made with hands, and in three days I will build another made without hands.'" The Resurrection finally brought home to the disciples the conviction which had gradually been forming in their minds with regard to the true nature of their Lord without their suspecting it themselves. It justified that extraordinary self-assertion of Jesus which is as much present in St Mark's Gospel as in the Gospel of St John, even if it be less explicit. What was this daring teacher, this strenuous healer of the sick, this binder and spoiler of the strong? "Who is this," the disciples might well ask, "that even the wind and the sea obey Him?"

The answers that Jesus gives in the Gospel of St Mark are not the answers of theological science, but they are rich in suggestions which theology can only endeavour to interpret. It is no mere man, though it is unmistakably a man, who moves before us in this primitive account. From the beginning to the end something is implied which is not uttered, and which is indeed unutterable. At the very outset the prophet John the Baptist, the greatest figure of recent Israelite history—and, according to the tradition which St Matthew and St Luke embody, pronounced by Jesus to be as great as any man that had yet been born—contrasts himself with the as yet unmanifested Jesus in terms which would be exaggerated and fantastic as applied to any merely human Messiah. "There cometh after me One stronger than I, whose shoe's latchet I am not fit to stoop down and loose." As the narrative unrolls, the strength of which John speaks is abundantly displayed.

Jesus is a man who deals with men as their sovereign and their master. Even His outward demeanour towards them shows Him as such. If He wishes to make an utterance public, He "calls the multitude unto Him." If He has something to say to a muttering group of scribes, He does not move towards them; He "calls them unto Him," and they come, as if they were bound to obey, even as His disciples do. He has no hesitation in dealing freely with the property of others. Swine by the thousand are lost to their owners at His fiat. "The Lord hath need of him" is the only reply which His disciples are to vouchsafe when they loose a stranger's ass for the use of Jesus; it is the way with kings to impress or commandeer what belongs to their subjects, and Jesus is at least a king[1]. Towards His disciples, and those in whom He sees the making of disciples, His imperiousness is unbounded. He bids them leave everything that they possess and follow Him. There is no sacrifice which He shrinks from imposing upon them. "Go and sell all that thou hast, and give it to the poor," He says to a rich young man. He warns the four disciples who elicited His last great prophecy that they would be betrayed to councils, and beaten in synagogues, and would have to stand before governors and kings for His sake; and He expected them to bear it bravely and willingly. He considered it not unnatural that men should leave "house, or brethren, or sisters, or mother, or father, or children, or lands" for His sake and the Gospel's. Would-be followers of His must be prepared to "deny themselves" in a sense beyond anything which our use of the term now denotes. They must "deny" themselves in the sense in which Peter "denied" Jesus, when he said, "I know not the man of whom ye speak." It seemed to Jesus no exorbitant demand upon men's faith to tell them to take up their crosses, like condemned criminals, and come after Him. He was prepared to see men lose their lives for His sake, and said that it was well worth their while to do so. To act otherwise would be to "lose their lives" indeed, with no possibility of retrieving them. It is not to the propagation of an idea that He summons them,—not to the championship of some impersonal cause,—but to devote themselves without stint to Himself. His own approval or disapproval is incentive enough. If anyone should be ashamed of Him and of His words, in the midst of an adulterous and sinful generation, He in turn would be ashamed of them, when He should come in the glory of His Father, with the holy angels.

---

[1] It is a tame interpretation, wholly unsuited to the occasion, which makes the words καὶ εὐθὺς αὐτὸν ἀποστέλλει πάλιν ὧδε a promise to restore the ass. The following words καὶ ἀφῆκαν αὐτούς are the fulfilment of καὶ...ὧδε, as καὶ εὗρον πῶλον is the fulfilment of εὑρήσετε πῶλον.

A variety of metaphors and incidental phrases in the Gospel of St Mark sets forth the relation which Jesus considered Himself to hold towards men. He is the physician whom sinners need to consort with them, even if those who think themselves sound can do without Him. He is the bridegroom in whose company mourning would be an outrage and an impossibility. He is the lamp, and has not "come" with the intention of having His light suppressed and obscured, but to set it where its rays will penetrate into all dark corners, till every secret thing is made manifest. He is the lord of the house, who is going away for a time, committing authority to His bondservants, and setting them their respective tasks, and expecting them to be on the watch for His return. He is the shepherd, who is the living bond which makes an integral unity of His flock, so that when He is smitten, they are scattered. In His actual intercourse with men, His tone is a paternal one. "My child," He says to the palsied man, "thy sins are forgiven thee." "Daughter," He says to the woman who drew healing from the touch of His garment, "thy faith hath saved thee." "Children," He says to His disciples when the rich young ruler turns sadly away from Him, "how hard it is to enter into the kingdom of God."

These various forms of expression are gathered up, we may confidently say, in the title by which Jesus chose, as a rule, to describe Himself. He is the Son of man. Learned volumes have been written upon the title and its origin and history. It is true that if we wished to translate "a human being" into the language which Jesus habitually spoke, we could find no other term for it than to say "a son of man." Perhaps no great part of the significance of the phrase would be lost if we were to admit that "the Son of man" means "the human being." But there is a vast difference between "a son of man" and "the Son of man." When Christ says that the Son of man can forgive sins, or that the Son of man is lord of the Sabbath, it is as absurd to interpret Him to mean that any and every man has these powers and prerogatives, as it would be to say that any and every man is homeless, or that any and every man's death has a redeeming value for others, because Christ says that the Son of man has not where to lay His head, and that the Son of man came to give His life a ransom for many. It is evident that Jesus lays claim to be "the human being" beyond all others. He represents humanity as no other can do. He claims to speak in the name of humanity, and to say what is good for man, and what is not, with a determination from which there is no appeal. He understands what mankind is, not merely with the complete knowledge which might belong to some higher order of intelligences, but with the broad and sympathetic insight of one in whom all that is truly human is gathered up and embodied and personified. It is for this reason that on the one hand His death has such a potency for men, and that on the other He is qualified to judge mankind, as again and again He affirms that He will hereafter do. He looks on to the end of things, and sees in Himself the fulfilment of that prophecy of Daniel, which doubtless suggested the title, where, in contrast with the monstrous and inhuman figures which represent the empires of the world, the kingdom of God appears in the form of a Son of man, brought near to the Ancient of Days upon the clouds of heaven.

Could any human being, who is human and nothing more, stand so far above his brother men as to be able thus to act and to judge for them? Is it possible that any could fancy such a position to be assigned to him? In an evangelical document which possesses as good historical authority as St Mark's Gospel does, Jesus warns His disciples that they are not to judge. We recognise that His warning is just. We are not qualified for the task. Any judgements of other men that we are compelled to form, even our judgements of ourselves, are only provisional, tentative, subject to endless reservations. But the judgements of Jesus Himself are final. What human being could without arrogance assume to himself this right of judgement which he refuses to other men, unless he were conscious of containing within himself something which made him altogether unique among men?

That Jesus had such a consciousness is discernible even in

the simple and untheological Gospel of St Mark. Jesus bears an unique relationship not only to men, but to God. It would not be safe, perhaps, to say so, if all our evidence lay in His assumption or acceptance of the title of "the Son of God." From one point of view that title is less significant than that of "the Son of man." There is good evidence that in the Gospel days it was a current and conventional description of the Messiah. As such, it had lost force and meaning, as all complimentary language does. The origin of the title lies, of course, in the promise made to David in the Old Testament concerning Solomon, "I will be to him a Father, and he shall be to Me a son," and in the Psalms which are based upon it. Thus the King who was expected to come was designated "the Son of God." "Rabbi," says Nathanael in the Gospel according to St John, "Thou art the Son of God; Thou art the King of Israel." It is not to be supposed that Nathanael at that early moment had recognised the Divine nature of Him whom he addressed. But it lies open for the Christian to believe that the promise was more completely fulfilled, and the Divinely prophetic phrase charged with a profounder meaning, than was understood by those who first uttered and received it, or by those later generations who singled it out and made a technical use of it.

To bring this out seems to have been the intention of Jesus on the famous occasion when, after enduring all the captious questionings of the Jews, He retorted upon them with a question of His own: "How say the scribes that the Christ is the Son of David?" It is the fashion in a certain school of modern interpreters to make out that Jesus, conscious of being Himself born of no such exalted lineage, yet unwilling not to be regarded as the Christ, was combating the received opinion that the Christ was to be descended from David. It is not necessary to resort to such an interpretation. The narrative which makes Him ask this question represents Him a few lines earlier as allowing a blind man to appeal to Him repeatedly in the words, "Son of David, Jesus, have mercy on me," "O Son of David, have mercy on me." It was not the intention of Jesus to deny the Davidic descent of the Messiah, to which so many prophecies pointed, but to make people think whether the prophecies—those of "David himself" included—were satisfied with a Messiah who should be nothing more than a reproduction of the glories of David, and whether they did not rather require one who should be to David, as well as to other men, the object, not of parental pride, but of humble obedience and adoring reverence. "David himself calleth Him Lord; and how is He his son?"

This was the final appeal of Jesus to a nation which rejected Him not because He claimed to be the Christ, nor even because He was prepared to be a meek and suffering Christ, but rather because the claims which He made for the Christ were so lofty and so Divine. It was because He demanded to be recognised in literal earnest as the Son of God. The words come too often, and the stress laid upon them is too great, for a critical reader to be content with the equation which makes "the Son of God" a simple synonym for "the Messiah." At the Transfiguration—where St Peter, in a moment of extraordinary elevation, proposed to erect three tabernacles, in which the religion of the Law and the religion of the Prophets and the religion of the Messiah should be concurrently and harmoniously enshrined side by side—the voice of God, reinforcing what it had declared at His baptism, set Jesus in a position, not of comparative superiority, but of absolute and incomparable majesty. "A voice came out of the cloud, 'This is My Son, My beloved Son; hear Him': and suddenly, when they looked around, they no longer saw anyone, but Jesus only with themselves." Moses and Elias, great as they were, had no place along with Jesus, in a syncretism combining all excellences. He alone was to be heard and seen. They, to use the language of one of the last parables of Jesus Himself, were but servants—bondservants—of the Divine Lord of the vineyard; Jesus was the one beloved Son.

As such He speaks and acts. If they ask at Jerusalem by what authority He does what He does, He refuses to put into words the truth which, if they had only been willing to be instructed, they would have learned with awe from the veiled language of John the Baptist. Those who receive Him, receive Him that sent Him. God is His Father. He is indeed the Father of all men; and once in the Gospel of St Mark Jesus uses the phrase which St Matthew has made so familiar to us; "that your Father which is in heaven may forgive you your trespasses." But Christ's consciousness of His Divine parentage goes beyond that of other men. Whether we hear Him in the anguish of the Garden pleading "Abba, Father," or predicting His return "in the glory of His Father," we are sensible that it is the "one Son, the beloved," who speaks. So entirely is this relationship to God the distinguishing and ultimate mark of Jesus, that He speaks of Himself absolutely as "the Son." It makes the dividing line not only between Himself and other men, but between Himself and those spiritual agencies above mankind who are sometimes described in Old Testament language as "the sons of God." The angels themselves are subject to the commands of Jesus: "He shall send forth the angels," He says, "and shall gather together the elect." They are His ministers; and it might be expected that knowledge should be withheld from them which was enjoyed by Himself. "But of that day or hour knoweth no one, not even the angels in heaven, nor yet the Son, save the Father." As all fatherhood is in God, so all sonship is in Jesus. The one title stands over against the other as its perfect correlative.

Beyond this the Gospel of St Mark does not carry us, nor was it necessary. Enough has been told us in this one swift narrative to take away any feeling of surprise that the writer of it should begin, as he clearly does, by speaking, quite simply and with no embarrassed attempt at justification, of Jesus as the "Lord," the Jehovah of the Old Testament: "Prepare ye the way of the Lord, make His paths straight[1]." But there is no intrusion of the Christology of a generation

[1] It is far from improbable that the Evangelist had the same thought in his mind when, after recording the words of Jesus to the demoniac whom He had healed, "Tell them how many things the Lord hath done for thee," he adds that the man published "how many things Jesus had done for him."

XI] *Christ in the New Testament* 455

later into the narrative of St Mark, or into the words of Jesus which it records. All is preparatory for the great conclusion which the Church attained by means of the Resurrection and of the coming of the Spirit, but the conclusion is not anticipated.

The Gospel of St Mark has been taken as the standard by which to judge of the life of Jesus as it first struck His original disciples. All investigators of the subject will agree to this selection. But there are other sources of information which are not less ancient nor less trustworthy than the Gospel of St Mark. Among them is that anonymous document which, as most students believe, has been employed by St Matthew and St Luke in common, and which may even have been in the hands of St Mark likewise. That venerable document contained the words which Jesus uttered on the return of the Seventy from the mission on which He had sent them. The mission had succeeded beyond their highest expectation, and the joy which they felt in its accomplishment was more than shared by their Master. Where they had seen a few evil spirits subject to them in His name, He had seen Satan like lightning fall from heaven. It was a foretaste of His universal redemption and sovereignty of the world. "In that very hour He rejoiced in the Holy Ghost and said, 'I thank Thee, O Father, Lord of heaven and earth, that Thou didst hide these things from the wise and prudent, and didst reveal them to babes; yea, Father, because so it seemed good in Thy sight. All things are delivered unto Me by My Father, and no one knoweth the Son, except the Father, neither knoweth anyone the Father, except the Son, and he to whomsoever the Son is pleased to reveal Him.'"

It has been reserved for a priest of the French Church to suggest that these words were never really uttered by Jesus Christ, but are the product of a later time, a specimen of the inspired "prophecies" of the primitive Church, which came by mistake to be attributed to our Lord Himself[1]. The suggestion is wholly without reason or probability. The saying contains nothing for which the self-revelation of Jesus

[1] Loisy, *L'Évangile et l'Église*, p. 74 f.

in St Mark's Gospel does not prepare us. Critics no less alive to a difficulty than M. Loisy have no hesitation in accepting it as genuine. But the import of the saying cannot be mistaken. It cannot mean that Christ's sonship consists in His knowledge of the Father, as has lately been contended. M. Loisy has pointed out that in that case it would be necessary to suppose that the Fatherhood of God consisted in His knowledge of Jesus as His Son; for the two statements are entirely parallel to each other. Christ has a knowledge of the Father which is altogether unique, and that knowledge is the natural result of an altogether unique relation. Christ is not the Son because He knows the Father; He knows the Father because He is the Son.

Many other particular sayings in St Matthew and St Luke bear out this language of Christ, besides the general tone and character of His teaching and action. He is a being of a greater kind than Jonas, greater than Solomon, greater than the sacred Temple itself. He and His are under no necessity to pay tribute, like other men, for the support of the Temple and its services, for He is the born child of the King whose palace it is, while the Jews at large are strangers. He is the bridegroom for whose marriage the Father makes world-wide feast. He is the Wisdom of God, by which even the crimes of men are overruled to bring about the Divine purposes. He is the Son, into whose name, which is one name with that of the Father and of the Holy Spirit, all nations are to be baptized[1].

If Jesus sometimes spoke of Himself in terms like these, we cannot feel it unnatural that He should have done so upon other occasions, unrecorded by St Mark, and unrecorded

---

[1] The famous phrase has not unnaturally been subjected to a good deal of criticism. It has been supposed to be an attempt to create support for the current practice of the writer's day by attributing the origin of it to the Founder of the Church. But the frequency with which Trinitarian formulae occur in the Epistles of St Paul and other New Testament writings makes it highly probable that our Lord should have spoken some such words as these. In themselves, they contain nothing that goes beyond what we find elsewhere in the Synoptic Gospels, though here it is in a highly condensed form.

by the other writer upon whom St Matthew and St Luke so freely drew. There is nothing in the teaching of St John's Gospel upon the person of Christ which is not really covered and justified by what the earlier documents contain.

There are indeed important differences between the aspect presented to us by the Lord Jesus in the pages of St John and that which He wears in the Synoptic Gospels. Had it been otherwise there would perhaps have been little need of a Fourth Gospel. It is hardly possible to doubt that the writer had before him, if not our three Synoptic Gospels themselves, at any rate the substance of them, and that he wrote with the express purpose of supplementing what he considered to be their deficiencies, and, in a few instances, of tacitly correcting their inaccuracies. But that he was satisfied in the main with the accounts of our Lord's life contained in them is shown by his not attempting, as St Luke or St Matthew did, to write a more comprehensive book, modifying, while incorporating, the earlier material which he found in use in the Church. He was content that the work of his predecessors should be read aloud and studied side by side with his own; he had no desire that it should be superseded. Thus he seldom gives a duplicate account of any passage in the Lord's life; and when he does so, as in the case of the feeding of the five thousand, it is in order to append to the account some great lesson founded upon it by Christ, which the Synoptic Evangelists were unacquainted with, or which it did not enter into their scope to set forth. It is only the most superficial criticism which imagines that St John was ignorant of the virgin conception, of the birth at Bethlehem, of the Transfiguration, of the institution of the Eucharist, of the agony in the Garden, of the great appearance in Galilee after the Resurrection, of the Ascension, because he does not mention them in the course of his narrative. His Gospel is a silent witness to the truthfulness and adequacy of the accounts which were already well known in the Church when he wrote. Had he considered them to be misleading, his own work would have given what he thought to be a better representation of the facts.

What St John—for no pretence is here made of doubting St John's authorship—has given us in his Gospel, is from one point of view a sketch of the history of the development of the disciples' faith, and of the unbelief of the Jews. It traces the gradual ascent of faith, from its first ventures, suggested by the utterances of John the Baptist, to its crowning intuition, of which Thomas was the spokesman, gained through the certainty of the Resurrection. It traces the growth of fatal unbelief from the first halting censures passed upon the mission of John, to that last moment when all the hopes of the nation were wildly flung to the winds, and "the chief priests answered, 'We have no king but Caesar.'"

But St John's interest in his story is far more than a historical interest. He has himself very plainly described his own purpose in writing. He says that he has deliberately offered but a small selection out of a great store of incidents which filled his memory; and his aim is to bring home to his readers—not, as M. Loisy has asserted, that Christ is the light and the life of souls, but "that Jesus is the Christ, the Son of God, and that believing" his readers "may have life through His name." The aim is in fact none other than that which the Synoptic Gospels have in view, though the method of reaching it is somewhat unlike theirs. St John is himself unconscious of wishing to present to his readers a different object of belief from that of the other Evangelists.

Nothing can be further from the truth than to assert, as is sometimes done, that the Christ of St John lacks the warm humanity displayed in the other Gospels. To mention but a single point, in no other Gospel is there so rich a display of human affection on His part. In none is Christ seen in such tender human relationships. In other Gospels, the Mother of Jesus, when His childhood is over, only appears in company with the not unkindly, but distrustful, brethren who come to force Him into a safe retirement. In St John's Gospel, she is His companion in life and in death : His first miracle is wrought at her intercession ; her welfare is His last solicitude upon the Cross. St John is not afraid to speak of the special friendships which bound Jesus to particular disciples. He "loved Martha, and her sister, and Lazarus." Among the Apostles themselves there was one who was specially favoured with his Master's affection. Though it is said of them all that He "loved His own which were in the world," and, on the last night of His earthly life, "loved them unto the end," so that love could go no further, yet one disciple was admitted that evening to a privilege beyond the rest. He was allowed to lean his head back upon the breast of the Master, and to draw forth from Him a secret which it seems that He would otherwise have kept hidden.

Such facts as these must be taken into account before we assent to the view that the Christ of St John is a passionless Divine being, moving stiffly and uneasily under a pretence of being human. It is the Christ of St John who sits weary at the well while His disciples go to buy Him food, and who asks for a drink of water from a woman and a Samaritan. It is the Christ of St John who confesses His dying discomfort upon the Cross, appealing to whatever relics of humanity might be left in those within earshot to assuage His thirst. It is the Christ of St John who sheds tears on the way to His friend's grave, and is convulsed with a strange trouble before He calls him back from the dead. It is the Christ of St John who more than once reels under the agitation of His soul as He draws near to the last conflict of all. "Now is My soul troubled, and what shall I say?" "Jesus was troubled in spirit and said, 'Verily, verily I say unto you that one of you shall betray Me.'" The humanity of his Christ is not a make-believe.

But it is true that St John brings out clearly some of the loftier aspects of the Lord's life and of the Lord's teaching that are not so explicitly set forth in the other Gospels. Nowhere else is the redeeming purpose of His life kept so constantly in view. The Baptist sets it forth in a riddle. Jesus hints at it publicly in His first manifestation of Himself at Jerusalem, when He speaks of the destruction and restoration of the Temple. He tells Nicodemus that He must be lifted up like the brazen serpent in the wilderness. As time goes on, references to His coming death are constantly upon

His lips. By means of it the grain of wheat will produce a harvest. By means of it all men will be drawn to the uplifted Christ.

The series of descriptions of His own place in the world which Christ gives in St John's Gospel has received and deserved much study. He declares Himself to be the living ladder which spans the distance between heaven and earth, and the medium of communication by which the needs of men are made known on high and the blessings of God are sent down to meet them. He calls Himself the bread of life which comes down out of heaven; it is impossible for anyone to know what life is without eating His flesh and drinking His blood. He is the light of the world; if it were not for Him, all men must walk in darkness. He is the good Shepherd, whose voice all good men hear, even if for the moment they do not know whose voice it is, and in whom one day they will all find their unity. He is the way, the truth, and the life; no one can approach the Father except through Him, but when once He is apprehended and appropriated, God stands revealed to the soul more truly than if heaven could be opened and God descried in His glory by the bodily eye. He is the true vine; the maintenance of a vital connexion with Him is the necessary condition of moral fruitfulness and of satisfying joy. He is the resurrection and the life; death itself, to those who are united to Him, ceases to be death. The Synoptic Gospels make it certain that Christ claimed to be the one and only mediator between God and men, but they do not set forth the claim with as much insistence and with so sharp a definition as St John's Gospel does. It is no exaggerated summary of the teaching of Christ recorded in it, when St John declares without any reservation in his Epistles, "He that hath the Son hath life, and he that hath not the Son of God hath not life."

If in the Synoptic Gospels Christ demands a full and ungrudging recognition of what was involved in the title of the Son of God, in St John's Gospel He does so more frequently and in a less reticent manner. At His first public visit to Jerusalem He already calls God "My Father" in a way that implies a relationship which others do not share. After His first violation of the traditional Sabbath law at Jerusalem He uses this language in so marked a manner that the Jews see what lay behind it. "The Jews sought the more to kill Him, because He not only destroyed the Sabbath, but spoke of God as His own Father, making Himself equal to God." A little later, their accusation against Him is, "that thou, being a man, makest thyself God." And Jesus never denied that they had drawn a right conclusion. He did not indeed Himself use the word which they used,—still less did He employ the peculiar phraseology of the Evangelist's preface to his work,—but all that forms part of the concept denoted in that word He freely applied to Himself. His action is the reflexion of the Father's. His words are the Father's words. There is a necessary bond between the Father and Himself which makes it impossible for Him to act independently of the Father; there is a law of love which makes the Father "show" the Son the whole of His own purposes and actions. It is the Father's will that equal honour should be paid to the Son as to Himself. Though the Father (as Jesus tells His disciples) is greater than He, yet He and the Father are one indissoluble entity. He does not say that They are one and the selfsame person, which would be absurd, but They are one and the selfsame entity. When the Jews angrily accuse Him of blasphemy for making these unheard-of demands upon their belief, Jesus draws their attention to expressions in the Old Testament which point towards a derivative Godhead, imparted from Its one eternal Source to those who receive His revelation. If they would only realise what possibilities were enshrined in those consecrated terms, they might be led to take a different view of what was meant by calling the Messiah, whom the Father had sanctified and sent into the world, the Son of God.

One thing is particularly prominent in St John's record of the self-revelation of our Lord. That He existed before His birth as man is only implied in the Synoptic Gospels, if it is implied at all, in such expressions as "I came not to call the righteous," "I came to send fire upon the earth." In St John it is far more frequently and more expressly spoken of. If Jesus is able to speak to Nicodemus about heavenly things as one who has seen and known, it is because He alone of all men has already had experience of a heavenly life. The Son was the object of His Father's love before the foundation of the world,—and that not in the sense in which all God's children are so, by virtue of the Divine predestination, but in the actual interchange of mutual love which never had a beginning. When Jesus ascends to God after His resurrection, it is a return to His former conditions; He receives once more the glory which He had enjoyed at His Father's side before history began. The course of human history had unfolded itself from the beginning under His eyes; the persons who had taken part in it were known to Him, and He remembered their longings and their joys. "Before Abraham was," He said, "I am."

St John's own conception of the person of Christ is concentrated in the title of "the Word." It is of no great importance to know whether anything of the speculations of Philo had reached St John in his old age, as it well might have done, or whether, historically speaking, his use of the term was derived wholly from its use in the rabbinic schools of Palestine. From whatever source he drew it, he employed it quite independently. It differs from Philo's use in at least one important respect, inasmuch as the Word of St John's Gospel is unmistakably a personal agent from the beginning, and the Gospel consists in a delineation of His personal life as a man on earth. It differs from the rabbinic use in being far more comprehensive. It at least includes all the processes by which this rational and ordered world of ours came into being and is sustained. It includes also all those explicit revelations which have ever come to man through the ministry of prophets and heaven-taught souls.

Nor was it in his Gospel, probably, that St John used the term for the first time. Christ in the Apocalypse is the same in every essential feature as in the Gospel of St John. While it is His redemptive sufferings which give Him the characteristic title which He bears throughout the book—a title which

Christ in the New Testament

St John the Evangelist first learned from St John the Baptist —the title of the Lamb, the Lamb is "the beginning of the creation of God," and shares with His Father the description of "the Alpha and the Omega," in whom all history has its origin and its goal. The Lamb is seated upon the throne with God His Father, and receives along with Him the adoration of all creatures. The water of life, which symbolizes the Spirit of God, proceeds from the joint throne upon which God and the Lamb sit. In one vision of the book He appears with the signs of victories already won, issuing at the head of His troops to win further victories, and distinguished by a threefold name. The first is one which is unintelligible to any except Himself. Upon His cloak, and upon His cuisses, or on the scabbard that hangs at His thigh, is the second name, "King of kings and Lord of lords," which in the Old Testament is applied to God. Whether inscribed upon His garments, or sounding around Him, the seer beholds or hears yet another name: "His name is called the Word of God." The abruptness with which the title is introduced makes it difficult to say for certain what meaning it is intended to bear. Perhaps the Word is especially considered as the decisive enunciation of the Divine will which carries all before it; "He spake the word, and it was done." But we cannot exclude from the title, when used to describe the Lord Jesus, the conception that the whole mind of God is gathered up and expressed, both to Himself, and to the world, in a single living utterance, personal, like the person from whom it proceeds.

The primitive writers did not first form their theory of the person of Christ, and then write their history to suit it— not even the author of the Fourth Gospel. They observed His life, and they put faithfully in writing what they had observed, though they did so in the light of the final conclusions to which observation and the Spirit of Christ led them. It is impossible to make history out of the Gospels if we start with the assumption that Jesus was nothing more than an inspired man. On that assumption, much that the Gospels contain must be discarded as most improbable, and the residue would fail to account for the beliefs concerning Jesus which were entertained and accepted by the first generations of Christians, as well as by those who came after them. Accept, on the other hand, the assumption that those beliefs were well grounded, and although difficulties still remain they are at least materially lessened. Endeavour to imagine God incarnate, and what could you desire to find in Him that you do not find in Jesus? What do you find in Jesus that you would desire not to find in God incarnate? We are incapable, indeed, of imagining exhaustively beforehand what an incarnate God would be like; but when the thing is before us, there is in us a power to discern the fitness of this circumstance and of that. "It became Him," says the Epistle to the Hebrews; and a similar phrase occurs more than once. We can judge, to a certain extent, what is becoming to God, when He has made us sensible of our needs, and of His attitude towards them.

The remark may apply to some things which do not form part of the primitive description of Christ's life, if by the primitive description we mean what is contained in the earliest form of the Gospel, used publicly in the apostolic Church.

It would, we feel, be not unbecoming for such a momentous entrance into human life as that of the Son of God, that the mode of it should be different from that of other men's birth. This is not the place to argue for the historical truth of the virgin birth of Christ; but, if it be assumed that Jesus Christ is what St Paul thought Him to be, then we can at least say with St Ambrose, *Talis decet partus Deum.* No one ever believed Jesus to be Divine, on the ground that He was born of a virgin; and it is most unlikely that He was first imagined to be born of a virgin because He was believed to be Divine. But, if He really was Divine, such a manner of birth was not unsuitable. It would not be a breach of natural laws in the same sense as if an ordinary man were to be so born. For a given man who was nothing more than man to be an exception to his kind in a matter of the sort would be a miracle such as perhaps no evidence could induce us to

XI]   *Christ in the New Testament*   465

accept. But in this case the person to be born, unlike His brother men, is already, on the hypothesis, an existing person before His conception, and that person is Divine. What wonder if, the conditions being dissimilar, the events should be dissimilar likewise? We cannot say that God could not have been incarnate otherwise; but we can at least say that, if He came in this manner, He gave a significant token of the new beginning which His birth effected in and for the race of men. "It became Him."

The Gospel of St Mark contains no mention of Christ's Ascension. It is not likely that it did so before its original ending was lost. More probably the original ending of St Mark's Gospel was almost identical with that of St Matthew's. The belief in Christ's Ascension, however, is universal in the New Testament. The Epistles of St Paul and of St Peter, the Epistle to the Hebrews, refer to it and make much of it. The Gospel of St John, though it gives no account of it, implies the knowledge of it more than once. St Luke offers two narratives of it, in his Gospel and in the Acts. Criticism may exercise its ingenuity upon the discrepancies or the harmonies of the two narratives; but that the sojourn of an incarnate God upon the earth should have ended in some such way as either of the narratives depicts is in accordance with our sense of the fitness of things. To continue His visible self-manifestations to the Church through an indefinite series of years would have created difficulties untold; to cease them without any signal that they were to cease would have left the disciples in a suspense which would have been cruel. But to appear to them for a last time, and to withdraw from them in a manner which indicated His return to His divine sphere, and at the same time His return in the human nature which He had assumed—which indicated also something of the character of the human body of the future, when it rises, like His, from the dead,—this was to act like Himself. "It became Him."

If Jesus was indeed God made man, "it became Him" to do and to live as all the four Gospels assure us that He lived and did. Had it been proclaimed aloud at the outset what He was, in a manner that none could mistake, to live with Him would have been impossible. His mother's hands would have failed her in her maternal offices. Such teachers as providence appointed for His youth would have been dumb before Him. The wholesome lessons to be gained by intercourse with the gracious Child would have been lost. "It became Him" that enough should be known, to those whom it concerned to know, to enable them to watch over Him with reverent and thankful care, but not so much as to paralyse and unnerve them. In like manner, when He grew up, and began His public ministry, "it became Him" not to disclose, even to His own disciples, at the beginning of their companionship with Him, truths which they were not yet seasoned to bear. Patiently He allowed them to learn for themselves. They began with the hope that they had found in Him the Messiah. So much they all, as it would appear, had learned from the Baptist, either directly or indirectly. But a supposition based upon an oracular authority is a very different thing from a conviction built up by experience. There was many an inward conflict, of which little record remains, before even this conviction became so firmly established as to be able to stand against all counter-theories with which other men's minds were filled. Christ bore with their slowness to believe. He welcomed and blessed each advance. He rewarded each step gained by giving them an opportunity of discerning something more. Little by little the wonder grew upon them, until at last one of the number—for whom the truth which was gradually emerging into view had at first been too stupendous to be so much as contemplated—cried aloud in an agony of penitence and joy, "My Lord and my God." Jesus blessed that disciple —or rather blessed all who should believe as that disciple believed, and who should not be so hard to persuade as that disciple had been. When that point was reached, the purpose of the earthly sojourn was accomplished, and the further stages in the education of faith were to be effected through the Spirit whom Christ sent down after His return to the right hand of His Father. Such a method of dealing with men "became Him."

It is one of the chief blessings which God has bestowed upon the present age, that Christians are beginning to learn more vividly than was the case in some earlier ages of Christianity, how truly and perfectly human the life of Jesus was. Certainly the Gospels portray it as a perfectly human life; but tendencies of thought within the Church led men at one time to look for other things in the Gospels than the tokens of a nature and of conditions wholly akin to our own. To rediscover the historical Jesus Christ has been the aim, and to a large extent the achievement, of our times. But it would be the defeating of the aim and the loss of the discovery, if, in working at the Gospel story, we were so to fix our eyes upon the human aspect as to lose sight of the Divine. The Gospels do not contain the record of a merely human life: to imagine it, shows as much blindness as to say that they contain the record of a life that is not human at all. It is the Divine in the human, it is the human united with the Divine, which is set before us by the Evangelists in their transcript from their own memory or from the memory of eye-witnesses. The formula at which one of them arrived by long and fruitful meditation, under the guidance of the Holy Spirit, alone satisfies the historic sense:—St Mark and St Matthew, St Luke and St John alike, they all tell of the dwelling among us of the Only-begotten come forth from the Father, with the Father's glory around Him manifested to those who had eyes to see. It was the life of the Word made flesh.

ESSAY XII.

CHRIST IN THE CHURCH: THE TESTIMONY OF HISTORY.

FREDERICK JOHN FOAKES-JACKSON, B.D.

SUMMARY.

I. THE PERSON OF CHRIST THE ESSENCE OF CHRISTIANITY.

The relation of our Lord to His followers being essentially *personal* the story of the Church is really a record of the education of the human race by Him. His greatness is seen, not in His satisfying the ideal of a single generation, but in his continuous appeal to all that is best in man.

II. THE GRADUAL UNFOLDING OF CHRIST'S INFLUENCE IN THE EARLY CHURCH.

The records of our Lord in the Synoptists, though inspired, are not a complete representation. His first disciples failed to comprehend instantly the significance of His Incarnation.

III. THE TRANSFORMING POWER OF CHRIST.

The impression created by our Lord on those who had not known Him during His Ministry is seen (*a*) in St Paul in a change of disposition : (*b*) in the early Gnostics by their realisation of the universal importance of the Incarnation : (*c*) in the early Apologists by their ideal of a 'new life.' But though the historic Christ in the early Church was at a later time somewhat obscured by the prominence given to the doctrine of the ' Logos,' the inner history of the Church shows that the example of the historic Christ was never completely forgotten.

IV. THE INFLUENCE OF CHRIST IN THE DARK AND MIDDLE AGES.

There was something in heathen civilisation that made it unable to survive the overthrow of the Empire in the West. Christianity was preserved in the Monastic movement, which even if it encouraged a false conception of life, was assuredly inspired by an intense desire to follow Christ. The 'City of God' of St Augustine was powerful as an ideal in mediaeval times because of its intense faith in the Divinity of Christ. It was due to the Spirit of Christ in the Church that modern civilisation emerged from the Chaos of the Dark Ages. In St Francis of Assisi a revival of the influence of Christ's personal example was manifested.

V. The Reformation.

By insisting on the personal relation of the believer with Christ the Reformation movement encouraged an endeavour to act in accordance with His will. The great progress of humanitarian views was due to the labours of those who laid special stress on the Atonement.

VI. Misapprehensions caused by the general acceptation of Christian principles.

This has led some thinkers to suppose that 'Faith' is no longer a necessity; yet, in a sense, every step in the progress of the world has been a triumph not only of 'Faith' but of the influence of Christ.

VII. The problem of the present age.

We desire to realise the Human Christ, but we can only do so by admitting the Divine as well. We must study (1) the Christ of the first Gospels, (2) of St Paul, (3) of St John. In these we see the Christ of the past, present, and future. Christianity is neither an organisation, a system, nor a sentiment; but as has been shown, the progressive guidance of man by Christ, Who is more fully comprehended by His servants as the ages advance.

"Not otherwise has the marvellous magnetism of Christianity called up from darkness sentiments the most august, previously inconceivable, formless and without life; for previously there had been no religious philosophy equal to the task of ripening such sentiments." Thomas De Quincey.

"The Church throughout the ages, in spite of faults and corruptions, was true to its mission as upholding the testimony to the presence among men of the Incarnate Lord. That presence wrought in divers ways among the hearts and consciences of men. It created a new sense of human relationship; it engendered new feelings of duty; it removed the hideousness of selfishness; it proclaimed the beauty of self-sacrifice. The world absorbed somewhat of its meaning, and its efforts grew nobler from what it learned."

Bishop Creighton, *Persecution and Tolerance.*

CHRIST IN THE CHURCH: THE TESTIMONY OF HISTORY.

"The action of Christ, who is risen upon the world which He has redeemed, fails not, but increases." Lord Acton, *Inaugural Lecture*.

I.

AT intervals in the history of the world certain men have arisen whose influence has exercised a permanent moral effect. Confucius, Buddha, Socrates, and the Hebrew prophets are among those who, by instruction and personal character alone, have aroused the conscience of mankind. Moses and Mohammed were leaders as well as teachers; and Julius Caesar, as the typical ruler, made an impression on the world which has stood the test of nearly twenty centuries. Others live in their written words; and, though their personality is as shadowy as that of Homer, they are still our companions and friends. But not one even of these great names has occupied the same sort of place in the hearts of men as Jesus Christ. He left no memorial of Himself in writing, His work on earth occupied but a very short space of time, His recorded sayings are comparatively few, yet, though the differences of opinion concerning Him are innumerable, there is an almost unanimous agreement among the most civilised races of mankind that no one ever approached Him in moral goodness or in knowledge of God.

From Jesus Christ emanated what is generally known as Christianity, the effect of which has been confessedly a benefit to mankind. But the appearance of Christianity is in some respects no unique phenomenon in history. The progress of the study of comparative religion is showing with increasing clearness how many features our religion has in common with other faiths. As we investigate the accessories of its organisation and practice more carefully, as we trace its gradual development, we see how much has been borrowed from extraneous sources. Christianity is in fact a system which, though possessing a very marked individuality of its own, has nevertheless many features which are to be found also in other creeds.

But the relation of Jesus Christ to Christianity differs entirely from that of all other founders towards the religions or philosophies which bear their names. Platonism, for example, may be defined as a method of philosophic thought derived from Plato ; Mohammedanism, as the belief in a revelation vouchsafed to Mohammed ; Buddhism, as the following of principles enunciated by Buddha. But Christianity is in essence adherence to the Person of Jesus Christ[1]. A Christian naturally asks not so much, 'What did our Lord command?' as 'What would He wish me to do[2]?' He regards Christ as an ever-present Master. The prominence of the Eucharistic Sacrament in nearly every Christian system shows how universally believers have recognised the necessity of keeping in touch with the Person of the Saviour.

The present essay is however mainly a consideration of actual results, and deals with the influence of Jesus Christ upon mankind chiefly from an historical standpoint. In ecclesiastical history we see as a rule the outward working of a system ; but we are seldom allowed to go below the

[1] Bishop Gore's *Bampton Lectures*, p. 9: "The personal relation to Himself is from first to last the essence of the religion which He inaugurated." Fairbairn, *Philosophy of Religion*, pp. 532-3 : "But Christ is not related to Christianity as are these creators (Mohammed and Buddha) to the religions that bear their names. The preeminence belongs to His Person, not to His words: His people live by faith, not in what He said, but in what He is; they are governed not by statutes He framed, but by the ideal He embodied."

[2] The popularity of Mr Sheldon's book, *In His Steps*, is significant. The title implies a widespread feeling that any practical difficulty in Christian life can only be arrived at by asking, not 'What did He say?' but 'How should one who desired to be like Jesus act under the circumstances?'

XII] *Christ in History* 475

surface or to discover the true significance of events. Regarded merely as the story of an institution the history of the Church often proves most disappointing. The human passions displayed, the apparent triviality of the causes which led to the most embittered disputes, the unfavourable light in which some of the most venerated names perforce appear, make the record of Christianity a sad one, and lead to painful disillusionment. But it is otherwise when once the clue to the mystery has been discovered. When we realise that through the Church, despite her errors, failures, and misconceptions, mankind is slowly and painfully progressing to a knowledge of the true meaning of the work of Jesus Christ upon earth, we are able to recognise a plan and a purpose, where formerly we saw only chaos. Throughout Christian history we seem to see, sometimes clearly and at other times more obscurely, the Person of Christ as a link binding events together, and maintaining an unbroken continuity.

The acceptance of the principle of evolution has caused great changes in our views regarding the history of Christianity, as it has in every other department of modern thought. The story of the Church in its highest sense is the record of the education of the human race by Jesus Christ, the principle of which appears to be progressive development. The parable of the grain of mustard-seed becoming a tree shows that there is no real antagonism between the evolutionary theory applied to the Church and the doctrine of Jesus Christ.

Yet this would have been difficult for our immediate forefathers to comprehend, trained as they were to regard the story of the Christian Church as a melancholy record of the declension of the faith from a state of primitive purity to one of such corruption that the original Gospel was almost forgotten. It was often taught that the only true believers were those who went back to antiquity and tried once more to revive the pure estate from which Christianity had fallen; that the true service of Christ had virtually disappeared for centuries, till restored at the Reformation; and that it was only by constantly looking back to the principles of the

Church of the New Testament and to antiquity that a similar declension could be prevented[1].

We, however, disciplined as we have been to regard things from an evolutionary standpoint, admit the principle of development in Church history. We can realise the impossibility of resuscitating the past. We can perceive that even in days of apparent retrogression the minds of men were being educated; that each age has something of its own to contribute; that, though we may have from time to time to reject many cherished beliefs, we nevertheless have gained something from every epoch. Our consciousness of develop-

[1] There is a very suggestive passage in Gardner, *A Historic View of the New Testament*, in which the width of English speculation is contrasted with the narrowness engendered by German specialisation. "I cannot believe," he says, "that in England we shall rest content, like the Ritschlians, with treating Christianity as if it were set apart from all other religions, and to be investigated without reference to them. Ritschl refused to see in conscience an immediate witness of God, would have nothing of a natural revelation, and regarded the suggestion of it as injurious to the Christian faith; and even Harnack seems to regard the adoption by the Early Church of Greek elements of religion as a forsaking of its mission to the world" (p. 263).

Does not Harnack's *History of Dogma* suffer somewhat from the overmastering influence of the same view? Dobschütz in his *Christian Life in the Primitive Church* makes a much-needed protest against emphasising the "secularisation" theory, at any rate in the sphere of morality. "It is a widely-spread idea that a period of deep decline follows a brilliant beginning, and that the post-apostolic age cannot be placed within sight of the apostolic. That may be right, if the concise spiritual power of St Paul's Epistles is compared with the rambling spiritual poverty of the apostolic Fathers. In our domain [*i.e.* in the domain of practical life], however, it is a totally erroneous view....The real moral status of the Churches is raised in spite of all so-called secularisation, *or rather, to some extent in consequence of the abatement of enthusiasm*. Excesses like those with which Paul had to contend in Corinth are to be met with only in quarters which the Church had cut off from herself. In the later literature there is hardly any mention of the sins of the flesh, falsehood, and so forth. This was not because such were considered indifferent, but because within the Churches there was now no occasion to discuss them" (pp. 372, 374). At the same time, since in every age the Church is tempted to regard her interpretation of her Lord as final and complete, a return to the historic Christ is a constant necessity, and the only cause of progress.

XII] *Christ in History* 477

ment is thus a stimulus to labour for the good of future generations.

It is in this spirit that we propose to deal with the subject before us. It is our purpose to look upon the work of Christ described in the Gospels, as St Luke teaches us to understand it, as one begun by Him, but not yet finished (Acts i. 1), regarding the Church as the means by which the Person of Christ is revealed in history. We shall frequently have to admit that we have received the record of our Lord's life and even many of His sayings modified by human hands[1]; that in the history of the Church we recognise much that is fallible; and that there is only a slow (though constant) progress towards the understanding of the Truth. But in this very progress, slow as it is, we shall discover, beyond that Figure in the Gospel narrative which is our necessary starting-point, the ever-present Person of Christ in history, leading mankind constantly forward towards the full perception of His will and Nature.

We should naturally desire to be able to trace in the history of the Church the constant recognition of the truth of St Peter's words that our Lord had left us an example that we should follow in His steps (1 Peter ii. 21). It would be a grateful task to show that in every age men set before themselves the ideal of the life of Christ as illustrated in His ministry, and that they endeavoured to conform themselves to this pattern. It would be a pleasing occupation to collect a series of quotations from the writings of the saintliest men of each generation, showing their appreciation of the life of the one perfect Man and their desire to conform all their actions to it. But in history it is rare to find what is expected, and still rarer to discover a confirmation of one's own theories as to what should have been the ideals of the past. In the case of Jesus Christ, moreover, it would be

[1] For example the accounts of our Lord's dealings with demons, of which Professor Whitehouse says (Hastings' *Dictionary of the Bible*, Art. Demonology), "We are dealing with the reports of chroniclers whose minds were necessarily coloured by the prevailing beliefs of the age, psychic and cosmic."

decisive against His Godhead to find that any age estimated Him exactly as any other. For that would imply that man could take in at one time more than one facet of the Nature of God. It is essential to His Divinity that He should satisfy the ideals and appeal to the best aspirations of nations and individuals in every age. That He is "the same yesterday, to-day, and for ever[1]" does not mean that His Person can only be rightly regarded in a single light; for as the unity of God implies infinity rather than simplicity, so the Person of Jesus Christ embraces all the best ideals of humanity, and exists, not for one generation, but for all ages.

In the enquiry before us we have to deal with the influence both of our Lord's words, and of His example. But beyond this there is the influence of a Person realised as ever present and Divine, and this is a factor far more potent and harder to define. Even the men who have most deeply moved their own contemporaries must have had something about them baffling all description, which those in contact with them have felt, but have never been able to explain. The charm that radiated from such a man as St Francis, the enthusiasm that the presence of Napoleon was able to evoke, the irresistible authority exercised over his followers by John Wesley, are examples of this. The power to gain ascendancy over others as displayed by such men is in some respects akin to that exerted by Jesus Christ on the men of His age. But the personal fascination which He exercised has renewed itself from age to age, and is perhaps stronger now than ever; whereas the influence of others has inevitably decreased as time went on. This may be considered as part of the historical testimony to the Divine Nature of Jesus Christ.

---

[1] Heb. xiii. 8. Bishop Westcott says of the following verse (v. 9), "The unchangeableness of Christ calls up the variety of human doctrines. The faith of the Christian is in a Person, not in doctrines about Him." *Commentary, in loco.*

II.

The four Gospels agree in representing the disciples as failing at first to understand our Lord's simplest teaching with regard to the nature of His mission. The twelve Apostles cherished the ideals of the Galilean Jews. They shared in the Messianic hopes entertained by the Jewish people during the interval which elapsed between the death of Herod and the Fall of Jerusalem. In some way (they knew not how) they felt that God was about to "restore the kingdom to Israel." They became persuaded by their constant intercourse with Jesus that He would accomplish this. But their comparative lack of imagination often made their conceptions of the future baldly literal. We learn, for example, from an incidental allusion in the first chapter of the Acts how little effect even the Resurrection of our Lord had in modifying their anticipations. If their belief in His power was increased, their ideas of His work were the same as ever. As soon as they had become familiar with the fact that Jesus was again with them they returned to the old method of questioning Him as to His intentions. Their "Lord, wilt thou at this time restore the kingdom to Israel?" (Acts i. 6) is but an echo of the questions so frequently asked during the ministry. It may be frankly acknowledged that the personal disciples of our Lord shared in the misconceptions of the age in which they lived; indeed the candour of this admission is characteristic of the Gospel narrative. Nor could the evangelists have left so divine an impression of the Christ had they not been truly inspired to record what they had "seen and heard." Yet the Gospels are the products of their age, and to appreciate them we must endeavour to assimilate the atmosphere of Palestine of the first century, and to put ourselves in the place of a Jew of that time. We must make due allowance for the limitations of the age as compared with the knowledge of nature to which we have attained[1].

[1] "Il est conforme à l'ordre des choses humaines que l'œuvre des plus grands, leur génie et leur caractère, ne puissent être bien appréciés qu'à une certaine distance, et quand ils ont disparu." Loisy, L'Évangile et l'Église, p. 21.

If our Lord made no attempt to correct errors or dispel illusions which time and increasing knowledge would remove, it was because He deliberately refused to complicate lessons on right doing, which men are glad to shirk, with lessons on controversial subjects, which men love, and concentrated His teaching on certain principles of life and conduct. Had He appeared in Galilee as a teacher of all the wisdom of the ages, had He laboured to show the world that the science, geography, and theory of government of His time were erroneous, He might have produced admiration and astonishment; but we can conceive of no abiding result following His appearance. But the object of our Lord's teaching was to implant in the hearts of men that which should bear fruit for all time, to give His disciples eternal principles, motives of action which should never fail to work, to instil truths capable of being realised more and more fully by every succeeding generation.

If many ideas in the Gospels appear to be limited by the circumstances of Palestine in the first century, the principles inculcated by Jesus Christ are more and more operative as the horizon of man is extended; and no real progress, no extension of knowledge, can be detrimental to their growth and influence. A survey of the history of the most advanced nations of the world will reveal an ever-growing appreciation of the meaning of Christ's message to humanity; and the waning of such appreciation is a sure sign of a decaying civilisation.

Even if we had to admit that some sayings and actions of our Lord have been misapprehended, it would still be a matter for surprise, not that Jesus was understood so imperfectly, but that He was understood so well. For in the Gospels we see practically nothing of the Twelve but their faults and failures. Incidentally this suggests that the Gospels are genuine Apostolic records. Had they been the work of a later generation we should expect to see a halo on the head of each Apostle. But instead of this no personal followers of any great teacher have faded so completely from the page of history as have most of the disciples of our Lord.

Except in the case of St Peter and St John, few records remain of their words and actions during His ministry, and these generally tell of their shortcomings. The silent part they played is in itself an indication that they, at least, realised the ideal of merging self in the service of Christ. To argue that their failure to comprehend instantly the meaning of His ministry is a proof that it had no significance is to misapprehend the whole method of Divine teaching as revealed in history; for that failure, even after prolonged study, is our strongest argument for the supernatural character of His work.

Nothing is more remarkable than the gradual manner in which mankind has advanced in the path of moral progress. The story of the Divine education of Israel, as it appears by the light of modern criticism, is a proof of the extreme slowness with which man grasps the most fundamental principles of morality. From Moses to Amos the Israelites were learning what seems to us the elementary truth that right conduct is more important than the performance of ritual acts of worship; Ezekiel proclaimed a startling novelty to many of his age, when he declared that every man is personally responsible to God[1]. But our Lord came to reveal to His disciples a view of duty far beyond anything of which the world had hitherto dreamed. He called upon men to make an unprecedented advance from formalism to spirituality, from laws to principles, from the tyranny of fear to the free service of love. But the true significance of the words or acts of any great person is rarely apparent at first, and important truths have scarcely ever been understood by the generation in which they first came to light. For since mankind is no more able than a child to see the purpose of its teachers in a moment, it has to assimilate its lessons before they can be appreciated at their true value. It is for the future that all great teachers have to work, and the more valuable their lessons the less rapidly are they comprehended. The 'immortals,' Homer, Plato, Virgil, Dante, Shakespeare, are still read because it is felt that they still have an un-

[1] Ezekiel xviii. 19, 20: but see also Jer. xxxi. 29.

revealed message to the world. What is true of them is
far more true of Jesus Christ, who, even regarded from the
naturalistic standpoint, is less easy to comprehend than any
human being who has hitherto lived on earth. The world has
not even yet learned its lesson; humanity is still striving to
attain the goal He set before it. No other life has exercised
a similar influence. No personality has had a similar power.
As Goethe truly says, "Let intellectual and spiritual culture
progress and the human mind expand as much as it will:
beyond the grandeur and the moral elevation of Christianity
as it sparkles and shines in the Gospels, the human mind will
not advance[1]." The Buddhist philosophy may have more
adherents, the rule of life prescribed by Mohammed may
have secured a more rapid recognition; but it is the Person
of Jesus Christ which is still a power on earth, and it is by
this means that the results of His life are seen in ever-
widening circles in the history of mankind.

III.

The conversion of St Paul is the great example of the
transforming power of the Saviour on one who had never
known Him on earth. It is moreover a striking demonstration that the meaning of the Incarnation might be more
plain to one who had not known Christ "after the flesh"
(2 Cor. v. 16) than it had been to His immediate followers.

It is frequently assumed that the conversion of St Paul
was a mere change in his convictions; but, if we compare
what the Apostle may reasonably be supposed to have been
before the great crisis in his life with what he unquestionably was after it, we shall find that it had a far deeper
significance.

St Paul describes himself in early life as being exceed-
ingly zealous for the traditions of his fathers (Gal. i. 14).
Zeal in a Jew of that age meant the fiercest fanaticism. It
could transform the pupil of the Rabbi, nay the Rabbi

---

[1] Harnack, *What is Christianity?* p. 4.

himself, into an intrepid warrior[1]. There seems little reason to suppose that St Paul was different from other enthusiasts of his nation, reckless of life when principles were at stake, ready to kill or to be killed if the interests of the ancestral faith demanded it. Such a man when he changes sides generally becomes the most uncompromising enemy of his former associates. Excessive zeal demands extremes, and in one respect St Paul showed himself true to his original character. Christ's teaching becomes to him the antithesis of Pharisaic Judaism. Yet he displayed no bitterness against the Jews. He desired their salvation above all things. He bore witness to their zeal for God. He professed a willingness to become *anathema* for their sake (Rom. ix. 3). In all his dealings as a disciple of Christ St Paul showed a regard for the scruples of others which a fanatic is incapable of displaying. As a Pharisaic Jew, again, he had been trained to adhere to his opinions without compromise, and his education was a stumbling-block in the way of his attempting to put himself in the place of another, or to view any subject save from the standpoint of a rigid observer of the Law. But while much of his theology is Judaic, while he shows the effect of his education in his treatment of nearly every subject he handles, his view of the Christian Society as a body preserved by the sympathy of every part, his broad and liberal treatment of such matters as the abstention from sacrificial meats, and his constant consideration for the feelings of others are inconsistent with his early principles. Such a change could only have been brought about by some external influence, and it can be attributed only to the overmastering power of the Person of Christ on a man of high intellect and resolute disposition. His Epistles reveal a character profoundly influenced by what he terms the meekness and gentleness of Christ (2 Cor. x. 1)[2].

---

[1] As in the case of Bar-cochab's revolt, of which the moving spirit was R. Akiba.

[2] To some extent Tertullian *de Patientia* is a parallel instance. He is terribly conscious that he, the fierce Tertullian, has no right to discourse about patience. Yet Christ has made him see that patience is the very nature of God (see end of

That he should have succeeded so completely in this respect shows that he had triumphed over the ingrained prejudices of early life and had become radically different in character. Consequently nothing can explain this transformation so justly as the Apostle's declaration that he had allowed his whole being to be absorbed by the Person of Christ; "I live, yet not I, but Christ liveth in me" (Gal. ii. 20).

Nor was it only in his life and character that he illustrated the personal influence of Christ; his writings first bring into prominence the power of Christ's death upon the individual. The thought of being crucified with Christ, which was destined to be one of the chief means of keeping the Person of Christ constantly before all Christians, is one of the keynotes of the Pauline theology.

The early Gnostics, whose views are at last receiving the intelligent appreciation so long withheld by Christian scholars, afford another remarkable testimony to the effect of the Person of Christ in the world. Representing as they did that part of educated society which was prepared to accept the Faith without abandoning philosophical methods, the numerous sects of Gnosticism show how tremendous a significance the appearance of our Lord on earth had for thinking men in the early days of the second century. In their wildest flights we can see how the Gnostics realised, as the earlier followers of the Messiah had failed to do, that not merely mankind, but the whole cosmos, seen and unseen, had been affected by the Incarnation. Even if they failed to interpret the true meaning of the Gospel story, they saw at least that it had a deeper meaning than the record of a man or prophet mighty in word and deed. The very fecundity of their systems shows how profound an impression Jesus Christ had made upon the world. Nor was Gnosticism blind to the moral beauty of the Saviour's life. The figure of the risen Teacher in the *Pistis Sophia* and the Christ of Marcion

c. 3: the words and sufferings of Christ, "probant patientiam dei esse naturam"). So as a Christian, Tertullian feels he must strive and pray for patience. Is it too much to say that the *de Patientia* is inspired by Christ? Tertullian could never have written it had he not been a Christian.

testify to the power of the Person of Christ in those outside the Church[1].

When we turn from the Gnostics to the Apologists, we may perhaps feel a certain disappointment in being unable to gain much information concerning the view taken by them of the personal Christ. Writing as they do for heathens, these authors show a natural reticence about Christian belief; and from the majority of them we learn rather the practice of the Church than the Christian opinion concerning our Lord. But a study of the Apologies swells the testimony that the Christians of the second century accepted our Lord as Divine; and even the description they give of Christian life throws a light on the influence of the Person of Christ in moulding the methods of thought and action in the Church. The first point is especially important, as in all early defences of Christianity the writer's object is to show that monotheism is the religion implanted in the heart of mankind, and that Christianity is a republication of the truths taught by Nature. Under such circumstances it would be reasonable to expect that Christ should be represented as no more than a wise man, and a teacher of the truth. To assert His Divinity was, as we learn from Justin Martyr's dialogue with Trypho, to weaken the claims of Jesus to be the Messiah and so to lose an advantage in argument with the Jews; and, as another result, to lay the Christians open to the retort that they themselves were guilty of the very thing they blamed the Gentiles for doing, namely, adoring a deified man[2]. The tendency of the age was all in favour of monotheism, and no charge was more damaging to the Jews than that brought by Aristides that their religion inculcated the worship of angels, and not a consistent service of the one True God[3]. But, although they would undoubtedly have made the preaching of Christianity more generally acceptable by teaching that Jesus was no

---

[1] "Harsh and unphilosophical as it (Marcion's system) was, it paid homage to Christ, and it professed to be built on Him. In the words of Christ and in the apostolic comments on them was to be found the only source of truth." Cruttwell, *A Literary History of Early Christianity*, vol. I. p. 238.

[2] Justin, *Adv. Tryph.* lxvii.; Minucius Felix, xxix.; Tertullian, *Apology*, xxi.

[3] Aristides, ch. xiv. (Syriac), "Nevertheless they too have gone

more than the prophet of the True God, so firm was their conviction of His Divinity, that the men of the second century made the worship of Him a characteristic of Christianity. The practice did not escape the notice even of a heathen governor like Pliny the Younger[1]. Except some of the Judaising sects, all Christians, Gnostic, Pauline, and Catholic, were agreed on this point. They explained the Divinity of the Person of Christ in different ways: but they were unanimous in acknowledging it. This general consensus of Christian opinion is an evidence of the impression created by His ministry on earth.

The new life entered upon by believers in Christ also illustrates the power of the memories of the Saviour's actual life on earth. The admission that He was Divine did not hinder the early Church from regarding Him as the Great Exemplar. No considerable body of men, it is true, tried to imitate Him literally[2]—His methods of teaching were not exactly followed—nevertheless the common object of the early Christian societies was to realise the 'new life in Him.' If we take the Apologists as our guides, we shall see that the chief features of the new life were hatred of idolatry, the practice of benevolence, and an enthusiastic admiration of personal chastity and purity. In each case we see an adherence to principles rather than the observance of fixed rules, and thus we have an example of the Person of Christ as a living force in the Church.

In the New Testament there are fewer warnings against the sin of idolatry than might have been expected. Coming as He did a Jew to Jews, our Lord never denounced that which all His hearers reprobated. With all St Paul's natural hatred of idolatry he lays down no precise rules for its avoidance.

---

astray from accurate knowledge, and they suppose in their minds that they are serving God, but in the methods of their actions their service is to angels and not to God."

[1] "Adfirmabant autem hanc fuisse summam vel culpae suae vel erroris, quod essent soliti stato die ante lucem convenire, carmenque Christo quasi deo dicere secum invicem."

[2] Harnack, *History of Dogma*, vol. I. p. 258. "Tatian's Encratism was an attempt to imitate the poor life of Jesus. This early conception of the *Imitatio Christi* was one of the many causes of asceticism in the Church."

XII] *Christ in History* 487

To him an idol was "nothing in the world" (1 Cor. viii. 4); and compliance with such social customs as the eating of meats used in sacrifices is only condemned by him if its observance proves a cause of stumbling to the weak. Yet in a very short time it became the distinguishing mark of a Christian to have no commerce with idolatry. And it appears from Pliny's Letter to Trajan that the abhorrence of Christians for the religion of the Empire lay in the fact that the worship of the gods or of the Emperor was regarded as disloyalty to Christ. If a man would 'curse Christ,' the act was accepted by the Imperial authorities as a final proof that he was not a Christian[1].

So much has been said of the benevolence of the early Christians and of their mutual love that there is but little need to dilate on the subject. Proofs are superfluous where a fact is admitted on all sides. Charity was a moving principle in the Christian community long before the Gospels were committed to writing; and here again the lines followed were in accordance with the spirit rather than the letter of our Lord's teaching. Kindness to the poor was in part an inheritance from Judaism; but Christian benevolence in early days surpassed anything that had hitherto been known. Its nature was never better exhibited than when the fugitive and persecuted believers crept back to the streets and squares of Alexandria and Carthage during the great pestilence of the third century to tend those heathen whom their panic-stricken relatives had abandoned[2]. It was the influence of the Person of Christ that made it impossible for any Christian community to exist without at least professing to recognise the duty of helping all who were in distress.

Few of the sayings attributed to our Lord are couched more distinctly in legal form than those which refer to the relations of husband and wife; and from the earliest times the Church set her face as unflinchingly against divorce as she did against idolatry. The sensitive purity of the primitive Christians may

[1] "Qui negabant esse se Christianos aut fuisse, cum...imagini tuae...supplicarent, praeterea male dicerent Christo quorum nihil posse cogi dicuntur qui sunt re vera Christiani, dimittendos esse putavi." Pliny to Trajan.

[2] Eusebius, *H. E.* VII. 22. Pontius, *Vit. Cypr.* ch. ix.; Abp Benson, *Cyprian—His Life, His Times, His Work*, p. 245.

appear exaggerated, and even injurious to family life, which was depreciated in comparison with the practice of celibacy. But neither exaggerations nor misconceptions can conceal the fact that Christianity raised purity to an importance hitherto unknown in the Roman world. The noble conclusion of Tertullian's treatise *Ad Uxorem* gives a beautiful description of Christian wedlock[1].

How little the endeavour to follow what the early Christians used to term "The way of Life" was due to a slavish adherence to legal precepts, or to a desire to reproduce in bare detail the lessons enshrined in the Gospel, may be seen in the argument of Tertullian's *De Corona Militis*[2]. It is there maintained that a soldier, who, more scrupulous than his Christian companions, refused to wear a wreath on the occasion of a military festival, and suffered in consequence, was worthy of praise because, not content with the precepts, he had endeavoured to conform his life to the spirit of the Gospel. Such a tendency, though, as in the case of Rabbinic Judaism, it might lead to excessive legalism, also makes for progress, when actuated by a desire to realise the ideal of obeying Christ as a Person, rather than His law as a code of morals. Christianity in this sense is an imitation of Christ, capable of constant development by being always directed towards a standard which becomes higher with increasing enlightenment.

The doctrinal part of early Christian Apologetic literature which made the greatest impression on the Church is the view of the Logos developed by Justin Martyr[3]. Justin, it will be remembered, was a philosopher whom no system of instruction would satisfy till he found a rest from all his doubts in Jesus Christ[4]. Justin identifies

[1] Tertullian, *Ad Uxorem*, ch. viii. "Unde sufficiamus ad enarrandam felicitatem eius matrimonii quod Ecclesia conciliat et confirmat oblatio, et obsignat benedictio?"

[2] Neander, *Antignostikus*. "In arguing against those who wished to adhere simply to the letter of Scripture, and were in danger of making a mere legal code out of it...Tertullian traces tradition and usage to an internal necessity, and found it in the Christian consciousness or the Christian reason." E. T., p. 268.

[3] His indebtedness to the Fourth Gospel is not here in question.

[4] Justin Martyr, *Dialogue*, chh. iii–vii.

XII] *Christ in History* 489

Christ with the Divine Wisdom manifested in all ages and amongst all people, the Teacher of Orpheus and Socrates as well as of Abraham and Moses[1]. To this writer the Incarnation is but the culmination of the many evidences of the presence of the Logos; wherever he saw goodness or wisdom, there he recognised the Person of Christ.

But although Justin's teaching with its constant allusions to the Gospel narrative may be due to the actual influence of Christ's ministry, the doctrine of many of his followers was moulded by the endeavour to connect our Lord's Person with the cosmological speculations of the age rather than with any practical bearing on human life. The theology of the Church after the contest with Gnosticism tended more and more to occupy itself with speculations concerning Christ as the Creator of the world and the revealer of the essence of the Godhead. The great sacrifice which the Church of Alexandria made to the necessity of exalting the Divine Nature of Christ was that, in accepting the Divine, she tended to lose her hold on the historical Jesus. Both Origen and Athanasius were deeply religious men, and to both of them religion was a very practical interest, but it cannot be denied that the Christ of their writings is not the Christ of the Gospel story so much as the revealer of the Divine Nature[2].

In the creed of Eusebius of Caesarea, which formed the basis of the Nicene symbol, Dean Stanley notices the words (καὶ ἐν ἀνθρώποις πολιτευσάμενον καὶ παθόντα[3]), "Who lived

[1] Justin, *Apology*, I. 46, II. 10. "We have been taught that Christ is the first-born of God, and we have declared above that He is the Word of whom every race of men were partakers; and those who lived with reason (μετὰ λόγου) are Christians, even though they have been thought Atheists; as among the Greeks, Socrates and Heraclitus, and men like them; and among the barbarians Abraham and Ananias and Azarias and Misael and Elias and many others."

[2] Harnack, *History of Dogma*, vol. IV. p. 45, speaks of the "notorious fact that the man (Athanasius) who saved the character of Christianity as a religion of living fellowship with God, was the man from whose Christology almost every trait which recalls the historical Jesus of Nazareth was removed."

[3] Stanley, *Eastern Church*, Lect. IV.

among men and suffered." If Eusebius and his followers were fighting for the retention of teaching concerning our Lord's life on earth, considering it to be endangered by the spread of Sabellianism in any form, the intense bitterness with which they opposed the Homoousians may be in some degree excused. The Antiochians of the fifth century maintained this tradition and saved the Church from accepting the transcendental Christ of Alexandria rather than the Christ of the Gospels. It is usual to justify Athanasius for the relentless stand he made against Arianism, but to regard the dispute concerning the Two Natures of our Lord as unnecessary; but, when the story of the latter comes to be written as sympathetically as that of the great Arian contest has already been, it is not unlikely that the verdict will be that the Monophysite heresy was every whit as dangerous to Christianity as ever Arianism had been. To its secret prevalence in the Church is due much of the degradation of Christian worship in the Middle Ages. The cultus of the Madonna, of the Bambino, and of wonder-working images, is traceable to the feeling that Christ's Divinity had absorbed His Humanity altogether.

Before we leave the Church of the East we may glance at one of the most attractive characters in Greek Christendom, the best product of Antiochian Christianity. Inferior in knowledge of mankind to Athanasius, in theological acumen to St Cyril of Alexandria, John Chrysostom stands absolutely alone as the finest moral character in the Greek Church. Other men won a title to sanctity by founding monasteries or refuting heresies; but Chrysostom dared to stand up boldly for righteousness against the practical Paganism of Constantinople. His story is that of a true Christian bishop, rebuking sin wherever he saw it, taking the side of justice and mercy wherever opportunity offered. In him, too, we find the most practical of the Christian preachers of his age. In days of controversy, when the natural acuteness of the Greek mind was stimulated to the utmost by theological disputes, John Chrysostom stands almost alone as the champion of practical religion. Sharing as he undoubtedly did in many of the prejudices of his age, he never lost sight of the fact that Christianity is a life and not merely a creed, and his episcopate at Constantinople is a noble and continued protest against the invasion of the Eastern Church by a corrupt secular government. He affords one of the few examples of a man of that century carrying out the duty of striving to imitate Christ in every relation of life. Nor can it be accidental that the theology of Antioch, which dealt so persistently with the fact that Jesus Christ is man as well as God, produced so beautiful an example of practical goodness.

In studying the History of the Church during the long Christological controversies which raged during the third, fourth, and fifth centuries, we inevitably tend to rate the importance of the leading men of the age by their influence on opinion. We are so interested in the great school of Alexandria as producing Christian philosophers that we are disposed to overlook the fact that its earliest masters regarded the Christian life as of infinitely more importance than the intellectual pursuits in which they excelled. It is only incidentally recorded of Pantaenus, the founder of the school, that he left his work of a teacher to become a missionary to the Indians[1], or that throughout his long life Origen looked on the martyr's crown, to which he almost attained, as the most glorious of rewards. Yet it was the practical service of Christ which attracted both, rather than the speculative doctrines of Christianity. If the zeal of Origen carried him on one notable occasion beyond the limits of discretion, it is but justice to remember that he and others of his school made it their object to manifest Christ's teaching by their lives[2]. That in Christianity their intellectual aspirations were satisfied is a testimony to the power of the Person of Christ to attract and compel the philosophers as well as the unlearned of the period.

[1] Eusebius, *H. E.* vi. 19.
[2] "Few men," says Dean Farrar of Origen, "have rendered to the cause of Christianity such splendid services, or lived from childhood to old age a life so laborious and so blameless." *Lives of the Fathers*, vol. i. p. 391; cf. Eusebius, *H.E.* vi. 38.

So again in the fourth century, were we to judge only from the historical records which have come down to us, we might imagine that the energies of the Church were entirely absorbed by controversy and monasticism. We picture to ourselves the bishops rushing hither and thither to attend councils for the purpose of deciding questions of doctrine, and devout men fleeing from the world to find peace in the seclusion of the desert. It is only as it were by chance that the letters of Julian, that bitter foe to Christianity, tell us that one of the secrets of the growth of the Church lay in her charitable institutions, her hospitals, her refuges, her schools; and that, in reforming heathenism, the Emperor could suggest no better example for his priesthood to follow than that of the Christians, whose first care it was to provide for the unfortunate[1]. Would anyone, reading about the troubled episcopate of St Basil of Caesarea, have imagined that he had leisure for aught but the Arian controversy and monastic and clerical reforms, were it not for the fact that the Arian Emperor Valens, when he paid his much dreaded visit to Basil at Caesarea in Cappadocia, inspected and approved the admirable charitable institutions provided by the bishop[2]? The stirring and exceptional incidents recorded by the historians of the Church are not the most important facts; it is the great work of beneficence, too often passed over in silence, which was the real essence of the life of the Christian Society.

IV.

From the consideration of the early Church we pass to an investigation of the influence of the Person of Christ on the civilisation of the nations which entered into the heritage of what was once the Western part of the Roman Empire. Before doing so, however, it is necessary to contrast what we term the civilisation of classical antiquity with that which has prevailed under Christian auspices.

Modern Christian Apologists have perhaps pressed too

[1] Julian, Epistle XLIX. to Arsacius, High Priest of Galatia.
[2] Socrates IV. 26; Sozomen VI. 16; Theodoret, *H. E.* IV. 16.

strongly the contrast between the morality prevalent in the days of Imperial Rome and that inculcated by Christianity. They dwell on such subjects as the harshness of the old Roman law, the cruelties sanctioned alike by law and by public opinion, the nameless corruptions of the society described by Tacitus, Juvenal, and Suetonius[1]. They point to the way in which Christianity has made impossible many things which were then tolerated and even applauded. But they seem not to recollect that there are certain periods in the history of the greatest Christian nations which rival the worst days of pagan Rome; and they neglect to point out that there was a constant protest even in the most evil days of heathenism against the corruptions of the age. Side by side with the crimes of Nero and the degradation of the Roman proletariat we must in fairness set the noble attempts of the legislators, who under the influence of the Stoic philosophy laboured to promote the cause of humanity and virtue.

On the other hand the enemies of the Christian faith accuse the Church of having undone all that Roman civilisation had done for the world. They maintain that a steady advance in ideas was already taking place when the progress of classical culture was arrested by Christianity, and accuse the Church of helping the barbarians to destroy civilised life[2].

We may concede that there were men and women living good and honourable lives under the Caesars, that philosophy was teaching many useful truths, inculcating benevolence and infusing a better spirit into legislation. We may admit the evidences we have that conjugal

---

[1] Brace, *Gesta Christi*, chh. ii–x.

[2] Hodgkin, *Italy and her Invaders*, bk. III. ch. 9. Dr Hodgkin, whose personal devotion to Christianity cannot be questioned, asks, "Would the Rome of the Fabii and the Scipios, the Rome which heartily believed in and worshipped Jupiter and Quirinus, Mavors, Ops, and Saturnus have fallen as the Christian Rome fell before the hordes of Alaric?" and adds "We are bound in our historical conscience to answer No"; but at the same time he quotes the weighty verdict of Mommsen, "It was no natural catastrophe which Paganism and genius might have warded off; it was old social evils above all, the ruin of the middle class by the slave proletariat, that brought destruction on the Roman commonwealth." See also Dill, *Roman Society from Nero to Aurelius*, bk. II. ch. 1; bk. III. ch. 1.

fidelity and natural affection prevailed in many homes, and acknowledge that St Paul's terrific enumeration of heathen wickednesses (Rom. i. 24—32) does not apply to every individual of his time. Yet, when we have granted all this, we cannot blind our eyes to the fact that the civilisation of Imperial Rome was remarkably wanting in recuperative moral energy. The Stoic lawyers did, it is true, apply new principles in their attempt to regenerate the world by improved legislation, but regrets for the past, rather than hopes for the future, are the chief features of the literature of the age. Great as were undoubtedly the virtues of ancient Rome, they were not such as could be revived in a totally different state of society. They were the virtues of a primitive civilisation, and they necessarily vanished when life became more polished and more complex. Religion and philosophy had nothing to offer in their place. We have in Seneca and Marcus Aurelius two men whose advocacy of righteousness gives them a right almost to rank among the best Christians of their times. Seneca indeed is in some respects worthy of the legend which makes him a friend of St Paul. His sentiments so often approach the morality of the Gospel that Tertullian can speak of him as '*saepe noster*[1].' That his whole life is not consistent with his writings would not necessarily prove his inferiority to many a Christian teacher, though his character, if marvellously elevated for a heathen, falls far short of a Christian standard. But even in Seneca's noblest exhortations to duty there is a detachment which is alien to the teaching of the Christians of his age. He is more inclined to recommend than to emphasise the imperative necessity to do right, which every Christian teacher perforce recognised; whilst his commendation of suicide shows how far his conception of human responsibility is from that presented by the Church. The reverence Christians had for his teaching is justified, but Tertullian's '*saepe noster*' is nearer the truth than Jerome's claim that Seneca was 'ours[2].'

---

[1] Tertullian, *De Anima*, xx.
[2] Jerome, *Adv. Jovinianum*, I. 49.
On Seneca's advocacy of the suffering classes see Lecky, *Rationalism in Europe*, II. 257.

The Emperor Marcus Aurelius is in many ways morally superior to Seneca; for, though he had not the same difficulties to contend with as the philosophic minister of Nero, he showed himself throughout his life consistently faithful to the principles he inculcated. Probably no better man ever ruled a great Empire; and the only blot on his reign is that he did not check the persecution of the Christians. But popular as his 'Meditations' deservedly are, they lack that quality which moves men deeply. We recognise even in the teaching of an emperor who lived for the benefit of his subjects a want of power to arouse an enthusiasm sufficient to arrest the moral decay of the age. He falls, we feel, short of the greatest of Christians, because though he seems unconsciously to have felt the life-giving touch of Christ, he lacked fuller knowledge of Him[1]. The world-wide civilisation of Rome was decaying; there was no power to progress, no motive to improve, and it was impossible to go back to a purer ideal. A debased, idle, city-bred proletariat, a vicious plutocracy, a disappearing middle class, a swollen bureaucracy, and an ever-shrinking population, was the complex result.

If tried by the test of actual events, the civilisation of classical antiquity is proved to have been a failure[2]. Those who defend it point after all to what might have been, rather than to actual facts. Even the best period of the Roman Empire, when its rulers were devoting their energies to the

[1] Renan in his highly appreciative account of Marcus Aurelius says, "But to keep himself always on the icy summit of Stoicism it was needful that he should do cruel violence to nature and cut out more than one noble part of it...sometimes the result...is something bitter and gloomy; the reading of Marcus Aurelius fortifies, but does not comfort." *Marc-Aurèle*, ch. xvi.

[2] Of the 1st and 2nd centuries, Dobschütz (*Christian Life in the Primitive Church*, pp. 364-5) says, "It was indeed a bloom-time of the highest culture....Yet it was a time of moral enervation, decrepitude and decay. There is no disproof of this in the fact that it received a new impetus and experienced, in a great religious renewal, a new moral birth, the last roses of autumn. All was swept away by the storms of national immigration: only what had its origin in Christianity lasted through the winter.".…"The net of Christian Churches spread over the Empire meant a powerful beneficent organisation in the centre of a world of egotism."

service of their people, was confessedly one of decay. History can hardly give another example of a succession of such excellent sovereigns as those who directed the Empire from Nerva to Marcus Aurelius; yet the process of degeneration went on unhindered. The overthrow of the Western Empire in the fifth century was inevitable long before Christianity had become a real power in the world[1].

Christianity on the other hand survived the Roman Empire because it was replete with motives for energy. Though it concerned itself with the life to come it enriched the present by providing something after which men could continually strive. In the teaching and example of Jesus Christ it set forth a high ideal which His followers were encouraged to make their own.

When we turn to the Eastern provinces to which the Empire was practically confined for nearly a thousand years, we witness a survival of the old system, a civilisation, strongly influenced, it is true, by the Church, but always dominated by the Imperial power. And the result, despite the vitality so often manifested by the government in Constantinople, was the complete destruction of Roman civilisation in the countries where it had lasted longest. In the West, on the other hand, the Church became and long remained all powerful. And there, though the provinces of the Empire were overwhelmed by ruin at an early period, Roman law and classical culture never perished utterly, and the germs of a society organised on a far sounder basis ultimately began to appear.

At the close of the fourth century Christianity, by entering into the monastic movement, was unconsciously preparing a means to survive the catastrophe which was about to happen in Western Europe. So repugnant is the ideal of the monk to the modern mind that it is not easy to realise that unless it had been adopted the Christian religion could scarcely have survived the overthrow of the Empire. Monasticism was, it is true, no part of primitive Christianity. The life of Jesus Christ was so entirely social that the Jews were offended at His readiness to associate with all classes of

[1] Hodgkin, *Italy and her Invaders*, bk. III. ch. 9.

men, and spoke of Him as "a gluttonous man and a winebibber, a friend of publicans and sinners[1]." The first Christians appear never to have withdrawn from the haunts of men, and even in the third century when Novatian seemed disposed to solitary asceticism he was suspected of being possessed by a demon[2]. Nor can it be denied that monasticism was borrowed from non-Christian sources, or at least had its counterpart in other religions. Still, so completely did its spirit incorporate itself in the Church, that for upwards of a thousand years it formed the ideal of perfect Christianity. It is necessary to appreciate this fact in order to understand Church History from the fourth to the fourteenth century. Almost every sincere Christian was a monk at heart. Many of the most earnest priests or bishops hoped that one day they might have leisure to make their peace with heaven in the monk's cell, and the best of the laity desired nothing better than to retire for a period of ascetic contemplation in their latter days; even the sinner nourished a secret hope that he might be converted and expiate his crimes before he died, as a penitent among men of 'religion[3].' It must be admitted that Christian monasticism, though it did not receive its primary impulse from the Gospel, owed many of its features to the Person of Christ. It was the desire to imitate His purity of life that, in the fourth century, drove men and women to take refuge in the desert from the secularised Christianity of the cities of the Empire[4]. Christ's advice to the young man who had great possessions and desired to be with Him wheresoever He went made St Anthony retire from the world[5]. Moreover, the Person of Christ proved strong enough to overcome that purely selfish ideal of individual salvation which in many cases lay at the root of the monastic impulse. The monks,—at least of the Latin and Celtic Churches,—were better than what we too hastily assume to have been the avowed object of their lives

[1] St Matt. xi. 19; St Luke vii. 34.
[2] Eusebius, *H. E.* vi. 42.
[3] Cotter Morrison, *Life of St Bernard.*
[4] Chrysostom, *Adv. Oppug. Vit.*

Mon., Stephens, *Life of Chrysostom*, p. 74. Dill, *Roman Society in the Last Century of the Western Empire*, bk. i. ch. 1; bk. ii. ch. 2.
[5] Athanasius, *Vita Antonii*, c. 3.

would imply. Their cloisters produced missionaries, preachers, reformers; their houses became centres of benevolent activity and learning; their best minds devoted themselves to the welfare of mankind, the Spirit of Christ driving them back to do battle with the world they had forsaken.

The age in which Monasticism first became a leading feature of Western Christianity witnessed the conversion of the most remarkable man who had appeared in the Christian Church since the days of the Apostles. To St Augustine more than to anyone else is due the course of Christian development during the Middle Ages. Long after his teaching had inspired the mediaeval ideal, its influence revived to become the moving spirit in the Reformation[1]. At the present time there is a disposition to depreciate Augustine somewhat unduly, partly because his clear and logical intellect was engaged in the task of setting forth the truths of Christianity with a definiteness distasteful to our modern notions, and partly because of the essentially monastic tone of much of his teaching. But the historian can never overlook the importance of the influence of St Augustine on his contemporaries and on subsequent ages; for, even if as a Christian teacher he falls short of St Paul in deep insight and sympathy, his personality is almost as interesting as that of the great Apostle himself. The story of his conversion told by himself is one of the most striking pieces of autobiography in literature. It is transparently honest and unaffected. We see in it the child, the school-boy, the university student, the man of pleasure, and the man of letters of the fourth century. We know both what drew Augustine to Christianity, and what repelled him. In some cases his perplexities are ours, and it is impossible not to feel a thrill of excitement when we reach the conclusion and are told how Augustine, overcome by an irresistible impulse, rushed forth into the garden, heard the child's voice say "Tolle lege," and took up the New Testament

---

[1] Harnack, *Monasticism and St Augustine*, p. 169, E.T., "Whenever in the following millennium and later the struggle has arisen against a mechanical piety, or the self-righteousness of jejune morality, there the spirit of Augustine has been at work."

to see the decisive passage, "Non in comessationibus et ebrietatibus, non in cubilibus et impudicitiis, non in contentione et aemulatione; sed induite Dominum Jesum Christum, et carnis providentiam ne feceritis in concupiscentiis[1]."

In this story we notice not only the influence of the monastic ideal, but also the power of the Person of Christ. It was, indeed, the account of St Anthony and the monks of Egypt that made Augustine decide to be a Christian[2]. Though never himself a monk, he was deeply imbued with the monastic spirit, and herein lay part of the secret of his power over men in the Middle Ages. But the far-reaching influence of his writings is chiefly attributable to his deep sense of the greatness of the work of Christ among men. The verses he read in the garden contained the command to 'put on the Lord Jesus Christ,' and his conversion meant no less than this to him. The strictness with which he interpreted the command was one of the chief reasons of his long delay to declare himself a Christian.

The book which produced the greatest impression on the Church of the West was Augustine's *De Civitate Dei*. To be appreciated it must be read through. A few chapters or even one or two books apart from the rest give no idea of its general scope. We are apt to read isolated sections, and, finding them devoted to what seems to us trivial or unimportant, to condemn the whole. But when these are taken as parts of the entire work, and we consider the thought and beliefs of Augustine's age, we have to admit that every chapter of the *City of God* has its purpose. The work is a truly great one, written with the fall of Rome sounding in the author's ears. The sack of the Imperial city by Alaric was the beginning of the end, the precursor of greater ruin. Augustine, on hearing the news that Rome—the city of man—had fallen, set himself to describe the City of God. The contrast caught the imagination of humanity, and the best minds of the West for generations strove to realise his ideal in the Christian state.

[1] Rom. xiii. 13, 14.   [2] Augustine, *Confessions*, VIII. 12.

But the hidden source of the hope of a *Civitas Dei* lay in the belief in the Divine Person of Jesus Christ. It is not, as might appear, a matter of no importance whether the barbarian conquerors of the Empire were orthodox or Arian. True, they were incapable of comprehending the nice points of the dispute. Their limitations, alike of language and intelligence, prevented their entering into the merits of the controversy. But between the Arian and the Catholic Christ there was to a barbarian this essential difference. The Arian Christ could be easily accepted by the barbarian as a new God or hero, like those whom his ancestors had revered ; but such a Christ could never be to him a real source of strength[1]. Difficult as it was for the newly converted warrior to understand the doctrine of a Son equal in all things to the Father, when once he grasped the dogma, it took too powerful a hold on his imagination to be shaken off. It was the firm belief in the Divinity of Christ which sustained the Church in her great struggle with barbarism, and made her in the face of every discouragement uphold the idea of a spiritual kingdom. The tide of heathenism might surge again and again over the devastated provinces, the work of martyr and missionary might be repeatedly undone, but the power of Christ as God and Judge of all sustained His servants. The story of the revival of the Church in the eleventh century shows the greatness of the recuperative power which she derived from the belief that, because Christ was God, His kingdom could be established on earth.

It is the habit of some writers to regard the history of the dark ages as the most vulnerable point at which the Church can be attacked. All the decay of learning, all the barbarism, ignorance, superstition, and oppression of those

---

[1] Gwatkin, *Studies of Arianism*, p. 263. "To the barbarian as well as to the heathen Arianism was a half-way halting place on the road to Christianity. Yet to the barbarian it proved only a source of weakness......it also blighted every hope of future growth. It was in the strength of orthodoxy that the Franks drove the conquerors of Rome before them on the field of Vouglé, and brought the green standard of the Prophet to a halt upon the Loire."

lamentable centuries are included in their indictment of Christianity[1].

Perhaps a summary of the facts generally admitted may help to remove some misapprehension. The barbarians who overran the Western provinces in the fifth century were not destitute of regard for the greatness of the Empire, or for its laws and institutions. Alaric and Theodoric, in its opening and closing years, were men full of respect for Rome. But the sixth century showed the weakness of the Gothic kingdom of Italy, which began with such promise and ended so disastrously. From this point we trace the rapid decay of civilisation till Charles the Great, and the temporary revival of the ancient glories of the Empire, now for the first time placed in German hands. How unstable were the foundations on which the power of the House of Charles the Great rested is sufficiently revealed by the dismal history of the ninth century. The invasion of the Northmen completed the ruin begun by the internal dissensions of Western Europe, and by the beginning of the tenth century "darkness had covered the earth and gross darkness the people." It is hardly possible to exaggerate the anarchy, savagery, and ignorance of Western Europe at that time. That order could be evolved out of such chaos appeared impossible. Yet out of this age of confusion and misery there was destined to emerge the most remarkable and progressive civilisation the world had yet known, the fruits of which are still ripening.

In many respects the task before the Western Church in the eleventh century must have appeared more hopeless than that which had hitherto confronted the Church of the East. The progress of barbarian invasion had been much slower in the Oriental provinces; for centuries Constantinople remained intact as a bulwark of Roman civilisation. But nothing survived the influx of the invaders of the West. By the end of the fifth century Britain, Gaul, Spain, Africa, and Italy had been overrun. By the middle of the sixth century Rome

[1] Cotter Morrison, *The Service of Man*, ch. vi. ('Morality in the Ages of Faith').

herself (if we may believe Procopius) had been depopulated[1]. All attempts to stem the tide of barbarism were unavailing, and the Christianity of the conquered people bore the brunt of the apparently hopeless battle. That the Church degenerated in the contest is undeniable. She shared in the ever-growing barbarism; nor could it possibly have been otherwise. Ambrose, Augustine and Jerome had all been educated under the splendid system of instruction which prevailed in the later Empire; but where were the schools in the devastated provinces to educate the clergy in the sixth and subsequent centuries? Their ranks were recruited by men brought up in savage homes with the fierce blood of barbarism hot within them; and how could the majority of them be free from the vices of their surroundings? They had to control men accustomed to yield to the wildest passions. Can we be surprised that they frequently utilised the credulity and superstition of their age? They lived amidst scenes of anarchy and bloodshed, and constant use made them callous to crimes from which we turn in horror. A bishop commanding armies appears to us incongruous; yet in lands devastated repeatedly by fire and sword no prelate could protect his flock without taking part in the actual warfare. The castle and the cathedral in close proximity seem strange companions, till we remember that it was in both that the trembling country side took refuge from the invading hordes.

It is impossible to understand the history of the dark ages and not to recognise the fact that the Church was fighting alike within and without a desperate battle with barbarism.

At times she nearly succumbed, and it cannot be denied that the majority of her clergy tolerated some of the worst abuses of their time. Yet the religious conscience, as expressed by the best Christians of the age, never ceased to protest. Nothing can be more honourable than the part the Church played in encouraging the recognition of the principles of law, and in humanising the ancient codes of the barbarian

---

[1] Gregorovius, *Rome in the Middle Ages*, bk. II. ch. 5, sec. 3. In 547 Procopius says that Totila departed ἐν ‘Ρώμῃ ἄνθρωπον οὐδένα ἐάσας, ἀλλ' ἔρημον αὐτὴν τὸ παράπαν ἀπολιπών.

conquerors[1]. From the first the better members of the clerical order fought the battle of the weak and helpless, and encouraged that care for the poor on which all true civilisation depends. Where the innate barbarism of the new converts proved so strong that its customs were retained after the adoption of Christianity, we almost invariably find that it was despite the protests made on behalf of the Church. It is unjust to reproach the clergy with encouraging judicial combats, ordeals and the like—at most they deserve the blame of failing to eradicate such practices completely or of lending them a partial recognition by connecting them with religious services. The best bishops protested repeatedly if they protested in vain[2]. It is only right to bear in mind that throughout the early Middle Ages the Church represented civilisation, and the civil governments barbarism, nor was it till the Papacy had won its greatest triumph in the complete humiliation of the German Empire at Canossa that there was any real progress in Western Europe. The moral victory of Hildebrand on that memorable occasion inaugurated a new era[3], and in the twelfth century the rise of mediaeval town life, the study of the Roman law, and the beginning of modern universities gave to the lay states a fresh impulse towards progress[4].

One creditable feature of Church life in the dark and the early Middle Ages, moreover, must not be overlooked, namely the zeal shown in missionary efforts. To brave the toils

[1] Guizot, *Civilisation en Europe*, Lect. VI. p. 166, "J'ai déjà parlé de la différence qu'on remarque entre les lois des Visigoths, issués en grande partie des conciles de Tolèdes et les autres lois barbares."

[2] Brace, *Gesta Christi*, ch. xiv.; cf. Triede, *Das Heidenthum in dem Christenthum*.

[3] Of the humiliation of Henry IV the German historian, Gregorovius, writes: "Nevertheless the weaponless victory of the monk has more claims on the admiration of the world than all the victories of an Alexander, a Caesar, or a Napoleon. The battles fought by mediaeval popes were not waged with weapons of iron and lead but with those of moral power, and to the use or effect of these spiritual means is due the fact that the Middle Ages occasionally attained a level higher than our own." *Rome in the Middle Ages*, vol. IV. p. 209, E.T.

[4] Lecky, *Rationalism in Europe*, vol. II. p. 31.

and dangers of carrying the Gospel beyond the frontiers of Christendom or of civilisation it is necessary that men should feel that they possess something which must, at any cost, be imparted to others. The power of Christ in the hearts of Christians inspired them from the earliest times with missionary fervour. Now there was an extraordinary and widespread renewal of the missionary spirit from the fifth century onward. It was felt in the struggling British Church in the far West, which in the day of her greatest need evangelised Ireland. It manifested itself among the Nestorian Christians, who, driven beyond the frontiers of the Empire, carried the Gospel to the inhabitants of the unknown nations in the remote East. It made Gregory the Great plan the conversion of the Anglo-Saxons whilst striving against the Lombards, who were at this time under the very walls of Rome. It impelled our own St Wilfrid to forget awhile his wrongs, and labour as a missionary among the heathen on whose shores he had been driven by shipwreck. It caused Ireland to send forth its evangelists to those whom continental Christianity had not yet succeeded in reaching. Amid all the fierce controversy and barbarism of the darkest period of European history the Christian missionary was at work, whether in the storm-swept islands of the West, in the dark forests of Germany, on the burning plains of India, or in the crowded cities of China;— a remarkable but sometimes neglected testimony of Christ's power.

It appears from a survey of mediaeval history that up to the middle of the twelfth century the Church in Western Europe had fought the battle of civilisation. Her attitude to the poor and oppressed might be ideally represented by the figure of a bishop, strong in spiritual or even temporal weapons, protecting them against brute force. But when her authority reached its highest point, her exercise of it began to be abused, and simultaneously a better ideal was presented to the world.

The victory over anarchy had been won; but in gaining the mastery the Church had abandoned many essential principles of the Gospel. She had become a secular power, and her weapons, if nominally spiritual, were actually carnal. She relied on her widespread organisation, her wealth, and her unrivalled diplomacy; and it was by brute force that she was now preparing to crush one of the most dangerous movements which had hitherto threatened her supremacy in Western Christendom. The Albigensian war, in which the Holy See let loose the ignorant fanaticism of Northern France on the intelligent inhabitants of Provence, was the crowning crime— a sure sign that it had abandoned its hold on the teaching of Christ.

Yet at this very period Francis of Assisi made his appearance, in the first instance as a lay reformer; and though the movement originated by him had been foreshadowed by similar ones, it is in many respects unique in history[1]. If his conversion was in itself no isolated phenomenon, his personality was unlike anything that had hitherto been known. His character and example were more far-reaching in effect than the order which bears his name. He brought men back to the long-forgotten view of the meekness and gentleness of Christ, to the facts of the Gospel of His sacred ministry among men.

Taken even at its best, religion at the opening of the thirteenth century was too often a sort of sublime selfishness. Heaven and Hell filled the minds of all men to the exclusion of other thoughts; and it has been aptly said by P. Sabatier that "they informed themselves about them with the feverish curiosity of emigrants who pass their time on shipboard trying to picture that spot in America where in a few days they will pitch their tents[2]": whilst the perpetual insecurity of life and property made the neighbouring monastery the sole haven of rest, where a man could live his life in peace and escape the fires of Hell. But Francis, though he felt the temptation to seek the peace of a life of contemplation, resisted it by refusing to separate the contemplative from the active life, thereby proving his superiority to his age.

---

[1] Sabatier, *Life of Francis of Assisi*, chap. 3 ('The Church about 1209'), also p. 100, E.T.; *Church Quarterly*, October, 1902.
[2] Sabatier, *Life of St Francis*.

The appearance of St Francis is truly one of the most astonishing facts in history. No religious leader ever showed greater originality, or possessed more power of attracting others. It may even be asserted that no life was more like that of the Saviour Himself. In entire absence of hypocrisy or even of self-consciousness, in all-embracing love, in tender solicitude for the poor and afflicted, in bright trustfulness in God, no saint has ever equalled the founder of the Order of Friars Minor. Passages in his life, sayings that fell from his lips, and acts recorded of him are, in beauty, almost equal to the stories of the Gospel. Yet what is related of him in the various 'lives' gives us the impression that we have no adequate portrait of the saint. "Reading the authors," says Paul Sabatier, "one feels every moment how the radiant beauty of the model is marred by the awkwardness of the disciple[1]." In days when religion had become formalised he was essentially unconventional in his piety, and whilst the bitterest passions were being aroused by religious controversy he himself, though humbly accepting the doctrine of the Church, was free from bigotry.

But the chief characteristic of the career of St Francis is that he broke with the traditions of his age and went back to the life and example of Christ. His originality consisted in his going straight to the model which men professed to reverence and trying thus to realise the Divine Life on earth. He restored the long-forgotten truth that to imitate Christ it was necessary to follow His example in helping others.

There can be no higher tribute to the greatness and goodness of this saint than the fact that it hardly seems irreverent to show in what respects he was inferior to Jesus Christ, not only in what he accomplished, nor in his shortcomings, but in his greatest virtues. It appears to be one of the many proofs of our Lord's Divinity that His words and works demonstrate His immeasurable superiority over one who, by following Him closely, succeeded in producing an effect on his own generation to outward appearances as

---

[1] Sabatier, *Life of Francis*, p. 145, E.T.

XII] *Christ in History* 507

great as that caused even by the earthly Ministry of the Saviour[1].

Like our Lord St Francis believed himself charged with a Divine message and acknowledged no human intermediary between himself and God. His precepts, like those of the Sermon on the Mount, inculcate principles rather than lay down formal rules[2]. Francis evidently desired to make love the bond of union in his society in place of any external compulsion. He appealed to the heart and conscience as no one, save Christ, had done before. But, great as was the result of his twenty years of labour, his principles were soon forgotten. There is no sadder fact in religious history than the reversal of the purpose of Francis by his order even in his own lifetime. That his followers should within a generation become, in place of simple, cheerful imitators of Christ, an ecclesiastical corporation famous for scholastic learning and an unwavering support of the papal policy; and that the skilful diplomacy of Cardinal Ugolino (afterwards Gregory IX) should convert the order which his friend had founded into an engine for furthering the schemes of Rome against the Empire, prove how much evil can sometimes result from a life lived with the noblest of aims[3]. If we enquire the secret cause of this failure we shall perhaps find it in that humility which is one of St Francis's most beautiful traits. With all his burning zeal he had the highest reverence for authority; and his patrons at Rome had the worldly wisdom to make

[1] Milman, *Latin Christianity*, bk. IX. ch. 10. "With the Franciscans and all under the dominion of the Franciscans, the lower orders throughout Christendom, there was thus almost a second Gospel, a second Redeemer, who could not but throw back the one Saviour into more awful obscurity. The worship of St Francis in prayer, in picture, vied with that of Christ."

[2] Sabatier, *op. cit.* p. 254. "Take away from it (the Rule of 1233) the passages which emanate from the papacy and......what remains is not a Rule, but a series of impassioned appeals, in which the father's heart speaks, not to command but to convince, to touch, to awaken in his children the instinct of love."

[3] Sabatier concludes the life of St Francis with the following remarks on the legend concerning him, "Begun in misapprehension, it ends by imposing itself upon the Church, which to-day guarantees it with its infallible authority, and yet in its origin it was a veritable cry of revolt against the decisions of Rome."

his devotion to the Church serve their own ends. But the humility of Christ was never the cause of a moment's weakness. We cannot conceive of any priest or Rabbi making our Lord do the work of the Sanhedrin at Jerusalem. Throughout His ministry He spoke unhesitatingly as the mouthpiece of the Father. He claimed absolute obedience from all who would follow Him. His "I say unto you" outweighed all authority, even that of the ancient Scripture. We are attracted by the humanity of Francis ; but we recognise Divinity in Jesus Christ.

V.

It is not easy for us to do justice to the work of the Reformation of the sixteenth century. Our forefathers saw in it a glorious emancipation, whilst amongst ourselves there are some perhaps who regard it as a time at which, if the old fetters were broken, new dogmatic chains were forged. The Confessions of Faith, Catechisms, Articles of Religion, which mark the course of the Reformation, are singularly out of harmony with the spirit of our age, and now that the facts are more accurately known neither Protestant nor Roman controversialists seem to emerge with much credit. We are perhaps now too disposed to regard the whole story as a record of theological rancour, an exhibition of the worst human passions, of tortuous diplomacy and ferocious cruelty. We lose patience with a century which opened with the rise of Humanism and ended with the division of continental Europe between the adherents of the Council of Trent and the Calvinists. "The Reformation," it has been recently said, "began with ideas and ended in force. In the Germany of the sixteenth as in that of the nineteenth century, an era of liberal thought closed in a fever of war,...and methods of blood and iron supplanted the force of reason[1]."

[1] *Cambridge Modern History*, vol. II. ch. VIII. p. 278 ('The Religious War in Germany'). See also the conclusion to ch. xviii ('The Church and Reform'). Lecky, *Rationalism in Europe*, vol. II. p. 42, may be consulted with reference to the intolerance of Protestantism.

Nor, if we allow for the condition of European civilisation at the beginning of the sixteenth century, is it possible to imagine that mere humanism would have saved it from sinking back into a state of unprogressive heathenism. The ethics of the religion of the age were none of the highest; but apart from religion men were absolutely unmoral. The most remarkable thing about the Borgias is that by their contemporaries they were regarded not as abnormally wicked but as exceptionally fortunate. The compatriots and contemporaries of Machiavelli were not shocked at his tone: on the contrary he was regarded by them as a philosopher and patriot rather than as a master of deceit[1]. But in the Reformation an awakening of conscience took place alike among its supporters and its opponents; for the Roman Church was itself the subject of almost as remarkable a reform as were the Churches of the northern nations. This twofold awakening was necessary to ensure the remarkable progress which has been made during the past three centuries. Yet the period of the Renaissance, though its interest lay in the human side of life as opposed to the Divine, also bears witness to the striving of the Spirit of God in man. The Person of Christ was not utterly forgotten in Italy even in the dreadful times which marked the close of the fifteenth and the opening of the sixteenth centuries. A Savonarola could make his message heard in Medicean Florence, and in the Rome of Leo X men were found turning once more to Christ[2]. In painting, even though the strong religious impulse given by Fra Angelico and his disciples was gradually waning, the inspiration of the Christian faith was still manifest in the great masters[3].

---

[1] Macaulay's *Essay on Machiavelli*.

[2] Ranke, *History of the Popes*, bk. II. ch. 1.

[3] Phillips Brooks contrasts the Sphinx and Raphael's Sistine Madonna as illustrative of the religions of the East and West: "One unites wisdom and power and claims man's homage for that conjunction. The other combines wisdom and love and says, 'Worship this.' The Sphinx has life in its human face written into a riddle, a puzzle, a mocking bewilderment. The Virgin's face is full of a mystery we cannot fathom, but it unfolds to us a thousand of the mysteries of life. It does not mock, but blesses. The Sphinx oppresses us with colossal size. The Virgin is not a distortion or exaggeration, but a glorification of

Outside Italy the new ideas, aroused by the discovery of fresh worlds and by the recovery of literature, were a powerful means of driving men back to the original Gospel and the historic Christ. Erasmus and Cardinal Ximenes gave the Western world the Greek Testament, and our English humanists deserted the schoolmen for the writings of the Apostles. The Person of Christ, long obscured by mediaevalism, was again attracting the attention of His servants.

The Reformation movement began on all sides with a return to Christ[1]; for the belief that man is justified by the merits of Jesus Christ and not by obedience to a complex system of ecclesiastical regulations was by no means originated by or confined to the German reformers. Even the Jesuits, the most formidable of the reactionaries, owed their initial success to the way they led their followers back to the contemplation of the Saviour[2]. The purely Christian element, which, though mingled with much else, undoubtedly existed in the movement begun by Ignatius Loyola, reveals itself in the zeal for missions to the heathen displayed by the Roman Church in the sixteenth century, as does also the revival of that movement in the direction of mysticism, which had been inaugurated by Gerson and Tauler in the fifteenth century. What is termed

---

humanity. The Egyptian monster is alone among the sands to be worshipped, not loved. The Christian woman has her child clasped in her arms, enters into the societies and sympathies of men, and claims no worship except love."

[1] Cf. Herrmann, on Luther and Christ ("Communion with God," pp. 133 and 116). "There can be no doubt...that to [Luther] the Person of Jesus was of far higher importance for the inner life of religion than it was when viewed from the old dogmatic standpoint. With Luther the Person of Jesus stands in the very centre of the religious experience itself. Jesus makes him certain of God, lets him see the Divine nature and life, becomes to him that manifestation of God's grace in which God enters into communion with him."..."Hence the attitude towards Jesus which Luther consciously held marks a step forward in the development of the Christian religion. We move forward in our Christianity only when the Person of Jesus gains a higher and more comprehensive significance for our own way of feeling and thinking."

[2] *The Spiritual Exercises of St Ignatius*. These, as we see from the *Testament of St Ignatius*, brought the founder of the Order on several occasions under the notice of the Inquisition.

'mysticism' preceded and followed the Reformation. It is not easy to treat this subject historically, since the mystical spirit is essentially a matter for the individual experience, and in many cases is not imparted but develops spontaneously in the heart; though we are far from denying that an impulse towards a mystical view of things may be communicated by intercourse with another. It is restricted neither to nation nor to creed, and may manifest itself at any time. Still there is a surprising similarity in all Christian mysticism even where there is no possibility of contact among those who feel its power. The deeply rooted antagonism between Catholic and Protestant in the sixteenth and seventeenth centuries did not hinder the mystics of each party from resembling one another in many essential particulars; and it is noticeable that all Christian mysticism seems to centre in the Person of Christ. St Teresa and St John of the Cross, the most prominent of Spanish mystics and the leaders in the ecclesiastical campaign against Protestantism, rivalled the Protestant teachers themselves in their exclusive devotion to Christ. Their ideal, like that of all Christian mystics, was 'Christ in us and we in Him[1].'

The scholasticism which at a very early period began to make Protestantism unattractive has a tendency to obscure the secret but powerful influence which Christ was exercising in the hearts of men[2]. But while Calvinist and Arminian were wrangling, and endless dreary works were produced on the mystery of Election and Free Grace or on questions of Church government, there was a steady development of the Christian conscience in the seventeenth and eighteenth centuries. The darkest Predestinarianism[3] could not prevent

---

[1] See Inge, *Christian Mysticism*.

[2] Phillips Brooks gives the following description of the views of the 17th century, "Its religion had grown strangely impersonal. It believed doctrines far more than it believed in the Son of Man. The seventeenth century believed in the Divinity of Christ, but its belief in the Divine Christ was weak, and the belief in the human Christ was well-nigh lost." *The Influence of Jesus*, p. 78.

[3] For a sympathetic account of the doctrine of election as held by the Puritans see Ritchie, *Natural Rights*.

such progress in humanity as no previous centuries had hitherto witnessed, as the conscience of man became more and more sensitive in regard to injustice and cruelty. Uninviting as Puritanism was externally, its insistence on the direct intercourse between man and his Redeemer was bringing the world into a closer relationship with Christ, and thereby strengthening the growing tendency to follow His precepts.

The close of the Middle Ages was distinguished by a callousness to human suffering, which at times was manifested by astonishing examples of cruelty. The brutality of the dark ages had been that of children, due to the unrestrained instincts of mankind. But the refinement of the fifteenth century makes its cruelty doubly repulsive. It was the age of ingenious tortures, when men delighted in the infliction of mental as well as bodily suffering. The ferocious character of the laws of the age caused almost as much misery as the anarchy of any earlier period. The claims of humanity were scarcely recognised except in the matter of charity to the poor.

This condition of affairs had perhaps been caused by the way the practice of religion had been reduced to a scheme of salvation. The mediaeval Church, with her elaborate classification of sins and virtues, her catalogue of penances, her doctrine of merits and indulgences, had to the majority of Christians made religion almost a matter of commerce. Nor did matters improve immediately after the Reformation. The overthrow of the power of the Church seemed to make things even worse; for whilst the stream of charitable gifts in many cases came to an end, there was little moral progress in other respects. The ruthless ferocity of the wars of the sixteenth century furnishes proof of the general and surprising indifference to human misery.

But the doctrine of the efficacy of the atoning sacrifice of Christ, which was so prominent at the time of the Reformation, gradually brought about a greater consideration for the human body. The answer of the sick man who, overhearing the physicians say "Fiat experimentum in corpore vili," replied,

"Non est corpus vile pro quo Christus mortuus est," is a declaration of a principle now universally recognised, that every human being has a claim to consideration. It is really the charter of individual rights.

No branch indeed of the Western Church can be refused the honour of having assisted in the progress of humane ideas, and non-Christians have participated largely in the work of diffusing the modern spirit of kindness; but the credit of the inception of the movement belongs without doubt to that form of Protestantism which is distinguished by the importance it attaches to the doctrine of the Atonement. No part of the Christian system has found less favour than this among the educated classes of our day, and many thoughtful minds have revolted against its apparent presentation of an unworthy conception of Divine justice. It has even been asserted that the thought of Christ's sufferings being a part of the Divine scheme of Salvation has in a measure sanctioned cruelty among Christians. But history shows that the thought of Christ on the Cross has been more potent than anything else in arousing a compassion for suffering and indignation at injustice. Early Puritanism, which occupied itself chiefly with such questions as the election of the saved by the Father, and left but little room for the work of the Son, was doubtless hard and unsympathetic. But the later Evangelicalism, which saw in the death of Christ the means of free salvation for fallen humanity, caused its adherents to take the front rank as champions of the weak, the feeling roused by their form of belief in the Atonement being summed up in the lines

"Thou hast done this for me:
What shall I do for Thee?"

Prison reform, the prohibition of the slave trade, the abolition of slavery, the Factory Acts, the protection of children, the crusade against cruelty to animals, are all the outcome of the great Evangelical revival of the eighteenth century. The humanitarian tendencies of the nineteenth century, which, it is but just to admit, all Christian communities have fostered, and which non-Christian philanthropists have vied with them in encouraging, are among the greatest triumphs of the power and influence of Christ.

VI.

At the present time Christianity is suffering from the very triumph of its principles. It is a noteworthy characteristic of the Apologetic of the eighteenth century that men are accused of wanting to be rid of Christianity in order that they may be free to live lives of self-indulgence. No such generalisation could be fairly made in our own times. How obsolete is this moral antipathy, how effectually, if insensibly, Christianity has coloured our predominant views of human responsibility we gather from indictments, presumably true when written, but to which to-day we can with fairness give but a very limited application. "The profound thinkers of this way," says Berkeley in his *Alciphron*, "have taken a direct contrary course to all the philosophers of former ages, who made it their endeavour to raise and refine human kind, and remove it as far as possible from the brute; to moderate and subdue men's appetites; to remind them of the dignity of their nature; to awaken and improve their superior faculties and direct them to the noblest objects; to possess men's minds of a high sense of the divinity, of the supreme good, and the immortality of the soul. They took pains to strengthen the obligations to virtue, and upon all those subjects have wrought out noble theories and treated with singular force of reason. But it seems that our minute philosophers act the reverse of all other wise and thinking men; it being their end and aim to erase the principles of all that is wise and good from the mind of man, to unhinge all order of civil life, to undermine the foundations of morality, and, instead of improving and ennobling our natures, to bring us down to the maxims and way of thinking of the most uneducated and barbarous nations, and even to degrade human kind to the level of brute beasts."

It would be impossible to write thus now, or as Butler did in 1736, "Accordingly they treat it (Christianity) as if in the present age...nothing remained but to set it up as a principal subject of mirth and ridicule, as it were by way of reprisals for its having so long interrupted the pleasures of the world[1]."

In our days it might rather be justly said that the Christian standard of morality has become so generally accepted by thoughtful men and women that they acknowledge it as a matter of course for their rule of life. The free thinker is not, as he is almost invariably depicted in the eighteenth century, a man who abandons Christianity in order that he may live an immoral life[2]; on the contrary many professed non-Christians are living lives by no means unworthy of servants of Jesus Christ, whose example, indeed, many of them are consciously striving to follow. We are witnessing at the present time the hitherto unknown phenomenon of a non-Christian nation, not only imitating Western civilisation with success, but also copying those virtues which it has been customary to suppose were the exclusive property of the most advanced Christian peoples. Even Europeans have only recently learned to mitigate the horrors of war by the recognition of the laws of humanity, and it is a truly remarkable fact that Japan has so readily followed their example in this respect. It is also noticeable that in British India not only do the inhabitants appreciate impartial justice, but, despite the proverbial venality of Oriental judges, natives who occupy judicial positions have adopted a high standard of honour in regard to their responsibilities. But it must not be forgotten that in our days non-Christian peoples have not developed the virtues of humanity and impartial justice without coming into contact with Christian civilisation; and wherever they have done so, it is no more than fair to ascribe the fact to the influence of the Person of Christ.

One consequence of the development of Christian

[1] Butler, *Advertisement* to the *Analogy*.
[2] A poet like Crabbe, a shrewd but not an uncharitable observer, seems to assume as a matter of course that a "free thinker" is a man who rejects religion because he desires to live an immoral life. See his *Gentleman Farmer*.

principles amongst individuals and nations who do not accept the Christian religion is that it is by no means uncommon to meet men who are convinced that while progress in the future will be on the lines of the principles inculcated in the Sermon on the Mount, Christianity, as a religion, will entirely disappear. It is even assumed that men are improving because Christianity is being gradually abandoned, and that their moral development will be even more rapid when they have completely divested themselves of religion. The state of the world in what is called 'the Ages of Faith' is contrasted unfavourably with its condition in an age of unbelief, and the improvement is attributed to the fact that 'Faith' is no longer regarded as of importance. But those who maintain this view make 'Faith,' *i.e.* belief about Christ, equivalent to belief in Christ and base their theories on the assumption that the men of the Dark and Middle Ages were distinguished by a genuine faith[1]. Despite many remarkable exceptions, the mass of mankind during this period seems to have been conspicuously wanting in what we should now term faith. The history of the Middle Ages is a record of boundless credulity combined with a widespread distrust of spiritual methods. If men believed in the constant intervention of the miraculous, they acted as though the very existence of the Church depended on her retaining her wealth and prerogatives. The rulers of the ecclesiastical state arrogated to themselves the highest spiritual powers, yet took good care to use every temporal advantage with consummate skill. The dread of increasing knowledge as a danger to the Faith was prompted by a secret distrust in the power of Christ. Persecution, which was most active when faith is assumed to have been strongest, was in reality a sure sign that those who employed it were themselves tormented by doubts. It was because men feared the power of Satan, and distrusted the goodness of God that witches were burned; and Galileo was silenced

[1] Cotter Morrison, *The Service of Man*. The result of his enquiry is, "That the Morality of the Ages of Faith was very low; and that the further we go back into times when belief was strongest, the worse it is found to be."

because the authorities of the Church feared that his theory might be detrimental to her interests.

It would be more just to say that the reforms which have done so much to humanise society in the present day are not so much triumphs of unbelief as of faith. Many, as we have already seen, were carried out by men with intense religious convictions, in the face of fierce opposition. The principles on which they acted are now upheld, not only by Christians, but by those who, while strong believers in righteousness, decline to be bound by the dogmas of Christianity. Again, there was never in any age perhaps a greater devotion to truth than in our own. In every department of learning the scientific spirit of our day has taught men to prefer truth to all other considerations. But there is no greater proof of a living faith than a fearless spirit in regard to the discovery of the truth at all hazards; and that this has prevailed among peoples who have long been disciplined by the faith of Christ may be said to be one of the crowning triumphs of His influence.

VII.

The religious problem of the day, however, is to bring back the realisation of the Human Christ. Men of the most different opinions are urging upon the Christian Church the need of laying aside all accretions and presenting the Christ of the original Gospel to the world[1]. The doctrine of the Divine Christ has, in the opinion of many, removed the man

[1] Dr Fairbairn, speaking as a Nonconformist, illustrates the present-day return to Christ by noticing the difference between the clerical library of to-day and that of fifty years ago. "Dogmatics and apologetics have almost disappeared... (while) lives of Christ by men of all schools, tendencies and Churches, abound, each using some more or less rigorous critical method. [Our age] knows [Christ], as no other age has done, as He lived and as He lives in history, a Being who looked before and after, within the limits and under the conditions of time and space, influenced by what preceded Him, determining what followed." (*Christ in Modern Theology*, pp. 18, 21.)

Ritschlianism is perhaps nothing more nor less than a determined attempt to find the whole content of Christianity in the Person of Christ.

Jesus so far from us that they desire to see Him divested of all that to them appears supernatural whether related in the Gospel narrative or attributed to Him by the reverence of His followers. They feel, in fact, that a Christ who neither claimed Divinity nor wrought wonders would better satisfy the needs of mankind; but they confess they find it most difficult to depict accurately this purely Human Christ. Those who reverence His Person, but cannot receive all that the creed of Christendom teaches concerning Him, are put to constant shifts in their attempts to describe Him. So many passages have to be explained away as not belonging to the original Gospel, so many words and actions of His have to be apologised for, that every attempt to tell the story of Jesus Christ from the standpoint of appreciative rationalism fails to commend itself to a candid mind[1]. We are as it were driven by the investigation of the Human Christ to acknowledge that He must be also Divine.

The lesson to be learned from History concerning Christ is not only that His appearance on earth is a fact of supreme importance in the past, but that by His Incarnation He became present in humanity for all time. If this be the case, the experience of nineteen centuries confirms the early belief in His Divinity. It has been already indicated that the doctrine of a Divine Christ has been frequently misapprehended. A superficial acquaintance with the history of the fourth century is sufficient to convince us that it would not be possible for us to see eye to eye with those who brought about the triumph of the Nicene Faith. Their standpoint, their methods, their interpretation of Holy Scripture are not ours; and though these *formulae* must be retained and cherished by the Church, the spirit in which we interpret them cannot be precisely the same as that of the age in which they were drawn up. But we may subject their conclusions to the test of time, and if history can show that, despite all the acknowledged failures

---

[1] This is strongly stated by J. M. Robertson, *A Short History of Christianity*, who decides that the only practicable course lies in the denial of the very existence of Jesus Christ.

of the Church, the presence of Christ has been constantly manifested in leading men forward to a higher conception of truth, humanity, and godliness, we have a further confirmation of St John's words, "The Word was made flesh and dwelt among us," and "the Word was God."

When, however, we speak of Christ as the Word of God, we are brought, not to a conclusion, but to a vista of fresh problems; and if, after considering the unique influence of our Lord on mankind in the past, we are led to acknowledge Him to be the manifestation of the Divine Logos, it is necessary to enquire what we mean by so tremendous a statement.

Let us then briefly recapitulate. We have, though necessarily abstaining from detail, traced the course of a constant development since the appearance of Christ to the present time. We have recognised therein the operation of a force in the world which has been continually transforming human nature. From the first we are conscious of the presence of a new impulse among mankind differing from anything which has gone before, a spirit of hopefulness and joy unknown to earlier generations[1]. The more we contemplate the action of a force, so remarkable and continuous as this has ever been, the more inevitably does the conviction follow that even the accepted narrative of the Gospel, with its supernatural events culminating in the miracle of the Resurrection, would not be sufficient to account for the undying influence of our Lord; for no memory of a life however pure and devoted, nor of miracles however astonishing, could have kept alive the belief that in Him mankind has the highest revelation of Divine goodness which it is capable of receiving, but for the fact that His power has been sufficient to enable Him to subdue death, and remain ever present in the world. Of this conviction, thus

---

[1] Hermas, *Mand.* x. 3, Ἔνδυσαι οὖν τὴν ἱλαρότητα τὴν πάντοτε ἔχουσαν χάριν παρὰ τῷ θεῷ, κ.τ.λ. See the remarks in Dobschütz, *Christian Life*, p. 319, E.T. "It is no dark apocalyptic picture that this story and these revelations give us. This however is not because Hermas the Encratite was naturally of a cheerful disposition, but because his faith had wrestled with him, and forced this inward gladness upon him." So far as I am aware this spirit is alien to that of the ancient world.

expressed, the chief significance lies in the word 'subdue.' It is justified by history taken as a whole, and by the general experience of mankind; nor is it possible for us to assign such a victory to any other man. However far reason or faith may lead us in extolling the capability of our common human nature, this one act remains unique. It underlies the existence of our hope in the capacities of humanity, the progress of which, as history demonstrates, depends on the belief in a triumphant Christ. Part of the difficulty that some feel to-day in admitting the Divinity of our Lord arises from our lately quickened sense of the Divinity of man; certainly the testimony of history agrees with the declaration of Scripture that through Christ we are "partakers of the Divine Nature" (2 Peter i. 4). All who acknowledge this admit that Jesus Christ is something more than man, that He differs from others not merely in degree but in some essential particular; in other words, that His nature is not merely Human but also Divine.

It has been said indeed with perfect truth that Jesus has taken His place in history as Man and not as God[1], and the realisation of this, never more vivid than at the present time, makes some look to the historical rather than to the Divine Christ. But as has been pointed out, the difficulties of accepting a Christ who is no more than human are almost insuperable. As the reality of the Christ seems to fade away when He is regarded only as a manifestation of Divinity, so the results of His life become inexplicable when we refuse to see Divinity in His Manhood.

A remarkable result of modern criticism is that, at the very time when the Human Christ is most earnestly sought for, the historic figure of Jesus is threatened with being relegated to the realm of myth. Few indeed of those competent to discuss the question have denied that Jesus of Nazareth is an historical character[2]; but the sayings of Jesus

---

[1] Loisy, *Autour d'un petit Livre*, p. 11, "C'est comme homme, non comme Dieu, que Jésus est entré dans l'histoire des hommes."

[2] Prof. A. S. Peake in a pamphlet *Did Jesus Rise Again?* mentions Mr Edwin Johnson's book, *The Rise of Christendom*, in which the author tries to show that Christianity is an invention of the monks of the Middle

have been declared to be but four, and these taken apart from any context are purely negative in character[1]; whilst several of the more moderate critics refuse to look for any words of His outside the Sermon on the Mount.

Though the tendency of the present day seems to be in favour of accepting the main outlines of the Gospel as they are generally received, the above views cannot be altogether disregarded. To the historian they appear to be even more incredible than they are to the literary critic, since the less that is known of Christ in the Gospels the harder it is to give an adequate reason for what has happened since the Incarnation.

And thus we are brought to the position assumed by St Paul and St John. To the former the power of Christ was not so much manifested by His actions or in the memory of His life, as in His presence in the heart and in the Society of the saints through the Holy Spirit: for, as he himself says, God revealed His Son not *to* him but *in* him (Gal. i. 16). Christ is thus for him the transforming power of life, dwelling both in the Church of which He is the Head (Eph. iv. 15) and in every individual Christian (Eph. i. 17). The Spirit of Christ is unfettered: where He is, there is liberty (2 Cor. iii. 17). Since the future is in the hands of Christ, the old order is passed away and all things are become new (2 Cor. v. 16, 17). Though the apostle alludes to the birth and humiliated life of our Lord, he dwells specially on the Crucifixion and the Resurrection, because we partake of the first when we die to sin (Gal. iv. 24), and the second is the earnest of all our hope for the future (Rom. viii. 11). The Christ of the present

Ages! The book is a veritable curiosity of literature. The same view is taken by Mr J. M. Robertson, who bases much of his argument upon the ignorance of our Lord shown in the Talmud. See *Christianity in Talmud and Midrash*, by R. Travers Herford.

[1] Matt. x. 17 ("Why callest thou Me good" &c.), Matt. xii. 31 f. (blasphemy against the Son of Man), Matt. xxiv. 36 ("Of that day and hour knoweth no man" &c.), Matt. xxvii. 46 ("My God, My God, why hast Thou forsaken Me"), are represented by Professor Schmiedel in *Encyclopaedia Biblica*, Art. "Gospels," § 139, as the only "absolutely credible" sayings. "These five passages, along with the four which will be spoken of (all refusals to work miracles), might be called the foundation pillars of a truly scientific life of Jesus"!

and of the days to come, and not the Christ of the past, is the dominant feature in the Pauline theology. The teaching of St John, though perhaps influenced by that of St Paul[1], takes us into an even wider sphere. We are taught to see in Christ something even more than the Spirit of God working in the present. In Him we see the mind of God, existing before all time, that expression of the Father's will which he terms the Word. The Incarnation is the manifestation of this Word to mankind. Life, light, truth, must have ever been and must continue to be inherent in the Word.

The teaching alike of St Paul and of St John, illustrated by the testimony of history, leads us to the acknowledgement that Christ is more than a great personality who played His part in the world long ago. We are, it would seem, compelled to confess that the Christ of these great teachers is in some respects more majestic than the beautiful conception of Him as transmitted to us by the Synoptic Gospels. In process of time, as the first century drew to a close, Jesus was better understood. And, if this be the case, there can be no finality about the knowledge of His Person. History and theology point to a fuller conception of Him in the future; according to our Lord's own words, as recorded in the Fourth Gospel, to see Him is to see the Father (St John xiv. 9). As this knowledge of God is the goal of all progress and belongs to the future, we can never know Jesus Christ by dwelling solely on the past.

We seem, however, to be in danger of being placed in a dilemma. On the one side we are directed solely to the historic Jesus and challenged to face the limitations of an age little versed in the field of scientific criticism. On the other we may be tempted so to fix our gaze on the transcendental Christ of St Paul and the Fourth Gospel as to neglect the gracious Figure of the Synoptists. The alternative may even be to choose between a Christ altogether Human and one altogether Divine. It is a phase of the old question between the Ebionites, with their Christ as a Jewish prophet, and the Marcionites, with their transcendental revealer of

---

[1] Gardner, *A Historic View of the New Testament*, Lect. VI.

the Supreme God of love; between Paul of Samosata, with his deified man, and Sabellius, with his 'economic' manifestation of God; between the school of Antioch, with its excessive insistence upon the humanity of Christ, and that of Alexandria, with its devotion to Him as the Divine Logos rather than as Man; between Professor Harnack, with Christ as the moral teacher of Galilee, and the Abbé Loisy, with the Jesus of the Gospels lost in the Christ-spirit working in the Catholic Church. But neither alternative can be accepted to the exclusion of the other. The instinct which leads men in all religious revivals back to the historic Christ of the Synoptists is indeed a sound one; for, in a certain sense, the Figure of our Lord taking upon Himself the form of a servant, and the glorified Christ of a later age are equally Divine. If we fail to recognise this, the reason lies in our own inability to realise that the essence of the Kingdom of God consists not only of a glorified Monarch in heavenly state, but also of a King tending, guarding, helping, toiling in and with His subjects. Our prejudices and our conceit make us blind to this truth. We criticise the Christ presented by the Synoptists, priding ourselves on our clearness and penetration; and we are in danger of ignoring the breadth, the fulness, the grandeur of the human Christ of Galilee. But even so, to dwell on Christ as man only, though it may result in pure life and right deeds, is not sufficient. It causes us to overlook His power to help, His eternal presence among us; to make Him an object of admiration, rather than the source of hope and love. A Christ who is human but not Divine cannot satisfy our requirements.

The acknowledgement of Christ's Divinity seems therefore to be the logical consequence of the contemplation of His Humanity; but in History such an acknowledgement is often characteristic of those periods of organisation which necessarily follow great outpourings of the Spirit of God. And, though the age of reflection, the epoch of the theologian and the interpreter, is necessary to the time of illumination, and completes the work begun by the quickening of the spiritual life; experience shows that it can bring forth evil instead of good fruit if once the original impulse is allowed to die. We cannot study the historic Christ without learning that God is revealed in Him; but pride, malice, and hatred have been proved by bitter experience to be capable of coexisting with an exclusive study of the relationship of the Son to the Father. To dwell solely on the connexion of Christ with the Unseen God may clear away heresy; but it also tends to put mere assent in the place of a vital faith, orthodoxy before a life in Christ, and to substitute for Christian freedom a scheme of salvation resting on a supposed bargain between God and man. We are led from the Human Christ to the Divine; but the next step is fraught with a peril, which can only be avoided by allowing the Divine Christ to lead us not to one who is no more than a dogmatic abstraction, but to Him Who is ever revealing Himself as the Source of Life.

The Church now as always must refuse the apparent alternative of sacrificing either the Human or the Divine Christ. The lesson of Christ in History appears to point to a solution in a Christology which shall be able to retain both. Three things are demanded: a Man who actually lived, worked, and suffered; a Divine Word Whose presence has always been in the world, but has been manifested with a special power since the Incarnation; and One, Human and yet Divine, Who is constantly revealing Himself with increasing clearness to the conscience of man. We want a Christ of the past, of the present, and of the future—of yesterday, to-day, and for ever.

It is this that Origen teaches us to look for in his study of the opening words of the Gospel according to St John. This writer deserves our confidence alike for his wonderful familiarity with the words of Scripture, and for the reverential spirit with which he treats it. He lays especial stress on the wealth of teaching in the Bible for those who are prepared to go below the surface and seek for its spiritual meaning. To him the Christ of the past is intended to lead forward to the higher conception of the Word of God. He shows how the reason (λόγος) inherent in all men leads to the contemplation of the Word (ὁ λόγος), Who in His turn brings us onward to the Source of all reason, the very Word (ὁ αὐτόλογος)[1].

No one can survey the past history of the Church without grave reflection concerning the future. At the present time it would appear as though we were passing through a crisis, in some respects resembling those of earlier times but with features peculiar to itself. A great change is coming over the thoughts of professed Christians. Many doctrines once regarded as absolutely essential are found to be no longer tenable in the present condition of knowledge. How few thinking people, to take but the simplest of instances, are now able to accept the Mosaic cosmogony as literally true, or to acknowledge the inerrancy of Holy Scripture in the sense which would have satisfied our forefathers. The question therefore that the men of our generation have to decide is briefly this: Does the surrender of these things imply the abandonment of Christianity? The answer to it seems to depend on what we consider to be the essence of the religion of Christ. If we consider that Christ is His own evidence and needs not that any man bear witness of Him, all these matters however interesting are unessential; and then we can survey the battle with the feelings of the commander whose lines of communication with an impregnable fortress and illimitable supplies are secure. But if we regard our Faith as a system of doctrines resting on the authority of the past, a scheme of salvation elaborately constructed out of infallible Scriptures, an ecclesiastical organisation fixed and unalterable since the days of the Apostles, or a stereotyped theory of the Universe, we are compelled to admit that the least fragment cannot be removed from the structure without endangering the whole[2]. On the other hand the acceptance

---

[1] *Com. in Johann.* tom. II. c. 3.

[2] "Does the Dean of Westminster," writes a correspondent of the *Daily Telegraph* of Dec. 24, 1904, "fully comprehend that in giving up the common-sense definition of Biblical inspiration he is surrendering not a mere outwork but the citadel itself?" It is this disposition manifested alike by defenders and opponents of Christianity that is to be deprecated.

of a living Christ, Who, as the Word of God, has been educating mankind from the beginning, and has worked in His Church in a special manner since the Incarnation, makes us able to look forward with confidence; since even though much once deemed to be of vital importance may have to be laid aside, it is only because we have something better to take in its place. For those who acknowledge this believe that in Christ mankind is advancing in every age to a more perfect knowledge, that in the end it may be filled "with all the fulness of God."

ESSAY XIII.

CHRISTIAN DOCTRINES AND THEIR ETHICAL SIGNIFICANCE.

JAMES FRANKLIN BETHUNE-BAKER, B.D.

ANALYSIS.

The current popular notion that conduct and ethical principles have nothing to do with creed and doctrines.

The question of the relation of creed to conduct is complicated by the fact that public opinion is usually taken as the guide and few men reason back to principles of any kind.

But the idea of 'duty' presupposes a theory of existence, of man's being and his place in the world, however the theory is derived and even if it is held unconsciously.

The recognition of the metaphysical basis of all ethics prepares the way for the consideration of the special question.

Christianity, though a practical way of life, is essentially a theory of being, and the theory of being is the source of all principles of action.

Jesus made Himself the basis of all His teaching; all His ethical teaching was a revelation of Himself. It is in this that the real novelty of His teaching lies. This is the distinctive feature of 'Christian' ethics.

The earliest Christians recognized in Him a new criterion of life and conduct; and subsequent generations drew their ethical conceptions from their doctrine about His Person.

No attempt to find any other basis for Christian ethics was made till modern times.

Variations in the relative valuation of ethical principles can be connected with variations in the form which Christian doctrines have assumed at different times.

The ethical significance of some doctrines is evident, but the true relation between doctrines and ethics can best be tested by reference to the fundamental doctrine of the Incarnation; yet to understand the real significance of doctrines their origin and the process by which they were evolved must be considered first.

The origin of Christian doctrines is to be found in the first attempts of contemporaries (unconscious metaphysicians) to understand who Jesus was.

Jesus Himself urged His disciples to these attempts, putting to them the question, "But whom say ye that I am?"

Examination of the three accounts of this question, and the answer, reveals the process by which doctrines were evolved.

The basis of all Christian doctrines is Jesus Himself, His own experiences, and the impression He made on His first followers and succeeding generations, fresh and fuller experience calling for wider inductions.

Present and actual religious experience has been the cause of all developments of doctrine, and must condition any future development.

Correspondence of doctrines with actual ethical and spiritual experience is the only possible test of their truth. The permanent value of the New Testament consists in its being the record of such actual experience.

The course of experience which led to the gradual formulation and modification of various Christian doctrines can be traced; but here the fundamental doctrines only can be considered, and that in their most general forms.

The doctrine of the Incarnation supplies at once a theory as to God's Being and as to man's being.

The ethical significance of the doctrine is best tested by consideration of the different ethical results of different theories as to the Person of Jesus, particularly the theory that He was mere man, the mere product of the natural evolution of the race.

The ethical implications of the doctrine of the Incarnation: the theory of life which it denotes, and the conception of sin, contrasted with the conception that follows from other views of the Person of Jesus.

The doctrine of the Incarnation supplies an authoritative ethical criterion and sets up an absolute standard, with an adequate motive—the love of God, the doctrine of 'forgiveness of sins' giving the needed stimulus to renewed moral effort.

The doctrine of the Trinity, similarly, based on spiritual and ethical experience, describes the highest form of existence, and furnishes the Christian conception of human personality, with its ethical consequences.

The doctrines of the Church and the Sacraments give more complete ethical expression to the same conceptions.

From these doctrines follow distinctive conceptions of the nature of evil, and of the relation between the 'material' and the 'spiritual,' with directly ethical corollaries, and they emphasize the true 'inwardness' of virtue.

The question whether Christian ethics can exist apart from Christian doctrine.

CHRISTIAN DOCTRINES AND THEIR ETHICAL SIGNIFICANCE.

THE subject of the ethical significance of Christian doctrine may seem to lend itself more readily to devotional than to scientific treatment. Of unscientific popular discussion it has recently at all events had its full share. Correspondence on the subject has filled the columns of a widely-circulated newspaper for several months, and seems to have incited comments in many pulpits; and the discussion of the question 'Do we believe?' has at least elicited the fact that there is a widespread feeling that the acceptance or non-acceptance of the Christian faith has little or nothing to do with principles of conduct: and that the only thing that really matters is what men do; while what they do is independent of what they believe.

Belief and conduct are set in antithesis. 'Christian' conduct, it is assumed and argued, may exist without Christian belief; as it is pointed out, Christian belief has often coexisted with conduct which few nowadays would be willing to call Christian. So that Pope, a century and a half ago (though another interpretation of the couplet is possible), is supposed to have said the final word upon the subject when he wrote:

> "For modes of faith let graceless zealots fight,
> His can't be wrong whose life is in the right."

It is not suggested that in morals a man may live 'from hand to mouth,' without fixed principles, but rather that the principles on which he rules his actions are independent of his religious beliefs—that Christian doctrines, if they have any meaning for him at all, have no influence on his outlook on life, and do not affect his action: that is to say, that Christian doctrines are devoid of ethical significance.

What, then, is the bearing of 'doctrines' on life? is the question to be considered. Does it make any difference to us, whether we believe or not, here in this life? This question of the relation of creed to character and conduct is at once complicated and simple. It is complicated, because of the contrast which is often seen between a man's action and the principles which he professes: a contrast which raises at once a difficult psychological problem. What is meant by belief? Do men believe what they think they believe?

To take an example. When a people professedly Christian tolerates institutions which are obviously in flagrant opposition to universally recognized Christian principles, is that people Christian in belief? We might find a country in which the belief in God the Father of all, one God for all men, is established:—a Christian country familiar with the thought that in Christ all earthly differences are done away, so that there is neither circumcision nor uncircumcision, neither Jew nor Greek, neither bond nor free, but all men are brothers: a country that professes the belief that all men are equal in His sight, and yet at the same time practically debars a negro, whatever his education, from all social and political rights. The contrast between doctrinal belief and social and political (or ethical) practice is so obvious, that if the belief is really held we have an instance of a people

"Whose life laughs through and spits at their creed,
Who maintain Christ in word and defy Him in deed."

Instances such as this could of course be multiplied in ordinary business relations, as well as in public and in private life.

On the other hand, the question is simple, because on the face of it conduct must depend on creed, if creed be understood. And the explanation of apparent anomalies is to be found in the fact that a creed is often accepted unintelligently, and not consciously realized. In such a case the supposed

XIII] *Ethical significance of Christian doctrines* 533

creed is not one's own, and then action is determined by other principles, which really constitute one's creed.

The prevalent idea of the chasm between doctrine and practical life has its source in the haziness and vagueness of thought—the logical and intellectual bankruptcy—in which men are content to live.

The needs of the moment are obvious. A theory of life is not called in to decide between two courses as to which is right and which is wrong. In practical experience the decision is not consciously made by reference to first principles. Public opinion—the opinion of a wider or of a smaller circle as the case may be—is the standard.

In some circumstances, no doubt, and for the mass of men, such an attitude commends itself as reasonable. When public opinion is sound and enlightened, when life is clean and pure, there is little need to trouble about the basis on which it rests. Englishmen at all events find it possible to combine with others for common ends, whatever their ideas and motives about other things may be : in politics, for national purposes ; in philanthropical endeavours in which religious differences are merged and men of all creeds unite ; in the ordinary routine—in families and schools and other societies which have a common corporate life. In a land "where faith is not afraid to reason, nor reason to adore"—the home of really free thought and expression, where respect for individual conscience reigns in a dual control with regard for the claims of the common weal of the society—this spirit, which ignores differences of principle (whether religious or political or ethical) among men who can agree in action, is seen to lead to excellent results. And there is always ready to hand the popular reading of the saying, "By their fruits ye shall know them," isolated from its setting, to support the view that religious opinions do not matter, and that conduct is all in all.

But it may with better reason be maintained that the prevalence of the idea that doctrines have no direct bearing on life is due to the fact that men do not commonly reason back to the real springs of action, and that in truth a theory, a doctrine, underlies all actions. The holding of such a theory may be unconscious, like the reflex action of a muscle in which conscious volition has no part. The particular act or course of conduct may be the result of habit, of long training, of social environment, if not of actually inherited tendency. Yet somewhere, however far back, there is as the source of a man's action a doctrine; and the theory of life on which it rests is his, though it is not his own invention and he may not be conscious of its influence on his acts. He may think, and say, that he has only done his 'duty.'

Probably no word is more often on the lips of men of high moral character and earnest purpose who care little about doctrine. The child learns the word in his Catechism, and all his life he goes on learning more exactly what it means. He finds it has many forms, and he has to use it in the plural; though all the forms go back to one conception. And he is happy if, as experience grows, he does not find that one duty clashes with another, and that in this 'conflict of duties' there lies the most perplexing moral problem which he has to face. To do his 'duty' in all the relations of life is supposed to be the highest end a man can achieve. It is an essentially practical end.

But how much belief the word involves! It implies a whole theory of life. It is only a short expression for a series of ideas relating to man and the world in which he lives. His conception of his 'duty' sums up his answer to the questions

> "What we are, and whence we came,
> Whence we came, and whither wending."

The word is essentially metaphysical, or doctrinal. It is meaningless apart from a fixed conception of the purpose of human life. It declares that man has responsibility, to himself and to others, to live his life in a particular way. There is a 'science of life' which it is possible for him to learn, and in accordance with its principles he must rule his course. The word 'duty' is essentially expressive of purpose, looking to an end, seeing the parts in the light of the whole, implying knowledge of what man is in himself and what his place in the universe is—knowledge of the final whole, and of the parts in relation to the whole.

He only knows what his 'duty' is, of whom it could be said that he

"Saw life steadily and saw it whole."

It makes no difference how this theory of life is framed or whence it is derived. 'Duty' may simply condense into a word the moral experience of previous generations, accumulated through past ages, or it may express the authoritative teaching of a special revelation which is believed to have been given from without, and to rest on more than human sanctions. In any case it is a theory of life, a science of life, that underlies the word. And the man who speaks of his duty in life has committed himself, whether he knows it or not, to a doctrine about life, which may of course be Christian or non-Christian, but cannot escape the necessity of dealing with the question of *being* as the basis of the law of *doing*.

Metaphysics—which is involved in the thinking creature's theory of himself, be it articulate or inarticulate—must thus, it would seem, be the basis of Ethics—the principles by which he endeavours to fulfil what he has already recognized as the end that is set before him. The process by which a man becomes conscious of his own personality is essentially a metaphysical process, and without the conscious recognition of personality there can be no sense of duty, no individual ethics. The same process leads to the recognition of other personalities, and is the basis of social ethics—the individual's duty to others—the duty of members of a society to one another.

These considerations are so obvious that the mention of them would call for apology, were it not the case that they are constantly ignored, and that the recognition of the metaphysical basis of all ethics prepares the way for the due appreciation of the ethical significance of the particular system of metaphysics which is expressed in Christian doctrines.

For though we are accustomed to say that Christianity is not a system, but a life; and it is true in one sense that all Christian doctrines are based on ethical experience, and that where the doctrines are not realized in life, there Christianity is not actual: yet beyond doubt they are metaphysical inferences from experience, and in their entirety make up a system of metaphysics. Christianity is, of course, a way of practical life, and has its system of ethics; but it is a religion which embodies the first principles and ultimate theories of existence and of knowledge. It was, doubtless, the language of metaphor and poetry, rather than of philosophy, that Jesus Himself in all His teaching employed, and the language of metaphor and poetry that His first interpreters after Him continued to use. But the very life of metaphor and poetry is the thought which they express. The true poet is not simply the cunning painter of meaningless pictures in word, or the weaver of subtle phrases and haunting cadences, but rather he 'who sees the infinite in things', and can give to his vision the most melodious and appropriate expression. No teacher of Hebrew lineage, to whom the Hebrew prophets were an inspiration, could fail to use the language of poetry. But at the back of it all was a philosophy of life, and the thoughts that found expression in poetry and metaphor were metaphysical. So that a recent saying, which seemed to some to be a paradox, "It is impossible to be a Christian on any rational grounds without first being a metaphysician," must be held to express a truth that is hidden from those who maintain that "the nearer the system of a systematic theologian approaches to metaphysics, the further it removes itself from Christianity." The attempt to divorce Christian doctrines from metaphysics, or metaphysics from ethics, leaves us in an intolerable and a hopeless position. A barrier is erected between Christian doctrines and that living experience out of which they grew: they are torn out of their historical environment and wrenched from their life-giving root; they become little more than a series of abstract propositions which have been supernaturally revealed, and are to be accepted, by a process in which the intelligence plays

XIII] *Ethical significance of Christian doctrines* 537

no part, to which no growth of human experience can contribute.

And ethics divorced from metaphysics would be deprived of their natural vital sustenance, and become a hard and barren code of laws. If the only function of religion were, as Matthew Arnold would have it, to deal with conduct, to inculcate morality, to elevate it out of a mere system of rule, to touch it with emotion: it would fail to fulfil even this allotted aim.

The view that Christian doctrine can only be regarded as obscuring and weakening the true meaning and force of Christianity as a religion—that the pathos, the charm, the eternal appeal of the Person of Christ as He moves through the gospel-tales are veiled and marred by the creeds of the Church—seems to be closely related to the view expressed in the second of these sayings, and to depend, like it, on a mistaken conception of Christian doctrines.

In early days it is clear that belief in the Incarnation was made the basis of all principles of conduct. In the teaching of Jesus Himself there is the closest connexion between His personal claims and the demand He makes on His followers for the particular way of life which He sets forth. The Christian's life is to be one of conscious service rendered to the Lord of life. Others indeed may unconsciously render such service, not knowing what they do, from mere humanitarian motives and instincts. But the stress which is laid on the fact that all such service, unconscious though it might be, is service to Him, does but bring out into greater clearness the essential basis of ethics, according to the conceptions and teaching of Jesus.

It is, indeed, just in this that the real novelty of His teaching lies. In the actual principles and rules of conduct, which saying after saying, parable after parable, and actions alike enunciate, there is very little that is new. Hebrew prophets and psalmists, and at least one great school of Greek philosophy, had insisted on the inwardness of all morality, and had turned men from the outward actions to the spirit which prompted them. Jesus was not the first to proclaim the need of control of thought, desire, imagination, will. He was not the first to insist on truthfulness and purity of heart as the test of truthfulness and purity in act. The supreme, if not the only, novelty, in His ethical teaching is to be found not in the contents of it, but in the basis which He gives it. The common people who heard Him noticed, with sure instinct, that He spoke not as the Scribes and Pharisees, appealing to an external standard, book or law or inherited tradition, but "with authority." When He took, as the text, as it were, of His teaching, some ancient command or maxim, He treated it as one who stood Himself upon a higher ground. He did much more than interpret it. And the new reading of the principle was to be accepted because it was His. He claimed and exercised absolute freedom. Every principle of life which He proclaimed was, and seemed to be, a revelation of Himself, the expression of His own unseen and inner life, in perfect correspondence with the visible life He led before the eyes of men. It was this that gave His teaching its authority. He spoke as one who had power over life. He made Himself the standard. He claimed men's hearts and minds. He bound them to Himself. The unparalleled words, "I am the Way, and the Truth, and the Life," are only a condensed expression of the claims which the earliest records of His life and teaching that we know imply. So far from the evidence is it to say that the earliest Christian tradition contained the record of the teaching of Jesus rather than a doctrine about Him, that it would be truer to maintain that all His teaching was conveyed in terms of Himself. It is impossible to get away from this personal claim. He based—the historical Jesus of the earliest tradition based—all His ethical teaching on Himself. It is this that gives it its peculiar character. His whole aim was to bring men to Himself, to bind them to Him. They are to lose themselves in Him, that they may find themselves. They are to make an absolute surrender to Him, in order that they may realize themselves. Apart from Him they can do nothing. It is in union with Him alone that they learn their true position and destiny, are able to bring to

XIII] *Ethical significance of Christian doctrines* 539

consciousness and actuality their latent capacities, and so attain that present peace and harmony which is salvation.

Out of their personal relation to Him, as a necessary consequence of it, is to spring the whole stream of their life.

No ethical teacher, before or since, has ever made himself the basis of his teaching.

Great thinkers and teachers, the master-minds of every age, have of course attracted to themselves disciples and something of the personal emotion that discipleship of every kind inspires. And the 'schools' that have grown up around them have naturally attributed to their founders that authority which is always conceded to extraordinary powers of mind and insight. What they could not have discovered, what they themselves had never thought or dreamt of, they have accepted on the authority of another. It was enough that he had said so. The αὐτὸς ἔφα of the disciples of one of the earliest masters represents the natural tendency of schools.

But Jesus was not content to win acceptance of this kind for His sayings. It was not to His words, but to Himself, that He claimed allegiance.

And His earliest followers, with a true perception of the facts, went forth to proclaim, not αὐτὸς ἔφα, but αὐτός: not what He said, but what He was. The Gospel was not words or sayings, but a Person—a life. He Himself was the good-news; He Himself the centre of all; He Himself all in all. It was Jesus Himself that they preached as the basis and the sum of all their hopes in this world and the next: and in the general reversal of standards which was implicit in the Gospel they proclaimed, with all the rules of life and generally accepted bases of morality so far at least discredited, they found in Him the standard of reference that was needed. The meaning of human life was revealed in Him. It was useless to look elsewhere for the principles on which it should be based. It was only necessary to interpret Him to fresh disciples and later generations, to draw out and apply to present conditions the law of life which He embodied.

We shall search the New Testament in vain to find any conception of the possibility of Christian life apart from Christ.

Doctrine and ethics go hand in hand together. Divorce of one from the other is not thought of. St Paul's most impressive appeals to moral principles and the moral consciousness are linked on to his most 'dogmatic' teaching. The ethical ideal is derived from the doctrine of the Person of Jesus, and the inferences which follow as to the nature of man and his place in the world. As ethical experience was at the very root of the earliest Christian doctrines, so Christian doctrines were presented from the first as themselves the source of the new way of life. The first condition was faith in Jesus. There, in Him, was to be found the standard of moral values and the proof of their validity. It is this direct and immediate dependence on the Person and Life of Jesus Himself that is the distinctive mark of Christian ethics. The antinomianism which threatened the life of the new society at an early date, and has at various crises invaded the Church in later times, is at least a standing witness to the conviction that the first essential is the doctrine. The antinomians of all ages have simply failed to draw from the doctrine they professed the natural inferences as to principles of life.

So it was in later times. Such an apologist as Justin expounded Christian doctrine and Christian ethics as a whole, and referred to the faith of Christians in Jesus—their ridiculous doctrines as they seemed to Roman statesmen and philosophers —as that which gave them power actually to live their lives in obedience to moral standards which seemed to others unattainable. He uses, that is to say, the admitted excellence of the ethical principles of the new religion as an argument by which to commend the doctrinal principles from which they spring: the appeal to results, which he makes by the way, is a concession to practical prejudice. He assumes that the excellence of the ethical principles which he recounts will be admitted by all: he is concerned to indicate, with regard to the most characteristic points, that for Christians their validity and authority are intimately connected with the beliefs they hold about Jesus Himself.

So close was this connexion supposed to be that no attempt was made to treat Christian ethics apart from Christian doc-

Ethical significance of Christian doctrines

trine. The Gospel offered the solution of the whole problem of human existence. The doctrine of the Incarnation carried with it the answer to every ethical question. In the first treatise which is professedly devoted to the exposition of Christian moral duties—the *De officiis ministrorum* of Ambrose—based though it is on earlier pagan conceptions, the 'four cardinal virtues' are dealt with as inseparable, and rooted in Christian doctrine: and Augustine a little later regards them all, along with the Pauline triad of graces, Faith, Hope, and Love, as simply different forms of manifestation of the one great principle of love to God, which depends directly on the Incarnation. And when the ethical system of the Church received complete scientific form at the hands of Thomas Aquinas, in spite of the influence on his thought of Aristotelian conceptions and Roman jurisprudence, it is doctrine that is still the basis of ethics. Though love is the formative principle and the vital energy of Christian life, the substantial basis of all morality is belief in Christian doctrine. The rejection of a single article of the Christian creed is the dissolution of the system of Christian ethics.

The work of Thomas Aquinas, 'indubitably the crowning result of the great constructive effort of mediaeval philosophy,' which, on the main point in view, carried on the earlier traditional conception, has exercised an enduring influence on Christian thought.

Apart from mysticism, with its comparative neglect of moral effort and freedom from doctrinal systems, no attempt was made to find any basis for morality independent of Christian doctrine till the seventeenth century, when the conflict of Church with Church, and sect with sect, and the new idea of natural law, led to the search for a new basis of ethics in the universal reason and moral consciousness of mankind—a permanent law of nature written in the constitution and experience of all men, which all could recognize and accept, without the aid or sanction of a revelation from without—or in the social and political needs of an ordered community.

So a severance between theology and ethics has taken

place, and the two sciences have been treated separately, with the result that is seen to-day.

It would be an interesting task to attempt to trace, in the history of Christian thought and practice in different ages, variations in the relative value assigned to different ethical principles, and to connect them with variations in the form which particular Christian doctrines have assumed from time to time[1]. In ages, for example, when a particular view of the doctrine of the Church and its authority has been most prevalent, 'obedience' has become almost the cardinal Christian virtue, and external compliance with rules has tended to supplant the true inwardness of Christian morality: particular theories of the Atonement have helped to determine the dominant conceptions of Christian principles of conduct: while, again, it would seem that a special type of character is commonly connected with a Calvinistic form of doctrine. But such variations in points of view of doctrine and of ethical principles correspond to what are merely passing phases of opinion, and to trace them out would take us away from considerations of more permanent importance.

Again, the ethical significance of some doctrines is self-evident. It makes all the difference whether we believe that personal existence is limited to this world, and that the final good is to be attained here if at all, or rather that "man has Forever" and that this life is only preparatory to a grander and larger sphere of existence, so that goodness is a process which is begun here, and all man's moral faculties are to be directed to the attainment of an ultimate end—"the heavenly crowning grace"—which can never be realized here upon earth. The doctrine of a future judgement by an omniscient Judge, from whom nothing can be hid, again, not only has supplied a powerful motive, but also points to the paramount importance of the secret things of the heart and mind—the unseen springs of action.

But passing over doctrines such as these and dealing with the question on broader grounds, the relation between

[1] The variations, which cannot be dealt with here, may be traced in W. Gass's, or Th. Ziegler's, *Geschichte der christlichen Ethik*.

XIII] *Ethical significance of Christian doctrines* 543

doctrines and ethics can, perhaps, best be tested by reference only to the leading doctrine of the Incarnation and such other doctrines as are most closely related to it. The question is, however, so largely determined by the mere consideration of the historical circumstances in which the doctrines arose that it is necessary first of all to consider their origin and the process by which they were evolved.

One aspect of the facts of which account must be taken is doubtless expressed when it is said that, "in the forefront of the teaching of Jesus Christ stands an ethical sermon," while "in the forefront of the Christianity of the fourth century we have a metaphysical creed"; and that "the one belongs to a world of Syrian peasants, the other to a world of Greek philosophers." But to say this is also to ignore the living experience, the Christian life, of the first and of the fourth century alike. In the forefront of the Christianity of the first century there stood neither ethical sermon nor metaphysical creed. Before the eyes of 'the world of Syrian peasants' loomed, larger than anything He said, the gracious and majestic figure of a Person who attracted to Himself their hearts and minds : while the conquest of life—the moral reformation of the Empire whose hostility had been at last overcome by the Christian life of the Church—was at least as much the task of the Christianity of the fourth century as was the adaptation of current philosophical terms to the expression of Christian thought[1].

It is no doubt true that to the gradual development and full expression of Christian doctrines much was contributed by the 'world of Greek philosophers,' to the influence of whose thought and phraseology attention has been fully directed in recent years. The great Christian thinkers who were most largely responsible for working out the doctrines would

[1] The anxiety for correct definitions of the Person of Christ, which was shown by the great champions of the Nicene Christology, was essentially due to their conviction that Arian theories endangered the Christian conception of Redemption, and left men still in their sins. Their interest in the controversy was primarily ethical. And the influence of Christian ethical principles shows itself at once in the moral reforms embodied in the legislation of Constantine and later Emperors.

probably have been the first to recognize the help they derived from earlier metaphysical thought in formulating the Christian theories of life and being. But to describe any such process as 'the Hellenization' of Christianity is to suggest a dramatic transformation-scene which has no place in history.

It is not to professed philosophers of any school or race, consciously attempting to build up a scheme of human life and solve the riddle of the universe, that we must look for the first steps in the process by which the fabric of Christian doctrines was built up, but to the untrained, unconscious metaphysicians who were to be found among the crowds who hung on the words of Jesus and marvelled at his acts.

For the origin of Christian doctrines we must go back to the 'world of Syrian peasants.' In the 'memoirs' that have come down to us under the name of one of them—the one by the way to whom we owe the fullest and most familiar report of the 'Sermon on the Mount'—we find an account of an episode, and appended to it a comment, in which we may see the first beginnings of doctrines. It is the account of the tempest on the lake, with the comment of the men, who marvelled, saying, "What manner of man is this, that even the winds and the sea obey him?" The account and the comment go back to the earliest tradition: they are contained both in St Mark and in St Luke: and a single verbal change which St Matthew makes in the comment[1] serves only to express more fully the thought in the minds of the men at the time. Their attention is fixed on the Person of Jesus. 'Who,' they wonder, 'of what tribe or nation is he? from what strange country—where in the world does he come from? what *manner of being* is this, that even the winds and the sea obey him?'

We may leave on one side the miracle. It is enough that something unusual had happened, something that formed a kind of climax in the new experiences of that little band of followers—those Syrian peasants. And it turned them into metaphysicians. In the moment in which the Syrian peasant

[1] Mk. iv. 36-41; Lk. viii. 23-25; Mt. viii. 23-27.

XIII] *Ethical significance of Christian doctrines* 545

put to himself that question, we need not say the peasant in him died, but at least the Christian theologian was born.

For all Christian doctrines are attempts to answer the question. All Christian doctrines are theories framed to interpret the Person of Jesus and actual Christian experience. From the facts which had come within the range of their own observation, the facts of their own experience, the earliest Christian theologians began to draw their inferences. In the fresh enthusiasm of the earliest days it may well have been that evangelists were content to state the stirring facts, as they conceived them, of the life of Jesus, and 'let them work.' But it was, of course, inevitable that something of their own interpretation should enter into their narrative; and it is clear that, before the Gospels which we have were committed to writing, thoughtful disciples, like-minded with those from whom at an earlier time in the earthly life of Jesus this question had been drawn, had begun to frame their theories by which to answer it. They had passed out of the stage of incipient unconscious metaphysics. They had gone behind the words and the teaching and the acts that made up the outer life of their Lord; they had tried to pierce the screen and penetrate into His inner being—so as to find an explanation of it all, and to get a definite theory of life. They had sought a clue to the solution of the problem of human existence as a whole from their actual experience of what life was in Him.

Had they not done this, it is just possible that we might still have had a code of morals based on the teaching of Jesus—collections of practical precepts and moral maxims, the 'bare bones' of the Christian religion; but we should not have had Christian theology or Christian ethics.

In essaying this work of interpretation and setting forth to others not simply the teaching of Jesus on conduct, nor simply Jesus, as He seemed to observers at the time during His ministry on earth, but rather Jesus as He seemed to them in the light of His whole career, as they could look back upon it with all their later experience—Jesus as they believed He really was in Himself,—the evangelists were acting in obedience to the demands which with one accord they represent Him as making during His life. He was not content that men should only give Him their hearts. He claimed the allegiance of their minds as well, gradually leading up the inner circle of His followers to the intellectual recognition of His person. He put to them the searching question, "But whom say ye that I am?" He encouraged them, that is, to try to formulate their feelings towards Him, to make inductions from the facts they had observed, to frame theories about Him. Metaphysics, doctrines, creeds are the inevitable consequences of compliance with His own suggestion. All three of the synoptists[1] record the question and the answer, though St Matthew alone exposes the full significance of St Peter's great confession—the intellectual profession of faith—by adding[2] to the earlier account the words of praise from Jesus which the confession won, and the declaration that the gates of Hades should not prevail against the church which was to be built on that foundation.

Throughout St Matthew's version of the incident the hand of the interpreter is plainly seen. The words of St Peter, recorded by St Mark, "Thou art the Christ," become in St Luke "the Christ of God," and in St Matthew, "the Christ the son of the living God." And the praise of Peter and the declaration concerning the church and the keys (interpolated by St Matthew before the injunction to silence and the prediction of the Passion, which follow in all accounts) must be read in sequence with the confession of faith by which they were prompted. Whatever St Matthew's source may have been, it is clear he means to emphasize the primary importance of the intellectual recognition of the Divine personality of Jesus to the existence of his church, and to imply that the first perception of this was an act of spiritual insight of the highest order, and that such spiritual insight alone could open the way to 'the kingdom of heaven' and discern upon earth, here in this life, the things which belonged to the kingdom from those which did not. St Peter is only a type

[1] Mk. viii. 27–33; Lk. ix. 18–22; Mt. xvi. 13–16.
[2] Mt. xvi. 17–19.

Ethical significance of Christian doctrines

of such spiritual insight, the first to proclaim the doctrine—the metaphysical faith—on which the Church was built. It was not the sand of sentiment, the shifting ground of emotion only, but the firm rock of the allegiance of the reason, the rock of the mind's conviction, on which the Church was built. To St Matthew at all events it is this doctrine—that Jesus is the Christ, the son of the living God—that is the one sure foundation of the Church, and of all for which the Church exists.

It is worth while to note, in passing, how in the three versions of St Peter's words which have come down to us, we have a conspicuous instance of the development of doctrine. St Mark no doubt records the actual words—"Thou art the Christ." The most impetuous of the apostles declared his conviction that the mysterious Person to whom the prophets of old were believed to have pointed had come. Jesus was the Messiah. The conviction was, in one sense perhaps, a flash of insight; but the question whether, or not, they were to see in Jesus the promised Saviour of their nation must have been already often in the minds of the disciples, and Peter was probably only giving enthusiastic expression to the inference to which they had come from the evidence of all that they had seen and heard. So, by this recognition of the Messiahship of Jesus, the first stage in the doctrine of His person was reached. St Luke's addition to the words of Peter is purely exegetical. It simply brings out more clearly the meaning of the phrase: 'the anointed of God.' The Messiah was in a special sense God's representative, His vice-regent in the world. But St Matthew's version seems to mark a further stage of reflective thought. The relation in which the Messiah stands to God is defined more nearly as one of sonship, and the words express a notable approximation to the doctrine of the Incarnation—an approximation which other evidence implies had not been made by the apostles at the time. The writer of the Gospel, from the standpoint of later experience, has drawn out the significance of Peter's recognition. He has not added to it, though he has expanded the form of words, so as to make them cover a later stage of thought. With historical inexactitude, but with doctrinal insight, he has read into the incident the meaning which he saw it had. It is a case of genuine development, due to the growth of living religious experience, such experience showing the need of a somewhat larger induction than had at first been made.

The facts preceded the doctrines. Just as at first men saw Jesus, His life, His works, and heard His words, and were set thinking, and trying to account for the impression which He made upon them; so it was when He was taken from them.

They saw that He treated God all through as a Father, and realized this relationship in every thought and act: and so they came to believe in the Fatherhood of God, and in the sonship of Jesus in a special sense. They saw that He treated man as His brother: and so they came to believe in the brotherhood of men. Through Him they found that they had access to God, that they received fresh spiritual strength, that they won tranquillity and peace: and so they came to believe in atonement effected by Him. And only afterwards did they reason how these things could be.

Only after they had observed these things in Him, and realized them in their own lives and practical experience as great realities, spiritual and ethical:—only then did they bring their metaphysical and intellectual faculties to bear upon them, to discover, if they could, the laws of being and of life to which they correspond, and to frame the doctrines which should express them.

The fact of the existence of Jesus—His experiences, His teaching, His life: the impression which He made upon men: the power by which He continued to sway men after His death: the experiences of His immediate followers, and the experiences of successive generations of men who in their own persons realized anew the same impression:—these are the subject-matter of Christian Doctrine. "That which we have seen and heard declare we...," "...that which we have heard, which we have seen with our eyes, which we have looked upon, and our hands have handled...."

Christian theology has simply carried on, and endeavoured to bring more and more towards completion, the work of

XIII] *Ethical significance of Christian doctrines* 549

interpretation which the authors of the gospels began. It has endeavoured, under varying conditions of life and thought, to give more and more adequate explanations of the Person and work of Jesus, to answer in new circumstances, and with more completeness, the question which was early answered in part by the narrative of the Nativity.

And the same process which began among His earliest followers in the lifetime of Jesus, and was carried further by the same men when they had to expand their earlier theories to include the fresh facts of His death, and all the spiritual and ethical experiences that followed—notably the unparalleled experience which has ever since been known as the Resurrection of Jesus:—the same process has gone on all down the centuries since.

Every great epoch in the development of doctrine has been produced by the insufficiency of current (earlier) doctrines to account for present and actual religious experience.

If, as may be, we are even now on the eve of another great development, it can only be in so far as the traditional explanations of the Person and work of Jesus, and of His and our relations to God and the universe in which we are placed, no longer seem to correspond to the realities of our intellectual, moral, and spiritual needs. And if, and so far as, this is the case, these explanations (which satisfied men in the past, because they could verify them in their own persons) are no longer true for us; and the Christian Society, taking account of the experience of the present as well as of the past, must seek some fresh inductions from the facts, which will obtain as wide recognition as the ancient doctrines have enjoyed. For "interpretation is of the present as well as of the past."

That these doctrines commended themselves to the minds of earnest and spiritual men of the past, as true to their experience, is the attestation with which they come at first to each fresh generation in turn. But they must be capable of verification in individual experience, as embodying a theory of life that works. So far as the theory, when honestly applied, is not found to work; so far, for the individual at least, it is in some way or other inadequate. Historical testimony, the accumulated experience of past generations, may commend it to him, and predispose him to accept it. The weight of such 'authority' must always be great in relation to a limited range of experience. Augustine himself declared that he could not have accepted the Christian religion had not the authority of the Church impelled him to believe it true—meaning the evidence which was furnished by the visible experience of the Christian Society, of men of all kinds and classes, in proof of the close correspondence between the theory of the Incarnation and the facts of life. But for each individual the final test of doctrines is their correspondence with his own experience. They must seem to him, when understood, to be the expression of something which he has realized in life, or which he knows that others are realizing, if he be himself without experience of the greater things of life; for even in these, the greater things of life, it is necessary at times to live 'at second hand': or else the doctrines are not true to him. Rooted in ethical experience as they were, ethical experience must attest them still. Does it, or does it not? This is the vital question, as regards the truth of the Christian conception of life, for each generation and age.

The question whether the Gospels record events as they actually happened, or not, is and always has been of secondary importance. For in any case it is certain that they and the Epistles of St Paul reflect the actual impression which was made by Jesus and His acts and teaching upon contemporaries and those of His followers who were nearest to Jesus in time of whom we have any knowledge; and nearer to the facts than the impression which they make we can never get. In any case it is certain that the source of Gospels and Epistles is in the actual life of a Society that realized, more vividly perhaps than they have ever been realized since, the experiences in explanation of which Christian doctrines were framed. The New Testament is, in any case, a witness to the play of ethical and spiritual forces on real life. It contains a large measure of speculative inference from facts; it reflects the earliest attempts at interpretation of the facts—whatever they were— of the life of Jesus, regarded from different points of view;

XIII] *Ethical significance of Christian doctrines* 551

it is written by men who had attained to a philosophy of life : but its ultimate *provenance* is not speculation, or interpretation, or philosophy, or any flights of imagination, but solid rock of experience of ordinary men and women living ordinary lives in the world, with ordinary tasks and occupations, who have somehow realized "the light that never was on sea or land" for men before, so that for them "all things have become new[1]."

It is easy to trace in the pages of the New Testament, and in the pages of the history of the Christian Society during the following generations, fragmentary though they be at first, the course of experience which led to the convictions that are represented by the fundamental Christian doctrines of the Incarnation, the Trinity, the Atonement, the Church and the Sacraments, and the Life of the world to come, in which the whole Christian philosophy of existence is summed up.

The time soon came, no doubt, when contact with other philosophies of life exercised a disturbing influence on the genuine development of Christian doctrine; and then appeal was made perforce to the experiences of the first generations of Christians, as embodied in the writings of apostles and evangelists, or in the unbroken tradition of the greater Churches and the practices and institutions which had come down from earlier times, to check the tendency to false development. But no such appeal could ever have been successful, unless the facts which it revealed had found support in the present experience of the Church at large. Even when the New Testament came to be regarded as the only test of the truth of doctrine, and the only court of reference, it was still from the particular circumstances of the period that particular doctrines assumed their varying colour and

[1] So, afterwards, the way in which Christians regarded themselves as a New People and were referred to as a *tertium genus* is striking testimony to the fact that the religion was regarded as a whole as something unlike any other. The whole conception of life, as well as the actual life which was led, separated Christians off from all other people. For Christians it was a new world, a world in which Love reigned,—and all because of Christ. They were one brotherhood, but only because they were united in Him.

out of the actual conditions of men's lives and thought that their new forms were shaped. And the new doctrines were often justified by isolating from their context particular images or even phrases, employed by writers of the New Testament, and treating them as an immediate source of doctrine in detail, ignoring the historical conditions in which the writings originated and by reference to which alone their evidence can be safely used.

The history of the doctrine of the Atonement, for example, affords abundant illustrations of the process in view and the principles involved. The history of the doctrine of the Church would furnish others.

But to trace the course through which Christian doctrines have gone is the object of this Essay only so far as it is necessary to realize on what foundation they rest, in order to appreciate their real significance. And the realization of the facts of the history of the development of Christian doctrines can hardly fail to carry with it the conviction that they are profoundly ethical in essence, and have the closest connexion with practical ideals of life.

Merely to set out in simplest terms a Christian doctrine is almost inevitably to write a homily. Plain exposition is the enunciation of principles of thought and conduct, and an appeal to the moral sense of men. If we take the fundamental Christian doctrine of the Incarnation, and state it as baldly as possible, this is evident at once.

In order to reveal to men the Divine life under the conditions of human life, the Son of God Himself became man —accepting whatever limitations were necessary in order that His life on earth as man should be a really human life. The life He lived on earth was one of service, entailing suffering— even a painful form of death. The whole purpose of it was ethical—to reveal to men the ideal life and so to stir in them the will to live that life, and give them power to carry out that will.

The doctrine presupposes certain axioms: the existence of man, the existence of the world, the existence of God. And at its back lies the conviction, which Christians inherited

XIII] *Ethical significance of Christian doctrines* 553

from Hebrew belief, that God was the creator of the world and of man, through whatever stages they had passed: that man was by nature and constitution designed for intimate fellowship with his creator, and endowed with power to determine the course of his life—to realize freely his destiny; but that by the assertion of his own self-will that fellowship was broken, the true knowledge of God was blurred and man's vision dimmed. The Divine order of the world was interrupted. The breach of this order was 'sin', and the responsibility was man's: yet he could not for himself restore what he had once destroyed. He was conscious of the schism in his nature, the disorder in the world, his alienation from God. But he could not find the way to set it right, till God, who had shown Himself in various ways, gradually training mankind by various methods, gave at last the full and complete revelation of Himself. To rescue men from sin, the Son of God becomes man, and shows the way through love and suffering that leads man to the goal.

Jesus, according to this doctrine, was no mere product of the natural development of man through long ages of growth and progress in nobility of aim and character—merely the crown of human evolution[1]. He was not one who by his own

---

[1] There is, of course, a sense in which Catholic Theology has recognized in Jesus the accomplishment of the last stage, so to speak, in a long process—the supreme expression of a perfectly developed and completed human nature. The modern theory of Evolution has perhaps for Christians emphasized, and may yet throw much more light on, this aspect of the Catholic doctrine of the Incarnation. Witness is borne to it by St Paul's conception of the summing up of all things in Christ, by the further working out of the idea by Irenaeus, and by the discussions of the question whether the Incarnation was, or was not, conditioned by the Fall; whether there would not have been an Incarnation independently of the Fall as the supreme Revelation of Himself by God, who had made partial and incomplete revelations of Himself in various ways which had served as preparations for the final and complete revelation in His Son. Every student of Christian doctrine will welcome fresh knowledge of any kind that helps him to draw out more fully the meaning contained in ancient definitions of the Person of Christ—meanings perhaps much richer than were present to the minds of the men who framed them. But the theory which is dealt with in this Essay, in contrast with the doctrine

peculiar virtue, or by the aid derived from the merits of his ancestors, could triumph over obstacles and mount to heaven. As man He was subject to the laws of human growth and development, but it was not so that He became man. There was no heightening of His natural powers, no exaltation to a higher sphere of life. It was not a case of the deification of mankind. It was all the other way. He was God before He was man. The process by which He became man was a condescension, a stooping, a coming down, a lowering, an emptying, a humbling of Himself, a forgoing of privilege.

Two simple ideas of profound significance for life are expressed in this doctrine. There is made in Jesus the revelation of God to man, and there is made the revelation of man to himself.

The revelation of God shows that Love is the law of the highest life, manifesting itself on the one side in self-sacrifice and on the other in active service. While, if God could enter upon human life, undergo a human birth and pass through the stages of human existence, without ceasing to be God, it follows that this human nature and life may be the expression of the Divine; since God could share it, it is not evil in itself; the potentialities of manhood are infinite: there is warrant for the noblest conceptions of human nature and human life that poets have pictured in the highest flights of their imagination.

"...flesh that I seek
In the Godhead! I seek and I find it."

Jesus became human, as Christians of old delighted to say, in order that we might become divine.

But, that we may come to closer quarters with the question of the ethical significance of Christian doctrines it will be well to consider the different consequences, in regard to ethical principles, of different theories as to the Person of Jesus.

of the Incarnation, is the theory that sees in Jesus only a particular man, and as such it is open to the objections which were urged against similar theories in earlier ages.

XIII] *Ethical significance of Christian doctrines* 555

The doctrine of the Incarnation had to compete from the days of the apostles onwards with various other theories of His Person, and the Catholic doctrine was worked out in detail under the pressure of controversy—controversy which has left its mark on the creeds in phrases, forced on the Church against its will, which sound to modern ears obscure, if not repellent. The old theories of the Ebionites, the Gnostics, the Sabellians, the Nestorians—that He was a man, yet supernaturally born : that He had no real human body : that He was a mere temporary mode of the existence of the one God, or that He was man with a special supernatural power of God indwelling in Him : or that His person was composite, a man and God being joined by some kind of mechanical process in one: or that He was somehow partly man and partly God, but wholly neither :—these and other similar theories, which were devised of old as explanations of His Person and influenced the phraseology and the final form in which the Church expressed its theory, are now for the most part of merely historical interest. It is, however, worth noting, as germane to the question, that such theories were regarded by the Church— the *communis sensus fidelium* which was in all these matters the ultimate court of appeal — not only as inadequate and false interpretations of the facts which had to be explained, but also as subversive of the recognized principles of Christian morality. False doctrine was supposed to poison the springs of life at their source. Heretics of all ages have been regarded not only as intellectually mistaken, or lacking in apprehension of spiritual things, but also as actually immoral. Such charges of immoral life as have been commonly brought by the 'orthodox' against the 'heretics' have often been, no doubt, mere vulgar slanders. But they witness to the close connexion which has been supposed to exist between sound doctrine and sound conduct, between true theories of being and true principles and practice in active life.

We need not, then, examine in detail the differences in ethical principles which would naturally follow from the different theories which were the subject of controversies that can now be described as dead battle-fields. It will be enough to take a broad differentiation, and to consider briefly, from two or three points of view, how ethical principles are affected by the two contrasted theories—the one, that Jesus was God incarnate, the other, that He was mere man. Does it make any difference, as far as ethical principles are concerned, whether the doctrine of the Divinity of Jesus is accepted or rejected? whether He is believed to be Very God become man, or simply a man with a special mission, as we say, a moral genius, man at the highest point of moral development that the human race has ever reached (for we may leave unconsidered, for the purpose of this comparison, any lower conception of His person)?

In the first place, in the doctrine of the Incarnation we have the expression of the principle of love as characteristic of the highest form of life. If God came down to earth to serve men, to save them by serving them, and in the process submitted to suffering and death as man, the love of God for man is exhibited in the plainest way—the very essence of Godhead is love. In the Incarnation there is made the revelation of the love of God as in no other way. In other words, love is seen to be the basis of life.

> "For life, with all it yields of joy and woe
> And hope and fear......
> Is just our chance of the prize of learning love,
> How love might be, hath been indeed, and is."

The prize is already in the hands of one who believes in the Incarnation.

And at the same time the ideal of perfect human life is set before the world with the strongest power of appeal. The specific motive of Christian conduct is given unmistakeably— the love of God for man awakening the love of man for God. The ethical value of an act done because it is regarded as right is fundamentally different from that of an act which is done from the motive of love. 'Good works' done in obedience to commands, to 'law,' leave us still 'unprofitable servants.' These are the works which St Paul declared could have no 'justifying' value. They leave us either self-righteous or cold and weary: we are still in the state of tutelage, and for us at

XIII] *Ethical significance of Christian doctrines* 557

least Christ has died in vain. When, however, 'good works' are the outcome of the spirit of love, then they have an ethical significance corresponding to the motive from which they spring. Under the influence of this motive a type of character is fashioned that is unique; while reference is made not to any external law or code of rules, but to an inner principle, and actions are the expression of the inner life. Such a difference of character and motive St Paul had always in mind. It is illustrated by the contrast which perhaps he meant to draw between the righteous man, who could not elicit the highest emotion, and the good man for whom another might be willing even to lay down his life. The righteous man may be essentially self-regarding while he respects the rights of others: the good man has no thought of self and so may draw out the love which answers to his own. So, too, St Paul's praise of love as the supreme Christian grace, in which he is at one with St John, has its source in belief in the Incarnation. "Though he was rich...he became poor." "He emptied himself."..."We love him because he first loved us."..."We know that we have passed from death unto life, because we love the brethren." These are phrases which express the essence of Christian ethics, both as to content and as to motive, in relation to the main idea of the Incarnation.

Historically, the principle that love is the constant activity and motive power of the highest form of existence is bound up with the doctrine, and it gives the ultimate criterion of ethics.

The question may be further tested by bringing it into relation to the conception of sin—the conception which separates ethical schools of thought more widely perhaps than any other. We need not dwell on the Christian conception of sin as a defect of will and a breach of the law of love, a defect and a breach for which the individual is responsible: an offence against a Person, a wound inflicted on a God of love. We need only ask whether they are the same ideas of sin that are suggested by the doctrine of the Incarnation, and by the theory that Jesus was merely the product of evolution.

If in the person of Jesus we have simply a man who has reached the highest stage of moral development; if He is merely the product of human development; then the moral ideals which He represents are merely the product of human development. They represent, to one who has reached this final stage of ethical development, the law of his being, and unswerving obedience to them is the condition of his life: if ever he falls below the standard which they set, he 'sins.' But of individuals, or races, who have not progressed so far, no such standard can be required. To the stage of ethical development which they have reached, quite other principles apply: different ethical standards set the law of their life, and only by them is their moral responsibility fixed. That is to say, what we commonly call 'sin' is grounded in the environment or the organism of human nature; it is a necessary stage in the evolution of the race, and as such it is in no sense 'wrong' in the earlier stages, though it may become wrong—as being an anachronism—in the later stages: what was at one time a natural instinct of self-preservation, and therefore necessary for the proper self-realization and development of individuals and of the race as a whole, may become in the course of growth detrimental to the development of higher qualities and faculties, and so may hinder the evolution of the highest form of human life. Much, it is clear, may be said for this conception of sin, as being in keeping with the main idea of natural evolution. There seems to me[1], however, to

---

[1] I only venture to say 'seems to me,' because the ethical implications of the theory of natural evolution have not yet been fully discussed in relation to Christian principles, and it is at present only possible to speak tentatively: and, though it seems to me that Darwinism when applied to ethics leads logically to Nietzsche's position, I am aware that there are some who think that the inferences that follow from the application of the Darwinian principles are not necessarily inconsistent with the ethical inferences from the doctrine of the Incarnation. I cannot offer any adequate discussion of the question, but in support of the position indicated in the above and following paragraphs I must add that it appears to me that distinctions in degrees of sinfulness, which are properly drawn from a Christian standpoint in regard to various states and stages of the moral development of individuals and races, are sometimes illegitimately

XIII] *Ethical significance of Christian doctrines* 559

be no doubt that it differs *toto caelo* from any estimate of sin which could be formed in the light of the doctrines of the Incarnation, the Atonement, the Cross.

Augustine tells us in his *Confessions* that he used in youth, long before his conversion, to pray for the gift of self-control; but, desiring still to enjoy pleasures that were incompatible

extended to cover distinctions of kind. For example, some distinction must doubtless be drawn between the infant's unchecked greed and temper and the adult's yielding to the allurements of the flesh, or between the 'action upon instinct' of primitive man and the vicious conduct of members of a civilized community. It is not reasonable to condemn defects of character in childhood as we condemn them in a full-grown man. When the conscience is really awake and mature, and the faculty of imagination has become one of the elements in our equipment of which we are fully aware, then beyond question such defects of character, and the acts or thoughts in which they find expression, must be distinguished from the child's or the savage's blind following of the promptings of his nature. But what is the nature of the distinction? To 'naturalistic' ethics it is absolute: there is a distinction of kind between the ethical character of the act or the thoughts of the savage or the child and the character of the same thoughts or act of the civilized man. The child or the savage is following the law of his physical growth and development, and therefore—if the word moral can be applied to him at all—he is obeying the moral law of his being and is doing 'right.' To Christian ethics the distinction is only one of degree:

it is a difference of more or less. The self-seeking of the child and the deliberate selfishness of the man are alike 'sinful.' All thoughts and acts must be referred to one absolute criterion. The moral failures of manhood are simply more sinful than the same moral failures of childhood. To fall below the absolute standard at any stage is 'sin': there is a fixed and permanent moral law. If it were not so, who could say when moral childhood ceased and moral manhood began? There would be no ethical answer to the man who dimly saw afar off a higher life to which he might some day attain, but felt that he had not yet reached the stage of ethical development to which its principles corresponded: those principles had not yet become the law of his being. If the illustration cited from Augustine's case seems to be rather an instance of one who sees and approves better things, but deliberately follows worse, it must be remembered that he felt that for him, as he then was, the life of continence was impossible: he was not yet morally capable of it.

The Christian ethicist, as I conceive him, sees sin universal in the world, but he does not say that it is not sin. In the recognition of it as sin, in every form and at every stage, there lies for him the only hope of the moral progress of individuals and the race.

with his prayer, he used to add "but not just yet." "Give me self-control, but not just yet." And again, when conscience seemed to call him to obey the truth, as he half-believed it to be, he used to answer, "Presently, O presently : let me be a little while." Such answers, it seems, might fairly be made by anyone who did not feel within himself constraint to follow the dictates of Christian ethics, if they represent only the law of life which applies to individuals who have already reached the highest stage of ethical progress, and if they are the mere product of the ethical evolution of the race, as they are on the theory before us. What the attitude is of one who has realized the conception of sin that corresponds to the doctrine of the Incarnation is shown by Augustine's condemnation of himself at a later time.

The conception of sin, then, that corresponds to the one interpretation of the Person of Jesus is different from that which corresponds to the other, and different systems of ethics are represented by the different theories of His Person.

The basis of ethics on the one assumption is found in the character and Being of God Himself and His relation to the human race—which is actually known to us by experience. On the other assumption there is no permanent basis; the standard is relative, always shifting, to be sought only in man himself.

From the point of view of evolutionist ethics the goal set before man is, of course, the realization of his true self ; but there is no canon to decide, among the conflicting tendencies of which he is conscious, which are evil and which are good. On the assumption of the Incarnation, however, we are in possession of an authoritative test of human life. The human life, which the Son of God lived, is the criterion by which all human lives must be judged. Not only is self-renunciation, in the form of active service, set before us as the character of the life of God, and the way to the realization of man's true self ; but, if the doctrine be accepted, the principles on which human life is to be moulded are expressed with an authority that leaves no room for questioning. There

XIII] *Ethical significance of Christian doctrines* 561

is, perhaps, a border land of uncertainty; there may be hesitation as to how the principles are to be applied to particular cases and circumstances as they arise: but about the principles themselves there can be no doubt. They are laid down absolutely in teaching and they are visibly carried out in life. And no distinction is made. There is not one principle for one class and another for another, or one for one time or stage of development and another for another.

All controversies as to egoism and altruism as ethical ends—as to the claims of self-realization and self-renunciation—are reconciled in the apparent paradox "He that will lose his life shall find it"—a paradox which was realized in the Person of Jesus. And the disciple of Jesus loses himself in Jesus. But in the process his sense of his own personality becomes the stronger. This is the note of true discipleship. St Paul's "no longer I, but Christ liveth in me" is the expression of the merging of one personality in another that results in the strengthening of the powers of the personality so merged, in the realization of the true self.

For others morality may be a matter of convention, deriving its principles and its sanctions from custom. Or it may be a matter of utility—the moral standards being fixed by careful consideration of what will promote the highest good of the individual or of the society of which he is a member. Or it may be a matter of knowledge—being therefore entirely relative to the intellectual capacity of the individual or the stage of experience which the society has reached. Others may follow this or that teacher and enrol themselves in various schools of ethics, or regard all moral principles as open questions, the answer to which is to be found by a nice calculation of *pro* and *contra*.

But one who accepts the doctrine of the Incarnation has an absolute ethical standard of reference. He knows that his moral ideas are spiritual in origin and belong to his very constitution: so they have an imperative validity and authority. He does not acquire them by any process of induction from experience, though it is by experience that they are called to consciousness. For him the distinction between right and wrong rests on an eternal foundation, and no compact of men among themselves can override the distinction : he does not depend on his own judgement or the judgement of any body of men as to what may be expedient and opportune. He knows that a man may be doing a thing that is wrong, even though he thinks it is right; and that the plea "they know not what they do" cannot win ethical justification. Though 'extenuating circumstances' may be allowed, and a sin of ignorance may be a lesser sin than a sin against light, yet it remains a sin ; and the person who commits it is responsible. "The servant who knew not his lord's will shall be beaten with few stripes"—is the expression of the absolute standard of ethics.

And just where this absolute standard would be felt with crushing weight, and might even paralyse all moral effort, the doctrine of the forgiveness of sins (one aspect of the doctrine of Atonement) comes in to remove the burden and give fresh stimulus to the will. "Forgetting the things which are behind, and stretching forward to the things which are before," with conscience at once freed from the past and quickened for the future, men are able through belief in this doctrine to make a new start on a higher plane of life. 'Forgiveness of sins' has indeed been styled 'Christ's greatest innovation in ethics,' and there can be no doubt about the ethical significance of a doctrine which is able to produce such practical results, and to effect such transformations of character as can be pointed to among the most certain facts of Christian experience—very miracles of the 'new birth.'

The doctrine that through Jesus, through His life and death, in union with Him, the alienation of man from God is done away, and access to God and communion with Him obtained—that is to say, the whole conception of Atonement and reconciliation—is essentially ethical. No other doctrine so vividly expresses at once the Christian idea of sin and the Christian motive of practical life. No conception exercises so powerful an ethical appeal as the conception that "for us men ...and for our salvation" He, by whom all things were created,

XIII] *Ethical significance of Christian doctrines* 563

came down from heaven, was incarnate, became man, suffered and died.

"...Love I gave thee, with Myself to love,
And thou must love Me, who have died for thee."

The doctrine of the Incarnation, then, gives validity to ethics. An ideal is set up and a criterion between right and wrong established. It makes an imperious demand on conscience. And it supplies an adequate motive. Man was made in the image of God : his destiny is to realize that image. The one Person in whom the realization was effected, is still a living force in the world, is still existent in the sphere of human consciousness; and in Him, by spiritual union with Him energized by love, it is possible for all men to realize their destiny.

Other doctrines in a sense subsidiary, though essentially correlated, to the main conception of the Incarnation, set forth one and the same theory of life.

The doctrine of the Trinity, for example, was arrived at primarily, no doubt, through the earthly experience of Jesus in His life as man—through His consciousness of union with the Father and of the working in Him of a spiritual force which was not dissociated from the Father and yet could be logically, in thought, distinguished from the Father. So His followers in turn became conscious of three ways in which they knew God. They were conscious of the working in them of a power to which they gave the name of Holy Spirit, as they were conscious of the influence on them of Jesus Himself, as Divine. And yet there was only one God—one Cause, one Principle, one Mind, one Will, one Life.

There were three ways in which God was known in human experience. Were there three ways in which He exists in Himself?

On the one side, popular Christian thought—the 'naïve Christianity' of the masses in all ages—might tend to an interpretation of these facts of experience that was tritheistic in effect. On the other side, it was argued that, as the

Godhead could not be conceived as other than one, it was only in relation to us that it was threefold : the trinitarian distinction was only to be admitted in respect of the working of God in the world, and had no existence in the real being of God Himself : it was only 'oeconomic,' a Trinity of revelation, the process by which He made Himself known to men.

But no theory of the Godhead which destroyed the unity of its Being, or which attributed a merely temporary and external existence to the three modes in which it was realized in human experience, seemed to the Church as a whole to satisfy the conditions of the problem before it. The experience and the teaching of Jesus, renewed in the consciousness of Christians generation after generation, required the recognition of a threefold activity—a threefold mode of existence—within the Godhead itself. Only if the one God existed eternally in three modes—in three relations or spheres of activity—only if the Being of God was trinitarian, could He be manifested in the three modes, Father, Son, and Holy Spirit.

This conception of a triune personality once formed, other lines of reasoning were called in to illustrate and support the conclusion. If man was made in the image of God, and this conception of God's being was true, there must be found in man too analogies that pointed to a Trinity. So, in accordance with the psychology of the times, analogies were found in such human triads as mind—knowledge—love, or memory—understanding—will. And above all note was taken of the fact that the fundamental conception of God as Love had a direct bearing on the question of His Being, and it was pointed out that this conception entailed the recognition of relations existing within the Godhead. The highest form of existence is conceived of as no dead abstraction but as in some sense 'social'—though words fail to express it : its character is not only the potentiality, but the living constant activity, of communion.

So from the doctrine of the Trinity follows, not only a particular conception of man's personality, but also the

XIII] *Ethical significance of Christian doctrines* 565

ethical principle that he cannot realize his true existence in isolation. He is a 'social' being, formed for communion. He does not exist as 'a distinct centre of being,' isolated and single by himself, but to the complex personality which is his must correspond a life of active relations to his fellows and to God.

The doctrine of the Church, as the organization through which the Christian theory of life is to be realized, and the Sacraments, as the material means by which the spiritual force of the living Jesus is conveyed to the members of His Church, and a real union with Him effected, stands for the same idea. All the disciples of Jesus are to be banded together in one Society, to support each other in the attempt to live the Christian life together, to carry out and realize the Christian ideal. The two great metaphors, or symbols, of the body and the members, and the Body and the Head, express the essential unity or solidarity of Christian life, of the members one with another, and of all together with Christ.

Only in social intercourse and in conscious relation to unseen spiritual forces can the highest human life be lived. The moral qualities which make for individual success and efficiency must give way, when necessary, to those which contribute to the well-being of the community. It is as a member of a community that man is called to live. He must recognize the worth of others. He will only reach a high development—only realize himself—through the development of the Society; but at the same time the individual is not lost in the Society: the well-being of the Society depends on each of its members realizing himself and consciously exercising his own peculiar functions.

No religion has emphasized so strongly the reality of evil in man and in the world, and at the same time so unmistakeably claimed man and the whole material universe for good. No religion has at once so exposed sin as a disease in human nature, and so hallowed earthly things and pointed to the beauties of nature and the possibility of joy in human life.

The most spiritual of other philosophies and religions, which have realized most vividly the sense of sin, have commonly found the origin of evil, the source of sin and suffering, in the material environment which is the setting of man's life, and have emphasized the antithesis between spirit and matter, and taught that the path to the realization of man's highest nature lay through emancipation from the body and all the material associations of his life on earth. The body and matter in all its forms were the root of evil and the sphere in which it worked; whether matter was regarded positively as an independent existence in itself, or simply negatively, as that which was farthest removed from real being. The ethical deduction from either conception was the same: the good cannot be attained except by withdrawal from active life, by crushing out the natural human feelings associated with the bodily nature of man, and fixing all attention on the free unfettered exercises of the intellectual or the spiritual faculties. 'Asceticism' thus becomes the principle of the highest life. The asceticism which from early times has found a home in the Catholic Church is, negatively at least, based on the same conception, and a divergence from Christian ideas; even if in its positive aspects, in some of the forms it has assumed, it may be justified as in ethical correspondence with Christian aims.

From the doctrine of the Incarnation and the Sacraments (the extension of the same conception)—from these doctrines and the belief in the life of the world to come and the resurrection of the body, the permanence, that is, of everything that is essential to the identity of the human person, an entirely different outlook upon life results. The dignity and worth of human nature and the whole universe are upheld. Every system of ethics is ruled out which is based on the disparagement of human nature, or on a dualistic opposition between the spiritual and the material, or on materialistic monism. The sacramental principle is the expression of the unity of life, in which things material are the instrument and the vehicle of things spiritual. Evil is not to be looked for in the bodily organism or in anything material. The body is the

XIII] *Ethical significance of Christian doctrines* 567

temple of the Holy Spirit, and "the earth is the Lord's and the fulness thereof." Evil is a disease of the will, immaterial, invisible, an intense reality in human experience, although it is no part of the eternal order.

The 'inwardness' which is always pointed to as essentially characteristic of Christian ethics is closely associated with this conception. All evil acts may be avoided, and yet the disposition—the character—may be evil. A man may abstain from all sins that find expression in any outward form, and yet be living a life of sin :—if his will be set towards sin, if his disposition be inclined to evil. So it is the direction of the will, of thought and desire, that is the object of Christian ethics. The avoidance of particular evil acts is only incidental. It is the formation of character that matters, and right action depends on right character. If the tree be good, its fruits will be good.

However narrow the conception of heathenism that prompted Augustine's famous description of the virtues of the heathen as only splendid sins, the saying—from his point of view—is in accordance with the doctrine that good works can only be done by one who is good. It is not the outward act, but the will and disposition and motive of the agent, that counts. An outward act, which would commonly be called a 'good' act, done from fear of punishment, or under some similar constraint of the reason or the will, and not really springing from the love of good in itself—the love of God—may have educational value and be of service in the gradual formation of habit and the building up of character ; but till the outward act is the free expression of the right disposition, it cannot be said to be really 'good.'

"For soul is form, and doth the body make."

These and other principles of ethics that have been reviewed may find parallels more or less close in the systems of non-Christian ethical thinkers and schools. That is not the question before us. The subject under investigation has only been the connexion between Christian doctrines and the ethical principles which are known to us as Christian. The examination of the relation between the two seems to suggest the inference, that no ethical principle can claim to be Christian which does not have its root in the doctrine of the Incarnation—a doctrine which gives at least a working theory of life, in the light of which human existence is transfigured.

A few lines, however, in conclusion, may be given to the question, whether, whatever the dependence of Christian ethics on Christian doctrines may have been in the past, it is not possible now for Christian ethics to be maintained without reference to the doctrine of the Incarnation : whether the elevation of the principles themselves is not sufficient to invest them with validity, and whether the beauty of the life of Jesus, regarded merely as a human example, does not make an appeal to the emotions strong enough to supply the requisite motive. For the philosopher there is the *testimonium animae naturaliter Christianae* : the ethical principles attest themselves and exercise an intrinsic cogency of their own. For the ordinary man and woman is not the *imitatio Christi* enough? Ordinary men and women can inspire friendship and love that knits to them others by the strongest of ties, and controls their thoughts and aims. Cannot a human Christ, unique among men, so capture men's hearts and master their wills that he can effect all that the theanthropic Christ of tradition could do?

No one who knows anything of the power of human love, the inspiring force of the great loyalties of life, could fail to have some lurking sympathy with those who would answer, 'Yes, the purely human Christ is enough : the Christ who was the child of Joseph and Mary, who never rose again except in the hearts of his disciples.'

It is, of course, impossible to set limits to the uplifting power of great ideas, which are in our experience as much realities as anything we know. It is impossible to deny that the example of a merely human Christ might arouse devotion

XIII] *Ethical significance of Christian doctrines* 569

enough to secure the triumph of the ethical principles which Jesus taught.

But that triumph is far enough off as it is, after centuries during which the appeal of the human Christ—the 'greatest friend of mankind'—has been reinforced by the claims of the Lord of Majesty, the suffering God, the Judge of all the world. Unique as was the impression He made on the Syrian peasants of old, on those who knew Him 'after the flesh,' the unique character of the impression which he has made on millions since has been at all events largely due to belief in the Incarnation, and incalculably fostered and sustained by the system of sacraments and worship which depend entirely on the doctrine.

Of Christian ethics divorced from the influence of Christian doctrine we have, as yet, had no experience. There have been no doubt conspicuous examples of noble lives, inspired by high ideals of thought and conduct, of men who rejected Christian doctrines and refused perhaps the very name of Christian; just as there have been great failures in life among those whose belief in Christian doctrine was apparently unimpeachable. But the men who furnish examples of 'Christian' ethics apart from Christian doctrine were themselves the product of a long line of predecessors whose Christian conduct was the outcome of Christian faith, who had grown up generation after generation under the influence—however imperfectly realized—of the doctrine of the Incarnation. Such men as these are what belief, not unbelief, has made them. Or, if it be doubted whether acquired characteristics and moral tendencies can have been transmitted to them, then we must at least take account of their social heredity :—the environment in which they are born, and in which they grow up, is one that has been and still is being profoundly influenced by Christian doctrine. Real isolation from Christian faith and Christian doctrine has been, and still is, simply impossible for any body of people in the Western world.

The moral philosophers who during the few last centuries sought an independent basis of ethics, and were divided among themselves by academic controversies as to the origin and the criterion of moral ideas, were agreed, as to the essential content of ethics, in upholding the traditional Christian morality[1]; and some of them at least maintained the traditional Christian beliefs. Until the days of Darwin it was generally believed that the world at large was governed by the same moral laws which were supposed to govern human society, that the general tendency of the cosmic process was in harmony with the accepted principles of the ethical progress of society. But Darwinism has put an end to this conception of the moral unity and order of the universe; and ethical evolution and natural evolution stand contrasted. The physiological criterion of progress is inconsistent with the moral standard: the prevalent humanitarian morality tends to counteract the effects of natural selection. Those who are faithful to the traditional moral conceptions speak of 'the harsh methods by which Nature has wrought out the variety and the perfection of organic life,' and look to humanity and civilization to mitigate their effect[2]. They declare that the ethical progress of society can only be achieved by actually combating the cosmic process[3]. On the other hand are those who, compelled to make their choice, declare themselves on the side of the cosmic process, and regard the ethical progress of the race as retarded by any action which is not in accordance with the laws that rule the evolution of Nature. Man is to be measured by the standard which applies to Nature. Morality, as commonly understood, is the 'negation' of life, the arch-enemy of the human race.

The evolutionist ethics of to-day, as represented by the teaching of Nietzsche, which is professedly anti-Christian in conception and frankly antagonistic to the received code of

---

[1] There are no doubt exceptions, at least in details. Thus, for example, Spinoza (in this respect anticipating Nietzsche) denied that pity (sympathy), humility, and repentance are virtues, as being pains and not arising from reason. But he recognized that, as men seldom live under the guidance of reason, humility and repentance bring more good than harm: which is to say that they *tend* to virtue. See *Ethics*, part iv. 50, 53, 54.

[2] A. J. Balfour, *Fragment on Progress*, p. 11.

[3] Huxley, Romanes Lecture on *Evolution and Ethics*, p. 33.

XIII] *Ethical significance of Christian doctrines* 571

morality, both in theory and in practice, proclaiming the need for a revision of the scale of moral values, are an actual instance of what may result in ethics from the abandonment of Christian doctrine[1].

But adequate evidence on which to form a judgement as to the possibility of Christian ethics maintaining their authority apart from Christian doctrine will be wanting till many a generation has passed away after all belief in the Incarnation has vanished from the world. It can, however, be said that, as there is no proof that the ethical principles have existed effectively in the past except in connexion with Christian doctrine, so there is little probability that they can ever exist in the future, for the mass of men at least, except in dependence on belief in a living Christ.

[1] Nietzsche himself ridicules those who imagine they have no more need of Christianity as a guarantee of morality, and give up Christian belief, while they cling more firmly than ever to Christian morality. See *e.g. The Twilight of the Idols*, Eng. Trans., vol. xi. p. 167.

ESSAY XIV.

THE CHRISTIAN IDEAL AND THE CHRISTIAN HOPE.

HENRY MONTAGU BUTLER, D.D.

ANALYSIS.

I. The "Christian Ideal and the Christian Hope" are considered mainly as to their *evidential* value. This in itself some lowering of their dignity. Then to whom is the evidence addressed? To Christians, not to unbelievers. The holy lives and faithful deaths of true Christians the great proof to Christians of the Christian Revelation and the Christian's Resurrection. Hebrews xi. quoted.

II. Christian lives examined; their wistful overpowering expectancy. Can it be an illusion? The spiritual growth from strength to strength. Dr Arnold's Sermon.

III. The *essence* of the Ideal and the Hope.

    A. A belief in the final victory of the Will of God.

    B. Attractive power of the Person of the Lord Jesus Christ, "Whom not having seen ye love."

    C. Adoration, the key-note of the Apocalypse.

    D. A belief in the supremacy of Love. This belief seems to be specially the conviction of our age. R. Browning, Tennyson, M. Arnold quoted.

IV. Responsibility of each Christian to increase, not to lessen, the evidence arising from the "Christian Ideal and the Christian Hope." "Earthy" lives, however estimable or attractive in many ways, tend to weaken such evidence. We can all be faith-makers and faith-refounders. J. G. Whittier quoted.

APPENDIX. Extracts from Sermons by Dr Whewell on his Wife's Death and Dr Arnold on "*The Moral Certainty of the true Christian's Resurrection.*"

THE CHRISTIAN IDEAL AND THE CHRISTIAN HOPE.

I.

THE subject which has been entrusted to me in this volume of Essays is, "The Christian Ideal and the Christian Hope"; and the aim of these Essays as a whole suggests at once and limits the special treatment of the subject. I wish to urge the evidential value of this Ideal and this Hope. They might of course be viewed and illustrated from many other sides. They have a history of their own, and biographies of their own, and poetry of their own, and, we might well add, picture-galleries of their own. It is not mainly in the arguments of books but in the beauty of lives that we find the Ideal and the Hope of those who have seriously and persistently taken the Lord Jesus Christ as their Master for life and death. If in this Essay, for which I am in many respects but ill fitted, I dwell chiefly on their evidential value, I shall not, I trust, be supposed to imply that I conceive this to be their only or their chief value. On the contrary, it is a relief to me to begin by confessing that in the very conception of 'evidential' purpose there is something lower than the highest.

In our highest and most truly inspired moods we put all thoughts of evidence out of sight. The mother with her babe in her arms does not reflect, though it is true, that her love is a proof of the love of the Creator. The soldier who rushes to the forlorn hope does not reflect, though it is most true, that his generous impulse is one more proof of the power of race, of patriotism, and of discipline. And, once more, when a Christian man or woman kneels beside some dying bed, or at some great Easter Communion, either in a grand cathedral or in a humble chapel, at the sacred moment of "the breaking of the bread," he does not reflect, though it is again sublimely true, that the joy, the human sympathy, the sense of Divine fellowship, with which his whole being is then penetrated, is a proof of the Presence of his Saviour, a proof of the fulfilment of the promise, "Where two or three are gathered together in My Name, there am I in the midst of them."

No, in our most exalted and our happiest moments we do not, we cannot, think of our exaltation and our happiness as proofs of anything. We have not the time, the mental or spiritual leisure, to make such reflexions. These things, these blessings, are themselves. In themselves is their value. They fill us, they pervade us, nay, they enrapture us, but they do not then prove anything. And so when we come to speak of the Christian Ideal and the Christian Hope as evidence either of the truth of the Christian Revelation as a whole, or of the life beyond the grave, we may admit that the task causes us something of a wrench. The theme, we feel, is less fitted for argument than for prayer, for poetry, for devout hymns. The Christian Ideal and the Christian Hope, so we say, are beautiful, august *facts*. They are there. They speak for themselves. They have the grandeur attaching to ancient monuments. Can we in any way add to their impressiveness, may we not seriously fear that we may detract from it, if we bring them to the bar of some human tribunal, and call upon them to give evidence of something beyond themselves?

The Christian Ideal and Christian Hope

That, I must confess, was my own instinctive feeling when it was first suggested to me that I should contribute to this volume a paper on the solemn words, "The Christian Ideal and the Christian Hope." And the feeling has hardly been lessened while I have attempted to fulfil my task. Again and again I have been haunted and almost checked by the misgiving, What you are saying is true. But in presenting the truth as a truth, are you not imperilling its beauty? Are you not making it less loveable even while you are insisting on its claims to be loved?

And another thought, akin to this instinctive misgiving, has throughout been close to my mind, 'For *whom* is the evidence in question intended? Is it for Christians, or for those who do not call themselves Christians? If for Christians, is it for them in those moments when intellect is for the time uppermost, or when the longing of the heart after its God prevails? Is it meant to put links into a chain of logic, or to put warmth into an appeal? Is it meant to convince, or, rather, to rouse and stir, and, if God will, uplift?'

Such questions either imply or create their own answer. Whatever the argument might be made in other hands, in the hands of some skilled theologian and "Christian Advocate," in my hands it is really no argument at all. I know that I have nothing to say which could either satisfy, or seriously move, any man who does not acknowledge God as his Father and Jesus Christ as his Redeemer. I know also that even to a Christian, and even a devout Christian, what I have to say may be little more than a pious truism, except in certain moments of his life when he looks less for a "sign" than for a renewed confirmation of his faith.

For myself, I have long felt that, next to the careful study of the words of the Scriptures and the words of Christ Himself, there was no proof of the Christian Revelation or of the Christian's resurrection to compare with that afforded by the holy lives and faithful deaths of true Christians.

The words of the Epistle to the Hebrews, impotent, if you like, as argument to an Atheist or an Agnostic, are to a Christian the one consoling evidence in a world full of mournful contradictions: "These all died in faith, not having received the promises, but having seen them and greeted them from afar, and having confessed that they were strangers and pilgrims on the earth. For they that say such things make it manifest that they are seeking after a country of their own. And if indeed they had been mindful of that country from which they went out, they would have had opportunity to return. But now they desire a better country, that is, a heavenly: wherefore God is not ashamed of them, to be called their God; for He hath prepared for them a city[1]."

These noble words, written of course respecting those who lived and died before Jesus Christ came in the flesh, seem to be the salt of all later and all present history, and to stand in the forefront of all Christian apologetics.

There are the men and the women who have cherished the Christian Ideal and clung to the Christian Hope. And more than this, they have represented, they have almost *been*, these two heavenly Powers. Since that portrait of the Children of Faith, seeing and greeting the promises from afar, was painted by that nameless Benefactor of mankind, it has been the "great sight" of history to gaze on the progressive making, the divinely ordered evolution, of pure and lofty Christian lives, lives of which "the world was not worthy." They are, if you will, the exceptions, nay, a mere handful out of the mass, whether you look for them in "kings' houses," or in the houses of the rich and the highly educated, or among the ordained pastors of Christ's Church, or, again, in "the streets and lanes of the city." A mere handful, I say, such lofty lives are, if compared with the great mass. Let the enemy make the most of it. Still *there* they stand; their "foundation is on the holy hills"; they ask to be interpreted; they invite criticism. If they are forced to bear witness and to explain themselves, we know beforehand what not one here and there, but what all will say: "Not unto us, not unto us, but unto Thy Name give the praise."

[1] Heb. xi. 13—16.

XIV] *The Christian Ideal and Christian Hope* 579

II.

Let us, then, look a little closely into such lives. We are struck at once, we are arrested, by their vast *variety*, and yet by their extraordinary resemblance. You may take your stand anywhere in the long course of Christian history. If you are a student of the Catacombs; if you are drawn to the times and the writings of great thinkers and great men like Origen, or Athanasius, or the first Augustine; if you have felt the charm of all that is purest and least worldly in what are called the Middle Ages, or, by a pardonable but grave exaggeration, the "Ages of Faith"; if, again, you are more at home in the age of Luther and Cranmer and Ignatius and Xavier and Calvin, and have tried to track the footsteps of the one Divine Spirit in intellects so various and tempers so antagonistic; or, if you have come nearer to our own times, and striven earnestly to see the marks of the Lord Jesus in such men as the two Wesleys, and William Wilberforce, and Chalmers, and Arnold, and Newman, and Keble, and Maurice, and Selwyn, and Thomas Erskine, and Stanley, and Westcott, and Dale, and Lightfoot, and Church, and Liddon, and Benson, and many a hard worker and dear friend who has truly fallen asleep in Jesus under our own eyes, and amid the criticisms—often how shallow!—of men whom we have seen and known; then you will have had the means of judging what that "power from on high" has been which has fashioned spirits so differently tempered and yet given them a unity both of present faith and of soaring hope.

Can you explain lives of that type, with their wistful, overpowering expectancy, except on one of two suppositions? The one is that they are *right*; that this confident on-looking and up-looking comes from God, and is stamped with the authentic seal of God's own truth. The other supposition is that they are *dupes*; that, from first to last, they have been dupes; that every "venture of faith," every sacrifice made for God in Christ, every *Imitation* of the mind of Christ, every straining forth to the unseen, every effort to join hands with

37—2

those who have reached what seemed the better country, "that is, a heavenly," has been one long and pitiful delusion. They have been throughout duped, duped either by some Person or by some indefinable force. If it be a Person, who can it be—"I speak as a man"—but He Who made them what they are? If it be an impersonal force, to which they owe their power of so hoping and so aspiring, nay, not the power only but the necessity, can there be, we ask, such cruelty, such mockery, in the universe? Can what we call Nature be stained by such a crime?

We will press the question further. We will not stay to defend ourselves against the charge of putting rhetoric in the place of argument. In such controversies as this rhetoric *is* argument. It is the voice of the heart, and it is to the heart that the appeal lies, the unbribed heart of mankind. But whether it be rhetoric or not, we press our plea. We point to a human life which is truly moving forwards. And, observe, we take this life not as a whole, not as a finished product. It is not from there that we make our start. No, we will take the same life higher up the stream, nearer its source, while it is still in the making, while its course is not yet free and buoyant, still less triumphant. And we still watch this life, so far as human eye can watch it. It may be the life of a great man, in some high place, in Church or in State; or it may be the life of some dear member of a private family, perhaps of our own. We watch this life with reverence and awe. We see that, like the universe itself, in spite of seeming to be at rest, it "still moves." It is making way. It is casting aside, one by one, "every weight." The temper is becoming sweeter, self is more and more put aside. The ideal of duty, always high, is ever rising. Great public causes, hitherto unknown or unmarked, become part of its daily interest, daily enquiry, and, as we can more than guess, daily prayer. The Bible becomes dearer. The examples of holy men and women, whether in the past or the present, become nearer and more rich in instruction. Illness and pain are patiently and even thankfully borne. "I certainly don't regret my illness," says one such sufferer; "besides showing me the marvellous

XIV] *The Christian Ideal and Christian Hope* 581

kindness of friends, it has, I hope, taught me much." Bereavement, again, is accepted not as a long farewell, but, to borrow a noble phrase of Robert Hall, as an "enlargement of our intercourse with heaven." And at last, as the earthly end of this life draws nigh, we more and more reverently watch it—not to criticise or to analyse but to revere, and, by God's help, to learn from it, and to gather from its unconscious teaching some memories that may last. And among these memories, never to fade from the heart and never to be quite forgotten or explained away by the intellect, is the sight of that "peace which passeth all understanding," that peace of one who has fought the good fight by a strength avowedly not his own, and, while enjoying earth to the full, declares plainly that he seeks a country, that father-land in which he was born and to which the loving Father now recalls him.

Again, I ask my Christian brothers and sisters, Can this assured peace, this onward look of certain expectancy, be all an illusion, a mockery? Can any Christian—I do not say any just man, or any clear-headed man, or any learned man, for I know that neither justice, nor clear-headedness, nor learning has any telescope for the inner courts of that City which God has prepared for His own—but I ask, can any *Christian* doubt that this constant growth in what we must needs call "holiness," and this intense looking forward to the nearer Presence of God in Christ and of His servants who have fallen asleep in Jesus, *must* be justified by solid fact, *cannot* be an idle hope, an empty dream?

More than fifty years ago it was my good fortune to read the sermon of Dr Arnold—I know not whether it is still in repute or whether it has passed out of common memory—on what he calls the "Moral Certainty of the true Christian's Resurrection." Not, observe, the absolute certainty of a general Resurrection, or of a Life beyond the grave for all alike—*that* great theme he does not there discuss—but the *moral* certainty, the certainty on moral grounds, that no true Christian can be left deserted by his Maker and his Saviour and be disappointed of the hope which has been his anchor through all "the waves of this troublesome world."

Arnold does not hesitate to make some grave admissions. He admits that it is not all lives, nor all lives for which the world is grateful, which can be appealed to as evidence for man's immortality. To the human eye, and almost to the human conscience, there are many lives which seem bounded by earth, limited to earth, and might be thought, without a shock to our moral judgement, to end with earth. Earth has given them, or denied them, their heart's desire, and that desire has never risen above the enjoyments, the comforts, the successes, the public services of earth.

But granted all this, what a different vision opens on our heart and conscience when we turn to the truly *Christian* life! There, as we have seen, earth has *not* been the all in all. Earth has less and less, as life went on, been its centre, its interpreter, its master, its satisfier. "I am a stranger upon earth; I am a stranger and pilgrim upon earth," has been the unspoken but the genuine utterance of each Christian soul. "I have a desire to depart, and to be with Christ, which is far better," has become at last its truest language, even amid all that makes earthly life lovely, delightful, or even sacred. And what we contend is that the sound of this heart-language, the sight of this eager expectancy, the receiving, as it were, of this legacy from the faith of those whom we have known and loved on earth, is to a Christian a *moral* proof that they have not been the dupes of their dearest hopes, or lost for ever the one joy for which they cared, and prayed, and strove, and suffered. It will be, I say, a *moral* proof to the *Christian*. Without believing this, he cannot retain his full belief in the love and the power of God and Christ. God is not the God into Whose Name he was baptized, Christ is not the Son of God Who rose victoriously from His grave at Jerusalem, if His servants who have so trusted, so believed, so striven to catch His likeness and to follow in His steps, have been all along mocked by a pitiless hope, which, as they would one and all have asserted, alone gave them this transforming power.

XIV] *The Christian Ideal and Christian Hope* 583

III.

And this argument will, it seems to me, be much strengthened if we examine more minutely in what the *essence* of "the Christian Ideal and the Christian Hope" may be said to consist. I say the *essence* of it, for, as we have seen, its *varieties* are clearly infinite. Not only does it vary in some important details at various periods in the growth of the Christian Society, but "at all times and in all places" it varies with different persons.

It is one for the man, another for the woman, another for the child. It is one for the man of action, another for the recluse, another for the poet or the philosophic student. It is one for the Eastern mind, another for the Western, another for the Northern. Is there, so to speak, any "common measure" between the barbarian just reclaimed from his tree-worship or amulet-worship or image-worship, and the man before whose mind, as, for instance, with a Max Müller, all the volumes of all Religions are unrolled and decyphered?

I believe that there is, but I am not equally clear that it can always be discerned. There may be too little evidence to catch the eye even of the most sympathetic explorer. And, generally speaking, as we search biographies, or personally observe Christian characters, we shall be more struck with their differences than their resemblances. The thought will come over us again and again, "One star differeth from another star in glory," rather than the thought that each star shines by a light not really its own, but given to it by the common Creator of all, as an efflux and a part of Himself.

If, however, we make it our aim to fasten on what is common to all Christians, on what I have called the *essence* of "the Christian Ideal and the Christian Hope," may it not find some utterance in such words as the following?

A. Every true servant of Christ looks forward, strains forward, to the final victory of good over evil, of truth over falsehood, of right over wrong. He keeps before his mind the Will of God as the final goal and arbiter of all human action and all human events. This Will must be supreme, and must prove its supremacy, even against all appearances. The obstacles may be of every kind, at every stage of man's development, and the power of each may *seem* to fall little short of omnipotence. But the Christian Ideal and the Christian Hope decide that it is *not* omnipotence; that omnipotence is to be found only in one Being, and that Being is God. The supremacy of the Divine Will, its unchangeableness, its gradual revealing of itself, its final victory—the faith in this appears to me the common heritage of all Christians. I could scarcely call by the name of Christian any man or woman to whom God had not granted this sure and certain hope.

B. Again, it seems to me that the *essence* of what we are now speaking consists in part, and in no small part, in an intense clinging to the Person of the Lord Jesus Christ. I do not know of any period in the last nineteen hundred years, or, again, of any country in the world where the Faith of Christ has made any lodgement, in which the great saying has not been found true, "I will draw all men unto Me." The "drawing" force, the wonderful "attraction," has lain largely of course in the teaching of Christ's messengers; largely in the system, if such a word is accurate, of the morals and duties inculcated; largely in the examples of the best men and women who called themselves Christians, and became, whether they knew it and meant it or not, representatives to others of the Faith of Christ. But, allowing for all this, the attraction, the "drawing power," as I have called it, has at all times lain far more in the Person of Jesus Christ, "Whom not having seen, ye love; on Whom, though now ye see Him not, yet believing, ye rejoice greatly with joy unspeakable and full of glory; receiving the end of your faith, even the salvation of your souls[1]."

[1] 1 Pet. i. 8, 9.

xiv] *The Christian Ideal and Christian Hope* 585

These words, familiar as they are, seem to me as marvellous, and, I will add, as prophetic, as they are confessedly beautiful. They fill me with wonder. I seem to see them reproduced not only in every period in Church history, but in every Christian nursery, every Christian school, every Christian village at home or abroad, every Christian ordinance. It is not in great Saints and Martyrs only, whether of the past or of the present, that you see this strange "attraction"—this fresh repetition, this constantly renewed birth, of the great saying, ὃν οὐκ ἰδόντες ἀγαπᾶτε, "Whom not having seen, ye love." You see it in the poorest cottage. You see it in the face and in the heart of the little child as she repeats the Hymn of Bernard of Clairvaux,

> Jesu, the very thought of Thee
> With sweetness fills the breast:
> But sweeter far Thy Face to see,
> And in Thy Presence rest.

You see it in the face of the manly schoolboy when, at Confirmation, or long before, the Person of the Christ, his own Saviour and Captain, first takes possession of his soul's affections.

Nor has there ever been a Missionary in any age or in any country who will not tell you, with a sincerity that admits of neither cavil nor refutation, that the Person of Jesus Christ takes captive one soul after another, with no distinction of rank, or race, or sex. It is not the evidences for the truth of the Sacred Books, it is not the wisdom or the poetry or the literary beauty of the words in those Books— it is not these, save in a very inferior degree, which draw the heart and overcome the prejudice or the indifference of man, or woman, or child. It is the Person—the Life, Past and Present and to come—of one Character in all history, the Lord Jesus Christ, the Jesus of Bethlehem, of Nazareth, of Capernaum, of Nain, of Caesarea Philippi, of Tyre and Sidon, of Bethany, of Jerusalem, of Gethsemane, of Calvary, of the Upper Chamber, of Emmaus, of the early morning by the Lake of Galilee, of the holy Mount of the Ascension—it is this Person, even more than His sacred teaching, Who has been the Ideal and the Hope "of every contrite" heart; this Person, "Whom not having seen," the poorest, the meanest, the guiltiest amongst us cannot choose but "love."

If I may borrow an impressive sentence from my old Trinity friend, Bishop Lightfoot, I would say: "Though the Gospel is capable of doctrinal exposition, though it is eminently fertile in moral results, yet its substance is neither a dogmatic system nor an ethical code, but a Person and a Life."

It is, therefore, no untruth, nor yet only a half truth, to say, If you wish to know what is the *essence* of "the Christian Ideal and the Christian Hope," Christ is that *essence*. Christ is Himself the Christian "Ideal." Christ is Himself the Christian "Hope."

And this language is not mystical only, it is in a high degree practical and fruitful. It may thrill hearts. It may stir and convince intellects. But, still more, it moulds and transforms lives. St John had before him but a small part of the history of his Master's Church when he wrote those words of confident and unerring insight[1]: "Beloved, now are we children of God, and it is not yet made manifest what we shall be. We know that, if He shall be manifested, we shall be like Him; for we shall see Him even as He is. *And every one that hath this hope set on Him purifieth himself, even as He is pure.*"

That is the effect, the natural, the proper effect of this hope, this "Christian Hope and Ideal." It was so in St John's day, before the Church of Christ had seen its hundredth birth-year. It has been so ever since, and is so to-day. That "Hope," that "Ideal," has been the one "salt" of the earth, the one purifying influence against "the corruption that is in the world by lust."

C. It is hardly a transition, it is but another step in the same Christward direction, to push our question a little further. We asked just now, "What is the *essence* of 'the Christian Ideal and the Christian Hope'?" Let us go on to ask, "What longing is there, what vision, which is common to every one who calls himself, or is called by others, a Christian?"

[1] 1 John iii. 2, 3.

The Christian Ideal and Christian Hope

As some answer to the first question, we have instanced, first, a settled assurance that the Will of God is supreme, and *must* in the end prevail; and secondly, a very lively sense, penetrating a man's whole being, of the attractive power of that gracious King and Saviour, "Whom not having seen, we" nevertheless "love."

And now may we not add to this lively sense, as a part of it, and an essential part of it, that *adoration*, that joyous pride of prostrate worship, which may be almost called the key-note of the Apocalypse? The whole universe, animate and inanimate, human and non-human, prostrate at the feet of Him through Whom all things were made, even of the Lamb Who, by His Blood, bought back, in some mysterious way, to His Father all that had been forfeited, all that had wandered from the fold—this is the majestic picture, this is the spectacle through the "open door in heaven," which presented itself to the eagle eye and the burning heart of the Seer in Patmos.

And is it not, in other words if you will, and other symbols if you will, the same great Vision that haunts and soothes and humbles and uplifts the minds and the hearts of all true Christians now? Christ the Conqueror, Christ the Opener of the Sealed Book, Christ the Solver of spiritual perplexities, Christ the Satisfier of spiritual cravings, Christ the Healer of all sores, personal, social, political, ecclesiastical, international—is not this the "Ideal," the longing, the far off but steadfastly cherished "Hope," of every true believer in Christ? Just so far as he enters into the Will and the eternal mind and purpose of his God, just so far as he sees in the Incarnate Word of the Father the final conquest over Death and Sin and men's hatred for each other, and over every form of lust and cruelty and wrong, just so far his heart and "all that is within" him will claim a part, a fresh and personal part, in that "new song" which must ever typify the highest adoration of which the spirit of man is capable: "Worthy art Thou to take the book, and to open the seals thereof: for Thou wast slain, and didst purchase unto God with Thy Blood men of every tribe, and tongue, and people, and nation, and madest them to be unto our God a kingdom and priests; and they reign upon the earth. And I saw, and I heard a voice of many angels round about the throne and the living creatures and the elders; and the number of them was ten thousand times ten thousand, and thousands of thousands; saying with a great voice, Worthy is the Lamb that hath been slain to receive the power, and riches, and wisdom, and might, and honour, and glory, and blessing. And every created thing which is in the heaven, and on the earth, and under the earth, and on the sea, and all things that are in them, heard I saying, Unto Him that sitteth on the throne, and unto the Lamb, be the blessing, and the honour, and the glory, and the dominion, for ever and ever. And the four living creatures said, Amen. And the elders fell down and worshipped[1]."

It might be too much to say that no one whose heart does not join in this Hymn of exalted adoration can claim "the Christian Ideal and the Christian Hope." We must allow for faint hearts and feeble minds, for doubts never cleared on earth, for wounds never quite healed, for tears that blind at times, and for long times together, the eyes even of the humblest faith. Still we claim that it is in this thirst for adoration, and in the certainty that it is one of the "things which must be hereafter" and one of the things which can "never be shaken," that the *essence* of both "the Christian Ideal and the Christian Hope" has been proved to consist. It has been proved age after age, and year after year. It is the transmitted heirloom of the whole Christian Society. It is the private treasure of each Christian soul. It is at once an age-long tradition and a daily power. It has always been, and we cannot conceive a day or an epoch when it shall cease to be.

And as to its evidential value, I do not say for "those that are without," but for Christians, who shall measure it? Is it not the sight of this, and the knowledge that it is always there, that in the hearts of thousands sustains and keeps alive faith in the unseen? We may, if we wish, live away

[1] Rev. v. 9—14.

XIV] *The Christian Ideal and Christian Hope* 589

from it. We may live out of it. We may exile ourselves from the "green pastures" of temperate social worship. We may fix our habitation, the habitation of both soul and intellect, in the frigid zone in which no faith can bloom, and we may there forget that we ever heard the great song of adoration, and that our own voices, now well-nigh frozen between our lips, were once contributors to its warmth and its joy. But our coldness can but slightly check the current of the adoration of others. We cannot freeze it at its source. We cannot, by our own isolated or even banded and confederate unbelief, snatch from others their undoubted or undoubting faith. *Securus iudicat orbis terrarum.* The perennial adoration of true Christians attests at once and ensures its perennially new creation.

D. There is yet another attitude of the Christian spirit which I dare to call part of the *essence* of its "Ideal" and its "Hope," I mean its constant tendency to own and to further the supremacy of *love.* This is a cold way of putting it, and we may well apologise for so putting it, but no one has ever questioned the evidential value of the Thirteenth Chapter of the First Epistle to the Corinthians, or of the almost contemporary utterance[1], "Love worketh no ill to his neighbour: love therefore is the fulfilment of the law"; or, again, of those later utterances which seem to be the native language of St John, and to bear witness to the very atmosphere which he habitually breathed[2]: "This is the message which ye heard from the beginning, that we should love one another...Beloved, let us love one another; for love is of God, and every one that loveth is begotten of God, and knoweth God...God is love; and he that abideth in love abideth in God, and God abideth in him."

Who can doubt that passages like these have created faith, have made Christians? They have been evidences to Christians of what the Faith of Christ is worth. They have made Christians nobly proud of their Faith. Every life that Christian men and women have observed and revered, whether in their own family, or among their friends, or in

---

[1] Rom. xiii. 10.   [2] 1 John iii. 11, iv. 7, 16.

biographies of the past or the present, every life, I say, that has breathed this spirit has been for them the confirmation of their Faith. It has made them sure that these lives are the true lives, the lives that God willed that men and nations should strive after, the lives that *must* some day, at what an Apostle calls[1] "the revealing of the sons of God," be acknowledged as the lives, whether few or many, which have not missed their goal.

And what St Paul and St John have done for all time by bearing witness to the supremacy of love as the one trustworthy bond, the one "building" force, of all human society, is what each Christian can do in a feebler way as he discharges his daily duties, bears his daily burthens, teaches, if he be a teacher, his daily lessons, conducts, if need be, his daily controversies. Every time that love appears as the chief object aimed at and the chief agent at work in any of these human operations, fresh evidence is laid before Christians that their Lord and Master spoke not vaguely but prophetically when He said, "By this shall all men know that ye are My disciples, if ye have love one to another."

And here I put a grave question both to myself and to any serious reader of these pages. Can we be mistaken if we believe that our own age, with all its materialism, and all its self-will, and all its levity, and all its scepticism, both profound and shallow, and all its downright disbelief in a special Christian revelation, has yet begun to grasp this great truth almost more than any ages which have gone before? No age, it seems to me, has ever so sickened at the *odium theologicum*; no age has been so weary of the ignoble Parliamentary wrangle, with its habitual imputation of low motives and incredible folly; no age has so honestly begun to discern that it is love alone which can speak the last, and perhaps also the first, word in the struggle between poverty and wealth, class and class, Church and Church, Nation and Nation. In no age before ours could the great singers and thinkers of mankind have left us such legacies as some of

[1] Rom. viii. 19.

those left by Browning and Tennyson and Matthew Arnold. For example:

> Our life, with all it yields of joy or woe,
> And hope and fear—believe the aged friend—
> Is just our chance o' the prize of learning love,
> How love might be, hath been indeed, and is;
> And that we hold henceforth to the uttermost
> Such prize, despite the envy of the world.
> *A Death in the Desert.*

Or, again, that noble haven of peace in *In Memoriam* after the passing storms of doubt:

> Love is and was my Lord and King,
> And in His presence I attend
> To hear the tidings of my friend,
> Which every hour His couriers bring.
>
> Love is and was my King and Lord,
> And will be, though as yet I keep
> Within His court on earth, and sleep
> Encompass'd by His faithful guard,
>
> And hear at times a sentinel
> Who moves about from place to place,
> And whispers to the worlds of space,
> In the deep night, that all is well.

Or, once more, those pathetic lines of the young Matthew Arnold, published more than fifty years ago, and as characteristic, I venture to think, as anything he ever wrote in the heyday of his fame:

> I too have long'd for trenchant force,
> And will like a dividing spear;
> Have prais'd the keen, unscrupulous course,
> Which knows no doubt, which feels no fear.
> But in the world I learnt, what there
> Thou too wilt surely one day prove,
> That will, that energy, though rare,
> Are yet far, far less rare than love.
> *Switzerland. A Farewell.*

Passages of this kind might easily be multiplied. The question is whether they are not characteristically modern. To my mind they reveal something of a new and a transforming spirit, the product in part, and the fulfilment in part, of "the Christian Ideal and the Christian Hope."

IV.

An Essay is not a sermon. It has no call to exhort or even to teach, but only to submit thoughts, and try to reveal to themselves and to each other those thinkers who share them. But it is hard to write on this subject without a wish to say something, if only to oneself or to one's friends, which may seem fitter for the pulpit than for the study.

If "the Christian Ideal and the Christian Hope," seen and read of all men in countless holy lives, have, for Christians at least, this strange evidential power; if other proofs of a teleological kind, and even proofs drawn from conscience, fail to impress on the general intellect of mankind a conviction that this earthly life of man is only the promise, and, as it were, the portal of a vaster life which begins, and cannot begin sooner, when earthly life has ended; "what manner of persons" ought we Christians to be when we can so live, and are in fact so daily living, as either to add, or not to add, to the proof of man's immortality, or, still worse, to disparage that proof and tend to make it incredible?

For it is no exaggeration to say that an apparently happy and successful life, into which the thought of God hardly appears to have entered, is to many a distinct difficulty in the way of the Christian Hope. They feel as the Psalmist felt when he said, in the perplexity of his soul[1], "I do see the ungodly in such prosperity; for they are in no peril of death, but are lusty and strong...Yea, and I had almost said even as they; but lo, then I should have condemned the generation of thy children." Such were the misgivings of the Hebrew poet, until he "went into the sanctuary of God," and there saw something of the temptations, the slips, the falls, and the earthly end of such men—yes, even the "fearful end."

[1] Ps. lxxiii. 3, 4, 14, 16.

XIV] *The Christian Ideal and Christian Hope* 593

With us, in our day, the perplexity is cognate, but by no means the same. We are not thinking of those whom we can bring ourselves to call "ungodly." That sombre word of the Old Testament means more than we mean, and much more than we wish to impute to either friend or foe. What we see, or think we see, is something of this kind. We see a man, in public or private life, going on, as it were, without God, and going on prosperously, if not gaily. He is upright, cheerful, good-natured, kind, staunch, courageous, and in manners delightful. And yet there is an earthiness about it all. The last day and the last hour of that life will come. There will be many regrets, many warm and genuine tears, many respectful and a few loving records, or, as we are coming to call them, "appreciations," of his career.

But there will be also a significant silence, not among enemies and critics but among those who loved the man best. Nothing will be said of him or implied which does not end with earth. You can explain him without bringing in a life beyond. *Here*, not *Hereafter*, is the thought, if not the word, engraven on his tomb. He has not added to the proofs which faith desires. You do not feel that a fresher and a more cogent force is added to the great words of old, "So that a man shall say, Verily there is a reward for the righteous; doubtless there is a God that judgeth the earth[1]."

And so again we come back to our solemn question, which we would leave, if we could, with all readers of this paper, whatever their age, their learning, their familiarity with moral and spiritual speculations, their contentment with earth, their disappointment with earth, their belief, or half belief, or disbelief in the Lord Jesus Christ. Our question is, "What manner of persons ought we to be in all holy living and godliness, looking for and earnestly desiring the coming of the day of God?[2]"

[1] Ps. lviii. 10.   [2] 2 Pet. iii. 11.

We can, if we will, be faith-makers in this great mystery. All men who have lived and died in faith have made it easier and more natural for others to live and die in the same. The Epistle to the Hebrews, with its bead-roll of the heroes of Faith is, as it were, being ever rewritten before our eyes. It has no last page. Almost as I write, I read in an unpublished work a tribute paid to a young and holy man whom Cambridge still freshly mourns: "A life like your brother's forms, I sometimes think, one of the strongest pledges of human immortality.... Such fitness for influence as he possessed is not acquired in a day, and just when its worth was being proved he was taken from us. Surely these gifts and graces are not now as if they had never been, or as if, once granted, they had been idly wasted! Can that earnest, patient cultivation really have been gratuitous, and the unselfish instinct that inspired it mistaken? Were it so, the whole universe seems out of joint. The more I consider such lives as that of your brother—lives, I mean, which, bearing promise of so rich a harvest, are yet cut off before the full harvest can possibly have been realised—the more my conviction grows that the passing of such men as he is not death but only the birth which we call death[1]."

Yes, as we said before, we can, if we will, be faith-makers and faith-refounders in this great mystery of life and death. We can also be faith-impairers and faith-destroyers, and all this not by argument, or by direct effort, but by sheer living— so living, on the one hand, that all who watch us, our aims, our omissions, our words, our silences, our simple standing aloof from works of mercy and ventures of faith, may see no reason to credit us hereafter with energies or emotions which earth has already exhausted; so living, on the other hand, that, in the hearts of all who see us—friends, children, servants, comrades, workmen employed by us, soldiers and sailors commanded by us, parishioners who come to our churches, scholars who come to our schools, young clergymen who come to our Ordinations—the hope of immortality, the belief

---

[1] *Letters of Forbes Robinson*, p. 182.

in immortality, the conviction of its supreme and incomparable importance and sacredness, may be year by year immeasurably increased.

Apart from the love and the call of Jesus Christ, I know of no more potent incentive to a holy life than this thought which is also a fact. We *can* so live as to help others to see not only no terror in death, but no darkness in the grave, no silence, no severance. Without a word, spoken or written, we can "comfort one another" in the chill hour of failure, in the wreck of cherished plans, in the agony of sudden bereavement. It is a wonderful triumph of what is open to all.

> The dear Lord's best interpreters
> Are humble human souls;
> The Gospel of a life like theirs
> Is more than books or scrolls.
> From scheme and creed the light goes out,
> The saintly fact survives:
> The blessed Master none can doubt
> Revealed in holy lives.
>
> J. G. WHITTIER, *The Friend's Burial.*

APPENDIX.

Any readers of my Essay will, I think, be glad to see two extracts from the writings of two great men, Dr Whewell and Dr Arnold.

The first is taken from a very touching Sermon preached in Trinity Chapel, February 3rd, 1856, after the death of Mrs Whewell; the second is taken from Dr Arnold's *Sermons*, Vol. III. Sermon xiii, p. 148.

A.

"Ought we not to act with the large views, the lofty purposes, the deep self-consciousness of immortal beings, if we *are* immortal beings?

"To think too much about Heaven is not a fault likely to be generally dangerous.

"Far different from this is the course, in this life, of the soul that aspires to the life eternal. Such a soul constantly desires, and by the grace of God, by supplication and prayer, by watchfulness and care, succeeds constantly more and more, in ejecting from its spiritual being all uncleanness, malice, wrath, pride, vanity, self-seeking, carelessness of others. It puts on more and more the raiment, or rather it is more and more pervaded by the spirit, of purity, meekness, charity, thoughtful kindness, self-denial, love of all, care for all, resignation, cheerfulness, heavenly hope, and heavenly trust. Those who seek Heaven, cherish such tempers as these. And if we see persons cherishing such tempers as these, and growing in them more and more, we cannot doubt that they are on the road to Heaven.

xiv] *The Christian Ideal and Christian Hope* 597

"Their heaven seems almost begun, even here on earth : and when their earthly tabernacle is dissolved, and they are translated to the region of Departed Souls—when the bodily frame which was interposed between the Soul and the presence of the Saviour is interposed no longer—the change must be as if one had been living in a region of light and of glorious sunshine, but immured in a close hut or prison-house which admitted only a few rays through its chinks ; and as if, by some mighty blast from above, awful and agonising for the moment, but yet gracious in its purpose and effect, the earthly hovel were blown down and carried away, and the happy tenant of it left rejoicing in the new-found glow of the celestial light, by which, though dimly seen, she had been so long in truth entirely surrounded.

" If we needed any proof that there is a hereafter for the souls of men : if we wished, as many of the most devout and sincere Christians have often wished, to find a confirmation of the promises made by Christ and His Apostles to men's souls, in a consideration of the nature and progress of the soul itself : if we desired to see how the economy of the world of grace is supported by the analogy of the economy of the world of nature : might we not find, in the aspect of such cases as I have just described, that which we seek ? For when a soul has reached such a stage—when, after a long course of discipline, of domestic teaching, of self teaching, of the teaching of experience and success ; of the teaching of pain and sorrow ; of the teaching of meditation and prayer ; when, after such a course of discipline, the soul has really reached a condition in which Faith, Hope, and Charity are habitual impulses of its being ; when it has attained a truly heavenly-minded unselfishness, and loving wisdom, and entire trust in the goodness of Him Who afflicteth :—can we suppose that the soul, when it has reached such a point, is to sink into nothingness ? When it has been so far matured, is it to be crushed for ever ? Can He Who unfolds the germ into the bud, and the bud into the flower, and the flower into the fruit, unfold the soul so far, and then consign it to destruction ?

"Can the same Lord of Creation—for He is the same Lord of Creation in the natural and in the spiritual world—be so careful to provide the means of perpetual progress in the lower sphere, and let progress in the higher sphere, after a short career—alas ! how short ! end in an utter blank ? Even if *some* men's souls seem as if they advanced not to any condition of worthiness why they should be continued in existence; if some buds of spiritual life are so little unfolded that they may seem not to be worth preserving; if there be some souls of which the lamentable course has been such that, if they should perish, nothing gained would be lost; yet still, in such other cases as I have referred to, where the gain has already been so great; where the spiritual life has already so marvellously budded and flowered; where the powers of the formation and development of a celestial life have already gone so far; in such cases we cannot think that what has been gained shall be at once and irretrievably lost; what has been done shall be utterly undone; what has been developed shall be annihilated; what seems so near to heaven shall be totally consigned to earth. To believe this would be to believe that we live in a world in which there is no Design, no Purpose, no Object, no Thought, no Wisdom, no Love. Even our natural reason, our contemplation of the general plan of the universe, may assure us that such flowers must have a corresponding fruit; that such spiritual powers must be further unfolded; that such heavenly life must have a Heaven in which it may breathe freely; that such a temporal being must have a corresponding eternal being.

"And the Gospel does but reverberate to us the spontaneous utterance of our own hearts, when it declares to us that such shall inherit the kingdom prepared for them from eternity; that such shall be received into the Heaven which the Son of God is gone before to prepare for them; that such shall be translated to a state in which there shall be no hunger or thirst, no pain or sorrow; where they shall be before the throne of God, and serve Him day and night though day and night like ours shall be no more."

B.

"But take again a third class of persons, who yet, like the other two, are dwelling constantly in the midst of us, whom we have seen and known—I trust also have admired and loved—and look at their lives, and think of their deaths, and then how infinitely impossible does it seem to conceive that these can have perished! So true is it that God is not the God of the dead, but of the living, for all live unto Him. Once think of anyone as devoted to God, as living principally in relation to Him, and it becomes as difficult to conceive of such a one that he has perished as to conceive of any other that

The Christian Ideal and Christian Hope

he will not perish. For here we have a man possessed with faculties and with affections that nothing on earth has satisfied or can ever satisfy; his life is imperfect; he seems to have been cut off most untimely if that God, Whom here on earth the very best men can only see, as it were, through a glass darkly, shall never be known to him more fully. And when we see such a man living to God continually, putting aside the objects which other men live for, and manifestly setting before himself another object, namely, the love of God in Christ—when we see him going on quietly, attracting no great notice or glory on earth, yet ripening continually in all goodness; suffering with cheerfulness, labouring with unwearied zeal, meek and forgiving, temperate, yet not severe; making the best possible use of earth and earthly things, yet ever looking beyond them; it is manifest that his conversation or citizenship, as St Paul calls it, is not here; and that if the grave close on him for ever, he who has lived better than any other class of men, will alone, of all men, never have reached the haven which he desired nor attained the end of his being. It is like those foreign plants, whose flowers and fruits will not come to perfection in our climate; but whose natural strength and beauty make us feel only the more sure that they must have, elsewhere, a better and more genial climate of their own."

THE END

www.ingramcontent.com/pod-product-compliance
Lightning Source LLC
Chambersburg PA
CBHW071216290426
44108CB00013B/1192